THINKING ABOUT OTHER PEOPLE
IN NINETEENTH-CENTURY
BRITISH WRITING

Nineteenth-century life and literature are full of strange accounts that describe the act of one person thinking about another as an ethically problematic, sometimes even a dangerously powerful thing to do. Adela Pinch explains why, when, and under what conditions it is possible, or desirable, to believe that thinking about another person could affect them. She explains why nineteenth-century British writers – poets, novelists, philosophers, psychologists, devotees of the occult – were both attracted to and repulsed by radical or substantial notions of purely mental relations between persons, and why they moralized about the practice of thinking about other people in interesting ways.

Working at the intersection of literary studies and philosophy, this book both sheds new light on a neglected aspect of Victorian literature and thought, and explores the consequences of, and the value placed on, this strand of thinking about thinking.

ADELA PINCH is Associate Professor of English and Women's Studies, University of Michigan.

CAMBRIDGE STUDIES IN NINETEENTH-CENTURY
LITERATURE AND CULTURE

General editor
Gillian Beer, University of Cambridge

Editorial board
Isobel Armstrong, *Birkbeck, University of London*
Kate Flint, *Rutgers University*
Catherine Gallagher, *University of California, Berkeley*
D. A. Miller, *University of California, Berkeley*
J. Hillis Miller, *University of California, Irvine*
Daniel Pick, *Birkbeck, University of London*
Mary Poovey, *New York University*
Sally Shuttleworth, *University of Oxford*
Herbert Tucker, *University of Virginia*

Nineteenth-century British literature and culture have been rich fields for interdisciplinary studies. Since the turn of the twentieth century, scholars and critics have tracked the intersections and tensions between Victorian literature and the visual arts, politics, social organization, economic life, technical innovations, scientific thought – in short, culture in its broadest sense. In recent years, theoretical challenges and historiographical shifts have unsettled the assumptions of previous scholarly synthesis and called into question the terms of older debates. Whereas the tendency in much past literary critical interpretation was to use the metaphor of culture as "background", feminist, Foucauldian, and other analyses have employed more dynamic models that raise questions of power and of circulation. Such developments have reanimated the field. This series aims to accommodate and promote the most interesting work being undertaken on the frontiers of the field of nineteenth-century literary studies: work which intersects fruitfully with other fields of study such as history, or literary theory, or the history of science. Comparative as well as interdisciplinary approaches are welcomed.

A complete list of titles published will be found at the end of the book.

THINKING ABOUT OTHER PEOPLE IN NINETEENTH-CENTURY BRITISH WRITING

ADELA PINCH

Department of English
University of Michigan

CAMBRIDGE
UNIVERSITY PRESS

CAMBRIDGE UNIVERSITY PRESS
Cambridge, New York, Melbourne, Madrid, Cape Town, Singapore,
São Paulo, Delhi, Dubai, Tokyo

Cambridge University Press
The Edinburgh Building, Cambridge CB2 8RU, UK

Published in the United States of America by Cambridge University Press, New York

www.cambridge.org
Information on this title: www.cambridge.org/9780521764643

First published 2010

Printed in the United Kingdom at the University Press, Cambridge

A catalog record for this publication is available from the British Library

ISBN 978-0-521-76464-3 Hardback

For Webb and Clara Keane

Contents

Acknowledgements

During the many years it has taken to write this book, I have been fortunate to have had the opportunity to share portions of it with colleagues at the following institutions: the North American Society for the Study of Romanticism, the American Conference on Romanticism, the North American Victorian Studies Association, the University of California–Los Angeles, the University of Chicago, Cornell University, the Graduate Center of the City University of New York, Harvard University, the Johns Hopkins University, New York University, Princeton University, Rutgers University, Vanderbilt University, Williams College, the University of Wisconsin, and Yale University; and, here at the University of Michigan, the Poetry and Poetics Workshop, and the Aesthetics Discussion Group. I wish to give my thanks to these institutions, to the individuals who made these occasions possible, and above all to the many people who kindly made comments on the project at these occasions; I have considered seriously all of your suggestions, which have helped make this book what it is.

For funding the time that has made the research and writing of this book possible, I thank the University of Michigan, the National Endowment for the Humanities, and the Center for Advanced Study in the Behavioral Sciences. The community of scholars at the Center for Advanced Study during 2003–2004 has my enduring gratitude for what proved to be a crucial, formative year. For important suggestions and conversations during that year, thanks go to Michael Bratman, Victor Caston, Philip Fisher, Dorothea Frede, Adele Goldberg, Alison Gopnik, Walter Johnson, Elaine Scarry, and Scott Shapiro. Special thanks in particular to Adele, for walking and talking in the Stanford hills; to Victor, who has continued to be an unfailingly generous resource; and to Scott, who on numerous occasions has massively re-shaped the direction of this project.

Many other colleagues and friends have made the writing of this book possible by reading parts of it, and through their suggestions, their criticisms, and their support. I feel very fortunate to have had the benefit of all of these things from the following people: Rachel Ablow, Amanda Anderson, Suzy Anger, Derek Attridge, Stephen Darwall, Kathryn Dominguez, Lynn Enterline, Gillian Feeley-Harnik, Jonathan Freedman, Julia Hell, Virginia Jackson, Andy Kirshner, Jonathan Kramnick, John Kucich, Kerry Larson, Marjorie Levinson, Michael McKeon, Tomoko Masuzawa, Dick Moran, Susan Najita, Jeff Nunokawa (who was party to a memorable dinner conversation in the autumn of 1997: more on that below), Alan Richardson, Stephanie Rowden, Sidonie Smith, Karla Taylor, Rei Terada, Martha Vicinus, Athena Vrettos, Ken Walton, Gillian White, Carolyn Williams, Elizabeth Wingrove, the late Merla Wolk, and Andrea Zemgulys. Sue Cutler and Karen Seeley – along with my former teacher, Mary Jacobus, and my former student, Wendy Katz – have generously clued me into the psychoanalytic concepts and conversations that bear on the topics of this book. On several crucial occasions over the years, Andrew Miller, Deidre Lynch, and William Galperin have taken the time to write me detailed (or, in Billy's case, oracular) comments on portions of the manuscript which I have returned to again and again. A special thanks to two of my Victorianist colleagues, Lucy Hartley and Danny Hack, who read chunks of the manuscript in the final phase. Other debts and thanks are recorded in my footnotes.

This book would not have been possible without the ceaseless encouragement, support, and advice of my husband, Webb Keane. Beginning with the crucial dinner conversation with Webb and Jeff in the autumn of 1997 that truly set this book in motion, conversations with Webb have constantly sent me running back to my desk with new ideas and questions. He has read every page of this book, often in multiple versions, as have my friends Yopie Prins and Don Herzog. Yopie's friendship, her generosity with her deep knowledge of Victorian poetry, and her feel for what is important, never cease to astound me. Webb, Yopie, and Don have each brought their own distinctive interests to bear on the topics of this book; I hope they know how much in it is owing to them.

Thanks to the generosity of the Department of English, the Horace H. Rackham School of Graduate Studies, and the Office of the Vice President for Research at the University of Michigan, I have had the good fortune to have a number of outstanding research assistants over the years: Caroline Giordano, Michael Gorwitz, Jill Lamberton, Casie LeGette, and Karen McConnell. For their exceptional work, and their shrewd, supportive presence during the last two summers of this book's writing, I would like to give special thanks to Casie and to Caroline: they made finishing it possible. Linda Bree and Liz Hanlon at Cambridge University Press have been a pleasure to work with. My enduring thanks to Phillip Mallett and another anonymous reader for their extremely helpful reviews of the manuscript.

I am indebted to Nicholas Roe and Jane Stabler for their kind hospitality during a research trip to St. Andrews; to Joanna Snelling, librarian, Corpus Christi College, Oxford, for graciously sending information from the Shadworth Hodgson library; and to the staff of the Harlan Hatcher Graduate Library at the University of Michigan for their patience.

Portions of Chapter 4 appeared in "Transatlantic Modern Love," in *The Traffic in Poems: Nineteenth-Century Poetry and Transatlantic Exchange*, edited by Meredith L. McGill (2008), pp, 160–82, and as "Love Thinking," *Victorian Studies* 50.3 (2008): 379–97. I am grateful to Rutgers University Press and to Indiana University Press for permission to use material here.

Finally: the first paragraphs that became part of this book were written in the autumn of 1997, two months before my daughter, Clara Keane, was born. To her, and to my husband Webb Keane, I dedicate this book, in thanks for having made the many years in which the rest of it was written so extraordinarily happy.

Introduction: Love thinking

We tend to feel that thinking about people we love is the next best thing to being with them. But the history of ideas about the powers of the mind is full of strange accounts that describe the act of thinking about another as an ethically complex, sometimes even a dangerously powerful thing to do. This book seeks to explain why nineteenth-century British writers – poets, novelists, philosophers, psychologists, devotees of the occult – were both attracted to and repulsed by radical or substantial notions of purely mental relations between persons, and why they moralized about the practice of thinking about other people in interesting ways. It explores why, when, and under what conditions nineteenth-century writers found it possible, or desirable, to believe that thinking about another person could affect him or her, for good or for ill. Such a study is designed to shed some light on our own beliefs in our mental powers: when does a belief in our mental powers over another seem delusional, and when might holding such a belief seem in fact an essential part of being a moral person? Studying the ways in which nineteenth-century texts account for the act of thinking about another person may, I propose, provide new insights into the logic of ideas about mental causation, practical ethics, and the sociability of the mind. When are we likely to conceive of "thinking," as did Samuel Taylor Coleridge (1801), "as a pure act & energy...*Thinking* as distinguished from *Thoughts*"?[1] How do we evaluate Elizabeth Barrett Browning's poetic agonies about whether it is right to think about her beloved ("I do not think of thee – I am too near thee," she admonishes) in her *Sonnets from the Portuguese* (1850), and strikingly similar musings in Hannah Arendt's powerful essay, "Thinking and Moral Considerations" (1971): "to think about somebody who is present implies removing ourselves surreptitiously from his company and acting as though he were no longer there"?[2] How might the climax of George Eliot's novel *Daniel Deronda* (1876), in which a woman believes she has killed her husband "in her thoughts," illuminate a long history of debates about thought crime?[3] How did nineteenth-century writers balance a commitment to mental freedom with a suspicion of mental force?

As these questions might suggest, I was attracted to the texts I discuss in this book, and motivated to write about them, by a set of philosophical – if that is not too grandiose a term – questions; but I also seek to contribute to our knowledge of the impact of certain ideas in nineteenth-century British culture. In this introduction I aim to sketch out both my philosophical motivations and the historical claims. Some readers may find that I skimp on one, or the other. In any case, the philosophical questions at issue in this study are thoroughly intertwined with its literary interests. For example: my introduction's title, "Love thinking," is borrowed from a long nineteenth-century poem more mocked than read, Coventry Patmore's *The Angel in the House* (1854–1856), a small, meditative section of which is titled "Love Thinking." Patmore's "Love Thinking" muses on the peculiar qualities, and ambiguous value, of a species of meditation about a beloved which does not result in any particular knowledge about him or her. The semantic ambiguities of that phrase, "love thinking" – and the way it confronts us with a choice about the relative weight we place on the first two syllables – will be considered in Chapter 4's discussion of thinking and knowing in the work of Patmore and George Meredith. Do we place emphasis on "love," which renders "thinking" a noun, and "love" modifying it, designating a species or kind of thinking? Or do we scan it differently, as "love *think*ing," in which case it seems to be a description of an act of thinking that Love (a personified being) is doing? Or is it an imperative, exhorting the reader to "love thinking"?

While all of these shades of meaning are at play in Patmore's poem, over the course of this book, "love thinking" comes to designate a set of beliefs about thinking about other people that emerges from the writings I discuss. It designates forms of thinking that are believed to be deeply social and embedded in passionate relationships to others, forms of thinking conceived of as forms of action, which produce not knowledge about but real effects on others. The writers treated in this book are rarely neutral about the effects of thinking. Some, such as the proponents of ethical thought-power we shall meet in Chapter 2 – the panpsychist James Hinton, the theosophist Annie Besant, the psychological mathematician Mary Everest Boole – enthusiastically believed in the power of thought to do good to others. Some, such as Coleridge and Barrett Browning, occasionally worried that thinking about another could constitute an act of domination and inflict damage. Patmore and Meredith were remarkably pessimistic about the value that thinking about the one you love could have, intimating that it could do more harm than good. Into these debates I introduce as well a group of thinkers who vehemently denied that thinking could have any effects on anything whatsoever: the Victorian epiphenomenalists. But by the end of this book – assisted in large part by a reading of Eliot's *Daniel Deronda* – I shall argue that this strand of nineteenth-century intellectual life reveals that, illogical as it may seem, there is a deep social and moral sense to entertaining the belief that thinking can affect, even harm, others. I shall elaborate on this idea not only later in this Introduction but also in my Conclusion.

I begin with two chapters that seek to establish a concern with the force of thinking in seemingly disparate kinds of nineteenth-century philosophical prose. The first chapter traces the career of ethical ambivalence about the act of thinking in nineteenth-century mental and moral sciences, focusing in particular on Scottish philosopher James Frederick Ferrier's *Introduction to the Philosophy of Consciousness* (1838–39). The writings of this philosopher may seem an unusual place to start, but it is precisely its writerly qualities that make Ferrier's *Philosophy of Consciousness* so compelling. I argue that Ferrier's strenuous conception of thought as a form of action results from the exemplary, historically significant intersections in his work among idealist and empiricist approaches to the psychology of mental action, and the literary possibilities of philosophical prose in nineteenth-century Britain. The chapter concludes by illuminating the link between British idealism in the 1830s and that decade's wave of interest in mesmerism, suggesting that it might be possible to view mesmerism as early anglophone idealism's social theory. The second chapter explores accounts of the sociability of the mind both in later nineteenth-century accounts of paranormal mental activity and in British idealist philosophy. Bringing together a diverse range of theorists of the force and the ethics of thinking along with innovative Victorian and fin-de-siècle philosophers such as Shadworth Hodgson and J. M. E. McTaggart, I seek in this chapter to provide a context for, and an interpretation of, Victorian debates about "epiphenomenalism": the question of whether the mind can, or cannot, cause things to happen.

The next two chapters examine nineteenth-century lyric poetry and poetic theory as articulations of ideas about thinking about a beloved person. Chapter 3 explores the relationship between poetic uses of second-person pronouns, and anxieties about intimacy. It focuses on the paradoxes that ensue when poets from Samuel Taylor Coleridge to Letitia Landon, Elizabeth Browning, Christina Rossetti, and Alice Meynell utter "I think of thee" – or more provocatively, "I do not think of thee." Chapter 4 explains how Victorian prosodists theorized the relationship between thinking about another and poetic rhythms. I evoke a context for an episode in Patmore's *The Angel in the House* in which a woman claims, rhythmically, "He thought I thought he thought I slept." I focus on the reverberations of this episode in George Meredith's *Modern Love* (1862) and in other poems of the era, and I explain its relationship to Victorian theories of poetic rhythm which viewed rhythm as the pulsation of thought from mind to objects.

In moving from philosophical prose to literary genres, this study does not give priority to philosophy over literature: this is not a study, by and large, of influence. The diversity of genres under scrutiny here is designed rather to establish the persistence of a concern with the effects of thinking of a person, as this concern takes shape in the distinctive genres – including philosophical prose – of nineteenth-century British writing. Indeed, in posing the questions "what are the ethics and effects of thinking about other people, and how did nineteenth-century writers give shape to this issue?" before a range of forms of writing, I have had several aims. The first is of course to underscore the intertwining of the literary and philosophical dimensions of my topics: the literary forms speak to philosophical issues, while the philosophical texts reveal the ways in which philosophical ideas happen in writing. As we shall see in Chapter 3, for example, an ethics of thinking about another person emerges in and through a poetics of address, while in Chapter 1 we shall see the ways in which James Frederick Ferrier's understanding of the agency of thinking unfolds in and through the agency of words. But my second aim is to open anew some questions about the work of genre, both in nineteenth-century culture, and in contemporary nineteenth-century literary studies. We may be inclined to view, for example, the work done by the shorter nineteenth-century poems discussed in Chapter 3 as fundamentally different from the work that the philosophical writers discussed in Chapter 2 cut out for themselves. However, we may be laboring under the weight of a twentieth-century understanding of "poetry" as a genre, with which the particulars of poetic practices may in fact be at odds.

Furthermore, as urgent as it is to think about the relation between the forms of philosophical prose and the forms of nineteenth-century verse, it is equally crucial to scrutinize the form of the Victorian novel in relation to the other forms of writing that took thinking about other people as their topic. It is for this reason that *Thinking about Other People* moves to the novel in its last chapter. My final chapter considers the intersections among ethics, psychology, and strategies of narration in Eliot's *Daniel Deronda*. I seek to explain why George Eliot regarded belief that thinking about someone might make something happen to them as simultaneously factually false and ethically efficacious. I demonstrate how Eliot's curious attitude towards the omnipotence of thought emerges in and through the novel's parsing of cause and effect, and through its ways of representing – and sometimes refusing to represent – the act of thinking. My analysis of this novel thus elaborates on two things that I find throughout this study: a tenacious pattern in nineteenth-century writing which could be described as a simultaneous attraction to and repulsion from belief in the belief that thinking about someone can affect him or her; and a persistent embedding of that ambivalence about thinking within the very forms of writing. *Daniel Deronda* renders vividly the ways in which thinking about not only other actual people, but also literary characters, can occasionally make them real.

HISTORICAL CONTEXTS: IDEALISM, IMAGINATION, LIBERALISM

The constellation of issues at the heart of this book – debates about the effects and the ethics of thinking about others, beliefs in mental causation and mental action at a distance – is manifestly not a set of concerns with a clear start date and termination, as my sense of these concerns as ongoing theoretical issues should imply. Nevertheless, the way in which the texts and authors discussed here range across the entire nineteenth century – from some of the early writings of Coleridge at the beginning of the century, to the writings of the philospher J. M. E. McTaggart at the end – requires some explanation. I shall argue throughout this book that one crucial context for the strand of thinking about thinking is the history in Britain of idealism: the philosophical tradition that emphasizes the priority of the human mind in accounts of knowledge and reality, and that is generally taken to designate the philosophy of Plato, Neoplatonism, and the writings of German philosophers who flourished at the end of the eighteenth century – Kant, Fichte, Schelling, Hegel. The distinctive history of the uneasy assimilation of continental idealist philosophy in England and Scotland begins – for better or for worse – with Coleridge, whose work remained throughout most of the century the most singular inspiration and source for generations of British intellectuals.[4] And it for all intents and purposes ends with the writings of McTaggart and a handful of others in the 1920s, after which idealism ceased to play anything more than a minor role in British intellectual life. The novelist May Sinclair began her *A Defence of Idealism* (1917) by professing some "embarrassment" over the timing of her task: "You cannot be quite sure whether you are putting in an appearance too late or much too early."[5] Throughout the century leading up to Sinclair's *Defence*, idealist philosophy – or philosophies – often seemed not only too late or too early, but always slightly external to what were often seen to be more authentically native, British modes of intellectual inquiry: empiricism, common sense, materialism, utilitarianism. The introduction of "German" ideas, both inside and outside of the universities, took place unevenly and uneasily: the low points in this history would include, for example, the travails of the philosopher James Frederick Ferrier – subject of my first chapter – at the University of Edinburgh in the 1840s and 1850s, when he had to defend himself against charges of being an un-Scottish Hegelian by claiming he couldn't understand Hegel himself.[6] My book is not a history of British idealism in the nineteenth century – indeed the most influential of the Victorian idealists, T. H. Green and F. H. Bradley, form very little part of the story; and it is emphatically not an account of the influence of any of the sources for nineteenth-century idealisms, neither continental philosophy nor Platonic revivals.[7] But the distinctive history of the uneven assimilation of idealism into British intellectual life provides a crucial context, and partial explanation, for some of the contours and motivating forces of debates about the power of thinking about other people in nineteenth-century writing. It is in order to explore and define this context that my first chapter focuses on Ferrier's *Introduction to the Philosophy of Consciousness* (1838–1839). Ferrier most frequently appears in literary studies as one of the leaders in the controversy over Coleridge's plagiarisms from Schelling in the *Biographia Literaria*, but he was himself a highly original, sometimes flamboyant philosophical writer. Through his early writing, I argue, we can see the ways in which the grafting of German idealist ideas about the priority of mind onto British empiricism resulted in some strangely literal accounts of the mind's power in and on the world around it.

Focusing on Ferrier, McTaggart, and other idealists as crucial parts of the context for beliefs about the act of thinking about another person has the advantage of reminding us how influential forms of idealism were in nineteenth-century British culture, in spite of our sense of their uneasy marginality. Romantic literature's relation to idealism and to philosophy generally is a hoary old yet enduring topic of scholarship and criticism, as is the debt to the German idealists (via Coleridge and Carlyle) of nineteenth-century American transcendentalism. Yet idealism's role in later nineteenth-century British intellectual life and literature has not often been on the agenda.[8] We have grown accustomed to thinking of

Victorian Britain as a realm of science, but it was also a realm of meta-physical speculation. To at least one Victorian observer, it seemed as if philosophical speculation had been accelerating throughout the century, and that "metaphysics" was on its way to becoming a household word. "The increase of attention to Speculative Philosophy in the British Islands during the last twelve years is very remarkable," wrote David Masson in his 1877 updated version of *Recent British Philosophy* (1865). And he went further to say that protests against philosophy's neglect that were "already antiquated in great measure before 1865…are now certainly quite past date." "The public have acquiesced more rapidly than might have been expected in such a matter," he marveled.[9] In our own era, literary criticism has unfortunately absorbed contemporary Anglo-American philosophy's disdain for most of its nineteenth-century precursors. There is little in nineteenth-century studies resembling the conversation between philosophy and literature that exists in eighteenth-century British studies. And while the philosophical writers discussed here – the idealist Ferrier, the unusual epiphenomenalist Shadworth Hodgson – may never be as familiar to literary scholars as Locke, Hume, and Adam Smith, they were implicated in the literary culture of their era as much as the eighteenth-century philosophers. Chapters 1 and 2, which focus primarily on the philosophical writers crucial to this study, may feel different in texture and emphasis from the chapters on poetry and fiction. At play are not only differences of genre, but also the differences between writing about poets amply familiar to readers, and philosophical writers less well known, not only to readers of literature, but also to historians of ideas. Because some of these writers deserve to be better known to literary readers, I have included more matter of an expository nature about their lives, careers, and ideas. It is hard to resist the appeal, for example, of a philosopher (Ferrier) who seriously proposed translating Tennyson's *In Memoriam* into prose in order to test its ideas. Tennyson, for one, was amused.

One of the singular features of the dissemination of idealist ideas in nineteenth-century British intellectual life, however, is the extent to which it actually took place through the writings of poets. This is a way to think about some aspects of the extraordinary uses, through to the end of the century, that readers and writers made of Coleridge and Shelley, both of whom hover throughout the chapters of this book. One nineteenth-century historian of American transcendentalism noted that in both England and America, Coleridge was "the source of more intellectual life than any individual of his time." He claimed that Coleridge had "disciples who never heard him speak even in print, and followers who never

saw his form even as sketched by critics. His thoughts were in the air."¹⁰
Later nineteenth-century disciples of Coleridge often expressed a personal
and passionate attachment to the man and his ideas: the Victorian epiphenomenalist Shadworth Hodgson dedicated one of his books to the
long-deceased Coleridge, calling him "my father in philosophy, not seen
but beloved."¹¹ Such personalization of a philosophical influence followed
Coleridge's own, distinctive tendency to cleave to philosophical ideas
as embedded in relations with others, which goes some way to explain
why he lurks so distinctly in the background of the strand of thinking
about thinking about others at the heart of this book.¹² As John Beer has
demonstrated, the Coleridge who was the object of fervent reverence and
love in the Victorian era was above all the later Coleridge of the *Aids to
Reflection* (1825).¹³ In that fragmentary, meditative prose work, Coleridge
counsels reflection upon the conditions of thought and language as means
to discovering the transcendent principles of Christianity within. But that
Coleridge was not separable from earlier Coleridges who are equally relevant to the strand of thinking about thinking studied here: Coleridge the
theorist of the imagination as "a repetition in the finite mind of the eternal act of creation in the infinite I AM"; Coleridge the theorist of ghost,
those manifestations of "the modes in which our thoughts…become at
times perfectly *dramatic*."¹⁴ Coleridge's writings will appear most extensively in this book in Chapter 3, where I discuss the vicissitudes of the
second-person addresses in his poem "This Lime-Tree Bower My Prison"
in the context of that chapter's analysis of thinking in the second person
in nineteenth-century poetry; but his presence will be felt intermittently
throughout Chapters 1, 2, and 3.

In Chapters 3, 4, and 5, it is Percy Bysshe Shelley who haunts some of
the authors I discuss. Shelley's Victorian reception was as passionate and
as diverse as was Coleridge's: relevant to the authors I discuss is a Shelley
who has been thoroughly spiritualized, idealized, and Platonized. Looking
back on her long life, the Catholic convert Alice Meynell noted, remarkably, that "the influence of Shelley upon me belongs rather to my spiritual
than my mental history. I thought the whole world was changed for me
thenceforth."¹⁵ In a publication of the Shelley Society in 1887, the Reverend
Stopford Augustus Brooke turned "Epipsychidion" – Shelley's defense of
extramarital sex – into a manifesto of the poet's "clasping at last its ideal in
the immaterial world of pure Thought."¹⁶ As we shall see, "Epipsychidion"
is the poem most frequently alluded to in later nineteenth-century texts
that ponder the ethics and effects of thinking about a beloved other. But
throughout the century Shelley's writing served as a kind of testimony to

the agency of thinking (in particular *Prometheus Unbound*, and *The Cenci*, in which "thoughts" themselves no less than people seem to have the power to murder). "I am as one lost in a midnight wood," says Giacomo, son of the evil Count Cenci, "who dares not ask some harmless passenger / The path across the wilderness, lest he, / As my thoughts are, should be – a murderer."[17] The significance of the figure of the drowned Shelley as a magnet for ideas about the murderous power of thinking about another person in George Eliot's *Daniel Deronda* shall be explored in Chapter 5.

If the long rise and fall of British idealism across the nineteenth century provides one framework for this study, a second, related framework is an arc that we can see stretching – again with Coleridge as our starting point – from the early nineteenth century to the early twentieth century, this time with Sigmund Freud as our end point. This is the arc of psychological theories of the agency of imagination from the romantic era to Freud's concept of the "omnipotence of thoughts." To begin at the end: in 1909 and 1910, very much under the influence of late nineteenth-century British anthropology – he cites Herbert Spencer, J. G. Frazer, Andrew Lang, and E. B. Tylor – Freud drafted the essays that became *Totem and Taboo*, a speculative work that considered whether some of the practices and beliefs of the "primitive" phases of mankind could be explained by psychoanalysis. The third essay, "Animism, Magic, and the Omnipotence of Thoughts," concerns magical practices used to make things happen: injure enemies, make people fall in love. In archaic animistic practices, Freud quotes approvingly from Frazer's *The Golden Bough*: "men mistook the order of their ideas for the order of nature, and hence imagined that the control which they have, or seem to have, over their thoughts, permitted them to exercise a corresponding control over things."[18] The psychological logic of such beliefs, argues Freud, is identical to that of neurotic patients who narcissistically overvalue psychic acts, and believe that evil wishes about another person "lead inevitably to their fulfillment" (87). The same belief, he observes, can be found in children: as is the case with many Freudian concepts, "the omnipotence of thought" is simultaneously rendered pathological and primitive, and admitted as part of a normal phase of human development. If it is common for children and "primitive" peoples to believe in the omnipotence of their thoughts only to lose this belief later, that is, the question underlying Freud's analysis is not "how could anyone come to believe that their thoughts have extrapersonal action at a distance?" but rather "how could anyone come to *not* believe that they do?" He opened the door to the possibility of viewing a belief in the power of thinking to affect others as an ordinary psychological phenomenon.[19]

There is every reason to resist the teleological pull of narratives which trace a direct line from romanticism to Freud. But it would be possible to see nineteenth-century discussions about the effects and ethics of the act of thinking about another person as pieces of a prehistory to the psychoanalytic concept of the "omnipotence of thought."[20] It allows us to situate Freud's treatment of thinking – which he sometimes termed "an experimental kind of acting"[21] – along a spectrum of manifestations of related concerns across the long nineteenth century. This study's strategy is to see the enormously influential vogues for mesmerism and other paranormal psychic powers in nineteenth-century Britain as points along this spectrum.[22] I integrate these topics into the study of British philosophy, not only British idealism (in Chapter 1) but also, as I shall discuss further below, Victorian epiphenomenalism (in Chapter 2). Some of the interest in the force of thinking to affect others derived, as did Freud's accounting of the omnipotence of thought, from nineteenth-century anthropological speculation on various forms of mind-magic – voodoo, witchcraft – discovered both abroad and among the rural at home.[23] Narratives of mind-power abound in nineteenth-century supernatural fiction.[24] In Thomas Hardy's beautiful, mournful tale "The Withered Arm" (1888), a forsaken milkmaid involuntarily jinxes her lover's young bride, whose arm withers under the force of her rival's dream of harm. "O, can it be," the milkmaid, Rhoda Brook, says to herself, "that I exercise a malignant power over people against my own will?" "The sense of having been guilty of an act of malignity increased," notes Hardy's narrator, "affect as she might to riddle her superstition. In her secret heart Rhoda did not altogether object to a slight diminution of her successor's beauty, by whatever means it had come about; but she did not wish to inflict upon her physical pain."[25] Hardy's emphasis on Rhoda's crushing sense of guilt renders "The Withered Arm" not so much a story of rural witchcraft as an account of the dread that your mind could – beyond your conscious control – inflict harm on another. It is a story that walks the road between supernaturalism and psychology.

A renewed sense of the extraordinary ethical value nineteenth-century intellectuals placed on the ordinary activity of thinking has come from literary scholars' recent re-evaluation of the culture of liberalism. Andrew H. Miller has emphasized how and why Victorian intellectuals put a premium on the *display* of thinking itself. Elaine Hadley has written of the ways in which, in the writings of some Victorian liberals – and that of some of their modern exegetes – liberalism itself comes to be defined by and as a "cognitive aesthetic." Victorian "habits of thoughtfulness," she summarizes, "generate what might be called a liberal cognitive aesthetic," "a model of habituated thoughtfulness that aspires to social order and decency – one mind 'operat-ing' on one mind at a time."[26] In the chapters that follow, I track the ways in which an aspiration that purely mental relations between two people – one mind operating on one mind at a time – could embody an ideal of mutual, equal relationship and could lead either to a cheerful optimism about men-tal power, or a pessimism about the ethics and the results of thinking about a beloved other. Particularly by the mid-to-later nineteenth century, I argue in Chapter 3, the pressures to make the mental relations between man and woman an ideal of democracy – articulated above all in John Stuart Mill's *On the Subjection of Women* (1869) – correspond to a heightened awareness of love thinking and its vicissitudes in the poetry of the period.[27]

This is a way of saying that one of the features of Victorian liberal-ism was a commitment to both the privacy *and* the sociability of mental life: a concern to integrate people's work of thinking about each other into the calculus of social relations. We can explore this issue by scrutin-izing carefully the status of "freedom of thought" in John Stuart Mill's *On Liberty*. Freedom of thought is the absolute center of liberty for Mill; the difficulty lies in parsing the ways in which freedom of thought is related to freedom of expression, to which it is always tethered. The dif-ficulties begin in a well-known passage from the "Introductory" chapter of *On Liberty*:

This, then, is the appropriate region of human liberty. It comprises, first, the inward domain of consciousness; demanding liberty of conscience, in the most comprehensive sense; liberty of thought and feeling; absolute freedom of opinion and sentiment on all subjects, practical or speculative, scientific, moral, or theological.

The inward domain of consciousness is fundamental – it is the chief terri-tory of human liberty, containing and holding dominion over conscience, opinion, and all mental freedoms. The passage continues by first curiously separating, then joining, freedom of thought and freedom of expression:

The liberty of expressing and publishing opinions may seem to fall under a differ-ent principle, since it belongs to that part of the conduct of an individual which concerns other people; but, being *almost of as much importance as the liberty of thought itself*, and resting in great part on the same reasons, is practically insepar-able from it.[28]

Here and as the discussion proceeds, freedom of expression is in fact sub-ordinate in Mill's conception to freedom of thought. The justification of freedom of expression is the cultivation and enlarging of mental freedom and the perfection of the human mind; the crime and the tragedy of the stifling of freedom of expression is the stunting of the individual intellect, "the sacrifice of the entire moral courage of the human mind," and the cramping of "mental development," which all conspire to "make[s] this country not a place of mental freedom."[29] Freedom of expression is an instrumental good, while freedom of thought is an intrinsic good.[30]

In Mill's discussion of the "liberty of thought and discussion" and in most of the flow of commentary on the freedom of expression that has come in its wake, however, much more has been said about freedom of expression than about freedom of thought, and the latter comes to seem subordinate to the former. In some respects this seems to be because of the basic epistemological problem of disambiguating peoples' thoughts from their words and deeds, which makes it difficult to hold them responsible for their thoughts. In the classical legal view of the eighteenth-century jurist Sir William Blackstone, for example: "as no temporal tribunal can search the heart, or fathom the intentions of the mind, otherwise than as they are demonstrated by outward actions, it therefore cannot punish for what it cannot know."[31] But once freedom of thought is bundled into freedom of expression, there remains a gaping question about whether, in Mill's view, freedom of thought is or is not subject to the fundamental principle governing the horizon of liberty, the harm principle. After initially differentiating freedom of expression from freedom of thought as "belonging to that part of the conduct…that concerns other people," Mill does not actually exempt thought from the harm principle in the fourth and fifth chapters of *On Liberty*. Mill defends a widening circle of the "inward domain of consciousness" as the essence of human freedom, and pushes back the horizon of harm to others that conditions justification for limiting an individual's freedom. But along that line where mental freedom and the harm principle meet there opens, in Mill's work, a space for taking a moral stance on thinking as part of social life with others. A commitment to mental freedom, paradoxically, invokes mental force.

It is crucial therefore to view Mill's defense of the freedom of thought, and the spectrum of the nineteenth-century beliefs about thinking as a practice with moral implications and practical force upon others, as related to each other. Nineteenth-century writers addressing political philosophy and writers addressing thought-power may not often have explicitly addressed each other – though we shall see, in Chapter 5, the ways in which Victorian legal theory on such matters may hover behind Daniel Deronda's response to Gwendolen Harleth's claims to have killed her husband in her thoughts. But the writers I discuss in this book are all engaged with an issue that Mill's defense of mental freedom raises.

The shared context of these Victorian texts in questions of whether persons should feel responsible for the effects of their thinking on others can be retrospectively illuminated by some recent essays in legal philosophy and moral psychology written in the long wake of the gray area opened by Mill's *On Liberty* – about the conditions under which we come to think about whether thoughts can harm. Herbert Morris points out, for example, that Blackstone's objection to punishing for thoughts – that you simply can't punish thoughts because you can't know them – is a thin one. There are all kinds of reasons for upholding the prohibition against punishing people for thoughts alone, yet the relationship between thought and action is intensely complex, and Morris notes that in ordinary moral judgments and even in legal reasoning thoughts are identified as origins for, at minimum, "harmful causal chains whose middle terms are actions or speech, thus creating a prima facie tension between the harm principle and the liberal commitment to the inviolability of thoughts."[32]

Meir Dan-Cohen goes further, suggesting that we do have reason to believe in "the extrapersonal effects of thoughts."[33] There are many ways in which we do care about people's thoughts, he argues, in contradistinction to their expression. It is possible to think of circumstances in which we feel that someone's lot in life is diminished or harmed by someone else's thoughts about him or her – instances of condescension, oppression. Dan-Cohen's goal is to pin down the circumstances in which, according to a kind of sliding scale of attribution of responsibility, it comes to seem "linguistically natural" (183) to ascribe extrapersonal effects to mental states. He argues that we do so by replacing talk of finding a "causal link" (181) between thoughts and effects on other people with a kind of logic we in fact use in everyday life – a recognition of what he calls "relational properties" (181) and the ways in which they constitute people's sense of self. If we are willing to grant (as most of us are) that our sense of self is in part constituted by our sense of what others think about us, then we ought to acknowledge that "a sense that is constituted by meanings is also susceptible to changes in them" (5). "On some occasions other people's attitudes towards us do serve as the relational terms that fix important features of ourselves" (190); hence "other people's attitudes and states of mind can accordingly affect a person's identity all by themselves without the mediation of action or expression" (5). It is in this way that Dan-Cohen claims to have documented "the logical possibility of a more active externalism: the mind can have direct, non-mediated, and non-causal effects on the world outside of it" (191).

Dan-Cohen's essay purports to prove that it is not so peculiar to believe that thinking about another person can harm them, because it can. There are other possibilities: I shall argue that, whether or not thoughts can actually have extrapersonal effects on others, it may make moral, psychological, and social sense to go about life as if one believes that they do. The power of thinking to affect others is a topic about which we may be likely to worry more than is warranted by the evidence. Nevertheless, Dan-Cohen's essay is a provocative response to the gap opened up between Mill's commitment to mental freedom, and his endorsement of the harm principle. It affirms that there are reasons to go back to the era of Mill in order to try to understand this gray area of moral psychology.

CONTEMPORARY CONTEXTS: SKEPTICISM, ANTI-SKEPTICISM, MENTAL CAUSATION, AND THE ETHICS OF THINKING

There are other ways in which the strain of nineteenth-century thinking about thinking about others I have identified can illuminate, and be illuminated by, twentieth- and twenty-first century ways of approaching the life of the mind. The significance of skepticism, and in particular skepticism about the knowability of other people's minds, for Victorian intellectual life and Victorian literature has been explored many years ago by Walter Houghton in *The Victorian Frame of Mind* and more recently in Andrew H. Miller's *The Burdens of Perfection*.[34] Miller eloquently documents the ways in which many Victorian texts turn to love and relationship as a way of overcoming skepticism, and he stresses the significance of skepticism about other minds for the development of crucial Victorian literary forms. The Victorian novel and the dramatic monologue can be seen as forms that respond to concerns about the knowability of others by giving readers access to other minds engaged in the actions of thinking.[35]

Thinking about Other People departs from this emphasis. It is not concerned with nineteenth-century attitudes toward knowing other minds, beliefs about knowing other minds, or skepticism about other minds. It is about the act of thinking about another person. The difference between a focus on the act of thinking about another person, and a focus on knowing another person's mind, may seem like a dubious distinction, and by insisting on it I may seem guilty of quibbling. Infirm this distinction may be, in that it is certainly impossible to imagine that thinking about other people, and imagining what's in their minds, don't have anything to do with each other. They often go together. In *Daniel Deronda*, for example, when Gwendolen Harleth thinks about Daniel, she often wonders what he is thinking: "Perhaps Daniel himself was thinking of these things."[36] As

I shall demonstrate in Chapter 5, the kind of guessing about someone else's thoughts represented by Gwendolen here, and the ideal of the transparent mind, are revealed in that novel as a kind of narcissism, a wishful thinking that doesn't help anyway – as the clairvoyant, mind-reading narrator of Eliot's story "The Lifted Veil" discovers to his peril. Casting thinking about other people as a concern about what's in their minds, Eliot sometimes seems to suggest, is often the least interesting, and least socially meaningful, way of thinking about thinking.

Thinking about Other People suggests that viewing the forms of nineteenth-century literature from the point of view of theories of thinking as action, rather than from the point of view of the problem of representing other minds, can illuminate crucial aspects of those forms. A focus on thinking as action will allow us, in Chapter 5, to question whether *omniscience* is the most salient term for understanding representations of thinking in the Victorian novel. It allows us to unravel, in Chapters 3 and 4, some of the distinctive features of Victorian metrical theory, and nineteenth-century poetry's distinctive ways of using the pronoun "you." Tethering our understanding of mental relations between persons, moreover, to questions of knowledge and knowledge transfer (an emphasis, I shall suggest, marking even the best scholarship on mesmerism, telepathy, and psychical research as forms of intimacy) puts limits on how we understand the sociability of minds. A great number of the texts I discuss here significantly subordinate questions of epistemology to a focus on thinking as a form of social action; they detach questions of knowledge from the action of thinking. In so doing, they theorize thinking about other people as a social act rather than an exercise in skepticism.[37]

The urgency of documenting the existence of anti-skepticism or non-epistemology-based accounts of thinking about other people is behind this study's emphasis on some writers and texts that have not played a prominent role in recent scholarship – on some writers who can, moreover, only be described as the losers in their era's struggles to define approaches to mind. The reasons why figures such as James Frederick Ferrier, and more marginal figures such as James Hinton and Mary Everest Boole, lost out in struggles between philosophy and psychology will be discussed in Chapters 1 and 2. But throughout this book I seek at least to partially suspend disbelief about some pretty implausible ideas about mental force in order to explore the patterns of our own interests and assumptions. As I discuss further at the end of Chapter 2, studying these writers allows us to imagine being in a world in which believing that thinking was a force that could affect others might seem more plausible, more normal, than does believing that thinking makes nothing happen. It allows one to imagine a situation in which the question to ask is not – as we might be inclined to ask – "how could anyone think that their thoughts could affect other people?" but rather, "how could anyone ever come to think that think-ing *doesn't* affect other people?" Trying on the second question turns out to be more than simply a kind of metaphysical historical-reconstruction thought-experiment, a trying-on of weird beliefs as if they were three-cornered hats. Rather, it is a way of getting at a complex aspect of moral psychology: that there may indeed be ways in which it makes a kind of moral sense for people to act *as if* their thoughts affected other people, and that in fact people do behave *as if* this were the case, all the time. As I shall discuss further at the end of the book, acting as if your thoughts could affect others, for good or ill, may be an ordinary part of social life.

Focusing on nineteenth-century conversations about thinking as a form of extra-personal action – whether in the writings of Victorian physicists interested in mental force; in fiction; embodied in theories of poetic form; in the writings of psychical researchers and occultists – also allows us to ponder the history, and the current disposition, of debates about mental causation. To believe that one person's thinking can make something hap-pen to another person, as did Annie Besant, Mary Everest Boole, and some of the members of the Society for Psychical Research, is to take a radical stance on the enduring philosophical question of whether the mind can cause anything at all to happen – a question that, for nineteenth-century intellectuals as for contemporary philosophers, cognitive psychologists and neuroscientists, seemed to get to the essence of the relation of body to mind, and of the "hard problem" of consciousness.[38] Can purely men-tal events – wills, intentions, wishes – be said to cause things to happen in the same way that physical entities and actions – an arm pushing, a ball rolling – cause other actions in the physical world? Or is causation purely the province of the physical world? It is for this reason that this study juxtaposes the Victorian mind-force theorists' most radical accounts of causation with the equally radical stance toward mental causation in Victorian epiphenomenalism – the philosophical view that consciousness has no causal effects, is merely a by-product of neurological events. In the writings of both sides can be found examples of extraordinary language, as the psychical researchers exhaustively catalogued "all classes of cases where there is reason to suppose that the mind of one human being has affected the mind of another, without speech uttered, or word written, or sign made," while the epiphenomenalists sought to argue that the mind's movements are "a mere foam, aura, or melody, arising from the brain, but without reaction upon it."[39] In Chapter 2, I shall demonstrate, through a close look at the work of the philosopher Shadworth Hodgson, the ways in which, surprisingly, an epiphenomenalist stance and a belief in psychic forces could in some instances converge in a resistance to reductionist, materialist views of the relation between body and mind, and an interest in preserving the domain of consciousness. It may be wishful thinking, but it would be nice to think that an understanding of the historical and intellectual contexts of Victorian epiphenomenalism – its emergence in an era of thought-power – might be able to add to the interdisciplinary conversation trying to refine what epiphenomenalism means, what is meant by mental causation, how to think about the brain, and how to make sense of our experience that our thoughts do make things happen.[40]

Thinking about Other People traces the ways in which nineteenth-century writers were especially attuned to the ethical issues at stake in thinking about thinking as a form of causation. That there is some kind of ethical dimension to thinking about another person becomes apparent whenever anyone has a reflex of guilt after thinking cruel thoughts about someone, or when anyone feels that saying "I'm thinking of you" to console a friend in difficulty is somehow the right thing to do. Chapter 3's discussion of nineteenth-century poetic versions of this proposition explores the formal and semantic paradoxes of such utterances. As strange as I often find some of the nineteenth-century writings about the ethics of thinking I discuss here, I have often found it instructive to keep an eye – often a quite skeptical eye – on discussions of the ethics of thinking closer to our own era, such as, for example, Hannah Arendt's eloquent and pessimistic essay "Thinking and Moral Considerations" (1971).[41] Arendt's turn to an ethics of *thinking* – at the end of a career of writing of action and the public sphere – has dismayed and perplexed many of her commentators.[42] The essay seems to devote much of its energy to minimizing the gains of thinking. Like many of the nineteenth-century writers discussed in this study, Arendt decouples thinking from knowledge (a gesture she attributes to Kant), and from judgment, and for much of the essay emphasizes thinking's disengagement from the world: "thinking as such does society little good." The essay then veers radically and unsettlingly at the end to suggest that in times of acute crisis, when everyone else is not-thinking, thinking becomes the only kind of meaningful action. Arendt concludes:

The manifestation of the wind of thought is no knowledge; it is the ability to tell right from wrong, beautiful from ugly. And this indeed may prevent catastrophes, at least for myself, in the rare moments when the chips are down.[43]

It is hard to fathom, given the rest of the essay, how Arendt can possibly suggest that thinking can "prevent catastrophes" – and given the essay's opening discussion of *Eichmann in Jerusalem*, she really means catastrophes – and it is hard to parse the qualification, "at least for myself." There is, in other words, a huge explanatory gap between the account of thinking as non-productive experience and this conclusion. Earlier, Arendt writes mordantly of the separateness of thinking from life:

For thinking's chief characteristic is that it interrupts all doing, all ordinary activities no matter what they happen to be. Whatever the fallacies of the two-world theories might have been, they arose out of genuine experiences. For it is true that the moment we start thinking on no matter what issue we stop everything else, and this everything else, again whatever it may happen to be, interrupts the thinking process; it is as though we moved into a different world. (164–65)

This separateness seems especially acute when we are thinking about another person:

In order to think about somebody, he must be removed from our senses; so long as we are together with him we don't think of him – though we may gather impressions that later become food for thought; to think about somebody who is present implies removing ourselves surreptitiously from his company and acting as though he were no longer there. (165)

In this passage, thinking about someone is truly not the next best thing to being with them; it is a retreat, a categorical inability to be with them.

While "Thinking and Moral Considerations" certainly, in the words of one recent commentator, "underperforms as moral philosophy,"[44] the essay interestingly dramatizes a crucial pattern of thinking about thinking about other people, in and through its own explanatory gaps. That is, in its leap from worrying about the separateness of thinking about another person, to presenting thinking as preventing disaster "when the chips are down," Arendt suggests not only that a kind of pessimism about thinking is the best thing we have, but that the practice of worrying about thinking's ethical effects – whether they are too much, or too little – is the best we can do. As we shall see, the nineteenth-century writer whose worrying about the ethics of thinking about another person most resembles Arendt's is, interestingly, Elizabeth Barrett Browning; but we will see related patterns in many of the authors under consideration. As I shall explain further at the end of this book, worrying, acting as if you believe – perhaps even actually believing – that thinking about another person can harm them or can damage your relation to them, is a strange but crucial way of acknowledging the place of thinking in social relations. Like other ways in which people instinctively take responsibility for things they are really not responsible for – apologizing to someone when you accidentally bump into them on a crowded bus, for example[45] – worrying about the effects of thinking about other people isn't something we'd want people not to do. It is a kind of reality-testing with questions of agency.

This book's argument about thinking about other people is that this kind of worry or belief – that thinking can harm – is the inevitable attendant upon the attitude towards thinking about other people I call love thinking: a commitment to thinking about other people as a crucial part of social life. At the heart of Arendt's essay is the contradiction that thinking about other people both seems like an interruption of life and is crucial to life itself. I wish to conclude this section by quoting at length a somewhat insane rant by a recent fictional person:

Not one of us thinks of anything else all day but men and women, the whole day is just a process one goes through in order to be able to stop at a given moment and devote oneself to thinking about them, the whole point of stopping work or study is nothing more than being able to think about them; even when we're with them, we're thinking about them, or at least I am. They're not the parentheses; the classes and the research are, so are the reading and the writing, the lectures and the ceremonies, the suppers and the meetings, the finances and the politicking, everything in fact that passes here for activity. Productive activity, the thing that brings us money and security and prestige and allows us to live, what keeps a city or a country going, what organises it, is the thing that, later, allows us to think with even greater intensity about them, about men and women…it's all that other activity that's the parenthesis, not the other way round. Everything one does, everything one thinks, everything else that one thinks and plots about is a medium through which to think about them. Even wars are fought in order to be able to start thinking again, to renew our unending thinking about our men and our women, about those who were or could be ours, about those we know already and those we will never know, about those who were young and those who will be young, about those who've shared our beds and those who never will.[46]

DEFINING "THINKING ABOUT ANOTHER PERSON"

One of the remarkable things about this monologue is its refusal to discriminate among kinds of thinking about other people. "Thinking about men and women" clearly includes romantic and erotic fantasizing about them, but that comes to seem beside the point. All kinds of thoughts, all qualities of thinking about manifestly all categories of people (including completely illogical ones – who are those who *will be* young?) are swept together. The nineteenth-century writers in this study have led me to understand both the strategic value of defining "thinking about another person" exceedingly broadly, *and* the compelling cases to be made for differentiating among kinds of thinking. James Frederick Ferrier – as we shall see shortly – railed against the neat taxonomies of mental "faculties" and functions – reasoning, imagining, remembering – in nineteenth-century psychology because he deemed them false distractions from what ought to be psychology's chief concern: the singular experience of consciousness. Coleridge was fascinated with making taxonomies of mental processes – as when he distinguished "*Thinking* as pure act & energy... *Thinking* as distinguished from *Thoughts*" – and then undoing the distinctions. In a slightly later *Notebook* entry we find him listing mental activities – "psychological Facts," he calls them: "1. We *feel*. 2. we perceive or imagine. 3. we *think*." "Never let me lose my reverence for the *three distinctions*," he vows. Nevertheless, in the same entry he cites approvingly Fichte's tendency to "resolve the 1st and 2nd into the third": "my *Faith* is with Fichte," he exclaims. And then he goes on to add a fourth: "shall we add a 4th, *willing*?"[47]

In my discussions of the nineteenth-century writings I explore in this book, "thinking about another person" deliberately embraces a wide spectrum of mental life: thinking about another person as trying to puzzle them out, certainly, but also thinking about another as reverie, attention, remembrance, or as mental picturing.[48] Sometimes "thinking about another person" consists of ratiocination, and something like propositional internal speech; sometimes it is something closer to an affect or emotion – something like a mental holding of another person, a mental preoccupation that may be experienced as simply the inability to think about anything else. The "about-ness" in "thinking about another person" is sometimes, as in the writings of the theorists of thought-power and thought-transfer in Chapter 2, strongly intentional. That is, it involves concentrated beams of thought directed at another person, as when members of a party at the Rev. Chauncy Hare Townshend's all "have striven silently and mentally to drive [an idea] into [an unwitting visitor's] thoughts."[49] At times, the "about-ness" of thinking about another person shades closer to the more philosophical sense of the intentionality of thought: to be thinking at all is to be thinking about something. My strategy in pulling together texts that reflect on thinking about other people so variously is to establish a wide spectrum of beliefs about mental action. Above all, in seeking to haul radical accounts of thought-power into a consideration of the ordinariness of everyday beliefs and worries about the sociability of thought, I follow the lead of some of the writers discussed here, who were interested in phenomena such as mesmerism precisely because they illuminated every-day thinking about other people. (As one commentator typically noted, "I hold that the mind of a living person, in its most normal state, is always, to a certain extent, acting exoneurally, or beyond the limit of the bodily person.")[50] Nevertheless, *Thinking about Other People* also identifies areas where a distinction among kinds of thinking about another person needs to be refined: in Chapter 3's discussion of second-person thinking, for example, I seek to distinguish what it means to think *to* someone from thinking about them.[51]

This book's emphasis on *thinking* about another is designed above all to explore accounts of thinking as – again, following Coleridge – a form of action, rather than as a synonym for "consciousness." There was of course a huge volume of writing on consciousness in nineteenth-century Britain, though what went under the umbrella of the term "consciousness" waxed and waned as well. For James Frederick Ferrier, as we shall see shortly, consciousness *was* – in his weirdly muscular, eccentric version of ideal-ism – "thinking as pure act & energy" itself. But for most nineteenth-century writers on mind and body, "consciousness" either covers all mental phenomena, or it has the narrower forces of "self-consciousness," an added awareness of self, an understanding familiar from Locke: "consciousness is the perception of what passes in a Man's own mind," and thus it "always accompanies thinking."[52] A book on the meaning of consciousness in nineteenth-century British philosophy, psychology, and literature would be very different from this one: *Thinking about Other People* is specifically focused on the interpersonal effects of thinking conceived as a kind of action, and I hope that the benefits of identifying and exploring a single strand of the incredibly densely woven discourses about the mind in nineteenth-century Britain will become apparent in these pages.

CHAPTER I

Thinking as action: James Frederick Ferrier's Philosophy of Consciousness

In nineteenth-century Britain, the story of thinking about other people was inseparable from the story of the struggle between the different intellectual disciplines that took thinking about other people as their proper business. The tension between psychology and philosophy – overlapping, but increasingly discrete, disciplines – forms a crucial context for this chapter and the next. This chapter explores how the Scottish philosopher James Frederick Ferrier (1808–1864) forged out of this tension an engaging understanding of thinking as a form of action.

The history of psychology in nineteenth-century Britain generally goes like this. Before the nineteenth century, the study of the human mind did not draw clear distinctions between philosophical and psychological speculation, nor did some aspects of human life – the emotions, or perception, for example – belong clearly to one or the other. The dominant intellectual traditions in England and Scotland – empiricism, associationism, and "Common Sense" realism – made the identity of psychology and philosophy particularly durable, well into the nineteenth century. Because, since Locke, anglophone philosophical speculation had largely concerned the origins of ideas in experience, and the laws by which the mind exercised its powers, philosophy was always in essence psychological in orientation: it focused on how the mind is shaped by its environment, and was at least in theory hospitable to empirical testing.

A stricter division between philosophy and psychology evolved gradually over the course of the nineteenth century, owing to a host of factors that included the movement of philosophy, under the influence of idealism and other continental trends, away from empiricist accounts of the mind; the development of the study of the brain within the medical sciences; the development of psychology as a clinical field devoted to the study and treatment of the criminally and mentally ill; the development of psychology as a laboratory science; evolutionary theory; and the general trend towards specialization of fields within the universities.[1] These developments were uneven and slow, and right through the first decades of the twentieth century the fields overlapped, and the words "philosophy" and "psychology" could in some contexts be used sometimes as virtual synonyms, and sometimes cast as sharply drawn antagonists.

In the preface to his massive *Dictionary of Philosophy and Psychology* (1901–1905), James Mark Baldwin gives an account of how the relationship between the two fields looked at the end of the century:

> The association between these two subjects is traditional and, as to their contents, essential. Psychology is the half-way house between biology with the whole range of the objective sciences, on the one hand, and the moral sciences with philosophy, on the other hand ... the rise of experimental and physiological psychology has caused the science to bulk large towards the empirical disciplines, as it always has towards the speculative; and the inroads made by psychological analysis and investigation into the domains where the speculative methods of inquiry, spoken of above, were once exclusively in vogue, render permanent and definite the relation on that side as well.[2]

While Baldwin's account here of the disciplinary promiscuity of psychology may sound familiar, and familiarly triumphal, the contents of the *Dictionary* may seem less so to us: here psychological and philosophical concepts rub shoulders with accounts of the mind – and of relations between minds – that have since been excluded from the disciplines. Here we find "muscle reading" (a kind of mind-reading popular in the 1880s and 1890s); telepathy; and other topics which "may be regarded as having some bearing on the question of the independent existence and activity of mind apart from body" and "of the nature and extent of any influence which may be exerted by one mind upon another, otherwise than through the recognized sensory channels."[3]

In this chapter and the next, I will argue that one of the curious results of the overlaps and, perhaps more important, the antagonisms between philosophy and psychology in nineteenth-century Britain were some lively debates about the power of thinking about other people. I hope to show that in the slow process by which psychology and philosophy got pulled apart from each other, like pieces of sticky taffy, there were strands of thinking that got stretched thin by the process. Some of these strands feature intellectual trends – continental idealism, mesmerism, telepathy – that were ultimately sidelined by psychology, but which sought, throughout the century, to claim a right to address the mysteries of the mind. In some of these we can see accounts of the act of thinking about another person that manifest a fascination with the power one mind might have over another in thought, accounts that seem either to celebrate or worry about a very muscular negativity in the mind's powers.

J. F. Ferrier's conception of thinking as action in his *Introduction to the Philosophy of Consciousness* (1838–1839) emerged from his attempt to rescue psychology from its dominant path in the 1830s. While Ferrier wrote well before the development of psychology as a discrete field of inquiry, the moral and mental sciences of the 1830s were largely shaped by writers who had their roots in eighteenth-century empiricism, and in particular in eighteenth-century associationism. Discovering the laws governing the relations among ideas in the mind was seen as the key to understanding human behavior. Especially tenacious in early nineteenth-century psychological thought was the Scottish, or "Common Sense," school, named by the Scottish philosopher Thomas Reid (1710–1796). In response to the skepticism of David Hume, Reid asserted that common sense rightly allowed us reliably to describe the mind's relation to the world it perceived. From thence, Reid and his enormously influential successors, such as Dugald Stewart (1753–1828), Thomas Brown (1778–1820), and Sir William Hamilton (1788–1856), devoted themselves to increasingly refined taxonomies of the faculties of the mind, focusing on cognition, sensation, and volition.[4] In 1830, Sir William Hamilton published a long essay in the *Edinburgh Review* reviving and defending Reid's "Common Sense" philosophy. This essay, which affirmed, following Reid, how really real are our perceptions of the world, seemed to establish the basic terms of speculative psychology for the decade.[5]

In the *Introduction to the Philosophy of Consciousness*, Ferrier viewed himself as conducting an internal critique of approaches to human mental life in the 1830s. Ferrier's thinking represents a possibility for psychology that went underground for decades: it sought to ground psychology in people's phenomenological experience of mental life.[6] His appeal to change the course of the development of psychology lost out, as psychology as a discrete field would be claimed, for some time to come, by inheritors (such as Alexander Bain, for example) of the empiricist, associationist school against which Ferrier defined himself in the 1830s. In his later work, Ferrier abandoned his attempt to reform psychology, and firmly placed himself on the side of philosophy. He tends to appear only in the footnotes to the history of philosophy, either as the writer who invented the word "epistemology" (in his 1853 *Institutes of Metaphysics*), or as among the first generation of anglophone philosophers who adapted themselves to the work of the German idealists. Thomas De Quincey described his work as "German philosophy refracted through an alien Scottish medium."[7]

Like De Quincey (whose relationship to Ferrier will be discussed in the next section), Ferrier was a fabulous prose stylist, and the style of the *Introduction to the Philosophy of Consciousness* was noted by contemporaries as something completely different from "ordinary metaphysical writing."[8] At least one contemporary shrewdly noted that the *Introduction*'s style was essential to Ferrier's interpretation of "consciousness" as action, and for this reason this chapter shall begin by placing Ferrier not only in the context of early nineteenth-century moral and mental sciences, but also in relation to the world of letters and literature. This chapter will end by considering the implications of Ferrier's conception of mental action for a social theory of thinking about other people, concluding by sketching the relationship between the understanding of mental action that emerges from Ferrier's work, and the controversies surrounding mesmerism in the 1830s and 1840s.

THE PHILOSOPHER AS MAN OF STYLE

The nature of Ferrier's philosophy is inseparable from his literary ambitions and peculiar prose style. The son of a successful Edinburgh lawyer, Ferrier lived at the center of Scottish literary and intellectual circles.[9] Sir Walter Scott was a family friend; the novelist Susan Ferrier (*Marriage*, 1818) was his father's sister; *Blackwood's Edinburgh Magazine* editor John Wilson was his mother's brother and the father of Ferrier's wife, Margaret. Ferrier's own early ambitions were literary. While an undergraduate at Oxford he published a long verse essay in Spenserian stanzas, *The Hope of Immortality* (1829), and he continued to publish on literary topics – reviews, translations, and an essay on translation – for most of his life. When – to settle accounts in a decades-old literary feud – *Blackwood's* needed to do a hatchet-job on Coventry Patmore's *Poems* (1844), Ferrier was their hatchet man. Ferrier thought hard about the relation between literature and philosophy: upon the appearance of *In Memoriam*, Ferrier seriously considered attempting to translate it into philosophical prose, to see if the poem's ideas held up unversified.[10]

After leaving Oxford, Ferrier had a brief career in law, but was drawn back to writing. This time it was philosophical writing, influenced by a trip to Germany in 1834, and a friendship with Sir William Hamilton, one of the few Scottish philosophers to have assimilated Kant. *An Introduction to the Philosophy of Consciousness*, published in seven installments in *Blackwood's* between February 1838 and March 1839, was his first philosophical work. Ferrier's academic career was

marked by conflict. On the success of the *Introduction* and the strength
of his friendship with Hamilton, he was appointed to the chair of Civil
History at Edinburgh, a position, commented a contemporary, "at that
time neither very laborious nor lucrative, and generally looked upon as
likely to be a stepping-stone to some more important professorship."[11]
Ferrier never ascended to that "more important professorship" –
namely, a chair in philosophy at Edinburgh. Though he was deputized
to hold his mentor Hamilton's Chair of Logic and Metaphysics during
Hamilton's illness in 1844–1845, he was not appointed Hamilton's successor upon his death in 1856. More bitterly, he was turned down for the
professorship in Moral Philosophy when that chair was vacated by his
uncle John Wilson's resignation in 1852. Both of Ferrier's candidacies
were foiled by Edinburgh politics, which brought civic controversies,
religious factionalism, academics, and Scottish nationalism together
in a noxious mixture. Ferrier spent the years from 1845 to his death
in 1864 as Professor of Moral Philosophy and Political Economy at St.
Andrews University. His incendiary failures at Edinburgh have seemed,
to those few partisans of Scottish philosophy who have studied his career, an "an academic tragedy" (in the words of his biographer), the event
that effectively closed the curtain on the Scottish Enlightenment and
plunged the Scottish academic world into a dark age of provincialism
and internecine conflict.[12]

One of the people who wrote on Ferrier's behalf for the Edinburgh
Moral Philosophy Chair in 1852 was the prolific, brilliant, but troubled
romantic prose writer Thomas De Quincey. Looking at Ferrier from De
Quincey's point of view provides an invaluable perspective on this Scottish
philosopher. It allows us to establish Ferrier's place in nineteenth-century
literary history, and provides a context and shape for some of the curious
features of his philosophy more effectively than can a retrospective view
of Ferrier from the point of view of the history of philosophy. Writing of
Ferrier, De Quincey's emphasis falls, tellingly, mostly on the philosopher's
prose style. After the first round of praise in his "Testimonial" for Ferrier's
philosophical works, he remarks that "universally, I ought to add by the
way":

These writings of Mr Ferrier, so remarkable for their Graeco-German subtlety,
drew no privilege of careless style from the weight of their matter; but, on the
contrary, were distinguished by the felicitous beauty of their illustrations, and
the precision of the language. These merits were not likely to be lost upon myself,
who have at all periods of my life carried to an excess, (if excess were possible,) the
culture of my mother tongue.[13]

Whatever his subject, De Quincey's writings almost always shade into autobiography, and as the typically self-aggrandizing and self-deprecating last sentence here suggests, this was certainly true of his writings on Ferrier. They are notable not just for their characterizations of Ferrier, but also for their author's identifications with their subject, and for a pathos that is De Quincey's own. The relation between the two must have been vexed, at least from De Quincey's perspective. As he points out in this "Testimonial," he had known Ferrier since the latter was a very young man, as the nephew of John Wilson. What he does not point out is that for part of this time, De Quincey was living in Wilson's house (as was Ferrier, intermittently), helping Wilson write his lectures as Professor of Moral Philosophy, a post for which Wilson was seriously underqualified.[14] De Quincey and Ferrier did similar kinds of writing – on philosophy and German literature – for *Blackwood's*, and De Quincey seems to have experienced the younger, more entitled man as his rival for the position of dutiful son and heir of Wilson. Throughout the "Testimonial," one can hear shades of resentment amidst the praise, not unlike the resentment one can hear in De Quincey's reminiscences of his more famous contemporaries, Wordsworth and Coleridge. De Quincey's characterization of Ferrier's work as "German philosophy refracted through an alien Scottish medium" is presented not as an account of Ferrier's own achievement, but rather as something he inherited along with his other advantages: "it was for Mr Ferrier an incalculable benefit that he was introduced, as if suddenly stepping into an inheritance, to a German philosophy refracted through an alien Scottish medium" (253–54). He was to the manor, or perhaps manner, born: Ferrier's very stylishness as a writer is attributed to fortunate family connections. He was able, De Quincey insinuates, to make room for style in philosophy by channeling the more severe logical philosophy of his mentor, Sir William Hamilton, along with the literary flair of his uncle, John Wilson (253).

It is, moreover, the very way in which Ferrier, at least in the early part of his career, hovered between professional philosopher and "man of letters" that prompts the deepest bitterness and self-recognition in De Quincey. In a manuscript essay probably written not long after the publication of the *Introduction to the Philosophy of Consciousness*, De Quincey speculates about what would have happened to Ferrier had he not become an academic. Speaking of some undefined time – perhaps precisely the time of the *Introduction*, which was well before he formally began what another contemporary called his "really philosophical life"[15] – at which Ferrier among the host of other scholars and

philosophers with "multiplied claims on my attention" attracted his
notice, De Quincey writes:

In this case I had no reason whatever for believing that Mr. Ferrier would dedicate himself to an academic life: and, unless it should be through books, I knew
of no way through which he could powerfully operate upon the philosophic
mind of the nation. But as I also knew the tendency of luxurious literary ease to
poison the wellhead of any large or systematic activity, such as was needed if the
whole machinery of his intellect were to be worked beneficially, I might gradually, through mere despondency as to any prospect so large as this, have suffered
the whole interest to droop in my own thoughts. Within his own library, and left
entirely to himself, I feared (which there might after all be really no reason for
fearing) that Mr. F would begin "to work short time"; that one loom would be
stopped after another; and not from any drooping of the central activity, but for
the very opposite reason – for an activity self-baffled by the mere infinity of its
objects.[16]

For De Quincey, to think about Ferrier was to think about himself. In
addition to his rueful admission about his own intimacy with what he
terms "the tendency of luxurious literary ease," the doubling between De
Quincey and Ferrier is also signaled by the two "droopings" of thought
here. The first is the probability that, without Ferrier's move to professor-
dom, De Quincey's interest in him would "droop" in his thoughts. The
second drooping is the probability that, without this move, Ferrier himself
would have foundered, not by "drooping" but via a syndrome De Quincey
knew well: losing himself in the undisciplined maze of thought. Without
the academic career, in other words, Ferrier would have become Thomas
De Quincey: philosopher manqué; failed systematizer; hack writer bur-
dened not by too few but by too many subjects; a broken loom; poisoned
by the luxury of the "literary ease" of the professionally unprofessional
man of letters.

Looking at Ferrier from the point of view of De Quincey thus provides
us with at least several valuable things. First, we must take seriously the
surprise De Quincey registers about Ferrier's turn of career: this is a genuine record of a life that *could* have unfolded differently, and of a difference
that must be seen as internal to Ferrier's writing. Second, De Quincey's
crazy prose registers with great suggestiveness the strange space in which
both his and Ferrier's writing takes place: this is a meditation on the relation of "philosophy" to prose, to the world of letters, and to labor and
industry – not only the machinery of the mind, but also the working of
the looms of a serialized publication such as *Blackwood's*, and the echoes
of the other looms clacking away, or striking, in the 1830s.

De Quincey's near-contemporary remarks thus illuminate the terms of Ferrier's self-fashioning in *An Introduction to the Philosophy of Consciousness*, as does the context of its publication in *Blackwood's Edinburgh Magazine*. Founded in 1817 as a more daring (and more Tory) foil to the *Edinburgh Review*, *Blackwood's* was, by Ferrier's time, not quite as intemperate as it had been in the teens and twenties. But it still was a magazine with a strong personality, that was, moreover, collectively dedicated to the creation of personalities.[17] Under the leadership of Ferrier's uncle Wilson, its style remained outrageous, scandalous, and inconsistent. In one episode of *Blackwood's* fictionalized bar-room conversation, the *Noctes Ambrosianae*, "De Quincey" remarks to "Hogg" (an exaggerated version of the actual poet and novelist James Hogg), "Sir, *you have no common sense*, and that in this age is the highest praise that can be bestowed on the immortal soul of man."[18] Ferrier's philosophical routing of "Common Sense" philosophy in the pages of *Blackwood's* must be seen as deriving some of its energy from the magazine's general refusal of received Edinburgh ideas.

The prose of Ferrier's *Introduction* is emphatically a *Blackwood's* style – polemical, flamboyant, highly metaphorical, and not unlike that of Thomas De Quincey, whose prose style clearly served as a powerful model and example. To his contemporaries, Ferrier remained a stylish "man of letters" (and also, apparently, a stylish dresser, a handsome dandy) as well as a philosopher throughout his life: "the signal example in Scotland of an alliance of artistic beauty with abstract philosophy."[19] For Ferrier, the will to philosophize is inseparable from becoming a man of letters. In the *Introduction to the Philosophy of Consciousness*, self, style, and argument are cognates of each other. Ferrier's philosophy describes the way men are made out of letters, as words, letters, and persons all become identical to each other, in order to animate the act of thinking.

DEMOLISHING "THE MIND"

Ferrier's essay begins as a witty, impassioned attack on what he sees as the fundamental folly of the moral and mental sciences of his day: the notion that there is such a thing as "the mind." The empiricist philosophy of mind that began with Locke and dominated English and Scottish thought in the early nineteenth century took "the mind" as its object of study, and sought to observe and to classify the mind's states, capacities, and powers. Ferrier's particular animus is directed at "our Scottish philosophers": Thomas Reid, Dugald Stewart, and above all Dr. Thomas Brown, author of the post-humously published, widely read *Lectures on the Philosophy of the Human*

Mind (1820). Brown's first premise is that the mind may be studied as a scientific object:

The mind, it is evident, may, like the body to which it is united, or the material objects which surround it, be considered simply as a substance possessing certain qualities, susceptible of various affections or modifications, which, existing successively as momentary states of the mind, constitute all the phenomena of thought and feeling.[20]

For Brown, the anomaly of the mental sciences – that the object of study is also the "instrument" of the science – provides their special interest and delight. In contrast to other sciences, he claims, "No costly apparatus is requisite – no tedious waiting for seasons of observation." "He has but to look within himself to find the elements which he has to put together, or the compounds which he has to analyze, and the instruments that are to perform the analysis or composition" (1.100–101).

Ferrier's position is that the mind "is altogether inconceivable as an *object* of thought."[21] To model the study of mental life on the study of matter, as Brown and other advocates of the "mental sciences" did, is a fundamental distortion. When the scientist of the mind claims to study "the mind," he effectively splits his mental apparatus into two: the I that thinks, and the mind that is thought about. Even worse, in "the current metaphysical language of the day," Ferrier declares:

Man consists of *three* elements, mind, body, and *himself* possessing both. This view of the subject may be disclaimed and protested against in words, but still it continues virtually to form the leading idea of the whole of our popular psychology. We may, indeed, be told that "mind" and ourselves are identical, but this statement is never acted upon to any real purpose … If it were, then "mind" would be altogether annihilated as an *object* of investigation. (23–24)

Studying "the mind" is both a grammatical and a logical impossibility, for to make an object of mind is to deprive it of consciousness. The scientist of the mind may wish to grant "consciousness" as a state or attribute to "the mind," and in writing about the mind's "varieties of 'feeling,' 'passion,'" and "states of mind," he effectively "vest[s] [the mind] with its own personality" (28, 30). And yet, when he says, "I think about the mind," "It will be found that the fact of consciousness clings on the one side of the inquiring subject ('I')" (30). When this happens, any consciousness attributed to the mind as an object gets sucked out, as in a vacuum.

Under these conditions, to think about "the mind" may be to "vest it with its own personality," but it is only a fictitious personality. The mind can only ever be an object "in a fictitious sense, and being so, is, therefore, only a fictitious object, and consequently the science of it is also a fiction and an imposture" (31). For Ferrier, to think about "the mind" is to think about a fictitious nobody, a monstrous character with no consciousness, neither the inquirer him or herself, nor anybody else. It is a fictitious being who stands between the human being and the world, a soul-less Frankenstein monster, a "mutilated skeleton" (12) who ought to "perish" (32). In a strange drama of animation and de-animation, the scientists of the mind are always killing "the human mind" in the act of establishing its very existence:

The human mind, not to speak it profanely, is like the goose that laid golden eggs. The metaphysician resembles the analytic poulterer who slew it to get at them in a lump, and found *nothing* for his pains. Leave the mind to its own natural workings, as manifested in the imagination of the poet, the fire and rapid combinations of the orator, the memory of the mathematician, the gigantic activities and never-failing resources of the warrior and statesman, or even in the manifold powers put forth in everyday life by the most ordinary of men; and what can be more wonderful and precious than its productions? Cut into it metaphysically, with a view of grasping the embryo truth, and of ascertaining the process by which all these bright results are elaborated in the womb, and every trace of "what has been" vanishes beneath the knife. (16–17)

Therefore, the way to establish a "philosophy of consciousness" is "by brushing away the human mind" (31): "our very first act will be to fling 'the mind' with all its lumber overboard" (54).

It is worth dwelling on the intensity, and on the rhetoric both polemical and nautical, of Ferrier's hostility to "the mind." For it may seem strange for a proponent of philosophy and a better psychology to be so hell-bent on demonstrating that the mind ("this hypothetical substance," he calls it [177]) doesn't exist: throwing the book at it. It can seem willfully anti-intellectual at times, a pyrrhic protest against the "common sense" that tells us that we ourselves as well as other people do indeed have minds we can make claims about, and do all the time. The negative energy of Ferrier's attack was not lost on his contemporaries. The theologian John Tulloch shrewdly argued that the force, the "*brusquerie*," of Ferrier's assault on Scottish philosophy was essential to clearing a new space. In turning to the *Introduction* "from ordinary metaphysical writing," Tulloch noted:

It is impossible not to be struck by its singular richness, life, and vigour, and a certain charm of enthusiasm which never allows the reader's interest to flag. It serves, moreover, to fix his starting-point in philosophy, both negatively and positively. From the first, it is obvious that he not only swerved aside from the path of the old Scottish philosophy, but ran right against it.

"But it is also obvious that it was no love of mere destruction which animated him," continues Tulloch.[22] The antagonistic stance is indeed
extremely productive for Ferrier. In revealing "the mind" to be a kind of
pseudo-personification, a monstrous person who logically stands apart from
the I who professes to observe it, and then attacking it mercilessly, Ferrier
mobilizes "the mind" as a kind of personification of the mental scientists –
Brown, Dugald Stewart, and others – that he is arguing with. "The mind,"
personified as a static, un-personed person – a hollow man, or some inverted
version of the Scarecrow from *The Wizard of Oz* (who has a personality, but
no brain) – emerges off the pages of Ferrier's text in and through his quarrel
with the associationists. The appearance of "mind" in the *Introduction* as a
non-person we can't think about is itself part of the fallout of the disciplinary divisions Ferrier is policing. However, it is also worth dwelling on the
emphasis on "first act" here ("our very first act will be to fling 'the mind'
with all its lumber overboard"). As we shall see, there is a strong connection
between Ferrier's polemicism and the *Introduction*'s concept of consciousness as primary action.

WORDS AND ACTS

Ferrier's alternative to the rule of "mind" consists of words and acts: words
as acts *as* thoughts. He begins with words, proposing a kind of ordinary
language test on "mind":

> The word "mind" is exceedingly remote and ambiguous, and denotes – nobody
> knows what. Let us then substitute in place of it that much plainer expression which
> everybody makes use of, and in some degree, at least, understands – the expression
> "I" or "me," and let us see how mind, with its facts and doctrines, will fare when
> this simple, unpretending, and unhypothetical word is employed in its place. (128)

Through a series of sentence-experiments in which he replaces the "mind"
in the sentences of mental scientists with "I" or "me," Ferrier builds his
case. As he demonstrates through these experiments, "I" is hardly a "simple, unpretending, and unhypothetical word" even though "every body
makes use of" it (128). In terms of determinate content, it is an extremely
thin word, a word of less semantic "meaning" even than "mind." Its significance lies exclusively in use, and in use it is a magic syllable:

> We have read in fable of Circean charms, which changed men into brutes; but
> here in this little monosyllable is contained a true and more potent charm, the
> spell of an inverted and unfabulous enchantment, which converts the *feral* into
> the *human* being. (109; emphasis in original)

Ferrier's emphasis on the speech act underwrites his story of human development, in which the fundamental transition takes place when the young child ceases to refer to himself [*sic*] in the third person, and "pronounces the word 'I.'" This is a word whose meaning, Ferrier insists, no-one can teach a child (106–9); he can only understand it at the moment he speaks it, and in speaking it, becomes it.

Ferrier's emphasis on "I" as a magic syllable that makes "*human* beings," moreover, has particular resonances in the pages of *Blackwood's* where the *Introduction* appears. As we noted earlier, the *Blackwood's* context for the *Introduction to the Philosophy of Consciousness* renders philosophy a mode of textual self-fashioning. *Blackwood's* in general was no stranger to the magical "I" in its pages, creating persons who had a real existence there who were only dubiously related to persons in the real world. This was especially true in a long-standing series of episodes that appeared in the magazine from 1823 to 1835, the *Noctes Ambrosianae*, a series of dialogues alleging to be transcriptions of lively evenings at Ambrose's tavern in Edinburgh attended by John Wilson, Thomas De Quincey, James Hogg, and others in Ferrier's circle. Mostly penned by John Wilson but many of uncertain authorship, these fictitious debates were later laboriously, filially edited by Ferrier in his edition of Wilson's *Works* (1855–1858). Ferrier acknowledged that "the *true* Ambrose's must be looked for only in the realms of the imagination" and that its characters, "although founded to some extent on the actual," existed only in the pages of the magazine. To Ferrier fell the responsibility of annotating the *Noctes*, translating the Scottishisms and local lore for a broader audience, and sorting out for that audience who were "purely fictitious characters," who were pseudonymous versions of real people, and who were speaking *in propria persona* (these three categories of persons often speaking together in a single dialogue).[23] In the pages of *Blackwood's*, the people made out of words are the close neighbors of the "unfabulous" human-being creating "enchantment" of the magical "I" of Ferrier's account.[24]

It is the act of saying or – as it emerges a bit later – more importantly *thinking* "I" that *is* consciousness. But just as what Ferrier means by "I" is not really ego, or self, or self-knowledge, what he means by "consciousness" is not what either Locke or most nineteenth-century British philosophical and psychological usages took it to mean: awareness of what is going on in our minds. Here is Thomas Reid's definition, from his *Essays on the Intellectual Powers of Man* (1785): "consciousness is a word used by philosophers, to signify that immediate knowledge we have of our present thoughts and purposes, and, in general, of all the present operations of our minds."[25] Contra Reid, Thomas Brown, and the other classifiers of static "states" of consciousness, Ferrier establishes consciousness as an act, the act of saying or thinking "I." It is synonymous with thinking itself. Thinking "this small word of one letter" supersedes the emphasis on saying, as Ferrier enlists Descartes on his side in an eccentric interpretation of Descartes' *cogito ergo sum*. For Ferrier, the *cogito* is significant because through it "the attention of psychologists was first distinctly directed to the only known instance in which ... *a thought* is the same as *a thing*" (140). The thought "I," moreover, is not only the same as the existence of "I," here defined as "consciousness, or the notion of self"; it creates it, brings it into being (139).

Ferrier vigorously denies the original import of Descartes' phrase in the *Discourse on Method*. There, Descartes is responding to questions of skepticism, questions about how we *know* we exist, about the difference between body and mind. As many commentators have pointed out, it contains a pretty thin notion of the "I": in Bertrand Russell's words, it is a mere "grammatical convenience."[26] Ferrier defends his novel interpretation of the *cogito* first by speaking for Descartes, and then introducing a character "Descartes" to speak for himself. In answer to the possible objection that the design of the *cogito* might have been "to prove his own existence," Ferrier declares, "Take our word for it, no such miserable intention ever entered into his head" (140). Then, as if to affirm that Descartes must have had a stronger commitment to the power of the thinking "I" to create itself, Ferrier has Descartes speak up *in propria persona* in dialogue with a skeptic who asks whether he has claimed to have created himself:

"No," replies Descartes; "I did not create myself, in so far as my mere existence is concerned. But, in so far as I am an *ego*, or an existence *as a self*, I certainly did create myself. By becoming conscious, I, in one sense, actually created myself." (141)

It is hard not to feel here that Ferrier has taken a page, as it were, from the *Noctes Ambrosianae* of his uncle Wilson and his circle, in which fictitious versions of real people are made to say all kind of ridiculous things (such as, "sir, *you have no common sense*"). The literary power of the "small word of one letter" is essential to Ferrier's conception of thinking as action that makes things happen.

NEGATION

Through his meditations on the word "I," Ferrier puts forth a conception of consciousness as a self-creating action. "The thought 'I' precedes and brings along with it the reality or existence 'I,' and ... this thought 'I' is an act." This is the "important truth in psychology," he declares (160–61). This act turns on its head the empiricist tradition which sees self as developed out of accumulation of sensations and reflections. For Ferrier, consciousness is actively antagonistic to sensation: "consciousness does not come into operation *in consequence* of these states [of sensation and feeling], but *in spite* of them: it does not come into play to increase and foster these states, but only actively to suspend, control, or put a stop to them." States of sensation exist, in fact "because unless they existed there would be nothing for it to combat, to weaken, or destroy" (79–80).

There are methodological, ontological, and ethical components to Ferrier's Terminator-like (put on this planet "actively to suspend, control, or … stop"; "to combat, to weaken, or destroy") conception of consciousness. It first of all has consequences for the nature of psychology as a discipline and a method. Methodology ought to follow reality: the psychologist or philosopher ought not start with the various faculties of "mind" which are, if they exist at all, "secondary in his actual development," but should begin his studies where the human being begins, with the act:

Therefore, in speculation he ought to follow the same order; and, copying the living truth of things in his methodological exposition of himself, should take this act as the primary commencement or starting-point of his philosophical researches. Such, in our opinion, is the only true method of psychological science. (161)

Cutting consciousness loose from sensation, moreover, Ferrier is pressed to explain where the act of consciousness, this original and first act, comes from: "how can a man *act* before he *is*?" (159). Prior to the act of consciousness, man does exist as a creature of God. Before the act there is an unconscious Being; with the act there is a personality:

We maintain, further, that this personality, realised by consciousness, is a new kind of existence reared up upon the ground of that act; that, further, there was no provision made in the old *substratum* of unconscious Being for the evolution of this new act; but that, like the fall of man (with which perhaps it is some way connected), it is an absolutely free and underived deed, self-originated, and entirely exempt from the law of causality; and moreover, in its very essence, the antagonist of that law. (160)

This "big bang" theory of the origin of consciousness establishes above all Ferrier's debts to the German idealists he had been reading since his journey there in 1834, in particular to Fichte. Fichte, whose *Wissenschaftslehre* (1794) was ranked by Friedrich Schlegel as one of the three world-shaking

events of the age (along with Goethe's *Wilhelm Meister* and the French
Revolution), proposed a transcendental account of the self that seemed too
extreme for most contemporary anglophone thinkers. Even for Coleridge,
who dismisses Fichte in the *Biographia Literaria*:

> Fichte's *Wissenschaftslehre*, or *Lore* of Ultimate Science, was to add the key-stone
> of the arch [of idealist philosophy]: and by commencing with an *act*, instead of a
> thing or substance, Fichte assuredly ... supplied the *idea* of a system truly meta-
> physical, and of a *metaphysique* truly systematic: (i.e. having its spring and prin-
> ciple within itself). But this fundamental idea he overbuilt with a heavy mass of
> mere *notions*, and psychological acts of arbitrary reflection.[27]

"Thus," concludes Coleridge, "his theory degenerated into a crude
egoismus."

Fichte's loyal defenders (then and now) can protest against Coleridge's
charge of crude egotism by detailing the incredible complexity and multi-
plicity of Fichte's *Ich*s. Fichte conceived of the I as a *Tathandlung*, a "deed-
action," something that absolutely "posits" itself:

> The I is what posits itself, and it is nothing more than this. What posits itself is
> the I and nothing more. Nothing else but the I is produced by the act we have
> just described; and the I can be produced by no other possible act except the one
> described.[28]

Fichte elaborated the self-positing I as a response to gaps in Kant: Kant's
inability to account for consciousness; the necessity for the transcendental self to be a spontaneous, *a priori* form of human knowledge; the gap
between the absolute self and any empirical self. Fichte's system (subjected
to many elaborations and revisions during his lifetime) does distinguish
between the absolute I and the empirical I; it was compelled by the paradoxes of self-consciousness to posit an I that is split and splittable.[29]

While Ferrier's approach to thinking is fundamentally Fichtean, the
Introduction to the Philosophy of Consciousness effects a drastic transformation. For Ferrier, there is no distinguishing among different kinds of "I."
Moreover, without the concept of *setzen*, or positing, to describe what it
is the self is and does, Ferrier's system curiously seems to put the weight
of self-creation on ordinary selves and the ordinary act of *thinking*. This
effect is also underscored by the extreme difference made by the context
Ferrier creates for his theory of consciousness: he is truly trying to effect
a method of proceeding for an experience-based *psychology*; and it matters
a huge amount that he describes his arrival at this account of the thinking self as a response to Scottish empiricist mental sciences, not to Kant.
We will address the net effect of Ferrier's channeling of German idealism

"though an alien Scottish medium," as De Quincey phrased it, in the next section. But first we must address Ferrier's emphasis on negation.

From the German philosophers, of course, Ferrier derived his concept of negation. The act of thinking "I" is in essence an act of negation. It is the bringing of the self or I into existence by negating all that is not I: "Unless a man discriminates himself as 'I' from other things, he does not exist as 'I.'"[30] Negation makes all other mental operations, including our perceptions of the outside world, possible. We could not perceive and know a rose if the rose were not discriminated from the self; negation renders the rose an object to our subjecthood (176). Ferrier thus defines consciousness not simply as an act, but as an act of negation: "consciousness ... is the discrimination between the *ego* and the *non-ego*; or, in other words, consciousness resolves itself, in its clearest form, into an act of negation" (144). Ferrier sometimes seems to fudge the relation between the act of negation, and the act of thinking "I," as for example in this passage: "We may say, if we please, that this act of negation is the *act* "*I*," but not that it arises out of the being "I" (181). We are likely to be thrown off by the diffidence of that "if we please" about what would seem to be such a crucial issue for the philosopher. But most of the time Ferrier refers to "the act of negation or consciousness" in one breath; the two are synonymous (182).

Ferrier's understanding of negation provides us with another example of how distinctive Ferrier's thought is, cut loose from its influence or sources. Like his understanding of thinking itself, Ferrier's negation involves a more dynamic negativity, not only establishing the difference between the I and the not-I, between ourselves and the rose, or between canceling and preserving (as in Hegel), but heroically reducing all that's made into a green thought in a green shade.[31] Ferrier really suggests that when we think, we are saying "no" to the world; here as elsewhere his emphatically linguistic turn on idealist philosophy makes word magic. His discussion of negation ends in wild philological speculation:

It is curious to observe how completely these views, in which we identify perception with a primary act of negation, are borne out by certain philological coincidences, which are, assuredly, not accidental, but based upon deeper reflection than we well know how to fathom. Thus, in Greek, there is the verb εω, I am: then, anterior to this, in the order of thought, there is νο-εω (primary meaning), I am – *with a negation*. (Secondary meaning) I *perceive*; showing how sensible the founders of the Greek language were, that all perception is ultimately founded on negation and identical with it; that an act of negation is, in fact, the very condition upon which perception depends. Our own word "know" also clearly betokens this – it is nothing but "no," and knowledge, from lowest to highest, is merely the constant alleging "no" of things, or, in other words, a continual process of denying them, first of ourselves, and then of one another: – of course we mean not only in word, but also in thought and in deed. Besides γινωσκω, in Greek, there is, in Latin, *nosco*, or *nonsco*, – all words denoting knowledge, and all carrying *negative* signs upon their very fronts.[32]

Needless to say, all of the etymologies in this passage are completely false; there is no basis in any language for Ferrier's assertion that "know" means "no" and "nothing but 'no'." But Ferrier's eccentric etymologies here allow him once again to animate little words, so that word and thought and deed are continuous. Here all knowledge words are not only falsely etymologized, they are also pseudo-personified. At the end of the passage this litany of words has become a kind of parade, a line of protesters or picketers, "all carrying *negative* signs on their very fronts." Like Wordsworth's blind beggar who wears "upon his chest / … a written paper," which "label was a type, / Or emblem of the utmost that we know," Ferrier's words carrying signs on their fronts get their force because they seem to blur the boundary between human forms and linguistic forms. Ferrier's concept of negation may nominally wear – a little like that other sign-wearing negative, Sigmund Freud's "no" which is a "certificate of origin" for repression – a tag that says "Made in Germany," but his strangely literal understanding of negation is all his own.[33]

FERRIER AND THE ETHICS OF THINKING

In spite of its idiosyncrasies, Ferrier's understanding of thinking as heroic action bears distinct affinities with that of another Scottish idealist, Thomas Carlyle. Writing *Heroes and Hero-Worship* (1841) around the same time as the publication of Ferrier's *Philosophy of Consciousness*, Carlyle similarly glorifies thinkers as well as thinking itself as heroic action:

It is the *Thought* of man; the true thaumaturgic virtue; by which man works all things whatsoever. All that he does, and brings to pass, is the vesture of a Thought. This London City, with all its houses, palaces, steamengines, cathedrals, and huge immeasurable traffic and tumult, what is it but a Thought, but millions of Thoughts made into One; – a huge immeasurable Spirit of a THOUGHT, embodied in brick, in iron, smoke, dust, Palaces, Parliaments, Hackney Coaches, Katherine Docks, and the rest of it! Not a brick was made but some man had to *think* of the making of that brick. – The thing we called "bits of paper with traces of black ink," is the *purest* embodiment a Thought of man can have. No wonder it is, in all ways, the activest and noblest.[34]

Carlyle's concern is with the exceptional "Thinker, the spiritual Hero" (20). However, for Ferrier, the ultimate justification of this extremely muscular view of consciousness is that it reveals the fundamental unity of psychology and moral philosophy. It reveals humans' essential freedom: if "consciousness is action," then it "is not itself derivative, but is an absolutely original act; or, in other words, an act of perfect freedom" (183). If the act of thinking is always an act of negating all that is not consciousness itself, consciousness is fundamentally antagonistic to nature, to sensation, and to passion, and thus the act of thinking is always a practical and moral act: "what act can be attended by a more practical result than the act by which we look our passions in the face, and, in the very act of looking at them, *look them down?*" (201).

To paraphrase Jane Austen, this may be strange morality to end with (*Persuasion*: "This may be bad morality to conclude with, but I believe it to be truth."). It is worth noting how very far Ferrier's moral philosophy is from that of the Scottish Enlightenment writers who preceded him. For David Hume and Adam Smith, moral philosophy was concerned with theorizing social relations, emphasizing how we think about other people through sympathy. For Smith in particular, sociability itself consists of mental acts. In the *Theory of Moral Sentiments* (1759), the acts of imagining, and representing to oneself, the feelings of other people are the bases of both moral judgment and the emotions of fellow feeling. The *Theory* begins, famously, by appealing to the problem of other minds, in particular the sufferings of another: "as long as we ourselves are at our ease, our senses will never inform us of what he suffers. They never did, and never can, carry us beyond our own person, and it is by the imagination only that we can form any conception of what are his sensations."[35] Sociability is founded on picturing the contents of other minds: the epistemological problem of knowing others is the center around which Smith's social and ethical theory is organized.

In Ferrier, this influential tradition seems to have gone (to use his colorful term) overboard – along with the idea of "the mind" itself.[36] If morality is linked directly to the primary act of thinking itself, there doesn't seem to be much room for other people. But the background of Scottish social theory is crucial to understanding how and why the act of thinking about another person might have been so much stranger for Ferrier and other nineteenth-century writers than for the epistemologically oriented eighteenth-century philosophers. "Thinking about another person" no longer necessarily refers to the mental picturing imagined by the Scottish Enlightenment social theorists: if to think about "the mind" is to suck consciousness, which "clings to the I," out of it, to think about another is to negate. In Chapters 3 and 4 of the current study, we shall explore the link between negativity, negation, and the act of thinking about another person in nineteenth-century poetry and poetics. Studying Ferrier alerts us to the role of early nineteenth-century British idealism in shifting the problem of thinking about other people in this direction. In British idealist philosophy itself, the articulation of a positive ethics and social theory did not emerge until the 1870s, in the work of T. H. Green (1836–1882) and F. H. Bradley (1846–1924). Emphasizing the ways in which the self is realized in social relations and social roles, Green and Bradley viewed their work as a corrective to both the shriveled sense of what a person is in Victorian utilitarianism, and the overly inflated sense of what a person is in Ferrier.[37]

But it may also be Ferrier's emphasis on word magic in his discussion of negation – Ferrier's strange and fallacious literalism about "know" and "no" – that suggests what may be most interesting for our purposes about the *Introduction to the Philosophy of Consciousness*. Ferrier's enlisting all the "no" words to wear the signs and do the work of negation ought first of all – like the other passages in the *Introduction to the Philosophy of Consciousness* where words, thoughts, and deeds fluidly merge together – to make us reflect again on the negative energy of his attack on the concept of the "mind." His polemical, colorful, throwing-the-mind-overboard language occurs in the context of a theory in which thinking creates through negating, and words do the work. The personality that is fashioned through the style of the *Introduction* – combative, polemical – *is* the personality of the all-negating "I" personified, fleshed out, as it were, through words. The antagonisms within the self – between thinking and sensation, for example – are the image, writ small (or, perhaps, large) of the antagonisms between the disciplines responsible for analyzing the mind. The passages of Ferrier's text most endowed with personality – such as the episode featuring Descartes, and the "know means 'no'" passage – also remind us that Ferrier's *Blackwood's* essays on consciousness are never simply channeling Fichte, but engaging in a stronger transformation. As German idealist ideas about thinking take shape in Ferrier's Scottish, worldly manner, they come to seem endowed with a kind of charisma, instinct with personality and with animistic power. Claims about the self-and-world positing powers of mind come to seem less idealist, less transcendental, and more like an account of the omnipotence of ordinary thinking.

As usual, De Quincey got it right. His memorable phrase for Ferrier's philosophy, "German philosophy refracted through an alien Scottish medium," points to a crucial constellation of contexts. His terms come, first of all, from optics, which was (as it happens) a lively field of scientific inquiry in Ferrier's world. De Quincey's terms would have resonated with the work of Sir David Brewster, who was Principal of St. Andrews University during Ferrier's tenure there (the two were often close allies). Brewster established crucial advances in optics, including the Laws of Refraction; he invented the kaleidoscope and the stereoscope, and was instrumental to early developments in photography. Both "refraction" and "medium" would have had optics as their primary context, as in this definition of "refraction," from Baldwin's *Dictionary of Philosophy and Psychology*: "the change of direction of rays of light, waves of sound, &c., which are obliquely incident to, and traverse a smooth surface bounding two heterogeneous media, or which traverse a medium of varying density."[38]

However, in nineteenth-century Britain, and in particularly in the 1830s and 1840s when De Quincey and Ferrier were writing, the phrase "alien [Scottish] medium" would also have resonated with a subject whose relation to science was less certain. Here is Baldwin's secondary definition for "medium":

A term applied, in connection with the phenomena of ANIMAL MAGNETISM, HYPNOTISM, and SPIRITUALISM, to a person whose speech and action are supposed to be controlled by a foreign personality or by a disembodied spirit, and who speaks from knowledge gained in some super-natural manner; also called "a sensitive."[39]

"Animal Magnetism" was a preferred term for mesmerism. One of the period's most influential treatises on mesmerism (which both De Quincey and Ferrier read), the Reverend Chauncy Hare Townshend's *Facts in Mesmerism, with Reasons for a Dispassionate Inquiry into It* (1840), refined the term "mesmeric medium" to designate not the person controlled by alien influences, but rather some kind of substance in the world, the existence of which he could only – but felt compelled to, by the evidence – infer, that permitted a mesmerist's mental action to influence another person.[40]

Following these leads, we could say that, in describing Ferrier's *Philosophy of Consciousness* as "German philosophy refracted through an alien Scottish medium," De Quincey was in part suggesting that Ferrier was capable of magically animating it. That Ferrier himself fashioned his own identity as philosopher on the model of medium or magician might be affirmed by turning to the opening pages of the *Introduction to the Philosophy of Consciousness*. There we find that Ferrier chose to open his philosophically essay with a parable: "Among the fables of the East there is a story that runs thus," the treatise begins. It is an Oriental tale about a youth who inherits a magic lamp, powerful enough to supply just money and jewels enough to satisfy his daily needs. Dissatisfied (of course) and wanting more, the youth seeks out a magician, who tells the youth that he can reveal ways to get endless wealth from the lamp, but warns him not to do it. The youth ignores (of course) the magician's warning, works the spell on the magic lamp, and is destroyed. "Reader!" apostrophizes Ferrier at the end of this tale. "This lamp is typical of thy natural understanding ... Therefore be not too inquisitive about it," he cautions, thus aligning himself with the magician in the story (4). The mind-magic of mesmerism was a crucial part of how nineteenth-century British writers imagined the act of thinking about another person.

FERRIER, MESMERISM, AND THINKING ABOUT OTHER PEOPLE

In 1838 and 1839, Ferrier's friend and mentor Sir William Hamilton held a private, advanced class in metaphysics which met at his home. According to one of the students (Alexander Campbell Fraser, later a rival of Ferrier's in one of his unsuccessful bids for a chair of philosophy at Edinburgh), "Ferrier was sometimes of the party on these occasions." Ferrier at that time was neither a professor nor a student, but still a lawyer and a writer; these occasions seem to have coincided with the writing and publication of the *Introduction to the Philosophy of Consciousness*. The instruction in metaphysics at Hamilton's included experiments in mesmerism. Fraser recounts Ferrier's involvement:

I remember the interest he took in phenomena of "mesmeric sleep," as it was called. An eminent student was sometimes induced for experiment to submit himself to mesmeric influence at these now far-off evening gatherings at Sir William's. To Ferrier the phenomena suggested curious speculation, but I think without scientific result.[41]

These experiments seemed to have gained Ferrier the antipathy of another one of his future enemies, John Cairns, a favorite student of Hamilton's who apparently received mockery from Ferrier at some of his outbursts "freed from the inhibitions of ordinary social intercourse" afforded by mesmeric trance.[42]

Everybody in the British Isles was interested in mesmerism in 1838–1839. Originally brought to England in the late eighteenth century by the writings and reputation of Franz Anton Mesmer (1733–1815), the Swiss doctor who claimed to have discovered a magnetic power that allowed one mind to place another into an altered state, mesmerism had a new life in the 1830s. Owing primarily to its partial rehabilitation by the French Royal Society in 1824, mesmerism had crossed the Channel again in the late 1820s and 1830s, and had become a craze. In 1838, under the auspices of the physician Sir John Elliotson, a committee of scientists at University College Hospital in London conducted a series of highly publicized demonstrations. Thomas De Quincey wrote that "animal magnetism" would produce "nothing less than a new world to the prospects of Psychology, and, generally speaking, to the knowledge of the human mind."[43]

This is the context in which the experiments in the philosopher Sir William Hamilton's parlor in Edinburgh took place, and this is the context in which Ferrier's *Introduction to the Philosophy of Consciousness* was written.[44] In her landmark study *Mesmerized: Powers of Mind in Victorian Britain*, Alison Winter demonstrates that mesmerism flourished precisely in an environment when the disciplinary lines between approaches to the mind were not yet drawn – in other words, in the same environment of overlap and antagonism among the moral and mental sciences, metaphysics and psychology that I've argued can be seen as having conditioned Ferrier's strong account of the mind's powers.[45] Like Ferrier's approach to psychology in the *Introduction to the Philosophy of Consciousness*, mesmerism's popularity waned in the later nineteenth century. It was both eclipsed by developments in approaches to mind in physiology and psychology, and absorbed into some of the practices and beliefs about mind-power that we shall turn to in Chapter 2.

Ferrier's interest in mesmerism may have been fostered by his acquaintance with John Campbell Colquhoun (1785–1854), whom he also met through Hamilton. As Winter notes, one of the reasons for mesmerism's extraordinary popularity and its richness for many nineteenth-century observers was its ability to accommodate a wide range of interpretations and explanations. To scientists like Sir John Elliotson, mesmerism clearly worked through some (yet unidentified) magnetic forces between bodies in proximity, and hence confirmed a materialist view of the close connections among mind, brain, and body. Yet other observers pointed to mesmerism to prove the immateriality of the mind and the existence of purely psychological forms of causality. J. C. Colquhoun was one of the latter, emphasizing mesmerism's immaterial essence in his *Isis Revelata: An Inquiry into the Origin, Progress, and Present State of Animal Magnetism* (1836). Mesmerism, in Colquhoun's optimistic view, ought to put to rest materialist approaches to mind:

There is no doubt, indeed, that, for a considerable period, our psychological theories have in general displayed a decided leaning towards materialism; they have …

relied too exclusively upon the mere acts of the material organization, as if there were nothing else deserving investigation.[46]

Colquhoun was fighting the same (losing) battle against materialism in psychology that Ferrier was, but his weapon was animal magnetism. Animal magnetism proves

incontrovertibly, the separate existence and independent activity of the soul of man, as well as its power over the corporeal organism ... and thus, by the most ample and irrefragable evidence ... set[s] for ever at rest that apparently interminable controversy between the Materialists and the Spiritualists. (I.45–46)

Even better, mesmerism provides the evidence of the truth of Kantian idealism – or perhaps we should say, according to Colquhoun, Kantian idealism expresses the truth of mesmerism:

A certain class of philosophers, deeply impressed with the mysterious intimations and manifestations of our spiritual nature ... have been led, independently of Revelation, to assume a two-fold world – a sensible and a supersensible, a two-fold life in man – the *phenomenal* and the *noumenal* ... The discoveries of Animal Magnetism have at length demonstrated that, in all this, there is more than mere metaphysical hypothesis, or poetical rhapsody. (Emphasis in original, II.171–72)

What would it mean to view mesmerism in the 1830s and 1840s as having been, among other things, the social theory of early nineteenth-century anglophone idealism? Mesmerism's account of the mind's powers over others is, at very least, a cognate extension into human relations of the view of mental action Ferrier arrived at in his attempt to challenge the empiricist picture of mind. The culture of mesmerism's countless experiments, demonstrations, written testimonials, and visual representations provided British observers with endless variations on the same tableau: two people, one person's mental action making something happen to the other: putting them to sleep, curing their physical or mental ills, causing them to beat time to the other's mental music.[47] These tableaux of intense mental relations between two people provided a strong argument about the powerful effects of thinking about another person; a set of instructions; and a training ground for thinking about thinking about another person.[48] Observers found the implications of mesmerism for ordinary life alternately exhilarating and terrifying. A *Blackwood's* essay called "What Is Mesmerism?" (1851) concludes with some trepidation about a future with mesmerism. "Whatever mesmerism is now, in its beginning," the author muses:

if it advances as fast as other sciences, what will become of us under its workings? ... It is frightful to think how rapidly time advances, and brings strange things to pass. In ten, twenty years, what a confusion the world will be in under its power – the consummation of "knowledge is power" all centred in mesmerism.

The author consoles himself somewhat from this worry ("what will become of us?") by adverting to an image of ordinary human contact. He resumes:

Electricity is probably its great agent. Philosophers say that, if you shake hands, there is an intercommunication of the electric fluid, a mutual participation of sentiment and all the phenomena of mind.[49]

As we shall see in the following, while the author's presentiments proved unwarranted, "in ten, twenty years" after this essay's writing, the place of "all the phenomena of mind" in social relations remained a deeply provocative question. But it is worth pausing here to stress again that viewing the 1830s craze for mesmerism through the lens of James Frederick Ferrier's strangely refracted idealism restores the role of idealism's strong accounts of psychological causation to the story of nineteenth-century accounts of mental relations.

CHAPTER 2

Foam, aura, or melody: *theorizing mental force in Victorian Britain*

In this chapter, I follow the thread of the previous chapter's investigation of nineteenth-century accounts of mental causation into the later decades of the century. The preceding chapter demonstrated that a focus on consciousness as a form of action could reveal strange philosophical bedfellows in the 1830s – a quirky but compelling idealist such as James Frederick Ferrier, and believers in mesmerism. As we move forward, the bedfellows just get stranger. A focus on strongly causal accounts of thinking reveals connections among Victorian physicists theorizing mental force in the new terms of their own discipline: a mystical woman mathematician; a weird but influential ear doctor; believers in phantasms; theosophists, Platonists, epiphenomenalists, pan psychists and positivists; and an idealist philosopher who articulated a compelling version of "love thinking": a particular kind of cognition that produces not knowledge but ethical, mystical bonds.

The development of ideas about mental force ought to be central to any account of nineteenth-century philosophy and psychology. However, by trying to tease out of the wealth of nineteenth-century writing on the mind a strand of thinking specifically about "thinking about other people," we are able to tell a particular story that casts a wider net, capturing writers and ideas from a broader range of fields. Like James Frederick Ferrier, the philosophical (and pseudo-philosophical) writers we meet in this chapter – such as the idiosyncratic metaphysician Shadworth Hodgson, the utopian polygamist ear doctor James Hinton, the philosophical ribbon-manufacturer Charles Bray, the psychological mathematician Mary Everest Boole, and even the fin-de-siècle idealist J. M. E. McTaggart – are by and large not mainstream figures. It is hard to trace their influence and progeny. However, reading them allows us to free ourselves from what Lisa Gitelman calls, in her history of outmoded nineteenth-century technologies, "the tug of teleology."[1] As we shall see, their attempts to describe how the mind affected the world lost out, in part because their vision of what philosophy or psychology ought to be lost out. Their writings represent attempts to solve problems about the place of thinking in social life, about the relation between mental freedom and mental force. And their solutions, however failed, outlandish, or wrong, may be more interesting, especially for readers who have the advantages, along with the disadvantages, of being outside the disciplines. Reading nineteenth-century philosophy and psychology as a literary scholar involves not only a willingness to blunder across disciplinary differences, but also a willingness to suspend disbelief about some pretty implausible ideas about mental force in order to find where the "tug" (to use Gitelman's word) on our own interests may be.

There is, then, a narrative unfolding in this chapter, a narrative about how and why a certain strand of nineteenth-century thought came to be so optimistic, despite challenges, about the effects of thinking about other people. But, again, this narrative is not one that one would find in the histories of philosophy or psychology. It may not be in step, either, with the narratives about the development of the study of the mind most familiar to scholars of nineteenth-century literature. Our attention has been preoccupied by the nineteenth century's treatment of the relationship of mind to body, and by the appearance of a growing consensus, beginning around mid-century, when a "mental physiology" – an understanding that psychological and philosophical issues need to be grounded in materialist approaches to the body – emerged in the work of Alexander Bain, George Henry Lewes, Herbert Spencer, William Carpenter, and others.[2] Bain, Lewes and others – as well as some of the major figures in the development of British ethical philosophy during this era – Mill, Sidgwick, Bradley – will make only shadowy appearances in this chapter, though their concerns with body and mind, and with ethics, respectively, do of course intersect with the interests of the writers featured here.[3] But my aim in focusing on theories of extrapersonal mental force is to show that there is a story that cuts across and complicates the narrative of nineteenth-century mind-study as the march of the materialists against the idealists. Putting some of the strange bedfellows together allows us to come to a number of discoveries about the currents of Victorian ideas about thinking, not least of which is the existence of a great number of Victorian writers and thinkers who were untroubled by, or saw themselves as transcending, any opposition between materialism and idealism. A broader context of diverse views on mental force permits us to come to a new interpretation of Victorian epiphenomenalism: the philosophical belief that thinking has no effect on anything whatsoever. And a broader context of ideas about mental causation can also provide a correction to some recent scholarship on one crucial area of Victorian belief in mental action at a distance: telepathy.

Throughout, we shall see a range of writers all devoted to studying what Coleridge called at the beginning of the century "*Thinking* as pure Action & Energy," "*Thinking* as distinguished from *Thoughts*"; thinking as an affectively, spiritually, and ethically charged act.[4] They sought to theorize thinking about another person as a social act, rather than as an exercise in skepticism about knowing other minds. By the end of this chapter we will begin to see the emergence of a conception of thinking we can call "love thinking" – a conception of thinking in which something like the strong, world-making account of thinking we found in Ferrier gets imbued with emotional and ethical significance: a kind of productive thinking about other people the ends of which are neither knowledge nor communication.

THEORIZING MENTAL FORCE

In the wake of the vogue for mesmerism in the 1830s and 1840s, many mid-nineteenth-century writers sought to theorize mental power as a form of extrapersonal action. The amazing effects of mesmerism pointed to facts about "ordinary thinking": "those extraordinary powers we are now considering are really not essentially distinct from the ordinary actions of the brain," one commentator typically noted. Or another: "I hold that the mind of a living person, in its most normal state, is always, to a certain extent, acting exoneurally, or beyond the limit of the bodily person; for most lucid persons…the exoneural apprehension seems to extend to every object and person round."[5] Such positions were illustrated with cheerfully optimistic anecdotes of everyday mind-power:

I have often been amused at a concert, or other place of meeting, to single out some person who has their back to me, and will them to turn their head in a given direction towards me, and generally I succeed…When I have been strongly wishing to see a friend it constantly happens that he appears.[6]

Some of the theorizing about the force and fate of ordinary thinking came from the desks of philosophers, but some of it came from the desks of physiologists and anatomists, and some from the armchairs of physicists. Crucial to the development of ideas about mental force were developments in physics, which underwent a transition around mid-century from a science of force which sought to explain "*all* natural phenomena from light to electricity and from astronomy to cohesion" in terms of action between discrete "point atoms over empty space" ("action at a distance"), to a new understanding of energy as distributed over a continuous field.[7] The terms "force" and "energy" did not remain clearly distinguished or defined, either within scientific writing or without, for some time; and the interpretations to which new scientific understandings of energy fields were put were highly variable. The move to theorize mental force in relation to physical force could cut both ways. That is, while some of the earlier nineteenth-century theorists of mesmerism saw mesmerism as evidence that mind-power was to be assimilated to matter (in the form of "animal magnetism," a pre-eminently physical force), mid-century developments in physics permitted some theorists to view the issue the other way around. As Roger Luckhurst puts it, "the invisible and supersensuous force of mind became the primary force of the universe, matter being regarded as merely one of its epiphenomenal and transient states."[8]

Two Scottish physicists, Balfour Stewart and P. G. Tait, spelled out the implications for a theory of thinking in *The Unseen Universe: or Physical Speculations on a Future State* (1875). Consoling and beautiful, *The Unseen Universe* takes the principles of the continuity and conservation of energy to mean that nothing ever dies. The energy that has temporarily settled into the visible world as we know it was somewhere before, and will go somewhere else – into a vastly extended and, to us, silent and unseen universe. The fact that *thinking* is a form of energy is essential to their understanding of spiritual survival and the existence of an afterlife. When we think, some of the molecules go back into our brain to form part of our own personal memories, but the rest move outward: "For every thought that we think is accompanied by a displacement and motion of the particles of the brain...we may imagine that these motions are propagated throughout the universe."[9] The universe is swirling with the motion of thinking.

We can find a particularly enthusiastic and creative interpretation of the physics of force in Charles Bray's *On Force, Its Mental and Moral Correlates; and On That Which Is Supposed to Underlie All Phenomena: With Speculations on Spiritualism, and Other Abnormal Conditions of Mind* (1866), the title of which indicates some of the philosophical attractions of a focus on mental force. Bray, a provincial industrialist and autodidact, an atheist and phrenologist, is best known now as an early intellectual mentor to George Eliot, whom he tried, apparently unsuccessfully, to hypnotize.[10] For Bray, the ultimate point of focusing on mental force is to affirm the identity of mind, spirit, and matter. Mental force is part of a force, or Force, with a capital F, which "rolls through all things." A passionate Shelleyan and Wordsworthian, a fan of Ferrier and of Fichte, Bray also drew on physics, and his interpretation of the science of energy is that Force renders the concept of matter "unnecessary": "this doctrine of the Persistence of Force seems to me, not only to make matter altogether unnecessary, but to exclude even the very idea."[11] Bray draws a picture of a universe liberated from matter and materialism; what appears as matter is merely the indication that force has been there, and the same force, as a bemused critic for the *Westminster Review* put it, "submitted to different organic conditions, becomes Shakespeare or a sheep."[12]

Bray's understanding of theories of the conservation of energy shapes his theory of thinking. Force comes into us; it must leave us too. Humans take in energy in the form of food; it feeds our thoughts; and our thoughts perforce must exit ourselves, because all forms of Force are always moving. "Heat and electricity are constantly passing off from the body; so is mind. We influence every one and every thing about us, and are influenced by them." He goes on, remarkably, "We photograph our mental states on all the rooms we inhabit."[13] In this striking phrase, the Coventry ribbon-manufacturer seems to conjure life as a giant Victorian mansion, with rooms and rooms wallpapered with the multiple exposures of people's mental states. As colorful as Bray's language is, this basic view of mental force was widely accepted. Here is J. S. Mill:

> It is known that the source from which this portion of Force is derived, is chiefly, or entirely, the Force evolved in the process of chemical composition and decomposition which constitute the body of nutrition: the force so liberated becomes a fund upon which every muscular and even every merely nervous action, *as of the brain in thought, is a draft.*[14]

The force of thought is a draft off the larger energies of the world.

Some doubts enter Charles Bray's ideas about how this process happens, and some fascinating complications and consequences too. Since Force is so protean and shape-changing, he is uncertain about whether, when we are influenced by the force of another's thoughts, that influence has the shape of thought. He muses, "Does thought passing from us become free thought, or does it join some odylic or other medium?" "Does it change its form, lose its consciousness, and thus no longer be thought and feeling?"[15] That Bray cannot answer these questions definitively, that he is willing to entertain the possibility that the mental force that photographs itself all over everything and everyone may be translated into an unintelligible form, reveals the difference between Bray's understanding of mental force, and the theories of "thought transfer" and telepathy so popular later in the century. That is, for Bray, mental force is truly, as for Coleridge, "thinking as pure action and energy…as distinguished from thought." It is a model of thinking as force rather than as a mental content or communication, a model, as we shall discuss later, which may be harder for us to grasp.

It also follows from Bray's understanding of thinking as force that a thought cannot be inside the mind, and elsewhere, at the same time. There is in Bray's account of the action of thought a barely perceptible, but fascinating, sequence of events: "When I speak then of a 'thought' atmosphere, a 'mental' atmosphere, or a 'general' mind, I mean either mind or sentiency *or that condition of force which immediately precedes mind or consciousness, and which must exist in the brain, when from a slight pressure upon it, consciousness ceases*" (82; emphasis mine). As Bray's contemporary critics were quick to point out, his writings did not exactly shed clarity on the relationship of brain to mind.[16] Any individual consciousness mysteriously emerges from, and then blips back into, a general "thought atmosphere." The "slight pressure" upon the brain that Bray refers to, which causes consciousness to cease, cannot, as drastic as it sounds, mean actual death. It is "slight": that is to say, it is a pressure that causes not consciousness itself, but a discrete thought or moment of consciousness, to die. Thinking, like life, is brief; our thoughts are only with us temporarily before they "pass off" (86) the individual. Indeed, the tenure of any thinking with any individual under this endlessly morphing world of force is so brief that it may be more accurate to say, as the skeptical *Westminster Review* critic did, that in Bray's account, "When we say 'I think,' we deceive ourselves. What we ought to say is 'Thinking is.'"[17]

But in the world of Charles Bray's *On Force*, no one is saying anything at all. It is a testimony to how generally removed Bray's vision is from a communications-based conception of mental action that the possibility that thinking might have force through its conversion into *language* seems never to occur to him. Once it passes off the individual, the force of thinking may morph into "free thought" or "some odylic or other medium" but never, it seems, into the medium of speech or language. The world of thinking, for all its global reach, is a silent world, sealed off from speech. Speaking and thinking seem strangely disconnected in *On Force*. This is brought home by the one time the topic of speaking comes up: as an example of something that can be done automatically, while thinking is going on. Referring to his old grammar book, Bray boasts, "from having been drilled hard in Murray in my school days, I can now repeat the whole of my adverbs, prepositions, and conjunctions, while thinking of something else" (184). This odd foreclosure of language or speech as one of the forms of force which thinking might "pass off" can contribute to our own picture of the complexity of Victorian theories of thinking. It highlights the often strange place of thinking in nineteenth-century Britain's culture of writing.

The notion that thought-action is carried out in silence had a corollary in the equally popular notion that extra-personal thinking does its work *unseen*. A giant unseen world radiates from human thinking, and presses on all sides our own world. If Charles Bray imagined thoughts photographed on the rooms in which we actually live, William F. Barrett, a physician and tireless member of the Society for Psychical Research (which we shall focus on soon), more typically held that our thought is written on a room-less, infinite unseen world. Yet this unseen world seems, if possible, more crowded and thought-stuffed than Bray's rooms. Barrett writes:

If in a more concrete manner than Longfellow meant,

> "No action whether foul or fair
> Is ever done but it leaves somewhere
> A record written by fingers ghostly."

If our thoughts and characters are faithfully and indelibly being written on the unseen, we are, in fact, involuntarily and inexorably creating not only in our own soul, but possibly in the invisible world, an image of ourselves, a thought-projection, that embraces both our outer and innermost life.[18]

We might wish to start with the end of this passage, and wonder, fruitlessly, what Barrett could mean when he says that our thought projections embrace not only our inner but also our outer life. In spite of what he says, Barrett's concept of thinking as a kind of unseen writing on the unseen is less concrete than Longfellow's; whatever concreteness there is here is on loan from Longfellow's already spectral image. Conceiving of thinking as action not only consigns speech to silence, but also ghostifies writing.

Discussions of mental force, then, often evoked a picture of an unseen world filled with the forms of our thoughts. Victorian discussions of mental force among even the most materially minded were influenced by, and in turn influenced, the revival of interest in Plato's philosophy in England from the 1850s onward, a revival which had become by the century's end, in the words of Frank M. Turner, "nothing less than a Platonic revival that far outshone that of the Renaissance."[19] Turner documents the huge upswing of translations of Plato, and commentaries on the texts, as well as the shifts in the teaching of Plato in the universities, in particular the enormous influence of Benjamin Jowett's introduction of Plato into the curriculum at Oxford. The discovery of the relevance of Plato's ideas to the concerns of serious Victorians seeking alternatives to materialism and utilitarianism was itself seen as proof of the transhistoric, transcendent power of thinking. "We begin to feel," reflected Jowett, "that the ancients had the same thoughts as ourselves."[20] As Turner and others have demonstrated, the Platonic revival was really a series of revivals, as Victorian thinkers sought to assimilate Plato to a range of concerns: Platonism as avatar or as alternative to Christianity; as part of Hegelian, or more frequently, Coleridgean idealism; as political philosophy undergirding different species of social reform. But just as we saw in Chapter 1 how Ferrier's North-British channeling of Fichte's idealism seemed to produce a strangely literal conception of mental force, so in some later-Victorian hands a Platonic realm of unseen intellectual forms comes perilously close to being a realm of thought-materialized ghosts; and mental force theorists were not averse to pointing out the analogies to Plato's philosophy. William Barrett, after the passage discussed above, insists that the unseen world of human thought-projection jived with Plato's idea "that the world of sensible things is only an image of the world of ideas existing in a supra-sensible world"; the physicist authors of *The Unseen Universe* cite Jowett's translation of the *Gorgias*.[21] Spiritualism and Platonism were all mixed up together, as there was a continuum of "unseen worlds" in which physicists, philosophers, and others all both borrowed glamour from, while also distancing themselves from, the more occult versions of the unseen. The "modern Victorian" writer May Sinclair joked in her philosophical treatise, *A Defence of Idealism*, that idealist philosophy suffered from its association with what she called "the powers of the Borderland" – mesmerism, telepathy, magic, mysticism: "I feel (to be disgustingly egoistic) that any reputation I may have is already so imperilled by my devout adhesion to the Absolute that I simply cannot afford to be suspected of tenderness, or even toleration for the professors of the occult."[22] Nevertheless, she joined the Society for Psychical Research, an organization to which we shall turn our attention shortly.

A focus on mental force is thus, as I argue throughout this book, a way to tell the story of the peculiar assimilation of various forms of idealism into British literary and intellectual culture. This late Victorian environment, in which a pseudo-Platonic unseen realm is made up of masses of oozing human thinking, also provides a context for understanding the extremely eroticized, aestheticized, and above all, personified version of the ideal in Walter Pater's Platonism. In "The Genius of Plato," Pater describes the intellectual realm as a realm of personal relations. For Plato, writes Pater, "all knowledge was like knowing a *person*."[23] "The peculiarities of personal relationship thus mould[ed] his conception of the properly invisible world of ideas" (134). The Platonist brings "into the world of intellectual abstractions" the experience of love, and the relation among the forms is like the relation "of *persons* towards one another, all the magnetism, as we call it, of actual human friendship or love" (140, emphasis his). We shall begin to turn to the place of love in theories of thinking in the next section.

MENTAL FORCE AND THE ETHICS OF THINKING ABOUT OTHER PEOPLE

Theories of extra-personal mental force proved attractive to a number of Victorian writers who in one way or another cast the power of thinking as highly voluntaristic, potentially altruistic, and cheerfully optimistic. We can see many of the different aspects of Victorian theorizing about mental force coming together in the ideas of James Hinton (1822–75). Hinton, an eccentric but charismatic physician, had a stellar career as a specialist in diseases of the ear but increasingly, especially after a spiritual crisis of some sort in the Azores Islands (which he termed his "moral revolution"), devoted his life to philosophical speculations. He published some of these during his lifetime, but left at his death a mountain of manuscripts, many on religious, ethical, and social issues, that over the next twenty years was mined and disseminated by his son Charles Howard Hinton, his friend the philosopher Shadworth Hodgson, and above all by a number of women in his circle: his wife Margaret; his sister-in-law (and perhaps lover) Caroline Haddon; the social purity reformer Ellice Hopkins; Edith Mary Oldham Lees Ellis (wife of Havelock Ellis); and the "psychological mathematician" Mary Everest Boole (widow of the mathematician George Boole). Hinton became, mostly posthumously through these devotees' editions of and commentary on his manuscripts, a surprisingly influential figure in the mixed-up soup of late Victorian socialism, sex radicalism, and sometimes spiritualism. Havelock Ellis described Hinton as having sought to do in morals what Walt Whitman did in literature (and elsewhere described him as having "the exalted temperament of a Shelley"); Edith Lees Ellis ranked Hinton with Nietzsche and Edward Carpenter as the three prophets of the modern world.[24] What Hinton's disciples and devotees learned from the odd otologist above all was an imperative to enact a kind of passionate altruism (the term itself he borrowed from G. H. Lewes' 1853 translation of Auguste Comte, but Hinton may be credited with popularizing the term in England), which he and his followers extended to members of the lower classes, and, most notoriously, to many members of the opposite sex.[25]

All of Hinton's devotees saw his ethical, social, and sex-radical ideas as emerging from what they termed his "metaphysics," and this is what is most interesting for our purposes. Hinton developed a form of pan-psychism, which he called "Actualism." It begins with a conception of the continuity of mental with physical force not unlike Charles Bray's (indeed Bray later cited an early essay by Hinton as an influence). If force is constantly passing between mental, organic, and inorganic entities, then it follows that consciousness can be said to have its home in inorganic entities as well as in humans: "all existence is truly active or spiritual, as opposed to inert or dead."[26] For Hinton, Actualism rendered meaningless a distinction between materialism and idealism, though his devotees would wrangle over whether his philosophy ought to be considered more of one or the other. For Hinton and his followers, the corollary of this brand of panpsychism is that all topics, from the molecular level to the social, were ethical issues.[27] This is truly ethics from the bottom-up, rather than from the top-down.

In Hinton's writings, thinking comes to be synonymous with the force, the "everlasting *action*," the process that animates the universe; his very notion of force is modeled on thinking. The force of thinking is eternal, intergenerational, transcendent, and, significantly for us, associated with error:

Here we see Life "written large" that we may read it; the long toil of thousands of men through thousands of years adding hour by hour new items of laborious search, or careful scrutiny, or scrupulous deduction, all collected into one great organisation, replete and pulsating with living force – *with living force of error*, be it noted [emphasis his].[28]

Hinton's posthumously published, incomplete *Chapters on the Art of Thinking*, from which this passage is taken, seeks to link this large, trans-historic view of thinking as the force of the universe with thinking as it is practiced by individual human beings. "Thinking, indeed," he proclaims in the chapter "Thought and Art," "is no mere mechanical process; it is a great Art, the chief of all the Arts; nay, it is both an Art and a work; it has the attractions of an Art and the positive results of a science" (43). "The perfect art of thinking must…be true to the whole of man's nature with all its faculties" (46). Hinton seems to have actually persuaded his friends and followers that he was indeed a kind of pure "thought-artist," in the words of Mary Everest Boole: he was an aesthete of thinking. "For the thought-artist," Boole declared, "no opinion is right or is wrong. The all-important thing is the conduct of the thinking-machinery." Boole along with other devotees insisted on Hinton's writings as somehow not really writing, but pure thinking. Whatever it was about, Boole insisted, "the *motif* was always the same – the Rhythm of Thought."[29] Ellice Hopkins stressed, similarly, that Hinton's manuscripts should be thought of not as writing, just as thinking: "It was a sort of mental photography, his MSS. being an accurate photograph of the processes of thought rather than a record of finished results." In Hinton as in Bray, there is a symptomatic privileging of thinking over both writing and speaking, an emphasis echoed in this assessment of Hinton as thinker by another of his female devotees, his sister-in-law, Caroline Haddon: "His thoughts were so completely undressed."[30]

Above all, the job of the thought-artist is to direct the force of his or her thoughts, like a hose on a garden, towards other people. One of the pieces of posthumous writing most frequently cited by Hinton's followers was an essay called "Others' Needs," published separately as a pamphlet as well as in *Chapters on the Art of Thinking*. Seen as the central statement of Hinton's ethical theory, "Others' Needs" articulates a pure altruism that seeks to overturn the tired debates about duty and utility in nineteenth-century ethical theory. Hinton ends the essay imagining God (and what Hinton meant by God, or thought about God, was much debated by his admirers, with Hodgson insisting he was a Christian philosopher, a judgment from which his more radical followers dissented) addressing humans: "Be different in your heart; cast out from them that which puts pleasure at strife with goodness; make the thought of others first."[31] Thinking about another person is in and of itself an ethical act: "If we can make our thinking too a giving, a loving, an escape from the death of trying to get, then eyes are opened – then we *know*."[32] In his later unpublished manuscripts, according to Havelock Ellis, Hinton agonized about the difficulties of thinking of others directly. "To think of others directly, instead of through the effect of thinking of the traceable, is really a delusion," he apparently wrote shortly before his death.[33]

While Hinton's elevation of thinking into an ethical good is fairly muddled (who can say what "the traceable" means?), it was quite influential.[34] For Hinton, ethics does not end with thinking about other people: it was interpreted by others as the beginning of a social practice, a practice that, as pursued by some of his devotees, involved variously social activism with the London poor, the sexually and socially abused, nascent socialism, and a battle against monogamy and domesticity as oppressive to women.[35] But for Ellis and others, the hinge between Hinton's pan psychism and his ethical and social views was a strong, emotionally and ethically invested conception of mental force as a powerful actor in human affairs. It is also no accident that two of the era's most enthusiastic theorists of mental force, Hinton and Charles Bray, were also charismatic social radicals who led complicated love lives, inside and outside marriage, for whom there seems to have been some kind of continuity between thinking about another person and sleeping with them. Hinton's thinking may have been undressed indeed. For Hinton and others around him, the art of thinking was not a route to knowledge, but a practice of endless doing, part of *"the living force of error,"* as Hinton emphatically described the collective universe of mental force in *Chapters on the Art of Thinking*.

The popularity of Hinton's ethics of thinking among women is also no accident. There is a considerable body of feminist scholarship which seeks to explain why nineteenth-century women, on both sides of the Atlantic, were attracted to spiritualist and occultist movements in such significant numbers. Such movements provided intellectual community and opportunities for leadership that bypassed educational and professional restrictions on women, while at the same time seeming to extend women's allegedly natural interests in matters moral, immaterial, and religious. The utopian potential of the promise of many such movements – the promise of contact across social boundaries, not excluding between the living and the dead – often allied such movements to the social and political movements – Fabianism, Suffrage – that were their contemporaries, and there were a number of women who played crucial roles in both movements, such as women's rights activist/socialist/Indian nationalist and Theosophist Annie Besant (1847–1933).[36] Besant, who took on the leadership of the Theosophist Society from the founder of this eastern-influenced body of occult belief, Madame Helene Blavatsky, synopsized her own views on the ethics and powers of thinking about other people in a slim, how-to book called *Thought Power: Its Control and Culture* (1900). Like James Hinton, Besant firmly believed that thinking was an art that needed to be learned and practiced: everyone nowadays wants to perform thought-transfer, she says, but first you must exercise your thought-power, just as an athlete exercises muscle power! Drawing heavily on yoga and meditation, *Thought Power* weaves together instruction on meditation, concentration, mental focus (cut way back on reading, she advises), with a powerful account of thinking about other people. Thinking for her is about relation – "thinking means," she pronounces, "the establishing of relations" – and it has its origins in the infant's desire for the mother's breast.[37] *Thought Power* ends with a chapter on "Helping Others By Thought," which gives an extremely benign account of how the student of thought-power can improve upon the good that thinking about another person always, in Besant's wonderfully literal account, can do. "A mere kind thought is helpful in its measure," she observes, "but the student will wish to do far more than drop a mere crumb to the starving" (120). As a first step the student of "thought-work" learns to surround a loved one with a thinking-blanket:

> A strong wish for his good, sent to him as a general protective agency, will remain about him as a thought-form for a time proportionate to the strength of the thought, and will guard him against evil, acting as a barrier against hostile thoughts, and even warding off physical dangers. (113)

But ultimately the thought-worker works towards the betterment of mankind: thinking is the essence of progressive social movements (121).

The metaphysical underpinnings and cognates of Victorian theories of thinking as extra-personal force were as attractive to some women as was its political potential. There is an untold story – or stories – about Victorian women intellectuals and innovative versions of idealism and panpsychism. In the words of May Sinclair: "Pan-Psychism has an irresistible appeal to the emotions."[38] Perhaps the most intellectually ambitious, and truly strange, of James Hinton's female disciples was Mary Everest Boole (1832–1916). Niece of the surveyor-general of India, George Everest, and married to the influential mathematician (and no spiritual shrug himself) George Boole, she was widowed in 1864 with five young daughters. She was herself extremely gifted in mathematics – a field closed to women – but through the influence of the philosopher and theologian F. D. Maurice she got a position as the librarian of Queen's College for Women at the University of London. During her tenure at Queen's College, she offered informal seminars in her lodgings on topics ranging from logic and mathematics to mental health, religion, and spiritualism, and wrote a book originally titled *The Message of Psychic Science to Mothers and Nurses* (it was eventually published in 1883, and later reprinted, modestly, as *The Message of Psychic Science to the World*). The contents of the book, which she showed in manuscript to Maurice, so dismayed him that he dissuaded her from publishing it, and he removed her from her post at the College. She then worked as James Hinton's secretary for the last two years of his life. One of her daughters married Hinton's son, Charles Howard Hinton, whose subsequent arrest for bigamy in 1885 helped tarnish the posthumous reputation of his father.[39]

From Hinton's death onwards, Mary Everest Boole became a prolific writer, churning out publications (some of them in Jewish periodicals, which she felt were more hospitable to her messages to the world) on a wide range of topics from education to mathematics to poetic meters. If what united Hinton's writings was, in Boole's words, "the rhythm of thought," what united Boole's own writing was a commitment to a version of "thought-power" that yoked everything from mathematical logic to mesmerism. She was committed both to psychologizing mathematics and to "algebraising...psychological material"; and she had a strong commitment to seeing all logic and thinking as fundamentally intersubjective and relational: "the relation in which we are...is a unit of thought. *Just while we are thinking of that relation*, but only for so long, it constitutes our Universe of Thought."[40] Like Annie Besant, Boole argued that thought power begins in infancy – all babies are born thought-readers, and then their minds start closing up.[41] Also like Besant, Boole was a strong believer in the cultivation of thinking to affect others, and she saw this as a power in which women were particularly adept: hence the "Mothers and Nurses" of her original title. "Every mother unconsciously mesmerizes her children, every nurse her patient, every teacher his pupils," she declares, "and this unconscious mesmerism is in all ordinary cases unquestionably more healthy than any other" (21–22). Boole's message to mothers and nurses is simply that they should understand the power of thinking about others that they are already unconsciously practicing so that they don't abuse it. However, unlike Besant, for whom a belief in the power of thinking to help others went hand in hand with political activism, Boole saw women's superior power of thinking about others as an argument *against* women's suffrage: "silent influence is on the whole more appropriate to the female line."[42] Boole's voluminous writings defy categories and sometimes strain comprehension, but they are a remarkable addition to the roar of Victorian writing about the silent power of thinking about another person.

THE SOCIETY FOR PSYCHICAL RESEARCH AND THINKING ABOUT OTHER PEOPLE

Nineteenth-century theories of mental force thus had enormous potential to alter visions of human relations. But what did it feel like to live in the rooms wallpapered with the thoughts of others? How did one, or could one, survive being thought about? As Besant warns, the mind not "steadied" will be "so easily thrown off its balance by the wandering thoughts from other minds, ever seeking to effect a lodgment, the vagrant crowd which continually encircles us."[43] The most vivid pictures of life in a Victorian world crowded with extrapersonal thought-energy are to be found in the voluminous records of the Society for Psychical Research, officially founded in 1882 by Henry Sidgwick, Frederick H. W. Myers, Edmund Gurney and others. An often uneasy alliance between confirmed spiritualists and skeptical but interested intellectuals, the SPR's mission was to document and scientifically evaluate the mounting evidence of "that large group of debatable phenomena designated by such terms as mesmeric, psychical, and Spiritualistic." Above all, they hunted after "all classes of cases where there is reason to suppose that the mind of one human being has affected the mind of another, without speech uttered, or word written, or sign made."[44] Like many of the other writers featured in this chapter, the members of the SPR were particularly concerned to find evidence of mind-power not in the extreme or altered states of mind acquired through mesmerism or even around the séance table, but in the course of ordinary life. Most of the SPR's writers were significantly more agnostic than some of the theorists of mental force about what caused the connection between one mind and another:

> The employment, therefore, of words like *force, impulse, impact*, in speaking of telepathic influences, must not be held to imply the faintest suspicion of what the force is, or any hypothesis whatever which would co-ordinate it with the recognised forces of the material world.[45]

They insisted that their subject matter was *"psychical"* experience only, whose causes remained a mystery (112). They sponsored and collected thousands of allegedly controlled experiments in "willing" (in which one person silently willed someone else to think, feel, or do something), thought-transfer, and thought-reading. But what they really liked were the anecdotes of "spontaneous" instances from ordinary life in which people's lives were altered by the force of someone thinking about them.

To read the first decades of *Proceedings of the Society for Psychical Research*, or the massive, moving book *Phantasms of the Living* (1886) is to be immersed in a world of people who are "thinking intently" about people they love, producing and receiving strange extrapersonal mental effects, and suffering such events as Myers' termed "invasions."[46] A Mr. B. wills a Miss V., living in a different part of London, to move about her house and remove a portrait from her dressing table; Miss V. writes back the next day about having been strangely compelled to do so: "I am *sure* you were thinking about me."[47] A Miss Martin "was sitting alone in the drawing-room, reading an interesting book, and feeling perfectly well, when suddenly I experienced an undefined feeling of dread and horror." It turns out that at just this moment, her "near and very dear" cousin, was dying (197). A dying mother's earnest wish to see her two grown daughters causes them both to leap out of bed in the middle of the night and order carriages to go see her.⁴⁸ This mother was always, the author of the report notes, a huge influence on her daughters. He adds that it was no accident that this event happened at night, "when the attention was not diverted by sights or sounds" (32). Love thinking, according to the SPR, is often a kind of night thinking. The extraordinary things that can happen when someone is thinking about you often hinge on the most minimal data of consciousness, such as the difference between sleeping and waking, living and dying.

The curious title of the SPR's publication *Phantasms of the Living* – principally written by Gurney, based on material collected in large part by Podmore, and with eloquent prefatory and concluding material by Myers – speaks to the authors' attempt to track the effects of being thought about by another person. They wished to focus on effects caused by the minds of the living, not visitations of ghosts of the dead. (And, by insisting on the word "phantasm" – which they acknowledge is merely an etymological derivate from "phantom" – the authors further emphasize that they are interested not in ghosts, but in a wider variety of mental effects, some of which take the form of visual materializations; others are purely internal disturbances, solely in the mind of the recipient.) They focused above all on visitations to the minds of the living from people who were, in fact, about to die, causing Myers to have to explain "why we have given the title of 'Phantasms of the *Living*' to a group of records most of which will present themselves to the ordinary reader as narratives of apparitions of the *dead*" (1: lxiii; emphasis his). But it means very much to the researchers that the apparitions and effects were caused when their agents were *not* dead: it is so that they can, in fact, attribute actual, thinking agents to the effects in the minds of their witnesses:

– Whether, that is, they do in fact correspond to some action which is going on in some other place or on some other plane of being; – or whether, on the other hand, they are merely morbid or casual – the random and meaningless fictions of an over-stimulated eye or brain. Now, in the case of apparitions at the moment of death or crisis, we have at any rate an objective fact to look to. If we can prove that a great number of apparitions coincide with the death of the person seen, we may fairly say, as we do say, that chance alone cannot explain this coincidence, and that there is a causal connection between the two events. (1: iii–lxiv)

Focusing on phantasms of the living, in other words, allows the authors to secure proof that they are not simply documenting, as Myers puts it, "the mere offspring of my own brooding sorrows" but rather effects of a verifiable "*agent.*" That some – though not all, they hasten to add – of the agents swiftly die ought not to reclassify them from the living to the dead, though the whole set-up does tie the power of thinking about another person tightly to questions of human survival and destruction. For Myers, whose interest in psychical research was driven above all by the search for proof of human immortality, the survival of human personality after death was ultimately a kind of echo of the idea of the survival of thoughts beyond the person.[49] Thus, the fact that the agent has such strong thought-power at the moment when his or her "psychical and physical energies alike seem reduced to their lowest limits" affirmed that human "intelligence" exists beyond the "limits of the phenomenal self."[50] Nevertheless, Myers held that the thinking that happened at the crisis of death was simply a heightened, more provable version of something going on all the time. "It is not unreasonable to suppose," he writes at the conclusion to *Phantasms of the Living*, "that the same telergy which is directed in a moment of crisis towards a man's dearest friend, may be radiating from him always towards all other minds, and chiefly towards the minds which have most in common with his own."[51]

It is in fact the broad range of the "phenomena" that the Society for Psychical Research took as grist for their mill that made their work so life-threateningly exhausting for some of their investigators, productive to think about, and maddening to study. Scholarship of the past several decades about the SPR and about the many other spiritualist and occultist movements of the era which were sometimes the Society's allies, sometimes their enemies, has amply documented not only the history of the SPR, its schisms and developments, and the particular intellectual interests of some of its best-known members and writers, but also its absolute centrality to Victorian intellectual, literary, social, and political life.[52] Emphasis has correctly been placed on the SPR's own emphasis on intersubjective and social bonds, and especially its links to utopianism: Pamela Thurschwell terms the SPR's experiments "experiments in intimacy." It has been common to see the SPR's work as centering on the discovery and investigation of "telepathy." In some sense, this is not at all a narrowing down of the Society's interests: as the authors of *Phantasms of the Living* note, "telepathy" – the term coined by Myers in 1882 – was designed to embrace a wide range of phenomena: "We thus get what we need, a single generic term which embraces the whole range of phenomena and brings out their continuity."[53]

Yet the nature of our scholarly focus on telepathy has rendered somewhat partial our picture of Victorian understandings of the act of thinking about another person. It is common to find in the scholarship on the history of investigations of parapsychological phenomena across the nineteenth century a narrative in which an interest in the power of one person's mind to control, or affect, another person (as in mesmerism) gradually gives way to an interest instead in the power of one person to *know* the thoughts of another person (e.g. telepathy).[54] Knowing thoughts is of course the focus of the endless, mind-numbing volume of "thought transfer–thought reading" experiments. It is thus no surprise that the theoretical paradigms most recently brought to bear on the study of the SPR have been paradigms emphasizing knowledge, communication, technology, and information. The spirits of Friedrich Kittler and Michel Foucault brood over both Pamela Thurschwell's *Literature, Technology, and Magical Thinking, 1880–1920* and Roger Luckhurst's *The Invention of Telepathy, 1870–1901*. Thus for Thurschwell, the SPR's work revealed "new ways of knowing," "an erotics of knowledge" (31), while Luckhurst ably demonstrates the complex emergence of "telepathy" out of the mix of the era's "interdisciplinary knowledges": telepathy is both fundamentally about "networks of knowledge" (5) as well as being situated within them.

In his history of the idea of communication, *Speaking into the Air*, John Durham Peters notes that the intense interest in telepathy, along with its cognate technological developments in the late nineteenth century, telephony and telegraphy, constitutes a crucial chapter in the development of a particular ideal of communication: an ideal of wordless transfer of information against which actual human discourse always seems to fall short. Peters' book is an eloquent critique of this ideal of communication, which, he writes, is always attended with a kind of "normative pathos," and which unnecessarily shrinks the nature of human relatedness to "communication" conceived as the transfer of the contents of one mind to another.[55] It is certainly true that the work of the SPR often confirms this content-based, epistemologically focused view of mental relations. However, to read the writings of the SPR in relation to the many other nineteenth-century theorists of thinking about another person as force is to find throughout their stories of "the effect of mind on mind" a remainder, a force of thinking about another person, which does not resolve into the transfer of a mental content, or a mind to be read. It is this remainder – an emphasis not on a mental content or information transferred but on the more elusive evidence of thinking about another person as a force – that we confront when we confront the gap, or lack of symmetry, between the SPR's stated emphasis on "all classes of cases where there is reason to suppose that the mind of one human being has affected the mind of another," and the mountains of "evidence" in their charts and graphs, which look like evidence of something else: guessing what is in someone else's mind.

Here is another way to think about that remainder, that longing for evidence of thinking as action beyond any particular information or content. William James was deeply interested in psychic phenomena; he was a member of the Society for Psychical Research, and a founding member of the American Society for Psychical Research. His brother Henry professed at least to be more skeptical, but in 1890 he reluctantly agreed to present William James' paper "A Record of Observation of Certain Phenomena of Trance" to the London meeting of the SPR while its author was detained in America. An amused William wrote to thank his brother in advance for this favor, and promised to think of him: "I will *think of you* on the 31st at about 11 a.m. to make up for difference of longitude."[56] William James' line, "I will *think of you*," is clearly designed in part to annoy his brother with its profession of psychic power. But does it not also draw on the kind of ordinary-language, folk-psychology ways in which we ourselves often use this phrase? And should not this usage be thought of as a milder version of the optimistic ethics of thinking about another person professed by Besant, Hinton, and others? James' "I will *think of you*" is a claim, whether serious or not, for some kind of consolatory efficacy. But it would be hard to say that William's proposed thinking of Henry is a communication or transfer to him of a particular mental content. The *letter* is the communication: the thinking promises an efficacy beyond content; it is a thinking as "pure act or energy" that stands outside of the letter. We shall have occasion to ponder further the relationship between writing "I will think of you," and actually doing it, in the next chapter of this book.

FOAM, AURA, OR MELODY: VICTORIAN EPIPHENOMENALISM

This chapter now turns to consider a strand of later Victorian thinking about thinking that would be seem to be the opposite of the strong accounts of mental causation and mental force we have discussed thus far: Victorian epiphenomenalism. Epiphenomenalism (the term itself was coined by William James in 1890 to characterize the position of some of his British contemporaries) is the philosophical position that mental events are totally immaterial and can have no effects at all on the physical world; can make nothing happen at all, not even our own movements, let alone extra-personal effects.[57] Hotly debated inside the halls of philosophy, psychology, and science, as well as without, from about 1874 through the 1890s, epiphenomenalism spawned a series of memorable images. The conscious, thinking mind was described variously as the foam on the crest of a wave; the scream of a steam whistle on a locomotive; a melody; and the shadow of the steps of a traveler.[58] All of these images were designed to underscore the inefficacy of thinking. So, for example, T. H. Huxley wrote that mental action is like the steam whistle on a locomotive because it "appear[s] to be related to the mechanism of [the] body simply as a collateral product of its working, and to be as completely without any power of modifying that working as the steam-whistle which accompanies the work of a locomotive engine is without influence upon its machinery."[59] So, Shadworth Hodgson, often cited as the first Victorian to lay out the epiphenomenalist position, says that in such a view "consciousness must be conceived by it in some such way as the foam thrown up by and floating on a wave, and having no reaction on the motion of the wave; so consciousness must float...on the surface of the brain"; consciousness, viewed as epiphenomenon, is "a mere foam, aura, or melody, arising from the brain, but without reaction upon it."[60] Victorian epiphenomenalism is a curious phenomenon: it says mental life is nothing; it says mental life is anything, a limitless series of beautiful metaphors.

In this section I sketch out a new context for, and a new interpretation of, Victorian epiphenomenalism. As a philosophical position, epiphenomenalism would seem to be everything the theories of mental force described in the previous sections of this chapter were not: dry, cautious, philosophically and scientifically respectable, sexless. But philosophically, epiphenomenalism also seems grim, hard-hearted, demoralizing, and just plain wrong. If there seems to most of us something obviously wacky about the strong accounts of mental action at a distance discussed thus far, we are also unlikely to assent to the position that our conscious thoughts have absolutely no effects in the world, even on our own actions. What could there possibly be to say in favor of a stance that reduces our mental efforts to nothing? The term has recently come back to life in contemporary philosophy, most often as a charge to be leveled at certain kinds of cognitive scientists and non-reductive physicalists and monists.[61] Looking back, Victorian epiphenomenalism seems either dark evidence of a historical moment in which men of science, such as Huxley, took the implications of the era's findings in evolution, materialism, and nineteenth-century brain science to their logical, dismal conclusions; or as premonitions of the current (dismal, but bracingly "real") findings of neuroscience. (Indeed, if Shadworth Hodgson is cited at all these days, it tends to be not in philosophy, but in neuroscience.)[62]

But Victorian epiphenomenalism merits a closer look, not least because of the ways in which this philosophical debate tossed up – as a wave tosses up sea-foam – some lovely literary language. How can we think about the relationship between this account of mind, and its images? What attracted some Victorian writers to such a stark account of the non-effectiveness of mental life? How did such a position become so paradoxically committed both to an extreme physicalism and to such an immaterial conception of thinking? I focus these questions on the work of Shadworth Hodgson (1832–1912), author of many of the metaphors above (and others: consciousness as the colors of the pebbles in a mosaic; as the hammers on the strings of a piano).[63] Hodgson was not a man of science, but rather an idiosyncratic, non-academic philosopher, who was a family relation of Thomas De Quincey, and claimed to have learned everything he knew from Coleridge. Hodgson allows us to see that the claims of the Victorian epiphenomenalist were highly specific, neither particularly materialist nor particularly neurophysiological. Victorian epiphenomenalism needs to be interpreted in the context of many other ways of thinking about thinking in order to reveal its surprising meanings.

Though he authored many of the memorable epiphenomenalist metaphors, Shadworth Hodgson's views on mental causation are quite complex, and changed across the course of his writings. A gentleman of independent means who never held an academic post, Hodgson was educated at Oxford, got married right after leaving the University, then lost his wife and only child three years later, and thereafter single-mindedly devoted the rest of his long life to the consolations of philosophy. He was one of the last serious professional non-professional philosophers, a writer for whom philosophy was a branch of literature. He belonged to many of the important intellectual London circles of the day, was crucial to the early years of the journal *Mind*, and was a founder and first president of the Aristotelian Society. If he is remembered at all today, it is mostly as a friend and interlocutor of William James; but he is more broadly important as a reminder of how diverse and unusual nineteenth-century British philosophical writing could be. In Hodgson's case, this involved a lifelong attempt to craft an alternative to both Victorian scientific materialism and German idealism, an attempt that resulted in a truly anomalous, innovative body of work that has struck a few commentators as prefiguring Continental phenomenology, especially the writings of Bergson and Husserl.[64] One of his goals, quite similar to James Frederick Ferrier's, was to wrest the study of consciousness away from what he saw as fallacies in the associationist tradition in psychology which dominated the psychological theory of his day with its talk of "the Mind" (capital "M") and its different faculties and logics of association, in favor of a purely subjective analysis of the experience of consciousness. In a letter to William James, he expressed his skepticism about psychology's hypothesizing of something called "the Mind" at all:

> Prove that there is such a thing, or any intelligible thing that answers to the word Mind, and I shall welcome the proof with joy, nay eagerness. As it is I suspect it is a mere *façon de parler*, a traditional hum, which has a basis neither in psychological construction nor in philosophical analysis.[65]

Hodgson's dispute with associationist psychology is in fact the context for the first articulations of the epiphenomenalist view, which in his first book, *Time and Space* (1865), it must be stressed, he describes in order to criticize. It comes up as he is arguing that associationist psychology, with its emphasis on the alleged "laws of association" that link chains of ideas, has no way of accounting for what Hodgson calls "spontaneous redintegration" – the kind of involuntary associations that happen in dreams. (Hodgson was an astute reader of his relative, Thomas De Quincey, and his interest in dreams as a test-case for mental causation can certainly be seen both as De Quincian, and as pseudo- or proto-Freudian.)[66] Old-fashioned associationism cannot explain the workings of the mind in "spontaneous redintegration" *except as* something meaningless, and inefficacious, as foam floating loosely on the surface of the brain. "The old theory therefore," he says, "is imperfect" in that it "requires the supplement of some psychological theory of the action of the brain," and in so doing consigns mental action to nothing.[67]

And yet, Hodgson's metaphors for this false theory of mental action seem to have had a life of their own: they were retroactively taken to describe his own position, and indeed in his next two books Hodgson adopted the doctrine his metaphors described.[68] It's worth paying close attention to why Hodgson adopts the position, and we can begin to do this by contrasting Hodgson's epiphenomenalism with Huxley's. Huxley's epiphenomenalism is (as you might expect) very much that of the Victorian man of science. In his 1874 lecture, "On the Hypothesis that Animals are Automata and its History," Huxley links epiphenomenalism to evolution (if we're willing to agree that, in animals, consciousness causes nothing, then we must extend that principle to human consciousness); to the evidence of current brain science (we have evidence that brain activity can cause changes in consciousness, but no evidence that thinking can cause the molecular changes that give rise to muscular motion). While defending

his embrace of epiphenomenalism against charges of fatalism, materialism, and atheism, Huxley blithely welcomes his audience into a brave new
world in which "we are conscious automata, endowed with free will" in a
limited sense and in which "in many respects we are able to do as we like,"
but in which we are, more importantly, part of the bigger series of causes
and effects that make up the sum of existence.[69]

But for Shadworth Hodgson, whom Huxley like everyone else credits
with starting the discussion, the move from using the epiphenomenal
image ("a mere foam, aura, or melody") to embracing actual epiphenomenalism has surprisingly little to do with evolution, or indeed with science at all. This emerges most clearly in his third (and most interesting)
book, *The Philosophy of Reflection* (1878). In this work, Hodgson justifies
his change of view from the beautiful negative metaphors of his first book
to a positively epiphenomenalist stance in his second book, *The Theory
of Practice* (1870). His explanation has less to do with science than with
purifying philosophy. In *The Philosophy of Reflection*, above all Hodgson
makes clear that in some respects he saw himself, and wished to be seen,
as in the tradition of radical empiricism of Hume, in which to claim that
anything causes anything is always a philosophical error, a reach beyond
what we can know. For Hodgson, to link questions of consciousness with
questions of causality, or with questions of conditions for emergence or
possibility at all, is philosophical death. It is to trespass into the terri-
tory of science: "The search after conditions, which is the life blood of
science, is the poison of philosophy."[70] For Hodgson (who, in the words
of one friend, "delighted to be called, and so always described himself, a
metaphysician"), the analysis of what it is to be conscious bars the door
to questions of what causes consciousness, or what consciousness can
cause.[71] And this is necessary in order to keep metaphysics separate from
science and in particular from psychology. Hodgson became an epiphenomenalist, above all, because:

This was in fact the step which enabled me to define the limits and relations
between a genuine philosophy and a scientific psychology, – I mean, the removal
of causation from consciousness, as such. Retain it there, and you must both
materialise philosophy (since the only known causation is material), and make
psychology illusory (since causation by consciousness is incalculable).[72]

Hodgson's emphasis on this point makes clear that Victorian epiphenomenalism was in some crucial cases only indirectly connected to the
rise of Victorian science, but was rather a chapter in the long history of
the prying apart of philosophy and psychology as disciplines over the

course of the long nineteenth century. Like Ferrier before him, Hodgson was fighting what was in Britain ultimately a losing battle to keep certain topics, such as the nature of consciousness, as the property of philosophy: a losing battle, because of the triumph of academic psychology on the one hand, and, on the other, the diversion of British philosophy into different (analytic) directions as the nineteenth century turned into the twentieth.

It is worth reflecting further on how drastic Hodgson's move – the embrace of epiphenomenalism to preserve consciousness for metaphysics – is. Epiphenomenalism competed in Victorian philosophy and psychology with a number of alternative views of the mind–body problem during this era, such as George Henry Lewes' dual-aspect monism (*The Physical Basis of Mind* [1877]); or various versions of interactionism (such as William Carpenter's in *Principles of Mental Physiology* [1874]); or what was called "mind-stuff" theory (e.g. William Clifford, "On The Nature of Things-In-Themselves," [1878]); or William James' agnosticism about the whole issue (in *Principles of Psychology* [1890]).[73] Some of these positions can seem more palatable to us than epiphenomenalism. Hodgson's turn to epiphenomenalism – his willingness to condemn consciousness to having no effects on the world, in order to purify and preserve the study of consciousness for metaphysics – can seem not simply throwing out the foam with the wave, but throwing out the baby with the bathwater. Hodgson seems to have exchanged the impotence of metaphysics for the impotence of the mind itself. A bad bargain for philosophy, we may feel, strangely unhumanizing, full of pathos.

However, it may be that for Hodgson, as well as for some of the more hard-core Victorian epiphenomenalists (not only Huxley, but also Henry Maudsley, G. J. Romanes, and others), there was also something strangely liberating in this view. Mental life was a mere nothing, but it was also, by the same token, more than everything: no longer tethered to the material laws of cause and effect, but working in its own ways. It is always instructive to consider the emotions lurking in philosophical writing (and especially in the case of Hodgson, who wrote tirelessly of the need to factor feeling into thinking); and the surprise of Victorian accounts of epiphenomenalism is that they don't feel grim, as the doctrine itself might warrant, but cheerful.[74] We can see this in the drive towards metaphorical language. There is a kind of intensity and giddiness in the proliferation of colorful mosaics, sea-foams tossing, pianos playing, shadows traveling, and so on: a kaleidoscope of agentless change, sound, and motion. The metaphors suggest that the idea that consciousness was totally immaterial, could make nothing happen, far from being grim, opened onto a kind of freedom. The language suggests that epiphenomenalism may have permitted Victorian writers to commit themselves to a hard-nosed materialism, while getting the stuff on top – the foam of thinking, the foam on the wave – for free.

Moreover, in the work of Hodgson at least, we can begin to see a surprising convergence between epiphenomenalism and some of the bodies of unorthodox thinking about thinking discussed in the preceding sections of this chapter. His epiphenomenalism must be viewed, for instance, in relation to his sympathy for the work of the Society for Psychical Research, several of whose members he counted as friends.[75] The young Roger Fry, for one, was apparently persuaded by Hodgson into a belief in the existence of spirits: after a weekend with the philosopher in the 1890s, Fry wrote to his mother, "There does seem some reason to think that there are spirits and that they exist in luminiferous aether," and he went on to note that Hodgson's was "much the most rational and collected account I have heard."[76] Though recent scholarship has demonstrated amply how absolutely central the vogues for spiritualism, mysticism, and the occult were to Victorian culture, the specific place of parapsychic beliefs in the history of nineteenth- and twentieth-century British *philosophy* may still be an incompletely told story. As we noted, the work of the SPR was to investigate "all classes of cases where there is reason to suppose that the mind of one human being has affected the mind of another, without speech uttered, or word written, or sign made." This is mental causation with a vengeance: a kind of anti-epiphenomenalism. The psychical researchers were divided on how to view mental causation: whether it was desirable to prove that the psychic world followed the laws of cause and effect of the natural world, or to prove that the psychic world lay outside those laws. While it may seem, in other words, hard to reconcile Hodgson's epiphenomenalism with his interest in parapsychic phenomena, *both* – both the anti-naturalism of Hodgson's brand of (metaphysically driven) epiphenomenalism, *and* the super-naturalism of the parapsychic – were equally departures from the naturalism of Victorian science.

Victorian epiphenomenalism, so extreme and unpalatable when viewed on its own, becomes much more interesting when seen as a point on the whole spectrum of beliefs about the powers of thinking in nineteenth-century Britain. It is best seen, perhaps like its opposites – strong beliefs in mental causation, whether from the point of view of idealism, or mesmerism, or any other of what May Sinclair called "the powers of the Borderland" – as a belief about the power of thinking whose significance lay in its wide-ranging social, emotional, and ethical implications, rather than in, say, its truth. Shadworth Hodgson's life and work would seem to have been ringed around by the presence of unseen others – the wife and child who died so shortly after the marriage, and to whom he seems to have dedicated *The Theory of Practice* fifteen years later ("Mortuis Meis"); and the dead Coleridge, to whom he dedicated *The Philosophy of Reflection*, in a fervently extravagant gesture of Victorian Coleridge-love: "To Samuel Taylor Coleridge, My father in Philosophy, not seen but beloved." In the Preface to that book, Hodgson claims that from his other philosophical influences and precursors (Hume, Kant, Salomon Maimon), he learned "(as it happened) nothing; from Coleridge everything."[77] He goes on to specify that what he learned from Coleridge included his belief in the inseparability of emotion and reason, the centrality of reflection as the highest form of thinking, the access to an unseen world via reflection, the indivisibility of subject and object, and the centrality of hope to cognition. However, Victorian Coleridge-love was a fascinating phenomenon, as susceptible Victorian readers somehow transformed the messy materials of posthumous STC into an idealized, coherent body of thought, and the last phrase – "not seen but beloved" – of Hodgson's dedication ought to make us pause.[78] Of course any reader in 1878 would know that Coleridge was "not seen" by Hodgson, nor ever had been (Coleridge died in 1834, when Hodgson was two years old). To address Coleridge in the realm of the "not seen but beloved" is to evoke a world in which the dead are living. For Hodgson, what survived after his reduction of thinking to epiphenomenon was not only a purified metaphysic, but also an intimation of consciousness as survival after death, and of the inseparability of philosophy from bonds of love between seen and unseen worlds.

It may ultimately, however, be the metaphors for consciousness tossed up by Victorian discussions of epiphenomenalism, like foam from a wave, that are the debates' most enduring legacy. They are figures for inert inefficacy that have lives and effects of their own.[79] Hodgson was a great lover of poetry, who published several astute essays on literary topics as well as verse translations from Greek and Latin authors. He proposed that the best test of philosophical writings would be to "bring them out of doors" and to translate them into poetry, which would "force them to assume their true shape."[80] Among his contemporaries, Hodgson was a great admirer of Swinburne; the structure and content of Swinburne's figurative language often seems to resonate with the *structure* of the epiphenomenalist image. Consider not only the imagery, but also the characteristic

floating detachment of vehicle and tenor in the simile in this stanza from
Swinburne:

> The wind is as iron that rings,
> The foam-heads loosen and flee;
> It swells and welters and swings,
> The pulse of the tide of the sea.[81]

CONCLUSION: J. M. E. MCTAGGART'S LOVE THINKING

This chapter has discovered that Victorian theorists of strong powers of
thinking and Victorian epiphenomenalists were linked in some curious
alliances, and shared some common concerns: a fierce allegiance to consciousness as a realm of power, freedom, intimacy, and "survival." But
another thing that, say, James Hinton and Shadworth Hodgson have in
common besides their unlikely friendship and weirdly shared intellectual values is their disappearance from the history of philosophical and
psychological ideas. Hinton and Hodgson, along with Bray and Boole,
and most of the other writers named in this chapter, are, for all of their
own emphasis on the survival of thought, names that have *not* survived
into our understanding of the history of ideas. Even the scholar committed to suspending judgment about who counts as a major or a minor
thinker can't help feeling uneasy about how unsurvived these people are,
no matter how influential (Hinton) or connected to the establishment
(Hodgson) they may have been in their own time. We may be tempted
to see their writings as epiphenomena of the dominant currents of their
time, floating loose from those more influential currents like foam on a
wave – "but without reaction upon it."

But there are a number of ways to think about their non-survival. First,
these writers allow us to imagine being in a world in which believing
that thinking was a force that could affect others – a force enabled by an
unseen world surrounding our own – might seem more plausible, more
normal, than does believing that thinking makes nothing happen. They
allow one to imagine a situation in which the question to ask is not –
as we might be inclined to ask – "how could anyone think that their
thoughts could affect other people?" but rather "how could anyone ever
come to think that thinking *doesn't* affect other people?" As I shall discuss
in later chapters of this book, trying on the second question turns out to
be more than simply a metaphysical historical-reconstruction thought-
experiment, a trying-on of weird beliefs as if they were three-cornered

hats. Rather, it is a way of getting at a complex aspect of moral psychology: that there may indeed be ways in which it makes moral sense for people to act *as if* their thoughts affected other people, and that in fact people do behave *as if* this were the case, all the time. Acting as if your thoughts could affect others, for good or ill, may be an ordinary part of social life. These theories about thinking about another person may open up possibilities for theorizing the place of mental relations in social life in ways that do not founder on epistemological problems about the knowability of other minds.

The theories of mental force discussed here, and the epiphenomenalism that would seem like their opposite, may be extreme ideas and massive failures: ideas that got pushed aside, along with their authors, by other developments in philosophy and psychology. But like a chemical catalyst that makes the solution turn purple, the body of ideas in this chapter shows up a cluster of beliefs which may be a persistent background presence in modern ideas about social life, only intermittently becoming visible. Another way, therefore, to frame the un-survivedness of these writers, and to think about the relations among them, is to see some strands of their ideas as in fact surviving on, woven together, in the writing of a slightly later, slightly – only slightly – less eccentric figure. The late Victorian, early twentieth-century Cambridge philosopher John McTaggart Ellis McTaggart (1866–1925) has not disappeared from the history of his discipline, or from ours: he was friends with Thomas Hardy (a friendship that began when Hardy wrote the philosopher a fan letter), and he makes guest appearances in literary criticism as an influence on T. S. Eliot, particularly concerning his famous concept of the unreality of time.[82] The last major figure in the tradition of nineteenth-century British idealism that began with Ferrier, McTaggart was less explicitly concerned with the ethical and social issues that preoccupied the other major figures in Victorian idealist philosophy, T. H. Green and F. H. Bradley, but his writings offer a vision of human relatedness and of thinking that is clearly affiliated with those of some of the other writers studied in this chapter.[83]

McTaggart had no patience with the Society for Psychical Research and its agonies over finding proof for human survival after death: not because he was against it, but rather because it seemed to him totally obvious. In his view, according to his friend and exegete Charlie Dunbar Broad, "the antecedent objections to human survival, drawn from common sense and natural science, are quite baseless."[84] A devout believer in spiritual survival but also a militant atheist, McTaggart devoted his career, from his amazing early essay "The Further Determination of the Absolute" (1893) (the writing of which he claimed "was like turning one's heart inside out"), to his final, incomplete work, *The Nature of Existence*, to working out a cosmology which purported to be Hegelian, but was mostly his own.[85] In his unorthodox elaboration of the Hegelian Absolute, the Absolute – that is, the abstract, eternal, ideal essence of reality – has to be thought of not as an idea, or as Spirit, or God. Rather, it has to be thought of as a society or "community of individuals like ourselves."[86] What binds together the individuals who make up the Absolute is love. And what McTaggart means by love, he tirelessly insisted, was really *love*: not some kind of generalized, abstract fellow feeling, benevolence or sympathy, but "intense and passionate" love, "that passionate personal affection which none of us in this life can feel towards more than a very few persons."[87] For further clarification, he says that what he means by love "is what it meant for Dante and Tennyson," and later specifies that this is the love of "the *Vita Nuova* and of *In Memoriam*."[88]

McTaggart knew that his philosophy of love sounded intensely flaky. Towards the end of his 1893 essay he stops to say: "it would be useless to attempt to deny that the conclusions I have endeavoured to support are hopelessly mystical" (271). It is a philosophy of love more radical than various Platonic or Neo-Platonic schemes to which it could be compared, in which earthly love is a kind of stepping stone to the Ideal.[89] For McTaggart, love actually *is* the Ideal. But McTaggart turns to love as the Absolute because it represents a kind of mental orientation towards another person that sets aside the claims of knowledge. "Knowledge" and "volition" are disqualified as routes to the Absolute. He concludes his essay:

The result of the whole investigation would seem to come to this – that it is by love only that we can fully enter into that harmony with others which alone constitutes our own reality and the reality of the universe…Knowledge and volition…only represent the true connection adequately in so far as they are approximations to and abstractions from love…Love is not only the highest thing in the universe, but the only thing.[90]

Just as McTaggart had to admit how flaky and mystical he sounded, I am compelled to confess how strangely moving it is to read McTaggart's otherworldly, outlandish ideas in his limpid, reasonable, and authoritative Cambridge prose. There's something delightful about this otherwise extremely abstract thinker going on about actual love being the meaning of the universe.[91] But I hope that throughout this chapter I have been able to demonstrate at least some of the seductiveness, for the literary reader, of a certain strand of "philosophical writing about thinking," from Bray to Hinton, from the physicists of force, to the epiphenomenalists with their metaphors. It is a strand of oddly moving philosophical prose that, as I've shown, casts thinking as a powerful but vacuum-sealed, silent force, strangely separate from speaking and writing. But it is also a prose with a consoling optimism about the force of thinking.

McTaggart's work shares the optimism about the power of thinking about other people we've seen in some of the panpsychic, mental force, thought-power prose discussed in this chapter. In McTaggart's case, this intense optimism about the continuity of human love and the Absolute seems to come along with no particular mandates for ethical or social behavior. As C. D. Broad notes, "the fact that the Kingdom of Heaven is a perfect society of intimately related persons gives us no guidance whatever in politics or ethics here and now."[92] In his later work, he elaborated further that love between people involved a particular kind of thinking or "cogitation." Love marks a union between cogitation and emotion; in love there cannot be one without the other: "We must hold that the cogitation of that to which the emotion is directed, and the emotion toward it, are *the same mental state*, which has the quality of being a cogitation of it, and the quality of being an emotion directed at it."[93] In "our present experience," moreover, cogitation is inseparable in some inevitable, but not particularly troubling, way from error. In *Truth, Love, and Immortality: An Introduction to McTaggart's Philosophy*, P. T. Geach notes that McTaggart's taxonomies of cogitation have, surprisingly, no place for "anything like acts of understanding or acts of knowing," and that "the problem of knowledge and belief" that exercised other philosophers "seems never to have worried him at all." On McTaggart's indifference to questions of epistemology and skepticism, Geach writes:

Problems of whether there is such a thing as *absolutely* certain knowledge, and whether acts of knowledge are distinguished from acts of believing by some introspective criterion – all of this seems to have bothered McTaggart extremely little.[94]

According to Geach, McTaggart's view was that "we live in a mixed state of knowledge and error"; his optimism about people's capacity for both error and for "correcting false steps" characterizes his attitude toward thinking (113). Yet in *The Nature of Existence*, Absolute reality must be thought of as a collection of minds linked through love because love is linked to the clearest kind of cognition, in which what love thinks equals a kind of tautological knowledge of itself. He concludes with this account of Absolute reality:

> We know that it is a timeless and endless state of love – love so direct, so intimate, and so powerful that even the deepest mystic rapture gives us but the slightest foretaste of its perfection. We know that we shall know nothing but our beloved, and those they love, and ourselves as loving them. (II: 479)

In the meantime, our connection to that Absolute is in the practice of love's union of cognition and emotion we could call a version of love thinking.

Throughout this chapter and the preceding one, there have been glimpses of an ongoing dialogue between philosophical prose and poetry. Reading Bray, Hinton, and Hodgson, it sometimes seems as if the entire story of Victorian beliefs about the act of thinking could be told as the story of the era's collective meditation on Shelley and Coleridge. James Frederick Ferrier seriously contemplated writing out Tennyson's *In Memoriam* into philosophical prose, while Hodgson thought that the truth of philosophy could be revealed by translating it into poetry. When McTaggart wishes to describe love in Absolute reality he refers, as we have seen, to Dante and Tennyson; when he wishes to describe love in this world he quotes Swinburne ("By The North Sea": see *The Nature of Existence* II: 157). In the next two chapters, we shall explore how Victorian poetry processed the power of thinking about other people. There may be no direct lines of influence between the prose writers that have been scrutinized in these first two chapters, and the poets – Coleridge, Landon, Barrett Browning, Rossetti, Meynell, Patmore, and Meredith – under consideration in the next two. It will be apparent how common are their concerns with the effects of thinking about another person. Nineteenth-century English poets thought seriously about the relations among thinking, writing, and spoken utterance, shedding light on the sequestering of thinking from the noisy world of language so curiously evident in discussions of mental force.

CHAPTER 3

Thinking in the second person in nineteenth-century poetry

What does it mean to say to someone, "I am thinking of you"? And what does it mean to write it? Do assertions of this kind betray our kinship, however distant, with the nineteenth-century evangelists of thought-power, believing with them that our thoughts about someone in need are a form of action that can bring restitution, assistance, or at least companionship? Or, is "I am thinking of you" just something we *say*, a proposition whose substance lies in its performance or communication? If so, does the thinking happen at all?

This chapter argues that nineteenth-century British poetry can provide us with insights into what it means to try to think in the second person, by complicating the difficult questions about what it means to say, *and* to write, "I think about you." Paying attention to the poetics of second-person address in nineteenth-century verse may teach us a great deal about how we know what it feels like to think about another person. Studying the poetics of address can demonstrate some of the ways in which what appear to be philosophical problems reveal themselves as literary forms.

That nineteenth-century poetry not only engages with philosophy, but also constitutes itself as a kind of thinking, is a notion that should require no special urging. We can begin by referring to Hegel's *Lectures on Aesthetics* (1832), which lined up "poetic thinking" with "*speculative* thinking," which transcends the limitations of both "*ordinary* thinking" and "the restricted thinking of the *Understanding*" which is the work of the "prosaic mind."[1] The distinctive, often uneasy assimilation of philosophical idealism into anglophone culture, which provides part of the context for the beliefs about the act of thinking about another person this book has been puzzling over, took place to a large extent through not only the work of poet-philosophers (such as Coleridge), but also the vehicle of poetry itself. The poems of Coleridge, Shelley, and others were thoroughly philosophized in later nineteenth-century England. In a publication of the Shelley Society in 1887, for example, the Reverend Stopford Augustus Brooke turned

"Epipsychidion" – Shelley's defense of extramarital sex – into a manifesto
of the poet's perennial "clasping at last its ideal in the immaterial world
of pure Thought."[2] But in our own scholarly climate, the proposition that
nineteenth-century poetry and poetics are themselves *forms of thinking* has
taken on a new life. The goal of Simon Jarvis' *Wordsworth's Philosophic Song*
is to take seriously the claims of Wordsworth (often cast as the great but
intuitive poet, in contrast to Coleridge the thinker) to think philosophically through poetry. "It might mean that a different kind of thinking
happens in verse," notes Jarvis: "that instead of being a sort of thoughtless
ornament or reliquary for thinking, verse is itself a kind of cognition."[3] We
may wish to proceed with skepticism about claims to ever really identify, or
understand, "kinds" of cognition. What we can study, I argue in this chapter and the next, are the ways in which aspects of poetry have historically
come to be associated with aspects of our experience of thinking.

The particular claim of this chapter is that nineteenth-century British
poets and poetic theorists often explicitly or implicitly linked poetic address
to beloved others to the act of thinking about another. They were not the
first poets ever to do so; nor did they always model second-person address
on the action of thinking; but there is a high correlation between poetic
address and the act of thinking in nineteenth-century British poetry, a correlation which this book's focus on thinking as a form of intersubjective
action makes highly conspicuous.[4] This may seem like an uncontroversial
or uninteresting claim to make but, as we shall see, the idea that second-
person poetic address has something to do with thinking has been overlooked by the emphasis of critical debates about "apostrophe," which have
largely proceeded as if writing "you" in a poem is unequivocally modeled
on speaking. As I hope to show, tracking the ways in which nineteenth-
century poets linked apostrophe to second-person thinking can alter or
clarify some aspects of the critical conversations about address, and clarify
our perceptions about its centrality to lyric poetry.[5]

This chapter will first ponder the writings of some nineteenth-century
poetic theorists who found the second-person pronoun to be the essence
of the poetry of their century. It then turns to consider a range of poems
spanning the century, from Coleridge's "This Lime-Tree Bower My Prison"
(1800) to Christina Rossetti's *Monna Innominata* (1881), which themselves
form a sustained conversation on poetical thinking in the second person. As this chapter proceeds it will, I hope, become gradually clear why
most of the poems I discuss here are by women, and why these poems by
women produce a somewhat less cheerfully optimistic picture of the power
to affect other people than that of the philosophical prose discussed in the

preceding chapter. We shall see emerging, in this chapter and the next, a deep ambivalence about the power of thinking about another person: a worry that thinking about another person may bring harm, may be a form of domination, or may be destructive to intimacy. I suggest that we can attribute some of these changes to an environment, by around the middle of the century, in which poetic forms came to represent the pressures placed on marriage to model ideal mental relations between two persons. This chapter will conclude by considering what is at stake when a poet, Elizabeth Barrett Browning – highly conscious of the vicissitudes and dangers of thinking about another person – declares, "I *do not* think of you."

NINETEENTH-CENTURY POETIC THEORY AND THE SECOND-PERSON PRONOUN

The mid-century theorizing of mental life as part of the force of the universe we surveyed in the preceding chapter had its correlates in approaches to poetry, and nowhere so provocatively as in Eneas Sweetland Dallas' *Poetics: An Essay on Poetry* (1852). Born in 1808 to Scottish parents in Jamaica, Dallas attended the University of Edinburgh where, like James Frederick Ferrier two decades before him, he was a student of philosophy under Sir William Hamilton, to whom he dedicated *Poetics*. Like Ferrier, he was interested in mesmerism. The influence of German idealists – in this case Schelling and Hegel – is as evident in Dallas' *Poetics* as it is in Ferrier's *Introduction to the Philosophy of Consciousness*, but as in the case of Ferrier's work, the result of "German philosophy refracted through an alien Scottish medium" (to cite again Thomas De Quincey's apt description of Ferrier) is an original, compellingly written work.[6]

Dallas' understanding of poetry is shaped by a conception of thinking deeply resonant with many of the mental action theorists discussed in the previous chapter. His *Poetics* begins by defining mental pleasure, which is, in essence, motion. To read the following passage in light of the writings of Bray, Tait and Balfour, and others is both to see anew a historical context for mental action theory, and to understand the emphasis on the silent work of force in some of those writers. Seeking to define the mental pleasure afforded by poetry as a form of activity, Dallas assures us that in the realm of the mind there is no incompatibility between repose and motion. Mental motion and the astonishingly swift motions of the modern world are figures for each other, as Dallas explains:

As railway motion is not only easy, but quick; as an eagle goes sailing athwart the sun with the swiftness of wind, and yet calm as a slumberer; as this ball of earth is rolled through the skies with speed at the uttermost, and yet seems as wafted with the softness of a feather on the gentle breath of evening; as wide nature, however still she may appear, is stirring ever and everywhere around us with unimaginable power; so the mind, for all its hush, may be up and doing at once with the strength of a giant, and the nimbleness of the fairy.[7]

In this fairy-tale of the mind (in which the mind is both giant and fairy), it initially seems as though this fast-moving train (as it were) of images is designed to explain mental motion. By the end of the passage, however, the effect is the other way around. It is only in the mind, and on the model of the mind, that all of these highly literary images of motion – Tennyson's eagle, Shakespeare's "ball of earth" (though who ever thinks of this ball of earth as wafted with the softness of a feather?) – come together as images of the union of motion and repose. As Dallas declares a bit later, "when we speak of activity, we must needs mean activity of the mind" (39). Motion itself – even the mechanized movement of the train experienced subjectively as easy motion by the passenger – is reconceived and modeled on the "hush," invisible world of mental action. Aestheticized in this passage and elsewhere, Dallas' conception of mental action is the essence of pleasure, and, as well, the opposite of knowing. The drive to know is for Dallas not a high form of mental action, but its crippler. Elaborating a concept of the role of unconsciousness in art that he derives from Coleridge, Schelling, and Carlyle, Dallas links too much seeking after answers to that killer of art, self-consciousness. Unconscious pleasure is the highest form of mental action, one that swells productively over its territory like the Nile. He quotes approvingly a passage from Hooker: "the mind, feeling present joy, is always marvelous unwilling to admit any other cogitation" (30). For Dallas, as for many of the writers surveyed in the preceding chapter, emotions fall under the heading of cogitation.

For Dallas, poetic address represents a particular kind of cogitation, one that refracts its objects into many parts. His remarks on the poetry of "you" emerge in Book 3 of *Poetics*, which is devoted to an ambitious classification of all world poetry into three major genres – dramatic, epic, and lyric – which correspond to distinct sets of historical, formal, and "philosophical" characteristics. The details of this endeavor, which culminates in an elaborate chart (119), and which for W. David Shaw betrays in Dallas "that distemper of learning which Bacon calls 'fantastical,'" need not concern us here.[8] But his discussions of the ways in which the different genres and ages of poetry orient themselves around particular pronouns – a characteristic he ranks under the category "philosophical" in his chart – is, while perhaps distempered, strangely revealing. While classical ("Antique,"

"Grecian") epic poetry is, unsurprisingly, characterized as a form of narration carried out in the third person, and lyric (which for Dallas is primarily "Eastern" or "Asiatic" poetry, by which he means the Hebrew Bible)
is a poetry of the first person, modern Western poetry – also classified as
"Romantic" – is for Dallas essentially dramatic, and essentially a poetry of
the second person.

The identity of the "you" around whom Dallas imagines modern poetry
to be centered is completely variable and yet, when viewed from Dallas'
sweeping, global perspective, all the same person wearing different clothing. When Dallas is alluding to properly dramatic works, "you" is any
or all individual characters, literary personages, and objects of address.
But the orientation of all modern poetry around "you" also represents its
self-conscious orientation towards that singular personage, "the reader."
"The whole literature of a dramatic era will look at things from the position and with the eye of the reader, constantly employing the second personal pronoun."[9] With the pronoun, Dallas gestures towards a familiar
theme: the ways in which nineteenth-century literature bore the imprint,
in unprecedented ways, of its huge and pressing reading publics.[10]

Nevertheless, the burden to justify the choice of "you" as the essential
pronoun of modern poetry leads Dallas down some unexpected paths. For
example: the division of poetic genres by pronouns corresponds to their
division according to time. Third-person epic poetry covers the past, and
lyric poetry in Dallas' definition is prophetically future-oriented. Modern
dramatic poetry takes place in the present tense. "Next," he continues,
"it may be shown that we think of You in the present tense, that He is
regarded as past, and that I project myself into the future."[11] Not only do
we "think of You in the present tense," but to think in the second person is, for Dallas, a curious form of thought that precludes apprehending
"you" as a "unity" (which is how we think about the first-person pronoun)
or as a "totality" (an honor accorded to a person who is thought about
in the third person). To think in the second person is to think of someone as a "plurality" (101). Like the later Victorian poet and critic Alice
Meynell's essay "Second Person Singular," to which we will turn shortly,
Dallas' discussion of the second-person pronoun makes much of the singular (as it were) historical fact that, of all modern European languages,
English does not distinguish between the singular and the plural second
person. For Dallas, the victory of "you" over "thou" signals not – as the
Quakers (whom Dallas dismisses as egotistical literalists) argue – hier-
archy and flattery, but rather the fact that the second person is inherently
dramatic, inherently plural, and thus inherently unknowable. "A man

seldom has doubts of his own identity," Dallas opines; whatever alterations or changes an "I" may undergo, "I am still the self-same being." However, he continues:

But you – when I see you pleased with what once gave you pain, and scorning what once you admired, what wonder if, not having a clue to these changes, I can hardly believe that you are one and the same person...I must (however unconsciously) regard you as not one, but more than one person; you are in yourself a host. (103–4)

While to think of a person in the third person implies "that our knowledge of him is past" (105), embalmed as a totality, thinking of someone in the second person gets at the person's essential freedom and their essentially transcendent nature. The meditation on "you" ends with the following thought-experiment:

You; what is my state of mind in calling upon You? I do not think of you as an Immortal, neither do I think of your Divine origin; but I think of you as now and here existent, a man of whose next thought, or word, or deed, I am uncertain, a man of Free Will....[In contrast]: He; we have nothing to do with his Immortality; as little do we think of His Freedom. (109)

As if to underscore that for Dallas number is intertwined with person, the shift from "you" to "he" is curiously accompanied by an unnoticed shift from "I" to "we." Unlike thinking of "he," thinking of "you" involves thinking of your free will, your Freedom with a capital F. The full weight of Dallas' "you" becomes clearest in the fourth, most Hegelian section of *Poetics*, "The Poet," in which dramatic art is revealed as the highest vocation in the growth of the arts, because of its approach to freedom ("It is in the exercise of Freedom that the human mind has a relationship and fellow-feeling with the Divine," [258]). We can see why for Dallas the configuration of the three great genres of poetry with the three personal pronouns is ranked as a philosophical, rather than merely a grammatical, matter. Thinking in the second person accesses the person's moral essence.

It may seem one of the more outlandish claims of this "perverse monograph," as W. David Shaw calls Dallas' *Poetics*, to load so much philosophical baggage onto a personal pronoun (and we shall have occasion to ponder some of *Poetics*' other outlandish claims, about the relationship of poetic meters to mental action, in the next chapter).[12] But the notion that the second-person pronoun has moral significance is not foreign to philosophy.[13] The significance of second-person thinking for ethics has most recently been explored, for example, by philosopher Stephen Darwall

in *The Second-Person Standpoint: Morality, Respect, and Accountability*.
For him, second-person ethics involves "practically directed and direct-
ive thought, thought that is addressed to, and that makes a claim on, a
free and rational agent."[14] Darwall's notion that thinking happens in the
second person, and can be addressed to, and can make a claim on, another
person, is deeply intriguing in the context of the current study. (Literary
scholars may be most familiar with the idea that second-person *address*
in itself may have an ethical dimension from Martin Buber's account of
I–Thou relations, the relevance of which to nineteenth-century poetry was
explored in Harold Bloom's book on Shelley.)[15] However, what reading
Darwall in conjunction with Dallas' philosophical thought-experiments
produces is an awareness of second-person address *as a mode of thinking*.
Developmental psychologists, meanwhile, have sought to prove that there
actually is a kind of primary second-person awareness that infants develop
before third-person, or even first-person awareness, and certainly before
language acquisition: accordingly, the second person is a form of thinking first and foremost.[16] Reading about second-person thinking can make
sense of our own experience of mental life, which often seems – if you are
like me – peopled with other people, and in which a great deal of what
feels like conscious thinking takes the form of inner address to others.

The significance of Dallas' "perverse" ideas about the second-person
pronoun in modern poetry might be confirmed by looking at Alice
Meynell's speculations on the same topic several decades later, in her essay
"Second Person Singular" (1898). Meynell also affirms that poetry plays a
particular role in Victorian thinking about thinking in the second person.
Her starting point is the absence, in modern spoken English, of a familiar
second-person singular form – the absence of a "*tu*" form distinguishing
itself both by number and by status from the "*vous*" form. The "modern
monotony of 'you'," for Meynell, stems from the "slovenliness of our civilization" in matters of language.[17] Like Dallas, she twits the Quakers for
hypocrisy and inconsistency (137–38) in their usage of "thee" and "thou"
when speaking with actually existing human beings. The great blessing of
modern English according to Meynell is that, in casting off the second-
person singular in ordinary speech (and she means throughout the *familiar* second-person singular), the second-person singular was preserved for
use – and for use only – in poetry and in religious experience. "The literary Genius was kind to its wayward chosen people, and kept for us a
plot of the language apart for the phrase of piety and poetry," she writes;
for poets and for the devout (and Meynell, a Catholic convert, was both),
the second-person singular pronoun is "our unique plot of disregarded

language that the traffic of the world passes by" (136, 137). The devolution and slovenliness of spoken English is thus a fortunate fall; the important thing about this "rude forefinger of a pronoun" is its silence.[18] Cut off from ordinary speech, "thou" is soundless and sequestered, the very index of modern poetry's essence, its affinity with spiritual aspirations. What Dallas' and Meynell's views of poetic second-person address share is an emphasis on poetry's "you"s as essentially non-speech. It is a theory of poetic address that belongs historically to a body of poetic theory that ponders, in new ways, the place of poetry in a silent world of print. We will do well to keep their views in mind as we move forward to consider more recent theories of "apostrophe" which imagine poetry as a voice.[19]

Moreover, if for Dallas thinking in the second person diffused and dispersed knowledge of the "you," for Meynell the virtue of the singular "thou" is hardly in its greater singularity, specificity (over the scatter-shot, pluralizing "you"), or its superior intimacy. As Emily Harrington has argued, Meynell conceived of intimacy as founded on the distance or separation between two people, and she knew that to think of someone in the second person is simultaneously to bring them closer and move them further into the distance.[20] Love and intimacy do the "thou" no favors; it is a thin kind of currency whose particular intimacy wears out in use:

It is by no means certain that the second person singular, with its single delight – the first – never to be renewed, has not to answer for the vulgar regrets of the world for the flights of its joys. "Toi," the first "toi," is an arbitrary, a conventional happiness, a happiness because it is single – it has no quality but that. The "many thousand" of "toi" are insignificant, and therefore it has no "poor last"; it sets a paltry example, therefore.[21]

And if Meynell knew that *saying* "toi" to a beloved wears out its singularity by the second time, even more did she know that poetic thinking in the second person renders the "thee" more multiple than singular, both everywhere and nowhere. In her sonnet "Renouncement," the "thought of thee" resides in the height of the sky and in the sound of a song; it is also "hidden" and "beyond":

> I must not think of thee; and, tired yet strong,
> I shun the thought that lurks in all delight –
> The thought of thee – and in the blue Heaven's height,
> And in the sweetest passage of a song.
> Oh, just beyond the fairest thoughts that throng
> This breast, the thought of thee waits hidden yet bright;
> But it must never, never come in sight;
> I must stop short of thee the whole day long.

> But when sleep comes to close each difficult day,
> When night gives pause to the long watch I keep,
> And all my bonds I needs must loose apart,
> Must doff my will as raiment laid away –
> With the first dream that comes with the first sleep
> I run, I run, I am gathered to thy heart.[22]

The urgency of the last line – "I run, I run" – betrays the fact that the action of the poem is of course purely mental: as Dallas would say, "when we speak of activity, we must needs mean activity of the mind."[23] The closest the speaker can get to the "thee" is in dreaming, which, as in some of the prose discussed in Chapter 2, is represented here as a kind of love thinking. We shall have more to say about Meynell's poem when we consider poems about not-thinking at the end of this chapter – and we shall revisit Meynell as a critic and theorist in the next chapter as well.

As odd and whimsical as Dallas' and Meynell's treatment of poetic second-person thinking can seem, both writers' understanding of *thinking* as the primary field of poetical "you"s and "thee"s comes from a deep reading of the practices of nineteenth-century poetry. Considering the poetry and the theory together, we can see why the question of "you" is not simply a grammatical question, but a philosophical and psychological one. We can bring our reading of Dallas and Meynell to a reading of this exceedingly minimal poem about thinking about another person by Samuel Taylor Coleridge's great grand-niece, Mary Elizabeth Coleridge (1898):

> Prisoned within these walls,
> I think of you.
> Lightly the snowflake falls,
> The rain too.
> Now it is rain, and now
> The snow again.
> Within – I know not how –
> 'Tis only rain.[24]

The "you" in this poem seems barely more than a grammatical marker. Compared even to Meynell's "thee" in "Renouncement" – a personage with at least a vague semblance of existence for us, having at least a "heart" the poem's "I" can get gathered to ("Renouncement," 14) – Coleridge's "you" is completely unspecified. This poem's mode of referring to "you" can scarcely be called an address: even to the extent that one can begin to infer a context, situation, or occasion for this poem, it is hard to imagine the poem as a communication or presentation to the "you," or even the fiction of one. A poem such as this one makes us acutely aware of the need for a discussion of poetic second persons that exceeds our understanding of "apostrophe" or even "lyric address." All we can say about Coleridge's "you" is that he has clearly absented him-self – for the sake of argument, let's call him a him – or wounded the "I," or is separate and suffering in some way. This poem is a drama of thinking in the second person, precisely not because it has anything to say *about* the "you," but because the "you" serves as a wavering place-holder that structures a poetic thinking. Only mentioned once, that is, the "you" sets up a series of oppositions, not only between "I" and "you," but also snow or rain, and "within" and outside, in which the "you" serves as a kind of moving wall. At first it would seem that "you" is outside, insofar as the "I" is emphatically "prisoned within these walls." But after that point, a perceptual uncertainty – snow or rain? Or snow and rain? – leads to a metaphorical certainty (in spite, or because of the disingenuous, perhaps disbelieving "I know not how") – that "Within… 'tis only rain." Inside is redefined as the tears within the speaker, and thus we come to feel that "within" is where the "you" actually is: not outside the walls, not outside anywhere, but being thought about. The perceptual-metaphorical progression puts the "you" in an inside that is modeled on the inside of the room. In a lovely essay called "A Note on the Use of the Word 'Internal'" (1941), Alix Strachey observed that sometimes we use the word "internal" to mean, simply, what is "mental," while sometimes – particularly in psychoanalysis – it refers more nar-rowly to "a mental space that is imagined as 'inside.'" M. E. Coleridge's "You" is what the psychoanalysts might call a "mental object."[25] Perhaps especially vividly, the deeply underspecified language of this slim poem clarifies the ways in which poetic thinking in the second person is not only "philosophical," as Dallas would have it, but also psychological.

I wish therefore to end this discussion of Victorian theories of think-ing in the second person by describing a parable from a piece of writing seemingly far afield – from D. W. Winnicott's stunning essay, "The Use of an Object and Relating Through Identifications" (1969), which may be seen, for our purposes, as an account of how other people intermittently become real in our thoughts. Winnicott distinguishes between two ways of thinking of others, which he calls "relating to" and "using." "Relating to" an object characterizes psychoanalysis' traditional domain: the way versions of and parts of other people inhabit our minds as mental entities, objects to our subjecthood. What Winnicott defines (rather counterintui-tively) as "using" an object describes the capacity to recognize and place the object – now no longer really an object – *"outside the area of subjective phenomena.*"[26] He is concerned to explore the relation between these two modes, in particular the passage from "relating to" to "using," which takes place only through what he calls the subject's – the infant's – "destruction" of the object, and that object's consequent survival: "It is the destructive drive that creates the quality of externality" (93). Winnicott gives his most vivid account of this process by ventriloquizing the (internal) voice of the subject as it addresses the object:

The subject says to the object: "I destroyed you," and the object is there to receive the communication. From now on the subject says: "Hullo object!" "I destroyed you." "I love you." "You have value for me because of your survival of my destruction of you." "While I am loving you I am all the time destroying you in (unconscious) *fantasy.*" (90)

This passage fascinates the student of poetic second-person thinking in that it suggests the ways in which – as we shall see in the next section of this chapter – an address to a "you" – "Hullo object!" – may be a way not of relating to another but of using. To address may be a way not to relate, but to destroy.[27] From Dallas' mid-nineteenth-century Hegelianism forward there is a thread of theorizing poetic thinking in the second person that is highly attentive to what we could call the productive negativity involved in thinking "you."[28] As we move forward, we shall see different poets thinking about this in different ways. Such poems goad us into a series of questions about thinking about another person as a form of action: is thinking about someone the next best thing to being with them, or only a pale and disappointing substitute? Does it bring a person closer, or push them further away? Does it create, or destroy them?

MENTAL PERSONS: "THOU, METHINKS"

A familiar romantic poem, Samuel Taylor Coleridge's "This Lime-Tree Bower My Prison" (1800), might help clarify some of the ways in which some of nineteenth-century poetry's most programmatic utterances orient themselves around some of the questions discussed above. Structured through a range of apostrophes and addresses to different – and different kinds of – yous and thous, "Lime-Tree Bower" can point us to some of the shortcomings of the ways we tend to view poetic second persons. This poem's addresses to persons and things come to us embedded in a dense history of communications and exchanges between Coleridge and his friends. Addressed poetically to Charles Lamb – who famously objected to the terms in which he was addressed – the poem first appeared in a letter addressed to Robert Southey; was used as a kind of currency as well in Coleridge's complex, triangulated relations with Thomas Poole, John Thelwall, and Charles Lloyd, among others; and may best be described as "as a poem silently addressed to Wordsworth."[29] It is a poem that emerges out of the intertwining, and mutual interruption, not only of personal relations and literary relations, but also of different modes of relating to other people. Contemplating this poem thus allows us to reflect on the ways in which poetic second persons may involve a curious interplay between actual relations with empirical persons who may intermittently appear "*outside the area of subjective phenomena*," as Winnicott put it, and mental relations with mental persons. "This Lime-Tree Bower My Prison" is among other things an exploration of the non-egalitarian nature of having another person *in mind*. This topic emerges through the poem's formal structures and modes of address, but also through the subtle pressure the presence of the friends – often by name, Lamb, but also, as "Friends," William and Dorothy Wordsworth – puts on the poem's programmatic statements about the freedom of the imagination to travel beyond the prison of our sight, and the faithfulness of nature – that "Nature ne'er deserts the wise and pure," and that "sometimes / 'Tis well to be bereft of promised good, / That we may lift the Soul, and contemplate / With lively joy the joys we cannot share."[30] The freedom of the imagination gets cast as something that may be at the expense of others. Readers have often treated the presence of the friends in the poem as more or less a vehicle for Coleridge's imaginings of absent and present landscapes, as the poem takes the form of the poet imagining the friends' seeing, from the inwardness of the landscape of the first verse paragraph, to the sublimity of the second, before the return to the beauties of the bower at the end.[31] However, by focusing our attention on the friends, we might turn this around and see the locodescriptive skeleton of the poem as a register of different modes of having others in mind.

In the first verse paragraph of "This Lime-Tree Bower," for example, Coleridge seems militantly to cast the friends as mental objects that can be moved about at will: "Friends," he calls them somewhat melodramatically, "whom I never more may meet again," a line that contains more than an element of melancholy vengeance (6).[32]

> Well, they are gone, and here must I remain,
> This Lime-Tree Bower my Prison! I have lost

Beauties and Feelings, such as would have been
Most sweet to my remembrance, even when age
Had dimmed mine eyes to blindness! They, meanwhile,
Friends, whom I never more may meet again,
…
Wander in gladness.

(1–6, 8)

But the exiling of the friends is the precondition for their endurance, the "still" of the rest of the passage. It brings them inward, into an inwardness which is expressed in the way Coleridge directs them, at first, into a landscape that enfolds them, that seems highly mental in its redundant dripping. The friends wander

To that still roaring dell, of which I told;
The roaring dell, o'erwooded, narrow, deep,
And only speckled by the mid-day Sun;
Where its slim trunk the Ash from rock to rock
Flings arching like a Bridge; – that branchless Ash,
Unsunn'd and damp, whose few poor yellow leaves
Ne'er tremble in the gale, yet tremble still,
Fann'd by the water-fall! and there my friends
Behold the dark green file of long lank Weeds,
That all at once (a most fantastic sight!)
Still nod and drip beneath the dripping edge
Of the blue clay-stone.

(9–19)

The nosing-forward movement of the lines – "ash…branchless ash," "ne'er tremble…yet tremble still," "drip…dripping edge," as well as the internal near-rhymes (gale, fall, file; long, lank) all conspire to make one feel as if what one is reading is not so much a description of a place (weird, remarkable, oozy, and inward as it is in itself) as the movement of the mind inventing an inside to contain its mental objects.

After he rescues the friends from the dripping weeds, Coleridge places them on a height, where the interplay of verb mood and address both clarifies and confuses how the poem imagines thinking about another person. Charles Lamb emerges here as the primary object of the poet's reverie, and as the poem's addressee, in a line we shall return to:

Yes! They wander on
In gladness all; but thou, methinks, most glad,
My gentle-hearted Charles! For thou hast pined
And hunger'd after Nature, many a year,
In the great City pent, winning thy way

With sad yet patient soul, through evil and pain
And strange calamity!

(26–32)

Compared to the barely-an-address "I think of you" of Mary Elizabeth
Coleridge's poem, discussed in the previous section, here we are distinctly in the presence of an actual poetic apostrophe: the "thou" form; the
exclamation point; the sudden turn to single out an individual for address;
the famously dubious epithet "gentle-hearted." It is a heightened poetic
gesture that is clearly affiliated with the genres of the seventeenth- and
eighteenth-century verse epistle and the ode. But there are several things
in the environment of this "thou" that we ought to pay attention to.

First, we note that the poem's "thou" becomes the sun, and by extension all the other natural elements who are invoked and addressed in the
imperative:

Ah! Slowly sink
Behind the western ridge, thou glorious Sun!
Shine in the slant beams of the sinking orb
Ye purple heath-flowers! richlier burn, ye clouds!
Live in the yellow light, ye distant groves!
And kindle, thou blue Ocean!

(32–37)

We might use this shift to refine our understanding of poetic address.
Some of the most influential treatments in twentieth-century lyric theory
focused on apostrophe as performance that renders all objects of address
more or less equivalent, or interchangeable. Here for example is Northrop
Frye in the *Anatomy of Criticism* on the essence of lyric:

The lyric poet normally pretends to be talking to himself or someone else: a spirit
of nature, a Muse, a personal friend, a lover, a god, a personified abstraction, or a
natural object…The poet, so to speak, turns his back on his listeners.[33]

Frye's list suggests that any differences among objects of address are completely subordinated to the basic fact of the fictitiousness of poetic address,
which is itself equated with the negation of empirical persons as a poem's
object of address. In his influential essay "Apostrophe," Jonathan Culler
similarly views apostrophe as a mode of constituting the poetic vocation
of the voice that calls. In this view, it doesn't much matter what kind of
thing that "I" is calling. Thus, romantic odes (his example is Wordsworth's
"Intimations Ode") which have multiple addressees apostrophize promiscuously in order to "bring together" heterogeneous addressees into a "single unreal space":

The fact that apostrophe involves a drama of "the one mind's" modifications more than a relationship between an *I* and a *you* emerges with special clarity in poems with multiple apostrophes. Wordsworth's "Immortality Ode," for example, brings together in a single unreal space "Thou child of joy," "ye blessed creatures," "Thou whose exterior semblance dost belie thy soul's immensity," "ye birds," and "ye fountains, meadows, hills, and groves." Brought together by apostrophes, they function as nodes or concretizations of stages in a drama of mind.[34]

But to apostrophize the sun and bid its inevitable set seems like a very different poetic gesture from addressing an empirical person whom one claims to know in a way that is both more intimate and less certain than the way one knows the sun will set. On the one hand, the conjunction of these two addresses makes the apostrophe to the sun seem preposterously grandiose in that, set next to Charles, the sun seems the object of a grossly uneasy familiarity. On the other hand, it makes the address to Charles seem impossibly, embarrassingly bossy too: as if the banality of the certitude with which one knows the sun will set when one bids it had lent a kind of fatuousness to one's confidence that the friend can be moved around. In this context, following on the apostrophes to the natural objects which simply ask them to exist – "live in the yellow light, ye distant groves" and, slightly more weirdly, "kindle, thou blue ocean" – the hypothetical descriptions of the friend's luminous experience of the Almighty ("So my Friend / Struck with deep joy may stand") feel imperative and domineering.[35] Indeed, the poet's power to make, in his mind, his friends perceive is mirrored in the characterization of the "Almighty Spirit" himself, "when he makes / Spirits perceive his presence" (42–43).

But the poem's record of the idea that thinking about the friend may involve a sublimely bossy sovereignty emerges most of all in the poet's retreat from the imagined open landscape into the description of the lime tree bower itself, in the third verse paragraph. While the plenitude of the bower can seem like the poet's reward for his imaginative beneficence to his friend, it is also a correction of it. We could dwell on the word "usurps" in the description of the deepening bower:

> And that Walnut-tree
> Was richly ting'd, and a deep radiance lay
> Full on the ancient Ivy, which usurps
> Those fronting elms, and now, with blackest mass
> Makes their dark branches gleam a lighter hue...
>
> (52–56)

A similar image of ivy – or foliage or flowers – usurping that on which it hangs will appear later in this chapter. Here as there, it is an image of an uneasiness about the relationship between thoughts about an object, and an object. It is a trope with a long history, and can be related, as we shall see, to an image in Andrew Marvell's poem "The Coronet" in which thoughts of God are likened to a garland that needs to be "shattered," stripped away from its object.[36] The uneasiness about thinking about the friend that is registered here emerges again at the end of the poem, which recapitulates in miniature the transition from the second to third verse paragraph, in a passage we could call "two ways of looking at a blackbird." Addressing (in all editions after 1800) Charles once more, Coleridge describes the last rook of the evening crossing his friend's path, and cannot imagine it just one way, but instead in two. He blesses the rook:

> deeming, its black wing
> (Now a dim speck, now vanishing in light)
> Had cross'd the mighty Orb's dilated glory,
> While thou stood'st gazing, or when all was still,
> Flew creeking o'er thy head, and had a charm
> For thee, my gentle-hearted Charles...
>
> (71–76)

Coleridge's "or" here between the sublime and the homely versions of crow encapsulates the pressure the friend puts on the poem. It replaces the bossiness of the second verse paragraph with a recognition that the friend's experience can only be an "or," a grammatical possibility.

"This Lime-Tree Bower My Prison" is thus a poem that is highly aware of the volatile nature of thinking about another person, self-conscious about the risks of domination, projection, aggrandizement, and reduction. Coleridge's intense overinvestment in other people made him more, not less, aware of the vicissitudes of thinking about other people: the way sometimes people loom in one's mind as inapproachably large and great, while others dwindle into "little Potatoes – i.e. *no great Things!* – a compost of Nullity and Dullity –."[37] That this awareness emerges in a complex politics of second-person address could be confirmed by dwelling further on the status of the addresses, imperatives, and pseudo-imperatives in this poem, and in particular on the conjunction in line 27 of "thou" and "methinks." As we noted, the proximity of different kinds of "thou"s in "Lime-Tree Bower" works to confer a conspicuous bossiness on Coleridge's addresses to Charles Lamb, an effect that can go unrecognized in approaches to poetic address that do not differentiate among kinds of objects. Furthermore, critical discussions of poetic address almost universally tend to treat it as a form of, in Frye's words, "pretending to talk to."[38]

But what does it mean to *pretend* to talk to some one? Coleridge's conjunction of "thou" and "methinks" casts "thou" as an act of thinking, not of speaking, and in so doing sets in play a series of paradoxes in which thinking and speaking become ghosts of each other, and poetic "thou"s and empirical addressees become virtual to each other. That is, if our theory of apostrophe imagines that we imagine the poet "turning his back on listeners," it becomes very hard to think about the poetics of address in relation to, say, this poem's own history as a medium of exchange in the intimacies between Coleridge and his friends. Once a poem stages an address to an actually existing person, that empirical person becomes virtualized – a "compost of Nullity" if not of Dullity –, part of the fictive fabric of the poem. At the same time, any actual reader of the poem – even the person to whom the poem is addressed – becomes virtual to the poem. Though the poem was "addressed" to him (explicitly so in its first publication, where it bore the subtitle "Addressed to Charles Lamb, of the India House, London," as if it were a letter with a postal address), the real Charles Lamb seems only to have read the poem after it was published in Southey's *Annual Anthology* in 1800, a reading which seems to have prompted his famous complaint:

> For God's sake (I never was more serious), don't make me ridiculous any more by terming me gentle-hearted in print, or do it in better verses. It did well enough five [*sic*] years ago when I came to see you, and was moral coxcomb enough at the time you wrote the lines, to feed upon such epithets; but, besides that, the meaning of gentle is equivocal at best, and almost always means poor-spirited, the very quality of gentleness is abhorrent to such vile trumpetings. My *sentiment* is long since vanished. I hope my *virtues* have done *sucking*. I can scarce think but you meant it in joke. I hope you did, for I should be ashamed to think that you could think to gratify me by such praise, fit only to be a cordial to some green-sick sonneteer.[39]

To read Lamb's protest in the context of the many different kinds of address surrounding the poem in Coleridge's circles to which we have access – what's in letters, what we can read in between the lines – is to see his protest as not so much about being called "gentle" as opposed to anything else (a little potato, for that matter) as about being pushed beyond the horizon of second-person poetical address, while at the same time being rendered internal to other relations. It is both typical of the writing practices of the Wordsworth and Coleridge circles, and curious, that Coleridge's poem addressed to Lamb appeared in three letters to other friends – Robert Southey, John Thelwall, and Charles Lloyd – several years before the poem made it into print. During these years, many of these friendships became alternately internal and external to each other. Here, for example, is the opening of a letter from Coleridge to Lamb from 1798:

Dear Lamb

Lloyd has informed me through Miss Wordsworth that you intend no longer to correspond with me. This has given me little pain; not that I do not love and esteem you, but on the contrary because I am confident that your intentions are pure. You are performing what you deem a duty, & humanly speaking have that merit which can be derived from the performance of a painful duty. – Painful, for you could not without some struggles abandon me in behalf of a man who wholly ignorant of all but your name became attached to you in consequence of my attachment, caught *his* from *my* enthusiasm, & learnt to love you at my fire-side, when often I have been sitting & talking of your sorrows & affections [afflic-tions], I have stopped my conversations & lifted up wet eyes & prayed for you.[40]

This particular misunderstanding was cleared up, but the way in which Coleridge tended to view his relationships with friends as nested within one another is a perennial feature of the letters. Such a context renders vivid the difference between poetic address – which could be sealed off, delivered not to the person to whom it is "addressed," nested in another friendship – and anything like speaking or writing. A look at the epis-tolary second-person addresses to Southey which resume right after the first appearance of "Lime-Tree" in a letter of July 1797 also helps us form a vivid contrast between Coleridge's practice of poetic address, and his prac-tice of addressing a friend in a letter. Right after the final lines addressed (in this version) to "you, my Sister, and my Friends!" he resumes, address-ing Southey:

I would make a shift by some means or other to visit you, if I thought, that you & Edith Southey would return with me. – I think, indeed, I am almost cer-tain that I could get a one horse chair free of all expence…And Wordsworth at whose house I now am for change of air has commissioned me to offer you a suit of rooms at this place … – & so divine and wild is the country that I am sure it would increase your stock of images – & three weeks' absence from Christ-Church will endear it to you – & …[41]

Different too is Coleridge's epistolary address to Lamb a year earlier, in his beautiful, eloquent letter to that friend shortly after the calamity – Mary Lamb's murder of their mother: "I look upon you as a man called by sorrow and anguish and a strange desolation of hopes into quietness, and a soul set apart and made peculiar to God!" That letter ends sim-ply "come to me" – an urgent imperative that feels very different from the mental people-and-cosmos-moving of the imperative apostrophes of "This Lime-Tree Bower My Prison."[42] We come to feel that by lodging this poem, along with others, under the heading "conversation poem," we have routed our ability to read Coleridge's poetics of address. In spite of the truly innovative, informal, perhaps "conversational" style of Coleridge's blank verse in these poems, their model for relating to others is not conversation: it is thinking.[43] We shall have occasion to consider the relationship between blank verse and thinking in the next chapter of this book.

Coleridge's own classification for the poems we call the "conversation poems" was "Meditative Poems in Blank Verse," and in his book *Coleridge's Meditative Art* Reeve Parker argues persuasively that "This Lime-Tree Bower My Prison" bears the influence of Coleridge's reading of seventeenth-century Puritan meditation treatises. Parker focuses in particular on Richard Baxter's 1650 *The Saints' Everlasting Rest* (in 1796, Coleridge wrote to Thomas Poole that Baxter was one of "*my men*"), tracing the echoes of that book on the poem's structure, style and world view.[44] One of the most striking implications of Parker's argument is that, if it is correct, it means that the poem's orientation towards Charles Lamb is, implicitly, modeled on the meditating Christian's orientation towards Christ. Parker quotes Baxter exhorting his readers to "*think* of Christ as in our nature glorified; *think* of our fellow-saints as men there perfected; *think* of the city and state as the spirit hath expressed it."[45] The traces of a text such as Baxter's on Coleridge's poem, like the traces of Marvell's "The Coronet" not only on Coleridge's poem, but also – as we shall see at the end of this chapter – on other nineteenth-century poems, opens a window onto a deeply important topic. This is the shaping of nineteenth-century attitudes and practices of thinking about other people by an entire Protestant tradition of forms of practice such as prayer and devotional meditation. It is impossible to do justice to this topic fully in the context of this book, but its presence in the poetry of the second person is palpable. As Meynell noted, the second-person singular was "set apart for the phrase of piety and poetry." Parker further quotes from Baxter's exhortation to the meditating believer:

Get the liveliest picture of them in thy mind that possibly thou canst; meditate of them, as if thou were all the while beholding them, and as if thou were even hearing the hallelujahs, while thou art thinking of them; till thou canst say, "*Methinks* I see a glimpse of the glory; *methinks* I hear the shouts of joy and praise; *methinks* I even stand by Abraham and David, Peter and Paul, and more of these triumphing souls! *Methinks* I even see the Son of God appearing in the clouds, and the world standing at His bar to receive their doom; *methinks* I even hear Him say, "Come ye blessed of My Father!"[46]

The echo of Baxter's repetitive, increasingly intense "methinks" in the "thou, methinks" of "This Lime-Tree Bower" affirms that Coleridge's poetic second person's closest model is meditation.

Coleridge's "Thou, methinks" thus requires a not-speaking that posits the "thou" as an entity that can never truly be spoken in the real beyond apostrophe's reach. Apostrophe here is concerned not with the fiction of voice, but with a non-voicing that gets cast as thinking.[47] We could even say that to *say* "Oh So and So, I am thinking of you" is paradox, because if you are saying it, you are not thinking, you are speaking. This may strike some of you, my readers, as an empirically preposterous claim: you may feel that you are capable of thinking about someone and talking to them at the same time. It may be an empirically preposterous claim, but there exists a logic of mutual exclusivity,[48] and lurking in nineteenth-century poetic practices of second-person mental address is a curious logic which posits thinking about someone and talking to them as not only mutually exclusive, but also ethically distinct. As we noted in Chapter 2, in an environment in which thinking is endowed with the power of action, thinking and speaking become detached. Again, we may find this counterintuitive, but we can find species of this logic – you can't really think about someone and talk to them at the same time, you can't really be thinking about someone and be with them at the same time – in a range of writings about ethics. Here for example is Hannah Arendt, in the late essay "Thinking and Moral Considerations" discussed in the Introduction to the present study:

> Thinking's chief characteristic is that it interrupts all doing...the moment we start thinking on no matter what issue we stop everything else, and this everything else, again whatever it may happen to be, interrupts our thinking process; *it is as though we moved into a different world*...In order to think about somebody, he must be removed from our senses; so long as we are together with him we don't think of him...to think about somebody who is present implies removing ourselves surreptitiously from his company and acting as though he were no longer there.[49]

The notion that thinking about someone involves moving into a different world from the one in which we can be with and think about him or her, and that we tend to think of thinking and speaking as mutually exclusive, can be found lurking in the background of Kant's counterintuitive thought-experiment at the end of the *Anthropology From a Pragmatic Point of View* (1798). Here Kant imagines a planet of alien beings who would *not* be able to think without at the same time speaking:

> It could well be that on some other planet there might be rational beings who could not think in any other way but aloud; that is, they could not have any

thoughts that they did not at the same time *utter*, whether awake or dreaming, in the company of others or alone. What kind of behavior toward others would this produce, and how would it differ from that of our human species?[50]

This, Kant, implies, would be truly another world: in our world, he implies, the norm is that our thoughts "toward others" are separate from our utterances. But Coleridge's "Thou, methinks," like other second-person poetic addresses, takes place in the in-between world of poetry. Perhaps we only know what second-person thinking feels like by reconstructing in our minds these forms of poetic address. In this way, we might redefine a philosophical problem as a literary practice.

"DO YOU THINK OF ME?": LANDON'S AND BARRETT'S QUESTIONS

Some of the topics highlighted in this reading of "This Lime-Tree Bower My Prison" – the inequality of thinking about another person, its relationship to meditation or prayer, its relationship to speech – became topics of debate in the decades that followed, in a conversation of poems by women in which second-person thinking serves as a kind of common currency. The theoretical center of this conversation – that is, the poem most committed to the notion that poetic second-person address is a form of thinking about another person, and to delineating its historical context – is Letitia Elizabeth Landon's "Night at Sea." This poem was published in the *New Monthly Magazine* in January 1839, only weeks after the news of Landon's death following her sea journey to Africa with her new husband in the summer of 1838 reached English shores. The poem thus seemed to come from the other side of the grave, the sea journey retrospectively the journey from which no one ever returns; and thus the second-person address that forms the poem's refrain – "My friends, my absent friends! / Do you think of me as I think of you?" – is effortlessly readable as an address to the reading public, the poem a dying poet's reflection on literary reception and posterity. As we shall see shortly, this is the basis on which Elizabeth Barrett responded to this poem in her elegy to Landon, "L.E.L.'s Last Question," and it is the primary set of meanings of a poem that Landon's poem itself consciously echoes, Felicia Hemans' "A Parting Song." In that poem, which concludes her 1828 volume *Records of Woman* (1828), Hemans echoes the final "song" of the dying Corinne in Mme. de Staël's novel: "rappelez-vous quelquefois mes vers." Hemans' poem begins "When will ye think of me, my friends? / When will ye think of me?"[51] Situated at the close of her volume, Hemans' Corinne-inflected question is clearly an appeal to the volume's readers. In this context, Landon's "Night at Sea" becomes legible primarily as a link in an artfully echoing chain of poems, a chain which puts into action the conditions of poetic reception and transmission for the work of the nineteenth-century Poetess.[52]

However, it is crucial to resist reading Landon's "Night at Sea" solely in the terms of the accidents of the temporalities of its reception: as a posthumous poet's address to her reading audience. This involves taking the terms of the refrain quite literally, and it involves reading the refrain within the context the poem itself creates. That context includes documenting the vastness of the global separation of addresser and addressee: this is a "night at sea" on a sea increasingly distant from the friends. "By each dark wave around the vessel sweeping / Farther am I from old dear friends removed," the poem notes, and the third stanza in particular spells out the implications of such a separation:

> The very stars are strangers, as I catch them
>   Athwart the shadowy sails that swell above;
> I cannot hope that other eyes will watch them
>   At the same moment with a mutual love.
> They shine not there, as here they now are shining,
>   The very hours are changed. – Ah, do ye sleep?
> O'er each home pillow, midnight is declining,
>   May some kind dreams at least my image keep!
>   My friends, my absent friends!
>   Do you think of me, as I think of you?[53]

There is no hope of a mutual, simultaneous experience: the "I" and the "you" are in different hemispheres, unable to see the same stars; they are in different time zones. While the first stanza of "Night at Sea" sets the "I" right at the onset of nightfall, in stanza three, over on the "home pillow," where the "you"s are, midnight is declining, and the "you"s are probably in bed. The best the "I" can hope for is that the "you"s might dream of her. Stanza Three makes quite clear that the "as" of the refrain – "Do you think of me, as I think of you?" – only marginally has the force of temporal simultaneity, inasmuch as dreaming of someone can be termed a form of thinking about them.

The global reach of "Night at Sea" is a notable feature of lyric poetry of the 1820s and 1830s, in which, in the hands of Landon and in particular of Felicia Hemans, a Byronic predilection for exotic locations combined with the realities of British overseas expansion in the first half of the nineteenth century to place a premium on lyric poetry that documented global travel and separation.[54] It could be argued that, in the first half of the nineteenth century, lyric genres and gestures of address – poetic second-person writings that did not belong to the post-office's traffic of letters – served as an imaginary technology for bridging transoceanic distances in the decades before the completion of, say, the first transoceanic cables. As we noted in Chapter 2, nineteenth-century ideas about thought power often emerged in relation to technological change. The Atlantic cable, for example, was represented poetically as a way of putting not language, but thought into motion.[55] We might recall the mock-exactitude of William James' *letter* to Henry at the end of the century discussed in Chapter 2, promising to time correctly his thinking about his brother across the Atlantic: "I will *think of you* on the 31st at about 11 a.m. to make up for the difference of longitude."

In the absence of anything *like* a transoceanic cable, Landon's "Night at Sea" theorizes poetic second-person thinking as the primary medium of a geographically distant relationship to another person. It evokes a crucial context for nineteenth-century interest in purely mental relations between persons and in thinking as a form of swift, silent, powerful interpersonal action: a globalizing Britain increasingly impatient with slow and watery mail. It is a poem that unfolds simply by elaborating that context for its refrain. "Do you think of me, as I think of you?" in its palindromical formulation provides no content to thinking. The "as," in this context, is not a marker of temporal simultaneity, but rather of formal, quantitative, and moral equivalence.

As the poem progresses, the refrain morphs slightly, and its status as a question – it was never much of one, but rather an aspiration or a wish – fades.[56] In its penultimate stanza, "Night at Sea" clarifies what it means to think about another person by means of an extraordinarily schematic dis-identification of the "I" with Coleridge's Ancient Mariner:

> On one side of the ship the moonbeams shimmer
>   In luminous vibration sweeps the sea,
> But where the shadow falls, a strange pale glimmer
>   Seems glow-worm like amid the waves to be.
> All that the spirit keeps of thought and feeling,
>   Takes visionary hues from such an hour;
> But while some fantasy is o'er me stealing,
>   I start, remembrance has a keener power.
>   My friends, my absent friends,
>   From the fair dream I start to think of you!
>
> (101–10)

On the first side of the boat is a shimmering but real perceptual reality; but on the second side, where the shadow of the ship itself falls on the water, is a freaky hallucination that clearly evokes the water snakes of Coleridge's poem ("Within the shadow of the ship / I watched their rich attire"). In that poem, of course, the vision of the snakes prompts a blessing from the Ancient Mariner which partially relieves him from his curse. But Landon's poem interestingly disavows this vision as "visionary," as "fantasy," and uses this Coleridgean moment as a manifesto for second-person thinking. Neither side of the boat holds permanent attractions for Landon's "I." She turns from the competing mental engagements of *both* perception (something she readily hands over to "the sailor" in the final stanza – it is he, not she who "well knows" the difference between chimerical clouds on the horizon, and the appearance of landfall in line 115) *and* fantasy and "start[s] to think of you!" Limned from both perceptual reality and fantasy, second-person thinking is accorded the status of a primary mental activity.

The extraordinary clarity of the understanding in "Night at Sea" of second-person thinking becomes even clearer when we compare it to Elizabeth Barrett Browning's response to the poem, "L.E.L.'s Last Question," written and published a few weeks later. This poem, in turning the refrain of "Night at Sea" into an urgent question, does two things that throw the significance of Landon's poem into relief. First, it converts the refrain of "Night at Sea" into a spoken utterance, and second, it interprets the "as" of the refrain as masking a fundamental asymmetry. Barrett's poem begins by putting Landon's refrain into quotation marks: quotation marks that do not simply attribute the line to Landon, but underscore Barrett's insistence on this line as something Landon *said*. The assertion that this is something Landon *said* is curiously emphasized in the second line of the poem:

> "Do you think of me as I think of you,
> My friends, my friends?" She said it from the sea,
> The English minstrel in her minstrelsy —[57]

Barrett's insistence on the refrain as speech surely emphasizes Landon's death: "She said it" embalms the refrain as the past-tense, singular utterance of a departed voice. By contrast, Landon's palindromic, reversible refrain in the context of "Night at Sea" seems oceanic and endless, desubjectivized, a thought with no determinate thinker. For Barrett, L.E.L.'s last question really is a question – something asked out loud – and it is, moreover, everyone's question: "We all do ask the same" (9); and everyone who loves does little "but sit (among the rocks?) and listen for" an answer (12). The crisis of L.E.L.'s death is also cast in auditory terms: the friends' "passionate response" – also termed a "cry" – "We think of thee" only happens when Landon is dead, "too deep to hear":

Bring your vain answers – cry, "We think of thee!"
How think ye of her? – In the long ago
Delights! – or crowned by new bays? – not so –
None smile, and none are crowned where lyeth she.

(43–46)

The exhortation to cry "We think of thee!" is, in "L.E.L.'s Last Question," the equivalent of the exhortation to weep in, say, *Lycidas* or *Adonais*.

"She said it from the sea": Barrett's insistence on Landon's refrain as a piece of iterable speech raises anew the question of the relationships among *saying* "I think of you," staging second-person thinking in a poem, and actually doing it. It is also a symptom of Barrett's suspicion of second-person thinking, something we shall encounter, at the end of this chapter, in the *Sonnets from the Portuguese*. But Barrett's emphasis on the refrain as a broken, non-reciprocated communication clarifies the extent to which Landon's poem models itself as non-communicative second-person thinking, for that poem is untroubled by a distinction between saying it, writing it, and doing it, as the latter two are tethered closely together. For Barrett's poem also poses itself as grimly dismantling the aspiration of "Night at Sea" to represent second-person thinking as a primary reality, and as a reciprocal one. The "as" of the refrain is revealed as deeply unequal. "L.E.L.'s Last Question" ends:

Do you think of me as I think of you? –
O friends, O kindred, O dear brotherhood
Of the whole world – what are we that we should
For covenants of long affection sue? –
Why press so near each other, when the touch
Is barred by graves? Not much, and yet too much,
This, "Think upon me as I think of you."

But, while on mortal lips I shape anew
A sigh to mortal issues, verily
Above th'unshaken stars that see us die,
A vocal pathos rolls – and HE who drew
All life from dust, and *for* all, tasted death,
By death, and life, and love appealing, saith,
DO YOU THINK OF ME AS I THINK OF YOU?

(50–63)

The reciprocity of thinking is not only interrupted by death in this case: it's simply too much to ask for.[58] If Landon's refrain is a covenant, it is too lopsided, and can only be referred to the voice who has the last word of the poem, the last version of the refrain, the voice of Jesus. The mortal sinner is thus enjoined not to think of other people but, like the readers of Baxter's *Saints Everlasting Rest*, to "think of Christ." It will not do, however, to see Barrett's objection to the "covenant" of interpersonal thinking as solely, or conventionally, theological. There is something quite remarkable about casting Christ's love for the human race as a transcendent version of the human act of saying "I'm thinking about you" – not to speak of casting Christ as quoting the alluring poetess L.E.L. Barrett's insistence, moreover, on converting Landon's thinking-poem into a poem of "vocal pathos" (60) is underscored by her own extravagant apostrophizing – "O friends…O dear brotherhood / Of the whole world" (51–52). On what grounds is Barrett so pessimistic about second-person poetic thinking in this world? That is my question about Barrett's "L.E.L.'s Last Question," and we shall return to this question at the end of this chapter.

THINKING IN THE SECOND PERSON AND THE MARRIAGE OF TRUE MINDS

To try to take seriously the status of address in nineteenth-century poetry – and to see it as an arena for an articulation of thinking about another person – is inevitably to invoke John Stuart Mill's seeming prohibition against direct address in his "Thoughts on Poetry" (1833).[59] Indeed, the contention that nineteenth-century British writers were concerned to bring poetic form to bear on the problems of two people thinking about each other, and that they may have brought together problems of intimacy, inequality, domination, and poetic form in similar ways, could be explored by reading well-known passages of that essay together with a passage from Mill's later work, *The Subjection of Women* (1869). In the latter text, Mill famously argues that the intractability of the inequality of the sexes lies in its embeddedness in the intimacy of marriage in particular. What distinguishes women from other classes of subjected peoples, he argues, is that "every one of the subjects lives under the very eye…of one of the masters – in closer intimacy with him than with any of her fellow subjects."[60] And he famously calls for the development of a psychology as a tool for understanding how inequality works. It is, he says:

a subject on which it is impossible in the present state of society to obtain complete and correct knowledge – while almost everybody dogmatizes upon it, almost all neglect and make light of the only means by which any partial insight can be obtained into it. This is, an analytic study of the most important department of psychology, the laws of the influence of circumstances on character. (23–24)

For Mill, the structure of marriage is such that intimacy and affection themselves are at odds with both communication (for Mill, "sincerity and openness") or the ability to think about the other (which for Mill does take the form of "knowledge" of the other's "actually existing thoughts and feelings" [24–25]). Even when, he writes – and he really means especially when – there is "complete unity of feeling and community of interests," and "true affection," a man and a wife's ability to address one another is distorted:

It often happens that there is the most complete unity of feeling and community of interests as to all external things, yet the one has as little admission into the internal life of the other as if they were common acquaintance. Even with true affection, authority on the one side and subordination on the other prevent perfect confidence. Though nothing may be intentionally withheld, much is not shown. (25)

This suspicion of intersubjective address in the intimacy of marriage could, if we squint hard, be seen as a curious counterpart to Mill's familiar distinctions in the "Poetry" essay:

Eloquence is *heard*, poetry is *over*heard. Eloquence supposes an audience; the peculiarity of poetry appears to us to lie in the poet's utter unconsciousness of a listener. Poetry is feeling, confessing itself to itself in moments of solitude.... Eloquence is feeling pouring itself out to other minds, courting their sympathy, or endeavoring to influence their belief, or move them to passion or to action. [But when a writer] *turns round and addresses himself to another person...*when the expression of his emotions, or of his thoughts tinged by his emotion, is tinged also by...that desire of making an impression upon another mind, then it ceases to be poetry.[61]

Reading the passages from this essay with those from *The Subjection of Women* could suggest to us the ways in which a poetics of address, of "turning round and addressing another person," was psychologized in the nineteenth century, situating Mill's suspicion of address as part of a general understanding of relations to others. In both cases what is imagined is an ideal of expression or communication that circumvents speech situations which seem inevitably distorted. Overhearing, eavesdropping, and voyeurism become the conditions of confidence, and intimacy is the enemy of knowledge. In this context, the possibility of purely mental relations would seem to be both ideal, and more highly charged.[62]

The conjunction of these two passages from Mill might also be suggestive for a reading in particular of nineteenth-century love poetry by women. Some of the issues in Coleridge's "Lime-Tree Bower" and Barrett's "L.E.L.'s Last Question" become more elaborated in these poems of erotic love,

which take up the questions of thinking about another in particularly pressing ways. Is being alone with your thoughts about a person akin to being
alone with him or her? Does thinking bestow the lover with knowledge,
consolation, or power? Does thinking "you" acknowledge, as E. S. Dallas
suggested in *Poetics*, the other's essential freedom? Or, is it possible that the
act of thinking about the other can constitute a form of damage to him or
her? The framework provided by Mill's *Subjection of Women* – the sense of
the urgency, and the difficulty, of putting together intimacy *and* equality in marriage – may provide a crucial context for women poets' particularly intense interest in mental relations. In addition, while – as we noted
in Chapter 2 – belief in thought-power was attractive to many Victorian
women writers, some of these poems articulate a flip side. The nexus of
thought and action may have stacked up differently for nineteenth-century
English women, for whom numerous restrictions on action may have grossly
enlarged a reliance on the domain of thinking. It is often the women in the
novels of the era who sit around thinking of the beloved. We shall scrutinize Gwendolen Harleth's modes of thinking about Daniel Deronda in
Chapter 5, but here is Lily Dale in Trollope's *The Small House at Allington*,
thinking of her faithless lover, "in the house, when I am all alone, thinking over it; – thinking, thinking, thinking."[63] Therefore, if thinking was
thought to be a form of interpersonal action, Victorian women writers may
have been particularly attuned to charges of excessive agency.

My final examples in this chapter will be drawn from some Victorian
sonnet sequences by women, which constitute part of a range of Victorian
experiments with genre to explore the vicissitudes and pressures on modern
love and marriage.[64] For John Addington Symonds, the sonnet – as opposed
to the lyric – was *the* form of modern passion which "seems to me," he
wrote to the poet Mary Robinson, "unavoidably 'raisonneuse'": "and here
it appears to me that the Sonnet is more fit for a complete expression of
all the [thoughtful anxieties] of passion than the lyric – for in lyrics you
cannot reason."[65] The sonnet as a genre always puts into motion the relations among construing, thinking about, and hailing the other. The sonnet seems to be the very *shape* of thought; and metrically "I think" or "I
thought" – as we shall see in the following chapter – are the perfect iambs.
In its dense, patterned form, the sonnet exteriorizes thought. And by exter-
iorizing thought, the sonnet de-psychologizes it, materializes it, alienates it
from the thinker as subject by placing any given sonnet about the beloved
other in a syntagmatic relation to all other thoughts about other beloved
others. In so doing, it puts the problem of thinking about others in a realm
other than psychology, or epistemology, or skepticism about other minds.

We might take our cue from Christina Rossetti's sequence, *Monna Innominata* (1881), which first of all makes clear that what lovers *do* is sit around thinking ("Thinking of you," one sonnet simply begins [9.1]). Here is the first sonnet:

> Come back to me, who wait and watch for you: –
>   Or come not yet, for it is over then,
>   And long it is before you come again,
> So far between my pleasures are and few.
> While, when you come not, what I do I do
>   Thinking "Now is when he comes," my sweetest "when:"
>   For one man is my world of all the men
> This wide word holds; O love, my world is you.
> Howbeit, to meet you grows almost a pang
>   Because the pang of parting comes so soon;
> My hope hangs waning, waxing, like a moon
>   Between the heavenly days on which we meet:
> Ah me, but where are now the songs I sang
>   When life was sweet because you called them sweet?[66]

Rossetti extends the notion that parting is such sweet sorrow so far that the beloved's absence turns out to be genuinely preferable to his presence. She delineates that absence as a lover's *practice*: "While, when you come not, what I do I do / Thinking." The line break after "what I do I do" invites the reader to pause and then to come to another pause after "Thinking"; what the lover does, what defines her practice as a lover, is thinking. "I do I do" also marks out a metrical pattern that doubles thought and produces thinking as practice. That the poem conceives of thought as practice or action – rather than as a particular content – is stressed not only by metrical marking but also by its highlighting of abstract markers of time at the expense of substantives: the prominence, for example, particularly as end rhymes, of "then," "when," and "again." In lines 6 through 8, the "you" – the beloved – gets assimilated to a "when": notice how the line endings set up a kind of apposition between "my sweetest 'when'," "of all the men," and "you." The assimilation of the beloved to a "when" also underscores the poem's revelation of thinking as productive practice rather than as, say, a reflection of a pre-existing object: the lover's thinking calls the beloved into being ("when") with the act of the poem.[67]

The things that make the first sonnet of *Monna Innominata* so striking are characteristic of this sequence as a whole and may even be said to be its themes: the ways in which thinking renders spectral or purely grammatical the "you" of address, the ways in which address performs not the bringing into presence of the other, but the other's attenuation. In spite of its increasingly elegiac tone, this sequence seems in fact content with the notion that writing is thinking is loving, and that where the beloved is, in consequence, is in the space of poetic address, neither here nor there.[68] In this respect. *Monna Innominata*'s way of thinking about thinking about the beloved is sharply different from that of the sonnet sequence that Rossetti wrote in response to Elizabeth Barrett Browning's *Sonnets from the Portuguese* (1850).[69] While Rossetti's poetics of absence opts out of confronting the politics – the possibilities of inequality – in mental relations, Barrett Browning confronts it head on.

To read *Sonnets from the Portuguese* is always to ponder the intertwining of empirical and virtual addressees, the intersection of what we can call, borrowing a phrase from Barrett Browning, "the poetical relation," and the epistolary relation between the real Elizabeth Barrett and Robert Browning.[70] It is impossible to avoid the oddity of the fact – as well as the myths built around the fact – that for Barrett and Browning courtship involved, with an extraordinary exclusivity (save for their fabled few meetings), the mutual interruption of writing to each other and thinking about each other. The Brownings' attitudes towards various kinds of thought-power theories differed widely throughout their relationship – they famously differed on mesmerism and spiritualism.[71] But the constraints of a courtship consisting entirely of writing and thinking prompted some professions on both sides about the powers of willing, wishing, and thinking. For instance, Robert Browning worried that a wind would make Barrett ill, and wished her good weather and good wishes the next day: "This sunny morning is as if I wished it for you – 10 strikes by the clock now – tell me if at 10 this morning you feel any good from my heart's wishes for you."[72] In her response, Barrett experiments with assimilating Browning's thoughts about her to an ill-or-good wind, and struggles with the difficulty of asserting the continuity of her thoughts about him, and his about her, as going on in between the episodes of writing:

If you did but know dear Mr. Browning how often I have written…not this letter I am about to write, but another better letter to you…in the midst of my silence, you wd not think for a moment that the east wind, with all the harm it does to me, is able to do the great harm of putting out the light of the thought of you to my mind, – for this, indeed, it has no power to do. I had the pen in my hand once to write, – & why it fell out, I cannot tell you. As you see…all your writing will not change the wind! You wished all manner of good to me one day as the clock struck ten, – yes & I assure you I was better that day – & I must not forget to tell you so though it is so long since. And *therefore*, I was logically bound to believe that you had never thought of me since...unless you thought east winds of me! *That* was quite clear; was it not? – or would have been, – if it had not been for the supernatural conviction, I had above all, of your kindness, which was too large to be taken in the hinge of a syllogism. In fact I have long left off thinking that logic proves anything – it *doesn't*, you know.[73]

She ends by throwing up her hands, but the fallout of the letter is a sense of Barrett's need to feel *thought about* by Browning, conjoined with an uneasiness about feeling that her existence depends on someone else thinking about her. To feel dependent on another's thinking is to feel both real and unreal.

In contrast to Rossetti's *Monna Innominata*, with its preference for virtual relations with a very disappearing addressee, Barrett Browning's *Sonnets from the Portuguese* makes the unease about having a relationship's survival contingent upon the two parties' continued thinking about each other absolutely central. It is dedicated to sorting out the relations among figures of address, mental persons, and empirical persons, in part by juxtaposing the logic of the sonnet sequence with the stuff of Victorian bourgeois intimacy: letters; locks of hair; expectations of sympathy, mutuality, and democracy.[74] The sequence is in some sense about Barrett Browning's struggle to make both herself and her addressee *real* at the same time.[75]

How is thinking and being thought about a struggle in the *Sonnets from the Portuguese*? Let me count the ways. First, the opening sonnet immediately establishes the lover as thinker. "I thought," she begins, "once how Theocritus had sung" – and casts love – in the form of a spirit who appears behind her and yanks her by the hair – as a violation of her scholarly and introspective musings. Love interrupts a certain kind of intellectualizing, an idea that comes up again in Sonnet 34 where the speaker confesses that when the beloved calls her by her childhood name, she responds more slowly than she did as a child: "When I answer now / I drop a grave thought."[76]

Second, when the poet does transfer her thoughts to the world of love, thinking comes to seem both a way of solving the problem of what it means to be in relation to another, and a problem *for* relation. The sequence as a whole ruminates on questions of proximity and distance, questions that are ultimately about what kind of "being with" a person it is to have them in one's thoughts. That is, I would argue that the sequence's obsession with spatial relations ("look up and see the casement broken in," e.g. *SP* 4.9), with questions of scale and size, with measuring which of the two lovers is greater, smaller, higher, lower, nearer, or further than the other, is in itself a symptom of the poem's musings, on a more phenomenological level, on what it might mean to have a person, literally, in one's mind. What does it mean to turn a person into a thought? Is fitting a person to one's mental space to miniaturize, or to aggrandize him?

Third, *Sonnets from the Portuguese* raises the stakes of such meditations by constantly putting into play the tensions among thinking, knowing, speaking, writing, and loving, never truly assimilating any one term to the others, as if by some chemical process the truth of an ideal, mutual relation could emerge. But in fact, these practices often seem mutually exclusive: for Barrett Browning, it seems as if you can't think about and write about someone at the same time; you can't think about and be with someone at the same time. If Barrett Browning's sense of the mutually exclusive nature of being with and thinking about another seems like a strange idea, we ought to consider again Hannah Arendt's "Thinking and Moral Considerations," which says much the same thing: "in order to think about somebody, he must be removed from our senses; so long as we are together we don't think of him." Sonnet 28, for example, in which Barrett ponders letters from the beloved, is riddled with ellipses, as if she were making room for unspoken, unwritten, even unthought blanks of intimacy even within the severely limited confines of a fourteen-line poem:

> This said,…he wished to have me in his sight
> Once, as a friend: this fixed a day in spring,
> To come and touch my hand…a simple thing,
> Yet I wept for it! – this,…the paper's light …
>
> (5–8)

Things come to a crisis in Sonnet 29, where the poet is struck by self-consciousness about her own thinking:

> I think of thee! – my thoughts do twine and bud
>   About thee, as will vines, about a tree,
>   Put out broad leaves, and soon there's nought to see
> Except the straggling green which hides the wood.
> Yet, O my palm-tree, be it understood
>   I will not have my thoughts instead of thee
>   Who art dearer, better! rather instantly
> Renew thy presence. As a strong tree should,
> Rustle thy boughs and set thy trunk all bare,
>   And let these bands of greenery which insphere thee
> Drop heavily down,…burst, shattered, everywhere!

> Because, in this deep joy to see and hear thee
> And breathe within thy shadow a new air,
> I do not think of thee – I am too near thee.
>
> (1–14)

While the imagery here – the clinging vine, the strong tree – and some of the sentiments might at first confirm some residual suspicions that *Sonnets from the Portuguese* is an embarrassing poem, it helps if we remember a similar image – that of the ivy-usurped tree – in Coleridge's "Lime-Tree Bower."[77] There, as here, this image represents thought as a kind of violence that chokes and conceals its object. In Barrett Browning's poem, it is particularly clear that this ethics of thinking about another person is at least in part modeled on a Protestant disciplining of meditations on Christ. It echoes most clearly Marvell's "The Coronet." In that poem, the speaker constructs a "garland" of flowers with which to adorn his Savior, only to realize that his garland turns out to be entwined with serpentine "wreaths of fame and interest."[78] He then turns to address Christ:

> But Thou who only couldst the serpent tame,
> Either his slippery knots at once untie;
> And disentangle all his winding snare;
> Or shatter too with him my curious frame,
> And let these wither.
>
> (19–23)

That this violence towards thought is also part of the sequence's engagement with its romantic legacy is signaled by its echo of an image as well from Shelley's "Epipsychidion": at the beginning of that poem, Shelley describes the beloved herself as striving,

> 'Till those bright plumes of thought, in which arrayed
> It over-soared this low and worldly shade,
> Lie shattered.[79]

There, as here, the poet seems worried about the possibility that thinking is a kind of zero-sum game or economy of scarcity in which one person's thinking can only occur at the expense of another's: thoughts are green leaves that obscure and distance all else.[80]

The net result in Barrett Browning's Sonnet 29 is an intense ambivalence: while she hates the thought of her thoughts smothering the beloved, the violence she directs at her own thoughts suggests a kind of defensiveness against separateness. It is the ambivalence of the vicissitudes of the omnipotence of thought. In its striking thematic clarity, Sonnet 29 makes clear that the intense pessimism about second-person thinking at stake for Barrett Browning is to be distinguished from an epistemological concern about misrepresenting or not knowing the object of one's affections. At issue here is not a concern with a fit between one's thoughts and one's objects. Nor is it a worry that the thinking subject might do herself wrong by ruminating obsessively about the object of her affections. It is rather an ambivalence about the act of thinking about the other itself, an ambivalence which opens up a vista of mental action, and mental sociability, as terrifyingly powerful and inimical to an ideal of mutual relation.

Barrett Browning's resistance to thinking in this sonnet, then, bespeaks a suspicion whose context is the pressure she puts on her sequence to imagine a mental relation between two people that could serve as a lived ideal of equality. The poet's experiment with "you" in a sequence about the marriage of true minds tests the limits of the ideal expressed in E. S. Dallas' account of thinking in the second person as access to the "you"'s essential freedom. Here, the pressures on marriage as a meeting of minds paradoxically make Barrett Browning aware of a negative potential in second-person thinking, a potential to diminish or to destroy. Barrett Browning's insight into the vicissitudes of the omnipotence of thinking emerges through a practice of second-person poetic address – that is, it is a philosophical position that emerges through the poetics of address, and is inseparable from it. I have argued here that women poets may have had a special interest in the poetics of second-person thinking. But in the next chapter, we shall see the ways in which two very different poems by Coventry Patmore and George Meredith also express a deep pessimism about the damage that can be done when a man and a woman think about each other. The ethics of beliefs about the power of thinking to affect another person, for good or for ill, is a curious, surprising thing: in the last chapter of this book, we shall see George Eliot turning the pessimism that has emerged from this chapter on its head, suggesting that there may be a moral virtue even in beliefs that your thinking can harm others.

Meanwhile, we might dwell, in conclusion, on the form that Barrett Browning's resistance to thinking takes in Sonnet 29 of *Sonnets from the Portuguese*, that is, on the movement this poem makes from its opening line – "I think of thee!" – to its last, which begins "I do not think of thee." If, as we discussed earlier, "I think of thee" presents a logical problem if we take poetic address as a pretending to speak, what does "I do not think of thee" mean? Especially in the logic of the poetics of address in an amatory sonnet? At first glance, "I do not think of thee" would appear to be a kind of Cretan's paradox. That is, saying "I'm not thinking of you" is not unlike saying "I am not lying" – or perhaps like saying (petulantly) "I'm not talking to you any more." Barrett Browning's final "I do not think of thee" could thus be compared to the opening line of Alice Meynell's sonnet "Renouncement," discussed earlier: "I must not think of thee." Barrett Browning's and Meynell's phrases are of course metrically equivalent.[81] Beginning "I must not think of thee," Meynell's sonnet makes quite clear that the poetic gesture of renunciation is really also its own opposite. The phrase "the thought of thee" is like a tic, present throughout the octet, even as it is being denied. In the first quatrain it literally interrupts its own denial:

> I must not think of thee; and, tired yet strong,
> I shun the thought that lurks in all delight –
> The thought of thee – and in the blue Heaven's height,
> And in the sweetest passage of a song.[82]

In this poem, the phrases "I must not think of thee" and "the thought of thee" are the tokens of thinking in the second person. "I must stop short of thee," the poem's "I" says (8), knowing that this is as close as it gets. As Freud declares in his essay on "Negation": "with the help of the symbol of negation, thinking frees itself."[83]

In this context, what then happens when we try to contemplate the utterance that would seem to be the opposite of Barrett Browning's and Meynell's pronouncements: "I think of thee"? Focusing on what poets are doing when they write "I do not" or "I must not think of thee" nicely illuminates what is at stake when they write "I think of thee." We could certainly say that to *say*, "Oh So and So, I am thinking of you" (as in the famous opening of Baudelaire's "Le Cygne": "Andromache, je pense à vous") is also a paradox. As we discussed earlier, there is a logic of mutual exclusion which pulls saying it and doing it apart. If we treat the beginning and ending phrases of Barrett Browning's sonnet – "I think of thee!", "I do not think of thee" – as spoken utterances, the differences between them start to evaporate, and we begin to feel that perhaps the heartfelt "I am thinking of you" offered to a friend in need is no mere thoughtless utterance. In the context of a poem, where the "thee" who is being addressed and thought about (or not) are, as this sonnet suggests, already incredibly flexibly located, always "already with thee" and yet, at the same time, never *really there*, in the no-place of the written page, "I do not think of thee – I am too near thee" is really not the opposite of "I think of thee." They are both a mode of second-person poetic thinking which is itself the opposite of the opposition between thinking and speaking; they are experiments in the intimacy and efficacy of writing, of the soundless words that feel like thought.

CHAPTER 4

Thinking and knowing in Patmore and Meredith

This chapter explores the work of two poets who were remarkably skeptical about the effects of thinking upon another person. Not from the point of view of the epiphenomenalists visited in Chapter 2, who flatly denied the existence of mental causation of any kind; but rather from the view that thinking about another – especially one you love – either does no good, or causes harm. They were attuned to the perils of diminishment, or destruction, attendant upon becoming an object of thought. Indeed, Patmore's and Meredith's pessimism conferred a great deal of agency on the act of thinking about another person, and hence deserves to be a part of this story as much as does the more optimistic view of the evangelists of thought-power discussed in Chapter 2. And, like the poets discussed in the latter section of Chapter 3, Patmore and Meredith made marriage the center and periphery of their speculations on thinking. In *The Angel in the House* and in *Modern Love*, they submitted marriage to intense scrutiny, parsing not only the complex relation between thinking about and speaking to an intimate other, but also the relationship between thinking about someone and knowing them.[1]

These poets ask us, in other words, to think again about some of the epistemological questions that this book explicitly set aside in the Introduction. Surely, we might stop to ask, nineteenth-century writers must have viewed the act of thinking about another person as, among other things, a means to knowledge and understanding. One of Patmore's favorite aphorisms was "All knowledge, worthy of the name, is nuptial knowledge."[2] The contexts of this aphorism, and the book in which it appears, *The Rod, the Root, and the Flower*, published the year before Patmore's death in 1896, include both the religious and the erotic preoccupations of Patmore's life. It stems from his increasingly anti-clerical, Swedenborg-inflected, mystical Catholicism. It was also written during the year of the painful waning of the married, elderly Patmore's intensely romantic friendship with the much younger, and also married,

Alice Meynell. Meynell's poetry was intimately tied to Patmore's poetics; they were excellent readers of each other's work. Curiously, she also was ultimately the recipient of his most celebrated work on marriage. In 1893 Patmore presented Meynell on her birthday with the sole extant manuscript of *The Angel in the House*, written decades before. Within a year or so, however, Meynell had withdrawn from their friendship, and accepted the increasingly devoted attentions of (the also aging, also married) George Meredith.[3]

Patmore's aphorism "All knowledge…is nuptial knowledge" speaks most immediately of the poet's understanding of human love as both part and type of the self's relation to God, which is the beginning and end of all experience and all knowledge. For Patmore, it suggests, the ability to know is derived from interpersonal relations, of which marriage is the exemplary form. The aphorism allows us, minimally, to view Patmore in a long tradition of thinkers for whom questions of epistemology are inseparable from questions of love. We shall return to reconsider the meaning of this aphorism at the end of this chapter. Meanwhile, however, its placement in the curious entanglement of the aging Patmore and Meredith in the 1890s may be seen as an epilogue to the curious engagement that we can discern in the poems both wrote in the 1850s and early 1860s, poems that grapple with the difference between thinking about someone, and knowing them, in courtship and in marriage.[4] One of the most perplexing poetic explorations of the perils of thinking about another person, *Modern Love* delineates the demise of a marriage. It is framed by what would seem to be the claim of a husband to know something about his wife: "By this he knew" is the poem's opening phrase; and the last phrase of the penultimate section of the sequence – just after the husband realizes his wife has taken poison – is "and he knew all."[5] It is, however, exceedingly difficult to say exactly what anyone knows at either of these moments, and even more difficult to say how the poem and its characters get from that first moment to the last. It is a text about which one feels that any attempt to paraphrase it into a coherent narrative falls apart upon closer scrutiny.

This chapter proposes a way of making sense of *Modern Love*, using the unlikely key of a small passage from Patmore's *The Angel in the House*. The link between these two poems allows us to see the ways in which both *The Angel in the House* and *Modern Love* crucially separate thinking about another person from knowing him or her. An even more unlikely key shall help us understand further what these poems have to say about thinking: Victorian metrical theory.

"THE KISS"

I will begin and end with a brief section of *The Angel in the House* called "The Kiss." *The Angel in the House*, which was published in two installments in 1854 and 1856 (with two sequels in 1860 and 1862), and was rearranged and revised many times, poses some structural, generic problems. Like many nineteenth-century long poems, it seeks to work out a relationship, not just between two people, but between its storytelling impulse, and its spurts of lyricism. Patmore formalized the opposition between narrative and lyric through the use of discrete narrative episodes, called "Idylls," that tell the story of Felix Vaughn's courtship of Honoria Churchill; these "Idylls" are prefaced by more meditative lyrics called "The Accompaniments" and "The Sentences" in the early editions, and later "The Preludes." These "Preludes" are often quite unconnected to the story but seem to illustrate its themes, and we can either locate them in Felix's head, as his thoughts during the long periods of waiting during his long, torturous courtship, or see them as commentary by another voice. Sometimes other people – not the poem's main characters – seem to appear in them. They are little puzzles embedded in the story. The interruption of the narrative by these lyric "Preludes" seems to heighten, rather than solve, the poem's fundamental problems: this is a story in which not much happens; the constraints of a Victorian courtship impose a kind of thinness on the narrative that seems embodied in the slow, interrupted way in which the poem unfolds. The contact between Felix and Honoria is minimal and strained; the relationship for much of the poem is all in his head; the pressure this creates causes a kind of repeated mental collapse, even after they're engaged. For example, Felix responds to Honoria's finally accepting his proposal by nervously going out the next morning and buying a gun: "I paced the streets; a pistol chose, / To guard my now important life."[6]

It is in one of the interludes from the main story that we find "The Kiss":

> "I saw you take his kiss!" "'Tis true."
>   "O, modesty!" "'Twas strictly kept:
> "He thought me asleep; at least, I knew
>   "He thought I thought he thought I slept."
>
> (183)

This is in some respects a pretty bad piece of poetry, but its badness is not the kind of badness that has often made *The Angel in the House* an object of derision: an overly earnest, highly sentimental idealizing of feminine

virtue and married bliss. The whole of "The Kiss" consists of two unattrib-
uted voices in quotation. But who is speaking here? – certainly not Honoria
Churchill and Felix Vaughn. To the extent that we have seen them speaking to each other at all, their dialogues have been chaste, discrete, and,
of course, interrupted: "'Honoria,' I began – No more. / The Dean, by
ill or happy hap, / Came home" (*Poems*, 104). The dialogue of "The Kiss"
resembles instead something from the popular nineteenth-century stage.
The imagination can supply us with, as the poem's two speakers, a female
ingénue who turns out to be not so innocent, and her anxious, upright,
exasperated suitor – or perhaps, à la *Sense and Sensibility*, an adventurous
young lady defending herself against the admonishments of a more prud-
ish older sister.

For "The Kiss" is funny, as well as bad; its funniness and its badness are connected; this is the badness of a cheap, cynical joke about a
cheap, cynical attitude towards sexual morality, about a woman who is
not as virtuous as she ought to be, and pretends to believe that being
asleep will get her off the hook. When the woman says the man *thinks*
she is asleep what she means, of course, is that she is not. Thinking here
is the opposite of knowing. The effect of the multiply embedded "he
thought" and "I thought" is certainly not the production of any kind
of "deep intersubjectivity," as George Butte has argued about similar
structures in nineteenth-century narratives from Jane Austen to Henry
James.[7] The effect is the opposite: this is shallow intersubjectivity; and
"knowledge" is merely a shared knowingness, a fleeting mutual com-
pact between the woman and the unscrupulous opportunist who kisses
her. An astonishingly tight little poem – it is not easy to pack a whole
drama into four short lines – "The Kiss" demonstrates the aptness of a
remark by Alice Meynell, whose intellectual – if not emotional – loyalty to Patmore was matched by her insight into his work. She compared Patmore's tightly packed quatrains to the tightly packed anatomy
of the human body. If you take the internal organs out, it is impossible
to stuff them back in:

Children are taught that if the frame of man were unpacked of its organs, no
hand of man would be able to replace them all within the space they had filled;
and in a like manner, a quatrain of Coventry Patmore's writings, if any one, by
fault of memory, should chance to spill its words and phrases, would baffle a
restorer. There is assuredly nothing tight or thronged or hard, but the fullness is
definite.[8]

The effects of this fullness in "The Kiss" are its layers of drama. What
seems ultimately most scandalous is neither simply the fact that the lady

has taken the kiss, nor solely her knowingness, but above all the fact that she admits it so freely.

The other thing that conspicuously makes this scrap of poetry both so funny and so "bad" is its meter, the way that the last line especially bumps rhythmically along: "'He *thought* I *thought* he *thought* I *slept*.'" This is certainly meter, if not modesty and sexual fidelity, being "strictly kept." Patmore's Victorian readers almost universally criticized his choice of this octosyllabic meter, in which the entire *Angel in the House* is written. The poem's defenders lamented that Patmore had chosen such a "humdrum," "jigging" meter for a subject – marriage – which he took so seriously.[9] Critics found the meter monotonous, "namby pamby," "garrulous," and "prattling"[10] and one review of the first installment took the form of a parody:

> From ball to bed, from field to farm,
> The tale flows nicely purling on.
> With much conceit, there is no harm,
> In the love-legend here begun.
>   – The rest will come another day
> If public sympathy allows;
>   – And this is all we have to say,
> About "The Angel in the House."[11]

Patmore spent the rest of his life energetically defending his choice of meter for his *Angel*, and lamenting that it had caused it to be taken less seriously. "Easy reading was often d – d hard writing," he grumped in his old age, and he threatened that he had half a mind to rewrite the whole poem in the loftier, more complex meters of his later "Odes" in order to get a better reception from the critics.[12] In a collection of 1878, in fact, we find that Patmore eventually wrote an entirely different poem also called "The Kiss."[13]

All metrical forms are of course subject to various uses and abuses, and different passages in the same meter can be either laughable or not. Patmore's use of the octosyllabic line in most of *The Angel in the House* is remarkably varied and modulated. "The Kiss," however, really does approach "doggerel," as George Saintsbury technically defined it in his massive *History of English Prosody*: strongly marked meter.[14] Particularly in the last line, the iambs bump out markedly because the semantic content, in particular the three repetitions of the word "thought," makes it impossible to read without seeming to exaggerate the meter:

> "I saw you take his kiss!" "'Tis true."
> "O, modesty!" "'Twas strictly kept:

> "He thought me asleep; at least, I knew
> "He thought I thought he thought I slept."

By the end of this chapter I shall attempt to explain this conjunction among a highly conspicuous meter, a proposition about the sociability of thinking, and sexual morality. But the apparent cynicism of the formulation of "The Kiss" – the vision of two lovers' practice of thinking about each other as leading to a mutual understanding only of the lowest kind – needs to be explored further.

Is Patmore simply having absurdist metrical fun, not only with sexual immorality, but also, à la Lewis Carroll, with a mathematical problem? In our own era, that is, mathematicians, logicians, and cognitive scientists have struggled to determine the best way to represent symbolically and to understand the structure of "common" or "mutual knowledge" situations which seem likely to regress infinitely: A knows that B knows that A knows that B knows, and so on.[15] Patmore's four-beat thinking line seems to cast a bemused eye, in anticipation, on some serious speculation about the rhythms of cognition. Some contemporary cognitive scientists who have studied our ability to process reports of such multiply embedded states of mind have argued that our capacity to keep track of the layers of embeddedness begins to falter dramatically at about four levels. If this is true, Patmore's "I knew / He thought I thought he thought I slept" measures out a significant boundary in human cognition. Some scholars in the "new field known as cognitive approaches to literature" have been eager to take the four-degrees-of-embeddedness limit as evolutionary fact, and to pursue the ways in which literary authors of the nineteenth century can be seen as "engaging with our evolved cognitive adaptations."[16] But we might wish to hesitate before taking as evolutionary fact conclusions drawn from, say, a study of seventy-seven University of Liverpool undergraduates' ability to process the mental states of others. And with Patmore's "Kiss" line in mind, we might wonder whether the fact that researchers see human ability to process "he thought I thought" statements to four or five levels of embeddedness rather has something to do with the fact that units of four and five are the backbone of English common meters. In a similar vein, as Kirstie Blair has demonstrated, nineteenth-century physicians determined that four beats or iterations marked out the natural human heart cycle.[17] The overwhelming place of the number four in English poetry and music has long inflected its appearance in British sciences, even the science of the sociability of human thought.

Perhaps, more accurately, the cynicism of "The Kiss" might be explained by its place in the narrative of *The Angel in the House*. "The Kiss" is one of the pieces that got moved around and revised slightly as Patmore rearranged the poem's second book, "The Espousals," which takes us from the moment of Honoria's acceptance of Felix's proposal to their wedding day. But it is always somewhere in the indeterminate middle between those two events, as Felix cycles through various stages of desire and ambivalence. In spite of the changes, it always comes shortly after a narrative episode called "The Revulsion" in which Felix tortures himself by imagining, much like the speaker in Wordsworth's "Strange Fits of Passion," Honoria dead:

> "What," I exclaimed, with chill alarm,
> "If this fantastic horror shows
> "The feature of an actual harm!"[18]

But the most provocative context Patmore provided for "The Kiss" is that which was put in place through a series of revisions that seem to have been mostly settled by 1858, in which "The Kiss" – newly titled, and newly stripped of the other "Sentences" that partnered it in its first location in the first edition of Book II – follows right after another, more meditative "Prelude," interestingly titled "Love Thinking." We may take that title itself to describe not only that poem, but also the dialogue that occurs between that poem and "The Kiss" – and some aspects of *The Angel in the House* as a whole. The grammar of the title itself is arresting, and shifts with emphasis: do we read it as "*love* thinking," "thinking" here as a noun with "love" modifying it, as a species or kind of thinking? Or do we scan it differently, as "love *think*ing," in which case it seems to be a description of an act of thinking that Love (a personified being) is doing? Or is it an imperative, exhorting the reader to "love thinking," as advertisements urge readers to "Drink Pepsi"? Either way, the title emphasizes thinking as an action or practice, an impression that is reinforced when we note that in other versions of *The Angel in the House* this particular poem, placed elsewhere – nowhere near "The Kiss" – and without the title, assumed the form of a letter from Felix to Honoria. In that version, it begins, "What lifts you in my thought so far / Beyond all else? Let Love be true!"[19] The version titled "Love Thinking" and placed before "The Kiss" recasts the "you"s as "she"s and "her"s, and the second-person letter becomes a meditation in and on the third person:

> What lifts her in my thought so far
> Beyond all else? Let Love not err!
> 'Tis that which all right women are,
> But which I'll know in none but her.
> She is to me the only Ark

Of that high mystery which locks
The lips of joy, or speaks in dark
Enigmas and in paradox.[20]

The revision of this poem, from second-person love letter, to third-person meditation, dramatically marks Patmore's interest in the difference between speaking to a beloved, and thinking about her, and stresses the poem's emphasis on purely mental relations between men and women.[21]

Newly set next to each other, "Love Thinking" and "The Kiss" begin a dialogue in which "Love Thinking" would appear to frame the practice of thinking about a desired other in a more serious, deeper way than does the funny "Kiss." That this "Prelude" has its origins within, rather than outside of, the earnest central narrative of *The Angel in the House* would seem to confirm this. Moreover, the language of "Love Thinking" is far loftier and more literary, indebted throughout in particular to Shelley's "Epipsychidion."[22] From that poem's image of the beloved's eyes "too deep / For the brief fathom-line of thought or sense,"[23] "Love Thinking" derives its final image of the results of the speaker's meditations on the question he had asked himself in the poem's opening lines:

And when, for joy's relief, I think
To fathom with the line of thought
The well from which I, blissful, drink,
The spring's so deep I come to nought.[24]

However, throughout "Epipsychidion," Shelley conceives of thinking about a beloved as a perilous leap into dizzying mystery, an activity that takes one to the brink "till those bright plumes of thought.../...lie shattered."[25] For the speaker in "Love Thinking," in contrast, it seems more like a perplexing retreat into ignorance. Advising the lover to be, like his heart, "content to feel and not to know" (15), "Love Thinking" defines love thinking as a mental practice that is completely unproductive of knowledge. It emphasizes love thinking's tendency both to create and to dissolve the object of thought,[26] as when the speaker describes his experience as the reverse of the mythological Ixion, who, in thinking he was embracing Juno, was only embracing a cloud-facsimile of the goddess set up as a trap by Zeus:

I kiss its cheek; its life divine
Exhales from its resplendent shroud;
Ixion's fate reversed is mine,
Authentic Juno seems a cloud;
I feel a blessed warmth, I see

A bright circumference of rays,
But darkness, where the sun should be.[27]

The original opening phrase of the poem that became, when placed next to "Love Thinking," "The Kiss" was not in fact "I saw you take his kiss!" but "I saw him kiss your cheek!": Patmore's revision may have been made to draw attention away from this echo.[28] Yet in charting thinking's tendency to turn even an "authentic Juno" into a cloud of insubstantiality, "Love Thinking," for all of its comparative loftiness, articulates a concept of thinking about another person no less thin, and no less negative, in its own way, than that of "The Kiss."

MODERN LOVE: TOO MUCH CONCEIVING

I'd suggest, however, that the strongest context, and the strongest reading of "The Kiss," is George Meredith's rewriting of Patmore's farcical quatrain in the harrowing opening lines of *Modern Love* a few years later:

> By this he knew she wept with waking eyes:
> That, at his hand's light quiver by her head,
> The strange low sobs that shook their common bed,
> Were called into her with a sharp surprise,
> And strangled mute, like little gaping snakes,
> Dreadfully venomous to him. She lay
> Stone-still, and the long darkness flowed away
> With muffled pulses. Then, as midnight makes
> Her giant heart of Memory and Tears
> Drink the pale drug of silence, and so beat
> Sleep's heavy measure, they from head to feet
> Were moveless, looking through their dead blank years,
> By vain regret scrawled over the blank wall.
> Like sculptured effigies they might be seen
> Upon their marriage-tomb, the sword between;
> Each wishing for the sword that severs all.[29]

First published in 1862, this sequence of fifty sonnet-like poems of sixteen lines was widely held to be a response to Meredith's first marriage to Mary Ellen Peacock Nicolls, which was as famously disastrous as Patmore's virtually concomitant first marriage, allegedly inspiration for *The Angel of the House*, was famously ideal. Mary Ellen Meredith left her husband in 1858 and died in 1861, and the poem was begun shortly thereafter. In the dense opening poem and elsewhere, however, *Modern Love* clearly exfoliates from, and rewrites, the play of thinking, sleeping, and sexual tension in "The Kiss," the elements of which are dispersed throughout Meredith's poem.[30] One episode recapitulates the scenario of "The Kiss": the husband catches his wife unblushingly receiving her lover's kiss on the forehead.[31]

Toward the end of this chapter, we shall return to consider how reading *Modern Love* as a rewriting of "The Kiss" helps us understand Patmore's quatrain. But reading *Modern Love* as a response to "The Kiss also provides something that may feel more urgent: a way to understand" Meredith's extraordinary poem. *Modern Love* was roundly condemned by its first critics, who were offended both by the poem's dense style and by its subject matter – "a grave moral mistake," intoned one reviewer, who felt that such a sympathetic treatment of marital discord was "one of the most disastrous calamities that can befall a nation" – though it was warmly defended by some readers, such as Swinburne.[32] Modern attempts to come to grips with the poem, while appreciative, have often foundered in following its illusion of narrative coherence. The poem seems to tell the story, begun *in medias res* in the midnight wake/watch of the first poem, of an unnamed man and woman facing a crisis of marital fidelity. The wife, who appears to be in an adulterous relationship, seems miserable, torn, and guilty; the husband, from whose point of view the story is mostly told, vacillates wildly between anger, self-incrimination, and nostalgia for an idealized past. The poem follows him through these moods, through charged and often wordless encounters with his wife; and it follows the pair as they go through the motions – at a dinner party, at a country house weekend – of appearing to the world as a happily married couple. About half-way through the poem (Sonnet XXII), the husband is distracted by a flirtation with another woman (always referred to as "Lady," in contrast to whom his wife is always "Madam"), with whom he becomes sexually involved (Sonnet XXXIX). The wife is then also racked with jealousy. At the end of poem, the husband and wife finally talk – but the effect of that talk is radically uncertain. The woman commits suicide: her husband finds her just before she dies, and comes up with an interpretation of her action of which readers, as we shall see, have reason to be skeptical.

As this summary may suggest – and as decades of commentary of the poem have pointed out – *Modern Love* gains its strength from the ways in which it conjoins novelistic plot and detail with form and language that hearken back to the Petrarchan sonnet sequence. In this regard it belongs in the company of the many other hybrid-genre poetic sequences of the nineteenth century, from Barrett Browning's *Aurora Leigh* to Clough's *Amours de Voyage*, and, of course, *The Angel in the House*. But *Modern Love*'s generic diversity also produces pitfalls: in particular, its language seems to hold out the possibility of a psychologically coherent narrative which it then consistently fails to deliver. In other words, readers are drawn to construct an account of psychological causality, an account of what particular psychological or characterological features of both the husband and wife have led them to this marital crisis.[33] Almost all such interpretations, however, ultimately feel like impositions on the poem – armed with such an interpretation, one returns to the poem only to realize that it doesn't quite fit. As Cathy Comstock has argued, *Modern Love* lacks the psychological glue that would bind the sonnets together into a coherent narrative: the poem "continually disturb[s] the hope of a progressive development of insight." James R. Kincaid similarly charges that critics of *Modern Love* "hide themselves behind a conception of the poem as a narrative," arguing that all readings of this remarkably resistant poem "naturalize" it.[34] It is a poem perhaps best read around, read obliquely, rather than interpreted directly. The approach here thus seeks to denaturalize rather than naturalize *Modern Love*, to cut across the poem's narrative, and to focus on isolating the constellation of concerns that emerge from *Modern Love*'s points of contact with Patmore's "Kiss."

For example, the Pre-Raphaelite circles in and out of which both Patmore and Meredith drifted in the 1850s and 1860s seemed to have been especially interested in the proximity of erotic life to the passage between waking and sleeping. We might think most obviously of Dante Gabriel Rossetti's intense, voluptuous sonnets from *The House of Life*, "The Kiss," and "Nuptial Sleep" (1869), both notoriously singled out by Robert Buchanan as "nasty" "trash."[35] In these sonnets, two lovers drift off to sleep in the ecstasy of their kiss in a manner both shockingly infantile and erotic. When the speaker reawakens from his wondrous, shimmering dreams, he wonders the more at seeing his lover sleeping next to him: "for there she lay."[36] Other renditions of this scenario, while still erotic, are less blissful. Patmore later published an agonizing version in "The Azalea" (1878), in which a bereaved speaker dreams that his wife is dead, awakens reassured by the belief that she is lying beside him, then remembers that she is, in fact, dead.[37] Most relevant to *Modern Love*'s vexed does-she-wake-or-sleep scenario may be some earlier poems by Coventry Patmore which Meredith would surely have known. In "The River" (1844), a young woman marries a man other than the one she loves. Her true lover responds by jumping in a river, an act that seems somehow to enter simultaneously the minds of the now-sleeping husband and wife:

> "Wake, wake, oh wake!" the Bridegroom now
> Calls unto his sleeping Bride:

"Alas, I saw thee, pale and dead,
Roll down a frightful tide!"
He takes her hand: "How chill thou art!
What is it, sweet my Bride?"
The Bride bethinks her now of him
Who last night was no guest.
"Sweet heaven! and for me? I dream!"

(13)

All of these poems allude to and revise of one of the Pre-Raphaelites' favorites, Keats' *The Eve of St. Agnes*, with its pairing of sleeping woman and wakeful man. But the lesson some of these mid-century poets seemed to have taken from that poem, or from Keats' concern with waking versus sleeping generally, was not so much about dreams and disillusionment as it was about the role of unconscious proximity in human intimacy. Here is the first stanza of another early Patmore poem, "Night and Sleep":

How strange at night to wake
And watch, while others sleep,
Till sight and hearing ache
For objects that may keep
The awful inner sense
Unroused, lest it should mark
The life that haunts the emptiness
And horror of the dark!

(54)

In his *Essay on Metrical Law* (1857), to which we will return at the end of this chapter, Patmore singled out this curious stanza about watching while others sleep as an ideal instance of the way in which a three-foot iambic line marks the slowest of all meters. The three beats, he argues, slow us down by creating a long empty pause at the end of each line. This effect is vividly demonstrated, he asserts, by the way in which the seventh line of the stanza – "The life that haunts the emptiness" – adds a fourth foot with the word "emptiness" – *"filling up"* the line in ways that make us aware of the emptiness of the other lines (emphasis his).[38] As we will discover in more detail later, there is a strong connection between a thematic interest in the rhythms of sleeping-with-another – what Meredith calls "Sleep's heavy measure"[39] – and the New Prosody of Patmore, which conceived of poetic meters as abstract phenomena made of ideal gaps and empty pauses rather than heard beats. It is a fascination with the rhythms of what we could call primary mental processes: those modes of thinking that are most tied to the unconscious, to dreams, rather than to the rationality of secondary-process thinking.[40] It is in this context that we can understand the many poems of this period that suggest that sleeping with someone is an ideal way of being with them.

But in contrast to Rossetti's or Patmore's versions of nuptial sleep, in *Modern Love* there is neither sleeping nor kissing; there is only thinking. And Keats' first-person question, "do I wake or sleep?" has been recast, crucially, as one person's thinking about another. As the poem opens, the husband and wife are lying together in bed, each trying to determine whether the other wakes or sleeps. The wife, weeping unrestrainedly, does so on the assumption that her husband is sleeping; the husband tries to figure out whether his wife is crying awake, or in her sleep. Suddenly the stakes of the "he thought she thought" game of Patmore's "The Kiss" seem much higher, as if we've moved from a cynical knowingness to a delineation of deep intersubjective understanding. That is, it might seem from the outset that Meredith casts the problem of thinking about another person as a question of epistemology, of the problem of knowing other minds.

And indeed, an orientation around epistemological questions is built into *Modern Love*'s engagement with form and style, as we can see by examining closely the sequence's first sonnet. Consider the striking opening line, "By this he knew she wept with waking eyes," which presents us with a claim to know that appears to be derived via inductive reasoning. By *this* – his wife's self-conscious cessation of her sobs – he knows she is awake: it is not so much the spectacular evidence before him, but his ability to reflect on it and bring that evidence to a conclusion, to turn it into a *this*, that is at stake. However, Meredith's opening "By this" signals immediately *Modern Love*'s turning inside-out of the tight ratiocination characteristic of the sonnet as a form: we recall J. A. Symonds' description of the sonnet form as "unavoidably *raisonneuse*" discussed in Chapter 3. The sonnets of Shakespeare typically lay out their reasoning and end with a "this": "If this be error and upon me proved" (Sonnet 116), or "All this the world well knows" (Sonnet 129). To begin at the end, as Meredith's first sonnet does, designates the fallibility and malleability of an empiricist theory of knowledge.[41]

The significance of the placement of *Modern Love*'s "By this he knew" is confirmed by considering its relationship to an early poetic fragment to which Phyllis Bartlett connected it in her outstanding edition of Meredith's poetry. The fragment, "Meeting," comes as close as anything to articulating an anti-*Modern Love*: it conveys Meredith's erotic ideal of non-reflective, non-communicative proximity to another. It begins, remarkably, "Say nothing":

> Say nothing: let us sit within arm's reach:
> The silent something passing to the skies

> From heartful earth, more spirit-rich than speech.
> And needing not the beam of tender eyes,
> Shall breathe between us, dearest soul, & be
> A viewless Angel born from you & me.

After the last line Meredith wrote, and then deleted, the following line: "By this we know we love."[42] The echo of this early, canceled line in the opening sonnet of *Modern Love* speaks volumes; it is a turn from paradise to paradise lost.

Furthermore, the term "this" in sonnets is frequently self-referential, as in "So long lives this, and this gives life to thee" (Shakespeare, Sonnet 18), or, "you live in this" (Sonnet 55): the poem is its own evidence and conclusion. Meredith's "By this he knew" inevitably feels like a deictic gesture that both affirms that pieces of knowledge have proofs in the real world, and, through its affiliation with the self-referential "this" of the sonnet tradition, dissolves proofs away. That the husband and wife of *Modern Love* are unable to know much, unable to know beyond the sonnet in which they live, is confirmed by the first sonnet's echoes of Milton's "On Shakespeare," and Meredith's choice for *Modern Love* of that poem's sixteen-line form. That poem supplies a model both for the slow, painfully attenuated cadence of the *Modern Love* sonnets, and for some of the funereal imagery of its opening. Milton's poem ends by imagining readers of Shakespeare as themselves the monument to the poet's fame:

> Then thou our fancy of itself bereaving,
> Dost make us Marble with too much conceiving;
> And so Sepulcher'd in such pomp dost lie,
> That Kings for such a Tomb wouldst wish to die.[43]

The first sonnet of *Modern Love* concludes by imagining the husband and wife made marble and lying side by side. It is a live burial:

> Like sculptured effigies they might be seen
> Upon their marriage-tomb, the sword between;
> Each wishing for the sword that severs all.

Like Milton's poem or Shakespeare's Sonnets, *Modern Love*'s first sonnet is itself the tomb that monumentalizes its inhabitants, the husband and wife who can be said to have made themselves "Marble with too much conceiving." It is a paralyzing echo chamber of thinking that produces no new knowledge.

We are, therefore, certainly asked to question the husband's "By this he knew" – much as we quickly learn the tragic irony of Trollope's title *He Knew He Was Right* (1869) – and thus asked to interpret *Modern Love* as a

poem about a failure to know another; and this can also be seen as one of
the lessons, and one of the causes of *Modern Love*'s cramped, dense style. It
is a restless style that piles figure upon figure, that prefers elaborate simile
over metaphor, and in which similes often lead to dead ends. The extended
simile of the husband and wife as sculptured effigies brings to an end a
sequence of figures that strain comprehension. In the first sonnet's first figure, the wife's sobs are compared to "little gaping snakes," an image whose
coherence is scrambled as the snakes are at once gaping, strangled (and
thus presumably disarmed), and, in the next line, "dreadfully venomous
to him" (6). It is as if the poem can't help following, all at once, all possible dimensions of a comparison of woman to snake, a comparison that
reappears throughout *Modern Love*; but the effect of Meredith's elaborate,
self-canceling similes is, as Isobel Armstrong has pointed out, to drama-
tize above all the dissonance between language and "the non-linguistic
world."[44] More difficult to parse is the jumble of figures of lines 8–13:

> Then, as midnight makes
> Her giant heart of Memory and Tears
> Drink the pale drug of silence, and so beat
> Sleep's heavy measure, they from head to feet
> Were moveless, looking through their dead black years,
> By vain regret scrawled over the blank wall.

The present tense of line 8 indicates that the "as" must be seen as inaug-
urating an extended simile that governs the entire sentence. The next line
introduces a train of partial personifications: a heart that drinks silence,
itself either a part of, or composed by, the fleetingly possibly personified abstractions "Memory and Tears." Finally, the image of the husband
and wife viewing their "dead black years" as a grisly graffiti consists of
an incomplete equation: if the "dead years" are a kind of writing, what
does the writing surface – the blank wall – imaginatively represent? It is a
vehicle with no tenor.

Such figures can be found throughout *Modern Love*. Here is the last
stanza of the poem:

> Thus piteously Love closed what he begat:
> The union of this ever-diverse pair!
> These two were rapid falcons in a snare,
> Condemned to do the flitting of the bat.
> Lovers beneath the singing sky of May,
> They wandered once; clear as the dew on flowers:
> But they fed not on the advancing hours:
> Their hearts held cravings for the buried day.

> Then each applied to each that fatal knife,
> Deep questioning, which probes to endless dole.
> Ah, what a dusty answer gets the soul
> When hot for certainties in this our life! –
> In tragic hints here see what evermore
> Moves dark as yonder midnight ocean's force,
> Thundering like ramping hosts of warrior horse,
> To throw that faint thin line upon the shore!
>
> (L.I–16)

These lines ask the reader to look into the poem ("here") to see *hints* of *something* (a "what" that is never identified) which is described via simile as moving as dark as the force of the ocean, which is itself described via simile as horses thundering on the shore. By the time one gets to the last line, one is hard pressed to say what it is that is throwing that faint thin line upon the shore, and what that shore, or that line, might be a figure for. As is often the case in *Modern Love*, this is a simile in which vehicles and tenors don't line up: Meredith's figurative language spins away from reference.

These lines' emphasis on an overpowering force that produces so little effect (a big ocean, a thin faint line) does indeed seem to refer to their own literary mode: an excess of figures that corresponds to only the faintest trace of reference. Furthermore, in gesturing towards its own representation of human relations ("in tragic hints here see"), this passage does seem to link excesses of figurative language with the problem of representing people's minds. It is tempting, in this regard, to see Meredith's figurative excesses as symptoms or indicators of an epistemological problem, as indicators of an ineluctable gap between language and experience, and even to see that gap as the very cause of the tragedy of the two individuals in the poem: language failed them in their attempts to communicate or to understand one another.[45] Representation has taken the place of knowledge.

Such an interpretation – of the tragic usurpation of understanding by acts of representation – is possible too at the level of plot. In the third-to-last sonnet (XLVIII), the husband and wife have an honest talk, the husband confessing his infidelity, to uncertain effect:

> Our inmost hearts had opened, each to each.
> We drank the pure daylight of honest speech.
> Alas! That was the fatal draught, I fear.
> For when of my lost Lady came the word,
> This woman, O this agony of flesh!
> Jealous devotion bade her break the mesh,
> That I might seek that other like a bird.
>
> (XLVIII.6–12)

In the sonnet that follows they have another encounter on the beach, and then a final, nocturnal, death-bed encounter:

> He found her by the ocean's moaning verge,
> Nor any wicked change in her discerned;
> And she believed his old love had returned,
> Which was her exultation, and her scourge.
> She took his hand, and walked with him, and seemed
> The wife he sought, though shadow-like and dry.
> She had one terror, lest her heart should sigh,
> And tell her loudly she no longer dreamed.
> She dared not say, "This is my breast: look in."
> But there's a strength to help the desperate weak.
> That night he learned how silence best can speak
> The awful things when Pity pleads for Sin.
> About the middle of the night her call
> Was heard, and he came wondering to the bed.
> "Now kiss me, dear! it may be, now!" she said.
> Lethe had passed those lips, and he knew all.
>
> (XLIX.1–16)

The question of what the husband knows, and what he thinks he knows, remains wide open, and the history of answers turns out to have its own love triangles and "he said she said"s. Wilfrid Blunt reported that Alice Meynell's husband, Wilfrid Meynell, read the poem to him, and "expounded it…as Meredith had expounded it to Mrs. Meynell. According to this the last two stanzas mean that the wife, 'Madam,' commits suicide so as to leave the poet free to marry 'My Lady.'"[46] Whether or not Meredith actually ever "expounded" thus to Alice Meynell, it is worth pausing to consider how strange it is that Meynell was positioned as the conduit of the truth of both *The Angel in the House* and *Modern Love* by the poems' authors. But this interpretation – that the husband of *Modern Love* understands his wife to have sacrificed herself to have freed him to marry his lover – is both supported by the poem and revealed as a distortion. It is buttressed by the husband's assertion in the previous sonnet that "Jealous devotion bade her break the mesh." But Sonnet XLIX itself tells a different story, suggesting that the wife takes her life in order to preserve the fragile return of her husband's trust and love that she experiences on the beach. The assertion that the husband knows "all" may amount to nothing.[47]

To summarize: the evidence of *Modern Love*, beginning with the first sonnet and extending to its denouement, may seem to point to a denunciation of how little Meredith's estranged pair know each other. They are reduced, in the first sonnet, to making the most minimal knowledge claim you can possibly make about another human being: judging the presence or absence of consciousness, and even that seems fraught with obstacles. But in fact, we learn throughout much of the poem, that the husband and wife in *Modern Love* actually know quite a lot about each others' minds, and, in spite of his rage, the husband is quite empathetic towards his wife, acutely aware of her intelligence and the premium she puts on insight into others. It is rather, however, that an excessive investment in insight, truth, and knowledge has brought them to this crisis.[48] Any knowledge they have about each other turns out to be neither more nor less helpful to them than the minimal knowledge about consciousness that is set up as a paradigm at the beginning. Indeed, Meredith seems to suggest that it is this very activity – lying around and thinking about each other – which is the problem: that it produces "knowledge" that makes only a minimal difference. *Modern Love* is fundamentally skeptical, not about people's ability to know one another, but about the value that psychological insight into or understanding of another person may have in an intimate relation, and even more, skeptical even of the value of *thinking* about one you love, at all. It is a painful refutation of the liberal, ameliorative belief that understanding, psychological insight, and attention can make things better, a belief soon to be enshrined in John Stuart Mill's plea for psychological understanding between men and women in *The Subjection of Women* (1869), a book Meredith allegedly devoured at a single sitting.[49] Expressing a more radical anxiety about the damage done by thinking about the beloved, Meredith subordinates psychology and epistemology to a conception of cognition as inseparable from loss and harm. Casting thinking as a part of intimacy that is its own undoing, *Modern Love* uses its negative energy to grope towards an ideal of non-reflective relation.

We can elaborate on *Modern Love*'s unusual stance toward thinking and knowing by looking at Sonnet xv which begins simply, "I think she sleeps":

> I think she sleeps: it must be sleep, when low
> Hangs that abandoned arm toward the floor;
> The face turned with it. Now make fast the door.
> Sleep on: it is your husband, not your foe.
> The Poet's black stage-lion of wronged love,
> Frights not our modern dames: – well if he did!
> Now will I pour new light upon that lid,
> Full-sloping like the breasts beneath. "Sweet dove,
> Your sleep is pure. Nay, pardon: I disturb.
> I do not? good!" Her waking infant-stare

Grows woman to the burden my hands bear:
Her own handwriting to me when no curb
Was left on Passion's tongue. She trembles through:
A woman's tremble – the whole instrument: –
I show another letter lately sent.
The words are very like: the name is new.

(xv.1–16)

The overwrought misogyny of the husband's actions and thoughts – he knows it's a joke to compare himself to Othello, but he does this kind of thing all the time – as well as the way in which the sonnet's staticky imagery gives way to the clarity and cruelty of the last two lines, is typical of the sequence as a whole. The most immediate antecedent of Sonnet xv, however, is neither *Othello* nor the history of the sonnet, nor even Satan at Eve's ear in *Paradise Lost*, but the first lines of *Modern Love* itself, in that once again the poem opens with the man trying to gauge whether the woman in bed wakes or sleeps. Here of course she's asleep until he cruelly wakes her in order to gain access to her first moment of consciousness.

However, the similarity and differences between the opening lines of Sonnets 1 and xv – "By this he knew she wept with waking eyes" and "I think she sleeps" – encapsulate the whole argument of *Modern Love* with respect to the relations between thinking and knowing. Not by distinguishing between knowledge and wakefulness in the first case, and thinking and sleep in the second, however: the most crucial difference between "By this he knew she wept with waking eyes" and "I think she sleeps" is the difference between the pronouns "he" and "I." One of the peculiarities of *Modern Love* is its shifts in pronouns and point of view. About one-tenth of the sonnets – clustered at the beginning and end of the sequence – describe both husband and wife in the third person, while the rest are narrated by the husband himself.[50] In this way, it might seem, the poem's concern with how the two protagonists know or think about each other is embedded in its narrative structure, enmeshed with questions about the nature of self-knowledge, omniscience, verification, and the tragic privacy of thought. But perhaps the difference between thinking and knowing – and the difference such a difference might make – just depends on the logic of the pronoun. Consider Wittgenstein's riddling explanation: "I can know what someone else is thinking, not what I am thinking. It is correct to say 'I know what you are thinking,' and wrong to say 'I know what I am thinking.'" He glossed this statement as "a whole cloud of philosophy condensed into a drop of grammar."[51] In *Modern Love*, Meredith often seems to take a similarly anti-psychological approach to thought and knowledge.

"Knowing" in *Modern Love* is never the attainment of some kind of truth, but is rather a kind of claim-making about another person: "he knew she wept," says some unknown claimer. "Thinking," by contrast, is a practice of the "I" who, if engaged in the ongoing practice of thinking, cannot logically be in the business of making knowledge claims about itself. In this context, the play of pronouns in Patmore's "He thought I thought he thought I slept," and his own revision of pronouns in "Love Thinking" opens onto, as Patmore himself seems to have known, several philosophical clouds.

Modern Love and *The Angel in the House*, in other words, reveal a stance on the relation between thinking and knowing that I have been pursuing throughout this book, a stance very different from both the earnest assumption that if you think about someone, you can claim to know them, and from a skepticism about knowledge of others. We may tend to view Wittgenstein's position, discussed briefly above, as an overturning of just such a Victorian earnestness about thinking and knowing. But in fact, nineteenth-century writing manifests a diversity of beliefs about thinking which often cast thinking as instinct with power, yet with claims separate from those of knowing. In the long view which the focus of this book affords, it is possible to see a curious point of convergence between, say, the curious bracketing of epistemology in the work of J. M. E. McTaggart, often viewed – as we noted in Chapter 2 – as the last figure of nineteenth-century British idealism, and the work of Wittgenstein, who changed the direction of anglophone philosophy for the twentieth century.[52]

In Meredith's *Modern Love*, however, the poet's furious negativity almost completely obscures any positive philosophical vision. If the poem is loud and clear in its pessimism about the effects of thinking about someone you love, what is Meredith's norm of relatedness? I noted earlier that the early poetic fragment "Meeting" begins to suggest what may be Meredith's ideal of intimacy: a non-communicative, non-reflective proximity to another. Its opening imperative, "Say nothing," is dramatically different from, for example, the superficially similar opening gambit of Donne's "The Canonization": "For God's sake hold your tongue, and let me love." Donne's speaker silences his lover in order to fill up space with his own eloquence. In contrast, Meredith's "Meeting" devolves into self-canceling silence:

> Say nothing: let us sit within arm's reach:
> The silent something passing to the skies
> From heartful earth, more spirit-rich than speech.
> And needing not the beam of tender eyes,

> Shall breathe between us, dearest soul, & be
> A viewless Angel born from you & me.
> ~~By this we know we love~~:

When Meredith's lovers meet, they sit "within arm's reach" but not embracing; they do not speak, nor do they gaze into each other's eyes. A "viewless Angel" – no Cupid, but an abstract "silent something" – is born of their very reticence.

A version of this ideal, non-reflective proximity is elaborated in Sonnet xlvii of *Modern Love*, the sonnet of which Swinburne claimed "a more perfect piece of writing no man alive has ever turned out":[53]

> We saw the swallows gathering in the sky,
> And in the osier-isle we heard them noise.
> We had not to look back on summer joys,
> Or forward to a summer of bright dye:
> But in the largeness of the evening earth
> Our spirits grew as we went side by side.
> The hour became her husband and my bride.
> Love that had robbed us so, thus blessed our dearth!
> The pilgrims of the year waxed very loud
> In multitudinous chatterings, as the flood
> Full brown came from the West, and like pale blood
> Expanded to the upper crimson cloud.
> Love that had robbed us of immortal things,
> This little moment mercifully gave,
> Where I have seen across the twilight wave
> The swan sail with her young beneath her wings.
>
> (xlvii)

The beauty of this sonnet begins with its first two lines, the plain declarative language of which forms such a sharp contrast to the anxious, posturing diction of most of the poem. Even the elaborate figure describing the merging of the flock of migrating birds with the sunset-tinged clouds (9–12) here serves only to heighten, rather than undo, the overwhelming emphasis on sensory experience. Crucially, the husband and wife here are absorbed in shared, parallel, sensory experience. It is an episode of shared not-thinking. Their minds neither return to the past, nor stray towards the future (3–4), but remain in "This little moment" (14). In this expansive little moment of sensory intensity, the husband and wife grow not closer together, but larger along parallel tracks – "Our spirits grew as we went side by side" (6) – and, curiously, become more married not to each other but to the moment: "The hour became her husband and my bride" (7). A detached, non-reflective parallel experience is the only ideal of relatedness held out by *Modern Love*.[54]

MENTAL METERS: HE THOUGHT I THOUGHT HE THOUGHT

We can now characterize that attitude toward thinking in *Modern Love* not as cynicism or even skepticism, but perhaps as a kind of stoicism about the minimal claims of knowledge, which conceives of love thinking as a kind of practice with indeterminate results. Seen as an interpretation of "The Kiss," *Modern Love* can clarify the attitude toward thinking about the beloved in *The Angel in the House*. *Modern Love* redirects us to Patmore's play of personal pronouns; and it also redirects us to the *Angel's* meter, or at least the meter of "The Kiss": what Meredith calls, in the opening of his poem, "Sleep's heavy measure" (1.11). Perhaps Patmore minimizes the yield of thinking about the beloved because he conceives of thinking as something like meter. Alice Meynell asserted, "When Patmore talked of his poems, it was of their metres."[55] So it may be worth taking a closer look at the meter of "The Kiss":

> "I *saw* you *take* his *kiss*!" "'Tis *true*."
> "O, *mo*desty!" "'Twas *strictly kept*:
> "He *thought* me a*sleep*; at *least*, I *knew*
> "He *thought* I *thought* he *thought* I *slept*."

I suggested at the beginning of this chapter that the passage seemed to exemplify everybody's worst impressions of the "namby-pamby" meter of the *Angel*, because the semantic content – especially in the last line – forces us to exaggerate the meter. Why would Patmore wish to exaggerate the "bad" meter of "The Kiss"?

Looking at the metrical effects of the last line more closely, we note that while the semantic content does seem to force the meter, it does not do so, because this is how we'd actually say this line in natural conversation. In real life, if you were saying something like this while telling a friend the story of a misunderstanding that happened to you during an embarrassing first date, you might say something like: "Well, it turned out that *he* thought that *I* thought that *he* thought that *I* thought …" You would stress the pronouns, not the word "thought," as you both emphasized and sought to untangle the confusion. An emphasis on the pronouns, rather than on the thinking, is what we find in the likely poetic source for Patmore's embedded thinking line, from Dante's *Inferno*:

> Cred'io ch'ei credette ch'io credesse.[56]

Describing a moment's confusion between Dante and his guide Virgil as they enter the forest of the suicides, the form of this line represented vividly for Leo Spitzer "the 'onomatopoetic' rendering of [Dante's] mental state of estrangement and confusion" and "the disruption of his mental communication with his master" through a brilliant "'adhesion' of language to the psychic content."[57] Though a recent translation has rendered this line "I think he thought that I thought,"[58] in its original, this celebrated passage places metrical stress on the two thinkers, rather than on the thinking.[59] In Patmore's "The Kiss," Dante's and Virgil's sublime confusion is translated to comic effect, in part because the English iamb emphasizes the act of thinking itself. The iambic force at the end of line 3 of "The Kiss," "at *least*, I *knew*," gathers force and carries over – assisted by the enjambment at the end of the line – to the next line: "He *thought* I *thought* he *thought* I *slept*."

The significance of the metrical stress on thinking, rather than thinkers, in Patmore's "two people in thought" line can be clarified by comparing it to a thinking-and-meter line from Wordsworth's "Anecdote for Fathers" from *Lyrical Ballads*, which Patmore must surely also have had in mind:

> My thoughts on former pleasures ran;
> I thought of Kilve's delightful shore,
> My pleasant home, when spring began,
> A long, long year before.
> A day it was when I could bear
> To *think*, and *think*, and *think* again;
> With so much happiness to spare,
> I could not feel a pain.[60]

As Cynthia Chase has noted, this thinking line empties content out of thinking:

The triple repetition of the infinitive "to think" compounds the difficulty of imagining what sort of reflection this line describes. To think again is to reverse a previous judgment, but to think again and again implies repetition rather than reversal or progression. Triple repetition describes a form of thinking that consists in repetition, and repetition is also what this line does. Hence the activity of thinking becomes indistinguishable from the activity of repeating the words "to think."[61]

We might want to add that thinking becomes indistinguishable from the meter of the words "to think," which is clearly what prompts Chase to write erroneously that the infinitive "to think" (rather than just the word "think" by itself) is repeated three times in Wordsworth's line. The iambic meter is crucially linked to the activity of thinking.

The Wordsworth of the "Preface" to *Lyrical Ballads* would have found the meter central to the claim of the speaker of "Anecdote for Fathers," that he has an inexplicable excess of happiness that allows him to bear painful thinking. In the "Preface," Wordsworth famously theorizes the pleasure of meter as the removal of pain:

There can be little doubt but that more pathetic situations and sentiments... which have a greater proportion of pain connected with them, may be endured in metrical composition.[62]

In contrast to Patmore's thinking line, in which the squeezing of two people thinking into a four-beat line causes estrangements of meter and sense, Wordsworth's thinking line bears no metrical pain. But to contemplate these lines together is to note the ways in which both Wordsworth's and Patmore's practices of linking meter, feeling, and thinking are fundamentally different from the understanding of the role of thinking and feeling in the lyric tradition that subtends a very different approach to poetry and thinking from my own, Helen Vendler's *Poets Thinking*. In Vendler's approach, the relationship between "poetry" and "thinking" is essentially dramatic: poems are scripts of the poet's process of thinking, much as, in the tradition of reading inaugurated by J. S. Mill's understanding of poetry as overheard "soliloquy," poems are read as dramatic scripts of a speaker. The job of the reader, in this view, is to reconstruct "the way thinking goes on in the poet's mind during the process of creation."[63] For Patmore and other Victorian prosodists, poetic forms were not the dramatic products of an anterior process of thinking; they were themselves the process of thinking.

Coventry Patmore had Wordsworth's "Preface" at hand when he wrote what was the most important nineteenth-century account of meter after Wordsworth, "An Essay on English Metrical Law" (1857), which he was thinking about and drafting at the same time that he was writing *The Angel in the House*. Highly influential, Patmore's "Metrical Law" marked the beginning of what came to be known as "The New Prosody" in part because of its emphasis on meter as something *purely mental*.[64] Reacting against the metrical theories of the Spasmodic poets of the 1850s such as Sidney Dobell, who viewed poetic rhythms as stemming from the physiological rhythms of the body, Patmore challenged the assumption that meter is about what you actually hear or say aloud, and argued instead that meter is important as an abstract idea in your mind against which you measure how the line would actually be spoken if it were spoken.[65] "I think it is demonstrable that, for the most part, *it has no material and external existence at all*, but has its place in the mind, which craves measure in everything."[66]

The contexts for Patmore's mentalizing of meter are the contexts for the theorizing of thinking as a form of action we have traced throughout this book: the rise of idealism in British philosophy; the prestige of psychology in the decades before its formalization as an academic discipline; and also, the situation of poetry in a world of print in which poetry was privately and silently read, in which the relationship of poetry to an actually speaking voice had become more attenuated.[67] The theorizing of meter drew upon the theorizing of thought force as flowing through the universe, as articulated by Charles Bray, Tait and Balfour, and others described in Chapter 2: poetic rhythms were of a piece with the pulse of the universe.[68] The eccentric philosophical mathematician Mary Everest Boole, whom we met briefly in Chapter 2, revealed to William James her theory that everything from poetry to mathematics to logic was based on what she termed "Adon rhythms": "that is the Force which comes into man at the contact of suitably differentiated poles...[as when] two contrasted ideas meet in one brain." The best poets, in Boole's view, are those that can translate the mathematical, abstract Adon rhythms into language.[69] In her essay "The Rhythms of Life," Alice Meynell's own conception of poetic rhythms embraced both poetry and life: both followed "the tides of the mind." "Periodicity rules over the mental experience of man," she wrote, "according to the path of the orbit of his thoughts."[70] The tides of the mind pulse through both waking and sleeping life, both unconscious and conscious mental processes. We may view the Pre-Raphaelite preoccupation with metricalizing sleep in the poetry as a corollary to the New Prosody's emphasis on poetic rhythm's origins in the deep structures of the mind.

In this context, in which poetic meter was increasingly elevated, generalized, and philosophized, nineteenth-century theorists increasingly fitted the activity of the mind to meter. "By some mysterious law, about which philosophers might have much to say," mused metrical theorist T. S. Omond, "rhythmical form is the vehicle through which alone a poet can express his thoughts."[71] In E. S. Dallas' *Poetics*, a book Patmore knew well, the motion – the "throbbing" – of the mind thinking was the source of meter; meter is a sign of the source of poetry in primary, unconscious mental processes:

When the mind in poetic mood is said to work unconsciously, it is not meant that self-consciousness is utterly extinct. If so, we were dead or in a swoon. We are always tied to self-consciousness and unable to escape, but we fly away from it as far as we can. Our thoughts would fain break away from time and wander through eternity, would leave the earth and soar through the unbounded heaven, would forget self altogether and be lost in the Divine. But because we cannot do so entirely; because, being held by a chain, there are limits beyond which we cannot go, if our minds on reaching these limits still retain the activity which carried them thither, the path which they describe – to speak mathematically – must needs be circular.[72]

Meter is caused by the circling rhythms of the mind as it first pulses out towards its objects and then gets pulled back into the self:

> The centrifugal force wherewith the mind rushes forth into the objective, acting on the centripetal force of self-consciousness, generates the circling numbers, the revolving harmonies of poesy – in one word, a roundelay. Thus the fine mechanism of verse goes round, wheel upon wheel, and wheel within wheel.[73]

In this context "I *think*" could come to seem the perfect iamb. There is a joke in the contemporary psychologists Alison Gopnik and Andrew Meltzoff's book *Words, Thoughts, and Theories* in which the authors recount the philosopher J. A. Fodor's skeptical comment on the notion of the stream of consciousness: when he's working, he is supposed to have said, his stream of consciousness – if he has one – is probably going something like, "Come on, Jerry. That's it, Jerry. You can do it."[74] For the Victorian metrical theorist, the "stream of thought" – a phrase that was soon to be enshrined by William James – would probably be something like the little engine that could: "I *think* I *can* I *think* I *can*."[75] Or, perhaps, "I think, therefore iamb." Victorian metrical theorists and poets treated iambic meters as the rhythm of thinking itself: in the words of John Addington Symonds, not simply as "a mere framework" for thinking, but "the organic body of a vital thought."[76]

Nineteenth-century metrical theory, then, was a field in which thinking was theorized as a primary mental practice, as a kind of rhythm that just keeps on going, wheel upon wheel, and wheel within wheel. In this context, one of the attractions of "The Kiss" for Patmore was as a metrical experiment. As the meter of the last line of "The Kiss" forces emphasis away from its natural place – the distinguishing pronouns – and onto "thought," it is the activity of thought, the shared activity of the man and the woman thinking, that comes to the fore. In *The Printed Voice of Victorian Poetry*, Eric Griffiths describes Patmore as having had a "conjugal understanding of prosody," much as the poet famously held a conjugal theory of knowledge.[77] However, his aphorism "All knowledge, worthy of the name, is nuptial knowledge" might best be understood not as a statement of confidence in the infallibility of conjugal understanding, but rather as an admission that all knowledge partakes of the uncertainties of love thinking. That Patmore – metrical theorist, and worshipper of the ideal relation between man and woman as the basis of all knowledge – should use a poem such as "The Kiss" to work out the relationship between his ideas about meter and his ideas about intimacy, requires no stretch of the imagination. As Griffiths demonstrates, his metrical treatise routinely makes links between the harmonies and discords of verse, and the harmonies and discords between persons.[78] We are now, I'd argue, better able to account for the puzzle of this seemingly anomalous passage from Patmore's long poem. Here, as throughout *The Angel in the House*, the cynical and the ideal are alluringly close together, and meter is the switch-point between them. In Patmore's words: "in metre, there is but half a foot between the ridiculous and the sublime."[79] Marking the rhythms of thinking, Patmore's and Meredith's difficult marriage poems pulse with a kind of intimacy, or proximity, in which men and women think with – perhaps not even about – each other, and do not presume to know much at all.

CHAPTER 5

Daniel Deronda *and the omnipotence of thought*

This book has tried to understand why nineteenth-century writers moralized about the practice of thinking about another person, and above all it has sought to understand under what conditions nineteenth-century writers found it possible, or even desirable, to believe that thinking about another person could affect him or her, for good or for ill. I have proposed that studying the way nineteenth-century texts approach what we can call mental action at a distance, or, following Freud, "the omnipotence of thoughts," can provide new insight into the history of ideas about mental causation, practical ethics, and the sociability of the mind.[1] I have also stressed the contemporary consequences, and contemporary value, of this strand of thinking about thinking: when, we might ask, does a belief that our thoughts might substantially affect other people seem seriously delusional, and when might behaving as if we had such powers be in fact an ordinary part of social life?

Throughout this investigation, I have explored how these questions took shape, for a range of nineteenth-century British writers, through specific literary forms and practices. The two preceding chapters focused on nineteenth-century poetry and poetic theory. Chapter 3 focused on the relationship between poetic uses of second-person pronouns, and the anxieties of thinking about a beloved other. I pondered the paradoxes that ensue when poets from Samuel Taylor Coleridge to Elizabeth Barrett Browning and Christina Rossetti write "I think of thee" – or, more provocatively, "I do not think of thee," proposing that nineteenth-century poets reformulated apostrophe from a poetic form of speaking-to-another into a form of silent thinking-about-another. Chapter 4 sought to explain how Victorian poets and prosodists theorized the relationship between thinking about another and poetic rhythms, focusing closely on an episode from Coventry Patmore's *The Angel in the House* in which a woman claims, rhythmically, "He thought I thought he thought I slept." I explained the relationship of this episode to Victorian theories of poetic rhythm which viewed rhythm as the pulsation of thought from mind to objects, and I demonstrated the deep reverberations of this episode in George Meredith's *Modern Love*.

Indeed the poetic preoccupations described in the previous chapters' readings of Patmore, Meredith, Barrett Browning, and Rossetti were not isolated phenomena, but in fact strands running through a range of Victorian texts. There is a significant body of poetry from the later Victorian period that seems to have been generated from the same nexus of concerns: an emphasis on the role of intellection in intimate relations; an emphasis on the embodiment of thinking about the beloved other in specific social, poetic, and linguistic practices and forms; an interest in the play of pronouns; and in the relationship between thinking and speaking. For example, Robert Browning's "James Lee's Wife" was begun shortly after the poet received a copy of the 1862 *Modern Love* volume as a gift from George Meredith. It consists of nine scenes, in nine formally varied sections, from the dissolution of a marriage. Patricia Ball has described "James Lee's Wife" as "a poem of shock and adjustment to shock, when love is discovered to be subject to time, likely either to go as it came or to remain with one partner as a dialogue suddenly reduced to soliloquy."[2] The sections of the poem creak under the strain of keeping the "you" (James Lee) and the "me" (his otherwise unnamed wife) aligned in rhyme and meter. In the first section, "James Lee's Wife Speaks at the Window," the speaker tries desperately to keep "you" and "me" together through a series of increasingly untenable syllogisms:

> Thou art a man,
>   But I am thy love.
> For the lake, its swan;
>   For the dell, its dove;
> And for thee – (oh haste!)
>   Me, to bend above,
> Me, to hold embraced.[3]

The tight, short-lined form, begun as emblem of a wished-for simplicity, comes to figure in the end the deprivation and narrowness of the marriage, and the forced rhyme of the parenthetical "(oh haste!)" with "embraced" expresses the speaker's desperate consciousness of the inexorable change in their relationship.

In Thomas Hardy's "She, to Him" sonnets, written at roughly the same time, a similar framework – an imaginary woman's consciousness of a lover or husband's defection – provokes a meditation on the disappointments of becoming an object of another's thoughts. The second sonnet finds the "She" proleptically imagining a future in which she has been reduced to a "thin thought":

> Perhaps, long hence, when I have passed away,
> Some other's feature, accent, thought like mine,
> Will carry you back to what I used to say,
> And bring some memory of your love's decline.
> Then you may pause a while and think, "Poor jade!"
> And yield a sigh to me – as ample due,
> Not as the tittle of a debt unpaid
> To one who could resign her all to you –
> And thus reflecting, you will never see
> That your thin thought, in two small words conveyed,
> Was no such fleeting phantom-thought to me,
> But the Whole Life wherein my part was played;
> And you amid its fitful masquerade
> A thought – as I in your life seem to be!⁴

In this poem, acts of thinking about another person produce a curious time warp: what is imagined is a fleeting future thought inspired by a hypothetical retrospective reflection, which is then said to contain, or to have contained, a "Whole Life" (12). The frame of real time – the time of a "Whole Life" – confronts the "fleeting" frame of thought-time (11). Lines 9–12 describe a sequence of nested thoughts: "Your thin thought" (10) contains her "Whole life," inside of which, in turn, "you" (13) is but "a thought" (14). As this train of embedded thought spirals down, real life becomes derealized, described in line 13 as a "fitful masquerade," even as the speaker protests against the discrepancy between his thought and her whole life. It is a spiral of diminishment, in which "thought" and thinness come to feel inextricably linked. The poem registers a feeling which legal philosopher Meir Dan-Cohen seeks to articulate in the essay "Harmful Thoughts," discussed in this book's Introduction: that there are instances in which it is possible to perceive that one person's thinking about another can cause harm.⁵

Both Browning's "James Lee's Wife" and Hardy's "She, to Him II" address the asymmetry in thinking about other people in the face of expectations of equality and reciprocity; and both trade on the pathos involved in male poets ostentatiously exploring such issues from a woman's point of view. It would be some time before women poets were able to rewrite Meredith's *Modern Love*.⁶ However, countless, lesser known Victorian poems absorbed its lessons. For example, Philip Bourke Marston's short dramatic poem "He and She" (1883) confirms the central insight of

Modern Love: that bad marital relationships could make for interesting poetic innovation. Marston's poem consists of parallel columns of verse representing the thinking of a "she" and a "he" – an adulterous wife and a tolerant but preoccupied cuckolded husband – the "she"s and "he"s and "you"s of whose thinking both are and are not each other. The problem of thinking about another person seems to involve not just twosomes, but awkward threesomes and foursomes – multiple "he"s "she"s, "we"s and "they"s – as thinking divides and multiplies people from themselves and others. The confusion of pronouns marks this poem's indebtedness to *Modern Love*, as does the fact that the husband's and wife's transparent knowledge of each other's condition makes them no happier. Marston's insistence that modern love poetry be understood as representing *thinking* as the hallmark of an intimacy that is both cripplingly claustrophobic and falling apart at the seams is signaled by the way in which he ends "He and She" with a couplet marked "(Aloud)."[7]

Moreover, the metricalization of thinking evident in the poetic theory of Coventry Patmore, E. S. Dallas, and others can be found throughout later Victorian poetry and poetics, even in a satiric poetic treatment of "modern thought," George Eliot's poem "A Minor Prophet" (1865). Like Robert Browning's Mr. Sludge, the Elias Baptist Butterworth of "A Minor Prophet" appears to be an unflattering portrait of an individual who belongs somewhere along the wacky end of the spectrum of nineteenth-century beliefs about the power of thinking examined in Chapters 1 and 2 of this book. He belongs with the mesmerists, spiritual mediums, muscle-readers, and believers of all sorts in the powers of the mind to affect others, to see into the future or beyond the grave or into other minds, and to make things happen. "I have a friend," the poem begins, "a vegetarian seer, / By name Elias Baptist Butterworth."[8] But Eliot's Elias – vegetarian, politically radical, and, as we shall shortly see, very metrical – is a more modern and more Shelleyan figure than Sludge. He prides himself on being an up-to-date, even scientific thinker, steeped in "Transatlantic air and modern thought" (23). For him, the "Rappings" at a spiritualist séance are not the handiwork of ghosts, but rather signs of a generalized, universal "Thought-atmosphere" (37, 43). To Elias all earlier forms of mysticism were merely versions, unacknowledged visitations, of the universal "Thought-atmosphere," descended to earth in order to "furnish weaker proof for weaker minds / That Thought was rapping in the hoary past" (48–49). Even the ancient Greeks might have been "edified...by raps," "if their ears / Had not been filled with Sophoclean verse," its poetry drowning out the universal rapping (50–52). In Elias' understanding, thought-power resembles a transcendental mind-rhythm not unlike that of Victorian poetic theorist E. S. Dallas. Elias looks forward to a puri-fied, millennial, vegetarian epoch when "Thought-atmosphere" will have its clearest manifestation, as pure rhythm: its highest truths "Will either flash out into eloquence, / Or better still, be comprehensible / By rappings simply, without need of roots" (59–61).

But as Charles LaPorte has noted, "A Minor Prophet" quickly modulates from its gentle satire of Elias' prophetic aspirations into a defense of the speaker's own ordinary modes of thinking as forms of prophecy: "the pro-phetic status promised by the poem's title is transferred from one character to another…the previously unrecognized character of 'A Minor Prophet' is plainly the monologist, who begins with wry deference to her friend… but who by the poem's conclusion has progressed to vatic utterances."[9] "Even our failures are a prophecy," the speaker professes (312), and then concludes in noble rhythms:

> Presentiment of better things on earth
> Sweeps in with every force that stirs our souls
> To admiration, self-renouncing love,
> Or thoughts, like light, that bind the world in one.

> (317–20)

Prophecy is interestingly redefined not as utterance at all, but as inner "force." What strikes one about "A Minor Prophet" is that its modula-tion of prophecy into ordinary thinking, its modulation from Elias to the speaker herself, is conducted through the medium, as it were, of the meter of Eliot's blank verse, which seems to affirm, especially in the poem's last passages, that rhythmic rapping and ordinary thinking may indeed be the same, and equally prophetic.

I have singled out Eliot's minor poem "A Minor Prophet" because its metricalization of thinking is inseparable from the ways in which it takes a polemical position on a debate about the power of thought that runs throughout the writing I've studied in this book. Eliot claims prophetic powers not for exceptional or magical thinking, or any of the many forms of mental extensions into the unknown that fascinated many of her con-temporaries, but for the beating in and through us of "ordinary modes of thought."[10] There is a strong normative claim for ordinary thinking at the end of "A Minor Prophet," a normative claim that can begin to indicate why Eliot is a fitting figure with which to conclude this book's investiga-tion of nineteenth-century accounts of the power of thinking about other people. We have seen throughout this study that the era's innovative for-mal means of representing the act of thinking about another person were intertwined with some curious moralizing, as Victorian writers sought to balance a commitment to mental freedom with a suspicion of mental force. I have puzzled over Elizabeth Barrett Browning's poetic agonies about whether it is right for her to think about her beloved at all; I have puzzled over the pessimism, or stoicism, about the gain, or the harm, that can be effected by thinking about a beloved that emerges in Patmore's *The Angel in the House* and Meredith's *Modern Love*.

In this chapter I will explore how the climax of a novel in which a woman feels she has killed her husband "in her thoughts" contributes to the discussion. Focusing on the intersections among ethics, psychology, and strategies of narration in *Daniel Deronda*, I seek to explain why George Eliot regarded the belief that thinking about someone might make something happen to them as simultaneously epistemologically irrational and ethically efficacious. There is by now a considerable body of critical literature on *Daniel Deronda* which has emphasized George Eliot's accommodation in this novel of the prophetic, the magical, the improbable, the non-rational, underscoring a consensus that at the end of her career Eliot was pushing beyond the boundaries of realism.[11] Much of the emphasis on the prophetic and the telepathic in *Daniel Deronda* centers on the indigent, ailing, Messianic Jewish scholar Ezra Mordecai Cohen, who seems truly to predict Daniel Deronda's advent in his life, shape his future, and read his mind: "You have risen within me like a thought not fully spelled."[12] I seek to shift the critical discussion slightly, however, and propose that we can best understand Eliot's position on the ethics of thinking about another person if we focus on those aspects of *Daniel Deronda* most akin to "A Minor Prophet": its modulation of mind power into ordinary, even failed modes of thinking ("even our failures are a prophecy," asserts Eliot in that poem). To do so will involve studying not only the most sensational part of the novel, Grandcourt's death and Gwendolen's sense of the deadly omnipotence of her thoughts, but also the ways in which the act of thinking about another person is structured into the fabric of the novel.

It should go without saying that in turning to Eliot in the last chapter of this book, I also seek to discover whether the discussions about poetry in the preceding chapters have any new news for the study of the form of the novel. It's hard to think about the nineteenth-century novel – particularly in its psychological-realist mode, of which George Eliot, and *Daniel Deronda*, would seem most exemplary – without thinking of it, unofficially, as a kind of machine for thinking about other people, and there is a long official critical tradition that ratifies that view. In his influential formulation, for example, J. Hillis Miller described the form of the Victorian novel as "a structure of interpenetrating minds," which unfolds through "a temporal rhythm made up of the movement of minds of the narrator and his [*sic*] characters."[13] In this formulation, the form of the Victorian novel might indeed be a version of Patmore's rhythmic "He thought I thought he thought," writ large.[14] In many such accounts, including Miller's, thinking about other people in the novel is constricted to a concern with the knowability of "transparent minds," the thick volume of Victorian fiction we hold in our hands as slabs of (someone's) gray matter.[15]

The notoriously split structure of *Daniel Deronda* casts a special light on the idea of the form of the Victorian novel as a structure of interpenetrating minds. Many readers have sought to resolve the problem of the novel's two plots, the Jewish plot and the Gwendolen plot, by focusing on the relationship between Daniel Deronda and Gwendolen Harleth. To do so is to further heighten the anomaly of this novel: it is a novel which, in a totally unprecedented fashion, places at its center a heterosexual relation between a man and a woman that cannot possibly be subsumed under any of the varieties of amatory plotting – courtship, seduction – known to English fiction. Gwendolen and Daniel are separated by ethnicity, illegitimacy, fortuity, fatality. But we can specify further the anomalous form of eroticism of their relation by noting that it is above all a relation constituted in and through their practices of thinking about each other. In the bulk of the novel, the actual encounters between Daniel and Gwendolen are, for all their strung-out intensity, spread pretty thin. They are seldom together on the same page.

I shall argue here that what holds *Daniel Deronda* together in spite of the famous divisions and entropic forces pulling its matter apart is, weirdly, the fictitious action of Daniel and Gwendolen thinking about each other. Their action of thinking about each other is neither completely reciprocal nor remotely equal. The content of their thoughts about each other may be, and often is, erroneous. It is, as Coleridge put it at the beginning of the century, their "*Thinking* as a pure act & energy," "*Thinking* as distinguished from *Thoughts*," which is the glue that holds together the parts of this book that seem otherwise on the verge of breaking apart, like a physical force field.[16] Moreover, I will argue, the glue or force field that is Daniel's and Gwendolen's thinking about each other strains at the boundaries of novelistic representation; it thus allows us to examine how the Victorian novel contributes to our everyday sense of how to parse the relationships among speaking, writing, and thinking.

This chapter starts off with an account of the place of Daniel's and Gwendolen's thinking about each other in the fabric of the novel, ending up with Gwendolen's final letter, in which she writes to Daniel, "Do not think of me." I then circle back to discuss the narration in the opening scene in the novel, then return to Grandcourt's drowning, and the omnipotence of thought.

THINKING ABOUT EACH OTHER

Scholars of George Eliot wishing to focus on the force of mental action in *Daniel Deronda* often devote their attention to Mordecai, whose prophetic tendencies make him at least a distant cousin to Elias Baptist Butterworth of "A Minor Prophet." In Mordecai, the power of effective wishful thinking comes together with biblical prophecy, "second-sight" (471), mind-reading, and the collective aspirations of Zionism. When Mordecai wishes something, it happens: his thinking is a form of "coercive" action (471). Of his wish to see Daniel: "in spite of contrary chances, the wish to see him again was growing into a belief that he should see him" (480). Mordecai's understanding of mental connection to another person resembles a form of thought-transfer, or file-sharing. He sees Daniel as a replenishment of himself, "so Deronda might receive from Mordecai's mind the complete ideal shape of that personal duty and citizenship which lay in his own thought" (512). On Blackfriars Bridge, where the two men find each other's glowing faces, sanctified by radiant sunset and "inward prophecy" (493), Mordecai seems truly to have materialized Daniel through thinking: "You have risen within me like a thought not fully spelled" (501). His magical thinking is endorsed as akin to scientific method:

His exultation was not widely different from that of the experimenter, bending over the first stirrings of change that correspond to what in the fervour of concentrated prevision his thought has foreshadowed. (493)

For George Levine, who notes generally that "Mordecai's mind lives outside the rules of causality, system, sequence," Eliot's approving endorsement of Mordecai's extraordinary modes of thinking, as in the passage above, is a sign of her accommodation of a new, more capacious understanding both of empiricism and of literary realism. For other readers, Mordecai's mind-power is, not unlike that of Latimer the mind-reading protagonist of Eliot's short story "The Lifted Veil," a symptom of an extreme version of Eliot's doctrine of sympathy, and a sign of the proximity of the Victorian novel to various fin-de-siècle psychological ideas which it prefigures. Omniscient narration is seen as intimately connected to mind-reading, telepathy.[17] Mordecai's mind-power, in this view, is the dream version of the novelist's own.

There are a number of reasons to shift away from this reading of Mordecai, and consequently from this view of the novel and of the novelist's aspirations. As Amanda Anderson has pointed out, the transparent "mind-meld" between Daniel and Mordecai that Mordecai seems not only to desire but to make real is not truly held up as an ideal by George Eliot.[18] The person in the novel for whom transparent thought-transfer does stand as an ideal is Gwendolen, whose modes of thinking are routinely discounted by just about everyone. What Gwendolen wishes for with Daniel is a total mind-read. "'I wish he could know everything about me without my telling him,' was one of her thoughts" (430). In a book full of wishes, this particular wish seems sadly infantile. It is a wish to be (passively) read, to be understood without any exertion on her part. Gwendolen's longing to be the object of Daniel's mind-reading is of a piece with her general assumption that she deserves to be taken care of, "princess in exile" (41) that she is, cared for, provided for, and, it seems, thought about. The narcissism of the wish is underscored by the attitude Eliot places Gwendolen in at this moment:

> "I wish he could know everything about me without my telling him," was one of her thoughts, as she sat leaning over the end of a couch, supporting her head with her hand, and looking at herself in a mirror – not in admiration, but in a sad kind of companionship. (430)

Formally, the first-person form of the wish makes it seem infantile and deluded, a mere personal wish, in contrast to which most of Daniel's and Mordecai's wishes are conferred with the dignity that free indirect discourse and the third person can give to the optative mode; and of necessity the concomitant forming of this wish as quoted internal speech – a mode of representing thinking that here as elsewhere represents the opposite of "deep thoughts." It is superficial thought (this just "was one of her thoughts" bouncing around in her mind), a flimsy internal non-utterance that barely substitutes for the out-loud telling she wishes to dispense with. Surely it would be a mistake to see George Eliot endorsing anything resembling this as either a moral or a narratorial ideal.[19]

However, it would also be a mistake to discount Gwendolen's practice of thinking about another, and to see it as fundamentally less substantial than Mordecai's.[20] Gwendolen's practice of thinking about other people – and particularly Daniel – may seem shriveled, epistemologically and morally. It is indeed narcissistic, mostly concerned with thinking about him thinking about her, as in the example above, or again on page 335: "perhaps Deronda himself was thinking of these things...always lurking ready to obtrude before other thoughts about him was the impression that he was very much interested in her." It could be argued that in spite of, or perhaps because of, the sticky narcissism of Gwendolen's thinking about Daniel, the accumulation of her "what is he thinking of me" thoughts do sediment out into a content of sorts: a conscience. Such is the implication of these well-known passages often adduced to prove that Daniel Deronda is a force for moral improvement in Gwendolen's life: "in some mysterious way he was becoming a part of her conscience" (415); "No chemical process shows a more wonderful activity than the transforming influence of the thoughts we imagine to be going on in another" (425). In this light, Daniel's influence on Gwendolen through her practice of thinking about him and of what he thinks of her is fundamentally of a piece with the influence he has on her through their highly charged meetings, and his famous words of advice (such as, "make your fear your safeguard").[21]

I wish to point out, however, that the novel asks us rather to see Daniel's and Gwendolen's mental relations, and Daniel's and Gwendolen's actual meetings, as two separate, and only strangely related, systems. The repeated shocks that both experience in their meetings is completely determined by the ways in which their existence for each other has been built up, over long stretches, in thought.[22] A persistent preoccupation of British object-relations psychoanalysis from its beginnings has been how to understand the connection of our "mental objects" – other people as they affect our mental lives – to real, actually existing people. The best writing in this tradition has wonderful things to say about how to think about the ontological status of the people we think about when they are in our minds.[23] Towards the end of *Daniel Deronda*, when the Grandcourts are about to anchor in Genoa, Gwendolen has a dream about Daniel Deronda, and then, shortly after awakening, sees him: "In an hour or so from that dream she actually met Deronda" (676).[24] Part of the force of the word "actually" here in this passage, which has deep roots that go down to Milton's account of Adam awakening in the Garden of Eden and finding Eve, comes from that tradition's association with the agency of dreams: she dreamed of him, then he appeared! But the casualness of "in an hour or so" in this passage suggests that the primary shock of "actually" here is that Deronda is in some sense *more real* for Gwendolen as a mental entity than otherwise.

The idea that a mental version of a person could in fact compete with his or her actual presence is cruelly mocked, early in the novel, as a possible explanation for Grandcourt's lack of lover-like attentiveness to Gwendolen: "this apparent forgetfulness might be taken for the distraction of a lover so absorbed in thinking of the beloved object as to forget an appointment which would bring him into her actual presence" (150). But a view of the vividness of mental persons over actual humans is corroborated by, of all people, the earnest Mirah, when she struggles to express to Daniel how she feels her lost mother's presence more in her absence: "When the best thing comes into our thoughts, it is like what my mother has been to me. She has been just as really with me as all the other people about me – often more really with me" (466). For Gwendolen thinking about Daniel, there is also a distinction to be made between the "really" and the "actually." The force of Eliot's "actually" is to remind us that for Gwendolen, seeing Daniel is the startling exception rather than the rule: the rule, the real (as opposed to the "actual") is having Daniel as an object of mind.

Gwendolen's "actually" meeting Deronda thus deserves to be set next to a parallel use of that word when Deronda goes from being a mental entity to a person for Mordecai on Blackfriars Bridge: "The prefigured friend had come from the golden background, and had signalled to him: this actually was: the rest was to be" (493). "Actually" here marks not the real, but simply a point on a timeline of prophecy, the current state of affairs differentiated both from what was and from what will be. Indeed, to borrow another phrase from the novel, we could say that one of the goals of *Daniel Deronda* is to make "actual Jews" (206) also *real*. To focus on the way characters in novels – in which there are no actual people – may become "real" to each other, without being shockingly "actual," may serve as a model for how fictional characters may become real (but not "actual") to readers (as in this thought-experiment: "Adela was reading *Daniel Deronda*. In an hour or so she actually met Deronda").

It must be stressed that to say that Daniel Deronda is more real in Gwendolen's mind is not to say that her thinking about him is in any way right or true. She is occasionally right. At times Daniel is indeed "very much interested in her" (336). But she is often sadly wrong about what his interests are; she has no idea what his life is actually like. When he does finally actually explain the huge changes in his actual life and its utter difference from anything Gwendolen could possibly think, her accession to knowledge is marked as a sublime cataclysm in which she feels herself reduced to a "mere speck" (803). Thinking and knowing are out of step, off the mark, out of rhythm: "it is the trick of thinking to be either premature or behindhand," the narrator notes (764). In *George Eliot and Blackmail*, Alexander Welsh writes eloquently of the ways in which thinking and knowing are disaggregated in *Daniel Deronda*, a novel he views as a critique of the social distribution of knowledge. Indeed, *Daniel Deronda* often seems to betray the kind of pessimism about knowledge I identified in Meredith's *Modern Love* in the preceding chapter of this book. Here, as there, access to knowledge about one's intimates seems to make minimal difference to how one feels. Gwendolen's knowledge that Grandcourt knows she knows about his past, for example, makes no significant difference to her misery in her marriage. It is an arid math problem. It is knowledge without thinking: as Welsh notes, "the loveless contentions of knowledge are oddly barren of thought."[25] However, Eliot differs significantly from Meredith (and I differ from Welsh) in valuing thinking without knowledge.[26]

The importance of Gwendolen's thinking about Daniel lies not in the accuracy of the contents of her thoughts about him but in the fact that she habitually does it. In her application of cognitive psychology's understanding of "mind-reading" to literature, Lisa Zunshine helpfully describes what cognitive psychologists mean when they refer to "effortless" mind-reading. To describe a person's mind-reading as "effortless," or even "successful," does not signify that she has an accurate picture of what's going on in another's mind. It is simply designed, rather, to indicate that she routinely behaves as if the other has a mind (something persons with autism, for example, cannot do), no matter how wrong she may be about what's in there.[27] Zunshine's discussion can suggest that cognitive approaches to fiction and fictional minds may in fact be helpfully a little less wedded to an ideal of omniscience or transparent knowledge of other minds than perhaps are other approaches to psychological fiction, from J. H. Miller's understanding of the form of Victorian fiction as the interpenetration of consciousnesses, to the critics who have linked the dream of the nineteenth-century novel to the (concomitant historical) emergence in telepathy. My aim here is to argue that such a model, whether we call it sympathy between minds, or omniscience, is far from being an ideal, moral or aesthetic, in Eliot's novel.[28] Rather, Eliot explores in *Daniel Deronda* the moral and aesthetic implications of thinking about another person as a form of substantial action, "effortless," wrong, or otherwise. Thinking about another person starts being most social when it is least omniscient, and most wrong.

Gwendolen's and Daniel's practices of thinking about each other is the rhythm of the novel, the melancholy remainder of a relationship that never "actually" happens (see Daniel's "if"s, 621). There are moments where Daniel's time is clocked out in thinking about Gwendolen: "Deronda found himself after one o'clock in the morning…with the consciousness that he had been in that attitude nearly an hour, and had thought of nothing but Gwendolen" (413). But their thinking about each other is not only not right, it is also never totally equal or reciprocal. It is quantified and compared: "And Gwendolen? – She was thinking of Deronda much more than he was thinking of her –" (547). Even in its unevenness, it is the action that holds together the two plots of *Daniel Deronda*. We see it as such, most visibly, in the line just quoted, which takes place right after a chapter break. We can perhaps get the best sense of the function of this line as a hinge, connecting vast expanses of unrepresented thinking, by comparing it to a sentence of Jane Austen's, which it resembles in its rhythm and substance, from *Mansfield Park*: "And Fanny, what was *she* doing and thinking all this while?"[29] In *Mansfield Park* this somewhat awkward question quickly comes to seem less awkward. It is patently rhetorical, a question the narrator poses in order to impress upon readers, early on in the story, that she has Fanny Price's complete confidence ("my Fanny," she later calls her). She totally knows what Fanny is thinking (and hence it is *not* like Frank Churchill's "Miss Woodhouse demands to know what you are all thinking" in the Box Hill episode of *Emma*). Before "And Fanny," Austen's narrator had been zipping quickly between and among the Bertrams and the Crawfords, registering their first and next-to-first impressions of each other. It is followed with an assertion of Fanny's silent thoughts about Henry Crawford ("as she still continued to think Mr. Crawford very plain, in spite of her two cousins having repeatedly proved the contrary, she never mentioned *him*"). Austen's "And Fanny, what was *she* doing and thinking all this while?" sutures the consciousness of a particular character into the fabric of a wandering omniscient narration; it is a move from the many to the one.[30]

Eliot's "And Gwendolen – what was she thinking?" is both like and unlike Austen's rhetorical question. It marks not a move from the many to the one, but from one to another. At the end of the preceding chapter, we were in Daniel's head, where the mental furniture he is moving around is, actually, the furniture with which he will furnish a new home for Mordecai:

Deronda's mind was busy with a prospective arrangement for giving a furnished lodging some faint likeness to a refined home by dismantling his own chambers of his best old books in vellum, his easiest chair, and the bas-reliefs of Milton and Dante. (546)

The best piece of furniture, mental or otherwise, that Daniel can think of is Mirah:

But was not Mirah to be there? What furniture can give such finish to a room as a tender woman's face? – and is there any harmony of tints that has such stirrings of delight as the sweet modulations of her voice? Here is one good, at least, thought Deronda, that comes to Mordecai from his having fixed his imagination on me. He was recovered a perfect sister, whose affection is waiting for him. (546)

Lest some of the sanctimoniousness of the phrasing lead one to feel the presence of the narrator's voice (which is alas occasionally capable of sanctimoniousness when it comes to Mirah), there are tags and pronouns that place this in Deronda's thoughts. The romantic Mirah-directed turn of Daniel's mind only makes the transition – "And Gwendolen?" – seem more wrenching, more conscious of the gulf between their thinking about each other (later, Mordecai and Mirah are mentioned as persons "whom Gwendolen did not include in her thinking about Deronda" [773]):

She was thinking of Deronda much more than he was thinking of her – often wondering what were his ideas "about things," and how his life was occupied. But a lap-dog would be necessarily at a loss in framing to itself the motives and adventures of doghood at large...(547)

Eliot's quantifying and qualifying the nature of Gwendolen's thinking (rather than just telling us, like Austen, what she's thinking) can seem cruel here. But the formulation wonderfully signifies a background of an economy of thinking, in which Gwendolen's and Daniel's thinking about each other is continuous enough to authorize such a comparative quantification.

The passages where Eliot draws attention to Daniel and Gwendolen thinking about each other are fairly few and far between, but passages such as this one depend upon the fact that we read as if we know it is going on all the time. Scholars of narrative have theorized the ways in which readers perceive, and respond to, the undertelling of aspects of a story, filling in or going on in spite of what's not there.[31] We should be able to admit that in *Daniel Deronda* it is the act of thinking about another person that is under-represented, all appearances perhaps to the contrary notwithstanding. In spite of all the endlessly detailed thinking about another person represented through internal quoted speech, free indirect discourse, and all of the other representational modes that seem to constitute the bulk of this vast book, there is a surplus: a rhythm of unrepresented thinking of Daniel and Gwendolen about each other, which we implicitly posit going on in the expanses of dense pages in between the verbal notations of their thinking.

It may indeed seem weird to propose the existence of unrepresented thinking in *Daniel Deronda*, a novel charged with excessive intellectualizing by everyone since Henry James.[32] But to contemplate such a thing is to focus our attention on thinking in the novel as a kind of action, rather than on thought as a kind of content. It is also a way to illuminate the paradox by which endlessly wordy psychological novels seem to have the ability to confront us with the possibility that thinking can go on without words. The notion that *Daniel Deronda* is structured to make us feel that there is even more thinking going on than is represented can help gloss a critical conversation about the novel that has cast reading it as an experience of silent, wordless thought-transfer. Gillian Beer has written, beautifully but obscurely:

The silence in which so much of *Daniel Deronda* takes place is a terrifying seal over the crowded and various discourses of the text. Here, the process of reading is assimilated very tightly to the silent movement of thought within us.[33]

What does it mean to say that thoughts move silently within us? And what is their relation to the writing we read? Are silent thoughts like "dark rays doing their work invisibly in the broad light," Eliot's famous (and very Shelleyan) description of the unconscious fantasies that move within Gwendolen "like ghosts," which Gillian Beer is clearly echoing?[34]

As odd as it is to focus on Eliot not-representing thinking, we might remember that *Daniel Deronda* houses at least one sublime passage devoted to the representation of not-thinking: the vacancy of Grandcourt's mind as he abstains from thought:

In this way hours may pass surprisingly soon, without the arduous invisible chase of philosophy; not from love of thought, but from hatred of effort – from a state of the inward world, something like premature age, where the need for action lapses into a mere image of what has been, is, and may or might be; where impulse is born and dies in a phantasmal world, pausing in rejection even of a shadowy fulfillment. (319)

Part of the fascination of this passage – for the reader and presumably for the writer – lies in the opportunity for filling up, with words, the lizard-like emptiness of Grandcourt's mind. Ordinary human thinking, such as Gwendolen and Deronda apply to each other, with all of its errors and narcissisms, goes on un- or under-represented, beating on in between those moments when Eliot puts it into writing.

"DO NOT THINK OF ME"

In Daniel's and Gwendolen's last meeting, at which Daniel announces his imminent departure for Palestine, he confirms that he and Gwendolen have in fact never "actually" been together much, and that therefore the nature of their relationship, being purely mental, will not change much by virtue of being separated by thousands of miles: it will be like gold to airy thinness beat. Indeed, it will be enhanced: "I shall be more with you than I used to be," he says to her, reasoning, "if we had been much together before, we should have felt our differences more, and seemed to get farther apart. Now we can perhaps never see each other again. But our minds may get nearer" (806). Daniel's reasoning should by this time seem truly in keeping with the nature of their relationship, in which thinking about each other seems in many ways alienated both from talking to each other and from representation in writing. He is not, that is, merely disingenuously rationalizing away her concerns.

What is lame and jarring, however, is what Daniel says to her right before this: "I will write to you always, when I can, and you will answer?" (805). And even stranger is Gwendolen's letter in the last chapter which follows. Gwendolen's letter – and the fact of Gwendolen's writing it – in the last chapter of *Daniel Deronda* deserves comment not simply because it is an intrusion of the "Gwendolen plot" into the last chapter which is otherwise wholly taken up with the "Jewish plot," thus bringing the novel to its extraordinary, future-oriented ending.[35] Gwendolen's disappearance into writing arrests us because in some ways she seems a character alienated from the culture of writing. She is at best a superficial reader (see her flippant discussion of literary topics with Mrs. Arrowpoint, 45–47; see also 547–48; see also her habit of treating people as "stale books," 430), and it is hard to figure her as a writer: her modes of self-presentation tend towards the dramatic and theatrical rather than the epistolary. Indeed letter-writing and letters seem generally alien to the world of *Daniel Deronda*, in which people's thoughts are flayed in the third person, rather than poured out in an epistolary first person. Grandcourt for his own reasons seems barely literate and can't even be bothered to write his own letters when he has to (320); people send telegrams rather than letters (709, 762). Grandcourt's cast-off mistress Lydia Glasher's epistolary bombshell (358–59) marks her as an unsettling visitant from another (sensational, gothic) literary genre. The only fluent, literate letters in the novel come from the pen of Daniel's artist friend, Hans Meyrick (641).[36] While Mordecai is a scholar and a writer, Jewish culture is as much associated with oral as with written culture in this book. Mordecai is much more interested in spiritually mind-transmitting his learning to Daniel than he is in having Daniel transcribe or publish what he has "actually written" (499).

Gwendolen's exit into writing at the end of the novel has an uncanny force, her letter arriving as it does on Daniel's and Mirah's wedding day, followed up by absolutely no commentary by the narrator:

But something more precious than gold and gems came to Deronda from the neighbourhood of Diplow on the morning of his marriage. It was a letter containing these words: –

Do not think of me sorrowfully on your wedding-day. I have remembered your words – that I may live to be one of the best of women, who make others glad that they were born. I do not yet see how that can be, but you know better than I. If it ever comes true, it will be because you helped me. I only thought of myself, and I made you grieve. It hurts me now to think of your grief. You must not grieve any more for me. It is better – it shall be better with me because I have known you. Gwendolen Grandcourt (810)

Gwendolen has been transfigured into italicized writing, a brittle form that seems far removed from her spectacularly physical presence throughout the novel. Not even Mrs. Glasher's curse comes in italics, though the inscription on the locket the Mallingers send to Mirah as a wedding present does ("*To the bride of our dear Daniel Deronda all blessings. – H.&L. M.*"): Gwendolen has become absorbed into inscription. Appearing after her exit from the pages of the novel, the letter hardly seems to come from her, in spite of the fact that it echoes some of the language she compulsively repeats in her final interview with Daniel in the pages before: "it should be better…better with me…for having known you" (805). It is strange to feel oneself, at the end of Eliot's intense explorations of thinking about another person in the third person, in the presence of a mode of address reminiscent of the posthumous letters of Clarissa Harlowe.[37]

But we should also dwell on the rhythm of the line, "*Do not think of me sorrowfully on your wedding-day.*" The epistolary imperative, "do not think of me" belongs in the company of the thinking/not-thinking-about-another-person second-person addresses of nineteenth-century poetry, some of which I discussed in Chapter 3 of this book: Elizabeth Barrett Browning's sonnet, for example, which begins "I think of thee!" and ends by reassuring the beloved, "I do not think of thee – I am too near thee." These second-person utterances, I argued, constituted a kind of meditation on the relations among thinking, speaking, and writing. They are experiments in thinking about another person as embodied in the specifically shifty territory of second-person poetic address, experiments in the intimacy of writing, in which the difference between "I think of thee" and "I do not think of thee" becomes minimal. Just as Barrett Browning's "I do not think of thee" necessarily strikes us as akin to the liar's paradox

("I'm not lying"), as a kind of orientation towards the addressee that must be a kind of thinking about him, so Gwendolen's "do not think of me sorrowfully" is an imperative the recipient cannot completely, and is never meant to, obey. It may be compared to something like Christina Rossetti's "When I am dead, my dearest / Sing no sad songs for me," an address whose posture of indifference ("and if thou wilt, remember / And if thou wilt, forget") burns it into the mind of the recipient. Gwendolen's exit into writing is thus a crucial emergence, on the far horizon of the novel, of a kind of second-person address that Victorian poetry was formulating into a bodiless, silent thinking about another person. To contemplate thinking about another person in *Daniel Deronda* is to confront, as we have throughout this study, the pressures on thinking in nineteenth-century cultures of writing, from the first, second, and third persons.

THOUGHTS THAT HAVE NO THINKER

The culture of writing in which George Eliot took on representing thinking was of course above all the culture of the third person: it is a world of "he"s and "she"s rather than "I"s and "you"s:

Perhaps Deronda himself was thinking of these things. Could he know of Mrs. Glasher? If he knew that she knew, he would despise her; but he could have no such knowledge. Would he, without that, despise her for marrying Grandcourt? (335)

But, as scholars of free indirect discourse – who have demonstrated more than anyone just how strange representations of the act of thinking in fiction can be – have shown, the third-ness of the third person pronoun in a passage such as this one is hardly stable. These urgent, anxious, self-justifying thoughts are "actually" Gwendolen's, slanted through the narrator via free indirect discourse: the "she"s and "her"s really "I"s and "me"s masquerading as the third person, or they are in-between first and third, neither fish nor fowl. Arguing on the basis of sentences like these, Ann Banfield sought to show how truly alienated from the world of speaking were the nineteenth-century novel's ways of representing thinking. They are "unspeakable sentences" in a language with no native speakers, that emerges in the eighteenth and nineteenth centuries, "not by contact with speech, but from universals of language common to both speech and writing" – the deep language of the mind.[38] Though the language of thinking in the novel may resemble ordinary spoken English, it points to a view of thinking as preceding speaking. In an analysis that is reminiscent of Beer's account of reading *Daniel Deronda* as silent thought-transfer, Banfield concludes:

The [historical] appearance of represented thought [her term for free indirect discourse] reveals that language represents thought, paradoxically, as inarticulated prespeech…In other words, represented thought is *an attempt to render thought as nonspeech through the medium of language*.[39]

One need not follow Banfield's Chomskian view of language to find her understanding of represented thought fascinating. It suggests that third-personish free indirect discourse in the nineteenth-century novel was, like the nineteenth-century poetic experiments with second-person address discussed in my Chapter 3, an experimental way of writing, a way to create soundless words that feel like thinking, thinking understood as cut off from the ordinary world of speech. The unspeakable sentences of free indirect discourse are dark rays doing their work silently in the chatter of broad light.

I hope to suggest in this section that, like the shadow cast by the partially represented or unrepresented thinking between Daniel and Gwendolen that structures the novel, the dark rays of indirectly narrated thinking have consequences for how Eliot views the ethics of thinking about another person in *Daniel Deronda*, and I will focus here on the novel's famous first scene: Daniel's and Gwendolen's wordless encounter at the casino of Leubronn. Gillian Beer correctly notes that the novel's opening, *in medias res*, has the effect of making Gwendolen's and Daniel's relationship seem more substantial than it "actually" is, in that the image of the two together lingers in readers' minds throughout the subsequent narration of the events leading up to this fateful moment:

In *narrative* time Gwendolen has prior claims. In *chronological* time Daniel has already a year earlier involved himself with Mirah's fate. But for the reader the relationship between Gwendolen and Deronda can never be dislodged from its primacy despite this later information, because *we knew them first*…the relationship between Gwendolen and Deronda appears to be the original one.[40]

The scene at Leubronn is truly a scene of origins. In its temporal structure it has many of the features of a "primal scene" as described by Freud: it seems to be chronologically primary, and thus the origin of something, but it isn't really chronologically pristine; the story begins elsewhere, and much of the significance is reconstructed in relationship to other, later events, as Gwendolen reverts again and again to this scene in her mind, canonizing it as an origin (e.g. 329, 404).

This scene also resembles a primal scene in that it is both a trauma, and an ideal. The opening scene of *Daniel Deronda* is a trauma for Gwendolen, of course, not only because her spectacular turn of bad luck at the gambling table, under the watchful eye of Daniel Deronda, seems to unleash a chain of misfortune, but also because Daniel's wordless scrutiny and his anonymous redemption of the jewels she desperately pawns are a stinging rebuke. But the episode also establishes the ideal form of Daniel's and Gwendolen's way of relating to each other. Daniel and Gwendolen do not meet here: they observe, and above all they think about each other.[41] Daniel famously watches Gwendolen as she plays at the roulette table, and tries to figure her out ("was she beautiful or was she not beautiful?"); Gwendolen notices Daniel paying attention to her, and thinks about him. Their eyes meet twice (10, 11) in the casino; they observe each other again later that evening; that is (famously) it.

Gwendolen views Daniel's thinking about her as a kind of telekinesis, or action at a distance. She comes to believe – as the scene unfolds, and on subsequent reflection – that Daniel's attention to her is what makes her luck turn at the roulette table. "You cast an evil eye on my play," she tells him at their first actual meeting three hundred pages later; "I began to lose as soon as you came to look on" (330). However, though Gwendolen first sees Daniel's *looking* as the agent of evil (she perceives him looking at her as she loses, and responds, theatrical creature that she is, by playing more recklessly, and losing more than perhaps she might otherwise have done), her emphasis on visual power is gradually shed, as looking, thinking, and acting become located on the same continuum. Later, his thinking and looking come to seem to Gwendolen indistinguishable from action, in that she mentally bundles in his silent watching her losses with his subsequent action of redeeming her necklace at the pawnshop. The whole of the episode at Leubronn is characterized as "that first interference of his in her life" (329). Gwendolen's understanding of what Daniel actually did to her at the beginning of the novel is thus not unlike her understanding of what she actually did to her husband at the end of the novel, which involves a strong sense of the continuity between thought and action.[42]

Daniel's activity in the opening scene is, moreover, explicitly not characterized as just looking, but as thinking about and evaluating what he sees. His thoughts are evaluative and undecided, rather than a reflex of an admiring gaze:

Was she beautiful or not beautiful? and what was the secret of form or expression which gave the dynamic quality to her glance? Was the good or the evil genius dominant in those beams? Probably the evil; else why was the effect that of unrest rather than of undisturbed charm? Why was the wish to look again felt as coercion and not as a longing in which the whole being consents?

She who raised these questions in Daniel Deronda's mind was occupied in gambling…(7)

What is represented from the outset is not the look itself, but the questions prompted by the look. This "inward debate" takes Daniel "farther and farther away from the glow of mingled undefined sensibilities forming admiration" (10). Looking and thinking are tethered to each other, but the latter activity tends to loosen the impact of the former.

Moreover, one of the reasons that in the opening scene and throughout the novel thinking about, observing, and admiring another and action get both rigorously distinguished from each other and blended into each other has to do with shifts in modes of narration. The extent to which thinking about another person can be a form of action in *Daniel Deronda* depends on modes of narration. Narrative agency and character agency slip in and out of each other, and it is here that questions of moral responsibility and questions of narration become implicated with each other. The opening pages of *Daniel Deronda* are fascinating as an example of the diversity and complexity of George Eliot's narrative modes, and in particular the issue of her narrative "omniscience." About the opening scene of the novel, Harry Shaw has observed that there is a genuine uncertainty of perspective: "for nearly a page, it's impossible to tell whether the figure who is observing Gwendolen and asking these questions will turn out to be the narrator, or an as yet unnamed character, or some mixture of the two."[43] Daniel Deronda is of course named after the first four questions, in a sentence that quickly places the four at-first-unmoored questions in his mind ("She who raised these questions in Daniel Deronda's mind was occupied in gambling"). But Shaw's point is generally correct. The very sentence that places the questions in Daniel's mind seems to zoom out to ruminate in a more omniscient way, speculating on a hypothetical gambling scene which is where Daniel and Gwendolen are not: she is gambling

not in the open air under a southern sky, tossing coppers on a ruined wall, with rags about her limbs; but in one of those splendid resorts which the enlightenment of ages has prepared for the same species of pleasure at a heavy cost of gilt mouldings, dark-toned colour and chubby nudities…(7)

It does not seem unreasonable to feel that the rhythms of the sentences, the weary knowing attitude, the animadversion to a scene that is not present to the characters' eye, and the super-pictorialism of the passage all conspire to make us feel that this is some kind of narrator thinking, no longer in Daniel's mind.[44] The question of whether we are with Daniel's thoughts or the narrator's gets a bit more uncertain in the next long paragraph describing the characters at the roulette table; the descriptions are increasingly marked as an observer's hypothetical speculation ("probably...surely" [9]; see also the rhythmic punctuation of the sentences by dashes and internal question marks). When the next paragraph begins "Deronda's first thought when his eyes fell on this scene," it strangely jars us into the notion that the preceding paragraphs were, precisely, *not* Daniel's thoughts – as we are now being told his "first thought" – and therefore belonged to someone else.

There is a critical literature on *Daniel Deronda* that has sought to explain some of Daniel Deronda's characteristics – his disabling thoughtfulness, for example – by seeing him as a freakish, walking, breathing embodiment of an omniscient narrator:

> In him, some critics maintain, George Eliot tried to incarnate her narrative persona by imagining the sort of life experience and psychology that might lead one to become a floating sympathizer...the mobile, detached condition that goes unremarked in an omniscient third person narrator becomes a psychological abnormality, rather than a literary device, when attributed to a *character*...giving character to a combination of readerly and narrative operations, in short, implicitly denigrates them as psychological quirks, as "too-much" thoughtful consideration, which diffuses regard, erodes personal desire, and undermines the will.[45]

However, lest we feel that the opening chapter of *Daniel Deronda* confirms the narrator's closeness to Daniel, or Daniel's to the narrator, we must note the similar slips between narrator's thoughts and Gwendolen's once the narration makes its extraordinary, unannounced shift, in the eighth paragraph, to Gwendolen's point of view. Up to this point Gwendolen has not only not been named, she has been emphatically a "she" ("was *she* beautiful or not beautiful?...*she* who raised these questions..."), a conspicuous third-person pronoun. We are given no "And Gwendolen? She was thinking ...": she is not yet a character differentiated from any other thinker here:

> But in the course of that survey her eyes met Deronda's, and instead of averting them as she would have desired to do, she was unpleasantly conscious that they were arrested – how long? The darting sense that he was measuring her and looking down on her as an inferior...(10)

The dash and the question at the end of the sentence marks this as free indirect discourse, a mode that wobbles in and out for the rest of the long paragraph, as Gwendolen's experience is narrated from both the inside and the outside.[46] Here as elsewhere we often feel that we are with Gwendolen, but just as often that the things that are said to "dart" through her mind are really more truly going through a narrator's.[47] These very fluid shifts make it more appropriate than ever to term the opening episode a primal scene, in that the characters of Daniel and Gwendolen seem to be in the process of being painfully and unevenly born out of a kind of narrative (and pronominal) ooze, at the same time that the narrator is being unevenly separated out from the characters.[48]

Throughout *Daniel Deronda*, there is a tremendous range of modes of representing both Daniel's and Gwendolen's thinking. They range from the kind of moralizing omniscient mode of assessing her characters that has opened Eliot up to charges of being overintellectualizing and controlling; to uses of internal quoted speech to represent some kinds of thinking that they do (as, for example, when Gwendolen wishes, in quotation, that Daniel could know everything about her); to a variety of forms of free indirect discourse.[49] It may be possible to make a taxonomy of Eliot's modes for representing consciousness, and to coordinate this taxonomy to a topography of the mind or of kinds of thinking, though one also suspects that the diversity of representational modes for thinking in Eliot would ultimately defy such an exercise.[50]

But in the opening pages of *Daniel Deronda*, the swift shifts between what seems like the narrator's thoughts and what seem like characters' thoughts can have a striking effect on the way we read the event being described. It is strange enough to contemplate Gwendolen's belief that Daniel's silent attention to her is what causes her luck to change (or least causes her to gamble recklessly), that his thoughts and judgments ("the darting sense that he was measuring her") can make something happen. But the way in which the thoughts and judgments of the first few pages loop between belonging to Daniel and belonging to the narrator can curiously make it seem as if the thinking that is making things happen to Gwendolen takes place not in her world but at the level of narration. Arrows of causation seem to poke through the floor that normally separates discourse from story. Many readers have noted that causality is oddly arranged in *Daniel Deronda*, which frequently, in the words of Cynthia Chase, reveals "a shifting of attention from the level of operation of the narrator...to the level of operation of the text or narrative as such," and makes us ponder, as Harry Shaw notes, "the possibility of movements between narrative world and story world."[51] If thinking is making anything happen here, who is thinking? In *Daniel Deronda*, the spectre of mental "action at a distance" is inseparable from the question of how things in fiction are understood to have been caused at all.

It may seem multiply odd to be constantly asking "who is thinking here?" of the opening sentences of *Daniel Deronda*. It is an odd question, first, in seeming to insist that there are in fact separate thinkers in the book that precede thinking, and second, in insisting on the sentences of the novel as representing thinking, whosoever's it may be. We might dwell for example a bit longer on one of the transitions from omniscient(ish) narration to free(ish) indirect discourse in the opening scene which is also the transition from Daniel's "inward debate" about Gwendolen, to Gwendolen's consciousness in their wordless encounter. The top paragraph on page 10 ends with a reflection on Gwendolen's demeanor, which is described as "too markedly cold and neutral not to have in it a little of that nature which we call art concealing an inward exultation"; the inclusive, knowing "we" of the phrase "that nature which we call art" conclusively (I would argue) identifies this as an omniscient narrator's sentiment.

But when the next paragraph picks up ("but in the course of that survey her eyes met Deronda's, and instead of averting them as she would have desired to do, she was unpleasantly conscious that they were arrested – how long?"), the dash that sets off the interrogative "how long?" precipitates us into the strange time warp of free indirect discourse.[52] There is no "tag" locating the phrase (such as "she wondered"). For a moment at least, a reader herself is arrested, suspended in the presence of thoughts that seem at least for a moment to have no thinker. In his curiously *Alice In Wonderland*-like "A Theory of Thinking" (1962), the British psychoanalyst W. R. Bion postulated the existence of "thoughts that have no thinker." He postulated that thinking as action emerges as something that has to be done with thoughts, which can exist prior to thinking (rather than being the products of thinking), as almost-objects in the mind: pieces of mental furniture. In so doing, he stressed thinking as something that needs to be done (and set into relief the specificity of what his patients were doing when they were not thinking their thoughts). Significantly, for Bion, to think is to be able to tolerate someone else's thinking.[53] Bion's notion of thoughts that have no thinker intrigues the reader of psychological fiction who feels that a novel such as *Daniel Deronda* is a machine for thinking about other people: not by giving us pictures of other minds, but by generating such sentences. The thoughts that have no thinker which are thrown up by Eliot's narrative technique are prompts for getting thinking about another person going, setting the novel in motion.

THE THOUGHT OF HIS DYING

Now we must contemplate whether thinking can make things happen in *Daniel Deronda* by focusing on the episode of Grandcourt's death by drowning, and on the novel's complex handling of Gwendolen's statements of beliefs about what happened on the boat: "You know I am a guilty woman" (689); "I did, I did kill him in my thoughts" (695); "I only know that I saw my wish outside me" (696). This episode is not only a place to think about the omnipotence of thought, but also about the agency of thoughts that have no thinker, or at least no certain one. As many of the novel's best critics have discussed, that is, we seem unable to think about what it would mean to consider Grandcourt's death as a result of Gwendolen's wishes that he might die, without also considering an author's ability to fulfill her own wishes in killing off characters. *Daniel Deronda's* deconstructive readers have been most persuasive in reading Grandcourt's drowning as a site for the confusion of author's and character's desires, and ultimately for revealing Eliot's stance towards the uncertain agency of writing. Grandcourt's death is, in Simon During's words, "a representation of an event…without agency." Marc Redfield notes:

> The problem of whose wish, if any, is being realized when Grandcourt drowns derives from the terms of Eliot's imaginative project.…[Casaubon's and] Grandcourt's deaths provoke the supplemental and less stable question of what it means for an "author" to "act" – that is, in this idiom, to kill a fictional character, or to identify with one, thereby seeing her wish outside her: murder, in other words, becomes the site for the staging of the question of what the act of fiction…is.[54]

Grandcourt's fall from the boat into the ocean off the coast of Genoa is, in this context, something like a dramatic version of the slips and falls from the level of narrative down to the level of story in the novel's opening chapter: falls into thoughts with no thinker (or sinker, perhaps). We could provide further context and suggest that in English literary history, and in particular for George Eliot (as also in *The Mill on the Floss*), death by drowning almost always raises the spectre of uncertain agency or responsibility, and of the murky waters of textual agency.

We could go further and suggest that when Grandcourt hits the water he undergoes a sea change into something truly rich and strange: Percy Bysshe Shelley, quotations and allusions to whose writings are scattered with increasing frequency over the pages leading up to the drowning. Shelley's own mysteriously drowned body of course actually washed up in 1822 on the shore not far from where Grandcourt drowns (but does not actually wash up: unaccountably, it is said that his body "had gone down irrecoverably," 686). Eliot and George Henry Lewes – himself an ardent Shelleyan in his younger years – visited Shelley's burial place in Rome in 1860. The novelist affirmed her allegiance to Shelley and his struggles against the world: "A spot that touched me deeply was Shelley's grave." "There," she commemorated, "lies the 'cor cordium' forever at rest from the unloving cavilers of this world, whether or not he may have entered on other purifying struggles, in some world unseen by us."[55] It would be preposterous to infer a connection in Eliot's mind between Shelley and Grandcourt: a less Shelleyan personage there never was. Rather, "Shelley" hovers in Book VII of *Daniel Deronda* as the patron saint of the agency of thought. The epigraph to Chapter 54 is from Shelley's verse drama *The Cenci*. It is a speech by Giacomo about his struggle with his fantasies about murdering his evil, incestuous father, Count Cenci:

> The unwilling brain
> Feigns often what it would not; and we trust
> Imagination with such phantasies
> As the tongue dares not fashion into words;
> Which have no words, their horror makes them dim
> To the mind's eye.[56]

It is the danger of thoughts sequestered from language he speaks of: such thoughts are "dim / To the mind's eye," but for that reason they have the force of action. A few lines later Giacomo urges Orsino not to dwell on the possibility of his father's death:

> I am as one lost in a midnight wood,
> Who dares not ask some harmless passenger
> The path across the wilderness, lest he,
> As my thoughts are, should be – a murderer.
>
> (II.ii.93–96)

Earlier, we find one of Mordecai's colleagues at the Hand and Banner reciting a passage from *Prometheus Unbound* on the power of thinking: "As thought by thought is piled, till some great truth / Is loosened, and the nations echo round" (522).[57] The dispersed presence of Shelley – martyr for the cause of the agency of thinking – in these chapters might be seen as tipping the scales in favor of Gwendolen's claims for the omnipotence of her thoughts.

To use the name "Shelley" as shorthand for the agent or cause of Grandcourt's drowning, however, does not solve the problem that it remains maddeningly difficult to say what "actually" happens on the boat between Gwendolen and Grandcourt. It is difficult to square Gwendolen's different statements about the event, or even to interpret them on their own terms. Here are Gwendolen's two main accounts, in which she expresses responsibility to Daniel:

"I did not want to die myself; I was afraid of our being drowned together. If it had been any use I should have prayed – I should have prayed that something might befall him. I should have prayed that he might sink out of my sight and leave me alone. I knew no way of killing him there, but I did, I did kill him in my thoughts." (695)

"...evil wishes were too strong. I remember then letting go the tiller and saying 'God help me!' But then I was forced to take it again and go on; and the evil longings, the evil prayers came again and blotted everything else dim, till, in the midst of them – I don't know how it was – he was turning the sail – there was a gust – he was struck – I know nothing – I only know that I saw my wish outside me." (695–96)

In her book *The Crime in Mind: Criminal Responsibility and the Victorian Novel*, Lisa Rodensky considers *Daniel Deronda* in the context of nineteenth-century British legal theory and practice, detailing the points both of convergence and of difference between the novel's ways of parsing interior states, intentions, causes, and responsibility, and the ways in which the law determined *mens rea*, or criminal intention. As she notes, "working out the relations between the interior life and the external acts and consequences of characters in the late novels of George Eliot is a humbling enterprise."[58] She argues that in the passages leading up to and following Grandcourt's death, Eliot refrains from giving us a very clear picture of Gwendolen's mind and Gwendolen's actions regarding the event itself (she beautifully points out how the text achieves clarity only on, for example, Gwendolen's "one act" [691]: tossing into the sea the key to a box with a knife in it), but rather gives a multiple and muddy picture in order to, so to speak, prevent literature from being an accessory to law.[59]

Rodensky points out that what is most difficult and most fascinating are not simply Gwendolen's seeming beliefs in the omnipotence of her thoughts and wishes, but Daniel's ways of responding to her beliefs. Here at length is the description of Daniel's reflections on Gwendolen's confessions:

Deronda felt the burden on his sprit less heavy than the foregoing dread. The word "guilty" had held a possibility of interpretations worse than the fact; and Gwendolen's confession, for the very reason that *her conscience made her dwell on the determining power of her evil thoughts*, convinced him the more that there had been throughout a counterbalancing struggle of her better will. *It seemed almost certain that her murderous thought had had no outward effect* – that, quite apart from it, the death was inevitable. Still, a question as to the outward effectiveness of a criminal desire dominant enough to impel even a momentary act, cannot alter our judgment of the desire; and Deronda shrank from putting that question forward in the first instance. He held it likely that Gwendolen's remorse aggravated her inward guilt, and that she gave the character of decisive action to what had been an inappreciably instantaneous glance of desire. But her remorse was the precious sign of a recoverable nature; it was the culmination of that self-disapproval which had been the awakening of a new life within her; it marked her off from the criminals whose only regret is failure in securing their evil wish. Deronda could not utter one word to diminish that sacred aversion to her worst self. (696, emphasis mine)

As Rodensky notes, Daniel's reasoning, and the very syntax of the sentences here, are tellingly knotty. She also notes that there is a confusion of reasoners here, as, for example, the sentence that begins "It seemed almost certain" is marked as Daniel's thinking, while the next sentence, with its talk of what can or cannot alter "our" desires, features the royal "we" of omniscient narration. These shifts have the effect of both collapsing and distancing narrator's and character's interpretations, a gap widened when we also realize that in some aspects of his reasoning Daniel is clearly wrong. The reader, who has been "on the boat" with Gwendolen and Grandcourt over the past few chapters while Daniel has been busy meeting his mother, knows that the murderous wish was no moment's "inappreciably instantaneous glance of desire," but obsessive, continuous thinking that had gone on until it smelled: thoughts "seemed now to cling about the very rigging of the vessel, mix with the air in the red silk cabin below, and make the smell of the sea odious" (675). It is a mistake to proceed as if Daniel were unambiguously a spokesperson for Eliot's views on beliefs about the extrapersonal effects of thinking.

Knottiest of all is the way in which Daniel's thinking in this paragraph entertains "the determining power" of Gwendolen's "evil thoughts," "the outward effectiveness of a criminal desire." What does it mean for Daniel to ponder that "it seemed *almost certain* that her murderous thought had had no outward effect"? Common sense conspires to make us supply a "middle term" in Daniel's thoughts, and read this as a rumination about whether or not Gwendolen actually translated the thought into an actual action.[60] But the sentence itself, read in its environment, actually entertains a proposition about mental causation, about whether thoughts can have outward effects, a proposition that, even though it is described as "almost certain[ly]" not true, is admitted as a possibility. As Rodensky notes, "the fear that Gwendolen's thought was as powerful as an act remains very much alive here."[61] While much has been written about the ways in which, in *Daniel Deronda*, George Eliot anticipated Freud's understanding of the unconscious and of the nature of human relationships, we might also wish to turn things around and view Freud as an attentive *reader* of *Daniel Deronda*, shaping his writing on "the omnipotence of thoughts."[62]

My interpretation of Daniel's response, however, does not take Freud as a guide – or does so only distantly. Rather, I seek here to take as my guide to interpreting Gwendolen's beliefs and Daniel's response the case for the sociable, productive effects of thinking about another person that I have been pursuing throughout my reading of the novel. In spite of the hint that he may be willing to entertain the possibility of the extrapersonal effects of Gwendolen's thoughts, Daniel on balance is certain that Gwendolen's statement that her wishes "had the character of decisive action" is unlikely to hold any truth.[63] Like Freud, Daniel sees a belief in the omnipotence of thought to be a delusion, but for Daniel, it is (as for Freud) an interesting and productive delusion. It is a delusion he is happy to tolerate. Indeed, the key to Daniel's response here, logically faulty though it is in some ways, is the way it resolves into relief: as the passage begins, "Deronda felt the burden on his spirit less heavy than the foregoing dread." I take the emotions of Deronda's response as central and interpretable, and take his tolerance of Gwendolen's belief – a belief he believes is mistaken – to be crucial. Gwendolen's deluded belief in the power of her thinking is an expression of guilt, responsibility, and remorse, which Daniel interprets as "the precious sign of a recoverable nature." It is "the culmination of that self-disapproval which had been the awakening of a new life within her." But what would it mean to find moral reassurance in a belief that is so patently false?

We can sharpen our sense of Gwendolen's false but significant claims of responsibility, and Daniel's strong response, by contrasting Gwendolen's mix of claims and feelings with those exhibited by Daniel's mother, the Alcharisi, in the chapters directly preceding Gwendolen's crisis. The dying actress, who has summoned Daniel to meet her for the first time, is practically remorseless as she narrates to her son her decision to abandon him as a child. Daniel repeatedly asks her why she has resolved to disclose all now. While the answers she gives all point to the possibility of "guilt" – she professes feeling compelled to obey her dead father's wishes, on the brink of her own death – this guilt does not seem remotely felt. "Oh – the reasons for our actions," said the Princess, with a ring of sarcastic scorn. "When you are as old as I am, it will not seem so simple a question" (628–31). Still the consummate actress, she is, Eliot suggests, completely incapable of feeling an authentic emotion on this or any other matter. Gwendolen thus appears to Daniel the inverse of his mother in this regard: while the Alcharisi feels no emotional accountability about what she is actually responsible for, Gwendolen feels responsible for an act – killing her husband in her thoughts – for which she is not.

Daniel's tolerance for Gwendolen's delusion points to something that moral psychologists have been writing about for some time: that people's ordinary judgments in matters of morality cast a pretty wide net. "If people genuinely do form irrational beliefs as a causal, but not intentional, result of their other beliefs, wishes, values and so on," writes Nomi Arpaly, "what are we to think when these irrational beliefs have moral import?"[64] Daniel's interpretation of Gwendolen's belief affirms the point of view that, in practice, people tend to approve of, or factor into views of what's moral, a wide range of beliefs, thoughts, and behaviors that don't seem particularly rational or true, especially when we factor emotion into accounts of ethics: and that, moreover, there many be practical reasons, rather than evidence-based reasons, for believing things. We might, for example, wish to extend Bernard Williams' concept of "moral luck" to make sense of Daniel's response to Gwendolen's guilty delusion.

Asking us to ponder the example of the dreadful, world-crushing emotions of guilt of the truck driver who has had the bad "luck," so to speak, to completely accidentally cause the death of a child, Williams famously pointed out that we tend to feel that it is understandable, and essential, for people to feel guilt about unintended harm to others. We'd feel there was something truly morally wrong about the truck driver who didn't.[65] Patricia Greenspan has explored what it would mean to see guilt as a positive way of making up for moral luck. She argues for viewing the claims of responsibility that people make in situations in which they've caused no harm intentionally as not-quite-beliefs: the feeling of guilt in such cases "serves as a way of holding an evaluative thought in mind."[66] Such thoughts, in her view, "resemble beliefs," but are more like an "'as if' version of the corresponding evaluative judgment" that we might experience more in the feeling than in the thought itself. Greenspan's argument suggests that the line between the feelings of guilt, and the thoughts and beliefs that the feelings bundle in, may be quite fluid. Her argument might make sense of the ways in which both Gwendolen's utterances and Daniel's interpretations fluctuate between a focus on obscure claims of agency ("I killed him in my thoughts…I saw my wish outside me"), and morally freighted emotions.

If guilt is a kind of thinking about another person, there is perhaps room to see a belief in the omnipotence of one's thoughts not as simply delusional, nor as infantile or atavistic (Freud), nor as a form of wacky magical thinking to be countenanced only by persons with a high (Victorian) tolerance for the gothic and the occult. I have been concerned throughout this book to demonstrate that there are some contexts in which holding a belief in our mental powers over another seems delusional, and others in which holding such a belief might seem in fact an ordinary part of being a moral person. As I have argued in this chapter, the possibility that thinking is most sociable when most in error is embodied as the structuring, formal principle of *Daniel Deronda*, in Daniel's and Gwendolen's thinking about each other. In this context, Gwendolen's deluded belief in the extrapersonal effects of her wishes, and Daniel's remarkable – and in its own way irrational – tolerance of her belief, may come to seem part of a larger picture of the act of thinking about another person that emerges here. As sensational (and wrong) as it is, Gwendolen's belief in the omnipotence of her thoughts about Grandcourt is on a continuum with all the other kinds of ordinary thinking "doing their work invisibly" in *Daniel Deronda*.

Pursuing this line of thinking – which suggests that thinking about another person may be a social good even when it's wrong – in relation to George Eliot might put us in a position of ascribing to her as a thinker a way of approaching ethics different from those commonly ascribed to her, so often described as the doctrine of sympathy, and an imperative to see into the life of others.[67] However, the ways of thinking about the ethics of thinking embodied in Gwendolen's belief and Daniel's tolerance of her belief may not be so much out of line with the critical focus on Eliot's commitment to an ethic of sympathy as a reason to broaden and complicate our understanding of her ethics. Detailing the ways in which *Daniel Deronda* organizes itself both formally and thematically around "*Thinking* as a pure act & energy," "*Thinking* as distinguished from *Thoughts*," thinking that is going on even when abstracted from representation and speech, shifts our view, and can give us new ideas about what the ethical force of a belief in the omnipotence of thought might actually be.

Conclusion: The ethics of belief and the poetics of thinking about another person

A close look at Daniel Deronda's response to Gwendolen's claims that she has killed her husband "in her thoughts," I suggested at the end of the last chapter, opens onto some larger areas in moral philosophy. It points to areas of debate about the ethics of belief and practical guilt in particularly illuminating ways. What are some of the "ideas about what the ethical force of a belief in the omnipotence of thought might be" that my reading of *Daniel Deronda* might lead us to consider?

The efficacy of beliefs justified on non-epistemic grounds was certainly an urgent issue for some nineteenth-century writers. The notion that there is an ethics to what one believes took particular forms in Victorian intellectual life: the topic often appears to us as part of the era's grand conflict between faith and science. We might begin by considering George Eliot's views. The position I've identified as Daniel Deronda's – that Gwendolen's belief is (probably) unfounded, but it is a sign of moral progress that she believes it – may seem to bear a family resemblance to Eliot's position on belief in God. Eliot tended to view religious belief as a potential means of moral development. Her career-long orientation around this position can be viewed not only in the sympathetic treatment of the faith of Mordecai and Mirah in *Daniel Deronda*, and in her sympathetic translations of Feuerbach's *Essence of Christianity* and Strauss' *Life of Jesus*, but also more programmatically in an early review of R. M. Mackay's *The Progress of the Intellect*, a sweeping, progressivist account of the history of civilization. Approvingly summarizing Mackay, she wrote: "divine revelation is not contained exclusively or pre-eminently in the facts and inspiration of any one age or nation, but is coextensive with the history of human development, and is perpetually unfolding itself to our widened experience and investigation."[1] Eliot animadverted on the advantages to be gained if religious thinkers were to get on board with this progressivist, moral-utility point of view.

It would be wise in our theological teachers, instead of struggling to retain a footing for themselves and their doctrine on the crumbling structure of dogmatic interpretation, to cherish those more liberal views of biblical criticism, which, admitting of a development of the Christian system corresponding to the wants and the culture of the age, would enable it to strike a firm root in man's moral nature, and to entwine itself with the growth of those new forms of social life to which we are tending.[2]

It may be objected that any similarity between Daniel Deronda's position on Gwendolen's belief in her thoughts' powers, and George Eliot's position on the moral utility of belief in God, disregards the necessity for discriminating among kinds of belief. A belief that your thoughts can go from point A to point B, or, in some other, less easily graphable, non-causal way, affect, harm, or diminish another person, is dramatically different from religious belief. It is not cosmological; it is a proposition about mental life and its relation to the world. It is manifestly different as well from believing that rain falls from the sky, or that humans tend to be interested in each other, but it is closer in propositional form to those than to religious belief. However, it was across broad, inclusive categories that debates about the ethics of belief were carried out in the Victorian period. Mathematician and philosopher W. K. Clifford's essay "The Ethics of Belief" (1877) takes on a wide range of kinds of belief, from a shipowner's belief in the seaworthiness of his vessel, to belief in prophecy, to a child's belief that fire will burn her finger, and applies to all his thundering conclusion: "it is wrong always, everywhere, for any one, to believe anything on insufficient evidence."[3] Our moral duty is to submit to "the universal duty of questioning all that we believe" ("Ethics of Belief," 344). Clifford's "Ethics of Belief" is a manifesto for the virtues of a scientific skepticism, but it also proceeds with certainty that any belief worth believing will be found to be grounded in sufficient evidence.

The ethics of Clifford's "Ethics of Belief" lies in our duty to believe what is epistemically true; we are ethically compelled to assent to beliefs only on grounds internal to the particular belief itself. Thus Clifford's "ethics of belief" has been termed a species of "intrinsic evidentialism,"[4] and thus William James' response, "The Will to Believe" (1896), can be termed an externalist, anti-evidentialist critique. James is bent on defending the idea that there can be good reasons, ethical and otherwise, to hold certain beliefs, reasons or considerations that are external to the content of the belief itself. Furthermore, to insist on the evidentialist standard for belief is to fly in the face of the ways in which beliefs work in people's lives – what James calls "the actual psychology of human opinion."[5] People's beliefs are, and are rightly, shaped by their emotions. "Evidently, then, our non-intellectual nature does influence our convictions. There are passional tendencies and volitions which run before and others which come after belief…*Our passional nature not only lawfully may, but must, decide an option between propositions, whenever it is a genuine option that cannot by its nature be decided on intellectual grounds*" ("Will to Believe," 19–20; emphasis his). To hold beliefs to the evidentialist standard is to risk abandoning beliefs to grave moral peril; it carries too high a risk: "*better risk loss of truth than risk chance of error*," he counsels, with a nod to Pascal's wager. To James, Clifford's evidentialism leads only to a shriveled sense of the ethical dimensions of belief.

Clifford and James represent the poles of the Victorian debate, and in this context, Daniel Deronda's tolerance for Gwendolen's false belief in the powers of her thinking falls closest to James' position. However, taking *Daniel Deronda* as a starting point enables one to glimpse an intriguing, complex vision of the ethics of belief, one that emerges not only within the starkest Victorian statements, but also within contemporary moral psychology. Even Clifford's "Ethics of Belief" merits a closer look. Though what Clifford means by the phrase "ethics of belief" is manifestly our duty to seek the truth of our beliefs, shadows of non-evidence-based moralism are visible in his essay as well. Such shadows are cast in particular by the richly textured fictional examples at the beginning of "The Ethics of Belief," which are often overlooked in the rush to come to Clifford's stark conclusions. In one of these fictions, Clifford sketches out an elaborate and obscure hypothetical fantasy: an island on which certain "professors" of an unorthodox religion bring grave, unfounded allegations against other islanders in the fervor of their religion. "They had sincerely and consciously believed in the charges they had made, *yet they had no right to believe on such evidence as was before them*" (341; emphasis his), Clifford insists: the accused were innocent. Clifford then asks us to consider: suppose the accused, upon a more thorough investigation, turned out actually to be guilty as charged? "Would this make any difference in the guilt of the accusers?" he asks (341). "Clearly not," is his rejoinder: "The question is not whether their belief was true or false, but whether they entertained it on the wrong grounds" (341). A space has been opened up between the epistemic truth of the belief, and the external moral rightness or wrongness of *the reason for* the belief. This is a space familiar to us now from our examination of Daniel Deronda's reasoning about Gwendolen's belief.

Debates about whether extrinsic, pragmatic, emotion-driven, or motivational justifications for belief are morally admissible have followed in the wake of the debate between Clifford and James. While some contemporary philosophers have sought to refine or defend an evidentialist ethics of belief, there is a good deal of sentiment on the side of broadening the ethics of belief in ways that might include reasoning such as Daniel Deronda's. For some, exploring the moral or pragmatic utility of irrational beliefs is a way to think about the place of irrationality in human affairs, or to broaden the account of what counts as rational.[6] Such accounts partially illuminate, and are illuminated by, the interesting puzzle of Daniel Deronda's response to Gwendolen, or more generally by the tolerant, reflective attitude towards believing in the effects of thinking on another person I have sought to cultivate in this book. However, most of the work on the pragmatic or moral utility of irrational beliefs – even when they take beliefs about relations between persons as their topic – has quite other goals. The philosophical literature on the ethics of irrational belief is full instead of a very different, but also very Victorian, example: the virtuous, trusting woman who persists – for the sake of the greater good – in believing that her lover is faithful to her, in spite of mounting evidence to the contrary – Trollope's Lily Dale.[7]

But perhaps my example from *Daniel Deronda* does not quite sit well with the philosophical literature on the ethics of belief, because belief is not entirely the right concept with which to talk about the attitudes towards thinking about other people that this book has explored. We would do well to remember the ambiguities of Gwendolen Harleth's obscure utterances: "you know I am a guilty woman"; "I saw my wish outside me"; "I killed him in my thoughts." For Gwendolen, or even for a real person in less melodramatic circumstances who has a reflex of guilt after thinking evil thoughts about someone, it may be grossly off the mark to assume that when someone feels those twinges of guilt, they actually hold a firm belief in the extrapersonal effects of their thinking. It may be a partial belief, a fleeting thought, or a feeling. At the end of the previous chapter, I discussed the possibility of reading Gwendolen's confession, and Daniel's response, as illuminating, and as provocatively illuminated by, Patricia Greenspan's concept of "practical guilt." For Greenspan and for other writers on this topic, the fact that people, in practice, often feel guilty even when they've committed no wrong poses an intriguing opportunity to contemplate rationality, morality, and emotion. In the words of Juha Raikka: "Cases of irrational guilt may be relatively common, but still most of us would say they are somehow strange."[8] Raikka and other philosophers have proposed explanations of what have become the canonical categories of irrational guilt – survivor's guilt, for example, or the vague guilt that a person brought up with a religious prohibition feels when violating that prohibition as a non-believing adult.[9] If something like survivor's guilt actually no longer seems so strange, but fairly easily explained, the phenomena this book has addressed – the range of ways in which thinking about another can become colored with guilt, from Arendt's assertion that if you are thinking of someone, you are necessarily absenting yourself from him or her, to more active suspicions of thinking about another as effecting diminishment or harm – do genuinely seem strange. And for Greenspan and Raikka, the value of such strange cases may be the ways in which they prompt reflection on the relations between emotion and cognition, and on the place of emotions in ethics. Of guilt or worry about harming, distancing, or diminishing someone in one's thoughts, we might say, following Greenspan, that "what it amounts to is a momentary object of (dispositional) attention, held in mind and allowed to influence thought and behavior as if it were believed, though unlike belief it would be discarded upon a moment's reflection."[10] Both writers see such instances of irrational guilt as revealing the ways in which emotions contain cognitive elements, and the way such feelings point to the fact that moral life may be governed by instances of feeling certain propositions, entertaining them, and trying them out without fully committing to belief in them.[11]

However, as provocative as these two philosophical discussions – about the ethics of belief, about irrational guilt – may be as contexts for pondering something like Daniel Deronda's response to Gwendolen's confession, neither really gets at the specificity of the provocative puzzle that emerges out of *Daniel Deronda* and out of the nineteenth-century material studied in this book as a whole. It is a puzzle made up of ideas about causation, ideas about ethics, ideas about the possibility of mental relations between persons; it is a puzzle that opens up new spaces for speculation within and among discussions of belief, guilt, and sociability. Furthermore, trying to find a place for the ethics of thinking about another person within current discussions in philosophy, even if trying to emphasize the point of view suggested by *Daniel Deronda*, that there may be something morally reassuring about the belief that thinking about another person can harm them, has another limitation: it focuses our attention exclusively on thinking as a form of harm. But as we've seen throughout this book, from the thought-power proponents of Chapter 2, to the folk-psychological accounts of statements such as "I am thinking of you" discussed in Chapter 3, the ethics of thinking about another person comes in more optimistic flavors. Such views find their way into modern discussions of causation and human relations, though they may do so in fugitive and surprising ways.

First, a whimsical example. In a charming essay called "Can You Help Your Team Tonight by Watching on TV?" designed to explain quantum mechanics to non-specialists, the physicist N. David Mermin introduces what he calls "The Baseball Principle."[12] Mermin, a fan of the New York baseball team the Mets, confesses that "somewhere deep inside," he feels not only that he should watch the Mets on television every time they play, but that "my watching the game makes a difference – that the Mets are more likely to win if I'm following things than if I'm not" (98–99). He describes this feeling as "completely irrational": he knows that "the outcome of the game doesn't depend in the least on whether I watch it or not. What I do or don't do in Ithaca, New York, can have no effect on what the Mets do or don't do in Flushing, New York," home of the Mets' stadium, hundreds of miles away (99). It is this rational position – that the outcome of any particular game does not depend on his watching – that he calls the Baseball Principle. Mermin scrutinizes the Baseball Principle, discussing, for example, the ways in which in fact it is impossible either to verify or to disprove in any individual instance, because you cannot both watch and not watch at the same time. He uses this problem as an opportunity to discuss the ways in which quantum theory has reopened questions about action at a distance, in an argument that I need not reproduce here. But it is first worth recalling how much nineteenth-century speculation about thinking as force and action was driven by the work of Mermin's predecessors, the Victorian popularizers of force-field physics. And second, it is worth noting that Mermin's essay ends completely immersed in its theoretical problem, and never returns to where he began: with the "feeling" that he "should" watch. Mermin's essay, that is, confirms that ideas about mental action at a distance continue to occupy the far reaches of conversations in philosophy and the sciences about causation in general: it is the limit case, deeply weird and mysterious, but, always, at the end of the day, deeply felt.

Mermin's passing confession that there's a feeling, one he can't easily shake, that he "should" watch the Mets on TV in order to help them win is thus an instance of the intuitive nature of the ethics of ideas about mental action at a distance. It could be said that Mermin's experience is simply a wish that he could make his team win, but the fact that it is felt and articulated as a belief – even a superstition – about mental action at distance merits our studying such feelings in those terms. Mermin's essay prompts us to consider whether there is a lingering ethics even in sophisticated discussions of causation, and whether this may be as true in twentieth- and twenty-first-century disciplines as in nineteenth-century writing.

The twentieth-century discipline most attuned to the notion of thinking about other people as a discrete part of human relatedness – attuned even to the idea that there may be a normative value to thinking that thinking about someone might affect them – is psychoanalysis. We may take this as another proof of the ways in which much of twentieth-century psychoanalytic theory has always seemed like nineteenth-century literary ideas, translated into theoretical form;[13] and this is another way of saying that I do not turn to psychoanalysis for its explanatory force, or as the last word, but as an instance of the persistence of a set of topics. As I noted in the Introduction to this book, it is possible to view some of the ideas about mental action in nineteenth-century writing as pieces of a prehistory to Freud's idea of "the omnipotence of thoughts." Moreover, Freud's discussion of this topic opens the door to seeing a belief in the omnipotence of one's own thoughts as a normative part of human development. Subsequent psychoanalytic theorists have taken seriously the possibility that the practice of thinking about another person can make things happen, that it is genuinely transformative both of the person who thinks and the person who is thought about. This is, in one view, a way of thinking of the relationship between analyst and patient: psychoanalysis is fundamentally about "the powerful mutual influence that two minds thinking closely together exert on one another."[14]

The psychoanalytic vision of the patient's and analyst's interlocking modes of thinking derives from its understanding of the place of thinking in the relation between parent and child. Psychoanalysis envisions the chains of embedded thinking between parent and child neither as an arid math problem ("he thinks she think he thinks"), nor as a cognitive limit (see Chapter 4), but as transformative. In the "mentalization" theory of Peter Fonagy and Mary Target, for example, the analyst "describe[s] a normative process in which an imagining other who thinks about the child's thinking and reflects this back to him enables the child to develop the capacity to reflect upon his inner world and to distinguish between his own psychic reality, the psychic reality of others, and external reality."[15] A particularly fascinating account of thinking itself – of the emergence of thinking *as* thinking about another – can be found in W. R. Bion's "Theory of Thinking," discussed briefly in Chapter 5. Bion's theory concerns the kind of thinking about another that characterizes both the "early emotional events between a mother and her infant," and the psychoanalytic session itself, and of course the relationship between those relations.[16] He stresses the way thinking is distributed between the infant and mother of his model – between "the rudimentary consciousness and the maternal reverie."[17] For Bion, "maternal reverie" is the mother's "capacity with love to think about her infant – to pay attention, to try to understand," above all to accept the infant's projections of his own thoughts and feelings into her: "her thinking transforms the infant's feelings into a known and tolerated experience." If all goes well, the infant "will introject and identify with a mother who is able to think, and he will introject also his own now modified feelings."[18] Thinking, that is, is a process of introjecting another person's ability to think about you. To think at all is to have thought with, of, and for another. At the center of Bion's account of thinking of another person lies the example of the mother's ability to contain in her thoughts the infant's thoughts that he might die: "If th[is] projection is not accepted by the mother the infant feels that its feeling that it is dying is stripped of such meaning as it has. It therefore reintrojects, not a fear of dying made tolerable, but a nameless dread."[19] The fascination of this example, which links the question of thinking of another person to the question of one's sense of survival, is compounded when we reflect that this uncanny scenario of thinking – the very notion of the infant thinking at all – is constructed in relationship to the speechlessness of infants. This is a scenario of thinking that emerges in the soundless corridors of the talking cure. As we noted in Chapters 2, 3, and 4, ideas and beliefs about the powers of thinking about another person often emerge as negative images of assumptions about speaking to another.

I have sought to argue here that, whether or not thoughts can actually have extrapersonal effects on others, it may make moral, psychological, and social sense to act as if one believes that they do. Further, I have sought to suggest in this Conclusion that while the moral, psychological, and social significance of attitudes towards thinking of others may be extended, and illuminated, by conversations in contemporary psychology and philosophy, contemplating attitudes towards thinking of others might also push such conversations in new directions. There is no single, discrete nineteenth-century discourse or discipline that bundles together the concerns of this book – thinking as a form of action, thinking's extrapersonal effects, and the ethics of thinking about another person; nor is there a straight-lined story to tell. However, I hope the chapters of this book have demonstrated that there are good reasons to investigate this cluster of topics historically, and that, moreover, there are good reasons to reflect on these topics outside of historical consideration. It is a cluster of topics that provide a way of unearthing unformed assumptions about how people view the role of mental life in social life. It is, as I suggested in the Introduction to this study, a way of reality-testing with questions about agency and responsibility, a way of valuing ordinary folk psychologies about the agency of thinking in spite of evidence to the contrary, and beginning to think through the problem from there. In a recent volume, *Does Consciousness Cause Behavior?*, essays by neuroscientists, psychologists, and philosophers contemplate the evidence offered by some experimental neuroscience that, in fact, consciousness does not cause behavior, is purely epiphenomenal, and appears to register belatedly the purely neurological chain that brings about, say, a motor action. A key point of a number of the essays is that such findings in no way absolve us from analyzing the ways in which we persist in acting *as if* consciousness is what causes behavior, and would continue to do so, in the face of even mounting evidence.[20] In the case of whether thinking about another person causes anything, the ratio of common sense to evidence to feeling or acting "as if" is distributed quite differently. While common sense, that is, may lead us to feel that our conscious thoughts have some kind of causal relation to our own actions, common sense is likely to reject the idea that thinking about another person makes something happen. But similarly, it is valuable to consider the ways in which people may sometimes feel as if their thinking about another person has "relational properties" – to borrow a phrase from Meir Dan-Cohen, the philosopher discussed in my Introduction most committed to arguing that thoughts can have effects on others – even if the evidence, by most standards, points the other way.[21] Entertaining the idea that thinking about someone may affect them is a way of acknowledging the place of thinking in social relations.

In the meantime, in our own era as in the nineteenth century, thinking about the place of thinking in social life is undertheorized, unevenly theorized, as likely to appear in literary forms as in the disciplines – philosophy, psychology – that would seem to be its proper domains. Chapters 3 and 4 of this book revealed the extent to which the ethics of thinking about another person were worked out in nineteenth-century poetry. I sought to provide a new context in which to read poems, such as Landon's "Night at Sea" and Elizabeth Barrett Browning's response, "L.E.L's Last Question," which intertwine questions about what it means to think about another person with practices of second-person poetic address. I suggested that these poems – and a host of others – can be viewed in relation to some of the most urgent political questions of the era: the vicissitudes of equality and inequality in intimate relations; the relationship of mental force and mental freedom unleashed by liberal political theory. We saw Landon and Barrett Browning disagreeing about whether the palindromical formulation of the refrain of "Night at Sea" – "Do you think about me as I think of you?" – is the formal equivalent of a substantial reciprocity in thinking; or whether purely mental relations are by nature highly unstable, asymmetrical, and unequal. While Landon aspired to the former, I argued, Barrett Browning wrote, not only in her response to Landon but in her other poetry as well, as if thinking always has the potential to diminish or infringe upon other people. Barrett Browning was highly attuned to the possibility of thinking's excessive agency, but highly conscious as well of both the need to feel thought about, and the dangers of becoming an object of thought. The poems featured in Chapters 3, 4, and 5 – including Barrett Browning's – also reveal the ways in which ideas about thinking about another person often derive from ideas about speaking to and writing to another. As I've noted throughout this study, the activity of thinking about another person is sometimes apprehended as a kind of internalized second-person speaking, and at other times theorized as something that happens when thinking is completely sealed off from the world of speech.

All of these issues are carried forward in a twentieth-century poem, Randall Jarrell's "A Sick Child" (1951), which, for our purposes, may be seen as a reflection on the nineteenth-century poetics of thinking about another person that has been at the center of this book. It is a poem about a mental conversation with a postman:

> The postman comes when I am still in bed.
> "Postman, what do you have for me today?"
> I say to him. (But really I'm in bed.)
> Then he says – what shall I have him say?
>
> "This letter says that you are president
> Of – this word here; it's a republic."
> Tell them I can't answer right away.
> "It's your duty." No, I'd rather just be sick.
>
> Then he tells me there are letters saying everything
> That I can think of that I want for them to say.
> I say, "Well, thank you very much. Good-bye."
> He is ashamed, and turns and walks away.
>
> If I can think of it, it isn't what I want. I want …
> I want a ship from some near star
> To land in the yard, and beings to come out
> And think to me: "So this is where you are!
>
> Come." Except that they won't do,
> I thought of them.…And yet somewhere there must be
> Something that's different from everything.
> All that I've never thought of – think of me![22]

Jarrell's poem is manifestly a portrait of the artist as a sick child, and what the sick child is sick of is, it seems, doing all the thinking and imagining he does. The only communication he receives from the outside world is a visit from a postman of his own imagining, who brings letters which are, of course, imaginary. The poem sets up a sliding scale of forms of address: from letters, to speech, to imaginary internal speech (as in line three, when the child admits that he doesn't really "say" anything to the postman – it's all in his mind), to a form of direct, unmediated second-person thinking. The latter is what the child wishes from the extraterrestrial "beings" from "some near star," whom he hopes will "think to me: 'So this is where you are!'" (14,16). (The "near star" from which these beings hail must surely be in the same galaxy as the planet described in Kant's *Anthropology*, discussed in Chapter 3, whose denizens cannot distinguish between thinking and speaking.) The fact that everything on this sliding scale of address is ultimately internal to the child's mind is both part of the poem's humor, and part of its pathos.

The child of "A Sick Child" is sick precisely of his inability to get outside his thoughts, to circumvent the moving wall between inside and outside that the poem's modes of address set up: "If I can think of it, it isn't what I want" (13). The letters the postman brings – "letters saying everything / That I can think of that I want for them to say" (9–10) – are his own wishes temporarily exteriorized. The child's cold brush-off, the postman's shame and hasty exit (11–12), are indications of the child's own disciplining of his own overweening imagination, which is an ongoing, never-completed task. The shame that clings to the postman may be seen, that is, as a projection of the child's own guilt over-excessive mental agency; it is a flag which marks the presence of an ethics of thinking. The poem's final appeal to "All that I've never thought of" makes us aware of the minimal difference between "all that I've never thought of" and the more idiomatic "all that I've ever thought of": in the realm of thought, everything and nothing appear as one and the same.

The sick child's last-ditch effort to interrupt the overweening agency of his own thinking takes the form of an interruption of his train of thoughts with an imperative address: "– Think of me!" (20). It is unclear to whom this appeal is addressed, just as it is unclear how to interpret the dash that precedes it, though one possibility is that this is an address and an appeal to, precisely, "All that I've never thought of." It is also unclear how to read the tone of these final words, whether they are on balance more imperious or more groveling, more self-pitying, or more earnest in their wishes. Nevertheless, they constitute an expression of a wish to be, instead of a thinker, an object of thought. For the sick child, becoming someone else's mental object would seem in no way to be a diminishment or derealization, as it often appears in Barrett Browning's poetry, or in Hardy's "She, to Him" sonnet discussed in Chapter 5. It offers the opposite: the possibility of being made real. In fact, the desire of the thinker to be contained in someone else's thinking is what makes life, and hence, paradoxically, more thinking, possible. We could confirm this by contemplating the ways in which the sick child's "– Think of me!" absorbs the reader of Jarrell's poem: it is minimally the reader who contains the sick child in her thoughts. The absorption of the reader into the poem, as one of its multiple addressees, begins as early as the parenthetical "(But really I'm in bed)" of line three, which the sick child "utters" as an aside – to whom else but us? – to highlight the mental nature of his address to the postman. Reading about another person and thinking about them become connected in this poem, and, just as poems, letters, and thoughts are curiously juxtaposed in "The Sick Child," so readers of the poem are curiously positioned as presumably welcome arrivals in the child's world, both like and unlike the postman who "comes" to him, and the visitors from "some near star" who think "Come" (1, 17).[23]

"A Sick Child," I am suggesting, may be seen as responding to the nineteenth-century poetic debate about whether becoming an object of someone else's thought is or is not an infringement or a diminishment, by suggesting that it is rather a kind of cure for excessive thinking. But we can take this interpretation of Jarrell's poem one step further by noting that it is most clearly a response to a specific kind of nineteenth-century poem, the legions of sick child poems published on both sides of the Atlantic throughout the century. In the nineteenth-century sick child poem (as well as in the related sub-genre, the dead child poem), speaker and addressee, adult and child, and living and dead, often exchange places in dizzying ways. In his recent re-reading of nineteenth-century American child poems, Kerry Larson asks us to notice the ways in which these manifestly sentimental (and often morbid) poems were in fact cool instruments for dramatizing a particular form of thinking: generalizing, democratizing speculation. Of the malingering children in the wildly influential, hopelessly generic poems of Lydia Sigourney – such as "Death of an Infant in Its Mother's Arms," or "The Sick Child" – Larson notes that the "stricken infants become the focal point for a kind of speculative musing as much as for outright dread and anxiety." "So marked is this speculative tone," he continues, "that it often becomes apparent that the more the mother contemplates the child, the more the two identities begin to mirror each other until they appear interchangeable."[24] In this reading, poetic speculation about the anonymous, generic child is a way of imagining equality.

Jarrell's "A Sick Child" would seem to be a rejoinder to such nineteenth-century sentimental verse. The sick child of his poem is no empty cipher, but rather a bratty (if also somewhat pathetic), precocious child who wishes you to know he has mastered hard words like "republic." But just barely, and he thus has his imaginary postman struggle with the word: "'This letter says that you are president / Of – this word here; it's a republic'" (5–6). However, "A Sick Child" is also implicated in the logic of nineteenth-century verse. Like not only the sick child poems that are its obvious precursors, but also the second-person thinking poems I've discussed in this book, "A Sick Child" links the practice of thinking about – and being thought about by – others to questions about equality and reciprocity.

It is funny to think of Jarrell's sick child as becoming the "president" of a "republic" – who would its citizens be? – because the world of the poem seems upon first reading very much an absolute dictatorship: the child seems so manifestly to be master of all he imagines. Becoming president of the republic is a responsibility he abdicates or at least defers, in any case (5–6). Yet, the appeal "– Think of me!" at the end of the poem puts things in a different light. It is, as I've argued, an imperative that aspires to put into motion a kind of thinking about another understood not only as action, but as action that might actually have salutary effects on the one who is to be thought about. It pulls the reader into a scenario of people thinking about each other, and being thought about, not as an exercise in skepticism (as in, people may think all they like but can never really know each other's minds) nor as an illustration of solipsism (as in, other people are in reality nothing but thoughts to us) but as a real relation. It asks us to think about mental relations as an ideal form of sociability, or perhaps as a part of ordinary sociability, a kind of relating that may have potential for reciprocity, for an equal exchange of thinking. It holds out for the possibility of a republic of thinking.

Notes

INTRODUCTION: LOVE THINKING

1. Samuel Taylor Coleridge, March 17, 1801, *Notebooks*, 1: 923.
2. Elizabeth Barrett Browning, *Sonnets From the Portuguese* XXIX.14; Hannah Arendt, "Thinking and Moral Considerations," *Responsibility and Judgement*, 165.
3. "'I did kill him in my thoughts'": George Eliot, *Daniel Deronda*, 695.
4. The vast scholarship on Coleridge and German idealism includes J. H. Muirhead, *Coleridge as Philosopher*; G. N. G. Orsini, *Coleridge and German Idealism*; Paul Hamilton, *Coleridge and German Philosophy: The Poet in the Land of Logic*. A re-evaluation of Coleridge as plagiarist of Schelling can be found in Tilar J. Mazzeo, *Plagiarism and Literary Property in the Romantic Period*.
5. May Sinclair, *A Defence of Idealism*, v.
6. James Frederick Ferrier, *Scottish Philosophy, the Old and the New*, 12–15; Arthur Thomson, *Ferrier of St. Andrews: An Academic Tragedy*.
7. Older historical studies of British idealism include G. Watts Cunningham, *The Idealistic Argument in Recent British and American Philosophy*; J. H. Muirhead, *The Platonic Tradition in Anglo-Saxon Philosophy: Studies in the History of Idealism in England and America*; W. J. Mander, ed., *Anglo-American Idealism, 1865–1927*. Recent scholarship has focused on the impact of Victorian idealism of British social and political thought: J. M. Milne, *The Social Philosophy of English Idealism*; Sandra M. Den Otter, *British Idealism and Social Explanation: A Study in Late Victorian Thought*.
8. Exceptions include Rosemary Ashton, *The German Idea: Four English Writers and the Reception of German Thought, 1800–1860*; Wendell V. Harris, *The Omnipresent Debate: Empiricism and Transcendentalism in Nineteenth-Century English Prose*; Diana Postlethwaite, *Making it Whole: A Victorian Circle and the Shape of Their World*; W. David Shaw, *The Lucid Veil: Poetic Truth in the Victorian Age*.
9. David Masson, *Recent British Philosophy*, 3rd ed. (1877), 262.
10. O. B. Frothingham, quoted in Ashton, *The German Idea*, 3.
11. Shadworth Hollway Hodgson, *The Philosophy of Reflection*.
12. Paul Hamilton, "Coleridge and the 'Rifacciamento' of Philosophy: Communicating an Idealist Position in Philosophy": "as a thinker...Coleridge

can only function when he is able to view the connections he makes with different discourses as kinds of relationship expressive of the person knowing as much as of the integrative process by which that person ascertains his or her knowledge," 417.

13. John Beer, "Coleridge's Afterlife," *The Cambridge Companion to Coleridge*, 231–44.
14. Samuel Taylor Coleridge, *Biographia Literaria*, 1.304; *The Friend*, 1.145.
15. Viola Meynell, *Alice Meynell: A Memoir*, 41.
16. *Epipsychidion by Percy Bysshe Shelley; a type fac-simile reprint of the original edition first published in 1821; with an introduction by the Rev. Stopford A. Brooke...and a note by Algernon Charles Swinburne*, xxix.
17. Shelley, *The Cenci*, 11.ii.92–96; *Shelley's Poetry and Prose*, ed. Neil Fraistat and Donald H. Reiman, 260.
18. Sigmund Freud, "Animism, Magic, and the Omnipotence of Thoughts," *Totem and Taboo, The Standard Edition of the Complete Psychological Works of Sigmund Frend (SE)* XIII: 83.
19. This is the view of psychologists Alison Gopnik and Andrew N. Meltzoff, who make a compelling case for seeing such theories in very young children – and in adults – as the result of a kind of category or domain mix-up, rather than neurosis. They argue that there is, even in ordinary adults, a wide range of ways in which people do things that involve the "overextension of the principles of psychological causality to complex objects." "The mistake in magical thinking is in selecting precisely the right domain to influence, and often, without higher level knowledge of the causal structures of domains" – that is, the knowledge of what parts of the universe can interact causally with what other parts, which young children lack – "the guess that psychological causality will apply is quite rational." Their examples (very adult ones) of such domain confusion: "if you can talk someone into a red-hot fury, why not talk them into a serious illness? If you can talk them into bed, why not talk them into becoming pregnant?" We might add, and if you can talk someone into a red-hot fury, why not think them into one? *Words, Thoughts, and Theories*, 141–2.
20. In *Imagining the King's Death*, John Barrell explores exhaustively the fate of the definition of "imagination" in the context of the trials for treason of British radicals in the 1790s. In these trials, a medieval English statute stating that it is treason "when a man doth compass or imagine the death of our lord the king" was put into play, the word "imagine" thus hotly contested in ways that both exceed yet, Barrell argues, undergird the literary and philosophical discussions of imagination from this era with which we are more familiar. At issue was whether "imagine" could mean not simply "picturing in the mind," but "intending," and/or a purely mental kind of doing. The nineteenth-century discussions of thinking of another as a form of harm may be viewed as a legacy of the political trauma at the end of the previous century. See also John Whale, *Imagination Under Pressure*.
21. Freud, "Formulations on the two principles of mental functioning," *SE*, XII: 221.

22. See Henri F. Ellenberger, *The Discovery of the Unconscious*; Maurice M. Tinterow, *Foundations of Hypnosis: From Mesmer to Freud*; Adam Crabtree, *From Mesmer to Freud: Magnetic Sleep and the Roots of Psychological Healin;* Alison Winter, *Mesmerized: Powers of Mind in Victorian Britain*; Roger Luckhurst, *The Invention of Telepathy*; Pamela Thurschwell, *Literature, Technology, and Magical Thinking 1880–1920*.

23. George Stocking, *Victorian Anthropology*, 188–96.

24. Nicola Brown, Carolyn Burdett, and Pamela Thurschwell, eds., *The Victorian Supernatural* (2004); Martin Willis and Catherine Wynne, *Victorian Literary Mesmerism* (2006).

25. Thomas Hardy, "The Withered Arm," *Collected Short Stories*, ed. F. B. Pinion, 60–62.

26. Andrew H. Miller, *The Burdens of Perfection: On Ethics and Reading in Nineteenth-Century British Literature*, 92–119; Elaine Hadley, "On a Darkling Plain: Victorian Liberalism and the Fantasy of Agency," 94. See also Amanda Anderson's emphasis on the Victorian cultivation of reflection in *The Powers of Distance: Cosmopolitanism and the Cultivation of Detachment*; and David Wayne Thomas, *Cultivating Victorians: Liberal Culture and the Aesthetic*.

27. Among recent scholars of Victorian liberal culture, Lauren Goodlad has most prominently discussed "the liberal ideal of mutual relations between autonomous actors," and "the intersubjective utopianism at the heart of prominent strains of liberal thinking," *Victorian Literature and the Victorian State: Character and Governance in a Liberal Society*, 23, 44.

28. John Stuart Mill, *On Liberty*, 15; emphasis mine.

29. *On Liberty*, 34; 35.

30. Daniel S. Malachuk, *Perfectionism, the State, and Victorian Liberalism*, 98.

31. Blackstone, *Commentaries*, Book IV, Chapter 2; quoted in Herbert Morris, "Punishment for Thoughts," *On Guilt and Innocence: Essays in Legal Philosophy and Moral Psychology*, 16.

32. This is Meir Dan-Cohen's summary of Morris; he correctly notes that after considering a wide variety of states of mind, Morris ends by narrowing thoughts to mean exclusively "intentions"; "Harmful Thoughts," 187.

33. Dan-Cohen, "Harmful Thoughts," 174. Subsequent references to this essay will be in parentheses.

34. W. E. Houghton, *The Victorian Frame of Mind*, 385ff; Andrew H. Miller, *The Burdens of Perfection*, 25 and *passim*.

35. Miller, *The Burdens of Perfection*, 92–119. The view that the formal features of the novel as a literary genre are designed to respond to the desire to know other minds underlies Dorrit Cohn's *Transparent Minds*, as well as cognitive approaches such as Alan Palmer, *Fictional Minds*, and Lisa Zunshine, *Why We Read Fiction*.

36. George Eliot, *Daniel Deronda*, 335.

37. The tradition of rendering skepticism about other minds a non-problem is associated with Wittgenstein, Gilbert Ryle, and J. L. Austin. Grounds for questioning the assumptions of skepticism about other minds has come not

only from philosophy but from more empirically oriented disciplines; see for example Alison Gopnik, "How we know our own minds: The illusion of first-person knowledge of intentionality" and Gopnik and Andrew N. Meltzoff, *Words, Thoughts and Theories*, 133. My aim is not to assert that Victorians didn't agonize about knowing other minds, but to explore and emphasize what can be learned by reading texts that seem to take a different stance. For an extremely useful account of Mill's grappling with other minds – which suggests that he was "the first philosopher properly to recognise the problem of other minds that arises from a 'relativity of knowledge' or Cartesian starting point" in his *Examination of Sir William Hamilton's Philosophy*, see Andy Hamilton, "Mill, Phenomenalism, and the Self," 160–72.

38. "Hard problem": David Chalmers, *The Conscious Mind: In Search of a Fundamental Theory*.
39. Edmund Gurney, Frederic W. H. Myers, and Frank Podmore, *Phantasms of the Living*, i.xxv; Shadworth Hodgson, *Time and Space*, 279–280.
40. See for example essays in *Does Consciousness Cause Behavior?*, ed. Susan Pocket, William P. Banks, and Shaun Gallagher.
41. The tradition of ethics following Emmanuel Levinas also addresses the topic of thinking about other people. Levinas stresses what he calls the subject's ideal "invocation" of the other, which is prior to thinking about him or her. "I call upon him. I do not just think that he is, I speak to him...nor does expression consist in *articulating* the understanding I already have... It consists, prior to any participation in a common content through understanding, in instituting sociality through a relationship that is, consequently, irreducible to understanding." "Is Ontology Fundamental?", *Entre Nous: On Thinking-Of-the Other*, 7–8. In this view, as Zygmunt Bauman comments, when the self realizes that "I am already *thinking*" (91), the incredibly precarious "moral party" of two is already over (*Postmodern Ethics*, 91). I find this body of work to be excessively phobic about thinking about another person.
42. Rei Terada, "Thinking for Oneself: Realism and Defiance in Arendt."
43. Hannah Arendt, "Thinking and Moral Considerations," 189. Subsequent references to this essay in this paragraph will be in parentheses. Much of the material in this essay was later incorporated into a series of lectures and a book which Arendt left unfinished at her death: *The Life of the Mind: Part I: Thinking*.
44. Terada, "Thinking for Oneself," 840.
45. Patricia Greenspan, *Practical Guilt*.
46. Javier Marias, *All Souls*, trans. Margaret Jull Costa, 63–64.
47. Coleridge, December 27, 1804, *Notebooks*, II: 2382.
48. On the waxing and waning of what counts as "thinking," see Susan James' account of how capacious was Descartes' conception of thinking, including emotion: *Passion and Action: The Emotions in Seventeenth-Century Philosophy*, 87–94. Recent scholarship on Victorian literature and psychology has paid particular attention to the role of specific forms of mental action in Victorian understandings of the mind, focusing on, for example, specific interest in

the period in habitual or automatic mental action, reverie, and memory. On habit, see Athena Vrettos, "Defining Habits"; on intuitive, non-deliberative modes of thought, see Vanessa Ryan, "Fictions of Medical Minds"; on reverie, see Nicholas Dames, "Reverie, Sensation, Effect"; on memory, see Vrettos, "Displaced Memory in Victorian Fiction and Psychology"; Sally Shuttleworth, "The 'Malady of Thought'"; Jill L. Matus, "Victorian Framings of the Mind."

49. Herbert Mayo, *Popular Superstitions and the Truth Contained Therein, with an Account of Mesmerism*, 3rd ed., 203.

50. Herbert Mayo, *On the Truths Contained in Popular Superstitions*, 190.

51. In his excellent discussion of the "display of thinking" in Victorian culture, Andrew H. Miller focuses on a distinctly defined strain of thinking about thinking: casuistry. *The Burdens of Perfection*, esp. 92–119. Sharon Cameron's *Thinking in Henry James* remains a remarkable rethinking of thinking in literature. Cameron reframes the discussion of the representation of consciousness in the novels of Henry James away from an emphasis on the contents of fictional minds and toward an understanding of how consciousness serves as medium of social relations – especially as an instrument of social power. "Thinking" is thus defined in terms of a Husserlian understanding of consciousness. Angus Fletcher's *Colors of the Mind: Conjectures on Thinking in Literature* is a wide-ranging study of the representation of thought in European literature.

52. Locke, *An Essay Concerning Human Understanding*, ed. P. H. Nidditch, 115; 335. Recent scholarship on Victorian psychology has amply explored debates about the definitions of consciousness, and unconsciousness, in nineteenth-century Britain: see Rick Rylance, *Victorian Psychology and British Culture 1850–1880*; Sally Shuttleworth and Jenny Bourne Taylor, *Embodied Selves*, 67–72; Taylor, "Obscure Recesses: Locating the Victorian Unconscious"; Jill L. Matus, "Victorian Framings of the Mind." My preference for *thinking* over *consciousness* stems as well from a desire to step back from an intellectual environment – our own – in which many academic disciplines are coming under the influence of the study of consciousness and cognition from the brain sciences. For a balanced meditation on possible relations among cognitive studies, philosophy of mind, and the study of the novel see Jonathan Kramnick, "Empiricism, Cognitive Science, and the Novel," 263–85.

1   THINKING AS ACTION

1. Daniel N. Robinson, *An Intellectual History of Psychology*; L. S. Hearnshaw, *A Short History of British Psychology 1840–1940*, Chapters 1–11; Rick Rylance, *Victorian Psychology and British Culture 1850–1880*; Graham Richards, *Mental Machinery: The Origins and Consequences of Psychological Ideas: Part I: 1600–1850*; Richards, *Putting Psychology in its Place: A Critical Historical Overview*; Nikolas Rose, *The Psychological Complex: Psychology, Politics, and Society in England, 1869–1939*; Kurt Danziger, *Naming the Mind: How Psychology Found*

its Language; William R. Woodward and Mitchell G. Ash, eds., *The Problematic Science: Psychology in Nineteenth-Century Thought* (1982); Edward Clarke and L. S. Jacyna, *Nineteenth-Century Origins of Neuroscientific Concepts*; Robert M. Young, *Mind, Brain, and Adaptation in the Nineteenth Century*; Kurt Danziger, "Mid-Nineteenth-Century British Psycho-Physiology: A Neglected Chapter in the History of Psychology"; Alan Richardson, *British Romanticism and the Science of the Mind*.

2. James Mark Baldwin, ed., *Dictionary of Philosophy and Psychology; including many of the principle conceptions of ethics, logic, aesthetics, philosophy of religion, mental pathology, anthropology, biology, neurology, physiology, economics, political and social philosophy, philology, physical science, and education* (1901–5), i: x.

3. "Psychical Research," *Dictionary of Philosophy and Psychology*, ii: 378.

4. James McCosh, *The Scottish Philosophy, Biographical, Expository, Critical, from Hutcheson to Hamilton*; Andrew Seth, *Scottish Philosophy*; George Davie, *The Scotch Metaphysics: A Century of Enlightenment in Scotland*; and Gordon Graham, "The Nineteenth-Century Aftermath."

5. William Hamilton, "Philosophy and Perception: Reid and Brown," *Edinburgh Review* 52 (1830): 158–207. On the prestige of psychology and its flourishing in criticism and in the poetry of Browning and Tennyson in the 1830s, see Isobel Armstrong, *Victorian Poetry: Poetry, Poetics, Politics*; and Ekbert Faas, *Retreat into Mind: Victorian Poetry and the Rise of Psychiatry*, 19–62.

6. George Davie, *The Scotch Metaphysics*, 3.

7. "Testimonial of J. F. Ferrier" (1852), *The Works of Thomas De Quincey*, 17: 254.

8. John Tulloch, "Professor Ferrier and the Higher Philosophy," *Modern Theories in Philosophy and Religion*, 358.

9. Elizabeth Haldane, *James Frederick Ferrier* in the *Famous Scots Series*, 1899; Arthur Thomson, *Ferrier of St. Andrews: An Academic Tragedy*, 1985; John Haldane, "Introduction," *The Philosophical Works of James Frederick Ferrier*, iii: xiii–xvi. A brief discussion of the relevance of Ferrier's writing to nineteenth-century poetry, particularly Tennyson's, can be found in W. David Shaw, *The Lucid Veil: Poetic Truth in the Victorian Age*, 48–53; Isobel Armstrong connects Ferrier's *Introduction to the Philosophy of Consciousness* to Tennyson's critique of sensation in "The Lotos-Eaters," *Victorian Poetry: Poetry, Poetics, and Politics*, 92–93. Ferrier's text makes a brief appearance in Matthew Campbell, *Rhythm and Will in Victorian Poetry*, 69–71, and Ekbert Faas, *Retreat into Mind*, 71–73.

10. James Frederick Ferrier, "The Poems of Coventry Patmore," *Blackwood's Edinburgh Magazine* 56 (1844): 331–42. The Tennyson anecdote is recounted in Elizabeth Haldane, *James Frederick Ferrier*, 58.

11. E. L. Lushington, "Introductory Notice," James Frederick Ferrier, *Lectures on Greek Philosophy* (1866), *Philosophical Works*, ii: xiv.

12. Thomson, *Ferrier of St. Andrews: An Academic Tragedy*; George Davie, *The Democratic Intellect: Scotland and her Universities in the Nineteenth Century*, 255–338.

13. "Testimonial of J. F. Ferrier" (1852), *The Works of Thomas De Quincey*, 17: 251. Subsequent references in parentheses.
14. Grevel Lindop, *The Opium Eater: A Life of Thomas De Quincey*, 165.
15. Alexander Campbell Fraser, "The Philosophical Life of Professor Ferrier," 194.
16. "A Review of a Philosophical Paper by Mr. Ferrier," *The Works of Thomas De Quincey*, 20: 296–97.
17. J. H. Alexander, *"Blackwood's Magazine* as a Romantic Form," 65; Leith David, Ian Duncan, and Janet Sorensen, "Introduction," *Scotland and the Borders of Romanticism*, 1–19; David Finkelstein, ed., *Print Culture and the Blackwood's Tradition* (2006).
18. *Blackwood's Edinburgh Magazine* 14 (1823), 495, emphasis in original; cited by J. H. Alexander, *"Blackwood's Magazine* as a Romantic Form," 66.
19. Fraser, "The Philosophical Life of Professor Ferrier," 194. On Ferrier as a man of fashion see Elizabeth Haldane, *James Frederick Ferrier.*
20. Thomas Brown, *Lectures on the Philosophy of the Human Mind*, 16th ed., 1: 90–91.
21. James Frederick Ferrier, *An Introduction to the Philosophy of Consciousness, Philosophical Works*, iii.29. All subsequent references will be in parentheses and will be to page number only.
22. John Tulloch, "Professor Ferrier and the Higher Philosophy," 358.
23. J. F. Ferrier, "Preface," *Noctes Ambrosianae* (1855), xii, xix.
24. Studies of the poetics of person-making in the *Noctes Ambrosianae* include Peter T. Murphy, "Impersonation and Authorship in Romantic Britain"; and Nicola Z. Trott, "North of the Border: Cultural Crossing in the *Noctes Ambrosianae.*"
25. Thomas Reid, *Essays on the Intellectual Powers of Man* (1785), 10.
26. Bertrand Russell, *A History of Western Philosophy*, 567. See also some of the essays in *Who Comes After the Subject?*, ed. Eduardo Cadava, Peter Connor, and Jean-Luc Nancy (1991); and for a reading of recent readings of Descartes, Rei Terada, *Feeling in Theory: Emotion after the "Death of the Subject,"* 22–31. On British romantic fictionalizations of Descartes' *cogito*, see Daniel Cottom, "I Think, Therefore I am Heathcliff."
27. Coleridge, *Biographia Literaria*, 1: 157–58.
28. J. G. Fichte, *An Attempt at a New Presentation of the Wissenschaftslehre* (1797/98), *Introductions of the Wissenschaftslehre and Other Writings (1797–1800)*, 108.
29. Andrew Bowie, *Aesthetics and Subjectivity: Kant to Nietzsche*, 58–67; George J. Seidel, *Fichte's Wissenschaftslehre of 1794: A Commentary on Part I*; Frederick C. Beiser, *German Idealism: the Struggle against Subjectivism, 1781–1801.*
30. J. F. Ferrier, "Introduction to the Philosophy of Consciousness," *Blackwood's Edinburgh Magazine* (August 1838), 144.
31. Laurence R. Horn, *A Natural History of Negation*, esp. 90–95.
32. Ferrier, "Introduction to the Philosophy of Consciousness," 244. This passage was silently cut from the posthumous *Philosophical Works.*

33. Wordsworth, *The Prelude (1805)*, VII: 612–619; Freud, "Negation," *SE*, 19: 236: "A negative judgment is the intellectual substitute for repression; its 'no' is the hall-mark of repression, a certificate of origin – like, let us say, 'Made in Germany'."

34. Thomas Carlyle, *Heroes and Hero-Worship*, 142.

35. Adam Smith, *The Theory of Moral Sentiments*, 9.

36. On the decline of the Scottish Enlightenment in the 1830s, see Anand Chitnis, *The Scottish Enlightenment: A Social History*, 238–46; Jerome Schneewind, *Sidgwick's Ethics and Victorian Moral Philosophy*, 63–88; and Gordon Graham, "The Nineteenth-Century Aftermath." On Scottish Enlightenment theories of society and ethics, see Christopher J. Berry, *Social Theory of the Scottish Enlightenment*, 23–47.

37. F. H. Bradley, *Ethical Studies* (1876); T. H. Green, *Prolegomena to Ethics* (1882); A. J. M. Milne, *The Social Philosophy of English Idealism*, 87–99.

38. Baldwin, *Dictionary of Philosophy and Psychology*, VII: 437.

39. Baldwin, VII: 60. In the 1830s and 1840s, the potential for connections among mesmerism, optics, photography, and philosophy were alive in many minds. Sir David Brewster was also the author of the popular *Letters on Natural Magic* (1832), which enthusiastically affirmed the powers of the human mind to produce effects that earlier, unenlightened ages had taken for either fraud or magic. Like many scientists, Brewster was highly interested in mesmerism. In a trip to London in 1851 (on which he was accompanied by Ferrier), he attended a "mesmeric séance" where, he wrote, "I saw things that confounded me" (*The Home Life of Sir David Brewster by his Daughter, Mrs. Gordon* [Edinburgh, 1881], 142).

40. Rev. Chauncy Hare Townshend, *Facts in Mesmerism, with Reasons for a Dispassionate Inquiry Into It* (1840), 409–540.

41. Alexander Campbell Fraser cited in Elizabeth Haldane, *James Frederick Ferrier*, 64–65.

42. Thomson, *Ferrier of St. Andrews*, 46; Alexander Macewen, *Life and Letters of John Cairns*, 92.

43. Thomas De Quincey, "Animal Magnetism," *Tait's Edinburgh Magazine* 4 (1834), 473.

44. The record of Ferrier's experiences with mesmerism in his writing is hard to parse. In the *Introduction to the Philosophy of Consciousness,* the matter comes up as a "miracle" that is nothing compared to the miracles of ordinary consciousness. He addresses the fans of mesmerism, mesmeric sleep or somnambulism (as the trance-like state into which mesmeric subjects were cast was called) and other paranormal phenomena: "Ye admirers of somnambulism, and other depraved and anomalous conditions of humanity! ye worshippers at the shrine of a morbid and deluded wonder! ye seers of marvels where there are none, and ye blind men to the miracles which really are! tell us no more of powers put forth, and processes *unconsciously* carried on within the dreaming soul, as if these were one-millionth part so extraordinary and inexplicable as even the simplest conscious ongoings of our waking life" (89). More provocatively,

Ferrier seems to have been the author of a "Postscript" – officially credited to John Wilson – to an article in *Blackwood's*, "What Is Mesmerism?" While the article is cautiously credulous, the "Postscript" is dismissive (*Blackwood's* 70 (1851), 83–85. A letter from Ferrier to Wilson asking for strict anonymity for the "Postscript" can be read as suggesting that the "Postscript" was above all designed to goad friends rather than to express Ferrier's own views. The letter expresses a desire to have the opportunity to hear the "Postscript" "well black-guardized by my mesmeric friends Colquhoun and Sir William Hamilton before telling them I wrote it." (Letters transcribed in The Papers of Arthur Thomson, MS. Box 38087; quoted courtesy of the University of St. Andrews Library). Ferrier's Victorian biographer, Elizabeth Haldane, suggests that Ferrier wrote elsewhere, and approvingly, on mesmerism in *Blackwood's* but no other articles on the subject can be definitively attributed to him (Haldane, *James Frederick Ferrier*, 66).

45. Winter, *Mesmerized*, 55–56. Studies of the impact of mesmerism on nineteenth-century British literature include Fred Kaplan, *Dickens and Mesmerism: The Hidden Spring of Fiction*; Sarah A. Wilburn, *Possessed Victorians: Extra Spheres in Nineteenth-Century Mystical Writings*; Martin Willis and Catherine Wynne, eds., *Victorian Literary Mesmerism*.
46. J. C. Colquhoun, *Isis Revelata*, 1: 43. Subsequent references in parentheses.
47. Townshend, *Facts in Mesmerism*, 312.
48. Compare Winter on "how mesmerism and its associated practices could become tools for modeling the nature of human interaction and social power…in certain circumstances mesmeric experiments had a significant impact on how people formulated claims about the nature of influence," *Mesmerized*, 5, 8.
49. "What Is Mesmerism?" [attributed to John Eagles], *Blackwood's* 70 (1851), 82.

2 FOAM, AURA, OR MELODY

1. Lisa Gitelman, *Scripts, Grooves, and Writing Machines: Representing Technology in the Edison Era*, 5.
2. Crucial texts include Herbert Spencer, *Principles of Psychology* (1855); Alexander Bain, *Mind and Body* (1873); G. H. Lewes, *The Physical Basis of Mind* (1877); William Benjamin Carpenter, *Principles of Mental Physiology* (1874); Henry Maudsley, *Body and Mind* (1873). On the emphasis on mental physiology and materialist approaches to mind in literary-critical approaches to nineteenth-century mental sciences, see for example Catherine Gallagher, *The Body Economic: Life, Death, and Sensation in Political Economy and the Victorian Novel*; Sally Shuttleworth and Jenny Bourne Taylor, eds., *Embodied Selves: An Anthology of Psychological Texts 1830–1890*.
3. In *Mesmerized: Powers of Mind in Victorian Britain*, Alison Winter makes a compelling argument for the value of studying what may appear to be fringe, disreputable, or discredited strands of the period's ideas about psychological and philosophical issues, not the least of which is that it crucial not to pre-judge which ideas were in the center and which were on the fringe, as the

border shifted radically. She points out that popular accounts of mesmerism may have had significantly more influence on how mid-Victorians were theorizing the mind than did Mill or Bain (136). Lucy Hartley similarly argues for the complexity of what did or did not count as "science" in the development of nineteenth-century approaches to mind in *Physiognomy and the Meaning of Expression in Nineteenth-Century Culture*, esp. 6–12.

4. S. T. Coleridge, March 17, 1801, *Notebooks*, I: 923.
5. H. G. Atkinson, quoted in "Appendix" to Charles Bray, *On Force, Its Mental and Moral Correlates; and On That Which Is Supposed to Underlie All Phenomenal: With Speculations on Spiritualism, and Other Abnormal Conditions of Mind* (1866), 152, 156; Dr. Herbert Mayo, *On the Truths Contained in Popular Superstitions* (1851): 190–91.
6. Dr. Charles Ede, quoted in William F. Barrett, "First Report on Thought-Reading," *Proceedings of the Society for Psychical Research* (1882), I: 32.
7. Crosbie Smith, *The Science of Energy: A Cultural History of Energy Physics in Victorian Britain*, 9; Mary B. Hesse, *Forces and Fields: The Concept of Action at a Distance in the History of Physics*, esp. 290–302; James Clerk Maxwell, "On Action at a Distance" (1876), *The Scientific Papers of James Clerk Maxwell*, II: 311–27.
8. Roger Luckhurst, *The Invention of Telepathy, 1870–1901*, 86.
9. Balfour Stewart and P. G. Tait, *The Unseen Universe; or Physical Speculations on a Future State*, 4th ed. (1876), 145.
10. On Charles Bray's life and his relationship with George Eliot, see Frederick R. Karl, *George Eliot: Voice of a Century*, 66–75; and Diana Postlethwaite, *Making it Whole*, 133–40. While Bray is often seen as Eliot's early "mentor," the influence went both ways; see Bray's use of *Adam Bede* in *On Force*, 105–6.
11. Charles Bray, *On Force, Its Mental and Moral Correlates; and On That With [which?] Is Supposed to Underlie All Phenomena: With Speculations on Spiritualism, and Other Abnormal Conditions of Mind* (1866), 5.
12. "Illusion and Delusion: The Writings of C. Bray," *Westminster Review* (January/April 1879), 235.
13. Bray, *On Force*, 86, 87.
14. J. S. Mill, *Three Essays on Religion* (1874), 147; emphasis mine. On G. H. Lewes and Herbert Spencer on force, see Postlethwaite, *Making it Whole*, 216–17.
15. Bray, *On Force*, 79.
16. See "Illusion and Delusion," and also Bray's own account of G. H. Lewes' "misunderstanding" of his work in *Phases of Opinion and Experience During a Long Life: An Autobiography*, 188.
17. "Illusion and Delusion," 234.
18. William F. Barrett, *On The Threshold of the Unseen*, 110.
19. Frank M. Turner, *The Greek Heritage in Victorian Britain*, 372.
20. Benjamin Jowett, quoted in Turner, 418.
21. Barrett, *On the Threshold of the Unseen*, 111; Stewart and Tait, *The Unseen Universe*, 90.

22. May Sinclair, *A Defence of Idealism* (1917), 263. See also Suzanne Raitt, *May Sinclair: A Modern Victorian*, 115; and Roger Luckhurst, *The Invention of Telepathy*, 261.
23. Walter Pater, "The Genius of Plato," *Plato and Platonism* [1893], 129.
24. Havelock Ellis on Hinton and Whitman: "Hinton's Later Thought," *Mind* (July 1884), 404; see also Ellis on Hinton and Shelley: "Preface" to Mrs. Havelock Ellis, *James Hinton: A Sketch*, xi. Comparisons to Shelley and to Coleridge were frequent. Hinton's manuscripts published posthumously by his circle include *Chapters on the Art of Thinking*, ed. C. H. Hinton, with an introduction by Shadworth Hodgson (1879); *The Law-Breaker and the Coming of the Law*, ed. Margaret Hinton (1884); *Philosophy and Religion: Selections from the Manuscripts of the Late James Hinton*, ed. Caroline Haddon (1881). Studies of Hinton by some of the same include Caroline Haddon, *The Larger Life: Studies in Hinton's Ethics* (1886); Ellice Hopkins, *Life and Letters of James Hinton* (1878; 8th ed. 1906); Mrs. Havelock Ellis [Edith Lees], *Three Modern Seers: James Hinton–Nietzsche–Edward Carpenter* (1910). As Seth Koven remarks, Hinton is, despite his considerable influence, practically invisible in contemporary scholarship, a notable exception being Koven's treatment of Hinton in *Slumming: Sexual and Social Politics in Victorian London*, 14–18. See also Willard Wolfe, *From Radicalism to Socialism: Men and Ideas in the Formation of Fabian Socialist Doctrines, 1881–1889*, 305–306; Stefan Collini, *Public Moralists*, 61; Phyllis Grosskurth, *Havelock Ellis: A Biography*, esp. 52–54.
25. On the scandal surrounding the sexual practices and views of Hinton's devotees, see Grosskurth, 98–104. On Hinton and Victorian "altruism," see Collini, "The Culture of Altruism," *Public Moralists*, 60–90.
26. James Hinton, "Preface" to *Philosophy and Religion*, xiii. On the revival of interest in panpsychism in contemporary philosophy, see David Skrbina, *Panpsychism in the West*; Galen Strawson *et al.*, *Consciousness and its Place in Nature*.
27. Haddon, *The Larger Life*, 21.
28. James Hinton, "On the Analogy Between the Organic and the Mental Life," *Chapters on the Art of Thinking*, 36.
29. Mary Everest Boole, quoted by Mrs. Havelock Ellis, *James Hinton: A Sketch*, 6, 7.
30. Ellice Hopkins, *Life and Letters*, 249; Caroline Haddon quoted in Mrs. Havelock Ellis, *James Hinton*, 33.
31. Hinton, *Chapters on the Art of Thinking*, 73
32. James Hinton, *The Life and Letters of James Hinton*, 130.
33. Quoted in Havelock Ellis, "Hinton's Later Thought," 397.
34. See also "Mental Physiology" and "The Art of Thinking," in Hinton's *Essays in Philosophy and Religion*, 100–162.
35. Koven, *Slumming*, 14–18.
36. Joy Dixon, *Divine Feminine: Theosophy and Feminism in England*; Marlene Tromp, *Altered States: Sex, Nation, Drugs, and Self-Transformation in*

Victorian Spiritualism; Alex Owen, *The Darkened Room: Women, Power and Spiritualism in Late Nineteenth-Century England.*

37. Annie Besant, *Thought Power: Its Control and Culture* (1900; 1918), 66, 41–42. Further references will be to this edition. Many thanks to Suzy Anger for bringing this book to my attention.

38. May Sinclair, *A Defence of Idealism*, vi.

39. For biographical information on Boole, see E. M. Cobham, *Mary Everest Boole: A Memoir with some Letters.* On C. H. Hinton's arrest for bigamy and its role in the scandal surrounding James Hinton and his followers, see Phyllis Grosskurth, *Havelock Ellis,* 101–103. A letter attesting to Hinton's character from the Oxford Platonist Benjamin Jowett led to a reduced sentence of three days in prison; afterwards Hinton, along with Mary Boole, emigrated first to Japan and then to America. C. H. Hinton (1853–1907) is the theorist of the "fourth dimension" of space – which, for example, in *A New Era of Thought* (1888) (edited by another Boole daughter, Alicia Boole) offers mathematical geometry as a means to access, among other things, better ways of under-standing human relations. "Our apparent isolation as bodies from each other is by no means so necessary to assume as it would appear" (*A New Era of Thought,* 67).

40. Mary Everest Boole, *Suggestions for Increasing Ethical Stability*, 12, 39.

41. Mary Everest Boole, *The Message of Psychic Science to the World*, 132ff.

42. Boole, *Suggestions*, 23.

43. Besant, *Thought Power*, 94

44. *Proceedings of the Society for Psychical Research*, I (1882), 3; Edmund Gurney, Frederic W. H. Myers, and Frank Podmore, *Phantasms of the Living* (1886), I: xxxv.

45. *Phantasms,* I: 112.

46. *Phantasms,* II: 176, 307.

47. *Phantasms,* I: 93.

48. *Proceedings of the Society for Psychical Research*, I:31.

49. Cf. Myers' posthumous *Human Personality and its Survival of Bodily Death,* I: 33.

50. *Phantasms,* I: 230–31

51. *Phantasms,* II: 302

52. Janet Oppenheim, *The Other World: Spiritualism and Psychical Research in England, 1850–1914*; Pamela Thurschwell, *Literature, Technology, and Magical Thinking 1880–1920*; Roger Luckhurst, *The Invention of Telepathy, 1870–1901*; Alex Owen, *The Place of Enchantment: British Occultism and the Culture of the Modern.*

53. Myers and Podmore, *Phantasms,* I: 11

54. See, in addition to above, Lisa Brocklebank's "Psychic Reading," 233–39.

55. John Durham Peters, *Speaking into the Air: A History of the Idea of Communication*, 8. For Peters' discussion of Myers, telepathy, the Society for Psychical Research, and the role of nineteenth-century spiritualism in the development of the modern idea of communication, see 5–9, 89–108.

56. William James to Henry James, October 20, 1890, *The Correspondence of William James*, II: 153. This remark is also quoted by Luckhurst, 20.
57. William James, *Principles of Psychology*, I: 129. For a fascinating account of the extraordinary salience of epiphenomenalism as a fad idea in Victorian popular culture, see Suzy Anger, "Are We Not Automata? The Mind–Body Problem in Late Victorian Literature."
58. Foam on a wave: Shadworth Hodgson, *Time and Space* (1865), 279; steam whistle: T. H. Huxley, "On the Hypothesis that Animals are Automata and its History" (1879), in *Method and Results* (1896), 240; melody: Hodgson, *Time and Space*, 278–80; shadow: William James, "Are We Automata?", *Mind* 13 (1879), 1.
59. Huxley, 240.
60. Hodgson, *Time and Space*, 279, 280.
61. Victor Caston, "Epiphenomenalisms, Ancient and Modern," 309–63.
62. Neuroscientist Ian Glynn treats Hodgson as a crude precursor in *An Anatomy of Thought: the Origin and Machinery of the Mind*, 8–10. See also *Does Consciousness Cause Behavior?*, ed. Susan Pockett, William P. Banks, and Shaun Gallagher (2006), 109.
63. Mosaic: *The Theory of Practice* (1870), I: 336; piano: *Time and Space*, 278.
64. The greatest wealth of materials can be found in *The Correspondence of William James*. Other contemporary reminiscences can be found in the letters of Leslie Stephen, who called Hodgson "the kindest, most simple of human beings & one of the most bewildering of philosophers" (letter to Charles Eliot Norton, December 25, 1882, in *Selected Letters of Leslie Stephen*, II: 295); and in James Sully, *My Life and Friends*, 252–53. Hodgson, along with Stephen and Sully, was a member of the London walking club, the Sunday Tramps, as well as of the small subset of Tramps, the "Scratch 8," who met regularly to discuss philosophical issues. The connection between Hodgson's philosophy and Bergson's was made as early as 1912 in H. Wildon Carr's obituary essay, "Shadworth Hollway Hodgson," *Mind* 84 (1912), 485. See also John L. Carafides, *The Philosophy of Reflection: An Examination of Shadworth H. Hodgson's Treatment of Experience*; Stuart F. Spicker, "Shadworth Hodgson's Reduction as an Anticipation of Husserl's Phenomenological Psychology," 57–73; Andrew J. Reck, "Hodgson's Metaphysics of Experience," 29–47.
65. Hodgson, letter to William James, April 8, 1887; also cited in John Beer, *Post-Romantic Consciousness: Dickens to Plath*, 53.
66. Hodgson notes his relation to De Quincey in "On the Genius of Thomas De Quincey" in *Outcast Essays*, reprinted in James Hogg, ed., *De Quincey and His Friends*, 316.
67. Hodgson, *Time and Space*, 279.
68. The error of taking Hodgson's images in *Time and Space* as representing his actual beliefs (which they did not, as yet) begins at least with William James ("Are We Automata?" [1879], 1), and persists to the present day. The only other writer who seems to have noticed this error is C. J. Ducasse, in *A Critical Examination of the Belief in A Life After Death*, 77.

69. Huxley, "On the Hypothesis that Animals are Automata," 244. Suzy Anger interprets Huxley's position as ultimately close to the one I assign to Hodgson; "Are We Not Automata?"
70. Hodgson, *The Philosophy of Reflection*, II: 23.
71. Carr, "Shadworth Hollway Hodgson," 32.
72. Hodgson, *The Philosophy of Reflection*, II: 65.
73. See Lorraine J. Daston, "British Responses to Psycho-Physiology, 1860–1900."
74. See for example Hodgson's comments on this topic in his "Introduction" to James Hinton's posthumous *Chapters on the Art of Thinking*: "the *emotional* nature of man must bear an equal part with his intellectual nature in determining his philosophical creed"; "Until…the emotions, those inner sensations which are the key to the character of nature as a whole, are given their due weight and place in philosophy, philosophy cannot be at unity with itself" (5, 6).
75. See the continuation of the letter to William James (on "the Mind"), quoted above: "and we are now having many prejudices….dispelled; and being forced to see that there are more things in heaving and earth, Horatio, &; chiefly by the labours, the pertinacity, of the Psychical Researchers, & and among them foremost perhaps our own friend Ed. Gurney" (quoted in J. Beer, *Post-Romantic Consciousness*, 53). The shelf-lists of Hodgson's library, now at Corpus Christi College, Oxford, reveal an extensive collection of books on psychical research and occult topics. Shadworth Hodgson is sometimes confused with *Richard* Hodgson, the SPR's Australian-born ghost-buster; he was no relation.
76. Roger Fry quoted by Virginia Woolf, *Roger Fry: A Biography*, 87.
77. *The Philosophy of Reflection*, I: 18.
78. John Beer, "Coleridge's Elusive Presence among the Victorians," 147–68.
79. On epiphenomenal consciousness as inert yet having a life of its own: William James caricatured the epiphenomenalist view of conscious life as something akin to the zombie seaman in "The Rime of the Ancient Mariner": "inert, uninfluential, a simple passenger in the voyage of life, it is allowed to remain on board, but not touch the helm or handle the rigging" ("Are We Automata?", 1).
80. He continues: "Do they still appear as truth, or have they donned a semblance of jest or dreaming?" (*The Philosophy of Reflection*, I: 22).
81. Swinburne, "A Song in a Time of Order. 1852," *Poems and Ballads* (1866), 4–8.
82. Thomas Hardy to J. M. E. McTaggart, May 23, 1906, *Collected Letters of Thomas Hardy*, III: 207. On McTaggart and Thomas Hardy, see Martin Seymour-Smith, *Thomas Hardy*, 336, 442, 444.
83. F. H. Bradley, *Ethical Studies*; T. H. Green, *Prolegomena to Ethics*. See A. J. M. Milne, *The Social Philosophy of English Idealism*, 87–99.
84. C. D. Broad, *John McTaggart Ellis McTaggart, 1866–1925*, 16.
85. J. M. E. McTaggart, note to "The Further Determination of the Absolute," (1893), in *Philosophical Studies*, 210.
86. J. M. E. McTaggart, "The Further Determination of the Absolute," *Philosophical Studies*, 215.

87. McTaggart, *The Nature of Existence, Volume II*, ed. C. D. Broad (1927), 148; C. D. Broad, *John McTaggart Ellis McTaggart*, 20.
88. McTaggart, "Determination of the Absolute," 266, 279.
89. Compare for example the place of love in the work of the seventeenth-century Cambridge Platonists: see Susan James, *Passion and Action*, 225–52.
90. McTaggart, "Determination of the Absolute," 266.
91. Cf. W. J. Mander on this "strange combination" in *The Nature of Existence*, its "potent mixture of detailed logic and deep passion," *Anglo-American Idealism, 1865–1927*, 13.
92. C. D. Broad, *John McTaggart Ellis McTaggart*, 14.
93. McTaggart, *The Nature of Existence* II: 146; emphasis mine.
94. P. T. Geach, *Truth, Love and Immortality: An Introduction to McTaggart's Philosophy*, 112–13.

3   THINKING IN THE SECOND PERSON IN NINETEENTH-CENTURY POETRY

1. G. W. F. Hegel, *Aesthetics: Lectures on Art*, II: 974–76.
2. *Epipsychidion by Percy Bysshe Shelley; a type fac-simile reprint of the original edition first published in 1821; with an introduction by the Rev. Stopford A. Brooke… and a note by Algernon Charles Swinburne*, xxix.
3. Simon Jarvis, *Wordsworth's Philosophic Song*, 4. See also Jarvis, "Prosody as Cognition," 3–15; and Jarvis, "Thinking in Verse." Cf. Oren Izenberg: "poetry is an extraordinary kind of thinking," "Poems Out of Our Heads," 217; Yopie Prins on nineteenth-century American poet Sidney Lanier's ambition "to make prosody itself into a form of thinking," "Historical Poetics, Dysprosody, and the Science of English Verse," 233; Jennie Jackson, "Thinking Emily Dickinson Thinking Poetry"; Jed Deppman, "Trying to Think with Emily Dickinson." John Schad's monograph on Arthur Hugh Clough seeks to explain the peculiarities (the alleged thinness) of Clough's verse as a symptom of that Victorian poet's obsession with thoughts at the expense of words: "words, for Clough, are merely the rubbish left over after the main event that is thinking"; *Arthur Hugh Clough*, 1. The most ambitious discussion is Stathis Gourgouris, *Does Literature Think? Literature as Theory for an Antimythical Era*, which poses "literature" as engaged in forms of thinking that exceed and resist what gets to count as thinking in "philosophy," understood as the project of western enlightenment. While it would be out of place here to seek to engage with the larger claims of this book – or to ponder extensively what Gourgouris is up to by seemingly personifying "Literature" as an entity that can or cannot think – his book provides a provocative framework for some of this work.
4. In the dramatic monologue, of course, second-person address most often is designed as a representation of speech. There are, however, a number of nineteenth-century dramatic monologues which interestingly trouble the expectation that an address to a "you" is spoken: for example, D. G. Rossetti's "Jenny," which unfolds as an unspoken mental address to a sleeping "you."

5. After at least a century of seeing the pronoun "I" as the essence of lyric poetry, the study of lyric has, in the past few decades, entered into a rich conversation about the ways in which the pronoun "you" is central to modern (romantic and post-romantic) lyric. Most of this conversation has focused on "apostrophe," and my own thinking on the poetic second person would be impossible without Jonathan Culler's ground-breaking essay, "Apostrophe." Critical responses to Culler include Alan Richardson's excellent "Apostrophe in Life and in Romantic Art: Everyday Discourse, Overhearing, and Poetic Address," which argues for broadening the category: that apostrophes and addresses are features not simply of poetic but ordinary forms of discourse, and urges an approach that focuses on the continuum between "natural" and heightened uses of such figures; and J. Douglas Kneale, "Romantic Aversions: Apostrophe Reconsidered," which argues for narrowing "apostrophe" more in line with its meaning in classical rhetoric – not any second-person poetic address, but a "turning away" from one object of address to another; and Michael Macovski's Bahktinian approach, *Dialogue and Literature: Apostrophe, Auditors, and the Collapse of Romantic Discourse*. I am also indebted to William Waters' *Poetry's Touch: On Lyric Address*, which focuses on the complexities of second-person addresses to real persons in modern poetry; and to provocative comments on apostrophe as an optimistic space of imagined proximity in Lauren Berlant's "Cruel Optimism." Related to this discussion as well are Anne-Lise François' extremely provocative comments on Thomas Hardy's mode of "inconsequential" address – addresses that are barely addresses – in his poems to his deceased wife, *Poems of 1912–13*. See François, *Open Secrets*, 180–94. Above all, as will become clear as we move forward, I am most indebted to Virginia Jackson's *Dickinson's Misery: A Theory of Lyric Reading*, especially pp. 118–65, "Dickinson's Figure of Address." Jackson is virtually alone, amid all the discussions above, in her insistence on treating poetic "you"s in the contexts of their material forms as forms of writing – forms which, in Dickinson's corpus, where the differences between a "letter" and a "poem" are both crucial, and ambiguous, are always highly specific. Finally, on terminology: as will also become clear as we move forward, I do believe it makes sense to distinguish apostrophes – dramatic rhetorical figures in which a poetic speaker turns to address an often imaginary, inanimate, or inaccessible being – from poetic "you"s in general, and will largely use the term "address."

6. Dallas is best known to modern readers as the author of several highly perceptive reviews of George Eliot's novels, and his second attempt at literary theory, *The Gay Science* (1866), has gained more attention, and is generally thought to be superior to *Poetics*. See Jenny Bourne Taylor, "The Gay Science: The 'Hidden Soul' of Victorian Criticism"; and Thomas C. Caramagno, "The Psychoanalytic Aesthetics of Eneas Sweetland Dallas." In *The Crisis of Action in Nineteenth-Century English Literature*, 65, Stefanie Markovits refers to *The Gay Science* and to Dallas as one of the "pioneers of psychological criticism"; Nicholas Dames elaborates this assessment in "Wave-Theories and Affective Physiologies: The Cognitive Strain in Victorian Novel Theories." Dallas is

discussed briefly in Ekbert Faas, *Retreat into Mind*, 501–51. A more exten-
sive and sympathetic account of *Poetics* can be found in Alba H. Warren,
Jr., *English Poetic Theory 1825–1865*, 126–51; and R. A. Forsyth, "'The Onward
March of Thought' and the Poetic Theory of E. S. Dallas"; W. David Shaw,
The Lucid Veil; Francis X. Roellinger, *E. S. Dallas: A Study in Victorian
Criticism*.

7. E. S. Dallas, *Poetics: An Essay on Poetry* (1852), 19.
8. W. David Shaw, *The Lucid Veil*, 253.
9. Dallas, *Poetics*, 99.
10. Dorothy Mermin, *The Audience in the Poem: Five Victorian Poets*; Garrett
 Stewart, *Dear Reader: The Conscripted Audience in Nineteenth-Century British
 Fiction*.
11. Dallas, *Poetics*, 101.
12. Shaw, *The Lucid Veil*, 252. Shaw is, however, intrigued by Dallas' remarks
 about the significance of the second person to modern poetry, and links it
 both to the Victorian dramatic monologue and to the centrality of second-
 person address in the poetry of Christina Rossetti (254–55). It is crucial to keep
 in mind that by "dramatic poetry" Dallas (unlike Hegel, from whom Dallas
 derived some of his scheme, but who really means just "drama") covers all
 modern poetry, even the poetry we might call "lyric." For Dallas, lyric poetry
 is a closed book: it refers almost exclusively to the poetry of the Hebrew
 Bible and other ancient and "Oriental forms," from fantasies of Chaldean
 shepherds to Sappho. In modern times lyric survives only in ballads, and
 in poets deemed to be closest to lyric's primitive origins – hence while there
 are scarcely any English lyrics (what we might call the English lyric, asserts
 Dallas, is really dramatic), there are Scottish ones (Beattie, Burns) (146–49).
13. Cf. S. T. Coleridge, "Essay on Faith": "there can be no I without a Thou, and
 [that] a Thou is only possible by an equation in which I is taken as equal to
 Thou, and yet not the same." *Literary Remains* IV: 428. See discussion of this
 passage in Anthony John Harding, *Coleridge and the Idea of Love*, 189–90.
14. Stephen Darwall, *The Second-Person Standpoint: Morality, Respect, and
 Accountability*, 9.
15. In his first book, *Shelley's Mythmaking*, Harold Bloom made extensive use
 of Martin Buber, *I and Thou* (orig. 1923). There exists a persistent current
 in continental philosophy which makes intersubjective relations founda-
 tional, of which Levinas is perhaps the best practitioner: see "Is Ontology
 Fundamental?" in *Entre Nous: Thinking-of-the-Other*, 1–11.
16. Vasudevi Reddy, "Experiencing Others: A Second-Person Approach to Other-
 Awareness," 123–44. For an overview of research on infants' capacity for second-person thinking, see Michael Tomasello, "Social Cognition Before the
 Revolution."
17. Alice Meynell, "Second Person Singular," in *Second Person Singular and
 Other Essays*, 133 (orig. pub. *Pall Mall Gazette*, April 20, 1898, 3).
18. The status of silence in Meynell's writing and in her reputation with her contemporaries is a vexed subject. As a number of recent critics have pointed

out, the frequency with which Meynell's many male admirers – Coventry Patmore, George Meredith, and Francis Thompson among others – praised Meynell for her expressive "silence" contributed to her reception as pre-eminently feminine writer. See Talia Shaffer, *The Forgotten Female Aesthetes* 159–96, and Maria Frawley, "The Tides of the Mind: Alice Meynell's Poetry of Perception," 62–76, for a discussion. Frawley's own view is to seek to rescue Meynell's interest in silence from its reception and to link it to Meynell's preoccupation with "thought processes" (74). Her emphasis on Meynell's "experiment[s] with addressivity" and with "the interconnectedness of poetic and cognitive processes" is related to mine.

19. On the challenges that Victorian poetry poses to ideas of poetry as a voice, see Yopie Prins, "Voice Inverse."

20. Emily Harrington, *Lyric Intimacy: Forms of Intersubjectivity in British Women Poets, 1860–1900*, 196–201.

21. Meynell, "Second Person Singular," 136.

22. Alice Meynell, "Renouncement," *The Poems of Alice Meynell: Complete Edition*, 69. This early poem was perennially singled out for praise by Meynell's admirers, including Ruskin and D. G. Rossetti. For an excellent discussion of the reception of "Renouncement" and the way this poem has been central to Meynell's reputation as a Victorian poetess, see Tracy Seeley, "'The Fair Light Mystery of Images': Alice Meynell's Metaphysical Turn."

23. Dallas, *Poetics*, 39.

24. Mary Elizabeth Coleridge, "Song," *Poems*, 1908, 56.

25. Alix Strachey, "A Note on the Use of the Word 'Internal'"; Meir Perlow, *Understanding Mental Objects*.

26. D. W. Winnicott, "The Use of an Object and Relating Through Identifications," *Playing and Reality* 86; emphasis his.

27. For a reading of Winnicott's use of address that is similar to my own, see Barbara Johnson, "Using People." I am also indebted to Jessica Benjamin's Hegelian reading of Winnicott's essay in "Recognition and Destruction: An Outline of Intersubjectivity," *Like Subjects, Love Objects*, 27–48.

28. On address, negativity, negation and destruction see for example Sanford Budick, "Tradition in the Space of Negativity." Treatments of apostrophe influenced by Paul de Man also emphasize the destructive nature of apostrophe: see e.g., Mary Jacobus, "Apostrophe and Lyric Voice in *The Prelude*."

29. The clearest account of the circulation – in letters to Southey, Lloyd, and Thelwall, and in its many printed versions – of "This Lime-Tree Bower My Prison" can be found in Jack Stillinger, *Coleridge and Textual Instability: The Multiple Versions of the Major Poems*, 43–51. Gurion Taussig promotes the idea that Coleridge's relation to his friend and neighbor Thomas Poole forms a crucial context in *Coleridge and the Idea of Friendship, 1789–1804*, 102. J. C. C. May's provocative comment, "as a poem silently addressed to Wordsworth, it is profoundly serious; the form of a public address to Charles Lamb concedes an element of exclamatory exaggeration," appears in his headnote to the poem: *The Collected Works of Samuel Taylor Coleridge, Volume 16: Poetical*

Works I: Part I, ed. J. C. C. Mays, 349. Relevant are several essays in the cluster "Coleridge, Friendship, and the Origin of Modernity, in *European Romantic Review* 14 (2003), especially Sophie Thomas, "Aids to Friendship: Coleridge and the Inscription of the Friend."

30. S. T. Coleridge, "This Lime-Tree Bower My Prison," 61, 65–68, *The Collected Works of Samuel Taylor Coleridge, Volume 16: Poetical Works I, Part I*, 353.

31. See for example Anne K. Mellor, "'This Lime-Tree Bower My Prison' and the Categories of English Landscape"; John Gutteridge, "Scenery and Ecstasy: Three of Coleridge's Blank Verse Poems"; Raimonda Modiano, *Coleridge and the Concept of Nature*; A.C. Goodson, *Verbal Imagination: Coleridge and the Language of Modern Criticism*. Approaches that take Charles Lamb's role in the poem seriously tend to break down between those who emphasize STC's "egotism" in using Lamb for his own purposes, and those presenting a more tolerant account of STC's dependence on vicarious experience and his genuine sympathy for Lamb. For the former, see Charles Rzepka, *The Self as Mind*; and A. Gérard, "The Systolic Rhythm: the Structure of Coleridge's Conversation Poems," in *Coleridge: A Collection of Essays*. For the latter, see Paul Magnuson, *Coleridge's Nightmare Poetry*; Kelvin Everest, *Coleridge's Secret Ministry*; Michael Raiger, "The Poetics of Liberation in Imaginative Power: Coleridge's 'This Lime-Tree Bower My Prison'"; and Adam Potkay, "Coleridge's Joy." For an approach to Coleridge that sees friendship – and conflicts between egalitarian and asymmetrical forms of friendship – as central to the poet's early writing, see Taussig, *Coleridge and the Idea of Friendship, 1789–1804*.

32. "Friends, whom I never more may meet again": Coleridge's evident desire to get the emotional force of this curious sentiment correct may be seen in the fact that he worried the word order of this line repeatedly; see Stillinger, 148.

33. Northrop Frye, *Anatomy of Criticism*, 249–50. Compare Virginia Jackson's similar argument about Frye, *Dickinson's Misery*, 130.

34. Culler, "Apostrophe," *The Pursuit of Signs*, 148. On the relation between the promiscuous apostrophizing in "Lime-Tree Bower" and in Wordsworth's "Intimations Ode": it would be possible to argue that this and other similarities are symptoms of the fact that Wordsworth and Coleridge were always thinking about each other. See Susan Eilenberg, *Strange Power of Speech*; Reeve Parker, "'O Could You Hear His Voice'," and Mary Jacobus, "Apostrophe and Lyric Voice in *The Prelude*."

35. For a related but slightly different reading of this conjunction of addresses, see Alan Richardson, "Apostrophe in Life and in Romantic Art: Everyday Discourse, Overhearing, and Poetic Address."

36. Thanks to Michael McKeon for suggesting the relevance of this poem.

37. "Little Potatoes": in the letter to Southey in which "Lime-Tree Bower" first appears, STC wrote: "Wordsworth is a very great man – the only man, to whom *at all times & in all modes of excellence* I feel myself inferior – the only one, I mean, whom I *have yet met with* – for the London Literati appear to me to be very much like little Potatoes – i.e. *no great Things*! – a compost

of Nullity & Dullity." STC to Robert Southey, circa July 17, 1797, *Collected Letters of Samuel Taylor Coleridge*, 1: 334.

38. But see the emphasis in Virginia Jackson's discussion of second-person pronouns in the writing of Emily Dickinson, *Dickinson's Misery*, 118–65, esp. 157–59.

39. Charles Lamb to STC, August 6, 1800, *The Letters of Charles and Mary Lamb*, 1: 217–18.

40. STC to Charles Lamb, Early May 1798, *Collected Letters*, 1: 403–404.

41. STC to Robert Southey, circa July 17, 1797, *Collected Letters*, 1: 336.

42. STC to Charles Lamb, September 28, 1796, *Collected Letters*, 1: 239.

43. The usage of the category "conversation poem" to designate "This Lime-Tree Bower" and others originates in George McLean Harper's 1928 essay, "Coleridge's Conversation Poems," *Spirit of Delight*.

44. Reeve Parker, *Coleridge's Meditative Art*, 28.

45. Richard Baxter, *The Saints' Everlasting Rest*, quoted in Parker, *Coleridge's Meditative Art*, 36 (emphasis mine).

46. Baxter, quoted in Parker, 37. As Parker notes, books such as Baxter's represent a complex attempt to render for Protestantism the practices of directed meditation so important for medieval Catholicism. For a provocative treatment of this tradition, in relation to broader cognitive and psychological issues, see Mary Carruthers, *The Craft of Thought: Meditation, Rhetoric, and the Making of Images, 400–1200*.

47. On the notion that thinking equals the death of one's own voice, see Giorgio Agamben, "Pascoli and the Thought of the Voice."

48. On the idea that there is a logic of mutual exclusivity, or a prohibition against thinking about someone, and being with and/or speaking to them at the same time: some neuroscientists claim to have demonstrated that some kinds of thinking are special brain activities that effectively shut out all the sensory world: R. Kawashima *et al.*, "Positron-emission studies of cross-modality inhibition in selective attentional tasks: closing 'the mind's eye'."

49. Hannah Arendt, "Thinking and Moral Considerations," 165 (emphasis mine).

50. Immanuel Kant, *Anthropology From a Pragmatic Point of View* [1798], 237, emphasis in original. Thanks to Deidre Lynch for bringing this passage to my attention.

51. Felicia Hemans, "A Parting Song," epigraph and 1–2, orig. *Records of Woman: With Other Poems* (1828), *Felicia Hemans: Selected Poems, Letters, Reception Materials*, ed. Susan J. Wolfson, 425.

52. On this chain of poems, see Angela Leighton, *Victorian Women Poets: Writing Against the Heart*, 71–77; Derek Furr, "Sentimental Confrontations: Hemans, Landon, and Elizabeth Barrett."

53. Letitia Landon, "Night at Sea," 11–30, orig. pub *New Monthly Magaine* 55 (1839), *Letitia Elizabeth Landon: Selected Writings*, ed. Jerome McGann and Daniel Reiss, 205.

54. Poems by Hemans featuring the scattering of loved ones across continents include, from *Records of Woman*, "Madeline, A Domestic Tale" and "The Graves of a Household." See Tricia Lootens, "Hemans and Home: Victorianism, Feminine 'Internal Enemies,' and the Domestication of National Identity."

55. See for example this commemorative poem:

> Though Nature Heaved the Continents Apart,
> She cast in one great mould the human heart;
> She framed on one great plan the human mind,
> And gave man speech to link him to his kind;
> So that, though plains and mountains intervene,
> Or oceans, broad and stormy, roll between,
> If there but be a courier for the thought –
> Swift-winged or slow – the land and seas are nought,
> And man is nearer to his brother brought.

With the advent of the cable, the poem continues, "Thought" has the power to "walk, like light, the ocean's bed, / And laugh to scorn the winds and waves o'er head!" John R. Ridge, "The Atlantic Cable," *Poems* 17, 20. I am grateful to John Picker for this reference. See also Picker, "Atlantic Cable."

56. Derek Furr terms the question of the refrain of "Night at Sea" a "rhetorical question," the answer to which is clearly, in his view, "no." He reads the poem as expressing Landon's regrets about aspects of the life she left behind: "it begs the reader to speculate about Landon's sorrows and private life and, thereby, to weep with her" ("Sentimental Confrontations," 41).

57. Elizabeth Barrett, "L.E.L.'s Last Question," orig. pub. *The Atheneum*, January 26, 1839; reprinted in McGann and Reiss, eds., *Letitia Elizabeth Landon: Selected Writings*, 365.

58. Angela Leighton sees Barrett distancing herself from her predecessor L.E.L. by casting Landon's refrain as "hopelessly narcissistic"; *Victorian Woman Poets: Writing Against the Heart*, 72–73. See also Dorothy Mermin, *Elizabeth Barrett Browning: The Origins of a New Poetry*, 106–7.

59. Recent readers of "Thoughts on Poetry" have suggested that it is in fact influential twentieth-century interpretations of Mill, such as Frye's, which have imposed upon us Mill's emphasis on the isolated speaking voice; see Jackson, *Dickinson's Misery*, 131–32; Harrington, *Lyric Intimacy*, 5–6.

60. John Stuart Mill, *The Subjection of Women*, 11.

61. Mill, "Thoughts on Poetry and its Varieties" (1833), *Collected Works*, 1: 348–49.

62. I am indebted to Stan Barrett for some of the formulations on Mill in this paragraph.

63. Anthony Trollope, *The Small House at Allington*, 457.

64. Studies of the Victorian sonnet include William T. Going, *Scanty Plot of Ground: Studies in the Victorian Sonnet*; Natalie M. Houston, "Affecting Authenticity: *Sonnets from the Portuguese* and *Modern Love*"; Amy Christine Billone, *Little Songs: Women, Silence, and the Nineteenth-Century Sonnet*.

65. John Addington Symonds, letter to Mary Robinson, November 14, 1884, *The Letters of John Addington Symonds*, II: 967. Thanks to Yopie Prins for this reference.

66. Christina Rossetti, *Monna Innominata* I.1–14, *The Complete Poems of Christina Rossetti*, II: 86–87.

67. For a related reading of this sonnet see Constance W. Hassett, *Christina Rossetti: The Patience of Style*, 185–86.

68. Important interpretations of *Monna Innominata* include William Whitla, "Questioning the Convention: Christina Rossetti's Sonnet Sequence, "Monna Innominata""; Anthony Harrison, *Christina Rossetti in Context*, 174–85 and throughout.

69. On the relationship of Rossetti's sequence to Barrett Browning's *Sonnets from the Portuguese*, see, for example, Marjorie Stone, "'Monna Innominata' and *Sonnets from the Portuguese*: Sonnet Traditions and Spiritual Trajectories," Tricia Lootens, *Lost Saints* 158–64.

70. Elizabeth Barrett to Robert Browning, February 3, 1845. *The Letters of Robert Browning and Elizabeth Barrett Browning, 1845–1860*, I: 14

71. Katherine H. Porter, *Through a Glass Darkly: Spiritualism in the Browning Circle*; Daniel Karlin, "Browning, Elizabeth Barrett, and 'Mesmerism'," Alison Chapman, "Mesmerism and Agency in the Courtship of Elizabeth Barrett and Robert Browning."

72. Robert Browning to Elizabeth Barrett, March 31, 1845, *Letters*, I: 47.

73. Elizabeth Barrett to Robert Browning, April 17, 1845, *Letters*, I: 47–48. On RB and EBB's ideologies of writing, speaking, and thinking in the courtship, see Daniel Karlin, *The Courtship of Robert Browning and Elizabeth Barrett*, 173–216.

74. Dorothy Mermin, *Elizabeth Barrett Browning: The Origins of a New Poetry*, 113–46.

75. David Reide argues unequivocally that *Sonnets from the Portuguese* marks EBB's acceptance of a real external object, as opposed to the phantasmal internal object of the early sonnets; *Allegories of One's Own Mind: Melancholy in Victorian Poetry*, 93–130. Needless to say, this is an oversimplification.

76. Elizabeth Barrett Browning, *A Variorum Edition of Sonnets From the Portuguese*, 1.1, 34.9–10.

77. Mary B. Moore refers to the imagery of Sonnet 29 as having "iconographic roots," but does not elaborate; *Desiring Voices: Women Sonnetteers and Petrarchanism*, 187. David Reide suggest that the vines in *Sonnets to the Portuguese* 29 have "biographical significance," "calling to mind the ivy that grew in her bedroom window" (*Allegories of My Own Mind*, 129). As Amy Billone points out, other readers have linked the vegetative imagery to the flower imagery of the last few poems of the sequence (*Little Songs*, 78–80). These readings do not do justice to the violence of the imagery. On the image of the palm-tree: in *A Variorum Edition of Elizabeth Barrett Browning's Sonnets from the Portuguese*, Miroslava Weir Dow notes that EBB frequently uses the palm – symbol of Christ's victory over death – in alluding in her letters to her and Browning's future life in Italy, 61.

78. Andrew Marvell, "The Coronet" (1681), *The Complete Poems*, ed. Elizabeth Story Donno, 16. 19–23
79. Percy Bysshe Shelley, "Epipsychidion," 15–17, *Shelley's Poetry and Prose*, ed. Donald H. Reiman and Sharon B. Powers, 374
80. Cf. Sharon Cameron, *Thinking in Henry James*, 171–72.
81. Meynell was an astute reader of Barrett Browning, and in particular very attentive to the earlier poet's uses of meter, admiring her work most when "pacing softly in the strictest measures of the bonds that all true poets so love – the bonds of numbers, stress, quantity, rhyme, and final shape." "Introduction" in *Elizabeth Barrett Browning: The Art of Scansion* (1916), quoted in Harrington, *Lyric Intimacy*, 223.
82. Meynell, "Renouncement," 1–4, *The Poems of Alice Meynell*, 69.
83. Cf. the following lines from Hardy's "The Walk," from the *Poems of 1912–13*: "And I went alone, and I didn't mind, / Not thinking of you as left behind" (*Variorum Edition of the Complete Poetry of Thomas Hardy*, 340). Though different from "I do not think of thee," these lines certainly share some of the thinking/not thinking logic of the examples by Barrett Browning and Meynell. As Anne-Lise François notes, "the carelessness by which he forgot her passes seamlessly into an equally heedless mode of inclusion," *Open Secrets*, 181.

4   THINKING AND KNOWING IN PATMORE AND MEREDITH

1. Discussions of the larger field of Victorian poetry about marriage include W. S. Johnson, *Sex and Marriage in Victorian Poetry*; Richard McGhee, *Marriage, Duty, and Desire in Victorian Poetry and Drama*; Patricia M. Ball, *The Heart's Events: The Victorian Poetry of Relationships*; Kerry McSweeney, *Supreme Attachments: Studies in Victorian Love Poetry*. See above all Isobel Armstrong's strong claim that Victorian poets focused on interpersonal relations as a framework for exploring political and philosophical concerns; *Victorian Poetry*, 7.
2. Coventry Patmore, *The Rod, the Root, and the Flower*, 73. J. C. Reid notes that Patmore had earlier penciled the phrase "all knowledge is nuptial knowledge" into his copy of Swedenborg's *Arcana Coelestia*; *The Mind and Art of Coventry Patmore*, 76.
3. On Patmore's beliefs about the love of God and sexual love, see J. C. Reid, *The Mind and Art of Coventry Patmore*, 117–47, and John Maynard, *Victorian Discourses of Sexuality and Religion*, 141–270. Maynard discusses the link between *The Rod, the Root, and the Flower* and Patmore's relationship with Meynell, *Victorian Discourses*, 270. On the poetic relationship between Patmore and Meynell, see Yopie Prins, "Patmore's Law, Meynell's Rhythm." Biographical accounts of Meynell's relationship with both Patmore and Meredith can be found in June Badeni, *The Slender Tree: A Life of Alice Meynell*. On the history of the manuscript of *The Angel in the House* presented to Meynell, see Patmore, *The Angel in the House*, eds. Patricia Aske and Ian Anstruther, II: xiii–xiv.

4. While it is clear that Patmore and Meredith knew each other's early work of the 1850s and early 1860s, and traveled in the same intellectual and artistic circles, most of the evidence of their responses to each other's work dates from the 1890s, the decade that saw not only their competition over Alice Meynell but also significant reprints of their early poetry. Meredith's letters contain some unkind comments about *The Angel in the House* inspired by a new edition (*The Letters of George Meredith*, II: 1222–23); at the time of his death in 1896, Patmore's library contained a copy of the 1892 reprint of *Modern Love* (Everard Meynell, *A Catalogue of the Library of Coventry Patmore*, 25).

5. George Meredith, *Modern Love*, I.I, XLIX.16, *The Poems of George Meredith*, I: 116, 144. Subsequent references to *Modern Love* will be to sonnet number and line number only.

6. Coventry Patmore, *The Angel in the House* Book II, Canto I, Idyll 2, in Patmore, *Poems*, 144. Unless otherwise noted, quotations from *The Angel in the House* will be to this edition, which is based on the 1886 edition, the last based on Patmore's own revisions. Due to the complex organization of this poem, most subsequent references will be to page number only.

7. George Butte, *I Know that You Know that I Know: Narrating Subjects from Moll Flanders to Marnie*.

8. Alice Meynell, "Introduction," *The Angel in the House Together with The Victories of Love by Coventry Patmore*, 22.

9. Edmund Gosse, *Coventry Patmore*, 58.

10. George Saintsbury, *A History of English Prosody, from the Twelfth Century to the Present Day*, III: 386; Basil Champneys, *Memoirs and Correspondence of Coventry Patmore*, I: 161.

11. *The Atheneum*, January 20, 1855; quoted by Ian Anstruther, *Coventry Patmore's Angel*, 76.

12. Basil Champneys, *Memoirs and Correspondence of Coventry Patmore*, I: 161; see also Patmore, *An Essay on English Metrical Law: A Critical Edition with a Commentary*, 27.

13. Patmore, *Poems*, 470.

14. Saintsbury, *A History of English Prosody, from the Twelfth Century to the Present Day*, I: 392–95.

15. Keith Devlin, *Goodbye, Descartes: The End of Logic and the Search for a New Cosmology of the Mind*, 230–31, 254–56.

16. Lisa Zunshine, "Why Jane Austen was Different, and Why We May Need Cognitive Science to See it," 276. Zunshine's argument is that Austen's innovation in fiction was to move narration of embedded mental states towards the cognitively challenging fourth level of embeddedness in unprecedented ways. For evidence of the limit of four levels, she draws on Robin Dunbar, "On the Origin of the Human Mind." A review of the actual experimental work of Dunbar and other "Theory of Mind" researchers, however, reveals that in their empirical work they do not entirely draw the conclusions Zunshine derives from them. See Peter Kinderman, Robin Dunbar, and Richard B. Bentall, "Theory-of-mind deficits and causal attributions."

17. Kirstie Blair, *Victorian Poetry and the Culture of the Heart*, 74.
18. Patmore, *Poems*, 179
19. Patmore, *The Angel in the House Books I & II: The First Editions Collated with his original Holograph Manuscript*, 1: 107.
20. Patmore, *Poems*, 182, 1–8.
21. The history of Patmore's revisions in the placement and text of "Love Thinking" and "The Kiss" within *The Angel of the House* can be summarized as follows. In the first edition (1856) of Book II, "The Espousals," the untitled, second-person version of the poem that became "Love Thinking" appeared in Canto V, "The Love-Letters," as the third of three "love letters" from Felix to Honoria. In the 1856 edition, the untitled poem which became, with some slight revision, "The Kiss," appeared as the first of three untitled "Sentences" in Canto VII, "Tete-a-Tete." For the second edition (1858), Patmore regrouped much of the material from the old Canto VII into a new Canto VIII, "The Koh-i-noor." This Canto begins, as do all of the Cantos from this version onwards, with three "Preludes," the second of which is "Love Thinking," and the third of which is "The Kiss." In most editions of *The Angel in the House* (1858, 1860, 1863, 1878, 1886), "The Kiss" is printed in isolation on a single page. In the holograph manuscript of *The Angel in the House* of uncertain date that Patmore presented to Alice Meynell for her birthday in 1893, "Love Thinking" appears in a later Canto, Canto IX, "The Regatta," but a note in pencil, again of uncertain date, says "In Koh-i-Noor" (*The Angel in the House Books I & II*, 2: 107). For an interpretation of Patmore's revisions, see Linda K. Hughes, "Entombing the Angel."
22. "Epipsychidion" was the particular focus of Patmore's ambivalence about Shelley, both his admiration for Shelley's style and for Shelley's idealization of love, and his deep disappointment that Shelley refused to see that love was nothing without marriage. See "The Morality of Epipsychidion," 113.
23. Percy Bysshe Shelley, "Epipsychidion," 89–90, *Shelley's Poetry and Prose*, ed. Donald H.. Reiman and Sharon B. Powers, 376.
24. Patmore, *Poems*, 182.
25. Percy Bysshe Shelley, "Epipsychidion," 15–17, *Shelley's Poetry and Prose*, ed. Donald H. Reiman and Sharon B. Powers, 67.
26. On the productive role of misunderstanding the beloved in *The Angel in the House* see Ablow, *The Marriage of Minds: Reading Sympathy in the Victorian Marriage Plot*, 30.
27. Patmore, *Poems*, 182.
28. Coventry Patmore, *The Angel in the House Books I & II: The First Editions Collated with his original Holograph Manuscript*, 1: 97
29. Meredith, *Modern Love*, 1.1–16.
30. It is conventional to see Meredith's *Modern Love* as an anti-*Angel in the House*. See for example Arline Golden, "'The Game of Sentiment': Tradition and Innovation in Meredith's *Modern Love*," 266. Isobel Armstrong writes eloquently of the need to read *The Angel in the House* together with *Modern Love*, but not of the intertextual connection between "The Kiss" and Meredith's poem. *Victorian Poetry*, 449.

31. Meredith, *Modern Love*, VI.
32. Unsigned review, *Saturday Review*, XVI, October 24, 1863; Swinburne, *Spectator*, June 7, 1862; both in Ioan Williams, ed., *Meredith: The Critical Heritage*, 106, 97–99.
33. Critical discussions of *Modern Love* that see the poem in psychological terms include Arline Golden, "'The Game of Sentiment': Tradition and Innovation in Meredith's *Modern Love*"; Phillip E. Wilson, "Affective Coherence, A Principle of Abated Action, and Meredith's *Modern Love*"; Dorothy Mermin, *The Audience in the Poem: Five Victorian Poets*, 126–44; Stephen Watt, "Neurotic Responses to a Failed Marriage: George Meredith's *Modern Love*"; Henry Kozicki, "The 'Unholy Battle' with the Other in George Meredith's *Modern Love*"; Pauline Fletcher, "'Trifles Light As Air' in Meredith's *Modern Love*"; Alan P. Barr, "How All Occasions Do Inform: 'Household Matters' and Domestic Vignettes in George Meredith's *Modern Love*."
34. Cathy Comstock, "'Speak, and I see the side-lie of a truth': The Problematics of Truth in Meredith's *Modern Love*," 129; James R. Kincaid, *Annoying the Victorians*, 139; see also John Lucas' account of the poem's failings and its resistance to interpretation, "Meredith as Poet."
35. Robert Buchanan, "The Fleshly School of Poetry," *The Contemporary Review* (1871); *The Rossetti Archive*, ed. Jerome McGann, 338–39.
36. D. G. Rossetti, "Nuptial Sleep," 14, *Poems* (1870).
37. Patmore, *Poems*, 361.
38. Coventry Patmore, *An Essay on English Metrical Law*, 27.
39. Meredith, *Modern Love*, I.11.
40. On primary-process thinking, see Jonathan Lear, *Open Minded*, 80–122; Linda A. W. Brakel, *Philosophy, Psychoanalysis, and the A-Rational Mind*.
41. Critical considerations of Meredith's use of other thematic and stylistic features of the Elizabethan sonnet in *Modern Love* include Cynthia Grant Tucker, "Meredith's Broken Laurel: *Modern Love* and the Renaissance Sonnet Tradition"; and Arline Golden, "The Game of Sentiment."
42. George Meredith, "Meeting," *The Poems of George Meredith*, II: 1049–50.
43. Milton, "On Shakespeare," 13–16, *Complete Poetry and Major Prose*, 64.
44. Isobel Armstrong, *Victorian Poetry*, 441.
45. The philosopher Ted Cohen's theory of metaphor would support the notion that there is a connection between *Modern Love*'s failed, jagged, incomplete, or excessively detailed figures and the poem's failures of knowledge. He argues that "the construction and comprehension of metaphors…requires an ability that is the human capacity for understanding one another," *Thinking of Others: On the Talent for Metaphor*, 1.
46. Wilfrid Blunt, November 7, 1905, *My Diaries*; quoted in *The Poems of George Meredith*, II: 1139.
47. Both Dorothy Mermin and Rod Edmond caution against taking the husband's point of view as the narrative truth of Sonnets XLVIII and XLIX; Mermin, *The Audience in the Poem*, 144; Edmond, *Affairs of the Hearth*, 222–24.

48. Mermin makes a similar point about the devaluation of knowledge in *Modern Love*: "clear-sightedness and unillusioned honesty do not bring marital happiness…the more husband and wife know each other, the more miserable they are and the more they diminish and harm each other." *The Audience in the Poem*, 142. More common is the view expressed by Kerry McSweeney, who sees the poem suggesting that "thinking clearly and rationally" would have solved the couple's struggles with "the vicissitudes of romantic love" (*Supreme Attachments*, 103).

49. John Stuart Mill, *The Subjection of Women*, 23–25. Phyllis Bartlett quotes *Fortnightly Review* editor John Morley's account of handing Mill's book to Meredith in 1869: "Meredith eagerly seized the book, fell to devouring it in settled silence, and could not be torn from it all day." Morley's explanation was, "He had more experience than Mill of some types of women and the particular arts, 'feline chiefly,' to which some have recourse to make their way in the world." *The Poems of George Meredith*, 1: 273

50. Critical accounts of *Modern Love* which stress the shifts in pronouns include Dorothy Mermin, *The Audience in the Poem: Five Victorian Poets*, 123–42; Arthur L. Simpson, Jr., "Meredith's Pessimistic Humanism: A New Reading of *Modern Love*"; William D. Reader, "The Autobiographical Author as Fictional Character: Points of View in Meredith's *Modern Love*"; and Natalie Houston, "Affecting Authenticity."

51. Ludwig Wittgenstein, *Philosophical Investigations*, 222.

52. On the encounter between McTaggart and Wittgenstein, see Brian McGuiness, *Young Ludwig: Wittgenstein's Life, 1889–1921*, 138.

53. Swinburne, *Spectator*, June 7, 1862; *Meredith: The Critical Heritage*, 99.

54. The ideal that emerges from *Modern Love* is not unlike that which Anne-Lise François has identified in Thomas Hardy's retrospective view of his first marriage in his *Poems of 1912–13*: a marriage in which there is not much communication, but rather a passive companionship. See *Open Secrets*, 180–94.

55. Quoted in Patmore, *Poems*, xii

56. Dante, *Inferno*, trans. Robert and Jean Hollander, XIII.25, 218.

57. Leo Spitzer, "Speech and Language in *Inferno* XIII," 98, 99.

58. Dante, *Inferno*, trans. Robert and Jean Hollander, 219.

59. J. C. Reid, *The Mind and Art of Coventry Patmore*, 110, expresses surprise, given Patmore's deep, life-long devotion to *The Divine Comedy*, that there are relatively few allusions to that text in Patmore's writing. He overlooks this passage. Patmore himself allegedly told D. G. Rossetti that "he meant to make *The Angel in the House* bigger than the *Divina Commedia*"; Edmund Gosse, *Coventry Patmore*, 54. In a Victorian translation that came out several years after *The Angel in the House*, John Dayman (1865) laboriously translated this line "I believe that he believed that I believed," but appended a note opining that the original line "is a specimen of the poet's mind too valuable to be diluted. Dante has often the air of a man too deeply engaged with things to concern himself about words" (quoted in Eric Griffiths and Matthew Reynolds, eds., *Dante in English*, 190). For a contemporary poetic

variation on the theme, see the refrain of Thom Gunn's 1954 poem "Carnal Knowledge": "You know I know you know I know you know" (Gunn, *Collected Poems*, 15–16).

60. William Wordsworth, "Anecdote for Fathers," 9–16; emphasis mine, *Lyrical Ballads, 1798*.

61. Cynthia Chase, "'Anecdote for Fathers': The Scene of Interpretation in Freud and Wordsworth," 204–05.

62. William Wordsworth, "Preface to Lyrical Ballads," *Prose Works*, 1: 147.

63. Helen Vendler, *Poets Thinking: Pope, Whitman, Dickinson, Yeats,* 6. On Vendler see Virginia Jackson, "Thinking Emily Dickinson Thinking Poetry," 211–13.

64. On Patmore and the New Prosody, see Taylor, *Hardy's Metres and Victorian Prosody*, 18–48; Prins, "Victorian Meters."

65. On the physiological understanding of meter of the Spasmodics, see Jason R. Rudy, "Rhythmic Intimacy, Spasmodic Epistemology," Kirstie Blair, *Victorian Poetry and the Culture of the Heart*, 85–102.

66. Patmore, *An Essay on English Metrical Law: A Critical Edition with a Commentary*, 15, emphasis his; see also T. S. Omond, *English Metrists in the Eighteenth and Nineteenth Centuries*, 152; Raymond Alden, "The Mental Side of Metrical Form."

67. See, in addition to Taylor and Prins, Eric Griffiths, *The Printed Voice of Victorian Poetry*; Matthew Campbell, *Rhythm and Will in Victorian Poetry*; Prins, "Voice Inverse."

68. Kirstie Blair, *Victorian Poetry and the Culture of the Heart*, 90–92. In *Hopkins' Idealism: Philosophy, Physics, Poetry*, Daniel Brown suggests that the metrical theory of Gerard Manley Hopkins was profoundly shaped by the conjunction of nineteenth-century idealism and physical force theory that I have identified as crucial to the era's understandings of thinking: Hopkins' "stress" was a mental reverberation of the physicists' "force." See especially 187–207.

69. Mary Everest Boole to William James, June 18, 1905, in *Mary Everest Boole: A Memoir with some Letters*, ed. E. M. Cobham, 117–18.

70. Alice Meynell, "The Rhythms of Life," 1.

71. T. S. Omond, *English Verse Structure*, 55–56. Earlier instances of such thinking exist: Kirstie Blair quotes J. Odell in 1806: "Man alone is sensible of a rhythmus in his motions…it regulates the pauses of both motion and of speech, and measures even the current of our thoughts." *Victorian Poetry and the Culture of the Heart*, 76.

72. E. S. Dallas, *Poetics*, 171; see also Kirstie Blair's discussion of Dallas on meter, *Victorian Poetry and the Culture of the Heart*, 84–85.

73. Dallas, *Poetics*, 171–72.

74. Alison Gopnik and Andrew N. Meltzoff, *Words, Thoughts, and Theories*, 22.

75. James, *Principles of Psychology*, 1: 224–90. The phrases "stream of thought" and "stream of consciousness" were current in Victorian psychology; "stream of consciousness" appears in G. H. Lewes' 1859 *Physiology of Common Life*. See Rick Rylance, *Victorian Psychology and British Culture*, 11–13.

76. Symonds, *Blank Verse*, 24. For a modern account of the association in English prosody between iambic pentameter and thinking, see Derek Attridge, *The Rhythms of English Poetry*, 125–29. See also Simon Jarvis, "Prosody as Cognition."
77. Eric Griffiths, *The Printed Voice of Victorian Poetry*, 198.
78. Griffiths, 198–99.
79. Patmore, *An Essay on English Metrical Law*, 27.

5 *DANIEL DERONDA* AND THE OMNIPOTENCE OF THOUGHT

1. Freud first used the term "omnipotence of thoughts" in *Totem and Taboo*, drafted 1909–10. He claimed to have borrowed the phrase from one of his patients, the "Rat Man." See *Totem and Taboo, The Standard Edition of the Complete Psychological Works of Sigmund Freud*, XIII: 85, and "A Case of Obsessional Neurosis," *SE*, X: 233.
2. Patricia M. Ball, *The Heart's Events*, 145.
3. Robert Browning, "James Lee's Wife," *Poetical Works 1833–1864*, 777. First published as "James Lee" in *Dramatis Personae* (1864), it was substantially revised and retitled "James Lee's Wife" in *Poetical Works*, 1868.
4. Thomas Hardy, "She, to Him II," *Variorum Edition of the Complete Poems of Thomas Hardy*, 15.
5. Hardy's interest in this phenomenon extended to at least one of his novels. "She, to Him II" was one of the early poems that he "prosed" in his first published novel, *Desperate Remedies* (1871). In the novel it forms part of an outburst by the grieved, conflicted Cytherea Graye, and in this context the social, ethical dimensions become starker. No longer a reproach against an unfaithful lover, it addresses the ways in which "our acquaintances" think about us: it is a lament about a fact of social life: "they will not feel that what to them is but a thought, easily held in those two words of pity, 'Poor girl!' was a whole life to me; as full of hours, minutes, and peculiar minutes, of hopes and dreads, smiles, whisperings, tears, as theirs; that it was my world, what is to them their world, and they in that life of mine, however much I cared for them, only as the thought I seem to them to be"; *Desperate Remedies*, 254; and note on 406.
6. On the influence of *Modern Love* on late nineteenth- and early twentieth-century American women writers see Pinch, "Transatlantic Modern Love."
7. The final couplet reads "Come, now, and play me some slow, sleepy tune, / And as you pass me, stay and kiss me, dear." Philip Bourke Marston, "He and She," *The Collected Poems of Philip Bourke Marston*, 247–49.
8. George Eliot, "A Minor Prophet," 1–2; *Collected Poems*, 1–2.
9. Charles LaPorte, "George Eliot, the Poetess as Prophet," 172–73.
10. The phrase is Freud's, quoted by André Green in "Psychoanalysis and Ordinary Modes of Thought," *On Private Madness*, 17. Eliot's own letters and diaries betray disapproval of some of her era's fads for extraordinary feats of mind: spirit rapping she famously called "odious trickery"; she and George

Henry Lewes left a séance at the home of Erasmus Darwin "in disgust"; *The George Eliot Letters*, III.359, VI.6.

11. George Levine, "*Daniel Deronda*: A New Epistemology"; Pamela Thurschwell, "George Eliot's Prophecies: Coercive Second Sight and Everyday Thought Reading"; Nicholas Royle, *Telepathy and Literature*, 84–110. Irene Tucker identifies *Daniel Deronda* as a book that announces itself as the point where "the history of English realism comes to an end," *A Probable State*, 35.

12. George Eliot, *Daniel Deronda*, ed. Terence Cave, 501. All references will be to this edition.

13. J. H. Miller, *The Form of Victorian Fiction*, 2, 6. The tradition of conceiving of the form of the novel as concerned with knowledge of consciousness goes back at least to Henry James, and finds an eloquent expression in Lukács' *Theory of the Novel*. A notable departure from this tradition is Sharon Cameron's *Thinking in Henry James*, in which thinking about others is conceived not as a form of knowledge but as a form of power.

14. See George Butte, *I Know That You Know That I Know: Narrating Subjects from Moll Flanders to Marnie*.

15. Dorrit Cohn, *Transparent Minds: Narrative Modes for Presenting Consciousness in Fiction*. On novels as thinking machines, cf. the unmotivated personification in the title of Nancy Armstrong's *How Novels Think*. On George Eliot and "the problem of other minds," see Kay Young, "*Middlemarch* and the Problem of Other Minds Heard." For a useful contextualization of the place of the novel in Victorian culture's emphasis on the display of thinking, see Andrew H. Miller, "Reading Thoughts: Victorian Perfectionism and the Display of Thinking."

16. S. T. Coleridge, March 17, 1801, *Notebooks: A Selection*, I: 923.

17. George Levine, "*Daniel Deronda:* A New Epistemology," 69–70. See also Alexander Welsh, *George Eliot and Blackmail*, 307; Sally Shuttleworth, "The Language of Science and Psychology in George Eliot's *Daniel Deronda*." On Mordecai and telepathy, see Nicholas Royle, *Telepathy and Literature*, 99–100; and Pamela Thurschwell, "George Eliot's Prophecies," 93.

18. Amanda Anderson, *The Powers of Distance: Cosmopolitanism and the Cultivation of Detachment*, 124; see also Daniel Hack, *The Material Interests of the Victorian Novel*, 169.

19. Eliot's skepticism about an ideal of perfectly readable minds is also expressed in a comparison the narrator makes when commenting, at a crucial moment, on the inexplicability of Gwendolen's and Grandcourt's erotic interest in each other: "The word of all work Love will no more express the myriad modes of mutual attraction, than the word Thought can inform you what is passing through your neighbour's mind" (301).

20. Here I differ from Thurschwell: "both Mordecai's and Gwendolen's wishes can be seen as making things happen in the world of the narrative, but their status as active (prophetic) and passive (hysterical) helps determine the way they are valued" (99). For a reading of *Daniel Deronda* that stresses similarities between Mordecai's messianism and Gwendolen's modes of thinking,

see Athena Vrettos, *Somatic Fictions*, 75; see also Jill L. Matus, "Historicizing Trauma: the Genealogy of Psychic Shock in *Daniel Deronda*," 67. My aim in taking seriously Gwendolen's modes of thinking is certainly related to the work of scholars who have linked her mental habits to currents in Victorian psychology. See, in addition to Thurschwell, Vrettos, and Matus, Sally Shuttleworth, *George Eliot and Nineteenth-Century Science*, 185–97. However, while, as Matus notes, many of these studies view Gwendolen in relation to mental disorders from hysteria, to monomania, to agoraphobia (see Matus, 74, n. 1), my emphasis is on those aspects of Gwendolen's thinking that are most ordinary, and least pathological.

21. Among readings that emphasize the therapeutic nature of Daniel's conversations with Gwendolen are those that liken their meetings to psychoanalytic sessions, including Peter Brooks, *Body Work: Objects of Desire in the Modern Novel*, 244–55; and Carl T. Rotenberg, "George Eliot – Proto-Psychoanalyst." Dissents include Ann L. Cvetkovich, *Mixed Feelings*; John Kucich, *Repression in Victorian Fiction*; Catherine Gallagher, *The Body Economic*, 145 and note 25.

22. Cf. Gillian Beer, "The tone of speech is lost…The characters act out much of their experience without speech. This has the effect of intensely dramatizing *encounter* when it does occur. So snatched scenes of conversation between Deronda and Gwendolen are imbued with a hieratic value," *George Eliot*, 214 (emphasis hers). On mental shock in *Daniel Deronda*, see Matus, "Historicizing Trauma."

23. For a helpful overview see Meir Perlow, *Understanding Mental Objects*.

24. Thanks to Jeff Nunokawa for bringing this line to my attention. The only other critical discussion of this line that I know of belongs to Nicholas Royle: his focus is rather on the oddness of Deronda being in Italy at all, and the way this "coincidence" ratifies the novel's commitment to the "acredbile," the non-logical, the telepathic (*Telepathy and Literature*, 96–98).

25. Alexander Welsh, *George Eliot and Blackmail*, 267.

26. On how feminine unknowingness may propel thinking and thus the form of the English novel, see Susan C. Greenfield, "The Absent-Minded Heroine: Or, Elizabeth Bennet Has a Thought."

27. Lisa Zunshine, *Why We Read Fiction: Theory of Mind and the Novel*, 16. The literature on autism and mind-reading includes Simon Baron-Cohen, *Mind Blindness: An Essay on Autism and Theory of Mind*; Shaun Nichols and Stephen P. Stitch, *Mindreading*.

28. Audrey Jaffe has theorized narrative omniscience as always only a fantasy of perfect knowledge in *Vanishing Points*.

29. Jane Austen, *Mansfield Park*, 38; emphasis hers.

30. Alex Woloch, *The One vs. the Many: Minor Characters and the Space of the Protagonist in the Novel*.

31. See for example Meir Sternberg, *Expositional Modes and Temporal Ordering in Fiction*.

32. Henry James "*Daniel Deronda* – A Conversation."

33. Gillian Beer, *George Eliot*, 214. Cf. Beer's earlier description of the novel as a "clandestine mental world of sequestered experience": "much of the book is preoccupied with thoughts – passionate thoughts which can for the most part find no pathway into action," *Darwin's Plots*, 175. See also Garrett Stewart, *Dear Reader: The Conscripted Audience in Nineteeth-Century Fiction*, 332. Alexander Welsh notes the ways in which *Daniel Deronda* seems to bear in its inwardness the pressure of "the silence of print culture" (*George Eliot and Blackmail*, 350). All of these comments are echoing, implicitly or explicitly, the "roar on the other side of silence." See John Picker's discussion of sound and silence in *Daniel Deronda* in *Victorian Soundscapes*, 82–99.

34. "The thought of his dying would not subsist: it turned as with a dream-change into the terror that she should die…Fantasies moved within her like ghosts, making no break in her more acknowledged consciousness, and finding no obstruction in it: dark rays doing their work invisibly in the broad light" (606).

35. Excellent discussions of narrative closure in *Daniel Deronda* include Garrett Stewart, *Dear Reader*, 301–28, and Gillian Beer, *Darwin's Plots*, 169–95.

36. Hans Meyrick's letter is of course the key to the novel in Cynthia Chase's essay, "The Decomposition of the Elephants: Double-Reading in *Daniel Deronda*," *Decomposing Figures: Rhetorical Readings in the Romantic Tradition*, 157–74. For a different assessment of the role of letters in *Daniel Deronda*, see Daniel Hack, *The Material Interests of the Victorian Novel*, 147–77. Hack argues that the letters, as opposed to bodily presence, are in fact an important form of influence in the novel.

37. On the relation of third-person modes of representing consciousness in the nineteenth-century novel to earlier techniques in epistolary fiction, see Joe Bray, *The Epistolary Novel: Representations of Consciousness*, and also William Galperin, *The Historical Austen*. On Gwendolen and the Richardsonian heroine, see Margaret Doody, "George Eliot and the Eighteenth-Century Novel." Reading, writing, and mental relations are more closely tied in *The Mill on the Floss*: cf. the epistolary mind space asserted in a letter from Philip Wakem to Maggie Tulliver: "I shall not go away. The place where you are is the one where my mind must live, wherever I might travel" (quoted in Royle, *Telepathy and Literature*, 193, n. 10).

38. Ann Banfield, "Where Epistemology, Style, and Grammar Meet Literary History: The Development of Represented Speech and Thought," 417. See also *Unspeakable Sentences: Narration and Representation in the Language of Fiction*. Benjamin Lee performs the miraculous task of summarizing Banfield's position: Banfield's "discovery is that of a unique type of 'unspeakable' sentence that severs the bond between communication and the linguistic representation of subjectivity. Although in ordinary discourse expressivity and communication are tied together, with the rise of novelistic fiction it becomes possible to separate the expressive and communicative functions of language. Banfield claims that the sentences of RST ['represented speech and thought,' the term she prefers for free indirect discourse] are not structured around the

speaker–hearer, I–you axis of speech communication but instead consist of 'unspeakable' sentences in which the expressivity and subjectivity normally attached to the speaking subject are transferred to a third-person subject. In addition, spatiotemporal deictics are corefererential now not with the present tense but with the past (the unmarked tense for narration)." *Talking Heads: Language, Metalanguage, and the Semiotics of Subjectivity*, 302. As Lee notes, Banfield's argument has been subjected to many cogent challenges.

39. Banfield, "Where Epistemology…" 449; emphasis mine. Banfield deems free indirect discourse to be relatively rare in George Eliot (443). Eliot certainly knew that there are times when thinking about another person feels like a voice in your head ("propositional internal speech"): "'I wonder what he thinks of me really? He must have felt interested in me, else he would not have sent me my necklace …' These questions ran in her mind as the voice of an uneasy longing…" (331).

40. Gillian Beer, *Darwin's Plots*, 194; emphasis hers.

41. For a reading of the opening scene that emphasizes looking and "mutual projection," see Audrey Jaffe, *Scenes of Sympathy*, 145–48.

42. For a discussion of the knotty relations between thought and action generally in Eliot, whose narratives often give "willing, judging, desiring, and feeling…the same ontological status as action," and specifically in *Daniel Deronda,* see Stefanie Markovits, *The Crisis of Action in Nineteenth-Century English Literature*, 87–128.

43. Harry E. Shaw, *Narrating Reality: Austen, Scott, Eliot*, 247. Cf. Beth Newman, *Subjects on Display: Psychoanalysis, Social Expectation, and Victorian Femininity*, 108.

44. This is especially true of the highly *composed* description of the casino in the next paragraph, and especially of the cameo appearance of the "melancholy little boy" who looks out at the viewer of the scene (8).

45. Gallagher, *The Body Economic*, 148–49; see also Neil Hertz, *George Eliot's Pulse*, 130–31.

46. In his reading of the opening scene Simon During focuses on the narrator's double relation to Gwendolen's consciousness; see "The Strange Case of Monomania: Patriarchy in Literature, Murder in *Middlemarch*, Drowning in *Daniel Deronda*," 98.

47. Cf. 135, during a meeting between Grandcourt and Gwendolen: "He stood perfectly still, half a yard or more away from her; and it flashed through her thought that a sort of lotos-eater's stupor had begun in him and was taking possession of her." One feels, more than is often the case, that this is really George Eliot's analogy, which has been put into Gwendolen's thoughts, rather than Gwendolen's "own."

48. Audrey Jaffe theorizes the ways in which omniscient narration defines itself in opposition to the bounded nature of the characters it manufactures (*Vanishing Points*, 12).

49. Such as D. A. Miller's wicked characterization of Eliot's omniscient narrator as "the mother," *Jane Austen, or the Secret of Style*, 32.

50. Cf. Dorrit Cohn, *Transparent Minds: Narrative Modes for Presenting Consciousness in Fiction*, 138–39.
51. Chase, "The Decomposition of the Elephants,"164; Shaw, *Narrating Reality*, 248.
52. Banfield, "Where Epistemology ..." 441–42.
53. W. R. Bion, *Second Thoughts*, 116, 165.
54. Simon During, "Strange Case," 100; Marc Redfield, *Phantom Formations: Aesthetic Ideology and the Bildungsroman*, 145, 154; cf. Neil Hertz, *George Eliot's Pulse*.
55. George Eliot, "Recollections of Italy, 1860," *The Journals of George Eliot*, 349.
56. Shelley, *The Cenci*, II.ii.82–88.
57. Markovits has discussed the significance of *Prometheus Unbound* to the novel, *The Crisis of Action*, 220–21.
58. Lisa Rodensky, *The Crime in Mind: Criminal Responsibility and the Victorian Novel*, 132. She clarifies that were the text to have clearly determined that if Gwendolen's only act was to have hesitated for a second before throwing Grandcourt a rope (696), Victorian legal thought would have indeed ruled her innocent, but she also recognizes that to focus on Gwendolen's failure to throw a rope is drastically to simplify the issues.
59. Rodensky, 160ff. As Rodensky discusses, Eliot was acquainted with legal theorist James Fitzjames Stephens. G. H. Lewes was interested in criminal psychology; Rodensky quotes his comment on thinking and doing oft-quoted in this context, "to imagine an act is to rehearse it mentally...hence it is that a long-meditated crime becomes at last an irresistible criminal impulse" (166).
60. Cf. Meir Dan-Cohen, "Harmful Thoughts," 187.
61. Rodensky, *The Crime in Mind*, 165. Susan David Bernstein sees Gwendolen's confession as itself a symptom of her powerlessness against masculine domination. She argues that the narrator and Daniel produce divergent accounts of Gwendolen's responsibility in order to point up the way in which Daniel's response is designed to shore up his masculine authority. *Confessional Subjects*, 131–34.
62. Freud read *Daniel Deronda* in 1882, when he was twenty-six. He wrote to his fiancée Martha Bernays expressing his admiration for the novel and specifically its representation of Jews. Ernest Jones, *The Life and Work of Sigmund Freud*, I: 174.
63. For a philosophical case for "a more active externalism" in which "the mind can have direct, nonmediated, and noncausal effects on the world outside of it," see Dan-Cohen, "Harmful Thoughts," 191.
64. Nomi Arpaly, *Unprincipled Virtue: An Inquiry into Moral Agency*, 12–13.
65. Bernard Williams, "Moral Luck," *Moral Luck: Philosophical Papers, 1973–1980*, 20–39. Andrew H. Miller alludes to the aptness of Bernard Williams' "moral luck" not only to Gwendolen's relationship to Grandcourt's death, but also to Neil Hertz's interpretation of Eliot, in which "the ethical judgments offered by the novel, however punitive, are seen as reprieves from a more painful skeptical condition in which agency is ambiguous," "Review of *George Eliot's Pulse*," 537.

66. Patricia S. Greenspan, *Practical Guilt*, 152.
67. See for example Suzy Anger, "George Eliot and Philosophy," 80. Many recent critical accounts of Eliot have noted Eliot's awareness of the limits of an ethics of sympathy, in *Daniel Deronda* in particular. Lisbeth During's "The Concept of Dread: Sympathy and Ethics in *Daniel Deronda*" finds in the novel a genealogy of morals that begins in dread, and is explicitly opposed to an ethics of sympathy.

CONCLUSION

1. George Eliot, "The Progress of the Intellect," *Westminster Review* 54 (January 1851); *Collected Essays*, 30.
2. Eliot, "The Progress of the Intellect," *Collected Essays*, 42; Eliot makes related arguments about the moral functioning of Christianity in others essays, such as "Evangelical Teaching: Dr. Cumming" and "Worldliness and Other-Worldliness: The Poet Young"; *Collected Essays* 187–88, 373–5. See also Eliot's review of William Lecky's *History of the Rise and Influence of the Spirit of Rationalism in Europe, Collected Essays*, 397–414. Discussions of Eliot's views on faith include Michael Davis, *George Eliot and Nineteenth-Century Psychology*, 161–70.
3. W. K. Clifford, "The Ethics of Belief," *Lectures and Essays*, 346.
4. Jonathan E. Adler, *Belief's Own Ethics*, 25–26.
5. William James, "The Will to Believe," 15.
6. On the evidentialist side of debates about the ethics of belief, see Adler, *Belief's Own Ethics*; see also David Velleman's critique of motive-based accounts of belief, "On the Aim of Belief," *The Possibility of Practical Reason*, 244–81. On the other side, see David Pears, *Motivated Irrationality*; Robert Nozick, *The Nature of Rationality*, 69–71; Jeff Jordan, "Pragmatic Arguments and Belief"; Pamela Hieronymi, "The Wrong Kind of Reason"; Andrew Reisner, "The Possibility of Pragmatic Reasons for Belief and the Wrong Kind of Reasons Problem."
7. See for example David Pears, *Motivated Irrationality*, 44–66.
8. Juha Raikka, "Irrational Guilt," 476.
9. See in addition to Raikka, David Velleman, "Don't Worry, Feel Guilty."
10. Greenspan, *Practical Guilt*, 159.
11. Justin D'Arms and Daniel Jacobson helpfully view Greenspan as part of a trend in contemporary moral philosophy they term "neosentimentalism," and contrast her view of the role of emotion in morality to that in Gabriele Taylor's influential account of guilt (*Pride, Shame, and Guilt*), which they see as excessively cognitivist; D'Arms and Jacobson, "The Moralistic Fallacy," 78–79. On neosentimentalism, see D'Arms and Jacobson, "Sentiment and Value," and Shaun Nichols, *Sentimental Rules*, 83–96.
12. N. David Mermin, "Can you help your team tonight by watching on TV? More experimental metaphysics from Einstein, Podolsky, and Rosen," 99. Thanks to Walter Cohen for bringing this essay to my attention.

13. On the continuity between nineteenth-century British literature and twentieth-century British psychoanalytic theory, see Mary Jacobus, *The Poetics of Psychoanalysis*, v–viii.
14. Lucy LaFarge, "The Imaginer and the Imagined," 622. See also H. W. Loewald, "On the Therapeutic Action in Psychoanalysis." Antonino Ferro pays particular attention to the ways in which the analyst's different modes of thinking – "operational thinking," "thoughtful reflection," "reverie" – operate in and with the patient's mental material: *Seeds of Illness, Seeds of Recovery: The Genesis of Illness and the Role of Psychoanalysis*. My thanks to Wendy Katz for these references.
15. LaFarge, "The Imaginer and the Imagined," 617; Peter Fonagy and Mary Target, "Playing with Reality"; "Playing with Reality III."
16. Edna O'Shaughnessy, "A Commemorative Essay on W. R. Bion's Theory of Thinking," 181.
17. W. R. Bion, "A Theory of Thinking," *Second Thoughts*, 116.
18. O'Shaughnessy, "A Commemorative Essay," 182.
19. Bion, "A Theory of Thinking," 116. For a fascinating reading of Bion's work, see Mary Jacobus, *The Poetics of Psychoanalysis*, 175–275.
20. Susan Pockett, William P. Banks, and Shaun Gallagher, *Does Consciousness Cause Behavior?* See especially essays by Gallagher, Ross, Pacherie, Bayne, Mele, and Malle.
21. Meir Dan-Cohen, "Harmful Thoughts, 181,
22. Randall Jarrell, "A Sick Child," *Complete Poems*, 53. Subsequent references will be to line number.
23. Stephen Burt has provocatively suggested that Jarrell's interest in psychoanalysis, in particular his absorption of the structure of the analytic process, may be seen as complicating question of how his poems construe their interlocutors or addressees. *Randall Jarrell and His Age*, 103.
24. Kerry Larson, *Imagining Equality in Nineteenth-Century Literature*, 86, 87.

Bibliography

Ablow, Rachel. *The Marriage of Minds: Reading Sympathy in the Victorian Marriage Plot.* Stanford: Stanford University Press, 2007.

Adler, Jonathan E. *Belief's Own Ethics.* Cambridge, MA: MIT Press, 2002.

Agamben, Giorgio. "Pascoli and the Thought of the Voice." *The End of the Poem.* Stanford University Press, 1999. 62–75.

Alden, Raymond. "The Mental Side of Metrical Form." *Modern Language Review* IX (1914): 294–308.

Alexander, J. H. "Blackwood's Magazine as a Romantic Form." *The Wordsworth Circle* XV (Spring 1984): 57–68.

Anderson, Amanda. *The Powers of Distance: Cosmopolitanism and the Cultivation of Detachment.* Princeton University Press, 2001.

Anger, Suzy. "Are We Not Automata? The Mind–Body Problem in Late Victorian Literature." Unpublished manuscript.

Anger, Suzy. "George Eliot and Philosophy." *Cambridge Companion to George Eliot.* Ed. George Levine. Cambridge University Press, 2001. 76–97.

Anstruther, Ian. *Coventry Patmore's Angel.* London: Haggerston Press, 1992.

Arendt, Hannah. *The Life of the Mind: Part 1: Thinking.* New York: Harcourt Brace Jovanovich, 1977.

"Thinking and Moral Considerations." (1971). *Responsibility and Judgment.* Ed. Jerome Kohn. New York: Schocken Books, 2003. 159–89.

Armstrong, Isobel. *Victorian Poetry: Poetry, Poetics, and Politics.* London: Routledge, 1993.

Armstrong, Nancy. *How Novels Think.* New York: Columbia University Press, 2005.

Arpaly, Nomi. *Unprincipled Virtue: An Inquiry into Moral Agency.* Oxford University Press, 2003.

Ashton, Rosemary. *The German Idea: Four English Writers and the Reception of German Thought, 1800–1860.* Cambridge University Press, 1980.

Attridge, Derek. *The Rhythms of English Poetry.* London: Longmans, 1982.

Austen, Jane. *Mansfield Park.* Ed. Jane Stabler. Oxford: Oxford World's Classics, 2003.

Badeni, June. *The Slender Tree: A Life of Alice Meynell.* Padstow: Tabb House, 1981.

Bain, Alexander. *Mind and Body: The Theories of Their Relation.* London: Henry S. King & Co., 1873.

Baldwin, James Mark, ed. *Dictionary of Philosophy and Psychology; including many of the principle conceptions of ethics, logic, aesthetics, philosophy of religion, mental pathology, anthropology, biology, neurology, physiology, economics, political and social philosophy, philology, physical science, and education.* 3 vols. London: Macmillan, 1901–5.

Ball, Patricia. *The Heart's Events: The Victorian Poetry of Relationships.* London: Athlone Press, 1976.

Banfield, Ann. *Unspeakable Sentences: Narration and Representation in the Language of Fiction.* London: Routledge and Kegan Paul, 1982.

"Where Epistemology, Style, and Grammar Meet Literary History: The Development of Represented Speech and Thought," *New Literary History* 9.3 (1978): 415–54.

Baron-Cohen, Simon. *Mind Blindness: An Essay on Autism and Theory of Mind.* Cambridge, MA: MIT Press, 1995.

Barrell, John. *Imagining the King's Death.* Oxford University Press, 2000.

Barr, Alan P. "'How All Occasions Do Inform': Household Matters and Domestic Vignettes in George Meredith's *Modern Love.*" *Victorian Poetry* 42.3 (2004): 283–93.

Barrett, William F. "First Report of the Committee on Thought-Reading." *Proceedings of the Society for Psychical Research* (1882): I: 13–34.

On The Threshold of the Unseen; an Examination of the Phenomena of Spiritualism and of the Evidence for Survival after Death. 2nd ed. London: Kegan Paul, 1917.

Barthes, Roland. *A Lover's Discourse: Fragments.* Trans. Richard Howard. New York: Hill and Wang, 1984.

Bauman, Zygmunt. *Postmodern Ethics.* Oxford: Blackwell, 1993.

Beer, Gillian. *Darwin's Plots: Evolutionary Narrative in Darwin, George Eliot, and Nineteenth-Century Fiction.* 2nd ed. Cambridge University Press, 2000.

George Eliot. Sussex: Harvester, 1986.

Beer, John. "Coleridge's Afterlife." *The Cambridge Companion to Coleridge.* Ed. Lucy Newlyn. Cambridge University Press, 2002. 231–44.

"Coleridge's Elusive Presence among the Victorians." *Romantic Influences: Contemporary – Victorian – Modern.* New York: St. Martin's Press, 1993. 147–68.

Post-Romantic Consciousness: Dickens to Plath. Basingstoke, Hampshire: Palgrave Macmillan, 2003.

Beiser, Frederick C. *German Idealism: The Struggle against Subjectivism, 1781–1801.* Cambridge, MA: Harvard University Press, 2002.

Benjamin, Jessica. "Recognition and Destruction: An Outline of Intersubjectivity." *Like Subjects, Love Objects.* New Haven: Yale University Press, 1995. 27–48.

Berlant, Lauren. "Cruel Optimism." *differences* 17.3 (2006): 20–37.

Bernstein, Susan David. *Confessional Subjects: Revelations of Gender and Power in Victorian Literature and Culture.* Chapel Hill: University of North Carolina Press, 1997.

Berry, Christopher J. *Social Theory of the Scottish Enlightenment*. Edinburgh University Press, 1997.

Besant, Annie. *Thought Power: Its Control and Culture*. (1918). Hollywood, CA: Theosophical Pub. House, Krotona, 1918.

Billone, Amy Christine. *Little Songs: Women, Silence, and the Nineteenth-Century Sonnet*. Columbus: Ohio State University Press, 2006.

Bion, W. R. *Second Thoughts*. London: Heinemann, 1967.

Blair, Kirstie. *Victorian Poetry and the Culture of the Heart*. Oxford University Press, 2006.

Bloom, Harold. *Shelley's Mythmaking*. New Haven: Yale University Press, 1959.

Boole, Mary Everest. *The Message of Psychic Science to the World*. London: C. W. Daniel, 1908.

Suggestions for Increasing Ethical Stability. London: E. W. Daniel, 1909.

Bowie, Andrew. *Aesthetics and Subjectivity: Kant to Nietzsche*. Manchester University Press, 1990.

Bradley, F. H. *Ethical Studies* [1876]. Ed. Richard Wollheim. Oxford: Clarendon Press, 1988.

Brakel, Linda A. W. *Philosophy, Psychoanalysis, and the A-Rational Mind*. Oxford University Press, 2009.

Bray, Charles. *On Force, Its Mental and Moral Correlates; and On That Which Is Supposed to Underlie All Phenomena: With Speculations on Spiritualism, and Other Abnormal Conditions of Mind*. London: Longmans, Green, 1866.

Phases of Opinion and Experience During a Long Life: An Autobiography. London: Longmans, Green, 1884.

Bray, Joe. *The Epistolary Novel: Representations of Consciousness*. London: Routledge, 2003.

Brett, George Sidney. *Brett's History of Psychology*. Ed. and abridged R. S. Peters. Rev. ed. London: Allen and Unwin, 1962.

Brewster, David. *Letters on Natural Magic, Addressed to Sir Walter Scott, Bart.* London: J. Murray, 1832.

Broad, C. D. *John McTaggart Ellis McTaggart, 1866–1925*. London: H. Milford, 1928.

Brocklebank, Lisa. "Psychic Reading." *Victorian Studies* 48.2 (2005): 233–39.

Brooks, Peter. *Body Work: Objects of Desire in the Modern Novel*. Cambridge, MA: Harvard University Press, 1993.

Brown, Daniel. *Hopkins' Idealism: Philosophy, Physics, Poetry*. Oxford: The Clarendon Press, 1997.

Brown, Nicola, Carolyn Burdett, and Pamela Thurschwell, eds. *The Victorian Supernatural*. Cambridge University Press, 2004.

Brown, Thomas. *Lectures on the Philosophy of the Human Mind*. 16th ed. Edinburgh: William Tate, 1846.

Browning, Elizabeth Barrett. "L. E. L.'s Last Question." orig. pub. *The Atheneum* January 26, 1839; reprinted in *Letitia Elizabeth Landon: Selected Writings*. Eds. Jerome McGann and Daniel Riess. Peterborough, Ontario: Broadview, 1997.

Browning, Elizabeth Barrett and Robert Browning. *The Letters of Robert Browning and Elizabeth Barrett Browning, 1845–1860*. Ed. Elvan Kintner. 2 vols. Cambridge, MA: Harvard University Press, 1969.

Browning, Elizabeth Barrett. *A Variorum Edition of Elizabeth Barrett Browning's Sonnets from the Portuguese*. Ed. Miroslava Weir Dow. Troy, NY: Whitston Publishing Co, 1980.

Browning, Robert. *Poetical Works 1833–1864*. Ed. Ian Jack. Oxford University Press, 1970.

Buchanan, Robert. "The Fleshly School of Poetry." *The Contemporary Review* 18 (1871) 334–50. The Rossetti Archive. Ed. Jerome McGann. 2000–2008. University of Virginia. February 25, 2008 http://www.rossettiarchive.org.

Budick, Sanford. "Tradition in the Space of Negativity." *Languages of the Unsayable: The Play of Negativity in Literature and Literary Theory*. Ed. Budick and Wolfgang Iser. New York: Columbia University Press, 1989. 297–322.

Burt, Stephen. *Randall Jarrell and His Age*. New York: Columbia University Press, 2002.

Butte, George. *I Know That You Know That I Know: Narrating Subjects from Moll Flanders to Marnie*. Columbus: Ohio State University Press, 2004.

Cadava, Eduardo, Peter Connor, and Jean-Luc Nancy, eds. *Who Comes After the Subject?* London: Routledge, 1991.

Cameron, Sharon. *Thinking in Henry James*. University of Chicago Press, 1989.

Campbell, Matthew. *Rhythm and Will in Victorian Poetry*. Cambridge University Press, 1999.

Carafides, John L. *The Philosophy of Reflection: An Examination of Shadworth H. Hodgson's Treatment of Experience* (Ph.D. diss, 1971).

Caramagno, Thomas C. "The Psychoanalytic Aesthetics of Eneas Sweetland Dallas." *Literature and Psychology* 33 (1987): 21–31.

Carlyle, Thomas. *On Heroes, Hero-Worship, and the Heroic in History*. Eds. Michael K. Goldberg, Joel J. Brattin, and Mark Engel. Berkeley: University of California Press, 1993.

Carpenter, William Benjamin. *Principles of Mental Physiology*. London: H. S. King & Co., 1874.

Carr, H. Wildon. "Shadworth Hollway Hodgson," *Mind* 84 (1912): 473–85.

Carruthers, Mary. *The Craft of Thought: Meditation, Rhetoric, and the Making of Images, 400–1200*. Cambridge University Press, 1998.

Caston, Victor. "Epiphenomenalisms, Ancient and Modern," *Philosophical Review* 106.3 (1997): 309–63.

Chalmers, David. *The Conscious Mind: In Search of a Fundamental Theory*. Oxford University Press, 1996.

Champneys, Basil. *Memoirs and Correspondence of Coventry Patmore*. 2 vols. London: George Bell, 1900.

Chapman, Alison. "Mesmerism and Agency in the Courtship of Elizabeth Barrett and Robert Browning." *Victorian Literature and Culture* (1998): 303–19.

Chase, Cynthia. "'Anecdote for Fathers': The Scene of Interpretation in Freud and Wordsworth." *Textual Analysis: Some Readers Reading*. Ed. Mary Ann Caws. New York: Modern Language Association, 1986: 182–206.

"The Decomposition of the Elephants: Double-Reading in *Daniel Deronda*." *Decomposing Figures: Rhetorical Readings in the Romantic Tradition*. Baltimore: Johns Hopkins University Press, 1986. 157–74.

Chitnis, Anand. *The Scottish Enlightenment: A Social History*. London: Croom Helm, 1976.

Clarke, Edward and L. S. Jacyna. *Nineteenth-Century Origins of Neuroscientific Concepts*. Berkeley: University of California Press, 1987.

Clifford, William Kingdon. *Lectures and Essays*. Eds. Leslie Stephen and Frederick Pollock. 2nd ed. London: Macmillan, 1886.

Cobham, E. M. *Mary Everest Boole: A Memoir with some Letters*. Ashingdon: C. W. Daniel, 1951.

Cohen, Ted. *Thinking of Others: On the Talent for Metaphor*. Princeton University Press, 2008.

Cohn, Dorrit. *Transparent Minds: Narrative Modes for Presenting Consciousness in Fiction*. Princeton University Press, 1978.

Coleridge, Mary Elizabeth. *Poems*. London: Elkin Mathews, 1908.

Coleridge, Samuel Taylor. *Biographia Literaria*. Eds. James Engell and W. Jackson Bate. *The Collected Works of Samuel Taylor Coleridge*. Vol. 7 Pts. 1 and 2. Princeton University Press, 1983.

Collected Letters of Samuel Taylor Coleridge. Ed. Earl Leslie Griggs. 6 vols. Oxford: Clarendon Press, 2000.

The Friend. Ed. Barbara E. Rooke. *The Collected Works of Samuel Taylor Coleridge*. Vol. 4 Pts. 1 and 2. Princeton University Press, 1969.

Literary Remains. Ed. Henry Nelson Coleridge. 4 vols. London: William Pickering, 1839.

Notebooks. Ed. Kathleen Coburn. 5 vols. New York: Pantheon, 1957–2002.

Poetical Works. Ed. J. C. C. Mays. *The Collected Works of Samuel Taylor Coleridge*. Vol. 16. Pts. 1–3. Princeton University Press, 2001.

Collini, Stefan. *Public Moralists: Political Thought and Intellectual Life in Britain, 1850–1930*. Oxford University Press, 1991.

Colquhoun, John C. *Isis Revelata: An Inquiry into the Origin, Progress, and Present State of Animal Magnetism*. 2 vols. 2nd ed. Edinburgh, 1836.

Comstock, Cathy. "'Speak, and I See the Side-Lie of a Truth': The Problematics of Truth in Meredith's *Modern Love*." *Victorian Poetry* 25.2 (1997): 129–41.

Cottom, Daniel. "I Think, Therefore, I am Heathcliff." *ELH* 70 (2003): 1067–88.

Crabtree, Adam. *From Mesmer to Freud: Magnetic Sleep and the Roots of Psychological Healing*. New Haven: Yale University Press, 1993.

Culler, Jonathan. "Apostrophe." *The Pursuit of Signs: Semiotics, Literature, Deconstruction*. Ithaca: Cornell University Press, 1981. 135–54.

Cunningham, G. Watts. *The Idealistic Argument in Recent British and American Philosophy*. New York: The Century Co., 1933.

Cvetkovich, Ann L. *Mixed Feelings: Feminism, Mass Culture, and Victorian Sensationalism*. New Brunswick: Rutgers University Press, 1992.

Dallas, E. S. *Poetics: An Essay on Poetry*. London: Smith Elder, 1852.

The Gay Science. London: Chapman and Hall, 1866.

Dames, Nicholas. *Amnesiac Selves: Nostalgia, Forgetting, and British Fiction 1810–1870*. New York: Oxford University Press, 2001.

"Reverie, Sensation, Effect: Novelistic Attention and Stendahl's *De l'amour*." *Narrative* 10.1 (2002): 47–68.

Dan-Cohen, Meir. "Harmful Thoughts." *Harmful Thoughts*. Princeton University Press, 2002. 172–95.

Dante. *Inferno*. Trans. Robert and Jean Hollander. New York: Doubleday, 2000.

Danziger, Kurt. "Mid-Nineteenth-Century British Psycho-Physiology: A Neglected Chapter in the History of Psychology." *The Problematic Science: Psychology in Nineteenth-Century Thought*. Eds. William R. Woodward and Mitchell G. Ash. New York: Praeger, 1982. 119–46.

Naming the Mind: How Psychology Found its Language. London: Sage Publications, 1997.

D'Arms, Justin and Daniel Jacobson. "The Moralistic Fallacy: On the 'Appropriateness' of Emotions." *Philosophy and Phenomenological Research* 61 (2000): 65–90.

"Sentiment and Value." *Ethics* 110 (2000): 722–48.

Darwall, Stephen. *The Second-Person Standpoint: Morality, Respect, and Accountability*. Cambridge, MA: Harvard University Press, 2006.

Daston, Lorraine J. "British Responses to Psycho-Physiology, 1860–1900," *ISIS* 69 (1978): 192–208.

Davie, George. *The Democratic Intellect: Scotland and her Universities in the Nineteenth Century*. Edinburgh University Press, 1961.

"Introduction." *Ferrier of St. Andrews: An Academic Tragedy*. Arthur Thomson. Edinburgh: Scottish Academic Press Ltd, 1985. ix-xv.

The Scotch Metaphysics: A Century of Enlightenment in Scotland. London: Routledge, 2001.

Davis, Leith, Ian Duncan, and Janet Sorensen. *Scotland and The Borders of Romanticism*. Cambridge University Press, 2004.

Davis, Michael. *George Eliot and Nineteenth-Century Psychology: Exploring the Unmapped Country*. Aldershot: Ashgate, 2006.

Deppman, Jed. "Trying to Think with Emily Dickinson." *The Emily Dickinson Journal* 14.1 (2005): 85–103.

De Quincey, Thomas. "Animal Magnetism." *Tait's Edinburgh Magazine* 4 (1834): 456–74.

De Quincey, Thomas. "A Review of a Philosophical Paper by Mr. Ferrier" (1842). *The Works of Thomas De Quincey*. Vol. 20. Ed. Edmund Baxter. London: Pickering and Chatto, 2001. 292–97.

"Testimonial of J. F. Ferrier" (1852). *The Works of Thomas De Quincey*. Vol. 17. Ed. Edmund Baxter. London: Pickering and Chatto, 2001. 250–54.

Devlin, Keith. *Goodbye, Descartes: The End of Logic and the Search for a New Cosmology of the Mind*. New York: John Wiley and Sons, 1997.

Dimock, Wai Chee. "Genres as Fields of Knowledge." *Publications of the Modern Language Association* 122.5 (2007): 1377–88.

Dixon, Joy. *Divine Feminine: Theosophy and Feminism in England*. Baltimore: Johns Hopkins University Press, 2001.

Doody, Margaret. "George Eliot and the Eighteenth-Century Novel." *Nineteenth-Century Fiction* 35:3 (1980): 260–91.

Ducasse, C. J. *A Critical Examination of the Belief in A Life After Death*. Springfield, IL: Thomas, 1961.

Dunbar, Robin. "On the Origin of the Human Mind." *Evolution and the Human Mind: Modularity, Language, and Meta-Cognition*. Eds. Peter Carruthers and Andrew Chamberlain. Cambridge University Press, 2000. 238–53.

During, Lisbeth. "The Concept of Dread: Sympathy and Ethics in Daniel Deronda." *Critical Review* 33 (1993): 88–109.

During, Simon. "The Strange Case of Monomania: Patriarchy in Literature, Murder in Middlemarch, Drowning in Daniel Deronda." *Representations* 23 (1988): 86–104.

Edmond, Rod. *Affairs of the Hearth: Victorian Poetry and Domestic Narrative*. London: Routledge, 1988.

Eilenberg, Susan. *Strange Power of Speech: Wordsworth, Coleridge, and Literary Possession*. New York: Oxford University Press, 1992.

Eliot, George. *Collected Poems*. Ed. Lucien Jenkins. London: Skoob Books, 1989.

   Daniel Deronda. Ed. Terence Cave. London: Penguin, 1995.

   Essays. Ed. Thomas Pinney. London: Routledge and Kegan Paul, 1963.

   The Journals of George Eliot. Eds. Margaret Harris and Judith Johnston. Cambridge University Press, 1998.

   The George Eliot Letters. 9 vols. Ed. Gordon S. Haight. New Haven: Yale University Press, 1954–78.

Ellenberger, Henri F. *The Discovery of the Unconscious*. New York: Basic Books, 1970.

Ellis, Havelock. "Hinton's Later Thought," *Mind* (July 1884): 384–405.

   "Preface." *James Hinton: A Sketch*. Mrs. Havelock Ellis. London: S. Paul, 1918.

Ellis, Mrs. Havelock [Edith Lees]. *James Hinton: A Sketch*. London: S. Paul, 1918.

   [Edith Lees]. *Three Modern Seers: James Hinton–Nietzsche–Edward Carpenter*. New York: Mitchell Kennerley, 1910.

Everest, Kelvin. *Coleridge's Secret Ministry: The Context of the Conversation Poems 1795–1798*. Sussex: Harvester, 1979.

Faas, Ekbert. *Retreat into Mind: Victorian Poetry and the Rise of Psychiatry*. Princeton University Press, 1988.

Ferrier, James Frederick. *An Introduction to the Philosophy of Consciousness*. In *The Philosophical Works of James Frederick Ferrier*. Vol 3. *Philosophical Remains*. Eds. Alexander Grant and E. L. Lushington (1883). Rpt. Bristol: Thoemmes Press, 2001.

Ferrier, James Frederick, ed. *Noctes Ambrosianae*. In John Wilson, *Works: Edited by his Son-in-Law Professor Ferrier*. Vols 1–4. Edinburgh: Blackwood, 1855.

Ferrier, James Frederick. "The Plagiarisms of S. T. Coleridge." *Blackwood's Edinburgh Magazine* 47 (March 1840): 287–99.

"The Poems of Coventry Patmore." *Blackwood's Edinburgh Magazine* 56 (September 1844): 331–42.

"Reid and the Philosophy of Common Sense." [Orig *Blackwood's Edinburgh Magazine* 1847] *The Philosophical Works of James Frederick Ferrier. Vol 3. Philosophical Remains*. Eds. Alexander Grant and E. L. Lushington (1883). Rpt. Bristol: Thoemmes Press, 2001.

Scottish Philosophy: the Old and the New. Edinburgh, Sutherland & Knox, 1856.

Ferro, Antonino. *Seeds of Illness, Seeds of Recovery: The Genesis of Illness and the Role of Psychoanalysis*. New York: Brunner-Routledge, 2004.

Fichte, J. G. *An Attempt at a New Presentation of the Wissenschaftslehre* (1797/98), *Introductions of the Wissenschaftslehre and Other Writings* (1797–1800) Ed. and trans. Daniel Breazeale. Indianapolis: Hackett, 1994.

Finkelstein, David, ed. *Print Culture and the Blackwood Tradition, 1805–1930*. University of Toronto Press, 2006.

Fletcher, Angus. *Colors of the Mind: Conjectures on Thinking in Literature*. Cambridge, MA: Harvard University Press, 1991.

Fletcher, Pauline. "'Trifles Light as Air' in Meredith's *Modern Love*." *Victorian Poetry* 34.1 (1996): 87–89.

Fonagy, Peter, and Mary Target. "Playing With Reality." *International Journal of Psycho-Analysis* 74 (1996): 217–33.

"Playing With Reality III: The Persistence of Dual Psychic Reality in Borderline Patients." *International Journal of Psycho-Analysis* 81 (2000): 853–73.

Forsyth, R. A. "'The Onward March of Thought' and the Poetic Theory of E. S. Dallas." *British Journal of Aesthetics* 3 (1963): 330–40.

Francois, Anne-Lise. *Open Secrets: The Literature of Unclaimed Experience*. Stanford University Press, 2008.

Fraser, Alexander Campbell. "The Philosophical Life of Professor Ferrier." *MacMillan's Magazine* XVII (1867068): 193–205.

Biographia Philosophica: a Retrospect. Edinburgh: W. Blackwood, 1905.

Frawley, Maria. "The Tides of the Mind: Alice Meynell's Poetry of Perception." *Victorian Poetry* 38.1 (2000): 62–76.

Freud, Sigmund. "Formulations on the two principles of mental functioning." *The Standard Edition of the Complete Psychological Works of Sigmund Freud*. London: Hogarth Press, 1953. 12: 213–26.

"Negation." *The Standard Edition of the Complete Psychological Works of Sigmund Freud*. London: Hogarth Press, 1953. 19: 235–39.

Totem and Taboo. The Standard Edition of the Complete Psychological Works of Sigmund Freud. London: Hogarth Press, 1953. 13: xii–162.

Frye, Northrop. *Anatomy of Criticism*. Princeton University Press, 1957.

Furr, Derek. "Sentimental Confrontations: Hemans, Landon and Elizabeth Barrett." *English Language Notes* 40 (2002): 29–47.

Gallagher, Catherine. *The Body Economic: Life, Death, and Sensation in Political Economy and the Victorian Novel*. Princeton University Press, 2006.

Galperin, William. *The Historical Austen*. Philadelphia: University of Pennsylvania Press, 2002.

Geach, P. T. *Truth, Love and Immortality: An Introduction to McTaggart's Philosophy*. London: Hutchinson, 1979.

Gérard, A. "The Systolic Rhythm: the Structure of Coleridge's Conversation Poems." *Coleridge: A Collection of Essays*. Ed. Kathleen Coburn. Englewood Cliffs, NJ: Prentice-Hall, 1967. 78–87.

Gitelman, Lisa. *Scripts, Grooves, and Writing Machines: Representing Technology in the Edison Era*. Stanford University Press, 1999.

Glynn, Ian. *An Anatomy of Thought: the Origin and Machinery of the Mind*. Oxford University Press, 1999.

Going, William T. *Scanty Plot of Ground: Studies in the Victorian Sonnet*. The Hague: Mouton, 1976.

Golden, Arline. "'The Game of Sentiment': Tradition and Innovation in Meredith's Modern Love." *ELH* 40.2 (1973): 264–84.

Goodlad, Lauren. *Victorian Literature and the Victorian State: Character and Governance in a Liberal Society*. Baltimore: Johns Hopkins University Press, 2003.

Goodson, A. C. *Verbal Imagination: Coleridge and the Language of Modern Criticism*. Oxford University Press, 1988.

Gopnik, Alison. "How we know our own minds: The illusion of first-person knowledge of intentionality." *Behavioral and Brain Sciences* 16 (1993): 1–14.

Gopnik, Alison and Andrew N. Meltzoff. *Words, Thoughts, and Theories*. Cambridge, MA: MIT Press, 1997.

Gordon, Mrs. *The Home Life of Sir David Brewster by his Daughter, Mrs. Gordon*. 3rd ed. Edinburgh, 1881.

Gosse, Edmund. *Coventry Patmore*. New York: Scribner's, 1905.

Gourgouris, Stathis. *Does Literature Think? Literature as Theory for an Antimythical Era*. Stanford University Press, 2003.

Graham, Gordon. "The Nineteenth-Century Aftermath." *The Cambridge Companion to the Scottish Enlightenment*. Ed. Alexander Broadie. Cambridge University Press, 2003. 338–50.

Green, Andre. "Psychoanalysis and Ordinary Modes of Thought." *On Private Madness*. Madison, CT: International University Press, 1986. 17–29.

Green, T. H. *Prolegomena to Ethics [1882]*. Ed. David O. Brink. Oxford: Clarendon Press, 2003.

Greenfield, Susan C. "The Absent-Minded Heroine: Or, Elizabeth Bennet Has a Thought." *Eighteenth-Century Studies* 39.3 (2006): 337–50.

Greenspan, Patricia S. *Practical Guilt*. New York: Oxford University Press, 1995.

Griffiths, Eric, and Matthew Reynolds, eds. *Dante in English*. London: Penguin, 2005.

Griffiths, Eric. *The Printed Voice of Victorian Poetry*. Oxford University Press, 1989.

Grosskurth, Phyllis. *Havelock Ellis: A Biography*. New York: Knopf, 1980.

Gunn, Thom. *Collected Poems*. London: Faber and Faber, 1993.

Gurney, Edmund, Frederic W. H. Myers, and Frank Podmore. *Phantasms of the Living* [1886]. 2 vols. Gainesville: Scholars' Facsimiles & Reprints, 1970.

Gutteridge, John. "Scenery and Ecstasy: Three of Coleridge's Blank Verse Poems." *New Approaches to Coleridge: Biographical and Critical Essays*. Ed. Donald Sultana. London: Vision Press, 1981. 151–71.

Hack, Daniel. *The Material Interests of the Victorian Novel*. Charlottesville: University of Virginia Press, 2005.

Haddon, Caroline. *The Larger Life: Studies in Hinton's Ethics*. London: Kegan Paul, Trench & Co., 1886.

Hadley, Elaine. "On a Darkling Plain: Victorian Liberalism and the Fantasy of Agency." *Victorian Studies* 48.1 (2005): 92–102.

Haldane, Elizabeth. *James Frederick Ferrier*. Famous Scots Series. Edinburgh: Oliphant, Anderson, and Ferrier, 1899.

Haldane, John. "Introduction." *The Philosophical Works of James Frederick Ferrier*. Vol I. Bristol: Thoemmes Press, 2001. v-xii.

Hamilton, Andy. "Mill, Phenomenalism, and the Self." *The Cambridge Companion to Mill*. Ed. John Skorupski. Cambridge University Press, 1998. 160–72.

Hamilton, Paul. *Coleridge and German Philosophy: The Poet in the Land of Logic*. London: Continuum, 2007.

    "Coleridge and the 'Rifacciamento' of Philosophy: Communicating an Idealist Position in Philosophy." *European Romantic Review* 14.1 (2003): 417–29.

Hamilton, William. "Philosophy and Perception: Reid and Brown." *Edinburgh Review* 52 (1830): 158–207.

Harding, Anthony John. *Coleridge and the Idea of Love: Aspects of Relationship in Coleridge's Thought and Writing*. Cambridge University Press, 1974.

Hardy, Thomas. *Collected Letters of Thomas Hardy*. 7 vols. Eds. Richard Purdy and Michael Millgate. Oxford: Clarendon Press, 1978–88.

    Desperate Remedies. London: Macmillan, 1975.

    The Variorum Edition of the Complete Poems of Thomas Hardy. Ed. James Gibson. New York: Macmillan, 1978.

    "The Withered Arm." *Collected Short Stories*. Ed. F.B. Pinion. London: Macmillan, 1977.

Harper, George McLean. "Coleridge's Conversation Poems." *Spirit of Delight*. London: E. Benn, 1928.

Harrington, Emily. *Lyric Intimacy: Forms of Intersubjectivity in British Women Poets, 1860–1900*. Ph.D. dissertation, University of Michigan, 2004.

Harris, Wendell V. *The Omnipresent Debate: Empiricism and Transcendentalism in Nineteenth-Century English Prose*. De Kalb: Northern Illinois University Press, 1981.

Harrison, Anthony. *Christina Rossetti in Context*. Chapel Hill: University of North Carolina Press, 1988.

Hartley, Lucy. *Physiognomy and the Meaning of Expression in Nineteenth-Century Culture*. Cambridge University Press, 2001.

Hassett, Constance W. *Christina Rossetti: The Patience of Style*. Charlottesville: University of Virginia Press, 2005.

Hearnshaw, L. S. *A Short History of British Psychology 1840–1940*. London: Butler and Tanner, 1964.

Hegel, G. W. F. *Aesthetics: Lectures on Art* trans. T. M. Knox. 2 vols. Oxford: Clarendon Press, 1975.

Hemans, Felicia. *Selected Poems, Letters, Reception Materials*. Ed. Susan J. Wolfson. Princeton University Press, 2000.

Hertz, Neil. *George Eliot's Pulse*. Stanford University Press, 2003.

Hesse, Mary B. *Forces and Fields: The Concept of Action at a Distance in the History of Physics*. London: T. Nelson, 1961.

Hieronymi, Pamela. "The wrong kind of reason." *The Journal of Philosophy* 103 (2005):437–57.

Hinton, C. H. *A New Era of Thought*. Ed. Alicia Boole. London: S. Sonnenschein & Co., 1888.

Hinton, James. *Chapters on the Art of Thinking and Other Essays*. Ed. C. H. Hinton. With an introduction by Shadworth Hollway Hodgson. London: Kegan Paul, Trench, & Co., 1879.

The Law-Breaker and the Coming of the Law. Ed. Margaret Hinton. London: Kegan Paul, Trench, & Co., 1884.

Philosophy and Religion: Selections from the Manuscripts of the Late James Hinton. Ed. Caroline Haddon. London: Kegan Paul, Trench, & Co., 1881.

Hodgson, Shadworth Hollway. "On the Genius of Thomas De Quincey." *Outcast Essays* (1881). Rpt. in James Hogg, ed. *De Quincey and His Friends*. London: Sampson Low, Marston, 1895. 314–60.

Outcast Essays. London: Longmans, Green, 1881.

The Philosophy of Reflection. 2 vols. London: Longmans, Green, 1878.

The Theory of Practice: An Ethical Enquiry. 2 vols. London: Longmans, Green, 1870.

Time and Space: A Metaphorical Essay. London: Longmans, Green, 1865.

Hopkins, Ellice, ed. *Life and Letters of James Hinton*. 8th ed. London: Kegan Paul, Trench, & Trubner, 1906.

Horn, Laurence R. *A Natural History of Negation*. University of Chicago Press, 1989.

Houghton, W. E. *The Victorian Frame of Mind*. New Haven: Yale University Press, 1963.

Houston, Natalie M. "Affecting Authenticity: Sonnets from the Portuguese and Modern Love," *Studies in the Literary Imagination* 35.2 (2002): 99–121.

Hughes, Linda K. "Entombing the Angel: Patmore's Revisions of *The Angel in the House*." *Victorian Authors and their Works: Revision, Motivation, Modes*. Ed. Judith Kennedy. Athens: Ohio University Press, 1991. 140–68.

Huxley, T. H. "On the Hypothesis that Animals are Automata and its History" (1879). *Method and Results*. New York: D. Appleton, 1896. 199–250.

"Illusion and Delusion: The Writings of Charles Bray," *Westminster Review* (January/April 1879): 488–503.

Izenberg, Oren. "Poems Out of Our Heads." *PMLA* 123.1 (2008): 216–22.

Jackson, Virginia. *Dickinson's Misery: A Theory of Lyric Reading*. Princeton University Press, 2005.

"Thinking Emily Dickinson Thinking Poetry." *A Companion to Emily Dickinson*. Eds. Mary Loeffelholz and Martha Nell Smith. Oxford: Blackwell, 2008. 205–21.

Jacobus, Mary. "Apostrophe and Lyric Voice in *The Prelude.*" *Lyric Poetry: Beyond the New Criticism*. Eds. Chaviva Hošek and Patricia Parker. Ithaca: Cornell University Press, 1985. 167–81.

The Poetics of Psychoanalysis: in the Wake of Klein. Oxford University Press, 2005.

Jaffe, Audrey. *Scenes of Sympathy*. Ithaca: Cornell University Press, 2000.

Vanishing Points. Berkeley: University of California Press, 1991.

James, Henry. "*Daniel Deronda* – A Conversation." (*Atlantic Monthly*, December 1876) *George Eliot: the Critical Heritage*. Ed. David Carroll. London: Routledge, 1995. 417–33.

James, Susan. *Passion and Action: The Emotions in Seventeenth-Century Philosophy*. Oxford University Press, 1997.

James, William. "Are We Automata?" *Mind*, 4.13 (1879): 1–22.

The Correspondence of William James. Eds. Ignas K. Skrupskelis and Elizabeth M. Berkeley. 12 vols. Charlottesville: University of Virginia Press, 1992–2004.

Principles of Psychology. 2 vols. New York: Henry Holt, 1890.

The Will to Believe and Other Essays in Popular Philosophy. Cambridge, MA: Harvard University Press, 1979.

Jarrell, Randall. *Complete Poems*. New York: Farrar, Strauss, and Giroux, 1969.

Jarvis, Simon. "Prosody as Cognition." *Critical Quarterly* 40.4 (1998): 3–15.

"Thinking in Verse." *The Cambridge Companion to British Romantic Poetry*. Eds. James Chandler and Maureen N. McLane. Cambridge University Press, 2008. 98–116.

Wordsworth's Philosophic Song. Cambridge University Press, 2006.

Johnson, Barbara. "Using People." *The Turn to Ethics*. Eds. Marjorie Garber, Beatrice Hannsen and Rebecca Walkowitz. New York: Routledge, 2000. 47–64.

Johnson, Wendell Stacy. *Sex and Marriage in Victorian Poetry*. Ithaca: Cornell University Press, 1975.

Jones, Ernest. *The Life and Work of Sigmund Freud*. 2 vols. New York: Basic Books, 1953.

Jordan, Jeff. "Pragmatic Arguments and Belief." *American Philosophical Quarterly* 33 (1996): 409–20.

Kant, Immanuel. *Anthropology From a Pragmatic Point of View*. [1798] Trans. and ed. Robert B. Louden. Cambridge University Press, 2006.

Karl, Frederick R. *George Eliot: Voice of a Century*. New York: Norton, 1995.

Karlin, Daniel. "Browning, Elizabeth Barrett, and 'Mesmerism'." *Victorian Poetry* 27.3–4 (1989): 65–77.

The Courtship of Robert Browning and Elizabeth Barrett. Oxford University Press, 1985.

Kawashima, R., B. T. O'Sullivan, and P. E. Roland. "Positron-emission tomography studies of cross-modality inhibition in selective attentional tasks: Closing the 'mind's eye'," *Proceedings of the National Academy of Science* 92 (1995): 5969–72.

Kincaid, James R. *Annoying the Victorians*. London: Routledge, 1995.

Kinderman, Peter, Robin Dunbar, and Richard P. Bentall. "Theory-of-Mind Deficits and Causal Attribution." *British Journal of Psychology* 89 (1998): 191–204.

Kneale, J. Douglas. "Romantic Aversions: Apostrophe Reconsidered." *Rhetorical Traditions and British Romantic Literature*. Eds. Don Bialostosky and Laurence D. Needham. Indiana University Press, 1995. 149–66.

Koven, Seth. *Slumming: Sexual and Social Politics in Victorian London*. Princeton University Press, 2004.

Kozicki, Henry. "The 'Unholy Battle' with the Other in George Meredith's *Modern Love*." *Papers on Language and Literature* 23.2 (1987): 142–60.

Kramnick, Jonathan. "Empiricism, Cognitive Science, and the Novel." *The Eighteenth Century: Theory and Interpretation* 48:3 (2007): 263–85.

Kucich, John. *Repression in Victorian Fiction*. Berkeley: University of California Press, 1987.

LaFarge, Lucy. "The Imaginer and the Imagined." *Psychoanalytic Quarterly* 73 (2004): 591–625.

Lamb, Charles. *Letters of Charles Lamb 1799–1801. The Letters of Charles and Mary Lamb*. Vol I. Ed. Edwin W. Marrs, Jr. Ithaca: Cornell University Press, 1975.

Landon, Letitia. *Selected Writings*. Eds. Jerome McGann and Daniel Reiss. Peterborough, Ont: Broadview Press, 1997.

LaPorte, Charles. "George Eliot, the Poetess as Prophet." *Victorian Literature and Culture* 31 (2003): 159–79.

Larson, Kerry. *Imagining Equality in Nineteenth-Century American Literature*. Cambridge University Press, 2008.

Lear, Jonathan. *Open Minded: Working Out the Logic of the Soul*. Cambridge, MA: Harvard University Press, 1998.

Lee, Benjamin. *Talking Heads: Language, Metalanguage, and the Semiotics of Subjectivity*. Durham: Duke University Press, 1997.

Leighton, Angela. *Victorian Women Poets: Writing Against the Heart*. Charlottesville: University of Virginia Press, 1992.

Levinas, Emmanuel. "Is Ontology Fundamental?" *Entre Nous: Thinking-of-the-Other*. Trans and eds. Michael B. Smith and Barbara Harshav. New York: Columbia University Press, 1998: 1–11.

Levine, George "*Daniel Deronda*: A New Epistemology." *Knowing the Past: Victorian Literature and Culture.* Ed. Suzy Anger. Ithaca: Cornell University Press, 2001.

Lewes, G. H. *The Physical Basis of Mind.* London: Truber & Co., 1877.

Lindop, Grevel. *The Opium Eater: A Life of Thomas De Quincey.* London: J. M. Dent, 1981.

Locke, John. *An Essay Concerning Human Understanding.* Ed. P. H. Nidditch. Oxford: Clarendon Press, 1975.

Loewald, H. W. "On the Therapeutic Action in Psychoanalysis." *International Journal of Psycho-Analysis* 41 (1960): 16–33.

Lootens, Tricia. "Hemans and Home: Victorianism, Feminine 'Internal Enemies,' and the Domestication of National Identity." *PMLA* 109.2 (1994): 238–53.

   Lost Saints: Silence, Genre, and Victorian Literary Canonization. Charlottesville: University of Virginia Press, 1996.

Lucas, John. "Meredith as Poet." *Meredith Now: Some Critical Essays.* Ed. Ian Fletcher. London: Routledge and Kegan Paul, 1971. 14–33.

Luckhurst, Roger. *The Invention of Telepathy, 1870–1901.* Oxford University Press, 2002.

Lukács, Georg. *The Theory of the Novel: a historico-philosophical essay on the forms of great epic literature.* Trans. Anna Bostock. Cambridge, MA: MIT Press, 1971.

Lushington, E. L. "Introductory Notice," James Frederick Ferrier, *Lectures on Greek Philosophy* [1866] *The Philosophical Works of James Frederick Ferrier* II: vii–xlviii.

Macewen, Alexander R. *Life and Letters of John Cairns.* 4th ed. London: Hodder & Stoughton, 1898.

Macovski, Michael. *Dialogue and Literature: Apostrophe, Auditors, and the Collapse of Romantic Discourse.* New York: Oxford University Press, 1994.

Magnuson, Paul. *Coleridge's Nightmare Poetry.* Charlottesville: University Press of Virginia, 1974.

Malachuk, Daniel S. *Perfectionism, the State, and Victorian Liberalism.* Houndmills and New York: Palgrave Macmillan, 2005.

Mander, W. J. *Anglo-American Idealism, 1865–1927.* New York: Greenwood, 2000.

Marias, Javier. *All Souls.* Trans. Margaret Jull Costa. London: Harvill Press, 1992.

Markovits, Stefanie. *The Crisis of Action in Nineteenth-Century English Literature.* Columbus: Ohio State University Press, 2006.

Marston, Philip Bourke. *The Collected Poems of Philip Bourke Marston.* 2nd edn. London: Ward, Lock, Bowden, 1892.

Marvell, Andrew. *The Complete Poems.* Ed. Elizabeth Story Donno. Harmondsworth: Penguin, 1976.

Masson, David. *Recent British Philosophy.* 3rd edn. London: Macmillan, 1877.

Matus, Jill L. "Historicizing Trauma: The Genealogy of Psychic Shock in Daniel Deronda." *Victorian Literature and Culture* 36 (2008): 59–78.

"Victorian Framings of the Mind: Recent Work on Mid-Nineteenth-Century Theories of the Unconscious, Memory, and Emotion." *Literature Compass* 4.4 (2007): 1257–76.

Maudsley, Henry. *Body and Mind.* London: Macmillan, 1873.

Maxwell, James Clerk. "On Action at a Distance." *The Scientific Papers of James Clerk Maxwell.* Ed. W. D. Niven. New York: Dover, 1952.

Mayo, Herbert. *Letters on the Truths Contained in Popular Superstitions.* Edinburgh: Blackwood, 1849.

Popular Superstitions and the Truth Contained Therein, with an Account of Mesmerism. 3rd edn. Philadelphia: Lindsay and Blakiston, 1852.

Mazzeo, Tilar J. *Plagiarism and Literary Property in the Romantic Period.* Philadelphia: University of Pennsylvania Press, 2007.

McCosh, James. *The Scottish Philosophy, Biographical, Expository, Critical, from Hutcheson to Hamilton.* New York: Robert Carter and Brothers, 1875.

McGhee, Richard D. *Marriage, Duty, and Desire in Victorian Poetry and Drama.* Lawrence: Regents Press of Kansas, 1980.

McSweeney, Kerry. *Supreme Attachments: Studies in Victorian Love Poetry.* Aldershot: Ashgate, 1998.

McTaggart, J. M. E. "The Further Determination of the Absolute." [1893] *Philosophical Studies.* Ed. S. V. Keeling. London, 1934. 210–72.

The Nature of Existence. Ed. C. D. Broad. 2 vols. Cambridge University Press, 1927.

Mellor, Anne K. "'This Lime-Tree Bower My Prison' and the Categories of English Landscape." *Critical Essays on Samuel Taylor Coleridge.* Ed. Leonard Orr. New York: G. K. Hall & Co., 1994.

Meredith, George. *The Letters of George Meredith.* 3 vols. Ed. C. L. Cline. Oxford: Clarendon Press, 1970.

The Poems of George Meredith. 2 vols. Ed. Phyllis B. Bartlett. New Haven: Yale University Press, 1978.

Mermin, Dorothy. *The Audience in the Poem: Five Victorian Poets.* New Brunswick: Rutgers University Press, 1983.

Elizabeth Barrett Browning: The Origins of a New Poetry. University of Chicago Press, 1989.

Mermin, N. David. "Can You Help Your Team Tonight by Watching on TV? More Experimental Metaphysics from Einstein, Podolsky, and Rosen." *Boojums All The Way Through: Communicating Science in a Prosaic Age.* Cambridge University Press, 1990. 95–109.

Meynell, Alice. "Introduction." *The Angel in the House Together with The Victories of Love by Coventry Patmore.* London: George Routledge and Sons, 1905. 1–26.

The Poems of Alice Meynell: Complete Edition. London: Oxford University Press, 1940.

"The Rhythm of Life." *The Rhythm of Life and Other Essays.* London: John Lane, 1897. 1–6.

"Second Person Singular." Orig. pub. *Pall Mall Gazette*, April 20, 1898. *Second Person Singular and Other Essays*. Oxford University Press, 1922. 133–40.

Meynell, Everard. *A Catalogue of the Library of Coventry Patmore*. London: Pelican Press, 1921.

Meynell, Viola. *Alice Meynell – A Memoir*. London: Jonathon Cape, 1929.

Mill, John Stuart. *On Liberty and Other Writings*. Ed. Stefan Collini. Cambridge University Press, 1989.

The Subjection of Women [1869]. Ed. Susan Moller Okin. Indianapolis: Hackett, 1988.

"Thoughts on Poetry and its Varieties." (1833) *Collected Works*. Vol 1. Eds. John S. Robson and Jack Stillinger. Toronto: University of Toronto Press, 1981.

Three Essays on Religion. New York: Henry Holt, 1874.

Miller, Andrew H. *The Burdens of Perfection: On Ethics and Reading in Nineteenth-Century British Literature*. Ithaca: Cornell University Press, 2008.

"Reading Thoughts: Victorian Perfectionism and the Display of Thinking," *Studies in the Literary Imagination* 35:2 (Fall 2002): 79–98.

"Review of *George Eliot's Pulse*." *Victorian Studies* 46.3 (2004): 537.

Miller, D. A. *Jane Austen, or the Secret of Style*. Princeton University Press, 2003.

Miller, J. H. *The Form of Victorian Fiction*. University of Notre Dame Press, 1968.

Milne, A. J. M. *The Social Philosophy of English Idealism*. London: Allen & Unwin, 1962.

Milton, John. *Complete Poems and Major Prose*. Ed. Merritt Y. Hughes. Indianapolis: Bobbs-Merrill, 1957.

Modiano, Raimonda. *Coleridge and the Concept of Nature*. Tallahassee: Florida State University Press, 1985.

Moore, Mary B. *Desiring Voices: Women Sonnetteers and Petrarchanism*. Carbondale: Southern Illinois University Press, 2000.

Moran, Richard. *Authority and Estrangement: An Essay on Self-Knowledge*. Princeton University Press, 2001.

Morris, Herbert. "Punishment for Thoughts." *On Guilt and Innocence: Essays in Legal Philosophy and Moral Psychology*. Berkeley: University of California Press, 1976. 1–29.

Muirhead, J. H. *Coleridge as Philosopher*. London: Allen and Unwin, 1930.

The Platonic Tradition in Anglo-Saxon Philosophy: Studies in the History of Idealism in England and America. New York: Macmillan, 1931.

Murphy, Peter T. "Impersonation and Authorship in Romantic Britain," *ELH* 59.3 (1992): 625–49.

Myers, F. W. H. *Human Personality and its Survival of Bodily Death*. 2 vols. London: Longmans, Green, 1903.

Newman, Beth. *Subjects on Display: Psychoanalysis, Social Expectation, and Victorian Femininity*. Athens: Ohio University Press, 2004.

Nichols, Shaun. *Sentimental Rules: On the Natural Foundations of Moral Judgment*. New York: Oxford University Press, 2004.

Nichols, Shaun and Stephen P. Stitch. *Mindreading: An Integrated Account of Pretense, Self-Awareness, and Understanding Other Minds.* Oxford University Press, 2003.

Nozick, Robert. *The Nature of Rationality.* Princeton University Press, 1993.

O'Shaughnessy, Edna. "A Commemorative Essay on W. R. Bion's Theory of Thinking." *Journal of Child Psychotherapy* 7 (1981): 181–92.

Omond, T. S. *English Verse-Structure (A Prefatory Study).* Edinburgh: David Douglas, 1897.

English Metrists in the Eighteenth and Nineteenth Centuries. London: Henry Froude, 1907

Oppenheim, Janet. *The Other World: Spiritualism and Psychical Research in England, 1850–1914.* Cambridge University Press, 1985.

Orsini, G. N. G. *Coleridge and German Idealism.* Carbondale: Southern Illinois University Press, 1969.

Otter, Sandra M. Den. *British Idealism and Social Explanation: A Study in Late Victorian Thought.* Oxford University Press, 1996.

Owen, Alex. *The Darkened Room: Women, Power and Spiritualism in Late Nineteenth-Century England.* London: Virago, 1989.

The Place of Enchantment: British Occultism and the Culture of the Modern. University of Chicago Press, 2004.

Palmer, Alan. *Fictional Minds.* Lincoln: University of Nebraska Press, 2004.

Parker, Reeve. *Coleridge's Meditative Art.* Ithaca, NY: Cornell University Press, 1975.

"'O Could You Hear His Voice': Wordsworth, Coleridge, and Ventriloquism." *Romanticism and Language.* Ed. Arden Reed. Ithaca: Cornell University Press, 1984.

Pater, Walter. "The Genius of Plato." *Plato and Platonism.* [1893] London: Macmillan, 1922. 124–49.

Patmore, Coventry. *The Angel in the House Books I & II: The First Editions Collated with his original Holograph Manuscript.* 2 vols. Eds. Patricia Aske and Ian Anstruther. London: Haggerston Press, 1998.

An Essay on English Metrical Law: A Critical Edition with a Commentary. [1857] Ed. Sister Mary Roth. Washington, D. C.: The Catholic University of America Press, 1961.

"The Morality of 'Epipsychidion," [1886] *Courage in Politics and Other Essays, 1885–1890.* London: Oxford University Press, 1921. 110–14.

The Poems of Coventry Patmore. Ed. Frederick Page. Oxford University Press, 1949.

The Rod, the Root, and the Flower. Ed. Derek Patmore. London: Grey Walls Press, 1950.

Tamerton Church-Tower and Other Poems. London: John W. Parker, 1854.

Pears, David. *Motivated Irrationality.* New York: Oxford University Press, 1984.

Perlow, Meir. *Understanding Mental Objects.* London: Routledge, 1995.

Peters, John Durham. *Speaking into the Air: A History of the Idea of Communication.* University of Chicago Press, 1999.

Picker, John. "Atlantic Cable." *Victorian Review* 24.1 (2008): 34–38.

    Victorian Soundscapes. Oxford University Press, 2003.

Pinch, Adela. "Transatlantic Modern Love." *The Traffic In Poems: Nineteenth-Century Poetry and Transatlantic Exchange.* Ed. Meredith L. McGill. New Brunswick: Rutgers University Press, 2008. 160–84.

Pockett, Susan, William P. Banks, and Shaun Gallagher, eds. *Does Consciousness Cause Behavior?* Cambridge, MA: MIT Press, 2006.

Porter, Katherine H. *Through a Glass Darkly: Spiritualism in the Browning Circle.* Lawrence: University of Kansas Press, 1958.

Postlethwaite, Diana. *Making it Whole: A Victorian Circle and the Shape of Their World.* Columbus: Ohio State University Press, 1984.

Potkay, Adam. "Coleridge's Joy." *The Wordsworth Circle* 35.3 (2004): 107–13.

Prins, Yopie. "Historical Poetics, Dysprosody, and the Science of English Verse." *PMLA* 123.1 (2008): 229–34.

    "Patmore's Law, Meynell's Rhythm." *The Fin-de-Siècle Poem: English Literary Culture and the 1890s.* Ed. Joseph Bristow. Columbus: Ohio State University Press, 2005. 261–84.

    "Victorian Meters." *The Cambridge Companion to Victorian Poetry.* Ed. Joseph Bristow. Cambridge University Press, 1999. 89–113.

    "Voice Inverse." *Victorian Poetry* 42 (2004): 43–59.

Raiger, Michael. "The Poetics of Liberation in Imaginative Power: Coleridge's 'This Lime-Tree Bower My Prison'." *European Romantic Review* 3 (1992): 65–78.

Raikka, Juha. "Irrational Guilt." *Ethical Theory and Moral Practice* 7 (2004): 473–85.

Raitt, Suzanne. *May Sinclair: A Modern Victorian.* Oxford University Press, 2000.

Reader, William D. "The Autobiographical Author as Fictional Character: Points of View in Meredith's Modern Love." *Victorian Poetry* 10 (1972): 131–43.

Reck, Andrew J. "Hodgson's Metaphysics of Experience." *Philosophy and Archaic Experience: Essays in Honor of Edward G. Ballard.* Ed. John Sallis. Pittsburgh: Duquesne University Press, 1982. 29–47.

Reddy, Vasudevi. "Experiencing Others: A Second-Person Approach to Other-Awareness." *Social Life and Social Knowledge: Toward a Process Account of Development.* Eds. Ulrich Muller, Jeremy I. M. Carpendale, Nancy Budgwig, and Bryan Sokol. New York: Lawrence Erlbaum Associates, 2008. 123–44.

Redfield, Marc. *Phantom Formations: Aesthetic Ideology and the Bildungsroman.* Ithaca: Cornell University Press, 1996.

Reid, J. C. *The Mind and Art of Coventry Patmore.* London: Routledge and Kegan Paul, 1957.

Reid, Thomas. *Essays on the Intellectual Powers of Man* [1785]. Ed. Baruch Brody. Cambridge, MA: MIT Press, 1969.

    Thomas Reid's Works, with Supplementary Notes and Dissertations. 2 vols. Ed. William Hamilton. Edinburgh: Maclachlan, 1846.

Reide, David. *Allegories of One's Own Mind: Melancholy in Victorian Poetry.* Columbus: Ohio State University Press, 2005.

Reisner, Andrew. "The Possibility of Pragmatic Reasons for Belief and the Wrong Kind of Reason Problem." *Philosophical Studies* 145.2 (2009): 257–72.

Richards, Graham. *Mental Machinery: The Origins and Consequences of Psychological Ideas: Part I: 1600–1850.* Baltimore: Johns Hopkins University Press, 1992.

    Putting Psychology in its Place: A Critical Historical Overview. 2nd ed. London: Routledge, 2002.

Richardson, Alan. "Apostrophe in Life and in Romantic Art: Everyday Discourse, Overhearing, and Poetic Address." *Style* 36.3 (2002): 363–85.

    British Romanticism and the Science of the Mind. Cambridge University Press, 2001.

Robinson, Daniel N. *An Intellectual History of Psychology.* 3rd ed. Madison: University of Wisconsin Press, 1995.

Rodensky, Lisa. *The Crime in Mind: Criminal Responsibility and the Victorian Novel.* Oxford University Press, 2003.

Roellinger, Francis X. *E. S. Dallas: A Study in Victorian Criticism.* Ph.D. dissertation, University of Michigan, 1938.

Rose, Nikolas. *The Psychological Complex: Psychology, Politics, and Society in England, 1869–1939.* London: Routledge and Kegan Paul, 1985.

Rossetti, Christina. *The Complete Poems of Christina Rossetti: A Variorum Edition.* 3 vols. Ed. R. W. Crump. Baton Rouge: Louisiana State University Press, 1979–90.

Rossetti, Dante Gabriel. *Poems.* 1st Ed. 1870. *The Rossetti Archive.* Ed. Jerome McGann. 2000–8. University of Virginia. February 25, 2008. www.rossettiarchive.org.

Rotenberg, Carl T. "George Eliot – Proto-Psychoanalyst," *The American Journal of Psychoanalysis* 59.3 (1999): 257–70.

Royle, Nicholas. *Telepathy and Literature.* Oxford: Blackwell, 1991.

Rudy, Jason R. "Rhythmic Intimacy, Spasmodic Epistemology." *Victorian Poetry* 42 (2004) 451–72.

Russell, Bertrand. *A History of Western Philosophy.* New York: Simon & Schuster, 1945.

Rzepka, Charles. *The Self as Mind: Vision and Identity in Wordsworth, Coleridge, and Keats.* Cambridge, MA: Harvard University Press, 1986.

Ryan, Vanessa. "Fictions of Medical Minds: Victorian Novels and Medical Epistemology." *Literature and Medicine* 25.2 (2006): 277–97.

Rylance, Rick. *Victorian Psychology and British Culture, 1850–1880.* Oxford University Press, 2000.

Saintsbury, George. *A History of English Prosody, from the Twelfth Century to the Present Day.* 3 vols. [1906–10]. London: Macmillan, 1923.

Schad, John. *Arthur Hugh Clough.* Tavistock, Devon: Northcote House, 2006.

Schaffer, Talia. *The Forgotten Female Aesthetes: Literary Culture in Late-Victorian England.* Charlottesville: University of Virginia Press, 2000.

Schneewind, Jerome. *Sidgwick's Ethics and Victorian Moral Philosophy*. Oxford University Press, 1977.

Seeley, Tracy. "'The Fair Light Mystery of Images': Alice Meynell's Metaphysical Turn." *Victorian Literature and Culture* 34 (2006): 663–84.

Seidel, George J. *Fichte's Wissenschaftslehre of 1794: A Commentary on Part I*. West Lafayette, IN: Purdue University Press, 1993.

Seth Pringle-Pattison, Andrew. *Scottish Philosophy; a Comparison of the Scottish and German Answers to Hume*. Edinburgh: Blackwood, 1885.

Seymour-Smith, Martin. *Thomas Hardy*. London: Bloomsbury, 1994.

Shaw, Harry E. *Narrating Reality: Austen, Scott, Eliot*. Ithaca: Cornell University Press, 1999.

Shaw, W. David. *The Lucid Veil: Poetic Truth in the Victorian Age*. London: Athlone, 1987.

Shelley, Percy Bysshe. *Epipsychidion by Percy Bysshe Shelley; a type fac-simile reprint of the original edition first published in 1821; with an introduction by the Rev. Stopford A. Brooke ..., and a note by Algernon Charles Swinburne*. Ed. Robert Alfred Potts. London: Published for the Shelley Society by Reeves and Turner, 1887.

Shelley's Poetry and Prose. Eds. Donald H. Reiman and Sharon B. Powers. New York: W. W. Norton, 1977.

Shuttleworth, Sally. *George Eliot and Nineteenth-Century Science: The Make-Believe of a Beginning*. Cambridge University Press, 1984.

"The Language of Science and Psychology in George Eliot's *Daniel Deronda*." *Victorian Science and Victorian Values: Literary Perspectives*. Eds. James Paradis and Thomas Postlewait. New Brunswick: Rutgers University Press, 1985: 269–98.

"'The Malady of Thought': Embodied Memory in Victorian Psychology and the Novel." *Australasian Victorian Studies Journal* 2 (1996): 1–12.

Shuttleworth, Sally and Jenny Bourne Taylor, Eds. *Embodied Selves: An Anthology of Psychological Texts 1830–1890*. Oxford University Press, 1998.

Simpson, Arthur L., Jr. "Meredith's Pessimistic Humanism: A New Reading of *Modern Love*." *Modern Philology* 67 (1970): 341–56.

Sinclair, May. *A Defence of Idealism: Some Questions and Conclusions*. London: Macmillan, 1917.

Skrbina, David. *Panpsychism in the West*. Cambridge, MA: MIT Press, 2005.

Smith, Adam. *The Theory of Moral Sentiments*. Eds. D. D. Raphael and A. L. Macfie. Oxford University Press, 1976.

Smith, Crosbie. *The Science of Energy: A Cultural History of Energy Physics in Victorian Britain*. London: Athlone Press, 1998.

Spencer, Herbert. *Principles of Psychology*. London: Longman, Brown, Green, & Longmans, 1855.

Spicker, Stuart F. "Shadworth Hodgson's Reduction as an Anticipation of Husserl's Phenomenological Psychology." *Journal of the British Society for Phenomenology* 2.2 (1971): 57–73.

Spitzer, Leo. "Speech and Language in Inferno XIII." *Italica* 19.3 (1942): 81–104.

Stephen, Leslie. *Selected Letters of Leslie Stephen*. Ed. John W. Bicknell. Columbus: Ohio State University Press, 1996.

Sternberg, Meir. *Expositional Modes and Temporal Ordering in Fiction*. Baltimore; Johns Hopkins University Press, 1978.

Stewart, Balfour and P. G. Tait. *The Unseen Universe; or Physical Speculations on a Future State*. 4th ed. London: Macmillan, 1876.

Stewart, Garrett. *Dear Reader: The Conscripted Audience in Nineteeth-Century Fiction*. Baltimore: Johns Hopkins University Press, 1996.

Stillinger, Jack. *Coleridge and Textual Instability: The Multiple Versions of the Major Poems*. Oxford University Press, 1994.

Stocking, George. *Victorian Anthropology*. New York: Free Press, 1987.

Stone, Marjorie. "'Monna Innominata' and *Sonnets from the Portuguese*: Sonnet Traditions and Spiritual Trajectories." *The Culture of Christina Rossetti: Female Poetics and Victorian Contexts*. Eds. Mary Arseneau, Anthony H. Harrison, and Lorraine Janzen Kooistra. Athens, OH: Ohio University Press, 1999. 46–74.

Strachey, Alix. "A Note on the Use of the Word 'Internal'." *International Journal of Psycho-Analysis* 22 (1941): 37–43.

Strawson, Galen *et al*. *Consciousness and its Place in Nature*. Exeter, England: Imprint Academic, 2006.

Sully, James *My Life and Friends: A Psychologist's Memoirs*. London: T. Fisher Unwin, 1918.

Swinburne, Algernon Charles. *Poems and Ballads*. 1866. In *Poems and Ballads and Atlanta in Calydon*. Ed. Kenneth Haynes. New York: Penguin, 2001.

Symonds, John Addington. *Blank Verse*. London: J. Nimmo, 1895.

The Letters of John Addington Symonds. Eds. Herbert N. Schueller and Robert L. Peters. 2 vols. Detroit: Wayne State University Press, 1968.

Taussig, Gurion. *Coleridge and the Idea of Friendship, 1789–1804*. Newark: University of Delaware Press, 2002.

Taylor, Dennis. *Hardy's Metres and Victorian Prosody*. Oxford: Clarendon Press, 1988.

Taylor, Jenny Bourne. "The Gay Science: The 'Hidden Soul' of Victorian Criticism." *Literature and History* 10 (1984): 189–202.

"Obscure Recesses: Locating the Victorian Unconscious." *Writing and Victorianism*. Ed. J. B. Bullen. London: Longman, 1997. 137–79.

Terada, Rei. *Feeling in Theory: Emotion after the "Death of the Subject."* Cambridge, MA: Harvard University Press, 2001.

"Thinking for Oneself: Realism and Defiance in Arendt." *ELH* 71 (2004): 839–65.

Thomas, David Wayne. *Cultivating Victorians: Liberal Culture and the Aesthetic*. Philadelphia: University of Pennsylvania Press, 2004.

Thomas, Sophie. "Aids to Friendship: Coleridge and the Inscription of the Friend." *European Romantic Review* 14.4 (2003): 431–40.

Thomson, Arthur. *Ferrier of St. Andrews: An Academic Tragedy*. Edinburgh: Scottish Academic Press Ltd, 1985.

Thurschwell, Pamela. "George Eliot's Prophecies: Coercive Second Sight and Everyday Thought Reading." *The Victorian Supernatural*. Eds. Nicola Brown, Carolyn Burdett, and Pamela Thurschwell. Oxford University Press, 2004. 87–105.

   Literature, Technology, and Magical Thinking 1880–1920. Cambridge University Press, 2001.

Tinterow, Maurice M. *Foundations of Hypnosis: From Mesmer to Freud*. Springfield, IL: C. C. Thomas, 1970.

Tomasello, Michael. "Social Cognition Before the Revolution." *Early Social Cognition: Understanding Others in the First Months of Life*. Ed. Pierre Rochat. Mahwah, N. J.: Lawrence Erlbaum, 1999. 301–13.

Townshend, Rev. Chauncy Hare. *Facts in Mesmerism, with Reasons for a Dispassionate Inquiry Into It*. London: Longman, Orme, Brown, Green, & Longmans, 1840.

Trollope, Anthony. *The Small House at Allington*. Ed. James R. Kincaid. Oxford: Oxford World's Classics, 1980.

Tromp, Marlene. *Altered States: Sex, Nation, Drugs, and Self-Transformation in Victorian Spiritualism*. Albany: SUNY Press, 2006.

Trott, Nicola Z. "North of the Border: Cultural Crossing in the Noctes Ambrosiane." *Romanticism on the Net* 20 (2000).

Tucker, Irene. *A Probable State*. University of Chicago Press, 2000.

Tulloch, John. "Professor Ferrier and the Higher Philosophy." *Modern Themes of Philosophy and Religion*. Edinburgh: Blackwood, 1884. 337–76.

Turner, Frank M. *The Greek Heritage in Victorian Britain*. New Haven, CT: Yale University Press, 1981.

Velleman, J. David. "Don't Worry, Feel Guilty." *Philosophy and the Emotions*. Ed. Anthony Hatzimoysis. Cambridge University Press, 2003. 235–48.

   The Possibility of Practical Reason. Oxford: Clarendon Press, 2000.

Vendler, Helen. *Poets Thinking: Pope, Whitman, Dickinson, Yeats*. Cambridge, MA: Harvard University Press, 2004.

Vrettos, Athena. "Defining Habits: Dickens and the Psychology of Repetition." *Victorian Studies* 42 (1999): 399–426.

   "Displaced Memories in Victorian Fiction and Psychology." *Victorian Studies* 49 (2007):199–207.

   Somatic Fictions: Imagining Illness in Victorian Culture. Stanford University Press, 1995.

Warren, Jr., Alba H. *English Poetic Theory 1825–1865*. Princeton University Press, 1950.

Waters, William. *Poetry's Touch: On Lyric Address*. Ithaca: Cornell University Press, 2003.

Watt, Stephen. "Neurotic Responses to a Failed Marriage: George Meredith's Modern Love." *Mosaic* 17 (1984): 46–63.

Welsh, Alexander. *George Eliot and Blackmail*. Cambridge: Harvard University Press, 1985.

Whale, John. *Imagination Under Pressure, 17980l832: Aesthetics, Politics, and Utility*. Cambridge University Press, 2000.

Whitla, William. "Questioning the Convention: Christina Rossetti's Sonnet Sequence, 'Monna Innominata'." *The Achievement of Christina Rossetti*. Ed. David A. Kent. Ithaca: Cornell University Press, 1987. 82–131.

Wilburn, Sarah A. *Possessed Victorians: Extra Spheres in Nineteenth-Century Mystical Writings*. London: Ashgate, 2006.

Williams, Bernard. "Moral Luck." *Moral Luck: Philosophical Papers, 1973–1980*. Cambridge University Press, 1981. 20–39.

Williams, Ioan, ed. *Meredith: The Critical Heritage*. London: Routledge and Kegan Paul, 1971.

Willis, Martin and Catherine Wynne, eds. *Victorian Literary Mesmerism*. Amsterdam: Rodopi, 2006.

Wilson, Phillip E. "Affective Coherence, a Principle of Abated Action, and Meredith's Modern Love." *Modern Philology* 72 (1974): 151–71.

Winnicott, D. W. "The Use of an Object and Relating Through Identifications." *Playing and Reality*. Routledge, 1971. 86–94.

Winter, Alison. *Mesmerized: Powers of Mind in Victorian Britain*. University of Chicago Press, 1998.

Wittgenstein, Ludwig. *Philosophical Investigations*. Trans. G. E. M. Anscombe. 3rd. ed. New York: Macmillan, 1958.

Wolfe, Willard. *From Radicalism to Socialism: Men and Ideas in the Formation of Fabian Socialist Doctrines, 1881–1889*. New Haven, CT: Yale University Press, 1975.

Woloch, Alex. *The One vs. the Many: Minor Characters and the Space of the Protagonist in the Novel*. Princeton University Press, 2003.

Woodward, William R. and Mitchell G. Ash, eds. *The Problematic Science: Psychology in Nineteenth-Century Thought*. New York: Praeger, 1982.

Woolf, Virginia. *Roger Fry: A Biography* [1940] San Diego: Harcourt Brace Jovanovich, 1968.

Wordsworth, William, and S. T. Coleridge. *Lyrical Ballads, 1798*. Ed. W. J. B. Owen. 2nd edn. Oxford University Press, 1969.

Wordsworth, William. *The Prelude, 1799, 1805, 1850*. Eds. Jonathan Wordsworth, M. H. Abrams, and Stephen Gill. New York: Norton, 1978.

Prose Works. Eds. W. J. B. Owen and Jane Worthington Smyser. 3 vols. Oxford University Press, 1974.

Young, Kay. "Middlemarch and the Problem of Other Minds Heard." *Literature Interpretation Theory* 14 (2003): 223–41.

Young, Robert M. *Mind, Brain, and Adaptation in the Nineteenth Century*. Oxford University Press, 1970.

Zunshine, Lisa. "Why Jane Austen Was Different, and Why We May Need Cognitive Science To See It." *Style* 41.3 (2007): 275–99.

Why We Read Fiction: Theory of Mind and the Novel. Columbus: Ohio State University Press, 2005.

Index

CAMBRIDGE STUDIES IN NINETEENTH-CENTURY
LITERATURE AND CULTURE

General editor
Gillian Beer, *University of Cambridge*

Titles published

Penguin Education

Britain transformed

V.T.J.Arkell

V.T.J.Arkell was educated in Ireland until 1950, and then at Bradfield
College, Berkshire, Queen's College, Oxford and Southampton
University. He has taught history in schools in Yorkshire and
Oxfordshire and is now a senior lecturer in history at Coventry
College of Education.

Britain transformed

The development of British society since the mid-eighteenth century

V. T. J. Arkell

Penguin Education

Design: Arthur Lockwood

Penguin Education
A Division of Penguin Books Ltd,
Harmondsworth, Middlesex, England
Penguin Books Inc., 7110 Ambassador Road, Baltimore, Md 21207, USA
Penguin Books Australia Ltd, Ringwood, Victoria, Australia

First published 1973
Copyright © V. T. J. Arkell, 1973

Made and printed in Great Britain by Butler & Tanner Ltd, Frome and London
Set in Lumitype Plantin

Contents

Preface

My aim in this book has been to help the reader understand Britain today by showing how much life in this island has changed during the last 200 years. So much of importance has happened during this period that everything cannot possibly be included. The knowledgeable reader therefore will detect some gaps in the text, as well as passages which are frustratingly brief. When I have departed from some traditional interpretations, as with Dr Arnold, I have certainly felt particularly the lack of space limiting my explanations.

In general I have tried to avoid giving the impression that the efforts of prominent individuals alone led to social and economic advance. Such developments rarely occurred in one year either, so that recording precise dates can be equally misleading. The knowledge that Cartwright, for instance, made a power loom of sorts in 1784 does not tell us when most cloth was woven first on power looms. And of the two facts, the latter, though vague, seems much more significant. In addition my dates normally record when measures took effect and not when Parliament approved them, e.g. Old Age Pensions began in 1909, not 1908.

Statistics drawn from the nineteenth century and earlier always pose problems. Some are demonstrably true, others reliable estimates and yet others too uncertain or incomplete to carry conviction. Shortage of space has prevented me from discussing in detail those I have included, but I have tried to ensure that they belong only to the first two categories. And where I have illustrated trends with figures, I have done my best to space them at regular intervals.

My quotations are not entirely authentic. I have left out some words without indication and altered others when I thought it clarified the meaning. I have also included many more contemporary descriptions of life and incidents in the eighteenth and nineteenth centuries than in the twentieth, because I felt the need to point the differences between life in more remote times and now.

Finally, I record most willingly my debt of gratitude to the Warden and Fellows of New College, Oxford, for awarding me in 1968 a School-master Studentship and to the Oxfordshire Education Committee for seconding me. I am also very pleased to thank again Miss Mary Worrall, Miss Elizabeth Barber and many of my other friends who encouraged me to persevere with this project.

Part 1   The eighteenth century

Chapter 1
Britain at work 1740s–1780s

Introduction

'God Save the Queen' is now established so firmly as our National
Anthem that it seems impossible to imagine the time when no one
in Britain could either sing it or repeat its words. But once this really
was true.

Although written at some stage during the seventeenth century, our
present national anthem remained almost entirely unknown until the
year 1745. Then the chain of events which were to bring it popularity
began on 25 July, when the attractive young prince, Charles Edward,

This engraving by Hogarth
shows the confusion as
soldiers prepare to march
nearly 400 miles to Edinburgh,
to fight Bonnie Prince Charlie.

landed on the west coast of Scotland in a bid to drive King George II from his throne. When the news of his landing reached London in the second week of August, the king was away in Germany and the government was utterly unprepared to crush the rebellion.

And so, for several months, Bonnie Prince Charlie swept all before him. In August the Highlands of Scotland fell to his control and before September was out he had captured Edinburgh and routed a small British army in a battle lasting little more than ten minutes. As the Young Pretender prepared to advance south, fear and panic swept the English capital. It was in this atmosphere that London's two main theatres, Drury Lane and Covent Garden, decided to perform 'God Save Our Noble King' at the end of every play. The song was received with thunderous applause and repeated every night until the rebels were defeated.

Now, the fact that Britain had no national anthem before 1745 is in itself of little consequence. But it does serve as a warning to anyone seeking to discover about our ancestors' way of life in the middle of the eighteenth century. Britain was then a very different country from today in all kinds of ways.

For a start, communication was very poor. No modern government, however badly organized, would have to wait a fortnight before it heard about an invasion in Scotland. But then, of course, eighteenth-century people had never seen a radio or telephone nor had they invented any means of using electricity.

There were far fewer people in Britain in the middle of the eighteenth century than there are now — less than eight million altogether. In other words, for about every eight people alive today, only one was to be found in the kingdom of George II. Or to put the same fact another way: now more people live in London alone than inhabited the whole of England, Scotland and Wales less than 250 years ago.

One natural result of this situation was that eighteenth-century towns were comparatively small and most people lived outside them. About three-quarters of the population lived in the countryside, mostly in villages of between 50 to 150 houses each. Where the soil was rich and fertile these villages were often no more than a mile or two apart, but in the northern counties especially the distance between the villages was rarely less than five miles. Judged by modern standards, Britain in the eighteenth century had few buildings and those which did exist were very small.

Land was then the main source of wealth and the landowners were by far the most important people in the community. Indeed, most of Britain was divided into estates of 2000 acres or more, which were owned by rich and powerful nobles and gentlemen. These were the people who governed the country and employed many of the lower orders. And so, from their wealth stemmed not just luxury, but power.

About three-quarters of the population of eighteenth-century Britain lived in the countryside. This Essex village is a cluster of houses dominated by the church.

11

How the wealth of the country was produced

Farming

The great wealth of the landowners was based on farming, which was by far the most important economic activity in Britain in the mid eighteenth century. The landowners' estates were generally divided into several farms of approximately 200 acres. One farm would supply a landowner's family with food. The rest were rented to tenant farmers for periods of perhaps fourteen years. The landlords were responsible for looking after the farm buildings, while the tenants provided their own seed and animals. Three-quarters of English farmland was farmed in this way. Farmers who owned or rented smaller holdings (of under 100 acres) cultivated less than a sixth of the land.

Most farms were mixed, growing corn, hay and vegetables and rearing cattle, sheep and hens. Naturally their soil and climate strongly influenced what they produced. Wheat was grown in most counties, but principally in the southern half of England. Barley too was found everywhere, but especially in Wales and the west. On the poorer soil north of the river Trent, the chief crop was oats. The less fertile regions were better suited to pasture farming. Many cattle were therefore raised on the hillsides of western and northern England and of Scotland, from where they were driven to be fattened in the fertile pastures near the towns. Scotland was one of the main centres for sheep, which were also reared increasingly in the English midlands.

On the heavier clay soils of the midlands in particular much farming was still organized as it had been for centuries. The crops were grown in large unfenced fields, subdivided into much smaller strips. Each village usually had three fields, one of which was left unsown every year to let the soil recover. The animals grazed in separate meadows and in the open fields after the harvest. Up to the mid eighteenth century this method of farming helped feed the people adequately. Keen farmers were anxious to see that the neighbouring strips were farmed properly and, since all the villagers had to plough, sow and harvest at the same time, the lazy ones were made to work.

But this open-field system also had its defects. Land was wasted, since gaps were left between the strips. They were difficult to drain, and weeds spread easily. The mating of selected animals was impossible because they mixed freely. No precautions could be taken against epidemics of infectious diseases like cattle plague which broke out frequently. Go-ahead individuals found it difficult to adopt many new practices.

However these disadvantages did not become serious until after 1750 when the population increased more rapidly. Then the demand for extra food raised prices and encouraged the farmers to produce more. Even so most farmers were naturally suspicious of new methods. They

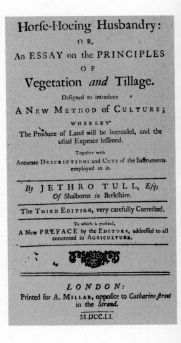

Jethro Tull was one of the first to advocate sowing seed in rows, but although this edition of his famous book was printed in 1751, ten years after his death, few eighteenth-century farmers copied his ideas.

wanted to be quite sure that they would gain before risking money which they could barely afford. They were further confused because some ideas seemed so foolish, like Jethro Tull's, an agricultural writer and farmer, who believed that manure was unnecessary and that wheat should be sown in rows at least a foot apart. Successful neighbours were the best advocates of new ways. And so, as farming became more profitable, the farmers at last took up generally the most productive methods which had become firmly established in some localities in the previous 100 years.

Many improvements in arable farming came from Holland in the seventeenth century. They were introduced to Norfolk and the surrounding countryside, from where they spread to other light-soiled districts, where previously most farmers had been unable to grow crops regularly on chalk, limestone or sand. They began by planting turnips, clover and sainfoin, which provided their animals with more fodder. The last two crops also restored nitrogen to the soil which, combined with the increased dung from the extra animals, made it much more fertile. Some farmers further increased the yield of their crops by mixing sandy soils with lime and clay and by irrigating fields which lay near streams. By the mid eighteenth century therefore some farmers on lighter soils were growing wheat more cheaply than those from the traditional clay regions. They also adopted more elaborate crop rotations which did not leave a third of the land fallow. These normally contained at least four different crops. Wheat, barley, clover and a root crop (perhaps turnips) were among the most common. Furthermore, by 1780 horses rather than oxen were generally used for ploughing.

Farmers on the heavy clay soils were slow to take up these improvements, which were often unsuitable for them. Because their grass grew

Farmers took to sowing their seeds in rows (instead of scattering it at random) very gradually, even though widely spaced rows saved seed and made the hoeing out of weeds possible. On this farm the four-wheel wagon has replaced the two-wheel cart, as was happening elsewhere, because it could carry a heavier load.

well, for instance, they had much less need of extra fodder for their cattle. Their main problems stemmed from the ground, which was too heavy, wet and cold. They had to wait until later in the spring before they could sow their seed, and implements like ploughs had to be stronger and pulled by more animals. These farmers badly needed proper drainage, which was a very difficult task. Therefore most advances in arable farming took place on the lighter soils, especially in those areas like the home counties, Norfolk and the Lothians from where the farmers could reach London and other large towns most easily. In east Kent, for instance, farmers specialized in growing fruit and vegetables as well as their usual crops. In Lancashire, Wales and Scotland they grew more and more potatoes.

Pasture farming also flourished. During the eighteenth century the number of sheep in Britain doubled to about twenty-five million. In Cheshire and Ayrshire in particular many farmers produced more milk and other dairy products. The number of cattle remained almost constant at under five million, but the farmers produced more beef because they fattened the beasts more quickly on the new crops and so slaughtered them younger. 'And though some have objected against the goodness of the flesh thus fed with turnips, and have fancied that it would taste of the root,' reported Daniel Defoe, 'yet upon experience 'tis found, that at market there is no difference, nor can they that buy

One outstanding landowner in the late eighteenth century was Thomas Coke of Norfolk, seen here inspecting his Southdown sheep. He not only improved the breeds of sheep and cattle in Norfolk, but also made his tenants use better crop rotations, and so the rents from his Holkham estates doubled in forty years.

Cattle and sheep being driven to market. Animals reared on hill pastures in remote areas often walked long distances to the towns before being fattened and slaughtered. The drover's job was a very responsible one, he not only had to look after the animals and deliver them safely, he also had to return with the money paid for them. There were special 'drove roads' which followed water holes and along which were inns for the drovers.

single out one joint of beef or mutton from another by the taste.' By the 1780s cattle and sheep were about one and a quarter times as heavy as they had been at the start of the century. Selective breeding was partly responsible for this development, but we know more about the breeding of race horses than of sheep until the mid eighteenth century. After then, Robert Bakewell's attempts to improve them were very well publicized.

Few great landowners were interested in pioneering new methods of farming in the early eighteenth century. When, like Viscount Townshend, they did devote themselves to farming they normally put other people's ideas into practice instead of trying out some of their own. Most pioneers were richer farmers with between 200 and 500 acres. Landowners took a greater interest in progressive farming when it became more profitable later in the century. They then spent more money on farm buildings and equipment in addition to their country houses and other luxuries. In Scotland, where much of the soil was less fertile and the farmers poorer, the landowners played a greater part in spreading new methods. They did this either by their own example or by providing their tenants with new buildings or by stipulating in their leases that certain new crops should be grown.

To help feed the growing population almost another three million acres were added by 1780 to the twenty-five million which were already

15

farmed in England and Wales in the early eighteenth century. This was done partly by draining marshy land, cultivating more hill-tops and taking over other waste land. Throughout the century more and more open fields were also enclosed by hedges or fences. This was normally carried out by private agreement among the villagers, but if several objected it could not be done until Parliament had passed a special act. This was a slow and expensive business, taking up to ten years to complete, and so very few were approved before 1750. Rising profits then encouraged the landowners and wealthy farmers to press on with enclosure where they had previously met with opposition. By the 1770s Parliament was passing sixty-five acts every year. Although new crops were sometimes grown in the open fields, enclosed farms were usually cultivated more efficiently.

Because farming was so important in the eighteenth century, most of the people worked on the land, often starting very early in life. Young children often earned a few pennies picking up stones in the fields or scaring birds away from crops, but boys rarely started regular work before they were eight. Then, for several years, they would trail around after the adults doing the odd jobs, for most farm work required strength and experience, neither of which they had.

The work of many farm labourers was involved with animals. Cattle, sheep and horses were valuable and had to be handled with care and sympathy. They could not be neglected for a day and those in charge worked seven days a week.

Farm labourers worked most unevenly throughout the year. At sowing, haymaking and harvest times they were kept very busy, often working from three in the morning to seven at night in the summer. In sharp contrast threshing was one of the few available winter jobs. Their wages, naturally, fluctuated according to the season, perhaps in this proportion: 5/– a week in winter, 8/– in summer and 12/– during the harvest.

Hay was mown with a scythe, which had to be kept very sharp. 'To look on, this work seems nothing,' wrote one contemporary, 'but it tries every sinew in your frame if you stand up and do your work well.'

A sickle.

16

Corn was usually cut by sickle, then bound into sheaves and stood in stooks to dry. Here one stook is still standing as the men load the wagon with sheaves, which will then be stacked in ricks. The women are busy gleaning – gathering for themselves the stray ears of corn.

Threshing with a flail was another back-breaking task. The thresher laid the corn on the barn floor and then for hour after hour swung the flail over his shoulder, aiming to hit the straw just below the ears so that the grains fell out without being crushed.

Eighteenth-century farmers usually hired their more skilled men, like shepherds and cowmen, for twelve-month periods at country fairs. In the north especially they often lived in the farmer's house, receiving board and lodging as part of their wages, but probably waiting for the rest in cash at the end of the year. Most other labourers were hired for shorter periods when there was extra work like hedging and ditching. Everyone's help, including the women's and children's, was welcome at harvest time.

In spinning the woman pulled out strands from the bundle of loose fibres above her and then twisted them with her fingers and a spindle turned by the spinning wheel into as even a thread as possible. Spinning created a lot of fluff, so this spinster is working with both door and window open. The basket on the floor contains skeins of yarn ready for weaving.

Industry

All Britain's other industries took second place to farming. Their total output was worth less than half the value of all farm products. There was also a very close connection between agriculture and industry, because the farmers provided many industries with their raw materials: wool for spinning and weaving into cloth, for instance, or hides for tanning into leather, and barley for brewing. And so a poor harvest might mean that manufacturers were left short. A good harvest, on the other hand, gave them a double benefit, for it brought plenty of raw materials and low food prices. Cheap food meant that people had more money left to spend on other goods.

All counties produced some woollen cloth, but three regions specialized in making the finer cloths: East Anglia, the West Country and the West Riding of Yorkshire. Making woollen cloth involved many different stages. It was a complicated industry to organize. Because so much work was done in people's homes, the material had to be moved many times before the cloth was finished. Often one merchant or clothier acted as the middleman who supplied perhaps twenty to fifty workers with the wool or cloth in the various stages which they required.

By 1780 the output of the woollen industry was worth a quarter of the value of all industrial products. Parliament recognized its importance by passing laws to help it. For a time, for instance, it was illegal to bury corpses in anything but woollen shrouds.

The other textile industries were not very important in the mid-eighteenth century. Of these linen was the most valuable. It was established in Lancashire and the Lowlands of Scotland. Cotton was made in the same regions. Until the 1770s pure cotton goods were illegal, so

The weaver, who was usually a man, first attached the yarn in close parallel lines from the front of his loom to the back; when he sat down he could open a gap between the alternate threads with his feet and through this he passed with his hands from side to side another ball of yarn wound round a shuttle.

cotton and linen were woven together to form a coarse cloth called fustian. Their manufacture was organized in a similar way to wool.

Silk-making was established in England towards the end of the seventeenth century, but it never competed successfully with the French or Italians. All its raw materials were imported and its fortunes fluctuated unpredictably as fashions changed. Nottingham and the east midlands were the centres for knitted stockings. Lace-making was established in the southern midlands. Where possible, these less fertile regions, which profited less from the latest farming techniques, took up such industries instead.

And so, towards the end of the eighteenth century, many people were engaged at home, making a wide range of goods with tools, or simple machines operated by hand. Those who had a spinning wheel, hand loom or knitting frame in their homes, together with the necessary materials and instructions on what to do, could soon acquire the skills needed in making textiles. Since these tasks usually entailed the endless repetition of a few simple movements they were very exhausting.

After being woven the cloth was far from finished. Linen (as shown below) and cotton were usually dipped in specially prepared solutions and then pegged out in the fields to be bleached for months by the sun and rain. Wool, on the other hand, was shrunk, hammered, dried, then cut smooth with large shears and finally dyed.

Since most workers had a set task to finish by the end of the week, they generally took life easily from about midday on Saturday to perhaps Tuesday, when they began to work really hard (up to sixteen hours a day) for the rest of the week. Often the whole family joined in, for, as with farming, children usually began to work as soon as they were able. The following account comes from a later period, but gives insight into the sufferings of some eighteenth-century children.

Little girls are kept up shamefully late if there is work, especially on Thursday and Friday nights, when it is often till eleven or twelve. They have to make two days out of Friday. Mothers will pin them to their knee to keep them to their work and, if they are sleepy, give them a slap on the head to keep them awake. If the children are pinned up so, they cannot fall when they are slapped or when they go to sleep.

Most masters supplied more workers than they needed and so few were kept busy throughout the year. After finishing their work for the week, therefore, they might have to wait a month or more not only for their pay but also for fresh materials. In the later eighteenth century, for example, once after eight months' unemployment Francis Place, a breeches-maker, was given a good supply of work. 'We now worked full 16 and sometimes 18 hours a day, Sundays and all. I never went out of the house for many weeks and could not find time for a month to shave myself.'

Iron was so scarce in the mid eighteenth century that people regularly returned nails to their blacksmiths to have them repaired. Nevertheless iron-making was Britain's most important metal industry.

Most of the work was done in wooded areas because large quantities of charcoal were used to heat the blast furnaces which extracted the iron from its ore. The molten metal was then run off into moulds.

A cast-iron cooking pot.

Charcoal-burning. The wood was stacked carefully in layers until the pile was eight or nine feet high. Then it was covered with straw or ferns and a layer of turf, lit, and left to smoulder for about a week.

The men on the right are pouring hot liquid cast iron into a mould to make cannon-balls. From the picture below you can see how they work the bellows to heat the small furnace.

Because this pig-iron still contained many impurities it was hard but brittle. Much was cast into simple shaped objects like pots and cannons. The rest was refined further in forges by reheating and hammering. This wrought iron was much tougher and more flexible, but it was very expensive because a lot of charcoal was needed to forge it. Slitting mills produced strips or rods of wrought iron from which nails and wire were made. The workshops which turned out locks, spades and other tools were all very small. Many were near Birmingham, even though much of their iron came from distant blast furnaces and forges.

Although eighteenth-century iron-makers suffered from a serious shortage of wood, they took a very long time to discover how to use coal instead without ruining the metal. Early in the century the Darby family succeeded in smelting pig-iron with coke in larger furnaces at Coalbrookdale in Shropshire, but they kept the process secret for nearly forty years. Because it raised the temperature in the furnaces and made

the metal more fluid, they could cast more delicate articles like buttons and door hinges. It was also cheaper. When the other manufacturers were at last copying their techniques in the middle of the century, the Darbys managed to forge wrought iron from coke-smelted pig-iron. Even so in the 1780s wrought iron remained very scarce and expensive. Copper, which was often turned into brass for kitchen utensils, helped fill the gap, but many things which we would expect to find made of metal were still made from wood.

In the eighteenth century coal was mined by men who hammered away with picks. When they had cracked the coal-face sufficiently, they usually used crowbars to prize it loose. They shovelled the loose coal behind them so that they could get at the face again. The miner did these operations kneeling and sometimes even lying on his side because many seams were about three feet high. He worked with very little light in most unpleasant conditions. The mines were often very damp, with water dripping down the rock face. The atmosphere was dusty, hot and stuffy. It was a job for very tough men who could really exert themselves for twelve hours or more every day.

From the pit-face the coal was either carried in baskets or pushed in wagons along low and narrow passages, often uphill, to the shafts. Women and children did this in many pits.

Coal output increased noticeably after 1750 even though dangerous gases and the risk of flooding prevented the miners from digging down more than a few hundred feet. Nearly all mines were sited in the countryside. The Durham coal-field was the most developed because it was by the sea and coal was so heavy that it could not be moved long distances on land. Most of it was still burned in people's homes rather than by industry.

Ironbridge, the first cast-iron bridge, built in 1779 over the Severn near Coalbrookdale. A three-mile stretch of the Severn Gorge, where the bridge still stands, is being developed into an open-air museum showing the origins of the industrial revolution.

22

A windmill.

A horse-gin at the head of a Welsh coal-mine. Pulleys used the movement of the horses, walking round and round, to pull up coal and miners from the pit below. Like Coalbrookdale, and most industrial sites, this mine is set in the countryside.

British industry expanded steadily but not rapidly in the middle of the eighteenth century. Further progress was held back by many things. Each major industry had serious technical problems by 1780. In textiles the weavers were frequently short of yarn because weaving was a much faster process than spinning. Wrought iron still had to be forged with charcoal. Coal miners could not reach the deeper seams.

Industry was still restricted by inadequate power. Some simple engines driven by water existed, but they were rarely of more than twelve h.p. and they could not be used all the time. As the iron-founder Samuel Walker of Rotherham complained: 'We have some works upon a river, which in general supplies us well with water; but in dry seasons we are much retarded for want of water.' Windmills were used extensively for grinding corn and pumping water, but they performed even more erratically. The only other available sources of power were the muscles of men and of animals. Horses walking round and round a gin could wind a cable on a drum which, for example, hauled coal to the top of a mine shaft.

Anyone who wanted to start a business found it almost impossible to raise the necessary money unless he could attract a wealthy backer or partner. Three brothers managed to establish themselves in the Lancashire cotton business in the following way. 'We got mother to go and see if she could prevail of old Mr Thomas Hoyle of Manchester (Printer) to lend us a hundred pounds. My grandfather was one of the Friends, called Quakers, as was also Thomas Hoyle. They were relations and fellow playboys.'

Because money was scarce, most businesses were small. They were run as private firms with very few employees by one family or by two or three in partnership. Usually buildings and equipment could only be paid for from their profits and so business expanded slowly.

Transport

Agriculture and industry were both hampered by poor communications. Most roads were little more than cart tracks riddled with ruts and pot-holes. When it rained mud made them almost impassable, so that travelling in winter was particularly difficult. Sometimes it was quicker for horsemen to ride through the fields than along the road. Many of the worst roads ran over deep clay. Arthur Young, a leading agricultural journalist, wrote in 1770 of a stretch in Lancashire:

I know not terms sufficiently expressive to describe this infernal road. To look over a map, and perceive that it is a principal one, one would normally conclude it to be at least decent; but let me most seriously caution all travellers who may accidentally purpose to travel this terrible country, to avoid it as they would the devil; for a thousand to one but they break their necks or their limbs by overthrows or breakings down. They will here meet with ruts which I actually measured four feet deep, and floating with mud only from a wet summer. What therefore must it be after a winter?

Riding on horseback was the fastest method of travelling, but long journeys were tiring for both horse and rider. Coaches were very bumpy and not much less exhausting, but it was the normal means of transport for those who could afford it. A typical journey from London to Yorkshire or Lancashire took as much as four or five days in the mid eighteenth century. Edinburgh and Glasgow were about an additional week away. Transport was both slow and very expensive.

By 1750 some main roads, mostly in the south-east, were looked after by about 400 Turnpike Trusts. Each controlled a stretch of about ten miles and levied tolls from all who used it. Sometimes they were so unpopular that riots broke out against them, yet they spread rapidly in the second half of the eighteenth century. Parliament had approved 1200 more turnpikes by 1780. Many were in the Midlands.

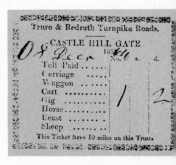

At the start of a turnpike stretch all travellers had to stop at a gate to pay their toll, which varied according to their means of transport. In return they received a ticket.

Travellers also had to pay to cross some bridges and this engraving by Thomas Bewick shows a farmer avoiding expense by driving his cow across a shallow part of the river.

Most toll-keepers lived in a small house on the roadside, so that they could easily see people approaching. Quite a number of toll-houses survive today.

In general the turnpikes improved the roads, although some concentrated on collecting tolls rather than maintaining surfaces. Yet the roads were still not good enough for moving most goods, as Thomas Telford's report to Parliament in the early nineteenth century shows:

With regard to the roads of England and Wales they are in general defective both as to their direction and inclinations; they are frequently carried over hills, which might be avoided by passing along the adjacent valleys; the drainage of the roads is quite as defective; there has been no attention paid to constructing good and solid foundations; the materials, whether consisting of gravel or stone, have seldom been sufficiently selected and arranged; and they lie so promiscuously upon the roads as to render it inconvenient to travel upon them.

Heavy or perishable goods could be moved only short distances in the eighteenth century. They were often carried by packhorses rather

A pack donkey was most suited to carrying textiles. They were strong; they could travel on rough land, and in bad weather conditions; and one man could tie several together and lead them in single file. But they cost a lot in food.

25

than by carts or wagons since the speed of wheeled traffic was about half walking pace. Moving fragile things was always a risky operation. Where possible goods were sent by sea or river, even though boats moved slowly and were often delayed by storms, drought, ice and other hazards. A Scottish professor, Adam Smith, explained why it was cheaper: 'Six or eight men, by the help of water carriage, can carry and bring back in the same time (three weeks) the same quantity of goods between London and Edinburgh, as fifty broad-wheeled wagons,

attended by 100 men and drawn by 400 horses.' It is less than sixty miles from Horsehay near Coalbrookdale to Chester, yet iron was still sent there in the 1770s down the river Severn and round the coast of Wales.

As the south applied itself more to producing food and many industries developed faster in the less fertile midlands and north, improved transport was needed to carry more goods between the different regions. As the century progressed more rivers were made navigable further upstream by dredging channels, cutting out bends and building locks by weirs. This also brought more areas within reach of London and the growing towns. Most southern and midland counties, however, together with much of Lancashire and Wales, were too far from the main rivers to benefit. There, industry had no adequate means of transport, and so they began to provide themselves with artificial waterways or canals from the 1760s. At first towns like Liverpool, Manchester and Glasgow were connected with their local coal-mines, but these canals soon carried iron, bricks, corn and other heavy or bulky goods as well. In the 1770s some longer canals were built, including the Grand Trunk Canal, which joined the rivers Mersey and Trent and thus linked (with a roundabout route) parts of Lancashire and Yorkshire to each other as well as to the Birmingham region (see map page 116).

Heavier and bulkier goods could be sent by slow-moving stage wagons. Their broad wheels were designed not to cause deep ruts, but they often ground the road surface to powder instead.

The Bridgewater canal, opened in 1761, astounded the people of Manchester with this 200-yard-long aqueduct which James Brindley built over the river Irwell.

Everyone travelling abroad went in all-purpose wooden sailing ships which were both slow and small by modern standards. (A voyage to America might well take six to eight weeks.) As yet there was no difference between passenger and cargo ships. At sea, of course, they were at the mercy of the wind and weather which could make voyages both uncomfortable and unreliable. The Austrian composer Joseph Haydn discovered why when he crossed the Channel on a visit to England later in the century:

I boarded the ship at Calais at 7:30 a.m. and at 5 p.m. I arrived, thank God! safe and sound in Dover. At the beginning, for the first four whole hours, we had almost no wind, and the ship went so slowly that in these four hours we didn't go further than one single English mile and there are twenty-four between Calais and Dover. Our ship's captain, in an evil temper, said that if the wind did not change, we should have to spend the whole night at sea. Fortunately, however, toward 11 o'clock a wind arose and blew so favourably that by 4 o'clock we covered twenty-two miles. Since the tide, which had just begun to ebb, prevented our large vessel from reaching the pier, two smaller ships came out to meet us as we were still fairly far out to sea, and into these we and our luggage were transferred, and thus at last, though exposed to a medium gale, we landed safely. The large vessel stood out to sea five hours longer, till the tide turned and it could finally dock. Some of the passengers were afraid to board the little boats and stayed on board, but I followed the example of the greater number. I arrived safely, without vomiting, on shore. Most of the passengers were ill, and looked like ghosts.

Foreign trade

In the mid eighteenth century ships took a quarter of the output of British industries abroad. About half these exports were woollens which went mostly to Europe. In addition increasing quantities of iron, brass and linen goods were exported to the British colonists in North America and the West Indies. In return the British imported timber, fur and fish from Canada and cane sugar, coffee, tobacco, cotton and rice from the warm American mainland colonies and the West Indies, where slaves from West Africa worked the plantations.

From India and the Far East, the East India Company shipped in tea, spices, silk and other fine cloths. The British did not consume all these semi-tropical products themselves, but re-exported much to other European countries; this made the European trade even more important.

After the Seven Years War (1756–63), when Britain captured several French and Spanish colonies, the re-export trade grew even faster. At this time many colonies were little more than trading posts, forts or naval bases. Europeans had settled in large numbers only on the American mainland and most of them won their independence in the 1780s, when they founded the United States of America.

Chapter 2
Life in the eighteenth century

Towns

Trade, either internal or overseas, usually accounted for the existence of towns in mid-eighteenth-century Britain. There were nearly a thousand altogether, but only a quarter of the population lived in them. Most had no more than about 250 houses or a thousand inhabitants. To us they would have appeared as merely large villages.

Nearly all had grown from villages into towns because they were on main roads and so were easy to reach. Some were situated where two roads crossed and others beside a ford or a bridge crossing a river. The farmers from the surrounding countryside normally took their spare produce to them to sell and also often bought the tools and cloth which they needed from there. Most towns had an open space, usually in the

Market day in Romford, Essex, has attracted many local farmers. The market was the main reason why most small towns existed.

A street in Liverpool. Water is being delivered to the houses from the water cart. Beyond is a sedan chair.

main street, where stalls were set up once or twice a week for the market.

The other streets were generally quite narrow. The houses were usually built in rows or terraces three or four storeys high. In a few towns, like Edinburgh, they were even taller. Apart from several churches and perhaps a small town hall, they had few buildings that were larger than ordinary houses. The inns and shops looked like houses from the outside, apart from entrances and ground-floor windows.

Towns with well over a thousand inhabitants were more than just market towns. In East Anglia and the west country in particular they were also centres for the making of woollen cloth. The simpler work like spinning was usually done in the villages, but much weaving and wool-combing was done in towns. The merchants who distributed the material to people's homes also lived in the woollen towns. When the cloth was finished it was sold in the larger towns like Norwich and Taunton. Two of the main centres for the cloth trade in Yorkshire were Leeds and Halifax. In the same way, metal goods were both made and sold in Birmingham. Thus every large town had at least one special reason for its growth.

Since heavy goods usually travelled by water, ports at the mouths of rivers controlled the trade between their valley and the rest of the country. The biggest ports, like Bristol and Glasgow, were centres for

29

Left: Dudley in 1775, Nottingham in 1784, and Birmingham in 1795. These views of three midland towns show how close most town-dwellers still lived to the countryside. At the end of the century only London was significantly larger than Birmingham.

trade with foreign countries as well as other parts of Britain. Exeter and York, for example, were towns that acted as local capitals for quite large regions as well as housing the law courts. Bath and a few others had become resorts for wealthy invalids and holiday-makers. Even though these towns were significantly larger, few had more than four or five streets. Most town dwellers therefore lived within a few minutes' walk of the countryside.

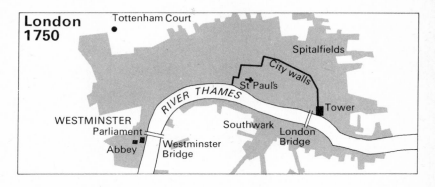

London, in contrast, was a giant (although not like London today). With two-thirds of a million inhabitants it was twenty times larger than any other town in England (and well over ten times the size of Edinburgh). Since the sixteenth century attempts to check its growth had failed. The two separate cities on the north bank of the Thames had already merged into one several miles across. Westminster was the centre for the country's government, but trade made the city of London even more important. Many of the goods sold in southern England passed through London. It was also the main port for trade with Europe and the East. There, too, many industries made silk, watches, and so on, on a small scale.

Part of Westminster Bridge, with Westminster Hall and Westminster Abbey in the background. Until it was opened in 1750 Londoners had to cross the Thames by London Bridge or by boat. It was regarded as one of the engineering wonders of the age.

Standards of living

The profits from farming, trade and industry meant that in the mid eighteenth century Britain enjoyed probably the highest standard of living in the world, having recently overtaken the Dutch. Yet by modern standards few were well off. Various estimates suggest that the annual average income in the 1750s may have been about £13 per head. However, this figure is almost meaningless because it takes no account of the fact that many families baked their own bread, brewed beer, grew some of their own food, gathered fuel and so on. In addition great landowners' families enjoyed several thousand pounds a year, while ordinary labourers' families shared perhaps £20 a year. Some labourers simply did not earn enough to live on, while others just could not find enough work. Gregory King, a statistician, estimated at the end of the seventeenth century that over half the population 'decreased the wealth of the kingdom', or were poor. A modern expert on the early eighteenth century, Dr J. H. Plumb, has concluded that 'probably a third of the population in England lived on the borderline of starvation'. When common lands were enclosed some suffered badly for they could not gather fuel or graze animals on it any longer.

Poverty invariably pinched most in winter, when the weather was coldest, and in spring, when food was most scarce. It also varied from one year to the next, depending on the harvest, and from one region

Bloomsbury Square in 1787. Many spacious and elegant squares were built in the west end of London where most rich landowners had a town house. Notice how milk was delivered.

Inside a fashionable London house. Only the wealthy could aspire to such furniture, porcelain, carpets, or plaster-work.

A Scottish interior. Notice the box-bed and the hens roosting in the rafters.

to another, according to how fertile the soil was. In the eighteenth century this affected most those living in the hilly parts of the north and west.

The poor have left behind them little evidence of their ways and places of living, but one can easily see how and where wealthy land-owners lived in the eighteenth century. Many of their country mansions are now open to the public. However, they were cold and draughty in winter and many families used them only during the summer. Normally they reserved the most imposing rooms for entertaining important guests. The inhabitants of such houses dressed magnificently. A Birmingham lady wrote in the 1780s:

At half-past seven the gentleman entered our drawing room, dressed in a suit of pale blue French silk, spotted with pink and green, the coat lined with pink silk plush, his hair in a bag, a white feather in his hat, a sword by his side and his ruffles and frill of fine point lace. My habit is made; it is dark blue, with a buff velvet collar and small gilt buttons; my waistcoat white with gold spangles; my ruffles and frills Mechlin lace; my hat black, with feathers, gold lace and gold fringe.

The style and colour of clothes did not change as rapidly as they do today, but new fashions were introduced continuously throughout the eighteenth century. The splendour of the clothes of the rich was

matched by the quantity of food they ate. For instance a Norfolk parson
was once visited unexpectedly by some friends. 'We were rather put
to for a dinner in so short a time,' he recorded later in his diary.
'However we did our best and gave them some beans and bacon, minced
veal, neck of mutton, roasted cold beef, steak pie and a Codlin (apple)
pudding.'

The richer people ate vast meals, as a French duke's son discovered
in the 1780s:

Dinner is one of the most wearisome of English experiences. The first two
hours are spent in eating and you are compelled to exercise your stomach
to the full to please your host. He asks you the whole time whether you
like the food and presses you to eat more, with the result that out of pure
politeness, I do nothing but eat from the time that I sit down until the
time when I get up from the table. All the dishes consist of various meats
either boiled or roasted and of joints weighing about 20 or 30 pounds. After
the sweets, the table is covered with all kinds of wine, for even gentlemen
of modest means always keep a large stock of good wine.

In the later eighteenth century landowners usually sat down to dinner
at about 5 p.m. Breakfast (at perhaps 10 a.m.) was their other main
meal. Their food at lunch and supper was cold and light.

The more successful farmers and lesser gentlemen were not so

These gentlemen in
Rowlandson's drawing are
indulging in a '2 o'clock
ordinary'. The absence of
ladies may explain their
manners.

HOT ROAST AND BOILED
EVERY DAY
FROM TWO TO FIVE.
Dinners drest on the
Shortest Notice

My Simili holds good to a title
Some Gorge while some scarce have a taste
But he that's content with a little
Enough is as good as a Feast.

A fine eighteenth-century farmhouse with the windows of the servants' bedrooms just visible behind the parapet.

A comfortable and well-furnished Welsh farmhouse kitchen, belonging to a wealthy farmer.

prosperous as the great landowners. Many of their houses still survive with their exteriors almost unchanged. Most northern farm houses were smaller than those in the south, east and midlands of England, but farmers' families did not have as much room as may appear, for servants and sometimes farm labourers lived with them too. Over a quarter of the families in Britain employed one servant or more. They were often hired, like farm labourers, at annual fairs and usually started work when they were ten or eleven. Most small farmers paid their servants about two or three pounds a year together with their food and lodging. In addition to their duties about the house, servants milked cows and helped gather in the harvest. What with the labourers and servants, the farm houses were often overcrowded by modern standards, for most had fewer than four bedrooms.

The kitchen was usually the main living room. It was warmest for sitting and talking and most convenient for eating. Its floor was probably brick or flagstones. All but the poorest farmers had, in addition, a parlour or drawing room and some even had two. With wallpaper or wooden panelling on the walls, boards on the floor and plastered ceilings, they were designed for entertaining guests, but in practice these rooms were rarely used. Behind the kitchen was at least one room where the family brewed beer, baked bread, made cheese and butter and also stored their food.

Most country dwellers lived in much smaller houses. In southern and central England all but the poorest had a two-storey cottage with three or four rooms. The larger ones normally had two bedrooms; the smaller only one. In the north, most people still slept on the ground floor. In Scotland and Wales they had even smaller houses – usually just two rooms, with recesses off the living room for extra beds. From the outside many cottages looked bigger than they really were because the cow houses were built beside them.

By the eighteenth century all but the very poor had glass in their windows and curtains to draw over them. Houses were no longer made of timber, but increasingly of brick or stone. Inside, the walls were nearly always whitewashed and the floors were beaten earth, covered with rush matting or more often old sacks. The furniture in most houses consisted of plain wooden chairs, tables and dressers made by a local carpenter, with a bedstead of brass or iron. Only in the wealthier homes were any of the chairs upholstered. As yet no house had a bathroom and only the rich had primitive water or earth closets inside.

Like the houses, the clothes of most countrymen were much less impressive than those of the rich landowners. In the north especially, eighteenth-century country dwellers would make most of their own clothes from homespun cloth. In the south they more often bought the cloth from which they made their dresses and shirts. Heavier garments, like coats, they acquired second-hand whenever possible. These practices spread northwards early in the nineteenth century. Colours were invariably plain and dull and many women used a strip of ribbon to enliven their dresses.

Most men wore a suit on Sundays, but they could rarely afford more than one or two in a lifetime. Nearly everyone had to make their clothes last as long as possible. Since washing helped wear them out, they were usually washed infrequently. They were also patched and darned many times and, when finally worn out, some part, like the tail of a shirt, could often be used to make a dress for a small child. Children rarely had new clothes. Normally they were passed on from one to another with parents nagging constantly not to get them torn.

Nearly all the eighteenth-century garments, including dresses, shirts and underclothes, were made from wool or linen. Beneath their dresses women invariably wore linen shifts or woollen petticoats, sometimes reinforced with horsehair. Some also had stays made of leather. Men might wear leather breeches or trousers of corduroy, but a linen smock was the usual dress for shepherds and many farm labourers until the end of the nineteenth century.

The food of countrymen was also simple. Most families ate three times a day. Their main meal was either at midday or on the husband's return from the fields in the evening, when many labourers had a

A one-storey country cottage.

The designs on a smock varied according to the occupation of the wearer and where he lived.

better dinner than the rest of the family. Bread formed the basis of most meals. In the eighteenth century it was darker and coarser than modern bread, but more nourishing. Most families baked it themselves. In the south of England the flour was milled from wheat, but in the north and west usually from barley, rye or oats. Often they ate it with cheese, onions, butter or lard. Sometimes they soaked it in gravy or, if very hard up, in hot water with salt and pepper. Potatoes too were eaten regularly in Lancashire and Cheshire, and porridge in Scotland and the north, with other foods made from oats. Most areas also had their own cheap and filling local dish, like Yorkshire pudding or Norfolk dumplings.

People normally had meat for their Sunday dinner, often in a stew. Beef and mutton were comparative luxuries, and only people like farmers and craftsmen were likely to afford them regularly. Most made do with bacon or pork, since many kept a pig. Tripe, haggis, faggots and similar dishes from animals' entrails were also common. Those who lived near the sea were likely to have smoked or pickled herrings from time to time. Inland they frequently killed blackbirds or sparrows and baked them in pies, even though about thirty sparrows were needed to make a pound of meat.

They could supplement their diet in summer and autumn with their own vegetables, which they normally cooked in stews and soups. In winter and spring, however, labourers and their families often went hungry. Whenever possible they washed down their meals with beer, cider and, in the north especially, milk.

A satire on some of the more absurd fashions of the rich in 1799.

Attitudes to others

The mean life of eighteenth-century labourers contrasted so sharply with the elegance of the wealthy landowners that they were hardly treated as if they belonged to the same species. 'I thank your ladyship for information concerning the Methodist preachers,' wrote one duchess to a friend. 'Their doctrines are most repulsive, and strongly tinctured with impertinence and disrespect towards their superiors. It is monstrous to be told that you have a heart as sinful as the common wretches that crawl the earth.' Only when their standards of living began to rise, did the idea that all people should be treated more equally win general acceptance.

In the second half of the eighteenth century over one-third of the men and more than half the women of England and Wales could not even sign their names. Many of the rest could read only simple passages and write with difficulty. No law compelled children to attend school. The extent of most people's education depended on the wealth of their parents. Few labourers' children stayed at school beyond the age of ten (if they went at all), while those with craftsmen or tradesmen for their fathers often remained several years longer.

The standard of education also varied greatly from one locality to the next, depending on the number and quality of schools available.

George Whitfield, a leading Methodist, preaching to an audience in Leeds (1749). He attracted the attention of non-churchgoers and the idle curiosity of spectators. His main audience was the mass of the working people.

Few schools had more than one or two teachers, who often taught the children in one large room attached to their house.

The schools were usually financed with money or land given by local landowners, together with subscriptions raised by the churches and fees from the parents. Well-endowed schools could educate some at least of their pupils free. The schools had various names like Free, Charity, Endowed, Parochial or Grammar Schools, but these were often unreliable guides to their activities and organization, for by the mid-eighteenth century many were run no longer according to their founder's intentions. Many grammar schools, for instance, were instructed originally to teach Latin and sometimes Greek to about thirty local boys whose parents could not afford to pay fees. But few grammar school masters knew the classics well and so they taught mostly reading and writing to the boys in their charge.

Since anyone could open a school without training, many teachers were elderly women who could barely read themselves. For a few pennies a week they usually took charge of children aged from about three to eight, whom they might teach to knit and sew and perhaps to read. Most parents expected nothing more; they were happy to have their children out of the way for a time.

Few landowners objected to this situation, since most were afraid that children who learned to read or add might not want to become labourers or servants like their parents. They were also very keen for the schools to teach good manners by, for example, making their pupils bow or touch their caps to their superiors, not to speak without permission and by beating those who lied or swore.

Such attitudes may not seem very Christian today, but in the later eighteenth century most English people belonged to the Church of England. Religion certainly comforted many in their pain and troubles,

Box-pews in a London church.

but there is no way of telling just how widely or sincerely their beliefs were held. On Sundays most landowners and people of importance attended the Church of England's services, but the number of those who joined them seems to have varied greatly. If a squire wanted his villagers to go or the parson was popular and respected, most would attend.

Eighteenth-century communities knew very little of what was going on in the outside world. Travellers were one source of news, but their stories were often about events at least several weeks old and might

Reading, in Berkshire, was one of the earliest provincial towns to acquire its own weekly newspaper. The Bill of Mortality applied to deaths in London only.

VOL. Numb. X.

THE Reading Mercury OR Weekly Entertainer.

Monday July 8, 1723. (To be continued)

READING:

Printed by W. PARKS, and D. KINNIER, next Door to the High-Street: Where all manner of Printing Business is handsomely Advertisements, Summons, Subpœnas, Funeral-Tickets, &c are done here after the best manner, with the Prints of proper Ornaments. Also Gentlemen may have their Coats Fancies curiously cut in Wood, or engrav'd in Mettal.

[Price of this Paper, Three-Half-Pence per W

The *Weekly* Bill of Mortality, *from* June 25, *to* July 2, 1723.

Abortive	1	Convulsions	134	Quinsie	1
Aged	30	Dropsie	13	Rickets	3
Apoplexy	3	Fever	50	Scald Head	1
Asthma	1	French-Pox	1	Small-Pox	42
Cancer	3	Gout	1	Stilborn	8
Canker	1	Griping in the Guts	12	Stoppage i'th' Stomach	3
Childbed	2	Horshoehead	2	Suddenly	1
Chin-Cough	1	Jaundies	3	Teeth	22
Chrisoms	1	Imposthume	3	Thrush	1
Colick	4	Measles	3	Tissick	5
Consumption	56	Mortification	5		

C A S U A L T I E S.

Cut his Throat at St. Giles without Cripplegate 1. Drownded 2, One at Waltham Abby (buried at St Helens near Bishopsgate.) and one at St. Dunstan at Stepney. Excessive Drinking 1. Kill'd by a Fall of a Wall at Allhallows Staining 1. Poisoned herself at St. Brides 1. Overlaid 2.

Christen'd 366. Buried 423 Decreas'd in the Burials this Week 86.

A Catalogue of BOOKS publish'd in *London* last Week.

The *Evangelical Union: Or, the blessed Harmony of a good Life, and sound Faith, being in Conjunction: A Visitation Sermon* preach'd at Lewes in Sussex. April 24, 1722. By Robert Wake, M. A (Dedicated to the Arch-Bishop of Canterbury) Price 1 s.

A *General Representation of Revealed Religion: in which the chief Prejudices that have been entertain'd against it, are examin'd, &c. By Tho. Rymer, Chaplain to the Lord Bishop of Norwich.*

The *History of Providence or the 6 Days Work of the Creation: In a Dissertation on the Sacred Writings.* Price 1 s.

Mahometism fully explain'd: Containing many surprizing Passages, not to be found in any other Author. By Mr. Morgan. Pr. 5 s.

Political Banishments. Occasion'd by Bishop Atterbury's Exile Being some Considerations thereon, and in what Case pronounc'd By Tho. Brisco, Price 1 s.

Th. *Royal Marriage; or King Lemuel's matrimonial Lectures.*

M.s. *Basker's Patch work Skreen, for the Ladies; or, Love and Virtue recommended: In a Collection of new instructive Novels: With Poems on the Pleasures of a Country Life. A Pocket Volume. Pr 2 s. 6 d.*

Cymbalum Mundi: Or, Satirical Dialogues on various Subjects. By Bonaventure dis Perriers. Done into English from the Original. Price 1 s. 6 d.

M U S I C K, *just publish'd.*

The *Opera's of Flavious, Otho, and Florident,* compos'd by Mr. Handell, the Opera's of Grisilda. Astartus and Camilla, compos'd by M Bononcini; also the favourite Songs in the Opera's of Muscus and Crispus; Solo's and Sonata's for a German Flute by Mr Pierro, Mr. Lully and Mr Shickard; Also great Variety of Musick for the common Flute, Violin, and Harpsichord in Genere.

40

well be only rumours. The deaths of important people were often reported while they were still alive and so it was always difficult to know what was true.

This situation changed slowly during the eighteenth century, when regular newspapers first appeared. In London a few were published every day, but in the other towns they usually came out once a week. However, their news was rarely 'new' because they gathered it by post. The *Reading Mercury* once announced:

A printing press, 1770.

They write from Chester that about a fortnight ago a schoolmaster discovered in an old ruinous building the body of the first Earl of Chester, who was nephew to William the Conqueror. The body was found to have been first wrapped in leather and then enclosed in a stone coffin. The skull and all the bones were very fresh and in the right position; and, what is more remarkable, the string which tied the ankles together was whole and entire, although it was more than 630 years since the internment of the body.

News from the Continent took even longer to arrive and *The Times* in 1805 amazed people when it managed to publish an account of the battle of Trafalgar only seventeen days after it was fought off the coast of Spain. As yet, few papers employed special reporters to look for news; they got their information from a variety of correspondents.

Health

News may have travelled slowly in the eighteenth century, but death and disease were all too frequent visitors. Around 1750 people probably died on average at about the age of thirty-five. Many, of course, lived much longer, because about a fifth of all babies died before their first birthday. Those who survived into their teens, therefore, could expect to live until they were about forty-five.

Our knowledge of why so many used to die so young is rather hazy, for the cause of most deaths was either not recorded or else the diagnosis was vague, like 'fever' or 'griping in the guts'. Smallpox had almost certainly been the most lethal disease among children until the mid eighteenth century, when it began to decline at last. Many young children died from measles and whooping cough and from infections which gave them sore throats or from diarrhoea, especially in hot summers.

Adults died from a greater variety of diseases. Consumption (or tuberculosis) probably caused about one death in six. Many more also caught it without succumbing. For them consumption was a long illness which might last several years and those who recovered rarely regained their full strength. Pneumonia was another illness which attacked the lungs and frequently proved fatal. A much smaller proportion than today died of heart complaints and cancer.

Those who were seriously ill suffered terribly. An aunt of the politician Charles Fox wrote to her husband in 1774:

My sister's stomach is wretched. She can keep nothing upon it. I hear it is such a constant symptom attending a cancerous complaint, that it is very alarming. It is now eight days she has been in this way, that she literally brings up a glass of water. Poor soul she suffers so, that I cannot conceive how she can hold it out long. [She did, however, for three months longer.]

These three days past my sister's sickness and pain have scarcely ceased day and night and the vexacious thing is that the Laudanum is losing its effect. God send her relief for she is indeed a most miserable creature from the pain she suffers. They think she cannot last many days.

Many endured long and painful illnesses which did not necessarily kill them. Some jobs were unhealthy. The dusty, damp or fumy atmosphere often affected the lungs of spinners, millers and many metal-workers. Weavers and others who worked by candlelight in winter were likely to suffer from failing eyesight. Many farm labourers suffered from ill health, according to one eighteenth-century doctor, because they were 'exposed to all the vicissitudes of the weather, which, in this country are often very great and sudden, and occasion colds, coughs, rheumatisms and other acute disorders. They are likewise forced to work hard, and often to carry heavy burdens above their strength, which, by overstraining the vessels, occasion ruptures etc.' Although the following passage describes the plight of a more recent farmer, in the eighteenth century others must have suffered similarly.

This man is probably taking a herbal medicine given to him by an apothecary. Herbal remedies were not necessarily effective.

When I were about 60, I suddenly got the gout come that bad as I couldn't stand, let alone walk, or hold anything in my hands, and the pain were terrible. I used to have to cling to the table with my elbows to get my balance to stand up at all before I could start to stumble along, and if I fell down I daren't put my hands down to catch myself because my wrists were gone stiff and felt as if they'd break off, so I used to let myself go and roll over like one of those acrobats you see sometimes. My wife was as full of rheumatics as I were of the gout and her knees wouldn't hold her up any more than my ankles would hold me.

Doctors could do little to help those who were ill. The only disease they could control was smallpox. From the 1730s they protected more and more people by giving them a mild dose of the disease; in other words, inoculating them. This was a method introduced from Turkey. However, some continued to die from the disease because no one really understood how inoculation worked, and they didn't always use it properly.

Otherwise, doctors contributed little to making people healthy. Surgeons, for example, performed only quick and simple operations, like amputating limbs. They could not stop blood poisoning, for they were just beginning to understand how wounds healed, as well as how food was digested and the lungs breathed air. They remained ignorant even longer about different types of blood, vitamins, glands and the functioning of most internal organs. When serious complications developed in childbirth they had to leave most women to die, often in agony. They could relieve some suffering with laudanum and various herbs, roots and barks, but doctors were probably most useful when giving general advice on what to eat or instructions to stay in bed and keep warm.

Pulling teeth was often done by a barber, for dentists hardly existed. 'Of all the aches and pains incident to the human body,' wrote one contemporary doctor, 'I do not know one more distressing than the toothache. I would always recommend extraction of the unsound tooth, rather than endure the pain for years and to be obliged to submit to the operation at last.'

Doctors also weakened many patients by bleeding. 'No operation of surgery is so necessary as bleeding,' pronounced one eighteenth-century medical book. 'Bleeding is proper at the beginning of all inflammatory fevers, as pleurisies, measles etc. It is likewise in all topical inflammations, as those of the intestines, womb, bladder, stomach, kidneys, throat, eyes etc, as also in the asthma, coughs, head-aches, rheumatisms, the apoplexy and epilepsy. After falls, blows, bruises or any violent hurt received either externally or internally, bleeding is necessary.'

Not surprisingly, perhaps, many families relied more on traditional remedies which were handed down like recipes from one generation to the next than on doctors. Those which used herbs were often quite effective, but others were useless and unpleasant. In one family, for example, those who had whooping cough ate a fried mouse, while asthma sufferers in another village swallowed young frogs. In spite of these remedies, most people recovered from such illnesses.

Amusements

Whatever their station in life, there were occasions when people could forget their troubles and enjoy themselves. The rich landowners, merchants and professional men went on holidays with their families. They visited inland spas, like Bath and Tunbridge Wells, both for amusement and to drink the local mineral waters for their health. But, important though these people were, their numbers remained very small. Later in the century some also began to frequent Scarborough, Brighton and other seaside towns. At first they drank the sea water on their doctors' instructions, but soon the visitors bathed in it regularly.

Rowlandson's picture of the Pump Room at Bath.

Scarborough, with its spa, became Britain's first seaside resort. The Pump Room is under the cliff on the left, and while some fashionable people parade on the beach, others swim naked in the sea.

The traditional country sport – hunting. A wood engraving by Thomas Bewick, one of hundreds of illustrations he made showing country life of the late eighteenth century.

Those landowners who preferred to stay at home had other amusements. As guns improved in the eighteenth century, they reared more and more pheasants and partridges for shooting and protected them from poachers with various devices. Their gamekeepers also tried to stop the villagers from killing them and other game, like hares and rabbits.

Hunting was even more expensive. By the later eighteenth century it could cost at least a thousand pounds a year to breed, feed and keep a pack of hounds and a stable full of horses. By then most gentlemen were giving up hunting hares for foxes, which ran straighter and so were more fun to chase on horseback. However, some districts were so short of foxes that they imported some from the Continent (and farmers were prevented from shooting them). The thrill of hunting was not confined to the landowners. Farmers who owned a suitable horse could also join in and others followed on foot.

Until the later eighteenth century horse races were often run between just two horses, usually on established courses like Newmarket and Doncaster. Then the numbers increased and often several heats were held to decide the winner. By modern standards the races were very disorderly. Many jockeys kicked or hit other horses with their whips and crossed in front of those just behind. Rules enforcing better behaviour were applied gradually. The Derby and the four other classics were all established between 1776 and 1814.

Joseph Haydn, the Austrian composer, recorded his impressions of a day at Ascot in the 1790s like this:

These horse races are run on a large field, especially prepared for them, and on this field is a circular track two miles long. It is all very smooth and even. Along the straight, stalls of various sizes have been erected, some of which hold 2 to 3 hundred persons. The places in these stalls cost from

1 to 42 shillings per person. The riders are very lightly clad in silk, and each one has a different colour, so that you can recognize him more easily. Each one is weighed in, and a certain weight is allowed him, in proportion to the strength of the horse, and if the rider is too light he must put on heavier clothes, or they hang some lead on him. The horses are of the finest possible breed, light, with very thin feet, the hair of their neck tied into braids, the hoofs very delicate. As soon as they hear the sound of a bell, they dash off with the greatest force. Every leap of the horses is 22 feet long. These horses are very expensive. The Prince of Wales paid £8,000 for one some years ago. Among other things a single large stall is erected, wherein the Englishmen place their bets. I saw 5 heats on the first day. In the first there were 3 riders, and they had to go round the circle twice without stopping. They did this double course in 5 minutes. No stranger will believe this unless they have seen it themselves. The second time there were seven riders. Just when you think that one of them is rather near the goal, and people make large bets on him at this moment, another rushes past him at very close quarters and with unbelievable force reaches the winning place. Despite a heavy rain there were 2,000 vehicles all full of people, and three times as many common people on foot. Besides this, there are all sorts of other things – puppet and horror plays – which go on during the races; many tents with refreshments, all kinds of wine and beer.

Whenever possible, horse races were held on public holidays, which were either prominent saints' days or closely connected with religious festivals like Shrove Tuesday, when people ate pancakes, and Palm Sunday, when they had figs if they could get them. Other special celebrations were held on 5 November, for instance, and 1 May, when most villages crowned their May Queen and the children walked in procession with her round the village. They often dressed the local well with flowers and danced too.

A race between two horses at Newmarket with spectators following as best they can.

Traditional village festivals, dancing round a Maypole on 1 May.

Plough Monday, the first Monday after Twelfth Night, was celebrated with dancing and foolery.

Several special days were closely connected with events on the farm. When the ploughing was about to start, they used to play pranks on their neighbours in some villages, as we still do on April 1st, as well as taking part in other ceremonies. The harvest festival, when 'all was safely gathered in', was much more of a red-letter day. Then the villagers not only flocked to church, but also feasted, drank, danced and played games.

Christmas too was celebrated with joy and feasting. Originally northern Europeans had celebrated on 25 December because the days had begun to lengthen. The evergreens which they brought into their houses were symbols of continuing life and the heat and light of the burning yule log contained a promise of summer. Not knowing when Christ

Harvest Home. These happy people are on their way to the harvest supper, after which they will be even more 'free and easy'.

Cock-fighting in Scotland at the turn of the century.

was born, the early Christians had adopted this festival to honour his birth.

Many families ate plum pudding on Christmas Day in the eighteenth century, but very few yet had turkey. Roast beef was a common Christmas dish, while others ate goose, chicken or duck. Mummers would come round to act short plays and the children completed the celebrations by playing various games in the evening. They did not send cards and rarely received more than two or three presents. On the next day employers usually gave their servants a coin or Christmas box and many tradesmen called on their patrons in the hope of receiving a box too. The Scots did not celebrate Christmas. Hogmanay, or New Year's Eve, was their great midwinter festival.

Some of the celebrations at traditional festivals would seem very strange to us. For instance, pairs of cocks often fought each other to death, perhaps on the village green. To prepare them for battle, their combs and wattles were cut off when young. Their beaks and spurs were sharpened with a knife, and those who could afford it tipped them with steel or silver. Poorer people rarely owned more than two or three, but some landowners bred up to a thousand cocks. Anyone could bet on the outcome of these matches, which were sometimes worth a hundred pounds to the winners. Often they were fought with forty-one cocks on each side, and might last several days.

Most villages and market towns celebrated one special day with particular gusto. At these feasts, which were usually called Revels in the west country and Wakes in Derbyshire and Staffordshire, jugglers, acrobats and animals often performed and stalls sold a great variety of goods. This advertisement for a revel in a Berkshire village on the Monday after St Anne's Day gives some idea of what went on:

This is to give notice that the Fair will be on Monday the first day of August, for buying and selling of cattle, hiring of servants, and all sorts of merchandize, and for the encouragement of gentlemen gamesters and others.

On the same day will be given an exceeding good Gold Laced Hat of 27s. value to be played for at Cudgels; the man who breaks most heads to have the prize, the blood to run an inch or to be deemed no heads.

In this sport the two combatants fought in a ring with a heavy stick, which had a guard to protect their hand, while their other arm was strapped to their waist. They drew blood from the top of their opponent's head (not his face) by hitting him with their cudgel. At another fair women fought, naked to the waist, with a coin in each hand. The first to drop one lost. Wrestling matches and kick shins were also held at these feasts. Participants in the latter assaulted each other with heavy hobnailed boots or iron-studded clogs.

Prize-fighting was even more popular. In the early eighteenth century the two fighters not only hit each other with their bare fists, but kicked, bit, pulled hair, carried stones in their hands and so on. For this reason they sometimes had their heads shaved completely. Gradually rules were enforced to cut out the most vicious of these practices, but fights could still last two hours or more, with short breaks between rounds, until the loser was carried senseless and bleeding from the ring. Fights between champions attracted large crowds and some noblemen in particular wagered big sums of money. Many leisure activities

Crib's second fight with Molineaux. Prize fights drew large crowds, and spectators betted on who would win.

Bull-baiting was sometimes part of festivals. After the bull was chained to a stake, any villager could set his dog on the bull for a small payment.

were cruel. Country boys, for example, enjoyed shooting at small birds with catapults and robbing their nests of eggs in spring.

Many of the sports which we know today existed in the eighteenth century. Football was played all over the country by boys and young men. Matches took place in the streets of many market towns on Shrove Tuesday and other feast days between teams from neighbouring parishes. Few rules governed the play and there was no limit to the number of players who rushed after the ball, which they could handle. Kicking and pushing opponents was all part of the game, which went on until one side scored a goal. This often took several hours. The 'ball' was sometimes a tin or a block of wood.

In the eighteenth century cricket was played almost exclusively in south-eastern England by ordinary villagers and a few gentlemen. The teams often consisted of a dozen players, one of whom acted as umpire, but sometimes there were as many as twenty-two. Many matches were played for money; some with stakes of £100 or more.

As today, the wickets were placed twenty-two yards apart, but the striker had a curved bat with which he tried to hit the balls that were delivered fast along the ground in overs of four each. To score a run he had to reach the other end of the pitch before the wicketkeeper popped the ball into a hole in the middle of the crease. Two men then recorded it by cutting a notch on a stick. There were no boundaries, so that all hits were run to the limit. In addition to retrieving the ball, the fielders could catch the batsman out. Until the 1770s batsmen were rarely bowled because there were only two short stumps about a foot apart. A third stump was then added in the middle and a straight bat adopted.

A cricket match in Marylebone fields in 1748. Notice the stumps and bats.

Government

In the summer of 1789 Britain's National Anthem attained an unprecedented peak of popularity. Earlier in the year King George III had recovered from a bout of madness, which was probably caused by a rare disease called porphyria. In June he set out for Weymouth in Dorset to regain his health and strength.

'The New Forest is all beauty,' wrote the novelist Fanny Burney in her diary; 'and when we approached Lyndhurst, carriages of all sorts lined the road-side, filled within and surrounded without by faces all glee and delight.' At Lyndhurst that evening the royal party

all walked out, about and around the village, and the delighted mob accompanied them. The moment they stepped out of the house, the people, with one voice struck up 'God save the King!'

These good villagers continued singing this loyal song during the whole walk, without any intermission, except to shout 'huzza!' at the end of every verse. They returned so hoarse, that I longed to give them all some lemonade. Probably they longed for something they could have called better! 'Twas well the King could walk no longer; I think, if he had, they would have died singing around him.

Such rapturous scenes continued after the king reached Weymouth.

The preparations of festive loyalty were universal. Not a child could we meet that had not a bandeau round its head, cap or hat, of 'God save the King'; all the bargemen wore it in cockades; and even the bathing-women had it in large coarse girdles round their waists. It is printed in golden letters upon most of the bathing-machines, and in various scrolls and devices it adorns every shop and almost every house in the town.

The King bathes, and with great success; a machine follows the Royal one into the sea, filled with fiddlers, who play 'God save the King', as his majesty takes his plunge! The King is everywhere received with acclamation. His popularity is greater than ever. Compassion for his late sufferings seems to have endeared him now to all conditions of men.

This was no exaggeration, but there was a second explanation for these scenes. In those days the king was still the most powerful man in the land. He appointed the ministers who governed the country, received from them detailed reports on what they did and finally dismissed them. If King George III's illness in 1789 had lasted much longer, people knew that his son, the Prince of Wales, would have replaced William Pitt and the other ministers with Charles Fox and his friends, who were not well liked. The public's joy at the king's recovery, therefore, also expressed their relief at being saved from unpopular ministers.

However, by then the king could not choose whomever he liked to be his ministers. Not only did they have to be members of one of the two Houses of Parliament, they also had to have some support

there. At most, therefore, the king's choice was limited to about 200 Lords and 550 members of the House of Commons.

The peers and bishops in the House of Lords belonged for life, but the members of the Commons were elected for seven years, or less if the king decided to dissolve Parliament. Even though they were of very unequal size, nearly all constituencies returned two members. They were also scattered unevenly throughout the country. For example, five south-western counties, with just over a tenth of the population, elected a quarter of the M.P.s. The electors were usually men who owned some property and so the great majority had no say in who governed them. Votes were recorded openly so that the candidates, who could spend what they liked, normally treated the electors to free beer, lavish dinners and even bribes to ensure their support. However, if they realized that they had no chance of winning, most candidates withdrew and so many M.P.s were returned unopposed. Because they were not paid, M.P.s had to be well-off. Some were wealthy merchants and lawyers, but most were landowners.

The First Lord of the Treasury was then becoming the chief (or prime) minister. As he supervised the other ministers more and more, the Chancellor of the Exchequer took charge of the country's money. The Foreign and Home Secretaries were created in 1782, but two Secretaries of State had shared their responsibilities before then. In

Open voting. The picture shows Hogarth's disgust at the corruption in politics, where idiots and cripples were carried to the booth to vote.

the cabinet the leading ministers were concerned mostly with Britain's relations with other countries, looking after the navy and army, regulating foreign trade and crushing riots or similar disturbances at home. They could not raise taxes without the consent of the House of Commons and also needed Parliament's approval for decisions like treaties with foreign countries. It came almost automatically from the House of Lords, but the Commons was not so subservient.

Local government

Even though Parliament also gave permission for canals and turnpike roads and allowed villages to enclose their common lands, decisions taken in London influenced people less than those of their local Justices of the Peace. J.P.s judged thieves, poachers and lesser criminals and settled disputes between neighbours. More serious offences were tried four times a year when all the J.P.s in a county met at its quarter sessions. They licensed public houses, appointed the parish constables, surveyors of the highways and overseers of the poor. They also supervised how these officials carried out their duties and collected the rates (or local property taxes) from the householders and sometimes settled wage claims too.

Since J.P.s had to own land worth £100 a year or more, this post was restricted to a tiny minority. As they were unpaid and few were trained or dismissed, the standard of their work varied tremendously. Many were conscientious, but others were stupid or uninterested. As a rule they punished poaching most severely but very rarely settled disputed wages or had the roads made up.

J.P.s had less power in those towns which had received a charter from the king entitling them to run their own affairs. By the eighteenth

A road mender at work.

A J.P. listens to the story about how this man became involved in a fight.

century there were over 300 of these boroughs, most of which were governed by a mayor and council. The councillors either appointed their own colleagues when a vacancy arose or else they were elected by some select citizens. Both methods had the same result: a few wealthy Anglican families dominated most English towns. Some had been left considerable wealth, part of which they spent on feasts and civic plate. The councils usually helped local trade by repairing bridges, harbours and so on, and seeing that their markets were properly run. The larger towns often set up Improvement Commissioners to pave and light the streets, lay drains or fight fires. They could levy rates from the householders, but most made little improvement apart from their town centres. The local constables and watchmen were even less successful in curbing riots and crime.

No new charters were granted in the eighteenth century, and so Birmingham, Manchester and other large and rapidly expanding towns did not govern themselves. However, the situation was not so bad as it sounds because Parliament could give them permission to appoint their own Improvement Commissioners.

Summing up

Towards the end of the eighteenth century, Britain was a prosperous and confident society, enjoying internal peace. The land was being cultivated more efficiently than ever before, while food production almost kept pace with the rising population. Many people were already engaged in various small-scale, but expanding, industries which were well supplied with the raw materials they needed, especially iron and coal. Britain's rivers and long coastline also enabled their goods to be transported fairly easily to most parts of the kingdom.

In addition some manufacturers realized that if they increased pro-

These London watchmen, along with the parish constables, constituted the police force of the time. The watchmen were elderly and not very effective.

54

duction, they could sell more goods abroad because Britain controlled a substantial empire. The opportunities to make larger profits overseas also encouraged some merchants to look for new ways of getting rich. Furthermore, British landowners were generally more keen than those elsewhere to make money by investing it in trade, transport, farming or mining rather than just spending it on themselves.

Lord Ashburnham, for instance, sent the following instructions to his agent, after coal had been found on his lands in Wales: 'That you will inform yourself of every circumstance that may either invite or discourage my immediate proceeding to open the pits and get on to work and that you will consider by what ways and means markets may be obtained to dispose of the coals. I am told that this undertaking may be of vast advantage and I therefore desire you to exert all you can in this affair and to give me an account of your proceedings.'

Thus, as the population increased in both wealth and number in the later eighteenth century, the British channelled more and more money and energy into developing their manufacturing industries. Eventually this resulted in fundamental changes in the country's whole way of life.

The butcher is the Prime Minister, William Pitt, who, because bread is so dear, has almost persuaded the speechless John Bull to pay five times as much for meat. Except for the odd bad year, prices had remained remarkably steady during the eighteenth century, until they shot up in the 1790s. In twenty years they almost doubled because of bad harvests, rising population and a long war, but afterwards they fell quickly.

Part 2 The nineteenth century

Chapter 3
The transformation of industry 1780–1910

Steam power

From about 1780 some British industries began to expand at a faster pace and on a greater scale then ever before. This transformation of industry was based on a new source of power – the steam engine. Eventually it provided man with a source of energy many times more powerful and reliable than he had ever had. Many people had experimented with a steam-driven engine in the seventeenth century, but the first effective one was not produced until about 1710 by Thomas Newcomen. His engine consisted of a piston in a vertical cylinder. It was driven by the condensation of steam and the pressure of the atmosphere. The piston was connected to one end of the beam, the other end of which was attached to the machinery. Three hundred or more were already at work by the 1770s, most pumping water out of the mines. They produced only about 5 h.p. and consumed huge quantities of coal.

From the 1780s these atmospheric engines were gradually replaced by a more efficient engine which burned less than one-third of the coal. Its inventor James Watt wrote: 'We have had many public trials made between our engine and the common engine and in some of them ours proved more than four times better and in none so little as three times better.' Watt was an instrument maker of genius who had been given the Glasgow University model of a Newcomen engine to repair. He realized that a lot of fuel would be saved if the steam was condensed outside the cylinder, which would not then have to be heated and cooled again for every stroke of the piston. Moving to near Birmingham, he was extremely fortunate in the people who helped him make his engines: his partner Boulton, his foreman Murdoch and the ironmaster Wilkinson who bored his cylinders so accurately that very little steam escaped. When in 1782 he used steam to drive the piston in both directions Watt had invented the steam engine. He continued to improve it with his foreman's assistance. Their next most important invention was a steam engine capable of driving all kinds of industrial machinery. By 1800 at least 1000 steam engines were in use, but most still pumped water in mines, breweries and waterworks.

Early in the nineteenth century better-made and better-designed engines, which could withstand steam at higher pressures, were pro-

Right: an atmospheric pumping engine made by Newcomen.
Steam is generated by heating water in boiler A. When valve D is opened steam fills cylinder B and drives piston C up to the top. Valve D is closed and valve E opened to spray cold water into the cylinder, where it condenses the steam and creates a vacuum so that atmospheric pressure on top of the piston forces it down. Valve D is opened to reheat the cylinder with steam and drive up the piston once more. The up-and-down movement of the beam operates pump rod F and raises water from the mine.
Far right: a rotative steam engine made by Watt. Steam from boiler A fills cylinder B, when valve D is open and valve E is shut. This drives down piston C, after which valves E and F are opened to let steam into the lower part of the cylinder and force the piston back up. Valve G is opened at the same time as valve D so that as the piston falls, used steam can escape into the separate condenser X. There it is cooled and turned

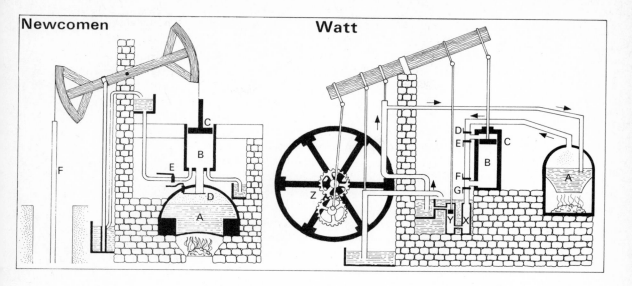

Newcomen

Watt

into water, which is removed from the condenser by pump Y returning to the boiler. When valve G is opened, a partial vacuum is also created in the cylinder which helps to pull down piston C. Two gear wheels Z turn the up-and-down movement of the beam into the circular motion needed to drive machines.

Trade token from a Cornish tin-mine, showing a beam engine.

A Buffery pumping engine.

duced by Trevithick and many others. Yet even so they caught on slowly. Because all machinery was made by hand, it took a long time to construct and was very difficult to repair when anything went wrong. This situation changed from about 1830 when mechanically driven machine tools like lathes were devised. Since they could make very accurately any number of screws and similar articles in standard sizes, better quality machines were assembled more quickly. Spare parts, too, became available.

The age of the mass-produced steam engine did not really begin until the 1830s. By then there were tens of thousands in use. Most were in the cotton industry. Even though they rarely generated more than 20 h.p. they were revolutionary because no other source of energy could compete with their power and reliability.

The steam engine was improved continually in the nineteenth century. Multitubular and fire-tube boilers made it more powerful. Triple expansion used the heat more effectively and so made it more economical. The crank replaced the beam as a more efficient method of connecting the piston to rotating machinery. By 1880 engines of 400 h.p. were quite common and a few giants of up to 10,000 h.p. existed.

Fixed steam-engine power

1840	0·35 m h.p.
1860	0·7 m h.p.
1880	2 m h.p.
1900	10 m h.p.

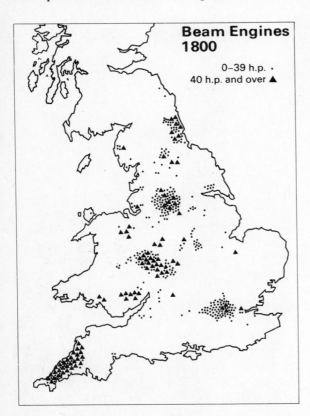

Beam Engines 1800

0–39 h.p. •
40 h.p. and over ▲

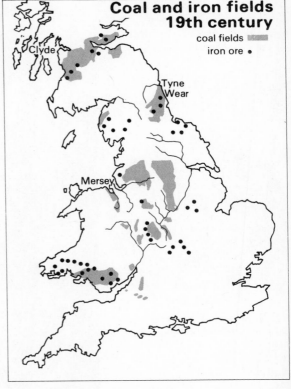

Coal and iron fields 19th century

coal fields ▨
iron ore •

Clyde

Tyne Wear

Mersey

The steam engine at this Staffordshire pithead has just raised a load of coal while lowering an empty trolley down the other shaft.

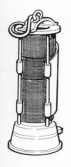

The flame of Humphry Davy's safety lamp burned blue when gas was present, but it did not explode because the gauze reduced the heat of the flame.

Coal

This rapid growth of steam power relied directly on large supplies of its only fuel: coal. There was a great increase in the amount of coal mined in Britain.

Coal was still cut by hand and the pits introduced few really new techniques. The increased demand was met by employing more miners and by making them dig deeper. This was made possible by more efficient steam pumps and steam-driven winding engines which used wire ropes to raise the coal to the surface, by better ventilation and by the miner's safety lamp which detected some dangerous gases. By the 1830s seams well below 1000 feet were being worked in south Durham and the inland coalfields of Lancashire and Staffordshire. Central Scotland and south Wales were mined more intensively later. By the end of the nineteenth century the best and most accessible seams were worked out. As the miners followed the eastern seams of the south Yorkshire–north midlands area, which dipped further below the surface, shafts of 3,000 feet were not uncommon.

Some of the work in mines was done by women and children. Boys and girls were often put in charge of the winding engines or of opening and shutting the trap doors which controlled the ventilation of the mines. Then they had to crouch all day in the same spot by themselves in the dark. When these evils were at last publicized in 1842 by a Royal

61

Trap-doors prevented the air from escaping from the coal face. Young children were employed to open them as the older ones pushed heavily loaded carts along the galleries. Lowering children down a coal-mine. Engravings like these illustrated the bad conditions in mines.

Commission, many mines no longer employed women, but Parliament made it illegal for them all. It also forbade them to employ boys under the age of ten. The limit, which was very difficult to enforce, was increased to twelve in the 1870s. Subsequently it rose with the school leaving age (page 281).

Mining was very dangerous. Loose rocks were easily dislodged and the risk of being killed or injured by one was always greater in the tall seams where they had further to fall. In the north of England fatal accidents were not even followed by inquests to discover why they had happened until after 1815. Few safety precautions were taken

Mining accident at Barnsley in 1866.

Coal-jagging in Wednesbury — delivering coal to houses.

before the mid nineteenth century. The mine owners insisted that they were not responsible. The men were most reluctant to put up enough props to prevent the roof from falling in and to inspect the winding gear and other machinery on which their lives depended. If they did, they spent less time mining and so earned less money because the miners' pay was based not on how long they worked but on how much coal they extracted. They preferred to take risks.

The deeper seams contained a dangerous gas called 'fire-damp' which could be exploded by the miners' candles. The safety lamp, which was invented in the early nineteenth century, did not really solve this problem, but it was often used to detect gas and so made the mining of deeper seams possible. There the air was more foul, the temperature higher (one pit paid the men an extra 6d a day for working in 130°F) and the risk of fire-damp even greater. In the 1840s a series of terrible explosions in the deeper mines led to stricter regulations, which inspectors helped enforce. The inspectors were particularly keen on proper ventilating machines and, although deeper shafts were sunk, they did not become more dangerous. However, many serious accidents still occurred.

To ensure that miners were not cheated by their employers, check-weighmen were appointed in the later nineteenth century to see that their output was recorded accurately and they were paid correctly. But still the miner could not rely on a steady wage, for if he came across a streak of rock in the seam which he was working, he might earn very little for a day or two. In addition, from about the age of forty, he could only do the less strenuous, and so the increasingly less well paid, jobs.

By the end of the nineteenth century most mines had machines at the pit head for sizing, sorting and washing the coal before it was transported. These jobs were usually done by the older miners.

Coal mined in Britain

1780	8m tons
1850	50m tons
1910	260m tons

Metals

Iron

The expanding industries of the nineteenth century needed plenty of iron as well as coal, since all new machines were made of it. But, because the existing furnaces and forges could not meet the demand, huge quantities of much needed wrought iron could only be produced by adopting several inventions on a large scale. Two men, Henry Cort and Peter Onions, perfected independently in the 1780s the long awaited invention of smelting it with coke. They heated the pig-iron in a reverberatory furnace, where it was kept separate from the coke to prevent new impurities from being added. The molten metal was then stirred or puddled with rods and, as the temperature dropped, most impurities were burned out. When it was cool, lumps were finally passed through steam-driven rollers which removed the remaining dross. This invention of puddling and rolling was indeed revolutionary. Good-quality wrought iron could then be made fifteen times more quickly and without using charcoal. The puddling and rolling process was adopted quickly during the wars against France (1793–1815) because Britain needed to produce as much iron as possible. Luckily there were abundant supplies of iron-ore near Britain's coal mines, particularly in Staffordshire, Shropshire, the area around Newcastle, south Yorkshire, south Wales and central Scotland. The number of

British pig-iron output

1780s	0·06 m tons
1850	2·5 m tons
1910	10 m tons

James Nasmyth's steam hammer, which delivered blows of great force. It could forge railway lines or the shafts of a giant paddle wheel.

Hammering rods of wrought
iron.

blast furnaces in action rose from thirty in 1780 to 300 in 1830.
Iron-works moved from the forests to the coal-fields, where they became
much larger. They used steam engines for several tasks, such as driving
the bellows in blast furnaces. In the 1830s the blast was heated before
it entered the furnace. This saved about half the fuel, since raw coal
and anthracite were then used instead of coke. The size of iron-works
continued to grow and new iron-fields were exploited from the middle
of the century: Lanarkshire, Cleveland and Cumberland.

As iron became more plentiful its price fell and more things were
made from it. Iron replaced copper in the manufacture of pots, pans
and bedsteads. It was also used to make other articles for people's homes,
like stoves and railings. The casings of machinery were constructed
in cast iron and the moving parts from wrought iron. Railway lines,
bridges and locomotives needed iron in vast quantities. The steam hammer, which Nasmyth invented in 1839, made it possible to forge long
bars and very large pieces of iron for the first time.

Steel

By the middle of the nineteenth century wrought iron could barely
withstand the growing stresses of fast-moving machinery and high-
pressure steam. Some men were therefore looking for a tougher metal
to replace it. One possibility was steel, which consisted of pure iron
and a small amount of carbon. It was already used for making knives
and clock springs, but it could be melted only in very high temperatures.
As a result it cost ten times as much as iron and very little was made.

Henry Bessemer discovered how to mass produce steel in the 1850s.
Using a cylindrical converter, he blew hot air into over twenty tons
of molten pig-iron. In his first successful experiment he actually produced wrought iron. This is how he described it later:

It is impossible for me to convey to my readers any adequate idea of what
were my feelings when I saw the incandescent mass rise slowly from the

mould. We had as much metal as could be produced by two puddlers and their two assistants working arduously for hours with an expenditure of much fuel. We had obtained a pure, homogeneous ten-inch ingot as the result of thirty minutes' blowing, wholly unaccompanied by skilled labour. No wonder, then, that I gazed with delight on the first-born of the many thousands of square ingots that now [1897] come into existence every day.

The Bessemer converter on the left is in blast, with flames roaring from its mouth. The hot molten steel (from which the impurities have been burned out) is being poured from the converter on the right into the giant ladle, which will be swivelled round to fill moulds in the front.

It took Bessemer several years to produce reliable steel and even then most ironmasters remained unconvinced that he had solved all problems. They would not spend a lot of money on building converters until they were certain that they would gain from them. The price of steel fell from about £60 to £13 per ton, but it still remained considerably higher than that of iron and so the Bessemer process caught on slowly. It was not until the railways began to realize in the 1870s that steel was worth the extra cost because it wore so much longer than iron that larger quantities were made. By then William Siemens had developed his open-hearth process which made better steel but not so quickly. He made the blast even hotter by using the escaping gases. Steamships were made from this type of steel from the 1880s. Since then nearly all new furnaces used the open-hearth method.

Both processes suffered from one serious drawback. Neither could remove the phosphorus which all British iron-fields, except Cumberland, contained. Therefore large quantities of non-phosphoric iron-ore were imported, mostly from Spain and Sweden. The amount rose from 30,000 tons in 1860 to seven million in 1910. This led to a great expansion of the iron and steel works near the coast, especially in the Cleveland–Newcastle area, Cumberland, the Clyde valley and south Wales. British steel makers were slow to adopt the Gilchrist Thomas invention which enabled them to make steel from phosphoric ores. This method, which put a basic lining of dolomite limestone in the furnace to absorb the phosphorus, was already well established in the USA and Germany when Britain turned to it in a big way after 1900.

All these new methods could produce only mild steel, which was unsuitable, for example, for very sharp or fast-moving tools. Nearly all the experiments to produce high-quality steel with new processes took place abroad. Yet even so the output of British steel increased remarkably from 250,000 tons in 1870 to 6,400,000 in 1910. By then steel completely dominated British metals, for the output of copper, tin and lead had declined sharply at the same time.

Engineering, which took over the job of making machinery and similar goods from millwrights and blacksmiths, expanded tremendously in the nineteenth century. In the first half of the century, engineering firms usually made anything that was ordered from them. About the middle of the century, however some firms began to make for example, nothing but machine-tools, and others only textile machinery. Eventually they produced a wider range of goods, including weighing machines and railway carriages and bicycles. They also used machinery to make revolvers, nails and small hardware goods, too. At the same time, shipbuilding moved to the northern iron- and coalfields. Giant shipyards grew up by the mouths of the Clyde, Mersey, Tyne and Wear.

A chain-making workshop at Cradley Heath in 1900, with almost all the work still being done by hand.

Cloth

Meanwhile cloth, for so long Britain's chief industry, had also been developing. The figures opposite of the total value of textile products show how they began to expand at this time and how cotton, whose output increased ten times between 1780 and 1800, replaced wool as the leading industry.

Cotton

The cotton industry was transformed from the 1790s, mainly because of Samuel Crompton's mule which adapted two earlier inventions (the spinning Jenny and the water-frame) to spin great quantities of strong yarn. As a result the amount which one spinner could produce eventually increased 200 times and the price of yarn fell from £2 per lb in the 1780s to 3/– in 1830. British cottons also became as fine as Indian muslins.

As the new spinning machines were driven by water wheels and were too large and expensive for people's cottages, they were housed in small mills or factories on the banks of streams and rivers. This also enabled the clothiers to supervise the work more closely.

Weaving became the next main problem because yarn could now be spun much faster than it was woven. This led to a great, but temporary, increase in the number of hand-loom weavers who were replaced

Value of textile products

	1770s £m	1830s £m
cotton	1	22
wool	8	17
linen	2	5
silk	1	6
	—	—
	12	50

Mule spinning. Women look after the threads while men supervise the machinery.

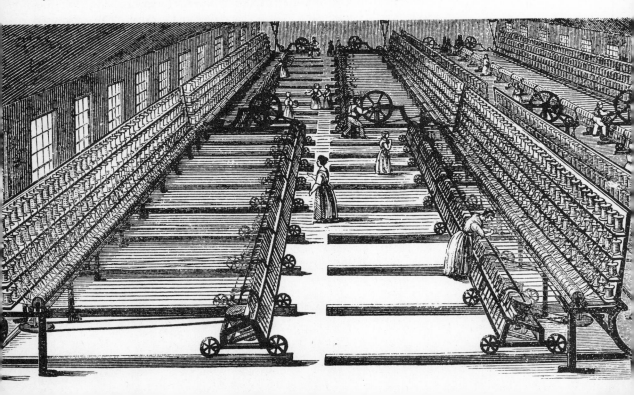

Raw cotton consumption

1780	8 m lb
1830	250 m lb
1870	1100 m lb
1910	2000 m lb

Raw wool consumption

1800	100 m lb
1850	200 m lb
1905	700 m lb

Power loom weaving worsted woollen yarn in 1844.

eventually by the power loom. A very unsatisfactory power loom appeared in the 1780s, and it had to be modified many times before more than a few cotton mills would use it. When they began to adopt it widely in the 1820s it was much more reliable and driven by steam, although it was not fully established until the 1840s. At the same time steam engines were harnessed to improved spinning mules and machinery for other processes. Revolving cylinders, for instance, were used to card the raw cotton and to print coloured patterns on the cloth after it was woven. The bleaching of cotton also became a much quicker and simpler process in the early nineteenth century when chlorine was used.

To cut the cost of transporting coal, the cotton industry moved into towns near the coal-fields of south-east Lancashire and the Clyde valley where the climate was most suitable and the ports well placed for receiving the raw cotton from America. At first the same firm both spun and wove, but gradually the processes were done separately.

British methods of making cotton changed little in the second half of the nineteenth century, apart from being speeded up. The USA pioneered mass production, producing the ring spindle in the middle of the century and the fully automatic loom at the end. In Lancashire the manufacturers were mainly interested in making finer cloths, like poplins and cambrics, for which the early ring spindles were unsuitable. However, even though ring spinning was not taken up generally until after 1900 the industry still prospered. The number of people employed in cotton mills rose from 100,000 in 1810 to 500,000 by the 1880s.

Wool

Though overtaken by cotton, the woollen industry remained one of Britain's leading industries in the nineteenth century. Because its consumption of raw wool rose it had to import increasing quantities from Australia and New Zealand. Wool was less suited than cotton to fast-moving machinery because it broke more easily. The worsted makers of Yorkshire were the first to use power looms from the 1830s. Most ordinary woollen factories did not adopt them until the 1850s and the 1860s when they had been improved. By then machines had been invented for all the other processes too. Combing was the last of these to be done by hand. By the second half of the century the industry was finally concentrated where coal was cheap and plentiful: the West Riding of Yorkshire. And the number of employees in the woollen mills reached their peak of 300,000 in 1890.

Linen

Linen was also less suited to machinery and suffered from the growth of cotton. After 1800 power-driven flax-spinning machines were introduced around Leeds, from where much of the yarn was sent to be woven in Scotland and Ireland. The industry declined in England from the middle of the century, and then in Scotland, where it was replaced by jute. It continued to flourish in Ireland. Silk-making also declined in the later nineteenth century.

Clothes

Until the 1860s nearly all clothes were made by hand and with very simple machinery. Then their manufacture was steadily revolutionized with the general adoption of some power-driven machines. They were applied to the knitting of stockings and underwear in the last third of the nineteenth century and to the production of boots and shoes, for which Northamptonshire was the centre. The sewing machine, which first appeared in America in the 1850s, made Leeds just as dominant in the clothing industry. Only poor-quality clothes were made by machines, since they could not cut very accurately nor could they sew complicated stitches. Therefore most garments had to be finished off by hand. Machinery was mainly restricted to the making of suits and coats until the 1890s, when it was used to turn out more hats and dresses as well.

The first Singer sewing machine (1854) was hand-turned by a large wheel.

Other industries

Power-driven machines completely changed many other industries in the later nineteenth century. Flour was ground by wind- and water-mills until the 1880s, when steel rollers replaced them. Since much of the grain came frome abroad, milling then moved to the ports. At the same time most breweries introduced steam-driven machinery.

The steam-driven paper mill was a French invention which the English copied early in the nineteenth century. Consequently they were

Soda crystals being produced in the 1840s.

Glass-blowing. The men extracted from the furnace a quantity of molten glass on the end of a long tube. They then blew it into the shape required.

Census of production 1907	
	£m
engineering/metals	165
textiles/clothing	160
mining	120
food/drink/tobacco	85
building	75
paper/printing	35
gas/electricity/water	30
chemicals	20
wood	20
others	30
	740
agriculture	120

able to meet the increased demand for all sorts of paper. It became even cheaper from the 1870s when it was made from wood pulp instead of rags. The first steam-driven printing-press produced *The Times* in 1814, but otherwise there were few changes before the 1870s. Then newspaper publishing adapted, from the manufacture of cotton, the idea of printing with two cylinders on a continuous roll. Type was no longer set by hand after the invention of automatic type-setting machines in the 1880s. Book printing altered much more slowly.

The chemical industry, which was almost a new one, flourished in the nineteenth century. Its main centres were in south Lancashire, Cheshire, Tyneside and Glasgow. It produced large quantities of chlorine for bleaching textiles and of soda for making glass and soap. The production of agricultural fertilizers was closely connected and so was the extraction from coal of gas, tar, dyes and drugs. The industry expanded most rapidly from the 1870s, when there was a great increase in chemical knowledge, but in this field the Germans always remained ahead of the British.

Few industries remained almost unaffected by technical changes. Coal-mining, as we have seen, was one. Building was another. Some new materials like concrete and iron were used for larger buildings, like railway stations and factories, but ordinary houses were still put up by hand in the traditional way.

In 1780 the total value of all industrial products had been £35 million. By 1907 it had risen to £740 million. Then the first census of British industries showed which were the most important.

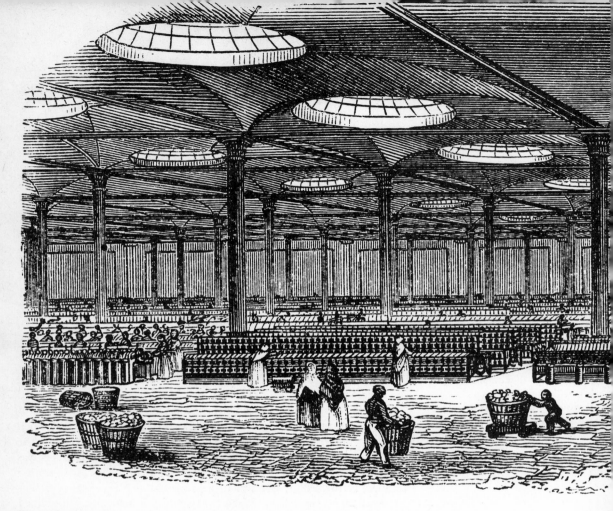

Factories

'Factory' in the eighteenth century meant a warehouse where goods were stored, but in the next it changed its meaning to a place where they were made. This does not mean that none existed before then, for some textiles were finished off in mills in the eighteenth century. Then the water-powered machines which were developed for spinning cotton, and later weaving, were also too large for private houses. In the Lancashire cotton mills men usually looked after the machinery and supervised the other workers, but the bulk of the work was done by women and children, who were cheaper, more docile, had nimbler fingers and learned new ways more quickly. The employers welcomed factories because they saved time and enabled them to supervise their 'hands' at work.

The work in the early factories was usually even harder and more monotonous than at home. The mill owners were anxious to make as large a profit as they could from their machinery and so they rarely

William Marshall's one-storeyed flax-mill at Leeds was built in the 1840s and covered nearly two acres.

Right This huge cotton factory near Preston in Lancashire was 158 yards long and contained 32,500 panes of glass. The building on the left is a reminder that most factories were much smaller.

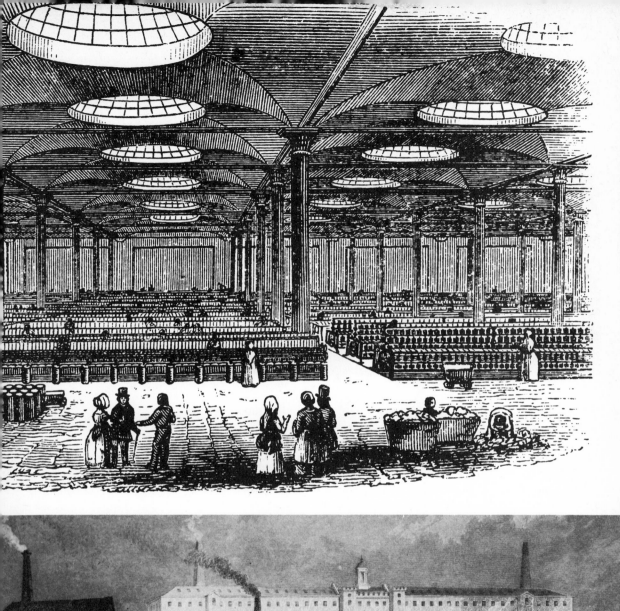

Needle-making at Redditch, near Birmingham, in the 1830s.

stopped it to give their workers a break. In booms the hours were especially long and in winter gaslight made work possible from long before dawn until well after dark. Except when trade was bad the hands worked for over twelve hours a day, six days a week. Since no one took naturally to this pattern of work, the early employers had to enforce very strict discipline. Those who arrived late or neglected their work were often fined between 6d and 2/– and some doors were even locked during working hours. To prevent the cotton thread from breaking, windows were kept closed and they often worked in temperatures of 80° F or more. Usually the smaller factories were the gloomiest and most crowded. Many families suffered because the children no longer worked with their parents. As one father lamented: 'My little girl has to go a mile and a half very early to her work and she comes home at half past eight. All that I see of her is to call her up in the morning and send her to bed and it almost breaks my heart.'

Although the early factories usually paid higher and more regular wages, few worked in them willingly. Most still preferred to work independently in irregular bursts even though a loom or spinning wheel often dominated their living room. From the 1840s the faster and more powerful textile machinery meant the employers could make substantial profits without making their hands work quite so long. By 1850 Parliament had reduced their working day to ten and a half hours and prevented the employment of children under eight.

Men in engineering

1850 100,000
1910 800,000

Until the middle of the nineteenth century most metal goods were made in small workshops, each employing a few men. Then many expanded into larger and larger engineering works, often with several hundred employees, turning out ships, machinery and so on. By the end of the nineteenth century nearly a quarter of the working population was engaged in a factory or workshop of some kind, although outside the textile and metal industries most were still small and employed perhaps ten to twenty men.

One result of the development of power-driven machinery was that the prices of many manufactured goods fell until eventually those who made them at home could compete no more. The number of hand-loom weavers, for instance, reached their peak of 500,000 in the 1820s. Then power looms cut their wages so drastically that many nearly starved and they were driven at last to find other jobs. In the second half of the nineteenth century machinery replaced hand work in so many industries that, by its end, very few people still worked at home, apart from those making clothes.

When the American journalist Jack London visited the East End of London in 1902, he discovered the miseries of their work. He was shown one room seven feet wide by eight long in which five men attached the tops of shoes to the soles with their own tools. They were kept fully occupied for only four months in the year when they worked flat out for nearly fourteen hours a day. 'In the winter a lamp burned nearly all the day and added its fumes to the over-loaded air which was breathed. There was barely room for the men to stand to their work for the rest of the space was heaped with cardboard, leather, bundles of shoe uppers and a miscellaneous assortment of materials. And yet I was given to understand that this was one of

Women stitching boots in the later nineteenth century. Shoemaking remained a hand process until the 1850s, when sewing-machines were introduced.

the better grades of sweating.' By then such work was called 'sweating' because the conditions were so much worse than in most other jobs. The Sweated Industries Exhibition of 1906 focused attention on these evils and within a few years Parliament removed the worst abuses.

The proportion of unskilled heavy labouring jobs was much higher in the nineteenth century than today, because there was much less machinery. Dockers, for instance, had to carry heavy sacks on their backs out of ships, while blast furnaces and gas works were stoked by hand and so on. Employment in these jobs was always uncertain, sometimes lasting for only a few days. The London dockers, for example, did not win the right to be employed for a minimum period of four hours until 1889. Towards the end of the nineteenth century unskilled labourers were employed less casually. Since then pneumatic tools, cranes, bulldozers and mechanical diggers have also made their work less exhausting.

Unskilled labourers could not expect to be employed for all the year during the nineteenth century and at times many skilled labourers were unemployed too. Those engaged in building, engineering and the manufacture of durable products were most likely to lose their jobs in a slump, together with those who made goods for export, like cotton. The proportion of unemployed declined significantly from the 1840s, but we do not know by how much. In bad years, like 1879 and 1886, at least ten per cent were out of work, but the proportion in the early nineteenth century was certainly much higher.

All workers alike were liable to lose their jobs through illness or accident, many of which were caused by fast-moving machinery, especially towards the end of the nineteenth century. People became careless when they worked beside them for long and it was all too easy to be slow in moving a finger, arm or even a head. The conditions in blast furnaces and most metal works were also very unhealthy and those who stoked boilers regularly suffered from the fumes. Some work in engineering shops and gas and chemical works was almost as dangerous as coal-mining. An Irishman employed at the British Alkali Chemical Works in Widnes in the 1890s reported:

I was working in a shed and I had to cross the yard. It was ten o'clock at night and there was no light about. While crossing the yard I felt something take hold of my leg and screw it off. I became unconscious; I didn't know what became of me for a day or two. On the following Sunday night I came to my senses and found myself in hospital. A nurse told me both legs were off. There was a stationary crank in the yard let into the ground; the hole was 18 inches long, 15 inches deep and 15 inches wide. The crank revolved in the hole three revolutions a minute. There was no fence or covering over the hole. Since my accident they have covered the hole with a piece of sheet iron. They gave me £25. Out of that I paid £9 for a machine by which to wheel myself about.

This bitter attack on sweated labour in 1888 supports the successful matchgirls' strike at Bryant and May's.

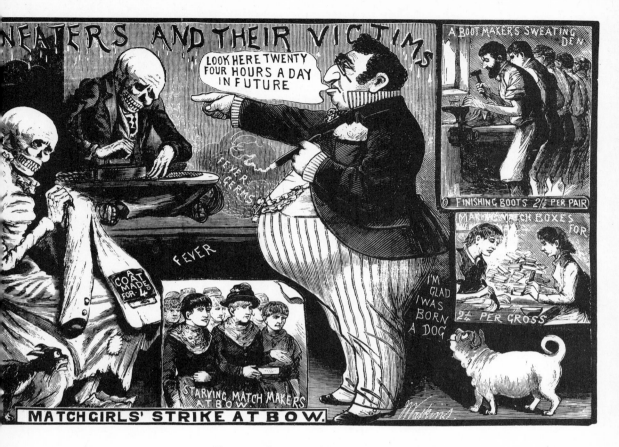

Few employers paid any compensation to their injured workmen before then. They refused to be held responsible for their mishaps, invariably claiming that accidents would not happen if their workers were careful. However, from 1897 most had to pay something when their employees were killed or injured, although before 1948 it was usually on a modest scale.

Factories had been inspected from the 1830s, but often with little effect before the end of the century, for the inspectors had little power to enforce the regulations.

Trade unions

In the eighteenth century discontented workers had very few effective means of preventing wage cuts or new machinery from putting them out of work. Occasionally when they were desperate they banded against their employers like the west-country weavers who 'cut all the chains in the looms belonging to Mr Coulthurst on account of his lowering of the wages'. In the early nineteenth century many textile machines were destroyed in similar outbursts, but they had no lasting effect. The southern farm labourers were more successful in 1830 when they frightened many farmers into not threshing by machine for some time. Despairing industrial workers continued to resort to violence in the 1840s. 'There have been many attempts to wreck workshops by using explosives,' reported Friedrich Engels. 'On Friday 29 September, 1843, an explosion caused serious damage to Mr Padgin's saw-making factory in Sheffield. The device used was a piece of piping filled with powder and sealed at both ends.'

By then skilled workmen very rarely used such methods. They could look after their own interests much better through trade unions. Since wages varied considerably in different areas, many crafts formed local unions, which often met in pubs, from the later eighteenth century. When all the tradesmen in one area agreed to accept only the union rate, they sometimes managed to get their wages raised. Frequently they tried to limit the number of boys trained in their craft and so prevent future unemployment. The brushmakers, shoemakers, west-country wool-combers and others helped unemployed members tramp to other counties to seek work. Many unions also paid out money to those who were too old or sick to work. Since most of these activities were illegal until 1824 (and Parliament made it easier to prosecute them from 1800) they often met secretly.

An attempt to form a union for all workers failed dismally in 1834, but trade unions were well established by the middle of the nineteenth

Police halting the march of Welsh miners on strike in 1889.

century, in particular among skilled workers in the building and metal trades. By the 1860s some had a full-time paid secretary and a few had a London headquarters which drew the local branches together. These unions tried to win concessions by negotiating rather than striking. As the carpenters' union secretary explained: 'We believe that nothing can be more advantageous than for the masters and men to meet and agree upon certain conditions.' Although the employers eventually accepted the existence of unions for the skilled, their position in law remained doubtful and so representatives from different unions met once a year from 1868 to discuss their common interests at the Trades Union Congress. At last in 1875 they obtained the undisputed right to strike peacefully.

Although one union leader insisted that 'employers, by their overbearing and tyrannical conduct, compel workmen to combine for their mutual protection', most attempts to form permanent unions among the less skilled workers failed before the later 1880s, apart from the Lancashire cotton workers and the coal miners in the north-east. Masters could usually replace unskilled labourers who threatened to strike and many flatly refused to employ union members anyway. The less skilled could often not keep regular accounts or run meetings in a businesslike way and were also short of money, especially in a depression. However, by the 1890s well-organized unions had at last grown up for dockers, railwaymen and other industrial workers in large concerns where the employers appeared to be remote and hostile men who exploited them. After 1910 these new unions attracted more members all over Britain.

This explosion of trade-union activity was partly the result of people working together in larger numbers and also a reaction against the employers' increasing determination to work their men as efficiently as possible. Impatient of success and short of money, for skilled workers were usually paid nearly twice as much, many of the newer unions regarded the strike as their main hope of winning concessions, especially if they worked in transport or other jobs where its effect was felt immediately. As one official asserted: 'I do not believe in sick pay, out of work pay and other pays, the whole aim and intention of this union is to reduce the hours of labour.'

Before the 1840s nearly everyone who was employed regularly expected to work for up to twelve hours a day. Then, when Parliament reduced the working day for women and children in textile mills, the unions fought for similar concessions for men without a cut in pay. In the 1870s some engineers won a nine and a half hour day and many others worked for about the same time by the early twentieth century.

Clerks, who wrote with quill pens, were not so well off. Paper work expanded as quickly as business in the second half of the century.

Many more letters and bills had to be written, as well as more complicated accounts kept. Clerks were therefore employed in increasing numbers in business and the civil service.

Most clerks worked under very strict discipline. They were expected to be very neat and punctual. They could not smoke nor talk to each other and the wall often carried notices like 'No clerk is allowed to leave the room without permission'. They could not even rely on being provided with a fire in winter, when they continued to work long hours. At the counting house of a London soap-maker, J. Knight and Sons, they had to arrive by six in the morning and stay until six in the evening. By the end of the century they were working from 7 a.m. to 5.30 p.m., but had lost half their dinner hour in return. Shop assistants, domestic servants and farm labourers also worked long hours, partly because unions were usually weakest among scattered workers who knew their employers personally.

Unions also fought to reduce week-end working, and Saturday afternoon off was enjoyed by textile workers and the employees of some London firms by the 1850s. In the next twenty years it was conceded to many other industrial workers in the provinces. However, most had to wait until the middle of the present century for all Saturday off and some still work a five and a half day week. Guaranteed holidays were another aim, but holidays with pay were reserved for the middle classes in the nineteenth century. Four bank holidays a year for all began in 1871.

All this union activity infuriated many employers, who fought back fiercely, often refusing to recognize the new unions. 'You might as well have a trade union in the Army, where discipline has to be kept at a very high standard, as have it on the railways,' argued one manager. They also dismissed prominent unskilled trade unionists and sometimes locked out all their employees when they threatened to strike. In 1898 these tactics humbled the engineers, the strongest union of all. Judges supported employers in several lawsuits and, following a rail stoppage in south Wales, strikes became very risky for five years from 1901.

Summing up

Thus industrialization brought both benefits and disadvantages. On the one hand, the new machines brought vastly increased production and much more wealth for the growing population to enjoy. But conditions in the factories where the goods were made were often very harsh, and many factory owners tended to exploit their workers, making them work long hours in unhealthy surroundings. This led the workers to found unions to try to improve their lot. The employers felt that their profits were threatened, and tried to suppress the unions. Thus the growth of factories often resulted in bitter conflict between employer and worker.

An illustration from a novel by Charles Dickens showing clerks with quill pen and typical high stools.

Trade-union members

1872	0·5 m
1892	1·5 m
1910	2·5 m

A docker's union membership card of 1891. It is signed by Tom Mann and Ben Tillett, the leaders of the successful London dockers' strike of 1889.

80

Chapter 4
Nineteenth-century towns

The growth of population

Britain's population grew dramatically after 1780. Farming could not provide many extra jobs for the increased numbers. The new industries, on the other hand, needed more and more workers. People therefore moved to the industrial areas, and to house them old towns were expanded and new ones built.

Almost all Britain's extra population since the 1780s has been packed into towns, unlike some other countries where their population grew much faster than their industries during the nineteenth century. A

Glasgow in 1864. Compare this panorama to the late eighteenth-century towns on page 30.

Population distribution		
	country dwellers	town dwellers
1740	6·5 m	1 m
1800	7·5 m	3 m
1850	10·0 m	11 m
1910	9·0 m	32 m

comparison with Ireland suggests what might have happened here if Britain's industries had not been transformed. Between the 1780s and 1840s the population of both countries doubled. However, the vast majority in Ireland continued to live in the countryside, partly because the English prevented industry from developing there, but also because they lacked raw materials. To keep themselves alive, the Irish were driven to growing more and more potatoes, which yielded more food per acre than any other crop. Disaster struck in 1845. Most of the potatoes were destroyed by blight. Many Irish died of famine in the next few years and even more fled to the USA and to towns in Britain, especially Liverpool. By 1900 Ireland's population was nearly halved and the total was little more than it had been in the 1780s. In the same period, several million people also left Britain, but here the population quadrupled. Without large towns and expanding industries this could never have happened.

In 1780 London and Edinburgh were the only towns in Britain with more than 50,000 inhabitants. By 1900 there were eighty more. This simple fact sums up one of the most important developments in the whole of British history.

London

London's expansion was amazing. It had over a million inhabitants by the early nineteenth century, when it surpassed the population of ancient Rome and became the largest city in the western world's history. Subsequently new citizens arrived at the rate of 300 every day.

Vast numbers of houses were built in streets and squares to shelter this constantly growing population. At first, London grew northwards and by the early nineteenth century the city's boundary ran roughly from Regent's Park to Islington. Madame Tussaud's, the British Museum and Euston Railway Station are now all in the part of London which was created around 1800. Streets of private houses were also built around Buckingham Palace. Because of the difficulty of crossing the Thames few Londoners lived to the south of the river until several bridges were erected across it early in the nineteenth century.

At first, successful merchants and other wealthy people who did not want to live in London moved away from the city to the nearest villages like Islington and Paddington. Then more and more houses were built along the main roads linking them with London. Finally the farmland in between was sold or rented, usually in small patches. Sometimes it was used for market gardening, sometimes for making bricks or brewing beer. Usually, however, the builders squeezed into their new estates as many houses as they could. They were laid out

'London going out of Town; or, the March of Bricks and Mortar.' Cruickshank's cartoon, drawn in 1829, remained topical throughout the nineteenth century.

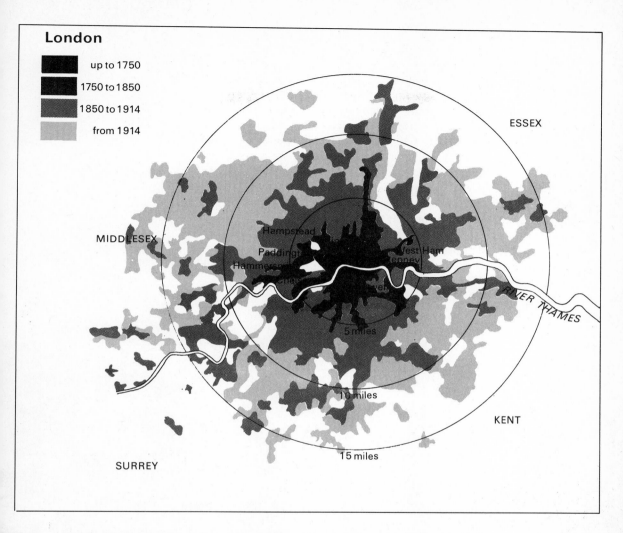

London

⬛	up to 1750
⬛	1750 to 1850
⬛	1850 to 1914
⬛	from 1914

ESSEX

MIDDLESEX

Hampstead

Paddington

Hammersmith

Chelsea

West Ham

Stepney

Camberwell

5 miles

10 miles

15 miles

SURREY

KENT

RIVER THAMES

The spread of London's built-up areas.

in squares and streets that sometimes followed the boundaries of former fields. Occasionally a large area like Camden Town was built at the same time, but most of London has grown up haphazardly in small sections like a patchwork quilt.

As London crept outwards, it swallowed up villages in all directions. They included Hampstead and Tottenham to the north, Chelsea and Hammersmith in the west, Stepney and West Ham in the east and Camberwell to the south. The district round Camberwell housed only a few people at the end of the eighteenth century. By 1900 nearly a quarter of a million people lived there. By then, London was a huge built-up area which had spread far into the neighbouring counties of Middlesex, Essex, Kent and Surrey. At one time, of course, they had

85

been covered by trees and fields, as one south Londoner complained: 'The old familiar field is cut up; the favourite blackberry hedge is cut down; the path along the mill stream is closed; the well remembered windmill has given place to a railway station; the footway across the waving corn is no more; the stream in which I bathed is bordered by terraces and villas; the little country alehouse at the corner has been covered with poverty-stricken houses.'

The east end developed somewhat differently from the other suburbs. As trade with other countries increased, more and more ships came to London. In the early nineteenth century special docks were at last constructed below Tower Bridge to make it easier for them to unload (see picture, p. 135). Then many industries like flour milling and sugar refining, which imported some of their raw materials, set up factories by the docks. Concurrently rows and rows of houses were built near the docks and factories for those who worked in them. Some of those near the river were erected on land which was originally a marsh. Almost all were packed in very close together.

London's food markets in the early nineteenth century. Smithfield for meat
(left), Covent Garden for fruit and vegetables (above), Billingsgate for fish
(below). Feeding the rapidly increasing number of London stomachs every
day was a mammoth task. Countrymen sent their produce to these markets
where it was bought, often early in the morning, by London's shopkeepers
or their agents, and by the servants of the wealthy. In 1830 a permanent
market building was erected in the centre of Covent Garden.

87

The sketches on these pages were drawn by George Scharf, a Bavarian-born draughtsman and lithographer who came to London in 1816. He took a great interest in the topography of London and made a vast number of drawings of the old buildings, street scenes and domestic life of the metropolis. The sketches are noted with area, date and even time of day, and show scenes such as the street traders – 'Strawberry Sellers', 'Chair Repairers'.

walk in and see the most wonderful sight

AN ENORMOUS FAT WOMEN

a boy born without arms and hands

The smallest man in the World

in Oxford Street
March 1843

London

Strawberries & Raspberries covered with cabbage and other leafs

Biscuits and sweet cakes

Other towns

The other towns expanded in a similar way but not on such a scale. Those which grew fastest first were in the regions of the newly mechanized cotton and woollen industries: Lancashire, the Clyde valley and the West Riding of Yorkshire. The construction of mills and factories from the later eighteenth century soon transformed small market towns like Bolton and Bradford when rows of houses were also packed tightly round them to accommodate the workers.

By the middle of the nineteenth century Liverpool, Manchester and Glasgow had become the largest towns outside London. Vast quantities of cotton cloth were made in Manchester and Glasgow, but all three were important primarily because they were centres for trade in cotton. The raw cotton came from America to Liverpool and Glasgow, which also exported the finished goods. From Liverpool most of the cotton for southern Lancashire was sent to Manchester, where the manufacturers from the surrounding towns bought it and later sold their cloth. As the century progressed most spinning was done in the towns within about a dozen miles of Manchester, like Bolton and Oldham, while weaving was concentrated a little further north in Preston, Burnley, etc. Each town tended to specialize in one particular thread or cloth.

One of the leading centres for the manufacture and sale of woollen cloth was Leeds. As it grew, however, it concentrated more on the trade of its neighbouring towns than on making wool itself. It also attracted many factories which made textile machinery and later ready-made clothes as well.

Leeds in 1840. By 1880 the population of the city had doubled.

90

Most textile towns went on expanding throughout the second half of the nineteenth century, and others like Birmingham and Sheffield, which were centres for the metal and engineering industries, grew even faster in the 1850s. Shipbuilding contributed to the rapid growth of some coastal towns, like Sunderland, later in the century.

Almost all these towns were on or near coal-fields. The industries on which they depended used steam engines and so needed large quantities of coal. The towns where it was mined were usually quite small and often sprang up close to each other, as in the valleys of south Wales. They grew larger only when another industry, like textiles, settled there as well. In general the largest towns of all were centres both for trade and for various industries.

As ships became larger, they could not use the smaller ports and so Hull, Cardiff, Bristol and other leading ports (including London) were among the fastest growing towns towards the end of the nineteenth century. Other seaside towns like Bournemouth and Blackpool also expanded as holiday resorts.

All towns did not expand at an even rate during the nineteenth century.

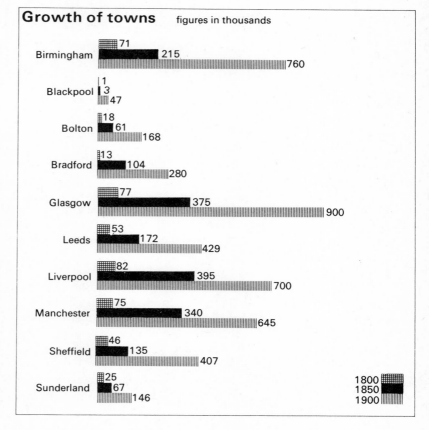

Growth of towns   figures in thousands

Birmingham	71 / 215 / 760
Blackpool	1 / 3 / 47
Bolton	18 / 61 / 168
Bradford	13 / 104 / 280
Glasgow	77 / 375 / 900
Leeds	53 / 172 / 429
Liverpool	82 / 395 / 700
Manchester	75 / 340 / 645
Sheffield	46 / 135 / 407
Sunderland	25 / 67 / 146

1800
1850
1900

91

Housing

Since most people walked wherever they went until later in the nineteenth century, they wanted to live as near to their work and the centre of their town as possible. At first, therefore, most builders wedged as many houses as they could fit into every available scrap of central land. Then they usually built more houses along the main roads leading out of the towns and finally in the fields behind. Factories and workshops also grew up in these suburbs. The large towns swallowed up neighbouring villages. Gorbals, for example, soon became an inseparable part of Glasgow.

Almost all these houses were built in terraces or courts. However, as the centres of their towns filled up, many of the wealthiest families, who could afford to run a coach, moved to the outskirts. There they lived in small villas or semi-detached houses in spacious gardens, usually on the south or west side of the town, away from the smoke. Later in the nineteenth century these exclusive areas were often engulfed by more houses and their occupants were driven even further out. When this happened several poorer families usually occupied a house which had been designed for one family and the garden was sometimes filled with more houses too.

The suburban house of a prosperous middle-class family in the mid nineteenth century.

The drawing room of a similar house in the late nineteenth century.

Prosperous Victorian houses built in Camberwell in 1866 and 1875.

In London the level of the streets where some of the finest houses were found had sometimes been raised at least several feet so that, from the front, the ground floor appeared to be a basement. Here was the kitchen and scullery, and coal was also stored. The front door admitted visitors to the next floor, where the spacious living and dining rooms were, with perhaps the main drawing room above. Servants almost always slept in attic rooms under the roof and the members of the family on the floor below.

From the mid nineteenth century, rows of terraced houses were built all over the country, nearly always in brick with perhaps slate roofs. Those for clerks and lower middle-class families usually stood back a few feet from the street with space for a small front garden. The door opened into a narrow hall. The front parlour often had a bay window. Beneath it there might be a coal cellar. Behind it there was a kitchen and maybe a scullery jutting out into the yard at the back, where the lavatory was normally built, perhaps beside the coal shed. Some skilled workers managed to rent similar houses, but the families of most manual workers lived in smaller two-storey houses. Their front door usually led straight into the living room, which might be no more than a dozen feet square. Those families who did not have a separate kitchen also cooked here. A narrow flight of stairs led to perhaps two bedrooms above – the front one often being reached through the back one. The better-off had three or even four bedrooms.

Not all families were as fortunate as these. Until the middle of the nineteenth century thousands of families in Liverpool and other south Lancashire towns occupied underground cellars, which were without light or proper ventilation.

Because ordinary working-class families could not afford to pay more than a few shillings a week for their houses, the builders put up most of them as cheaply as possible. A report in the 1840s said:

An immense number of the small houses occupied by the poorer classes in the suburbs of Manchester are of the most superficial character. New cottages are erected with a rapidity that astonishes persons who are unacquainted with their flimsy structure, having no foundation. The walls are only half brick thick (4½ inches) and the whole of the materials are slight and unfit for the purpose. They are built back to back and, like a honeycomb, every particle of space is occupied. Double rows of these houses form courts with, perhaps a pump at one end and a privy at the other, common to the occupants of about twenty houses.

Right Some members of the upper classes showed concern about the housing conditions of the labouring masses, but Prince Albert still expected four families to live in this model house built in 1851 for the Great Exhibition.

But such ideas led to better houses which were built in more spacious estates (*below right*) for some artisans (or skilled workmen) who could afford them.

Smaller Victorian houses in Camberwell, built in 1879 and 1900. Similar houses appeared in most towns throughout Britain.

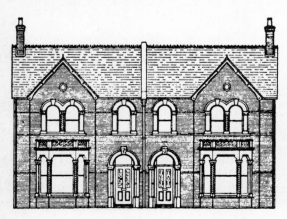

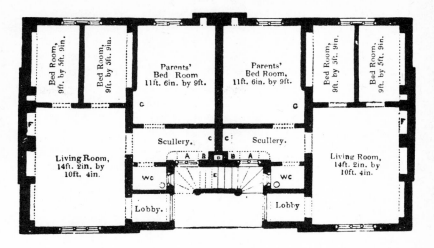

Bed Room, 9ft. by 5ft. 9in.

Bed Room, 9ft. by 5ft. 9in.

Parents' Bed Room 11ft. 6in. by 9ft.

Parents' Bed Room, 11ft. 6in. by 9ft.

Bed Room, 9ft. by 5ft. 9in.

Bed Room, 9ft. by 5ft. 9in.

Living Room, 14ft. 2in. by 10ft. 4in.

Scullery.

Scullery.

Living Room, 14ft. 2in. by 10ft. 4in.

WC

WC

Lobby.

Lobby

Back-to-back houses were especially common in Leeds and the industrial towns of Yorkshire, while back-to-earth ones were built against the hillside in the narrow valleys of the Pennine woollen towns. Many of these houses survived at least until the 1930s, when George Orwell described some of them. This one in Sheffield was typical: 'Back to back, two up, one down (i.e. a three-storey house with one room on each storey). Cellar below. Living-room 14 × 10 feet and rooms above corresponding. Sink in living room. Top floor has no door but gives on open stairs. Walls in living room slightly damp. House is so dark that light has to be kept burning all day. Six in family, parents and four children.'

Writers wanting to shock their contemporaries into taking action naturally described only the worst houses. Many nineteenth-century town houses were better than these, but unfortunately we have no reliable guide to the general housing situation before 1891. Then the census counted the number of houses for the first time. It revealed that over one-tenth of the English lived in houses with more than two people to a room. (This means at least seven in a three-roomed house.) In towns like London and Bradford overcrowding was twice as bad, while over a third of the inhabitants of Durham and Northumberland also lived more than two to a room. Scotland had so many one- and two-roomed houses that half the Scots were overcrowded and a tenth were packed at least four to every room.

Working-class houses were built in terraces – usually as cheaply and as close together as possible. The more prosperous could easily turn their front rooms into shops, but many dwellings were too small. In the bottom right picture the outside stairs indicate that at least five families lived here. Several households would share one outside toilet, situated in the back yard.

The maps show crowded back-to-back houses and dreary rows of tunnel-back houses built at the end of the nineteenth century in Birmingham.

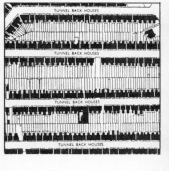

Urban health

The houses of poor families often caused ill health. They were over-crowded, badly ventilated and frequently damp, dirty and draughty too. Those without cellars or thick stone walls found it difficult to keep food cool and so prevent it from going bad in summer. Flies, TB germs and so on flourished in these conditions, and when animals were housed nearby, their fleas and lice added to the risk of infection.

Animals were packed into towns as well as people, for many horses were needed to pull coaches, carts and buses. Cows were kept for milk before the railways carried it swiftly from the country. Since meat could not be frozen, animals were killed in slaughter-houses near to where they were eaten. Other hazards to health in crowded towns were overstocked graveyards, the obnoxious waste of some factories and tanneries, and smoke. The air over most towns was usually heavily polluted, especially in winter.

Few town-dwellers could bury their refuse and excrement. Dumping it in near-by streets was often their only means of getting rid of their rubbish. Most towns collected it, but they piled it on dunghills close to the houses. They also cleaned their streets irregularly and inefficiently, especially away from the main roads. The latter were swept about once every two or three weeks in many towns, but the side streets were cleaned so rarely (perhaps twice a year) that they were nearly always filthy. A survey of Manchester's streets in the 1830s revealed that there were 'heaps of refuse, stagnant pools, ordure etc.' in over half. Similar sights could be seen in almost every town. 'There is not a street, lane or approach to Inverness that is not disgustingly defiled at all times, so much as to render the whole place an absolute nuisance', declared a report in the 1840s.

Much of the trouble stemmed from the fact that 'there are very few houses in town which can boast of either water-closet or privy'. Similar reports came from other towns. In Birmingham 'many privies were without doors and overflowing with filth', while in parts of Leeds 'the privies are few in proportion to the number of inhabitants. They are open to view both in front and rear, are invariably in a filthy condition, and often remain without the removal of any portion of the filth for six months.'

Some lavatories drained into cesspits, which often leaked and so they contaminated nearby wells. In addition they were emptied so rarely that those which did not leak usually overflowed. Also the drains were so wide that they could not be cleaned properly. Toilets close to streams and rivers drained directly into them so that in the large towns they became little more than open sewers. The Thames at London, for instance, became so unpleasant in the hot summer of 1858 that it was known as the 'Great Stink'.

Water supply was another vital problem for the large towns. Most

Nightmen removing excrement, or night-soil as it was often called.

Faraday the great scientist presenting his card to Father Thames.

98

streams and rivers were barely suitable for washing, yet many town-dwellers had no alternative but to use them. The river water at York, for example, was very cloudy in the nineteenth century, but after letting it settle for a day or two, the inhabitants still drank it. The suburbs were usually shortest of water, for they had fewer wells, springs and streams. Their inhabitants were often supplied with water at perhaps a halfpenny a bucket by men who came round with carts.

London was the first town to get extra water from outside – through hollowed-out tree trunks. It could only run downhill and private water companies piped it into the basements of those who could afford their charges. In the nineteenth century iron pipes enabled them to pump water faster uphill and in larger quantities. More and more towns therefore followed London's lead. Some companies also erected standpipes in the streets for the poorer inhabitants. Water gushed out of them for perhaps an hour on three evenings a week. Since fifteen to twenty houses might share a pipe, their occupants queued up with buckets and sauce-pans to collect enough water for the next few days. Even these facilities, however, were not at all widespread until after 1850.

Until the later nineteenth century the amount of water which people used varied greatly according to their wealth and where they lived. In a few favoured towns like Preston nearly everyone had about eight gallons a day (which is about half what we use today). But the normal daily ration in London and elsewhere was two or three gallons and some had even less.

Even though eighteenth-century London had shown that huge towns were outstandingly unhealthy, many rapidly growing cities in the early nineteenth century were totally unprepared for the sanitary problems which nearly overwhelmed them. Most wealthy Victorians never went near the homes of the poorer workers and so they knew little of conditions in the worst parts. A few individuals, like Edwin Chadwick and John Simon, tried hard to make them realize just how bad they were. They publicized figures, for instance, showing how much longer people lived in Rutland or Wiltshire than in Liverpool and Manchester. The average age of death in 1840 was:

Queuing for water in a London alley.

	professional persons, gentry and their families	tradesmen, shopkeepers, farmers and their families	labourers, mechanics, servants and their families
Manchester	38	20	17
Liverpool	35	22	15
Rutland	52	41	38
Wiltshire	50	48	33

However, such statistics left most people unmoved, so Chadwick and his friends then tried rousing their consciences with vivid reports on the worst places (see page 99).

The sudden appearance of an Indian disease called cholera stirred public opinion much more effectively. We know now that between 1831 and 1866 four epidemics killed about 200,000 Britons, mostly in big ports like Newcastle and Liverpool and the poorer areas of the large towns. At the time people everywhere were very frightened because they had no idea where the disease would strike next, how long it would last and how many victims it would claim. Nor could they take any precautions because they did not know how it was spread. Some doctors surmised that impure water was the agent, but not until the 1880s did a German, Robert Koch, prove that cholera germs were usually carried by water contaminated by the excrement of its victims.

Typhus also brought a sudden and painful death to many adults.

A crowded London court in 1852 with a large refuse heap gave children a chance to play, adults to scavenge and disease to spread.

The Fleet was originally a river flowing into the Thames, but long before the nineteenth century Londoners had turned it into an open sewer.

The 'Deluge' Patent Washdown Pedestal. Water-closets could be found only in the homes of middle-class Victorians. This splendid model cost over £10 – as much as many labourers earned in three months.

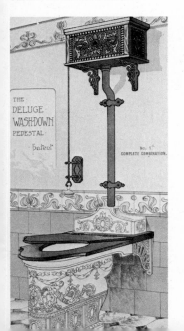

Lice carried its germs and it often struck in epidemics. One of the last major ones in the British Isles killed many starving Irish in the 1840s. Cecil Woodham-Smith described an attack of typhus in her book *The Great Hunger*:

The patient becomes all but unrecognizable. His face swells and he turns a dark congested hue; he raves in delirium [and] throws himself about; as the fever becomes intense and his body burns he is apt to jump out of the window, or plunge into a river in search of coolness; the rash appears from which typhus derived its former name of 'spotted fever'. Meanwhile the patient is in acute pain – he vomits, develops agonizing sores and sometimes gangrene, followed by the loss of fingers, toes and feet.

Typhoid was another fever with similar symptoms. Its germ was usually carried by water (and sometimes milk) but did not kill nearly so many victims as typhus.

Ignorance was not the only reason why the towns were slow to tackle their sanitary problems. Large-scale improvements cost a lot of money and so, when the experts disagreed on what should be done, those who had to pay usually plumped for the cheapest rather than the most effective schemes. Since they also interfered with people's rights and property town councils could rarely act until new laws were passed giving them permission.

Liverpool, where living conditions were among the worst in the country by the mid nineteenth century, was one of the first to tackle its problems vigorously. From the 1840s it prevented people from living in underground cellars by filling in many with sand. It also paved many more streets and footpaths, which were easier to clean, laid new sewers, built public conveniences and even saw that slaughter-houses were cleaned from time to time. Manchester was one of the few towns to put a stop to the building of back-to-back houses, but many more followed Liverpool's example and widened some streets.

Because of the rapid growth of most towns the situation was not improved until the 1870s. Some, like Newcastle, took even longer to make progress.

Few lavatories were flushed with water before the mid nineteenth century. Then more and more water closets were built, following the discovery that narrow drainpipes made of earthenware carried away the sewage quickly and cleanly. But the town councils still did not know how to dispose of it. London, for instance, had a system of main drains by 1865, but they just poured it into the Thames. In the 1870s Parliament made it illegal to connect new drains with a river, but it had little immediate effect. The lower part of the Thames was still described as 'black, putrid sewage for its whole width' ten years later.

Improvements came more certainly from the 1870s, when the whole country was divided into sanitary districts, each with a medical officer of health and a sanitary inspector. Liverpool and London had already had medical officers for twenty-five years, but Birmingham and most other towns did not appoint them until they were forced to. These officials were responsible for spotting outbreaks of infectious diseases, leaks in drains, impure water, the pollution of rivers, nuisances caused by factories and the dumping of refuse, and for taking remedial action.

At first many were rather slack in carrying out their duties, but progress came steadily in public health, for more and more new laws from the 1870s forced, and no longer just permitted, the councils to take steps to protect their inhabitants.

By the early twentieth century all the great cities still had insanitary areas, but the smaller mining towns in south Wales, Durham and Yorkshire were then the most unhealthy. Since then they too have collected their refuse more efficiently and cleaned their streets more thoroughly. Eventually special sewage works were also built inland to make it harmless, but seaside towns continued to pump their sewage into the sea.

When most town councils took over their local waterworks in the second half of the nineteenth century, they gradually made the water purer by filtering and adding chlorine and other chemicals. As the large towns continued to expand, they built special reservoirs to provide them with more water. And so the habit of washing regularly with soap and warm water spread among the poorer classes from about the 1880s. Thus, by the end of the nineteenth century, the health problems of towns were on the way to being solved.

Deepening the Fleet Street sewer, with brick-built tunnels.

The Prince of Wales opening London's main drainage works in 1865.

Manchester's two town halls. The first one was built during the 1820s in the classical style and the picture shows it in 1842 surrounded by an angry Chartist crowd. By the 1870s Manchester had long outgrown this building and so it erected the impressive Gothic Hall to reflect the city's size and importance.

Amenities

Not only did towns become healthier, they also became more imposing. At the end of the eighteenth century only the capital cities of London and Edinburgh had many large public buildings and several wide streets. The centre of London was made even more impressive in the early nineteenth century, when Regent Street and Trafalgar Square were laid out and Buckingham Palace and the British Museum built.

The centres of most other towns changed little before the railways in the 1840s. Nearly all smaller ones could build a station within a few minutes' walk of the main part of the town, but the large towns often had to pull down some houses to create convenient sites for their stations.

From the middle of the century, as they prospered, most towns provided themselves with various public buildings too. By the end all important towns had at least one hall of which the local citizens were often very proud. At the opening of the St George's Hall in Bradford the mayor had boasted: 'We are eleven feet wider than the hall in Birmingham and about as much longer.' However, Leeds possessed an even larger hall within a few years and other towns rivalled Leeds soon after. Some erected quite imposing post offices and stock exchanges too.

In the second half of the nineteenth century many banks and offices were built and large central houses were adapted to accommodate them. Until department stores appeared at the end of the century, nearly all shops were small enough to fit into the ground floor of ordinary houses and they were not built specially. The ports and main trading towns, like Manchester, also squeezed in many warehouses for storing goods near the centre. Most factories, however, needed more land and so were usually found in the suburbs.

Towns changed their appearance further by making up, and perhaps widening, their main roads, laying pavements and installing gas lights. A few, like Birmingham, even rebuilt whole sections of the town. By the end of the nineteenth century, therefore, fewer people lived in these central areas. More and more travelled there to work and shop and sometimes for entertainment too.

Small shopping centres usually developed on the site of former villages in the suburbs. Some builders left a space for a church when they laid out a large housing estate, but even so the town centres had many more churches and chapels. The suburbs had fewer public houses, even though many corner houses were converted into them or small general shops. Schools and hospitals were normally built on the nearest available land when they were required.

The inhabitants of small towns can reach the countryside so easily that many rapidly growing towns, like Manchester, did not realize the advantages of leaving open spaces near their centres until they had little central land left. From the middle of the nineteenth century, therefore, many had to use cemeteries and small gardens as parks while they created larger ones on the outskirts. Around London, areas like Wimbledon Common and Epping Forest were not preserved until the 1870s, for example. Sports grounds and recreation centres were also established on the most acceptable of the remaining sites.

So much for the growth of industrial towns in the nineteenth century. By 1900 society was beginning to be able to organize life in towns far bigger than those of a hundred years before. The lesson had not been learned easily, and many had suffered and died in the process. But the slums of earlier years still stood and the problem of poverty in towns was far from solved.

Inside the children's section of a town library. The Libraries Act of 1850 made it possible to set up libraries out of rates.

Sunday morning in a London street in 1856. When the pub opened drink provided the fastest escape route from these surroundings.

Urban poor

On a summer evening in 1902, an American journalist disguised as a sailor, walked along streets of the east end of London with two old men.

Both kept their eyes upon the pavement as they walked and talked, and every now and then one or the other would stoop and pick something up, never missing the stride the while. I thought it was cigar and cigarette stumps they were collecting, and for some time took no notice. Then I did notice.

From the slimy, spittle-drenched sidewalk, they were picking up bits of orange peel, apple skin, and grape stems, and they were eating them. They picked up stray crumbs of bread the size of peas, apple cores so black and dirty one would not take them to be apple cores, and these things these two men took into their mouths, and chewed them, and swallowed them.

Jack London, who reported this incident, was amazed to see it in one of the wealthiest cities in the world, but sights like this could have been seen in any British town throughout the nineteenth century. 'A very great number are unable to provide for themselves and their families a sufficiency of food of the plainest and cheapest kind,' disclosed a report on the hand-loom weavers of Lancashire in the 1830s. 'They are clothed in rags; they have scarcely anything like furniture in their houses; their beds and bedding are of the most wretched description and many of them sleep upon straw.'

105

A poor family's home in 1875
— one attic room.

Equally disturbing scenes were recorded in Glasgow in the 1840s.

We saw half-dressed wretches, crowding together to be warm; and in one bed, although in the middle of the day, several women were imprisoned under a blanket, because so many others who had on their backs all the articles of dress that belonged to the party were then out of doors in the streets. This picture is so shocking that, without proof, one would be disposed to doubt the possibility of the facts; and yet there is perhaps no old town in Europe that does not furnish parallel examples.

At the same time Friedrich Engels described more vividly part of Manchester, where some 4000 people lived in about 200 cottages:

A horde of ragged women and children swarm about the streets and they are just as dirty as the pigs which wallow happily on the heaps of garbage and in the pools of filth. The inhabitants live in dilapidated cottages, the windows of which are broken and patched with oilskin. The doors and the door posts are broken and rotten. On the average twenty people live in each of these little houses, which consist of two rooms, an attic and a cellar. Not only the cellars but even the ground floors of all the houses in this quarter were damp.

It is possible that these descriptions are exaggerations. By the 1830s, for instance, the hand-loom weavers were a special case. With power looms, their wages had fallen sharply. Some also treat Engels as an unreliable witness because he was a friend and sympathizer of Karl Marx, the founder of Communism. However, other accounts throughout the nineteenth century confirmed that many Britons were desperately poor.

At the time people accepted this as normal. In church they were sometimes reminded of Christ's saying: 'Ye have the poor with you always.' However, although they frequently thought they knew how many lived in poverty and why, in fact they had little detailed information to guide them until the later nineteenth century and so they could only guess.

The situation began to change in the 1880s, when a leading socialist, H. M. Hyndman, claimed that a quarter of the population was poor. Charles Booth, a wealthy Liverpool merchant and shipowner, was one of the many who maintained that this was both untrue and dangerous. To prove that Hyndman was wrong, he organized a survey of every house in the east end and centre of London.

By 1889 Booth was indeed able to put Hyndman right, but not in the way he expected. Hyndman had actually underestimated the amount of poverty. Booth found that just under one Londoner in three was poor. In addition a quarter of those (or nearly ten per cent altogether) lived in extreme poverty. (Of course some districts contained few poor people, but two-thirds of the population were poor in parts of Southwark.) In the next twenty years investigations in York and elsewhere confirmed Booth's conclusion. Without doubt at least a quarter of the population lived in poverty.

But what did poverty mean?

For Booth 'my poor may be described as living under a struggle to obtain the necessaries of life and make both ends meet; while the very poor live in a state of chronic want'. The other investigators' definitions were equally vague. And yet their figures for those living in poverty were amazingly precise. Booth himself concluded that 30·7 per cent of all Londoners were poor. In 1899 Seebohm Rowntree discovered that 27·84 per cent of the citizens of York were poor.

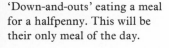
'Down-and-outs' eating a meal for a halfpenny. This will be their only meal of the day.

Before their surveys the investigators calculated to the nearest penny what people needed to feed and clothe themselves. Working on the

assumption that an adult ought to spend 3/– a week on food and 6d on clothes, while a child needed 2/3 and 5d respectively, Rowntree concluded that 'for a family of father, mother and three children, the minimum weekly expenditure upon which physical efficiency can be maintained in York is 21/8'. Larger families of course needed more and smaller ones less.

However, those who were living just above this poverty line were probably no better off than those just below. A survey of Reading in 1912 shows just how difficult it is to estimate how many really were poor. This inquiry concluded that 20 per cent did not earn enough to feed, clothe and house themselves adequately even if they spent every penny wisely. The families of another 20 per cent received less than 5/– a week over the bare minimum considered necessary to maintain 'mere physical efficiency'. Most of these spent some money on drink, bus or tram fares, birthday and Christmas presents, food which they liked and clothes that were not always plain and hard-wearing. Therefore many more than those which Booth, Rowntree and others placed below the poverty line were badly housed and underfed.

Why were people poor?

Many Victorians assumed that it was because they were lazy, drank or did not save. As one judge argued: 'poverty could be prevented if you could prevent weakness and sickness and laziness and stupidity and improvidence, not otherwise.' 'That drink leads to beggary as well as to crime is a commonplace,' added another writer. But the researches of Booth, Rowntree and others showed convincingly that the great majority were not poor because of their own failings. Although few families were poor for just one reason, Booth and Rowntree estimated the prime causes of their poverty like this:

Booth: 66%   low wages and lack of regular work for father
           21%   too many children or one parent seriously ill
           13%   drink and thriftlessness

Rowntree: 52%   father received too low wages
           22%   family too large (more than four children)
           21%   death or illness of the father
            5%   father out of regular work

According to Rowntree drink and gambling, ignorant or careless housekeeping all aggravated poverty, but they rarely caused it. Although many families spent over a sixth of their income on beer, for instance, they would still have been poor however they had spent it. Jack London was sure that people usually drank because they were poor.

When a family is housed in one small room, home life is impossible. A brief examination of such a dwelling will serve to bring to light one important cause of drunkenness. Here the family arises in the morning, dresses and makes its toilet, father, mother, sons and daughters, and in the same room, shoulder to shoulder (for the room is small) the wife and mother cooks the breakfast. The father goes to work, the older children go to school or into the street, and the mother remains with her crawling toddling youngsters to do her housework – still in the same room.

Here she washes the clothes, filling the pent space with soapsuds and the smell of dirty clothes, and overhead she hangs the wet linen to dry. Here, in the evening, amid the manifold smells of the day, the family goes to bed. That is to say, as many as possible pile into the one bed and the surplus turns in on the floor. This is the round of their existence, month after month, year after year.

Now such a room as I have described is not home but horror; and the men and women who flee away from it to the public house are to be pitied, not blamed. There are 300,000 people in London divided into families that live in single rooms. Wretchedness squirms for alleviation, and in the public house its pain is eased and forgetfulness is obtained.

Many Victorians knew better than Rowntree and Jack London – Demon Drink was the main cause of the misery of the working classes and prevented them from reporting regularly for work.

INTEMPERANCE,
IS IRELAND'S BANE! ENGLAND'S CURSE! and SCOTLAND'S WOE

Drink even exalts them, and makes them feel that they are finer and better, though at the same time it drags them down and makes them more beastly than ever.

When one hears that between a third and a quarter of the population lived in poverty, it is easy to assume that two-thirds were unaffected. But this was not so, partly because many labourers did not earn enough to keep a family of several children. In Reading one person in five was judged to be poor in 1912, but this included one child in three. Furthermore over half the children in the town had lived in poverty for some time at least before they left school at fourteen.

Rowntree explained how this affected many people's lives:

The life of a labourer is marked by five alternating periods of want and comparative plenty. During early childhood, unless his father is a skilled worker, he probably will be in poverty; this will last until he, or some of his brothers or sisters, begin to earn money and thus augment their father's wage sufficiently to raise the family above the poverty line. Then follows the period during which he is earning money and living under his parents' roof; for some portion of this period he will be earning more money than is required for lodging, food and clothes. This period of comparative prosperity may continue after marriage until he has two or three children, when poverty will overtake him.

The curse of many poor families was too many children. These children are waiting to be hired for work.

110

This period of poverty will last perhaps for ten years — until the first child is fourteen years old and begins to earn wages; but if there are more than three children it may last longer. While the children are earning, and before they leave home to marry, the man enjoys another period of prosperity — possibly, however, only to sink back again into poverty when his children have left him, and he himself is too old to work, for his income has never permitted his saving enough for him and his wife to live upon for more than a very short time.

A labourer is thus in poverty and therefore underfed:

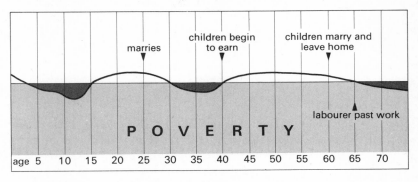

(1) In childhood, when his constitution is being built up;
(2) In early middle life, when he should be in his prime;
(3) In old age.

It should be noted that the women are in poverty during the greater part of the period that they are bearing children.

The Salvation Army providing farthing breakfasts for pauper children, 1880.

Of course the lives of all labourers did not follow this pattern. A few never married, some had no children and others did not earn enough in their forties and fifties to rise above the poverty line again. Yet even so, Rowntree's cycle was true for many and so was his conclusion: 'The proportion of the community who at one period or another of their lives suffer from poverty to the point of physical privation is therefore much greater than would appear from a consideration of the number who can be shown to be below the poverty line at any given moment.'

Rowntree also noticed that women usually suffered most: 'We see that many a labourer, who has a wife and three or four children, is healthy and a good worker, although he only earns a pound a week. What we do not see is that in order to give him enough food, mother and children habitually go short, for the mother knows that all depends upon the wages of her husband.' An accident or illness might kill or disable the chief wage-earner at any moment and plunge his family into poverty without warning. The threat of poverty therefore hung over the heads of almost all members of the working classes, especially if they survived into old age.

111

None was paid a pension and few managed to save much money. Therefore the longer they lived after they became too old to work, the poorer they became. Booth found very few who were not reduced to poverty by their mid seventies and concluded that 'old age stands out plainly as the prevailing cause of pauperism after sixty-five'.

To state that 30·7 per cent or 27·84 per cent lived below the poverty line at the end of the nineteenth century is misleading. It is more accurate to say rather vaguely that about half the population was either afflicted or threatened by poverty for most of their lives and perhaps a tenth were destitute. But we must not make the mistake of assuming that poor people were always miserable. As Booth observed: 'Although their lives are an unending struggle and lack comfort, I do not know that they lack happiness.' Usually people make the most of the circumstances in which they are brought up.

The Poor Law

Nor did the poor suffer entirely unaided. Until the 1830s each parish had been responsible for looking after its old and sick, widows, orphans and unemployed. Some had been sheltered in poor houses or workhouses, but many parishes had saved money by helping as few as possible. Whenever they could they had set them to work, found jobs for their orphans in other parishes and sometimes sent away unmarried mothers-to-be in the late stages of pregnancy.

All parishes were not so mean, especially towards the end of the eighteenth century when prices and the population had risen and with them the numbers seeking relief. Increasingly they had paid allowances to poor families with three children or more, widows and, mostly in the south, some labourers on inadequate wages. Some fathers were made to contribute to the upkeep of their illegitimate children. By

The casual inmates in this London workhouse, 1860, slept in very primitive conditions.

the early nineteenth century this more generous treatment of the poor meant that in some parishes a fifth of the population was given some relief, though rarely more than a few shillings a week.

Wealthy householders grumbled so much about having to pay higher rates that, although it was untrue, many people eventually believed that the poor labourers had larger families and worked less hard as a result. And so a new Poor Law was introduced from 1834. It grouped the parishes together in unions, which were ordered to build and run their own workhouses and save money by helping only those who went to live in them. But in practice most unions went on paying outdoor relief (of about 2/– a week) to many old and sick people and to some able-bodied too, especially in Lancashire and Yorkshire.

Life inside most workhouses was rarely as harsh as *The Times* and novels like *Oliver Twist* made out. Usually the paupers were fed adequately, but they were treated little better than criminals and made to feel so inferior that everyone avoided the workhouse until they were really destitute. Dread of the workhouse persisted in the later nineteenth century after their conditions improved. By then fewer than one per cent of the population was to be found inside a workhouse at any one moment (while over twice as many received relief), but about a quarter of the adults in Britain died in a workhouse or hospital run by the Poor Law.

This picture, from the 1890s, brings out well the prison-like atmosphere of the large workhouse, with the men separated from the women even for meals. A countless number of destitute people inhabited every Victorian city.

Chapter 5
Communications and trade

Coaches and canals

On Friday, 25 August 1826, at ten o'clock in the morning the popular journalist William Cobbett left Hurstbourne Tarrant in Hampshire on horseback to visit a village some fifteen miles away. After reaching his destination safely, he described some incidents on the way:

I never knew the flies so troublesome in England as I found them in this ride. I was obliged to carry a great bough, and to keep it in constant motion, in order to make the horse peaceable enough to enable me to keep on his back. It is a country of fields, lanes, and high hedges; so that no wind could come to relieve my horse; and, in spite of all I could do, a great part of him was covered with foam from the sweat. In the midst of this, I got, at one time, a little out of my road in or near a place called Tangley. I rode up to the garden-gate of a cottage, and asked the woman, who had two children, and who seemed to be about thirty years old, which was the way to Ludgarshall, which I knew could not be more than about four miles off. She did not know! A very neat, smart, and pretty woman; but she did not know the way.

'Well, my dear good woman,' said I, 'but you have been at Ludgarshall?' – 'No.' – 'Nor at Andover?' (six miles another way) – 'No.' – 'Nor at Marlborough?' (nine miles another way) – 'No.' – 'Pray, were you born in this house?' – 'Yes.' – 'And how far have you ever been from this house?' – 'Oh! I have been up in the parish and over to Chute.' That is to say, the utmost extent of her voyages had been about two and a half miles! Let no one laugh at her, and, above all others, let not me, who am convinced that the *facilities* which now exist of *moving human bodies from place to place* are amongst the *curses* of the country, the destroyers of morals and of happiness. It is a great error to suppose that people are rendered stupid by remaining always in the same place.

The fact that Cobbett was so surprised to find a woman who had travelled so little, means that she was exceptional. Most people by then visited at least their local market towns fairly often. Many changed jobs and moved house quite frequently, but they normally stayed within the region in which they had been born.

The 'facilities' for moving human bodies which Cobbett disliked so much were not railways but stage coaches, which had improved

114

The mail coach was the fastest kind of stage coach. It had an armed guard, carried no passengers outside and ran strictly to time. John Palmer started this service in 1784.

remarkably since the later eighteenth century. The coaches had been made more comfortable with, for example, better springs. Along the routes between the main towns, coaching inns had been established at intervals of less than twenty miles. There, with efficient organization, the stage coaches could change to fresh horses in little more than five minutes. They took advantage of the harder and smoother road surfaces, which engineers like Telford and Macadam provided for many turnpike trusts, to maintain average speeds of ten m.p.h., even on long journeys. By the 1830s someone in London could reach Yorkshire in one day and Edinburgh in two. Stage coaches had become the fastest method of travelling in the world.

By then there were about 3000 coaches in Britain. They rarely carried more than a dozen passengers and were also very expensive. Few men, for instance, earned as much as a pound a week, yet that was the price of a ticket from Birmingham to London. In addition travellers had to buy an expensive meal at an inn on the route and give about another five shillings in tips. Most people, therefore, continued to walk wherever they went.

The great expansion of industry and mining coupled with the growth of towns led to an ever-increasing demand for better means of moving goods as well as people. Not many canals had been opened before the 1790s, but then there was a rush to build them when it was shown that they could make handsome profits.

New canals appeared mainly in central and southern England, where they were run by private companies. By the 1830s over 4000 miles of canals and navigable rivers were in use. They had replaced pack-horses, for from the tow path one horse could pull by water a load of at least forty tons. And yet the boats travelled at only two m.p.h. for, in the midlands in particular, the canals were narrow and shallow.

Not all canals were successful. In the mainly agricultural regions there was not enough traffic to make them pay. In hilly districts many locks and aqueducts had to be built. This made canals awkward to use and expensive to run. And so they really flourished only in flat industrial areas. The most successful ones were in Lancashire and the west midlands where Manchester, Birmingham and other inland towns were linked with the main rivers and the sea. Here transport costs were often cut by half and on the most popular routes they fell by even more. Many industries came to rely on the canals for their supply of raw materials and for opening up more markets for their finished products.

Canals completely changed communications in the centre of England. The needs of canals even created a new town, Stourport, and many others expanded as cheap transport encouraged industrial activity.

Rivers

navigable rivers about 1750

Manchester

Birmingham

London

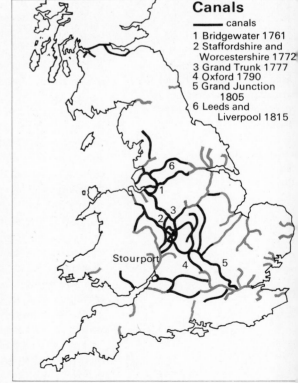

Canals

canals
1 Bridgewater 1761
2 Staffordshire and Worcestershire 1772
3 Grand Trunk 1777
4 Oxford 1790
5 Grand Junction 1805
6 Leeds and Liverpool 1815

Stourport

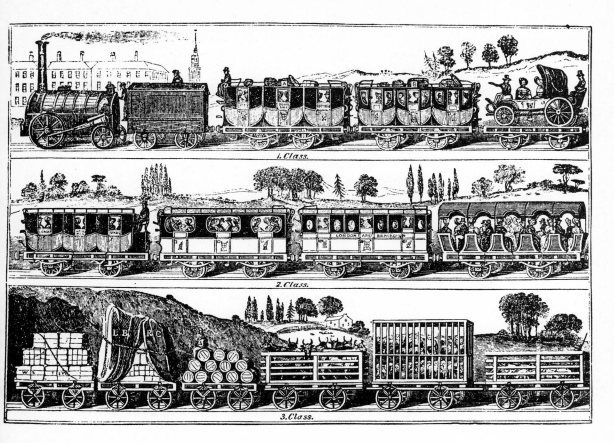

1. Class.

2. Class.

3. Class.

The earliest trains on the London to Birmingham railway. At first upper-class families travelled separately in their own carriages to avoid mixing with strangers, but the attraction of enclosed coaches soon dispelled their scruples. From the start the railway carried goods and animals as well as people.

Railways

As the canal and stage-coach systems were reaching their peaks, they were challenged almost immediately by a faster and more convenient form of transport – the railway. And so when the railways swept the country in the 1840s, coaching in particular declined very quickly.

Railed ways had existed in some seventeenth-century coal-mines near Newcastle, where horses pulled trucks for short distances along wooden lines. In the eighteenth century they were improved with cast-iron rails and devices like pulley wheels to draw the wagons up slopes. However, even Watt refused to believe that a moving steam engine would ever replace the horse. It was far too heavy and cumbersome, would break up the track and create a host of other problems.

Nevertheless these were solved gradually from about 1800. A rim or flange on the inside of the wheels kept the trucks on the lines. The rails, which rested on sleepers, were eventually made of smooth wrought iron and placed 4 feet 8½ inches apart. When better boilers led to lighter machinery, mobile steam engines no longer smashed the

117

track. By 1830 horses were being supplanted. The engineers continued to produce more powerful and reliable locomotives. Their inventions included bogie wheels, which helped them pass round curves more freely. But they were reluctant to use brakes. The horse, some argued, had no brakes so why should a locomotive! The opposition of people like landowners, who thought that their interests would suffer from the railways, also had to be overcome.

The planning and building of railways was left to private companies which were formed to make a profit. Many were very small. Their original intention was to run them like canals and roads, with everyone paying a toll and using their own wagons. But this proved to be impracticable and so the company which laid the track also ran the services. The building of railways entailed huge engineering works. Roads and rivers had to be crossed and routes cut through hillsides or laid on treacherous clay or marshy ground. Many stations, bridges, tunnels, viaducts and embankments were also created.

The line from Manchester to Liverpool was opened in 1830 and the one between London and Birmingham in 1838, but most industrial towns were not linked by rail until the 1840s. By 1850, 6,000 miles

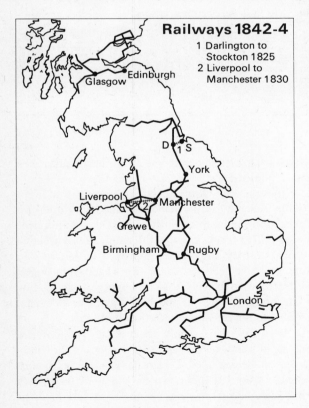

Railways 1842-4

1 Darlington to Stockton 1825
2 Liverpool to Manchester 1830

Glasgow
Edinburgh
D 1 S
York
Liverpool
Manchester
Crewe
Birmingham
Rugby
London

Railways 1852

A view of the Liverpool to Manchester railway across Chat Moss. The embankment, built on marshland, was designed by George Stephenson.

Handbill for a day trip from north Staffordshire to the sea. The train shown is about thirty years out of date.

of track were open to traffic and the railways were moving perishable as well as heavy and bulky goods all over the country at speeds of twenty m.p.h. or more. However, some lines were never profitable. Competition between rival companies or unjustifiable optimism led to their being laid unnecessarily.

The railways went on developing after 1850. Steel rails replaced iron from the 1870s. Four tracks were laid on busy main lines. Many more branch lines were opened. The block signalling system, which divided the line into sections and only allowed one train in each section at a time, made travelling safer and faster. So did improvements in the design of locomotives. Britain's railways were at their peak after 1900, when their combined length was 20,000 miles. All the important trunk routes were controlled by fourteen large private companies. In the 1890s Parliament restrained them from putting up their goods prices, which helped maintain the big increase in the amount of freight carried by the railways, from ninety million tons in 1860 to 500 million fifty years later. Some heavy goods were still sent by sea round the coast, but no other land transport could compete with the railways.

Although built originally to carry heavy goods like coal, from the start railways were popular with travellers, whom they carried at about half the cost and more than twice the speed of the stage coaches. At first the companies devoted themselves to looking after the wealthy passengers who could travel in their own carriages tied to flat wagons. Soon the railway compartments became more comfortable and all first-class ticket holders travelled together. From the 1870s some lines ran even more luxurious Pullman carriages. From the 1880s in winter the compartments were heated with steam from the engine. For the wealthier passengers dining cars were also added to many long-distance trains.

'It is a great mistake to believe in the speed and excellent management of the British railways,' wrote a Frenchman in the 1850s. 'The

Building St Pancras, the
London station, which was
opened in 1868.

The Forth bridge, completed
in 1890, was one of the first
to be made of steel. This
impressive achievement of
J. Fowler and B. Baker still
carries the railway north from
Edinburgh.

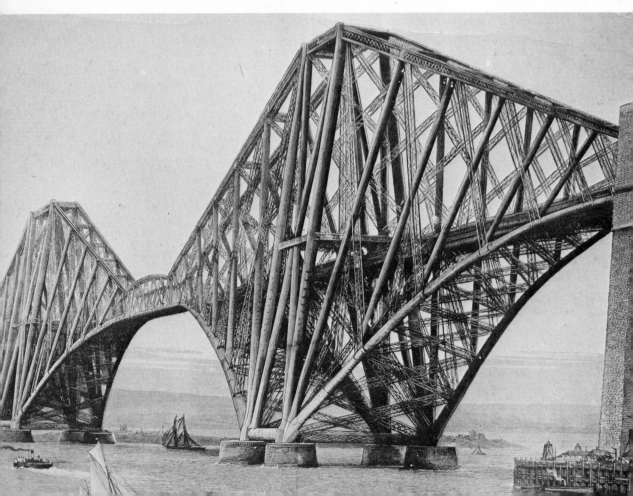

Railway journeys made

1850	70 m
1870	300 m
1890	800 m
1910	1300 m

cheapest seats are mostly uncovered, and in a country where it rains perpetually can one imagine anything more barbarous? The second-class compartments have wooden benches and back rests, no upholstering of any kind. The windows are unglazed and only provided with wooden shutters. These carriages are so dirty that it is difficult to believe they are ever swept.'

Until the 1870s many trains, especially the faster ones, ran without third-class carriages and sometimes without second-class as well. From then, however, the poorer travellers did not have to wait for the slower trains which many companies had run specially for them since Parliament in 1844 had made them cater for all classes. In the later nineteenth century their carriages were fitted with glass and their seats given a little padding. At the same time the railways also ran specially cheap trains in the early mornings and evenings for workmen to get to and from their work and special excursion trains to the seaside and the large towns. By the 1890s long-distance trains were provided with corridors and the average speed of some expresses had risen to around fifty m.p.h. From London people could reach Edinburgh, for example, in a little over eight hours. With all these improvements the number of individual journeys made on the railways rose every year.

From the middle of the nineteenth century the railways influenced profoundly how towns grew. They made it easier for travellers to reach them and for farmers to feed the town-dwellers. Railways also helped supply the factories with their raw materials and carry their finished goods to be sold in other towns. And so some towns, which were not linked to the railway, like Stamford, were barely affected by industrial development. Nearby Peterborough expanded instead.

Other new forms of transport had an even greater effect on travelling inside towns.

Special workmen's train about to leave Liverpool St Station, London, in 1884.

The horse bus was established first in London and then spread to other towns from the 1840s. However, it had serious limitations because it rarely went faster than walking pace, could not climb hilly streets and inside the passengers were packed in tightly. In addition only clerks and other middle-class people could afford regularly its fares of 3d or more. This is an omnibus of 1865.

Horse-drawn trams appeared first in the 1860s and were operating in most large towns within ten years. Running on rails reduced the friction, and so they went faster (about 6 m.p.h.) and carried more passengers at cheaper rates. Thus many skilled workmen could afford to travel on them regularly and so live further from their work. But to lay the rails was costly, and they were therefore limited to main roads.

Towards the end of the nineteenth century some companies tried harnessing the steam engine to the tram. But the steam tram never caught on, partly because it remained obstinately slow in picking up speed and because it was dirty.

Right Fleet Street, London. As more people lived away from their work in the late-nineteenth century, the volume of urban traffic increased very rapidly. City streets had never been designed to cope with so many buses, cabs and carts.

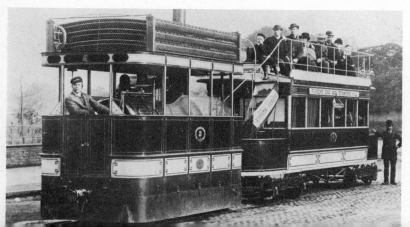

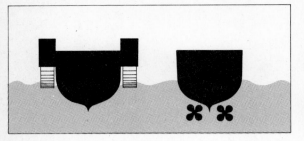

Steamships

The steam engine took much longer to conquer the water than the land. In the early nineteenth century the first steamships were used to ferry people across the mouths of rivers like the Clyde and Thames. By the 1820s steam ferries were sailing regularly between Calais and Dover. Longer voyages were impossible at this stage because they consumed so much coal and the ships' paddles needed calm water. Also British canals were too narrow and their banks too weak to risk letting barges travel any faster.

At sea steam provided a source of power independent of the unpredictable weather, but steamships did not begin to cross the Atlantic until the 1840s. The 2000-ton liners which were run by companies like Cunard took a fortnight over the journey and were nearly four times as large as most sailing ships. Even so, for some time they carried only passengers and letters because the coal took up so much space that there was little room left for cargo. Sailing ships remained much cheaper and also became more streamlined so that until about 1870 clippers were the fastest ships afloat (see picture, p. 135). However, sailing ships could not use the Suez canal after it opened in 1869 and so steamships finally gained an overwhelming advantage on the eastern route. By then more efficient screw propellers had replaced the clumsy paddles and a number of other technical advances completed the triumph of steamships. They were made of iron from the middle of the century and of steel from the 1880s. Compound engines, which used the steam more than once, cut their coal consumption by more than half. Ships designed specially for different funtions appeared: tugboats, grain, cattle and passenger ships among them. They became bigger and stronger and, whereas a vessel of 1000 tons was thought to be large in 1850, one of 10,000 tons was not unusual by 1910. Indeed, several transatlantic liners of over 20,000 tons could reach New York in well under a week by then. Larger, faster ships were able to charge much less for the passengers and cargoes which they carried.

The figures opposite of the tonnage of ships built in Britain record the change-over from sail to steam. Sailing ships had not disappeared by 1910, but steamers carried most goods and nearly all passengers.

Screw propellers were much more efficient than paddles in rough water. Screws, however, needed a more powerful engine to drive them.

Right: Brunel's gigantic steamship *Great Eastern*, on her maiden voyage in 1860. Driven by paddles, screws and sails, she was over 220 yards long. In spite of the space and comfort inside, *Great Eastern* never attracted enough passengers to make a profit and so within a few years she was relegated to laying telegraph cables across the Atlantic.

Tonnage of ships built in Britain

	sailing ships	steam ships
1790	1·3 m	—
1860	4·2 m	0·5 m
1910	1·0 m	10·5 m

Postal services

'Dear Robinson,' wrote the author, William Hazlitt, from Wiltshire to London in 1809, 'I did not receive your friendly letter till this morning. There is sometimes a delay of one or two days in the post, and I shall therefore send you this in a parcel by the coach, so that you will have it tomorrow.'

Such complaints show that by then the mail coaches had given the country a very efficient postal service. They were the fastest means of delivering messages. The receiver, not the sender, paid for letters carried by mail coach. They were charged according to distance and were very expensive. For less than fifteen miles the cost was 4d, and for fifty miles it was 8d. Most people, therefore, did not send letters. Talking was their only means of communicating with others.

The Post Office eventually realized that its postmen wasted much time asking for money before they delivered each letter. From 1840, therefore, the sender paid for the postage by sticking an adhesive stamp on to his letter. Rowland Hill, who was responsible for this change, also reduced to one penny the charge for sending a letter to any part of Britain. It cost more only if it weighed over half an ounce. The railways then carried the mail much faster than the stage coaches and special carriages were devised for sorting letters on board the trains. Steamships also took them to Europe and North America and later to the rest of the world.

People posted their letters at a post office until the 1850s when letterboxes were first erected in the streets. The Post Office then extended its services by carrying post cards for a halfpenny from the 1870s and parcels from the 1880s. At the same time postal orders made it safer for men to send part of their wages, for example, back to wives or mothers at home and the registered mail looked after other

Penny black, carrying a portrait of Queen Victoria (1837–1901). Until 1854 stamps were not perforated but had to be cut out with scissors.

London's first letter box, erected on the corner of Fleet Street in 1855.

Sorting letters inside the
London Post Office, 1875.

valuables. These and other developments led to a remarkable increase
in the number of items delivered by inland post.

By the later nineteenth century mail was often delivered on the
day it was posted, since some towns had up to six deliveries a day.
Complaints like this letter in *The Times* again reveal how efficient
the postal service had become. 'I posted a letter in the Gray's Inn
Post Office on Saturday, at half-past 1 o'clock, addressed to a person
living close to Westminster Abbey, which was not delivered till next
9 o'clock the same evening; and I posted another letter in the same
Post Office, addressed to the same place, on Monday morning before
9 o'clock, which was not delivered till past 4 o'clock in the afternoon.
Now, Sir, why is this?'

Post offices were opened in most villages as well as in every town
before the end of the nineteenth century. They made it much easier
for business men to place and receive orders all over the country.
They also influenced people's lives in many other ways, as Flora Thompson discovered when she worked in a small country post office in
the 1890s. 'She knew the girl in love with her sister's husband whose
hands trembled while she tore open her letters from him; and the
old mother who had not heard for three years from her son in Australia,
but still came every day to the Post Office, hoping; and she knew
families which were being dunned for the payment of bills, and what
shop in London supplied Mrs Fashionable with clothes, and who posted
the box containing a dead mouse to Mrs Meddlesome.'

Letters, parcels and postal orders were not the limit of the Post
Office's work. The telegraph, which was invented in the 1830s, used
electricity for the first time to send messages along wires. An American,
Samuel Morse, devised a code to translate into letters the way in which
an electric current, controlled from one end of a wire, could move

Items delivered
by inland post

1840	90 m?
1880	2,000 m?
1922	5,600 m
(1970	13,600 m)

a needle at the other end to the right or left. Later the messages were received in long or short buzzes on a special buzzer.

The telegraph wires were built first beside the railway lines to warn the stations when a train was coming or when one had been delayed. Then, from the 1850s, private companies made it possible for business men and others to send telegrams. Cables were also laid across the bed of the Channel and the Atlantic, but they were of such poor quality at first that most soon became useless. By 1870, however, telegrams were being sent to India as well as to America. The Post Office had taken over the telegraph in the previous year and has been responsible for telegrams ever since.

The lower classes used telegrams almost exclusively to announce deaths and bad news to the rest of their family, but not so the wealthy. As Flora Thompson wrote of the 1890s: 'Cycling was considered such a dangerous pastime that the members of the earliest cycling clubs telegraphed home news of their safe arrival at the farthest point in their journey. Or perhaps they sent the telegrams to prove how far they really had travelled, for a cyclist's word as to his day's mileage then ranked with an angler's account of his catch.' At the start of the twentieth century eighty-five million telegrams were sent in Britain every year, but the service has declined steadily ever since. A superior method of sending messages, which also used electricity, gradually superseded it.

Reading morse code signals from a buzzer, 1888.

The first vessel to lay cable on the bed of the sea, 1843. The early cables often broke or perished, so that many stretches were laid several times.

'We publish in another column,' announced *The Times* in 1879, 'the extraordinary new uses of which the telephone has been found capable. By its means the human voice can be conveyed in full force from any one point to any other five miles off, and with some loss of power to a very much more considerable distance still.' An invention which lets you talk to someone even five miles away is clearly superior to one that sends short messages in code. *Right* A table telephone, 1890.

American business men were quick to use the telephone service, which its inventor, Alexander Bell, opened in New York in 1878.

Newspapers

The way in which news was circulated changed after 1800. Groups of working men used to club together in the early nineteenth century to buy weekly periodicals and pamphlets which were strongly critical of the government. Written by William Cobbett and others, some sold 10,000 copies or more. The daily newspapers were also expensive and were bought almost entirely by the middle classes. Even when their price fell to about a penny in the middle of the century, most people still had neither the time nor the inclination to read them. The articles were generally long, with only a small heading, and you had to read them like a book.

Before the 1850s no daily paper, apart from *The Times*, sold more than a few thousand copies a day. Then the *Daily Telegraph* made good use of the invention after which it is named and raised its circulation to over a quarter of a million. At the same time many more daily papers were started, especially outside London. They included the *Manchester Guardian* and the *Yorkshire Post*. Even more people read the Sunday papers. Detailed reports of violent crime, sex and sport in, for example, *Lloyd's Weekly* and the *News of the World* appealed to them on their day of rest.

From the 1890s the number of newspaper readers rose at an even faster rate for several reasons. In the early nineteenth century the presses were operated by hand and printed less than 250 copies an hour, but by the end of the century, machine-driven presses could turn out 10,000 copies an hour. With the telegraph and telephone the papers received their information almost at once. Then the railways distributed them so quickly that they still described recent events. Also, more people could read (see page 169).

Daily sales of
weekday papers

1850s	100,000
1890s	1,000,000
(1970s	13,000,000)

A newspaper press printing *The Graphic*, in 1884, one of the earliest illustrated magazines. Compare this with the eighteenth-century hand press on page 41.

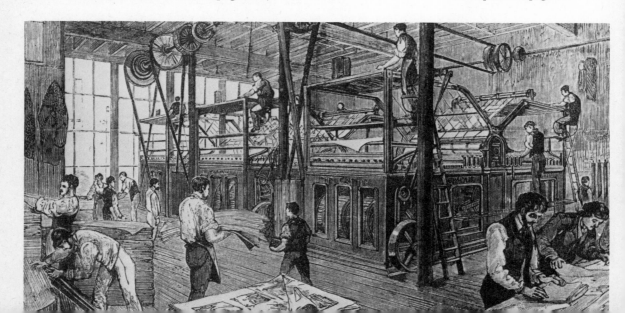

Copy of verses on the Appalling

Murder of Mary Da[vis]

By her husband in Moor-street, Birmi[ngham]
Tuesday October 12, 1847.

Come all you tender Christians
List' to my mournful song,
I'll tell of a dreadful deed,
And that before its long,
Committed was in Birmingham,
As you shall quickly hear.
By Mathew Davis his wife,
Without any dread or fear.

She had bound him down to keep the peace,
Which he had broke before,
And he upon this fatal day,
Was to be bound once more,
He said will you go against me,
To which she said, I will!
Then with an oath he cut her throat,
Her precious blood to spill.

Now is he bound in prison strong,
And to Warwick sent with speed,
And to await his trial,
All for this dreadful deed.

There is three poor chil[dren]
Deprived of a mothe[r]
All by a thoughtless fat[her]
O, drinking, friends [...]
Do not indulge in passi[ng]
It never leads to goo[d]
It oftentimes unmans th[e]
And ends in deeds o[f]

What tongue can tell what pencil paint,
The hardships that she bore,
But now alas! the die is cast,
And her troubles are all o'er,
And may this deed a warning be,
With all men and their wives,
May quarrels cease with lasting peace,
The remainder of their lives.

Now in this dark and gloomey cell,
I bitterly do weep,
The midnight bell and thought of death,
Deprive me of my sleep.

THE BOY'S OWN PAPER

No. 1.—Vol. I.   SATURDAY, JANUARY 18, 1879.   Price One Penny. [ALL RIGHTS RESERVED.]

MY FIRST FOOTBALL MATCH.
BY AN OLD BOY.

IT was a proud moment in my existence when Wright, captain of our football club, came up to me in school one Friday and said, "Adams, your name is down to play in the match against Craven to-morrow."

I could have knighted him on the spot. To be one of the picked "fifteen," whose glory it was to fight the battles of their school in the Great Close, had been the leading ambition of my life—I suppose I ought to be ashamed to confess it—ever since, as a little chap of ten, I entered Parkhurst six years ago. Not a winter Saturday but had seen me either looking on at some big match, or oftener still scrimmaging about with a score or so of other juniors in a scratch game. But for a long time, do what I would, I always

"Down!"

seemed as far as ever from the coveted goal, and was half despairing of ever rising to win my "first fifteen cap." Lately, however, I had noticed Wright and a few others of our best players more than once looking about in the Little Close where we juniors used to play, evidently taking observations with an eye to business. Under the awful gaze of these heroes, need I say I exerted myself as I had never done before? What cared I for hacks or bruises, so only that I could distinguish myself in their eyes? And never was music sweeter

Nineteenth-century presses produced not only closely printed newspapers for the leisured middle classes and magazines for their children, but also lurid broadsheets for the masses.

The Times.

No. 21,898.   LONDON, TUESDAY, NOVEMBER 14, 1854.   PRICE 5d.

Foreign trade

Britain's improved communications helped the increase in foreign trade which accompanied the growth of industry. Without this trade, cotton and other leading industries would hardly have existed, for they imported most of their raw materials and also sold many of their finished products abroad.

British foreign trade began to expand quickly in the 1780s. In twenty years its total value doubled and it continued to grow very rapidly throughout the nineteenth century. And so, whereas it had been worth £22 million in 1780, the total had risen to £1200 million by 1900.

The pattern was already fixed by the end of the eighteenth century. Britain exchanged her manufactured goods for some food and raw materials, but with the expansion of industry the types of goods changed. In 1830 textiles, especially cotton, accounted for two-thirds of all exports, but their share had fallen to just over a third by 1910. By then, substantial quantities of machinery, metal goods and coal were also being sent abroad. In the first half of the nineteenth century the amount of imported raw cotton expanded very rapidly (see page 69) and so, later, did the quantities of raw wool and timber. At the same time, grain, meat and butter replaced sugar and tea as the main imported foods.

Throughout the nineteenth century the British imported more than they exported, without running into debt. This was because 'invisible' exports more than covered the deficit. They were of two kinds. Those countries which borrowed large sums of money in England to pay for the building of railways, for instance, paid interest to their creditors in return. The fact that the British owned half the tonnage of the world's merchant ships and earned money abroad by carrying goods from one foreign country to another is equally important. By 1910 they received £300 million a year from 'invisible' exports – half the value of their visible exports.

During the eighteenth century the government had tried to protect British industry by regulating foreign imports with customs duties and other restrictions. Indian textiles, for example, were both better and cheaper than Lancashire cottons, and, without government help, the industry would probably have collapsed. By the first half of the nineteenth century, however, many British industries were so superior to their rivals that few still needed protection. Indeed some government regulations actually hindered them. Many manufacturers, realizing that customs duties made their raw materials more expensive, tried hard to persuade the government to abolish them. Others supported them, hoping that if British tariffs were removed, other countries would follow suit and so import more from Britain. Manchester manufacturers led this campaign for free trade. In their struggle against the landowners who were very keen to retain the duties on foreign corn, the free

The opponents of the Corn Law repeal were convinced that the end of protection spelt ruin for farming. This picture, by Richard Doyle, made in 1849, is captioned: 'A banquet showynge ye farmers friend impressynge ye agricultural interest that it is ruined.' In it, Disraeli is attempting to convince affluent farmers of their fate.

traders made good use of the writings of Adam Smith. He had maintained, among other things, that only a few manufacturers gained from customs duties and that Britain should not make what other countries produced more cheaply.

After most duties and restrictions were eventually removed in the 1840s and 1850s, nearly all British manufactured goods sold well abroad. Britain appeared to be gaining handsomely from free trade, but in fact this was the reward for becoming the first major industrial country. Until the 1870s Britain produced more coal and pig-iron every year than the rest of the world put together and two-fifths of all exported manufactured goods were British.

From then on Britain faced increasing competition. In Germany, which was not united until 1871, the technicians were particularly well trained and the government actively encouraged heavy industry. The USA, which expanded very rapidly after the civil war ended in 1865, perfected many new automatic machines, like the ring spindle, through necessity: there was an acute shortage of skilled workmen. By 1910 Germany was producing twice as much steel and machinery as Britain and the Americans more than three times as much. In France, Italy and Japan industry was also advancing. The USA and Europe, therefore, no longer needed so many British goods, on which they charged higher customs duties. This drove the British merchants to trade more with the remoter parts of the world, especially with their colonies in Africa and Australasia and with Argentina and the Far East. By 1910 Britain's share in the world's trade of manufactured goods was still a quarter.

Most Britons still remained well satisfied with their achievements. One small island could not dominate the world for ever and it was only to be expected that other countries would catch up. Britain still ranked as one of the world's three leading industrial nations and was unchallenged in some fields, like shipbuilding.

Though trade expanded during the nineteenth century, the pace of growth was very uneven. Sometimes trade boomed and the factories easily sold all they could manufacture. At other times, trade suddenly slumped, goods were almost impossible to sell, factories closed and people were put out of work, not knowing why or for how long. Not all slumps were equally severe. Some were confined to a few industries or a few counties, while others affected the whole country. They also lasted different lengths of time, but never more than a few years. One of the worst depressions began in 1839 and was over by 1842. Most Victorians came to accept booms and slumps as inevitable, almost as certain as birth and death. The Prime Minister, Lord Liverpool, argued in 1819 that the government could do nothing to halt a slump: 'Whatever the cause of the present distress might be, it could not

A shipyard in 1865. Steamships gave British shipbuilding a new lease of life, and the proud pose of these prosperous Victorian shipbuilders reflects the fact that they have recently outstripped their American rivals.

A tea clipper, the fastest of sailing ships, approaches London from the East in 1858.

Tea clippers in the East India Company's London dock, 1892. It was one of four major docks built in the Thames estuary early in the nineteenth century.

be ascribed, in any degree or in any way, to the government or legislature of this country.' Most followed this opinion.

The weakness of the emerging capitalist system was the main cause of booms and slumps. Industrialists could sell what they made only to those who wanted to buy, but the demands of the public for their goods were neither even nor very predictable. When interest rates were low and money was plentiful, there was usually a considerable demand for British goods. Most manufacturers, eager to earn as big a profit as possible, were encouraged to produce all they could. But this did not continue steadily. At some stage more goods than were wanted were made and some merchants were unable to sell all they held. If the manufacturers then produced less, dismissed some of their workers, and waited for the demand for goods to pick up, a slump had begun. Mrs Gaskell described one in Manchester in her novel *Mary Barton*. 'Cottons could find no market and goods lay packed and piled in many a warehouse. At every mill some were working short hours, some were turning off hands, and for weeks Barton was out of work, living on credit.'

Fluctuating supply and demand was not the only cause of slumps. Harvests still affected the economy in the first half of the nineteenth century. When the harvest was bad the price of food rose sharply and people had less money to spend on other things. Wars also upset

the economy. They prohibited trade with enemy countries, and when they were over, many industries might be disorganized if huge orders for weapons and uniforms stopped suddenly. A crisis or change of government in a foreign country could also injure the interests of merchants and manufacturers. The cotton industry, for example, was seriously dislocated by the American Civil War (1861–5). A period of falling prices, like 1873–95, might discourage some manufacturers, for they often had to accept smaller profits. But these slumps must not make us forget that, over all, the British economy expanded in the nineteenth century on a scale which had never been seen before.

Business organization

Businesses remained very small in the first half of the nineteenth century. Nearly all consisted of either one man, one family or a few partners. They continued to expand slowly, mainly because if a company went bankrupt, all its partners were responsible for paying its debts. Even their private property could be sold to ensure that the debts were paid in full.

This situation began to change from the middle of the century when the laws affecting joint stock companies were altered. They were run by a board of directors who split their capital into a number of portions

This cartoon is titled 'Bubbles for 1825, or: fortunes made by steam'. Most joint-stock companies were prohibited by the Bubble Act of 1720, so that when it was repealed in 1825 a host of new companies sprang up, both sound and unsound. Feverish speculation in shares led inevitably to many bankruptcies before the end of the year.

Victorian coins. Silver coins (genuine silver, not nickel) were crown, four shillings, half crown, florin (introduced in 1849 as the first step towards decimal currency), shilling, sixpence and threepence. The sovereign was gold.

Farthing

Halfpenny

One penny

Groat
(Fourpence)

Florin

Sovereign

or shares, which could be sold to the public. Every year they then paid interest or dividends to their shareholders. A special charter or Act of Parliament was needed before a new joint stock company could be formed, but the demand for railway companies in particular increased so much from the 1830s that the laws governing them were altered several times. By the 1860s it became so easy to found one that many unsound and dishonest companies were formed. Only half those registered in the 1860s and 1870s survived longer than five years. The regulations controlling them were tightened up eventually. At the same time the protection of limited liability made them much more attractive. If the company went bankrupt, the liability of each shareholder was limited to the money which he had invested in it. He could not lose anything else.

Shares were bought and sold at the Stock Exchange by stockbrokers who acted as agents for the public. The Stock Exchange did so little business in the eighteenth century that it met in a London coffee house. By the beginning of the nineteenth century it had moved into a building of its own. Stockbroking work increased steadily from the 1840s with the railway boom and the growth of joint stock companies.

Very few manufacturing firms formed themselves into limited liability companies before the 1880s. Then more intense competition and the increasing use of larger and more expensive machines persuaded many to change their minds. Joint stock organization enabled the larger firms to raise extra money. Most smaller companies, however, remained private and kept their shares in the family. For them the chief attraction of limited liability was its legal protection. By 1910 two-thirds of all British firms had become limited liability companies.

Banking

The growth of industry and trade depended on safe and efficient banking services. Even before the industrial revolution bankers were necessary. Gold and silver coins were the only legal money in the eighteenth century and people who had some to spare were often glad to lend it to a banker. Not only was he likely to keep it more safely, but he also paid them interest. He could do this because he then lent it to someone else at a higher rate of interest. Usually the banker gave only a note or promise to pay a certain sum when asked. A reliable banker's 'promissory note' satisfied most people because it was easier to carry and store than gold or silver. In this way banks created a system of paper money.

The Bank of England dominated banking in England, for it was the only bank whose notes were valid in London. Although run privately, it had gained this privileged position in the eighteenth century in return for managing the National Debt and for arranging the large loans which the government needed to pay for its wars against France.

There were only twelve country banks in the English provinces in 1750, but they had risen to nearly 600 by the 1820s. They were usually run in partnerships of two or three men, most of whom were originally merchants dealing in commodities like wool and corn. Nearly all issued their own notes which were valid only in their own locality. They contacted each other through the London bankers. With their help many traders and farmers saved, bought materials and paid their debts.

Many of these banks, however, were unstable. Their resources were small, and since all issued more 'promissory notes' than they had cash on deposit, when many people tried to withdraw their money at the same time, they sometimes did not have enough in reserve. These banks therefore went bankrupt and all who had left their money with them suffered. This happened particularly in 1814–16 and 1825. In *John Halifax, Gentleman*, Mrs Craik described the predicament of one country banker in 1825:

He was at this moment perfectly solvent and could meet both the accounts of the gentry who banked with him, together with all his own notes now in the county – if only both classes of customers would give him time to pay them. 'But they will not,' he lamented. 'There will be a run upon the bank, and then all's over with me. It's a hard case – solvent as I am – ready and able to pay every farthing – if only I had a week's time. As it is, I must stop payment today. Hark! they are at the door again! Mr Halifax, for God's sake quiet them!'

In the eighteenth century the Scots had had larger and more secure joint stock banks, but in England they did not replace private family banks in large numbers until the 1830s. No bank formed after 1844 was allowed to produce its own notes and so, by the end of the century, the Bank of England issued virtually all notes in England and Wales. Because the amount of paper money was restricted by the quantity of gold which the Bank of England had in reserve, banking became less risky. In addition fewer bankruptcies occurred from the last third of the nineteenth century because the Bank of England at last concentrated fully on looking after the cash reserve of the joint stock banks, supporting deserving firms when a crisis threatened and providing the country with enough notes, backed by increased gold reserves, to transact its business.

Payment by cheque became increasingly common in the second half of the nineteenth century after the joint stock banks joined the London Clearing House, which made it easier for them to settle what they owed each other. Cheques were safer and more convenient than gold or notes. As the banks also provided their customers with other services, which included loans by overdraft, the deposits in British banks rose from about £180 million in 1850 to £1200 million in 1914. They

Stone and Stoke

BANKS.

WE, the undersigned, having full Confidence the Responsibility and Resources of Mr. MOOR[E] Do hereby declare our readiness to take his Note in payment as usual.

Dated 20th December, 1825.

William Horton,	John Cartwright,	George Bentley,
John Horton,	John Bromley,	J. Salt,
William Elley,	Bamford and Shaw,	John Marsh,
Thomas Mottershaw,	George Jackson,	William Southern,
Henry Somerville,	Arthur Morgan,	Anne Hughes,
Joseph Lovatt,	Luke Lakin,	Thomas Partridge,
Edward Clarke,	Robert Silvester,	John Hammersley,
W. & G. Keen,	Thomas Turnock,	James Cramer, jun.
T. M. Hubball,	J. Dickenson,	William Bullock,
Edward Knight, M. D.	Robert Turnock,	James Dudley,
Francis Hughes,	Benjamin Keeling,	William Bentley,
Betty Perry,	Joshua Drewry,	William Dearn,
William Fowke,	Charles Dudley,	William Tagg,
Jane Hughes,	Thomas Bostock,	John Wynne,
Edward Worsey,	Jane Wiggin,	Richard Abberley,
Joseph Boulton,	Richard Hart,	Edward Peake,
John and Thomas Boulton,	Joseph Cliff,	John Beckett,
Edward W. Horton,	Charles Chester,	John Wilkes,
William Churton,	Charles Kenderdine,	John Butler,
Thomas Eld,	Richard Trubshaw,	Samuel Ray,
Samuel Walker,	Joseph Painter,	Thomas Till, sen.
Charles Wright,	Thomas Hammersley,	Richard Simkin,
Charles Dawson,	Joseph Pickin,	John Shallcross,
Peter Rock,	William Gregory,	John Shaw,
Thomas Ward Pemberton,	James Miller,	William Cook,
George Webb, Mercer,	Leightons and Hughes,	William Guinan,
Henry Webb & Co. Cornfactors,	Isaac Kenderdine,	William Morris,
John Griffin,	William Kenderdine,	Robert Smith,
Francis Burgin,	Thomas Kenderdine,	George Humphrey,
William Kenderdine,	Thomas Woolley,	John & Richard Wil[...]
James Turnock,	Thomas Swift,	John Rogers.
William Jones,	Joseph Sillitoe,	
	William Beckett	

DREWRY, PRINTER, STAFFORD.

An attempt to save a Stafford bank in 1825. It would survive only if those who feared it might collapse did not withdraw their money.

Approximate purchasing power of £1
(1790 about 85p)

1810	50p
1820	70p
1830	85p
1840	70p
1850	95p
1860	75p
1870	85p
1880	90p
1890	105p
1895	125p
1900	100p
1910	90p

Customers inside the Bank of England depositing and withdrawing their cash at the start of the nineteenth century.

also opened more branches in different parts of the country. Amalgamation helped the individual joint stock banks grow larger, and so fewer (120 in the mid nineteenth century, thirteen in 1920). By the early twentieth century Barclays, Lloyds, the Midland, National Provincial and Westminster banks dominated most ordinary banking business in England and Wales. With great resources, headquarters in London and branches all over the country they were almost as safe as the Bank of England itself. (By 1914 Scotland had eight joint stock banks which still issued their own notes.)

By the end of the nineteenth century, because of Britain's industrial and commercial supremacy, most foreign countries turned almost automatically to London when they wanted to borrow money. The Bank of England, therefore, tried to keep the British economy stable for the sake of both world trade and Britain. This was a difficult job. Since much business was conducted with borrowed money, it was always affected if the rate of interest paid on bank loans and deposits was altered. The lower this bank rate was, the cheaper money was to borrow and so the more business flourished both at home and abroad. But when it was very low, foreign countries were encouraged to borrow large quantities from London. If much gold was lost in this way, the British economy could be upset seriously. Thus one of the chief concerns of the Bank of England was to adjust the bank rate so skilfully that it was high enough to keep the pound absolutely stable without discouraging trade and industry at home.

Thus, by the end of the nineteenth century Britain had developed the means of communication, banking and company organization necessary to cope with the vastly expanded business and trade.

Chapter 6
Aspects of country life

Introduction

'We thought we would let you know that we are getting on right well,' wrote one labourer from Sheffield to his former home in Norfolk in the 1870s, 'for instead of working for 13s. a week we get 22/6; and instead of working with bread and cheese, and sometimes with bread and nothing with it, we get a thumping bit of beef with it, and we like it much better; for we have had more beef this week than we had in three months at home. Tell our poor fellow-men not to stop there and be starved and ruined by Mr Farmer, for they can live here, and that is more than they can there.'

After the middle of the nineteenth century so many more left their villages for the towns, that the numbers living in the countryside

A shooting party poses for a photograph in 1869. Country estates were often maintained for their sporting facilities.

Price of wheat per quarter	
1810s	95/–
1830s	55/6
1850s	54/–
1870s	51/–
1890s	28/–

A small market town in Suffolk celebrating Queen Victoria's Golden Jubilee, 1887. Notice the umbrellas which are keeping off the sun. During the nineteenth century sunburnt faces were considered unattractive, especially in a lady.

actually declined, especially in the more remote areas like Cornwall and the Highlands of Scotland. The result was that, by the opening of the present century, for the first time in the world's history less than a quarter of the citizens of an important nation dwelt in its countryside (see table, page 84).

For those who remained behind life changed, but never so rapidly as for the inhabitants of the new towns.

Farming

As Britain's population grew, the country's demand for food increased. Yet until about 1870 only a quarter of all the food eaten in Britain came from abroad. In other words British farmers almost succeeded in feeding the rapidly growing population.

The high price of corn until 1813 encouraged them both to grow more wheat and to cultivate the less productive clay soils and hillsides. Then, as prices fell, the farmers changed slowly to rearing more animals. Meat and dairy produce gained from the railways in the middle of the century, because, unlike grain, they needed fast transport to the towns. Even so almost all farms in the south and east (light soils) also grew corn and so remained mixed until at least the 1870s.

By then the railways and steamships had combined to open up the American prairies and huge quantities of foreign corn were imported

because its price fell sharply. It was the food which could be moved long distances most easily, but the British government refused to protect with customs duties those farmers who relied most on growing corn. Even though increasing quantities of frozen meat also came in from Australasia, where possible these farmers turned to raising cattle. By 1910, when the British imported two-thirds of their food, many farms were specializing in the production of milk, eggs and other foods which could not travel far and three-quarters of the output of British farms came from rearing animals. The figures of the value of British farming's output record its uneven progress.

The fortunes of the farmers on the wet and heavy clay lands fluctuated most. They were hit hardest by falling prices in the early nineteenth century because they had one of the most expensive soils to farm. From the 1840s it could at last be drained properly with cheap cylindrical tile-pipes, which were much stronger than the previous ∩-shaped ones and were laid about three feet deep. However, this was often done inefficiently and by the 1870s only about a fifth of the land which would have benefited had been drained. And then, when the price of wheat slumped, many of these fields were abandoned.

The yield of crops grown in Britain increased for various reasons in the nineteenth century. From the 1830s nitrate of soda and other manures were imported from South America. Then chemical fertilizers like phosphorus were also extracted from the waste slags of steelworks and distributed by the railways.

Arable farming also benefited from many new implements and machines. However, since most farms did not use them until long after they were invented, it is often difficult to say exactly when they were introduced. More crops were also grown for animals. Mangels, kale and the hardier Swedish turnip were added to the ordinary turnip and clover. Later the railways helped increase the consumption of cattle cake, which consisted of imported beans or linseed.

Shorthorns replaced Longhorns as the most important cows in the early nineteenth century. Two of the pioneers who developed them were the Collings brothers from near Darlington. Many more cattle, like Ayrshires, Devons and Herefords, were also bred specially for milk or meat. Paintings of monster animals can be very misleading, for they were often advertisements which exaggerated the size of the farmer's largest beast, which was usually old as well. In fact the improved animals rarely became much larger. Some weight was moved from their shoulders to their rump or udders where it was wanted. British breeders were so successful that by the end of the century they supplied many other countries with their pedigree stock.

As their animals became more valuable, the farmers took better care of them. A Wiltshire natural history writer noted early in the nineteenth century: 'The cows in this district used to be Longhorns

Value of farming output

	£m
1780	65
1830	80
1870	130
1910	120

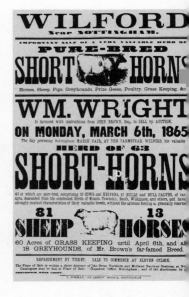

These two oxen weighed over a ton each, but the artist has tried to make them appear even larger, by shortening the man's legs and by putting bantam cocks in the foreground and a village in the far distance.

which remained in the meadows all the winter, with no better shelter than hedges and bushes. But now Shorthorns have come, and cattle are housed carefully.' Farmyards were built for them, sometimes in brick. Larger barns were also erected to house all the straw and food which the cattle needed. Much elaborate machinery was devised to make butter and cheese in the dairy. Even so, a shortage of suitable buildings helped prevent an even greater turnover to pasture farming at the end of the century.

Britain's shortage of land drove many farmers to adopt the new techniques which enabled them to increase their output or reduce their costs. Yet, in spite of the development of Agricultural Shows, changes in farming came more slowly and much more unevenly than in industry. In part this was because local conditions varied so much. Since a farmer's earnings depended on food prices and the yield of an unpredictable harvest, it was very difficult for him to plan ahead. In addition some farmers and landowners were not really interested in farming improvements. The depression from the 1870s, however, forced many of the most incompetent arable farmers to give up.

In many ways British farming was still the most technically advanced in the world in the early twentieth century, but it was clearly no longer the country's chief source of wealth. The value of all its produce was worth less than one-sixth of industry's total output (see Table on page 71). In addition the number of people engaged in farming, which reached a peak of two million in the 1850s, declined partly because the railways made it so much easier for young countrymen to find work in the towns. From the 1880s farmers saved money by hiring fewer un-skilled labourers and working those they retained more efficiently.

However, the conditions of those who remained improved slowly. Various machines eased the burden of their work. The threshing machine was one of the first, but because it left even less work for winter it was most unpopular. Horse-drawn reaping and mowing machines were much more of a boon at harvest time. Machinery led to less work for women, spread it out more evenly over the year and raised wages too. By the second half of the nineteenth century almost all labourers were hired for the year, except specialists like sheep shearers and threshing machine operators who travelled round the farms.

A seed drill

A harrow

Because labour was cheap and plentiful most farmers did not begin to use these machines until long after they were invented.

Jethro Tull's seed-drill of the early eighteenth century was most unsatisfactory until it was improved from the 1780s. Then some farmers used it on light soils, but it was not taken up generally until the mid nineteenth century.

Stronger harrows made of mass-produced iron also appeared in the first half of the nineteenth century. They broke up the clods of earth left after ploughing.

The horse-drawn mowing machine, like the reaping machine, first became popular on the larger farms in the 1850s. (They cut hay and corn respectively.) Before the end of the century the reaper and binder also tied up sheaves of corn with string.

Primitive threshing machines emerged in the later eighteenth century, but not until the 1860s could steam-driven threshing machines clean the grain and grade it in sacks. With flails, these men would have taken six months to thresh as much grain as this machine could do in a week.

Attempts to move heavy steam engines in the fields were much less successful, although some farmers did plough by steam in large, flat and regularly shaped fields from the 1850s.

A mowing machine

144

A threshing machine

A steam plough

145

Country society

Money could still be made out of farming for most of the nineteenth century, and the great landowners with their vast estates continued to enjoy all the power and luxury that life could provide. At the same time most farmers also lived quite well. Their houses for instance were improved steadily with more comfortable furniture and better decoration. The new kitchen ranges made cooking easier. Water closets were also installed upstairs in some farm houses, but since they were often flushed with rain water from the roof they were of little use in dry weather.

Yet the country gentry did not feel really secure, for they were aware that in the towns money was being made by business men, some of whom were of very humble origin. Some of the most successful of these men actually bought a country estate, and even when they did not they tended to consider themselves as good as many gentlemen. There was much ill feeling against such upstarts, for country society still tended to take it for granted that everybody should know his place. In many Anglican churches labourers and their wives sat on separate benches at the back or side. Joseph Arch, who was brought up in Warwickshire in the 1830s, discovered that: 'In the parish church the poor man and his wife were shown pretty plainly where they came among their fellow-creatures. The parson's wife used to sit in state

Above: a door-to-door salesman.
Left: a rabbit-warrener. These men were not casual trappers. They worked in specific areas, paying rent for the use of the land. The landowners would, in return, also protect the rabbits from foxes for the warrener.

'Brusher' Mills, a snake-catcher, photographed in 1895 outside his home, a charcoal-burner's hut. He made his money in several ways: the New Forest authorities paid one shilling a head for adders; he also sold adders' fat as a remedy for sprains, rheumatism and for adder-bites; and he sold all kinds of snakes at fairs, markets and even to the London Zoo. He would catch the snakes by trapping them with a two-pronged stick and picking them up with large tweezers.

in her pew in the chancel, and the poor women used to walk up the church and make a curtsey to her before taking the seats set apart for them. They were taught in this way that they had to pay homage and respect to those "put in authority over them".'

In fact the lot of farm labourers improved very slowly during the century. Indeed, if we are to believe William Cobbett, by 1831 they were actually worse off:

All of you who are 60 years of age can recollect that bread and meat, and not wretched potatoes, were the food of the labouring people; you can recollect when the young people were able to provide money before they were married, to purchase decent furniture for a house; you can recollect when a bastard child was a rarity in a village; you can recollect when the young men did not shirk about on a Sunday in ragged smock-frocks with unshaven faces, with a shirt not washed for a month, and with their toes peeping out of their shoes, and when a young man was pointed at if he had not, on a Sunday a decent coat upon his back, a good hat on his head, a clean shirt and a pair of handsome Sunday shoes. There were always some exceptions to this; but I appeal to all those of you who are 60 years of age whether this be not a true description of the state of labourers of England when they were boys.

Cobbett was looking at the past through rose-coloured spectacles, but his evidence does not stand alone.

147

Inside an Orkney cottage.
Notice the box beds at the
back, the furniture and the
kettle hanging over the fire
in the middle of the room.
The clock is placed so that
people outside can tell
the time.

Grinding corn by quern in the
Orkneys; a very old, slow and
tedious method.

Most labourers' cottages were not improved until the second half of the nineteenth century, when the new ones were larger and more stoutly built. However, many continued to live in the three-roomed ones. There several children normally slept in one bed, sometimes across and not down it to fit more in. Some mothers still cooked on open fires. Few labourers had many belongings. Of one Suffolk village, G. E. Evans wrote recently: 'Each family has its own nest of possessions – a pair of china dogs, a few old photographs, a couple of old chairs and a few pieces of old-fashioned china and a nineteenth-century clock.' They did not take long to arrange when they moved into a new cottage.

This reminiscence of a country boy shows how few toys many children had. 'One morning as I poddled along to school by myself, I had a find. It was a little bodkin case, made of brass. No children of our sort ever had any sort of toys, as you can imagine, and anything a little bit out of the ordinary was a treasure to us. So you can realize what sort of state I was in that morning, and as soon as school had started, I was caught by the teacher playing with my toy under the desk.'

During the first half of the nineteenth century several significant changes occurred in country people's diets, although by modern standards most remained inadequately fed. For a start more and more families began to drink tea regularly. It was expensive and so they

The interior of a farm labourer's cottage in Dorset, 1846.

made it very weak; few mixed it with milk, but most sweetened it with sugar. Although not so nourishing as beer, tea did add warmth to cold meals like bread and cheese.

Potatoes were grown more widely in the northern part of the country and in most southern counties too. They had three main attractions. They were cheap, they were eaten hot and a small garden could produce a lot of them. 'For years past their daily diet is potatoes for breakfast, dinner and supper and potatoes only,' concluded a report on the Somerset labourers in the 1850s. But this was unusual, for in most areas they still came second to bread.

Most families in the midlands and south (apart from Suffolk and Devon) bought their bread instead of baking it. By then it was made from wheaten flour almost everywhere, which made it whiter and easier to eat without butter. The labourers in the north were generally better fed than those in the south, but there were many local variations. Dorset was one of the worst counties. This was a typical labourer's diet there in the 1850s:

Some landowners used devices like this 'humane' mantrap to protect their property from poachers in the early nineteenth century.

> After doing up his horses, he takes breakfast, which is made of flour with a little butter and water from the tea-kettle poured over it. He takes with him to the field a piece of bread and cheese to eat at midday. He returns home in the afternoon to a few potatoes, and possibly a little bacon, though only those who are better off can afford this. The supper very commonly consists of bread and water. Beer is given by the master in hay-time and harvest.

And even though countrymen lived longer than town-dwellers (see page 99), life in the village was not particularly healthy. Although they buried much waste, many villagers also kept piles of refuse turning into manure quite close to their cottages. These, together with primitive methods of sanitation, also spread disease.

> Many and many a cottage didn't have a W.C. at all. They just 'went broadcast' in the fields. Them as did have closets weren't a lot better off. They had a vault dug somewhere near the house, with a wood structure over the top. In the seat there'd be a big hole cut, too big for any child to sit over. So the children didn't use the closet till they were nearly growed up. They'd just go anywhere, but mostly along by the side wall of the house. Once a week somebody would take a shovel and a barrow and clean the leavings up.

This description is of the fens in the later nineteenth century, but it gives a good idea of how most labourers' families lived earlier.

Some cottages had wells in their gardens, but most did not. Many inhabitants therefore collected rain from their roofs in barrels, but in dry weather it was soon used up. Drinking water came from the village well or spring. Those who lived near streams or rivers fetched some in buckets, but often the water was not very clean and they only washed with it. In winter, or if it was some distance away, they saved carrying by using very little. Most people therefore washed both themselves and their clothes infrequently, often without soap. It was also normal for several to wash in the same water.

In the nineteenth century the farm labourers furthest away from the industrial towns were worst off. By the middle of the century their wages in some south-western counties like Wiltshire were still about 7/6 a week, which was no higher than they had been eighty years earlier and was less than half the pay of many industrial workers. Some farmers certainly gave their men milk, eggs and even meat when they had some to spare, but these extras were not given regularly and were rarely worth more than 2/6 a week. Opportunities for regular poaching were also rare.

The pump of a Warwickshire cottage in 1895. It was much easier than drawing water from a well.

At the time people often assumed that there were fewer poor in the countryside than the towns. Surveys of villages like one of Ridgmount in Bedfordshire in 1903 showed how wrong they were. There, investigators using the same standards that were applied to London and York by Booth and Rowntree found that forty per cent of the population were not properly fed, clothed and housed. And this forty per cent who were poor included nearly all the children in the village. Now, Ridgmount was no ordinary village. The wealthy Duke of Bedford, who lived nearby, employed twenty of the villagers and had rebuilt many of their cottages. In other words the inhabitants of many other villages were even worse off than those of Ridgmount.

The towns contained more poor people because they had many more inhabitants. The proportion was certainly no higher. But since their poor were crowded together in slums, they were noticed much more.

Flora Thomson's recollections of a small village near Buckingham in the 1880s confirm this. There all the farm labourers earned 10/- a week. Their families usually ate cabbage and potatoes for their main meal with a 'square of bacon, amounting to little more than a taste each'. For other meals they depended largely on bread and lard.

In nearly all the cottages there was but one room downstairs, and many of these were poor and bare, with only a table and a few chairs and stools for furniture and a superannuated potato-sack thrown down by way of hearth-rug. Coal and paraffin for lighting *had* to be squeezed out of the weekly wage; but for boots, clothes, illness, holidays, amusements and household renewals there was no provision whatever. But in spite of their poverty and the worry and anxiety attending it, they were not unhappy.

Model labourers' cottage in Derbyshire. Particularly in the 1850s and 1860s many landowners built better dwellings for their tenants.

These men and women dressed in their best clothes are waiting to be hired as servants or farmworkers for the year. The hiring fair was a common means for getting work in rural areas throughout England and Scotland. This is one in Warwickshire in 1872.

Driving pigs to market in Birmingham in 1903. In most places this was still the normal way of getting livestock to market. If the animals held up the traffic, that was too bad for the traffic.

Aspects of country life in the 1890s. *Left:* Haymaking with everyone helping out. Mechanical methods were not widespread, and it was still hard work. Felling trees in Devon (*below left*). The axe and saw were the only means of getting timber.

Right: Thatching the roof of a cottage. In those days it was easy — farmers often thatched their hay-ricks; and it was cheap — they would use the leftovers of the corn harvest.

Below: Inside a blacksmith's forge. Shoeing horses was his main task, but he also made to order all sorts of equipment in wrought iron.

Superstitions

It was among the country people that the old superstitions lingered
longest. Living comparatively short and insecure lives, which depended
so much on the weather and the seasons, and knowing little about
germs and the world outside their immediate locality, belief in spirits
and omens seemed quite reasonable. In the fen country, for instance:

most women and a lot of men believed in signs and omens, especially about
death. There were all sorts of signs when anybody was going to die. Most
people had their private signs, like hearing footsteps, or finding a coffin-shaped
crease in a sheet when you unfolded it, or dreaming of lice. Some omens
everybody believed, and if any of these happened they brought real terror
with them. If a robin came into a house it was a bad sign for a death somewhere
in the family, but if an owl sat on the roof, or flew up against a window
at night, that meant a death actually in the house. A clock stopping suddenly
for no reason sent everybody cold with terror; so did a dog howling.

Long winter evenings spent in badly lit houses with a flickering
fire and perhaps one candle made ghosts and demons, witches and
fairies appear more real. They wanted protection from them too.

'Hag-stones (flints with holes in them) were at one time accounted
a safeguard against fairies or witches,' G. E. Evans discovered in Suffolk. 'They were hung on doors or carried in pockets as witchcraft
preventatives. It is still a common practice to tie a key to one of these
small holed flints. If iron was joined to the stone its potency as a
protective charm was increased; and the iron of the key united with
the hag-stone to form a powerful safeguard, preventing all evil from
entering the house.' In the same way horseshoes protected doorways.

'On one of the farms here,' Mr Evans continued, 'there is a field
with a holly tree standing somewhere near its centre. The field would be
much easier to farm if the tree were removed, but the farmer will
not have it touched as he believes that cutting down a holly tree is
always followed by bad luck.' Many farmers also spared elder trees
because they believed that witches lived in them. Other superstitions
about trees and plants included not taking some indoors. These taboos,
of course, were not to be found in all parts of the country.

Mrs Gaskell described a very different superstition in her novel
North and South. The heroine was surprised to learn that a woman
in a southern village had burned her neighbour's cat alive. She
explained that she had lent her husband's Sunday clothes to a gypsy
who had not returned them. 'Alarmed by their non-appearance and
her subsequent dread of her husband's anger and as, according to
one of the savage country superstitions, the cries of a cat, in the agonies
of being boiled or roasted alive, compelled the powers of darkness
to fulfil the wishes of the executioner, resort had been had to the
charm.'

Telling the bees about deaths
and events in the family was a
very old superstition. Holding
the key was part of the ritual.

156

A corn dolly, plaited from the last sheaf of the harvest. By traditional belief, the dolly would ensure a good crop in the following year.

Often people tried to foretell the future rather than control it. This belief, for instance, was dying out about a hundred years ago. 'In Gander Lane we saw in the banks some of the "Midsummer Men" plants which my mother remembers the servant maids and cottage girls sticking up in their houses and bedrooms on Midsummer Eve, for the purpose of divining about their sweethearts.' Another guide to the future was the pattern of tea leaves left in someone's cup. The time when people were born was commonly thought to influence the rest of their lives too. Many old sayings record these beliefs. 'Never be born on a Friday, Choose some other day if you can' was one. 'Always be born in the morning ' was another.

Many of these country superstitions still survived in Leeds in the 1930s, according to Richard Hoggart. 'To put shoes on the table, to walk under a ladder, to spill salt, to bring holly into the house before Christmas, to break a mirror, to give a knife without receiving a coin, are unlucky: to have a black cat cross one's path, to put on stockings the wrong way out, to touch wood after tempting misfortune, all these are lucky.' All superstitions were by no means silly. Killing spiders, for instance, could bring bad luck to those who lacked chemicals to destroy flies.

In the nineteenth century then, though farming techniques improved and new crops were grown, society changed much less than in the towns. If a man alive in 1750 could have been transported to a late nineteenth-century village, he would have found much that was basically familiar. But a large industrial town would have appeared to him a totally strange and terrifying place.

Chapter 7
Religion and education

The churches in the nineteenth century

All was not well with the Church of England in the early nineteenth century, as the Rev Francis Kilvert discovered later, when talking to a parson in Dorset.

> The Vicar told us of the state of things in his parish when he first came to it (in the 1820s). There were 16 women communicants and most of them went away when he refused to pay them for coming. One day there was a christening and no water in the font. 'Water, sir!' said the clerk in astonishment. 'The last parson never used no water. He spit into his hand.'

Of course, this case was quite exceptional. The Church's main failing was that about half its parsons did not live in their parishes; poorly paid curates usually performed their duties instead. And so the unsatisfactory state of the Church of England accounts, at least in part, for the success of the Nonconformist churches during the nineteenth century.

While most Scots were Presbyterians, in England the Baptists, Congregationalists and other Nonconformists formed perhaps ten per cent of the population in the 1780s. When John Wesley finally broke with the Church of England in 1784, he had under 100,000 followers. However, after his death seven years later the Methodists increased rapidly even though they split into several different sects in the early nineteenth century. One of their ministers reported their influence in East Yorkshire in the 1840s.

> Thousands who had sunk to a level of dull monotony, unbroken from year to year, except by fairs, races, fox hunting etc., found, in our oft-recurring means of grace – soul stirring preaching services, fervent prayer-meetings, lively class-meetings and hearty singing – a life, a freedom, and a joy to which they had been strangers. Existing wrongs, injustices and estrangements between families and neighbours were corrected, and there was created and fostered a neighbourly solidarity which changed the spirit of whole villages. Indeed, Methodist chapels have long been the centres around which the religious life of these villages has revolved. They feel at home *there* as they do not at the Parish Church.

A middle-class family pose on their way to church, around 1900. The class of most worshippers was revealed by their 'Sunday best' clothes.

Townsmen who wanted to be considered respectable were naturally drawn to Nonconformist churches, which were seldom dominated by landowners and rarely made the middle ranks of society feel inferior. And so all the other Nonconformists gained much support. By 1851, when the first and only religious census was taken, the Protestant worshippers in England and Wales were divided almost equally between the Nonconformists and the Church of England. The former flourished in most industrial towns and some rural areas, like Wales, Cornwall and Bedfordshire. The Church of England remained unchallenged in much of the countryside, especially in the west midlands and the counties between Dorset and the Wash. But in the large towns it had become merely one of several active churches. Altogether about half of those aged over ten stayed away from church on 30 March 1851 and seventy-five per cent or more were non-attenders in some leading towns. 'The masses of our working population are never, or but seldom, seen in our religious congregations,' concluded the census.

Proportionate allegiances changed little during the second half of the nineteenth century, but the number of practising Christians failed to increase at the rate of the total population.

The Bible was the foundation of all Protestant beliefs until at least the middle of the nineteenth century. In their services the clergymen read passages from the 'Word of God' and explained them in lengthy

Religion 1851

Church of England	$3\frac{1}{2}$ m
Methodist	2 m
other dissenters	$1\frac{1}{2}$ m
Roman Catholic	$\frac{1}{4}$ m
non-attenders	$6\frac{1}{2}$ m

sermons. Nearly all agreed that less than 6000 years ago, God had created the world in six days and that it had changed little since. They also believed that this life was a preparation for the next and that both prayer and good behaviour helped them reach Heaven.

The Anglicans (Church of England) generally sang more psalms and listened to duller sermons than the Nonconformists, whose preachers often described vividly the terrors of Hell. They also stressed the comforting belief that repentance to Christ could save them from their sins. This message was repeated in their hymns.

Originally the Nonconformists were much more enthusiastic about their religion. Strict Methodists, for example, prayed and read their Bibles daily and condemned dancing, card playing, alcohol drinking, the wearing of ornaments and so on, especially on Sundays. Some Nonconformists even disapproved of cooking and travelling on Sundays. Many also became anxious to help only their unfortunate neighbours and not drunkards, divorcees, or unmarried mothers. Anglicans gradually observed the Sabbath more rigidly too and laws were passed prohibiting the Sunday opening of shops, theatres, parks and museums and restricting the playing of games.

Nor was religious observance confined to one day in the week. 'In the autumn of 1816,' wrote the daughter of a duchess, 'mama first began to have family prayers of a morning in her room with her maids and ourselves. Afterwards she made arrangements for family prayers, including the men servants as well as female servants, for evening as well as morning prayers.' Grace was said in many households before and after meals.

Although the Church of England had bishops and organized its services differently, their basic beliefs differed little from most Noncon-

Popular Nonconformist preachers attracted huge congregations to the large urban chapels in the 1850s.

A typical Methodist chapel in Cheadle.

formists until the second half of the nineteenth century. Then, some, but by no means all, Anglican clergymen began to insist that, without the help of a priest, ordinary people could not approach God. They also claimed that He was actually present in the Bread and Wine of the Communion Service, which these parsons celebrated much more frequently. They wore more elaborate garments too, dressed their choirs in surplices, installed organs and some even burned incense like the Roman Catholics.

These and similar changes divided the Church of England and upset many Anglicans, but the Nonconformists eventually lost touch more with their congregations. Already in the 1890s a Congregationalist minister was complaining: 'Christian parents no longer forbid their children to read novels or to learn dancing. Some of them accompany their sons and daughters to the theatre and in many Christian homes billiards and cards are allowed.' As people lived longer and more comfortable lives, they ignored increasingly condemnations of such innocent pleasures together with threats of hell. The gradual acceptance of the theory of man's evolution from animals, and the scholars who discovered mistakes in the version of the Bible translated into English, also prevented most people from believing that every word was literally true.

By 1900, then, religion was no longer the force it had been. Gradually it came to play a smaller part in education too.

Sunday schools provided many urban children with their only means of education. Yet not many of their pupils even learned to read fluently.

RULES
OF THE LEEK WESLEYAN METHODIST
SUNDAY SCHOOL.

FIRST.—The Scholars must all come clean washed and combed, at Nine o'Clock in the Morning, and half-past One at Noon.

SECOND.—They are not to go out if they can possibly avoid it; nor at all until the change has taken place. When they go they must take a permit from the Teacher.

THIRD.—Not one word must be spoken in School Hours to any body but the Teacher. No looking off books, or getting lessons aloud are permitted.

FOURTH.—The Girls are not to walk with their pattens on in the School.

FIFTH.—Those who write, must shew every line as they write it to their Teacher before they begin upon another.

SIXTH.—If a Scholar neglect coming to School, or sending a reasonable excuse for not coming two Sundays together, such Scholar's name will be liable to be crossed out of the List.

SEVENTH.—Those who are not present when the names are called over, will be marked for late attendance.

EIGHTH.—If a Scholar be convicted of cursing, or swearing, or quarreling, or wilful lying, or calling nick-names, or using indecent language, they shall be admonished for the first offence, punished for the second, and excluded for the third.

NINTH.—If a Scholar be found guilty of a misdemeanor which may not be here particularly specified, and the offence is considered of so capital a sort as to require exemplary punishment, he shall be forthwith expelled from the School.

TENTH.—When the Scholars are dismissed they must go straight home without loitering in the Streets, and if any be seen running, jumping, or playing at any play or game, or in other respects misbehaving themselves, they will be treated as in the 8th Rule.

ELEVENTH.—Those Scholars who can read the Bible, and repeat the Wesleyan Catechism No. 1, will be taught to write (providing their own paper,) and those who have made a proficiency in reading and writing, and whose good conduct recommends them to notice, may learn accounts on Saturday Evening's.

TWELFTH.—When the Children go to Chapel they must walk regularly, two and two along the Street, neither thronging or pushing each other, nor speaking one word from the time they leave the School to the time they come out of Chapel; they must go reverently and quietly to their seats, not

Elementary schools

To the 1840s

As the population rose rapidly, many Sunday schools were opened from the 1780s, mostly in the growing towns. Older children who worked during the week could still attend these schools. They were also cheap to run and it was much easier to find teachers on Sundays.

The wealthy Christians who contributed towards Sunday schools naturally wanted the poorer children to hear about the life and teachings of Christ. They were also anxious for the children to learn to behave better. 'If I were a good girl I should go to heaven – if I were bad I should have to be burned in brimstone and fire; they told me that at school yesterday. I did not know it before,' reported one girl. Stories and hymns also described the fate of bad people in the Old Testament, like the children who teased the prophet Elisha:

God quickly stopped their wicked breath
And sent two raging bears
That tore them limb from limb to death
With blood and groans and tears.

Some schools overcame the children's natural reluctance to rise early

Ragged schools, like this one in Edinburgh, 1851, were often held for poor children in the towns.

on their only day of rest by, for instance, paying a penny to everyone who arrived on time on four successive Sundays. They might get another penny for reciting a chapter from the Bible. Even though most still attended Sunday school so irregularly that they learned little, many would have remained unable to read had they not gone at all.

Early in the nineteenth century some church weekday schools in the towns adopted a new method of teaching that enabled one teacher with very few books to instruct several hundred pupils. First, he taught the lessons to the older children who were called monitors, some of whom were as young as eight. These monitors then repeated the lessons like tape recordings to groups of about ten children. Lesson time was very noisy because all the groups were taught in the same room under the teacher's supervision.

Since the Bible was often the only book available, lessons like this were based upon it. 'There were seven days between the birth of Jesus and his circumcision, and five days from that event to His Epiphany, the time when the star led the Gentiles to worship the holy child. How long was it from the Nativity to the Epiphany?'

Moral lessons were taught as well as mechanical skills. Those learning to read in these monitorial schools spelt out sentences like: 'BAD MEN ARE FOES TO GOD.' The group began by repeating together the letters after the monitor; then the whole word and finally the complete sentence. Since the schools had so few books and writing paper was even more scarce, the children learned nearly everything by heart. They chanted phrases over and over again after the monitor, who then tested the children.

One well-planned lesson concluded like this:

Monitors at work among pupils.

Monitor: Spell Bee.	Pupils: B-E-E.
What is a bee?	A little insect.
What is it fond of?	Sugar. Flowers.
What sort of flowers?	Roses, tulips, buttercups.
What else is a bee fond of, what does it like to do?	Work.

Since the pupils had to give exact answers to the questions as in a television quiz, the monitors could teach subjects which they did not understand. Those who learned the right answers might not understand them either. A visitor to one school discovered this when he questioned in an unexpected order a boy who had just answered correctly:

Who was Moses?	Apostle of Christ.
Who was Peter?	An angel.
Where was Christ crucified?	England.
Who was Jesus Christ the son of?	Son of David.
Who then was David?	Son of Jesus.

Because there were so many children to control, the discipline was very strict. Yet those who misbehaved were rarely beaten. They were much more likely to be kept in for half an hour or publicly disgraced by having to wear their coats back to front. Dirty ones sometimes had their hands and faces washed in front of the whole school. Those who worked and behaved well received merit tickets, eight of which were worth a penny.

From the 1830s the government gave the churches some money to help them build more schools. It also appointed a committee and some inspectors to supervise how they spent it. Soon the inspectors found these elementary schools sadly wanting. One inspector reported:

In three or four instances only have I found a schoolmaster occupied in teaching on suddenly entering a school of the common class. I have far oftener found them reading an old newspaper, writing a letter or bill, probably for some other person, reading a magazine or doing nothing of any sort.

A commission in the 1840s confirmed this.

Of the very small proportion of those who could read fluently, very few, when questioned, were found to have any conception of the meaning of the words they uttered; so that great numbers of these children were as little benefited, after years of so-called tuition, as if they had never been at any school.

However, the upper and middle classes were quite satisfied with these limited achievements because most were afraid of the consequences of giving these children a better education. Therefore schools which taught a little reading, together with spinning and sewing for the girls and cobbling or carpentering for the boys, pleased the wealthier classes best. These included the schools founded by Hannah More. 'My plan of instruction is extremely simple and limited,' she had explained earlier. 'The children learn on week-days such coarse work as may fit them for servants. I allow of no writing for the poor. My object is to train up the lower classes in habits of industry and piety.'

In spite of all the new schools that were opened, until the 1840s the provision of education in the country barely kept pace with the rapidly expanding population. Indeed, in some of the fastest growing towns, the children's chances of going to school actually declined for a time. One-third of the bridegrooms and a half of the brides could still not sign their names in 1840.

However, children who learned little or nothing at school did not always suffer, because very few acquired at school the skills and knowledge that they required for earning their living. As one Warwickshire woman explained: 'All the children then spent more time with the men and women than they would later, for no one thought of school as carrying the real burden of their training.'

Illiterate bridegrooms 1840

London	12%
Northumberland	20%
Essex	50%
Bedfordshire	55%

Elementary schools

1840–1900

The development of industry gradually changed this situation because the employers needed more and more workers who could read and write with some fluency. Also in the days before typewriters they increasingly wanted clerks who could write and add quickly and neatly. Industrialists came to value schools for another reason: their strict discipline trained people to work steadily and to do as they were told without question.

In the 1840s Dr Kay, the secretary to the committee which distributed the government grants, helped develop a new system to replace the monitorial schools. At thirteen some children became apprentices or pupil-teachers for five years. They took classes during the day and were taught by their headmaster in the evening. At eighteen a few went on to college for a year or two to be trained as teachers.

However, improvements came slowly and education in England continued to lag behind that of other industrial nations. Nearly all children went to school by 1860, but most did not stay long enough to learn much. By then the government was contributing nearly £1 million a year to the church schools and was determined to get value for money. From 1862, therefore, it gave a school a grant of 12/– a year

In school the infants were expected to behave just like the older children.

for each pupil only if its buildings were approved by an inspector and if the child attended regularly and passed an annual exam in reading, writing and arithmetic. This new system became known as Payment by Results.

After leaving the infants at the age of seven or eight, the children went into a class called Standard 1. At the end of the year they were tested by an inspector. Those who passed moved up to Standard 2. If they failed they stayed in the same class and took the same exam a year later. Altogether there were six, and later seven standards. In the towns the classes rarely had less than seventy pupils and were often considerably larger. Several sometimes shared one room. In small schools one teacher taught at least several standards at once.

Lessons in reading, writing and arithmetic dominated each day. The beginners read books written in words of one syllable. Shakespeare and Milton were among the authors read by Standard 6. The children read aloud in turns, and since each standard had only two or three books, they often knew long passages by heart by the end of the year. For Joseph Ashby, who went to school in south Warwickshire in the 1860s: 'Reading was worst; you might wait the whole half-hour of a reading lesson while boys and girls who could not read stuck at every word. If you took your finger from the word that was being read you were punished by staying in when others went home.'

In the lower standards the children wrote on slates with special pencils. They started to use pen, ink and paper in Standard 4, when they had to copy out letters and sentences like this without making mistakes or blots:

aabbccddeeffgghhijkkllm

Such samplers were completed by generations of schoolgirls all over the country – to improve their minds as well as their needlework.

They also had spelling tests, dictations and learned many long words.

In arithmetic they tackled increasingly difficult sums. By Standard 4 they might reduce 3196 years to seconds or $10\frac{1}{2}$ miles to inches. Some also learned tables and rhymes like the following:

Two pints will make one quart,
Four quarts one gallon strong.
Some drink too little, some too much,
To drink too much is wrong.

Few elementary schools owned a piano, but many taught singing. Children usually learned a song by listening to their teacher and repeating it after her. Most also learned to draw. After first copying patterns, they eventually drew objects like buckets, but they did not compose their own pictures. Girls, who were still taught separately whenever possible, also learned sewing.

166

ABCDEFGHIIJKLMMOPQRSTUVWXYZ*12345

Jesus permit thy gracious name to stand
As the first effort of an infants hand
And while my fingers o'er the canvas move
Direct my tender thoughts to seek thy love
With thy dear children let me have a part
And write thy name thyself upon my heart

Mary Clench Aged 11 years   1835   I hope my work will please my
Chelmsford Essex   Is so then I have gain'd my end

Elementary school children rarely played games. Apart from walking to school, their only exercise was probably marching in formation in the school yard. Towards the end of the century they did various exercises with their arms, legs and bodies. All moved together in rows.

At the same time most schools began to teach one or two new subjects, like history and geography, to the higher standards. In geography, for example, they learned the names of a country's main towns in alphabetical order and its rivers or capes in the correct order round the coast, usually without seeing a map.

If a child did not attend school regularly and if he failed his exams at the end of the year, the school received a smaller grant and his teacher's salary might also be cut. And so those who played truant were beaten as soon as they returned to school. (Some therefore stayed away an extra day to postpone the agony.) The nearer they came to examination day, the more likely the teacher was to beat them whenever they made a blot or spelling mistake, stumbled in their reading or got a sum wrong. (Most parents beat their children just as frequently at home.) On the day itself, according to Flora Thompson: 'The very sound of the inspector's voice scattered the few wits of the less gifted, and even those who could have done better were too terrified in his presence to be able to collect their thoughts or keep their hands from trembling.'

Battle of the Alphabet, 1850
From the 1840s Parliament debated many proposals for involving the state more in education, but until 1870 all were defeated. Most clergymen preferred to leave a child uneducated than to have him taught the wrong religious doctrine. Here, Nonconformist, Church of England and Roman Catholic ministers are fighting over a child.

School attendance officers
were needed to enforce
compulsory education for all.

Men and women unable
to sign at their weddings

England and Wales

	M	W
1841	33%	49%
1861	25%	35%
1881	14%	18%
1901	3%	3%

Scotland

	M	W
1861	11%	21%
1881	7%	14%
1901	0%	0%

Even though many hated their schooldays and soon forgot most of what they learned, this Payment by Results system was, in its way, effective. When it was abandoned in the 1890s, few children were still illiterate. One perceptive inspector noticed other achievements: 'Anyone who can compare the demeanour of our young people at the present day with what it was 25 years ago, must notice how roughness of manner has been smoothed away, how readily and intelligently they can answer a question, how the half hostile suspicion with which they regarded a stranger has disappeared; in fact how they have become civilized.'

Both the government and churches were responsible, but they would have made even greater progress had the various churches not squabbled over what religion the schools should teach, whenever the government tried to intervene more directly. Eventually it overcame their opposition in 1870 and passed an Act creating School Boards, which were instructed to build schools where there were not enough already and to teach only the basic Christian truths inside them. As a result the Church of England quickly built as many new schools as it could, but huge gaps still remained in most towns and some country districts for the School Boards to fill.

By 1880 the government made it compulsory for all children to attend school between the ages of five and ten, but many areas were still short of schools and so this was not always possible. In addition children often stayed away from school to earn money. In the country-side, for example, they often helped with the harvest, scared birds and picked up stones in the fields. In the poorer districts of the towns especially many parents could not afford the fees of 3d to 6d a week. When most elementary schools stopped charging fees after 1891 these children attended more regularly and by 1900 most stayed until they were twelve.

Six million children attended elementary schools by then – three times as many as in the 1860s. They came almost entirely from the working and lower middle classes. Almost half went to schools run by the Church of England and most of the rest to board schools. The religion that was taught there had pleased the Nonconformists so much that they had handed over most of their own schools to the School Boards. Since the latter had more money than the churches, board schools generally had larger buildings, more equipment and more fully trained teachers, although there were many exceptions, especially in slum and country districts. They also tended to use, for example, more reading books and models, blackboards and maps.

Some town schools taught the older children more advanced subjects like algebra, science and French. Indeed by the 1890s in London and large industrial cities like Bradford and Manchester, those who had passed Standard 7 and wanted to learn more went to separate Higher

Grade schools. There they learned commercial and practical subjects. Although this was just what British industry needed these schools did not last long. They were closed by an Act of Parliament passed in 1902 and most technical instruction since then has been given to boys after they have left school.

Despite strong protests from the Nonconformists, by the same Act Church of England schools received more money but still remained free to teach their own religion and to appoint their own teachers. It also abolished the School Boards and handed over the elementary schools to the much larger county and borough councils – except in Scotland where the School Boards survived until the 1920s.

As the table on page 169 showed, the Scots were more literate than the English. Yet even so, a Commission which inquired into Scottish elementary schools in the 1860s found them in little better state than the English ones. Many parishes had no school. At the rural schools, where the roofs often leaked and there was hardly any furniture, most pupils learned little. In the more efficient schools the masters tended to concentrate on the brightest and to ignore the less able. When yearly examinations in reading, writing and arithmetic were introduced, the teachers were forced to attend to all their pupils. In Scotland education was made compulsory to the age of thirteen earlier than in England, but it was very difficult to enforce the law. In the north and west in particular the people lived on very scattered farms and so many children had to walk long distances to school.

With large classes discipline had to be very strict. Here certain words of command tell the class exactly when to put away their work and prepare to leave the room.

'Return slates'
The slate should be smartly lifted and placed in the groove in front of the desk.

'Raise desks'
The edge of the flap should be grasped. The flap should be raised quickly without noise.

'Stand out'
Scholars should rise smartly with arms straight by their sides. Scholars at the right end of the desk should take one step to the right and one step forward. Scholars at the left should take one step left and one step to the rear.

A Lambeth school in 1874.

The 1870 Act made great demands upon school-building needs. School Boards built large and imposing schools in many towns, but they were frequently overcrowded, so that some temporary classrooms were also erected.

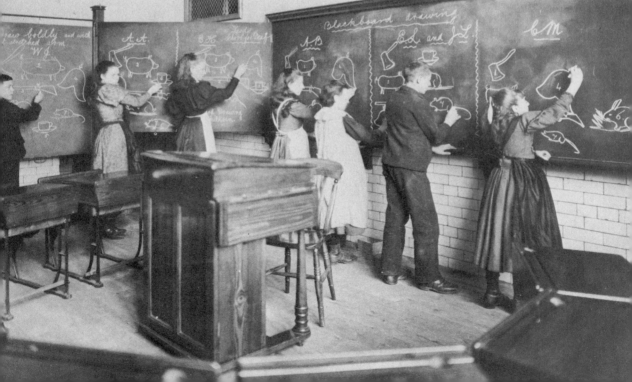

Scenes from board schools in Leeds. *Left:* Mid-morning Assembly – note the children's boots and heavy clothes. *Right:* Playtime – but without the girls.

Left: Deaf children all copying the same drawings. *Right:* A piano lesson – wind and string instruments were rarely taught. *Below:* Physical education was then called drill, when boys and girls were still kept separate.

Secondary schools

Comfortably-off middle-class parents did not send their children to elementary schools. In the nineteenth century a whole range of secondary schools grew up for them and the upper classes. Although many grammar schools had sunk to the level of elementary schools by then, a few were so popular that the master, who was usually a clergyman, had to engage several assistants to teach the junior forms. At some, like Leeds, they were not only taught the classics in a more interesting way, but also subjects like English, French, mathematics and even science. However, most grammar schools charged fees for these extra subjects and so all pupils did not study them. 'Not infrequently when questioning the highest class of a school on geography or history,' reported one inspector, 'I have noticed a number of children preserve a dead silence, and on inquiring further, have learned that they were pupils who did not pay for the particular subject and therefore did not learn it.'

Some headmasters increased their salaries by taking boarders who paid fees, but they tended to neglect the local boys for their private pupils. A few energetic headmasters, like Dr Thomas James of Rugby, had transformed their schools by attracting several hundred boarders. The boys travelled to them by stage coach and, later, railway. If they did not engage a private tutor by the early nineteenth century, most wealthy landowners sent their sons to Eton, Rugby, Westminster or a similar leading school. Because their pupils were not confined to one locality, they were called rather misleadingly 'public schools'. Their fees were usually too high for the newly prosperous merchants, civil servants and so on, so that many cheaper public schools were formed from the 1840s. By the end of the century there were over a hundred, mostly boarding schools, which educated about 30,000 sons of the wealthiest people in the country. Most refused to admit the sons of clerks and tradesmen, for whom many private day schools developed.

Several grammar school headmasters followed the example of Dr Thomas Arnold and excluded all the free local children. Eventually these schools became afraid that the government would prevent them from spending on the sons of the rich money which had been left for the education of the poor. Led by Uppingham, they therefore formed the Head Masters' Conference which preserved their independence in the 1870s. It also provided a more precise definition of a public school. New schools, like Cheltenham and Marlborough, whose headmasters attended the conference, were accepted as public schools.

Most ex-grammar schools founded separate˜schools for their local shopkeepers, craftsmen and clerks at the same time. When this happened at Oundle one clergyman 'warmly approved of the elimination from the Upper School of a lower class element, composed chiefly of day boys from the neighbourhood, now provided for in an entirely separate

The dormitory of Christ's Hospital, a boarding school founded originally for orphans. The pupils wore a distinctive uniform of long blue coats.

174

school. The Upper School, which is a first grade Public School, is now composed exclusively of sons of gentlemen, almost all being boarders. This judicious separation of classes by the present headmaster has proved a decided success.' Thus these exclusive schools contributed to making their pupils regard themselves in later life as being superior to others. Some public schools were also founded for girls from the 1850s. They were run quite separately and, like the London Collegiate School, were mostly day schools.

After attending a small private school or being prepared by a local clergyman, boys arrived at their public school at about eleven and stayed until they were sixteen or older. In class they spent about three-quarters of their time studying Latin and Greek. These classics were not intended to train anyone to earn his living. Their main purpose was to give a general education to landowners' sons — and to prepare boys for the universities.

Most boys learned page after page of grammar by heart and wrote prose and verse compositions in Latin nearly every day. When they read books by Virgil or Caesar they usually translated each sentence word by word first and then in more polished English. Finally they analysed its grammar before moving on to the next sentence. Only a few boys in schools like Winchester read the books quickly. None but the able ones appreciated the ideas and culture behind the classics they read. For the great majority the classics were always heavy going.

A commission which enquired into the public schools in the 1860s reported that many even left school at nineteen unable to analyse a simple passage in Latin or Greek without the help of a dictionary. Also most knew very little about other subjects, even though they usually read a few English books and were taught divinity and some mathematics as well. At least until then, many schools taught French and science, like music, optionally in the boys' free time. This recollection shows how limited their education could be:

What my brother Tom learned at Shrewsbury was clear enough: Latin and Greek with the ancient history and geography pertaining to them. The only English literature that reached him were lines put into Latin verse, while Milton was used for punishment. There is a pencil note in his copy of *Paradise Lost*: 'Had to write 500 lines of this for being caught reading *King Lear* in class.' The only modern geography he knew was the map of Scotland because this too was chosen as a punishment.

Cheltenham and some other new schools did devote more time to modern subjects, often for those entering the army or the professions. By the end of the nineteenth century most fifth and sixth form boys had some choice in what they studied, although this often meant that those who could not cope with the classics took up modern languages, history, maths and (natural) science instead.

175

Originally all the boys were taught together in one big school-room. Classes of forty to fifty were quite common, but they were rarely taught together. Instead the masters normally set the boys work and tested them one by one. Hence most did not work very hard.

In the second half of the century the classes became smaller as the schools appointed more masters, fewer and fewer of whom were clergymen. Most forms were also given their own classroom where their master usually described or explained things to everyone together and the boys competed against each other for marks. Almost all headmasters before the later nineteenth century were great floggers and many junior masters kept order only with frequent beatings. At times this drove the boys to rebel, and once the masters at Rugby had needed soldiers to bring the school back under control.

Before the later nineteenth century the boys rarely saw their masters outside the classroom. They lived together in long dormitories, often with separate cubicles for the older ones. Left to themselves, they frequently fought, bullied the weaker ones and gave cruel nicknames to the deformed or highly sensitive. The older boys dominated the others, making the youngest ones clean, cook and run messages for them. Headmasters accepted this situation officially by appointing some sixth form boys prefects to help run their schools. The young boys were still treated harshly. Usually they were not allowed to put their hands in their pockets, even in winter, and at Westminster they had to run wherever they went. At another school in the early twentieth century, those who were cheeky to the prefects walked along a passage while the older boys kicked their bottoms.

In nearly all schools the boys began each day by attending a service in chapel and concluded it with another service, but religion seems to have had little effect on their behaviour. Their companions

The School Room at Harrow (1816) contains several different classes. The master at the end is testing the boy standing beside him while the others get on with their work.

influenced them much more. They encouraged each other not to tell tales, but to endure injustices in silence. They also learned that one of the best ways to avoid being teased or bullied was to dress, talk and behave like everyone else and not reveal it when they were pleased or upset.

Until about the 1860s most boys had a lot of free time in which they walked, fished or poached and played rough games. These usually involved kicking a ball around a playground or hitting it with bare hands against a wall. They had few rules and there was no limit to the number of players who struggled to get near the ball. The older boys gradually imposed more rules and the schools eventually took up soccer or Rugby. In summer they all played cricket (page 210).

At first the masters took little part in this development, but from about the 1870s most schools made their boys play a recognized game every weekday. They realized that it helped keep them out of mischief, especially when they organized regular matches against other schools, forms and dormitories. And games in which they had to play for their team and not themselves discouraged selfishness. Thus by the later nineteenth century the boys had almost no time to spend as they liked, apart from a few hours on Sundays. Every day was strictly regulated from the moment they got up to the time they went to bed. This unchanging routine encouraged them to accept the world as they found it and not to think critically.

By the end of the nineteenth century parents usually kept their sons at public school from the age of thirteen for approximately £100 a year. By contrast most private and grammar schools charged their day boys between £3 and £15 p.a. This big difference divided the schools sharply between the different classes.

Boys playing cricket at Charterhouse. Wellington's famous statement, 'The battle of Waterloo was won on the playing fields of Eton', sums up the spirit of 'sportsmanship' to which the upper classes adhered in all aspects of their lives.

In general the grammar schools in Scotland were more efficient than those south of the border. The Commission investigating Scottish schools in the 1860s had discovered one teaching mostly classics in nearly every town. The Scots also had many private schools and academies. Some of these taught mathematics, commercial subjects and modern languages extremely well, but there was no common pattern of study and children arrived and left at different ages. The grammar schools were so poor that they had to charge fees to nearly everyone. However, these were so low that few middle-class parents could not afford to pay them. From the 1870s the School Boards ran most grammar schools as well as the elementary schools and so the Church of Scotland lost its control of education.

The English grammar schools began to revive from about the 1870s as the demand for cheaper secondary education increased. The Charity Commission also began to see that those schools which had been left land and money used them properly. A few, like Manchester and Bradford, compared well with most public schools, but many were still very small and could not afford all the books and equipment they needed. Nor could they pay their teachers adequately even though most pupils were now charged fees. And so by 1900 very few who attended grammar schools in England and Wales were sons of manual workers.

University education in the nineteenth century was reserved for the children of the wealthy. At first only the sons of gentlemen or those training to become Anglican parsons went to the colleges at Oxford and Cambridge, and the cartoon satirizes their life there.

Reforms from the 1850s raised the standards of work and admitted the Nonconformists, but the colleges remained so expensive that four-fifths of their students came from public schools. Women were also admitted for the first time, only to make life duller, according to this cartoon.

New Universities also grew up in London and the industrial towns, often to teach new subjects, like engineering or English, to some students from the lower middle classes.

In general grammar schools had become pale reflections of public schools. They played the same games, but not so well because they had poorer facilities and day boys had less time to practise. They appointed prefects, who were less effective in a day school. They studied similar subjects, but not to such a high standard, because most children left at sixteen or earlier and their junior classes in particular were considerably larger.

High or grammar schools for girls were opened in Leeds, Nottingham and Oxford, for instance, in the 1870s, but most other towns had to wait for one somewhat longer. As yet few women were trained to teach to a standard comparable with that found in boys' schools.

By the end of the nineteenth century, then, the government had acted to make primary education more efficient. As a result practically the whole population could read, write and do simple calculations. This was the minimum necessary to survive in the new and more complicated world which was developing. Secondary education was a different matter. The sons and daughters of the rich could go to good schools which trained them to take their places as defenders of upper-class values. Lower middle-class children often went to grammar or private schools, which were generally less efficient, but still offered a fair secondary education. Unless they were very clever and lucky, the children of labourers received no secondary education at all.

Chapter 8
The Victorian way of life

Incomes and prices

Did people living in the nineteenth century gain or lose from the revolution in industry?

Such simple questions are rarely easy to answer, because different people's experiences varied so much. When Victoria became queen in 1837, many hand-loom weavers' and some southern farm labourers' families had been driven to the brink of starvation by the economic changes of the previous generation. In addition many others suffered at least temporarily from unemployment or the loss of their common lands. On the other hand, the growth of trade and industry had already brought a marked rise in wages in most industrial counties together with handsome profits for many merchants and manufacturers, farmers and landowners.

By the 1840s the situation was summed up neatly by the philosopher J. S. Mill. 'Hitherto,' he wrote, 'it is questionable if all the mechanical inventions yet made have lightened the day's toil of any human being. They have enabled a greater proportion to live the same life of drudgery and imprisonment and an increased number of manufacturers and others to make fortunes.'

As he was writing, however, things were changing and since then the country's standard of living has risen remarkably. The increase in the total British national income is not very informative because it ignores both changing prices and the rapidly rising population. However, by recording the average income per head (recalculated at the prices of 1913–14), the figures opposite take both into account.

Since these figures are averages, they give only a vague idea of how living standards improved. Unfortunately everybody did not share equally in the growing wealth. As we have seen many families were still poverty-stricken at the end of the century, and even though the proportion of those who were poor fell during the second half of the nineteenth century, their total number actually increased, because the population grew so fast.

British national income

1850	£500m
1880	£1,000m
1910	£2,000m

Average annual income per person

1851	£20
1861	£22
1871	£27
1881	£31
1891	£40
1901	£47
1911	£49

A middle-class family group in the 1890s.

Dudley Baxter's estimates of incomes in England and Wales in 1867 show what an enormous gulf still separated rich from poor.

	proportion of families	approx. annual income
upper class	0·1%	over £5000
upper class	0·4%	£1000–5000
middle class	1·5%	£300–1000
lower middle class	8·0%	£100–300
lower middle class	15·5%	£50–100
skilled manual workers	14·0%	£70–100
semi-skilled	26·0%	£55–85
agricultural and unskilled	24·5%	£30–60
wageless	10·0%	£15–30

Note on class The upper classes normally mean the substantial land-owners, but already by 1867 a few manufacturers, merchants and bankers had similar incomes. In general these latter groups formed the wealthier or upper middle class, together with lawyers, doctors and the successful members of other professions. Most clerks, shopkeepers and school teachers were included among the lower middle classes. Craftsmen and skilled workers enjoyed a comparable standard of living and security to many of them, but the lower strata of the working classes lived very differently.

Four years after Queen Victoria died in 1901, L. C. Money estimated that the following groups in England and Wales each shared a third of the national income.

people	annual income
1·4 m	over £700
4·1 m	£160–700
39·0 m	under £160

George du Maurier was a writer and illustrator whose drawings provide a detailed record of the changes in Victorian fashion as well as making satirical comment on the attitudes and ideas of the middle and upper classes. His work appeared in magazines and books from the 1860s to the end of the century.

These drawings come from *Punch*, the humorous magazine started in 1841. Those on the left are from a series that show English society at home. *Top left:* 'An awkward incident in fashionable life.' Mrs Vavasour Belsize, thinking the reception at Brabazon Hall would take place on the ground floor, has come in a skirt of such fashionable tightness that it is impossible to mount a single step to reach the reception, which is on the first floor.
Bottom left: A musical evening with the famous new tenor, Signor Jenkini. Mrs Ponsonby de Tomkyns is determined to persuade her husband to secure him for her own musical evening in two weeks' time.

BARBAROUS TECHNICALITIES OF LAWN TENNIS.

Woolwich Cadet (suddenly, to his poor Grandmother, who has had Army on the Brain ever since he passed his Exam.). "The Service is awfully severe, by Jove! Look at Colonel Pendragon—he invariably *Shoots* or *Hangs*!"
His Poor Grandmother. "Good Heavens, Algy! I hope you won't be in *his* Regiment!"

IT'S NOT SO DIFFICULT TO SPEAK FRENCH, AFTER ALL.

Mistress (fluently). "Oh—er—Françoise, il faut que vous alliez chez le Chemist, dans High Street, pour le Gargle de Mademoiselle Maud; et chez le Toy-Shop, pour le Lawn-Tennis Bat de Monsieur Malcolm; et n'oubliez pas mon Waterproof, chez le Cleaner, vis-à-vis l'Underground Railway Station; et dites à Smithson, le Builder (dans Church Lane à côté du Publichouse, vous savez), que le Kitchen-Boiler est—est—est——"
Françoise (who has been longer in England than her new Mistress thinks). "Est Burrrst! Très bien, Madame."

Food

The feeding habits of the nation changed. During the first half of the nineteenth century the wealthy took their dinner progressively later: by the 1850s rarely before 7.30. As a result, lunch became a cooked meal served at 1 o'clock or soon after. Breakfast was then eaten earlier and consisted of only a few dishes kept hot on the side. For important parties in large houses, however, it remained an elaborate meal until the early twentieth century. Porridge, kidneys, eggs, ham, chops, cod, potted game, stewed prunes, scones, rolls, toast, bread, butter, marmalade, jam, tea, coffee, cream and milk might all be served. Mid-afternoon tea drinking became fashionable among the upper classes from the 1840s.

In addition to banquets, when a dozen or more different meat courses might be served, the wealthy consumed huge quantities of beef, mutton, venison, pheasant, salmon and trout throughout the year. Before the late nineteenth century they ate few vegetables with them. 'The Victorian upper classes came to be as fond of good food as they were of other sins of the flesh,' wrote the historian Dr J. Burnett in *Plenty and Want*. 'Probably no civilization since the Roman ate as well as they did. The achievements of modern science combined to place the delicacies of the world on the tables of the rich. In nothing was the contrast between wealth and poverty more obvious than in food.' The

A satirical view of an upper-class dinner-party. There are more servants present than guests.

184

A leisured breakfast in 1886 after father has left for the office. Sailor suits were then popular among middle-class boys.

A well-laid supper table designed by Mrs Beeton, whose *Book of Household Management*, first published in 1861, contained much advice for the middle classes on how to feed and behave.

comfortably-off middle classes ate substantially too, enjoying perhaps bacon and eggs for breakfast and a meat dish and suet or pastry pudding at most main meals. Novels about life in Victorian times often describe them tucking into solid meals. In Arnold Bennett's *Old Wives' Tale*, for instance, the family of a prosperous draper have cockles, mussels, toast and tea in the afternoon, followed by cold pork, apple pie and cheese for supper.

It is much more difficult to find out how the working classes fared in the growing towns, because their standard of living was so varied – as Engels discovered in Manchester in the 1840s:

The better-paid workers, especially those in whose families every member is able to earn something, have good food as long as this state of things lasts; meat daily, and bacon and cheese for supper. Where wages are less, meat is used only two or three times a week, and the proportion of bread and potatoes increases. Descending gradually, we find the animal food reduced to a small piece of bacon cut up with the potatoes; lower still, even this disappears, and there remains only bread, cheese, porridge and potatoes until, on the lowest round of the ladder, potatoes form the sole food.

An investigation in the 1860s which compared the weekly diets of poorly paid Derbyshire weavers, among others, with those of several hundred farm labourers, confirmed that some adults in the towns (perhaps a third) fed even worse than most farm labourers.

	weavers	farm labourers
bread	12 lb	12 lb
potatoes	4 lb	6 lb
meat (mostly bacon)	12 oz	16 oz
sugar (and treacle)	11 oz	7½ oz
fats (butter, dripping, suet)	3½ oz	5½ oz
cheese	4 oz	5½ oz
tea	½ oz	½ oz
milk	1¼ pts	1½ pts

As wages rose from the middle of the century, more town-dwellers ate boiled mutton and similar meat dishes regularly. But in London and the large towns those who sold and produced cheap food had increasingly taken the opportunity to make larger profits by adding other substances. Milk and beer were watered down, boiled potatoes mixed with flour and baked into bread, chestnut or ash leaves added to tea, sand to sugar and so on. Pure cheap food was a rarity in the leading towns by the 1850s because so much was adulterated in ways like these.

Often the adulteration was skilfully disguised. The small quantities of chalk and alum which made the bread whiter were relatively harmless, but poisonous dyes coloured inferior tea and made sweets look brighter too. Effective action was taken at last in the 1870s. By the next decade housewives could be sure that the bread, tea, sugar and so on in the shops were pure. Only beer and milk remained watered down until the early twentieth century.

In the 1880s the prices of most common foods fell by up to a third. Most people therefore enjoyed a more varied and purer diet.

The main cause was the import in huge quantities of cheap foreign wheat and meat (page 142). The early tinned meat was coarse, stringy and unappetizing, usually containing a large chunk of unpleasant-looking fat. However, it sold at half the price of most fresh meat and many families bought it happily. Soon, frozen, and later chilled, beef and mutton from Australasia and the Argentine were almost as cheap and clearly of much better quality than tinned meat. Fish was also

A bitter comment on adulterated food.

Many working-class families had no oven at home, so the local baker cooked their Christmas (or Sunday) dinner for them.

Eating ice-cream Greenwich, London, in the 1890s.

preserved in ice and so, in addition to herring, by the end of the century, a lot of cheap cod was eaten, often fried with chips.

By then most families ate meat fairly regularly – hot on Sunday, cold on Monday and rissoles from the scraps by Wednesday was a common pattern. They could also afford more eggs, fruit, vegetables and dairy produce. The price of cheese and butter fell when the factories produced them in large quantities, together with more and more jam, cakes, biscuits and chocolates. The Co-operative stores whose food was always reliably pure, and multiple grocers cut the prices of many of these foods further. In 1889 Lipton, for example, reduced his packet tea from 2/6 to 1/7 a pound. And whenever prices fell, consumption rose.

Margarine, a newly invented substitute for butter, was first imported from America and Holland in the 1870s. It was originally made from beef fat, but from the 1890s the British used more and more vegetable oil which contained fewer vitamins. At the same time the demand for ever whiter bread led millers to remove from the flour the wheat-germ with the bran. Since the germ contains most of the goodness of a grain of wheat, most white bread has given little nourishment.

By 1900 the working classes spent about 2/– to 4/– a week on food for every member of the family, while the comfortably off middle classes enjoyed between 10/– and 30/– each.

A grocery shop at Dudley in 1900.

SKINNER'S SPECIALITIES IN LADIES' TOURNURES.

PRINCESS BEATRICE.

"SKINNER's well-known Specialities are perfection."—Englishwoman's Domestic. "SKINNER's Specialities are so highly appreciated here that they are universally worn; the designs are beautiful, and I am sure will be highly appreciated by all Spanish ladies."—Spanish Review of Dress and Fashion.
SKINNER'S PRINCESS BEATRICE are entirely without steel, and are made in three qualities. No. 1. Especially suitable for walking or visiting costumes. No. 2, Slightly larger, and fitted also for occasions of demi-toilette. No. 3 is larger and suitable for promenades or garden parties. Each quality is made in white French horsehair, trimmed rose-colour; white, trimmed white; and in grey French Horsehair, trimmed silver check and dove colour.

PRINCESS COLLAPSING.

SKINNER'S PRINCESS COLLAPSING are made in fine French Horsehair, on very light steel springs, fastened at the points by a new method, which completely prevents the steel points from moving or working through the horsehair. This Tournure Improver or Bustle, or by whatever name one pleases to call it, collapses the moment it is pressed, as in sitting down, and expands when its wearer rises, thus throwing out the folds of the dress when walking or standing, and yet taking up no room when sitting down or lying upon the sofa. The sides of this elegant Tournure are flat, so as to allow the tablier ends to fold smoothly under the folds at the back of the dress. We feel sure every lady will approve of this Tournure, which lends grace and elegance to the toilette.

SKINNER's PRINCESS COLLAPSING are made in three qualities : No. 1 is especially suitable for walking or visiting costumes; No. 2 larger, more deployé, and fitted for wedding fêtes and occasions of demi-toilette; No. 3 is longer, and finished with flounces, and is especially designed for evening wear and for balls; it throws out the dress, and yet allows it to fall gracefully. Each quality is made in white French Horsehair, trimmed rose-colour; also white, trimmed white; and in grey French Horsehair, trimmed dove colour.

THE GREAT QUESTION OF JUPON AND TOURNURE.

The Tournure which has been discarded for the past few months has brought its own downfall, and proves that no exaggeration, no sudden change, can be elegant. The Tournure is now worn more than ever ; the curve is gradual from the waist ; they are much gored—en bias—down the centre of the back. Steels are run in vertically and one down each side to keep it from rising or going out of shape ; they reach just across the back only. Skinner's Tournures are especially designed for the latest fashion to slope from the waist and to throw out the dress, and yet allow it to fall gracefully ; these styles are greatly in favour with the leading élégantes, and are much sought after.

SKINNER'S DUDLEY and SUTHERLAND are great novelties; they can be made narrow or wide at any particular part, according to the option of the wearer. They are specially designed for carriage toilettes, afternoon receptions, toilette de visite, evening dresses, concert, dinner, or opera wear. SKINNER'S DUDLEY is made in Oxford and Cambridge stripes and white brilliante. SKINNER'S SUTHERLAND s

made in a pretty fancy Horsehair, trimmed dove colour, grey French trimmed dove, white trimmed white, and white trimmed rose. To be had of all respectable drapers and ladies' outfitters through the principal wholesale houses. If not in stock ladies should ask them to procure through their wholesale house, either in London, Manchester, Glasgow, Dublin, or Belfast.

DUDLEY.

SUTHERLAND.

SKINNER & CO. call ladies' special attention to their Name and Trade Mark, which is on every article ; any not having Name and Trade Mark are not genuine, but only imitations of these Celebrated Goods.
REGISTERED AND MANUFACTURED BY
SKINNER AND CO., 1, Cox's Court, and 1, Montague Place, Little Britain, London, E.C.

An advertisement in *The Queen* magazine, dated 1876, for ladies 'tournures', or improvers. Look at the pictures on the next page. Under which dresses would they have been worn?

Clothes

The rapid expansion of the cotton industry meant that people no longer had to wear mainly woollen or linen clothes. In the 1840s Engels was convinced that this had led to a change for the worse. 'The clothing of the working people of Manchester is in very bad condition,' he complained. 'Wool and linen have almost vanished from the wardrobe of both sexes and cotton has taken their place. Shirts are made of bleached or coloured cotton print goods and woollen petticoats are rarely to be seen on the washline.' Cotton clothes are not so warm as woollen ones, but Francis Place detected one of their advantages in the 1820s: 'As it was necessary to wash cotton clothes, cleanliness followed almost as a matter of course. The extension of the cotton manufacture has done all but wonders in respect to the healthiness of women.' Cotton clothes were also cheaper, and so before the end of the nineteenth century all women wore knickers and usually changed them regularly. Some cotton dresses had gay patterns too. From the 1850s people could also buy more and more ready-made clothes, but for some time they were little improvement on home-made ones.

Shoes were the biggest problem in most families. Few people had more than one pair. If they were stout and heavy, cleaned regularly and repaired about once a year, they might last for up to three years. Children often went barefoot. Many also wore boots, but they might well be little better off, according to a woman brought up in the Fens at the end of the last century.

The boots we had were all made of strong, stiff leather to last a long while and to stand up to the stony road. They got stiffer and heavier through being wet and dried quick overnight, standing on the hearth, and they chafed our heels raw. The boys had to have their boots hobnailed to make them last longer, but it made them so heavy they could hardly get one foot afore the other.

In the Lancashire cotton towns some people wore wooden clogs, which were cheaper. Both sexes usually wore long woollen stockings, knitted at home. Even as late as 1900 silk stockings cost 10/– a pair.

Fashions for the richer Victorian ladies remained as fanciful as ever and at the end of the century people could still normally tell someone's position in society by glancing at their clothes.

Working men's clothes at the turn of the century. Scarves hid the shirt worn without a collar. Everyone had a hat, and bowler hats were common.

1808

1830

Ladies' changing fashions: Such clothes kept the dress-, hat- and glove-makers very busy.

190

Above: A selection of clothes
for boys and young gentlemen.

1862

1888

191

Health

In the early nineteenth century people lived a little longer on average than their grandparents had done. By 1840 a baby could expect to live for about forty years.

We have already seen on page 99 that country-dwellers were healthier than the inhabitants of the largest towns. Those figures also showed that the wealthier classes lived significantly longer than the poorer, and that the labourers in Wiltshire, who were among the worst paid in Britain, died about five years earlier than those in Rutland.

Upper-class women often hired wet nurses to suckle their infants, but other children rarely had sufficient milk. Some whose mothers could not feed them were even silenced with a mixture of flour and water. Thus many were so weak that an attack of measles was often fatal. Furthermore, undernourished children invariably grew up into adults who were more vulnerable to other germs.

Although fifteen per cent of all infants still died before their first birthday throughout the second half of the nineteenth century, in general people's lives began to lengthen again from the 1870s. Boys who were born just before Queen Victoria died could expect to live until they were about forty-five and baby girls a few years more

A more precise way of recording this lengthening of life is to give the number of people per thousand who died every year. But the table below shows that rich and poor still did not share a common fate. In

Crude death rate per thousand

1800	about 25
1840–70	22
1900	17
(1970	11)

Comparative death rates per thousand

London mid eighteenth century	nearly 50
England and Wales 1840–70	22
large industrial towns 1840s	25–30
country areas 1840s	about 20
Liverpool 1856	30
Liverpool 1856 (worst area)	39
York 1890s (richest area)	14
York 1890s (poorest area)	28

Comparative death rates of infants per thousand

England and Wales 1840–1900	about 150
some country districts 1875	110
Liverpool 1875	220
Leeds 1875	200

his study of York, Rowntree demonstrated again how the wealthier were healthier. In 1899 thirteen-year-old boys from the poorest homes were on average 11 lb lighter and $3\frac{1}{2}$ inches shorter than those from the better-off working-class ones, while upper middle-class boys were even heavier and taller.

The gradual improvement in health towards the end of the nineteenth century was due in part to better food, clothes and housing

Gillray's cartoon of 1808 attacks the alarmist propaganda of the Anti-Vaccine Society.

Thirty-three years after Gillray's attack, in 1841, the relative merits of innoculation and vaccination were still being debated.

and to work done in cleaning up large towns (see pages 101–2). But it was also due to advances in medical knowledge and techniques.

The first of these completed the conquest of smallpox. Early in the century inoculation was replaced by a new method developed by a Gloucestershire doctor, Edward Jenner. Acting on a local belief that milkmaids who caught a mild disease called cowpox never subsequently got smallpox, he proved that those who were vaccinated artificially with cowpox were also made immune from smallpox. Vaccination therefore soon became widespread. Partly because of this lucky discovery small-pox claimed few victims in Britain after the mid nineteenth century, apart from one epidemic around 1870.

By then doctors were also being trained better and had thermometers and stethoscopes to examine patients more efficiently.

Following the work of a Frenchman, Louis Pasteur, doctors at last began to understand the real nature of diseases. When teaching chemistry, Pasteur had studied in detail the fermentation of wine and beer. He discovered that they sometimes went sour when invaded by microbes which were so small that they could be seen only under a microscope. He detected a great variety of these bacteria in the air. Some were harmful and turned cuts septic.

After studying several diseases which attacked silkworms, chicken, cows, sheep and dogs, Pasteur was eventually able to prove that each was caused by a different bacteria or germ which usually entered the animal's bloodstream. He made another even more important discovery. Not only did those animals which survived one attack of a disease rarely catch it again, but those which were injected with a weakened form of the germ also became immune. Thus, when Pasteur found ways of weakening the germs and then injected his animals with the vaccine, as it was called, he was able to immunize them from certain illnesses.

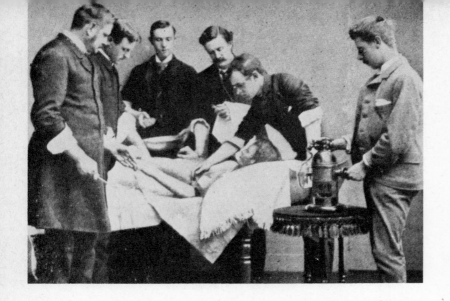

An early operation. The surgeons are wearing their everyday clothes and are not wearing masks. The machine on the right, invented by Lister, issued a spray of carbolic acid to kill infection.

From the 1880s Robert Koch and several other doctors used Pasteur's discoveries to protect people. They identified the germs of T.B., cholera, typhoid and diphtheria among others and were soon able to immunize people against them too. They did not always need a vaccine, for sometimes a few drops of blood from a person who was already immune gave sufficient protection.

Many germs, however, eluded them until later. Some, like those which caused measles, polio and flu, were so small that an ordinary microscope could not detect them. Even so, the doctors did know how most diseases were spread and so they were able to give the medical officers of health precise advice on what precautions to take. Milk, for instance, was one of the main carriers of T.B. germs and so it was made safe by Pasteur's method of killing germs in wine by heating it briefly to about 150° F.

A street 'doctor' selling patent medicines and pills at the front door.

Even though most larger towns had hospitals by 1800, people who were too ill to be looked after properly at home did not go to them automatically until the present century. The early hospitals were so crowded that they often had two patients in one bed. They were not kept very clean and usually smelled unpleasantly. Their nurses were not trained. Therefore those who entered a hospital were less likely to be cured than to catch a disease from another patient. The rich were always treated at home and many poorer people avoided hospitals if they possibly could.

Surgeons were of little use until the middle of the nineteenth century, for they could not make their patients unconscious and all operations were very painful. Then the Americans started using ether and soon after British doctors discovered that chloroform was a more satisfactory anaesthetic. One of its first uses was to deaden the pains of women in childbirth. Operations also became less rushed, but most patients' cuts still went septic. In many hospitals nearly half died from blood poisoning or gangrene until the 1870s.

Therefore, even with anaesthetics surgeons could not perform more complicated operations than amputating limbs until a Scot, Joseph Lister, showed them that they could gain from Pasteur's work on bacteria. Lister sprayed the cuts with carbolic acid to kill the germs and prevent infection. He also kept his hands and instruments as clean as possible. At first most other surgeons laughed at Lister, but so few of his patients died of blood poisoning that they eventually copied his methods. Even so, operations for appendicitis were about the most complicated performed by the end of the century.

All classes did not benefit from these medical advances. Many families could afford neither doctors' fees nor the cost of their treatment. And so working-class women, for instance, continued to have their babies at home, attended only by an experienced older woman.

Such advertisements encouraged the late Victorians to cure themselves without spending money on a doctor — but not all were equally convincing.

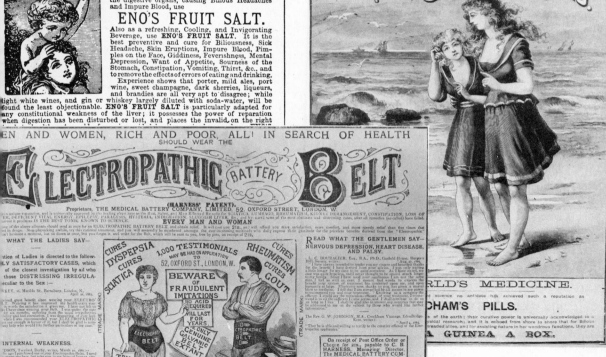

Domestic service

The health and comfort of the better-off Victorian families depended to a large extent on their servants. Twenty or more were employed in the wealthiest houses, while women whose husbands had incomes of about £500 a year could afford three full-time servants – enough to relieve them of almost all housework. The wives of most tradesmen and clerks and of some skilled workmen who earned nearly £100 a year usually had one girl for most of the heavy work, while they cooked and looked after their children themselves. Few families with lower incomes kept full-time servants, although many did employ women for particular tasks like washing.

Servants had plenty to do in houses which had neither running water nor electricity, where most rooms had a coal fire and where food was cooked on an open fire or kitchen range throughout the year. They often had to carry buckets of coal or water up steep and narrow staircases. Those leading down to the kitchen were usually the steepest of all. They were often unlit too, so that maids had to feel for the steps with their feet and still keep the tray or whatever it was they were carrying perfectly balanced. 'They build these houses as though girls wasn't human beings,' grumbled Mrs Kipps in a novel by H. G. Wells. 'Some poor girl's got to go up and down, up and down and be tired out, just because they haven't the sense to leave enough space to give their steps a proper rise. And no water anywhere – every drop got to be carried. It's houses like these wear girls out!'

Maids also emptied chamber pots, laid fires and carried away the ashes, kept the range and fireplaces clean with black lead, dusted and swept the rooms, scrubbed the floors, made the beds, polished shoes, brass and silver, and washed, darned and patched clothes. They peeled potatoes, sliced beans and washed up. When there were two servants one usually worked in the kitchen and the other in the rest of the house. The more servants, the more specialized their work became.

Most employers tried to organize their week in a strict schedule to fit in as much work as possible. Six a.m. was a normal time for a maid to get up and she was usually kept working until she went to bed at about 10 p.m. Apart from a fortnight's holiday when she could go home to see her family, she rarely had more free time than an afternoon a week and the odd hour when her mistress did not want her.

The domestic servant in Arnold Bennett's *The Old Wives' Tale* 'lived seventeen hours of each day in an underground kitchen and larder, and the other seven in an attic, never going out except to chapel on Sunday evenings, and once a month on Thursday afternoons. On rare occasions an aunt was permitted as a tremendous favour to see her in the subterranean den. Everybody, including herself, considered that she had a good place and was well treated.'

Servants sought employment from the readers of *The Times*. These advertisements appeared in 1854.

A group of servants from a large household in the 1880s.

Underground kitchens were usual. They were often very gloomy because they had few windows. They rarely had more furniture than a table, a few wooden chairs and the odd cupboard. The kitchen was at least warm, unlike a maid's bedroom which was usually in an attic and was often icy cold in winter. 'The places in which some maids are asked to sleep are a disgrace to civilization,' declared the *Woman's Book* early in the twentieth century. 'Underground bedrooms, besides being dark and airless, are sometimes damp and insanitary as well.' Servants often ate plainer food than the rest of the family and many employers kept the tea, sugar, butter and so on locked up so that the servants could not help themselves when their backs were turned. Life was especially lonely and dreary for those who worked alone.

Conditions of work, of course, varied considerably in different houses, depending on the layout, number of other servants and the employer's wealth. But the mistress's personality probably affected them most of all. Some were kind and helpful, treating the young maids almost as if they were their own daughters. Others, however, were very strict and bossy, keeping them occupied with all sorts of jobs and complaining whenever they slipped up. A maid's chances of obtaining another situation depended on a good reference from her previous employer, and so she could rarely afford to risk offending her by saying what she thought of her treatment.

The daughters of most ordinary labourers began as single general servants or maids of all work. By the later nineteenth century they rarely started before they were twelve, when their usual wage was about £8 to £10 a year. If their employer took the trouble to train them well they stood a better chance of promotion later. They usually obtained their situation through personal contacts or perhaps advertisements in a newspaper or shop window.

Girls generally preferred to work in big houses, where they had more companions and men from the stables and gardens with whom they could mix and relax. They were probably treated better, paid more and might also receive some of their mistress's cast-off clothes. If their master's family was of some importance they were also more likely to take a pride and interest in its affairs.

They also had a chance of promotion. Young girls who started as scullery maids soon discovered that there were many rigid distinctions of rank between the different servants. Everyone was their senior and it would take them years to work their way up through under and upper kitchen maid to even the lowest grade of cook. In the main part of the house there were often several types of housemaid below the housekeeper and lady's maid. The housekeeper was paid about the same as a cook – perhaps £50 a year. Few, however, reached the top. As soon as they married they stopped work.

By the end of the nineteenth century one girl in every three between the ages of fifteen and twenty was a domestic servant. Altogether there were over one and a half million.

Kitchen-maids, from a children's counting book of 1860.

Cleaning windows and scrubbing steps at a Domestic Economy school in 1908.

Victorian women

Most domestic servants were female and this fact reflects the low status of women in the nineteenth century.

Children soon became aware that they were being brought up in a man's world. Their father was the head of their family. They carried his name and their position in the world depended entirely on his job and wealth. His duty was to provide them with enough to live on and to punish them when they misbehaved.

Their mother alone was responsible for running the home, feeding, clothing and cherishing all the family. Everything a wife owned, even her clothes, and the money she earned were legally her husband's property. In practice she was almost as much under his control as she had been earlier under her father. She was also expected to obey his commands. Even if he beat her she could do little to prevent him. Most people accepted without question St Paul's description of the relationship between the two: 'Wives submit yourselves unto your husbands, as unto the Lord. For the husband is the head of the wife, even as Christ is the head of the Church. Therefore as the Church is subject unto Christ, so let the wives be to their own husbands in everything.'

Upper-class women were normally fully occupied supervising a houseful of servants, arranging dinner parties and entertainments, writing letters to their relations, walking, riding, breeding dogs and so on. They never took jobs outside their homes. And neither did women in middle-class families who could afford not to. As one who lived to be

An early typewriter, 1867.

Women at work in a telegraph exchange in 1871.
Such machinery provided more and more women with the chance to work outside their homes in the late nineteenth century.

a hundred explained: 'Papa, as a true Victorian gentleman, felt it was rather a slur on him that a lady of the family should go out to work; ladies should live on an adequate income supplied by father, husband or son.'

Such women never became politicians, lawyers, doctors or clergymen, like their brothers, nor did they often help with running the family business. Indeed by the second half of the nineteenth century subjects like politics, finance and sex were generally considered too difficult or too unsuitable for women, and gentlemen were taught not to discuss them in their presence. Thus ladies rarely had a thorough education. Instead most learnt to embroider, to play the piano, dance and draw. Restrictions on their behaviour included not smoking in the presence of others and taking extreme care over how they dressed. In the 1890s, for example: 'One of our governesses, thinking to be very modern and dashing, once ordered a new skirt, which cleared the ground by quite two inches. But when it came she was too bashful to wear it. For, of course, ankles ought never to be seen at all, and, if they were, the lady they belonged to was not quite a nice lady.'

The young sometimes found this attitude puzzling. In 1892 a girl wrote:

Why do old people always disapprove of anything which they didn't do when they were young? Two ladies — or, as Grandpapa says, two shameless females — in bloomers bicycled through the village yesterday, and some of the women were so scandalized that they threw stones at them. I didn't dare say so, but I thought that they looked very neat, though I don't think I should like to show my own legs to the world like that. Still, it's all a question of what one is accustomed to.

Most people put a high value on 'respectable' behaviour. Older women or chaperons accompanied the younger ones in the evenings to ensure that they behaved respectably. They had to remain above reproach while waiting for an eligible bachelor to propose marriage.

Until recently there were fewer men than women, so that while about ten per cent of the men who grew up in the nineteenth century never married, nearer fifteen per cent of the women remained spinsters. Then, as now, husbands nearly always married wives a few years younger than themselves, yet few women married in their teens. Most couples started a family quite soon after marriage. Indeed, in the nineteenth century over a third of the brides were pregnant by their wedding day (and about one baby in twenty was born out of wedlock). When one partner died leaving the other with a family of young children, widowers usually married again quite quickly, but widows found it more difficult to attract another husband.

Few marriages ended in divorce because before the 1850s it cost at least several hundred pounds. Thus only the wealthiest couples could

A 'Scorcher' showing herself off, a pin-up picture of 1897.

A wringing and mangling machine eased the burden on washing day.

afford to be parted by anything but death. Then the cost was reduced to about £50, but the law continued to favour men blatantly. If a husband could prove that his wife had committed adultery once, for example, he could obtain a divorce, but even if he lived openly with a mistress she could not divorce him. A wife had to prove that he had either been cruel to her as well, or deserted her for at least two years, before she could win her freedom.

These conditions for women began to change in the later nineteenth century, when several Acts of Parliament strengthened a married woman's legal rights. Some, of which the most important was passed in 1882, enabled her to keep control of all her property when she married. At the same time many of the younger husbands whose wives had no servants started to give them some help about the house by carrying, for instance, buckets of coal or water. In addition, as standards of living rose, not quite so many wives had to pinch and scrape all the time, spinning out every penny, cooking none but the cheapest meals and darning and patching all the family's clothes. Since more women were illiterate at the start of the nineteenth century they gained more than men in at least one important respect from the improvement in education (see page 169).

But all these changes did not come about of their own accord. Some women struggled very hard to hasten notable advances.

The arguments that women were unsuited to the world of politics was undermined by the suffragettes. Here, one puts the case for votes for women in Trafalgar Square in 1908. (They were given the vote in 1918, see p. 304.)

Amusements

Before the twentieth century, most working-class homes were much too small and plain for anything but eating, sleeping and working. The adults went elsewhere for most of their amusements, like drinking, singing and playing in brass bands.

Only families with servants could relax in their own homes. The better-off invited their friends in for dinner parties and dances. A pianist usually provided the music, sometimes accompanied by a violinist or cornet player. The lower middle classes entertained their friends to supper parties, when they might act charades or play various card and other games, like forfeits. They also read novels and the women frequently passed the time with embroidery and fine needlework.

The picture opposite shows some of the toys of children born into families that were comfortably off. Hide-and-seek was also great fun in large and well-furnished houses. The sons and daughters of traders, clerks and skilled workmen enjoyed some of these pleasures, but not so many. Children from ordinary working-class homes usually had to make do with dolls made of rags and blackbirds or starlings as pets. Many could not even afford marbles and so played with chestnuts instead. They also played games like hop-scotch which needed no equipment. These appealed most to girls, who often chanted simple rhymes as they played. In north Oxfordshire, for example:

Prince Albert with the royal Christmas tree in 1848.

A pretty, graceful game to watch was 'Thread the Tailor's Needle'. For this two girls joined hands and elevated them to form an arch or bridge, and the other players, in single file and holding on to each other's skirts, passed under, singing:

> Thread the tailor's needle,
> Thread the tailor's needle.
> The tailor's blind and he can't see,
> So thread the tailor's needle.

As the end of the file passed under the arch the last two girls detached themselves, took up their stand by the original two and joined their hands and elevated them, thus widening the arch, and this was repeated until the arch became a tunnel. As the file passing under grew shorter, the tune was quickened, until, towards the end, the game became a merry whirl.

From about the 1840s Christmas festivities in England began to change noticeably. German merchants who settled in towns like Manchester and Bradford introduced the custom of bringing into the house a fir tree, which they covered with candles, decorations and presents. Queen Victoria's German husband also helped popularize the Christmas tree. Christmas cards appeared soon after the penny post. People sent them to their special friends and distant relatives from about the 1860s.

Blindman's Buff in a Victorian drawing room.

Snow scenes made attractive pictures and so these cards spread the romantic idea that Christmas should be white. It was strengthened from the 1870s as carols like 'Good King Wenceslas' became increasingly popular.

The tradition of eating turkey was established even later in the century. So was the widespread giving of presents. Although people in some European countries had long believed that St Nicholas gave gifts to good children on his feast day, 6 December, the Americans invented a jolly Santa Claus with a red robe and a white beard, who distributed presents on Christmas Day.

Much entertainment could also be found outside the home. In the larger towns the better-off attended plays and concerts, and by the middle of the nineteenth century most smaller towns also held varied

Mummers acting a traditional story at Christmas time.

St Giles Fair, Oxford in 1885.
Travelling shows attracted
their audiences by troupes of
performing dogs and monkeys,
marionettes and other side-
shows. At the turn of the
century a new feature was
added – the cinema.

entertainments, which included lectures, readings of prose and poetry, comic and serious songs and short melodramas.

The towns were visited by travelling circuses which performed inside tents. In a ring in the centre the animals executed their tricks, like picking out the biggest rogue in the audience. Acrobats walked along tight-ropes or stood on two moving horses at the same time. Clowns added to the popularity of these circuses in the later nineteenth century. So did the side-shows in which people saw puppets, rare animals in cages and freaks like dwarfs.

And yet, drink remained the main recreation of most poorer men. It was the easiest means of forgetting their cares, at least for a while. In the second half of the nineteenth century the average annual consumption of beer was about thirty gallons per head. Most public houses and working men's clubs were very plain and unattractive places. To attract more customers and to keep them longer, especially on Saturday nights, some landlords engaged acrobats, clowns and dancers. Nearly all these performers also sang and acted many songs, usually with attractive tunes and a chorus for the drinkers.

These entertainments became so popular from the 1850s that some landlords in London and other large towns built large halls beside their pubs to accommodate all their patrons. From the 1870s these music halls were built like theatres, and rather than present a

205

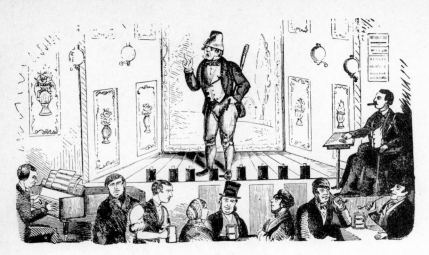

From small beginnings the music halls blossomed into entertaining and exciting spectacles. Union Street, Southwark, 1859.

Part of a poster advertising the exploits of Leotard, 'the man on the flying trapeze', at the Alhambra Palace, Leicester Square, London, 1860.

continuous run of different turns throughout the evening, they started giving two set programmes every night. Some songs were sung by women dressed as men or by men impersonating women. Songs in which the audience joined remained one of the main attractions and a vast number were written specially for the music halls. In this one the chorus revealed the identity of the solo singer:

You don't know who you're looking at; now take a look at me!
I'm a bit of a nob, I am — belong to royaltee. . .

chorus: I'm Henery the Eighth, I am!
Henery the Eighth, I am, I am!
I got married to the widow next door,
She's been married seven times before.
Ev'ry one was a Henery —
She wouldn't have a Willie or a Sam.
I'm her eighth old man named Henery,
Henery the Eighth I am!

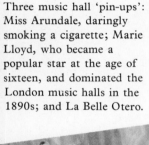

Three music hall 'pin-ups': Miss Arundale, daringly smoking a cigarette; Marie Lloyd, who became a popular star at the age of sixteen, and dominated the London music halls in the 1890s; and La Belle Otero.

Others included: 'Pack up Your Troubles in Your Old Kit Bag', 'All the Nice Girls love a Sailor' and 'She was Poor but she was Honest'.

The words of many songs were coarse or suggestive and the performers' jokes were often dirty. But audiences revelled in them and

Street entertainment in the 1890s. Pavement quartet. Monkeys on a barrel organ. Gipsies with a travelling bear.

even shouted abuse or threw missiles at those they disliked. Nevertheless sports were becoming less violent. By the 1860s, when it was made illegal, prize-fighting had been in decline for a generation. Then the Marquis of Queensberry's rules transformed it into modern boxing. Cock-fighting disappeared at about the same time, but bull-baiting and fighting with cudgels had been suppressed about thirty years earlier, when the number of special festivals also began to decline. They disrupted the regular pattern required for industrial work. These sports were all exciting to watch, but they were also cruel. In the second half of the nineteenth century they were replaced at village fairs by harmless races in sacks or with eggs in spoons, bowling for pigs and cheese and so on. But other sports were developed for the regular entertainment of the town dwellers.

Children improvise their own games round a gas lamp.

Games

Originally football was a rough and unorganized game played on village greens, but the public schools changed it in the mid nineteenth century. There the older boys gradually imposed more rules on their disorganized playground scrambles and so football became more ordered and skilful. Most made it illegal to trip an opponent and to handle the ball. They also limited the number of players who could take part. Rugby started to follow this example, but then allowed their players to run holding the ball in the 1840s. Some schools like Marlborough also adopted Rugby's rules, but most continued to play according to their own rules for another generation or more. However, this made it almost impossible for the schools to play matches against each other or for old boys from different schools to play together when they went up to the same university or lived in the same city.

By the 1860s standardized rules had become essential, but attempts to reach a compromise failed. Two different games therefore emerged eventually. In soccer the ball was moved towards the goal by dribbling, but in Rugby handling and tripping were permitted, although iron-tipped boots had been banned. The number of players was reduced first to twenty and finally to fifteen, but Rugby remained a very rough game until the 1880s at least. Then referees started to control the matches. They began to penalize those who tripped or seized an opponent by his throat and so the players had to resort to tackling each other round their legs as they do today. Rugby remained a very dull game to watch because there was very little passing. Most of the time was taken up in scrummages in which the two sides shoved against each other while trying to hack the ball forward. These forwards did not begin to pass it back between their legs until some time later.

Football at Kingston-upon-Thames in 1846. On feast days, like Shrove Tuesday, matches were often played between neighbouring towns or villages and all who wanted to joined in. Handling, kicking and pushing were part of the game, which usually continued until one side scored a goal.

There was much more movement in soccer, which had developed more towards its modern form by 1871 when the game was played between eleven players (one of whom could handle to protect the goal) and play lasted for ninety minutes. 1871 was the year in which the F.A. Cup competition was started and until the 1880s teams of ex-public school boys dominated it almost entirely.

Then at last football was affected profoundly by the growth of towns. There boys had usually played rough-and-ready games on waste patches of ground or in side streets, but they had rarely played organized football on proper pitches. Even the playgrounds of most elementary schools were too small for football. Furthermore Sunday was the only day of rest for most working men until the later nineteenth century, but rigid observance of the Lord's Day prevented them from playing organized games on Sundays.

From the 1870s, however, local clergymen and other well-intentioned Victorians founded many football clubs for working-class lads in the towns. Some, like Everton and Aston Villa, were formed originally to help keep the members of a congregation or Sunday school out of mischief on a Saturday afternoon. Southampton's connection with its local parish church, St Mary's, is perpetuated in its nickname of the Saints. Arsenal, West Ham, Manchester City and other clubs were formed towards the end of the century for the employees of one works or factory. The number of clubs attached to the Football Association rose very rapidly (from fifty in 1871 to 10,000 in 1905) and many more played rugby too.

The Aston Villa team posing for a photograph in 1887, the year in which they first won the FA Challenge Cup.

The two main reasons for this great development were that more and more workers were not working on Saturday afternoons (page 81). Higher wages also enabled them to pay something for their entertainment.

Many did not want to play football; they were quite happy to watch. And so by the end of the century they flocked in their thousands to see Saturday football matches throughout the winter. The numbers attending the Cup Final show how rapidly the game became popular. In 1881 there were 4000, and in 1901, 111,000.

The Football League was founded in 1888 to give more point to the regular Saturday matches of the leading teams. At first only twelve clubs from Lancashire and the midlands took part, but others from all over the country joined soon after. Leagues for less skilful teams were also formed later. Since the spectators paid for admission they enabled more clubs to pay their players. These professionals then had more time to practise and so they became fitter and more skilled than all but the outstanding amateurs, who therefore formed their own separate competitions early in the twentieth century.

Soccer was a fast-moving and exciting game to watch, but rugby provided spectators with few thrills. Nevertheless robust and healthy men enjoyed the everlasting scrummages and in the industrial parts of Wales, Lancashire and Yorkshire all sections of the community took it up enthusiastically. Elsewhere rugby remained almost exclusively an ex-public school sport. The men who controlled it refused to let clubs pay their players and so in the 1890s the northern clubs broke away and founded what later became the Rugby League. It permitted professional players, reduced their number to thirteen and altered the laws in other ways to encourage more passing and so make the game more attractive to watch. Like the leading soccer clubs, the Rugby League clubs then played competitive matches throughout the winter, cheered on by masses of regular supporters. Between them these two forms of football provided almost ideal entertainment for the men of the crowded industrial towns.

Outside Wales, rugby union remained almost entirely a middle-class game in which competitions were rarely held. Even when the laws were changed to open up the game, only the international matches attracted large crowds.

Cricket also 'came of age' in Victorian times. Batting improved considerably early in the nineteenth century and so some bowlers resorted to delivering the ball with their arm at shoulder level. Later they raised it even higher so that by about the 1860s overarm bowling had become quite general. Boundaries were also introduced by then and batsmen were protecting themselves with thin pads and gloves.

Cricket became increasingly popular from the middle of the nineteenth century when matches were played regularly between a number of counties, although the county championship was not organized until 1873. Many leading players in these teams, of whom a Bristol doctor called W. G. Grace was the most outstanding, were sons of landowners or of the prosperous middle classes. Nearly all had learned to play at their public schools, where it became very popular in the second half of the nineteenth century, and many had then gone on to Oxford or Cambridge.

Thousands of cricket clubs were established in all the industrial towns in the later nineteenth century and then many local leagues were formed for them to compete against each other on Saturdays. Outside Scotland, cricket became the undisputed national summer game in both town and country until at least the middle of the present century. Few players were paid, but the newspapers reported the county championship matches in full and news of a Test Match held people from every social class spellbound.

The other sports which the wealthy Victorians created did not become nearly so popular. For long they were played almost exclusively by the middle classes who had enough money and free time.

Golf was confined almost entirely to Scotland a hundred years ago. Then some of the wealthier English middle classes took it up. Courses

Dr W. G. Grace (1848–1915) played in his first important cricket match at the age of fifteen, and by the time he retired forty-five years later had helped turn the game into a national institution.

By modern standards Victorian golf courses were rather rough.

were first created for them by the seaside. Later they appeared inland on the outskirts of towns. It was an expensive game, partly because it needed so much land, but many successful men in business and the professions as well as politicians were quite happy to pay the high subscriptions of their clubs.

Rowing was organized on competitive lines at Oxford and Cambridge in the first half of the nineteenth century. Since the 1850s their annual race has been one of the main highlights of the year for all rowing enthusiasts. Otherwise, until the present century, rowing was confined almost entirely to a few public schools like Eton and Westminster which were sited near substantial rivers. Only those who were not 'by trade or employment a mechanic, artisan or labourer' were allowed to compete in the other principal rowing attraction – the Henley Regatta.

The Greeks had held athletic competitions well over 2000 years ago and, as far as we know, races had been run over long distances even earlier, but the modern form of athletics is little more than a hundred years old. It developed from a meeting at Oxford in 1850 when racing over hurdles was revived. However, few people took athletics very seriously before the present century, even though the public schools regularly organized large-scale cross-country runs and steeple-chases.

Henley Regatta at the end of the century.

Two other games became much more popular with the middle classes, partly because they could play them in their own gardens. These were croquet and lawn tennis (see the picture on page 183).

The Victorian middle classes developed even more games. Like hockey, the majority were played in teams. Betting was prohibited and the players were usually expected not to want to win, but only to enjoy the game. In the 1908 Olympics, for instance, when a Dutch rowing crew bumped into the side of the course their British opponents waited for them to continue the race.

The Olympic Games had been revived in 1860 and soon played the leading role in giving athletics a world-wide appeal. Rather than invent their own, most other industrial countries took up some, at least, of the sports devised by the British town-dwellers and wealthier

Croquet was one of the few games which Victorian women could play on equal terms with men. At first they played with very wide hoops.

A ladies' hockey match in the 1860s.

A penny-farthing bicycle race organized by Colchester Cycling Club in 1886. At first cycles were used only for racing and recreation, but after the safety bicycle appeared in the 1880s with a brake, a chain and pneumatic tyres, people began to ride them to work and to the shops, although they still used them for fun (see p. 200).

middle classes. Association football, for example, spread first to Europe in the later nineteenth century. Then the South American countries and other less-developed nations adopted it with enthusiasm and it eventually became the world's leading game. Only in the USA did it make little headway. There some colleges took up Rugby, but they soon changed the rules and American football turned into quite a different game. Rugby and cricket were established mainly in those countries like Australia and South Africa where the British settled. Instead of cricket, the USA adopted another English game, baseball (which they claimed later to have invented). Tennis and golf quickly became more popular in the USA than in Britain, where most people could not afford the equipment or the clothes required for such games.

The age of optimism

Their great material progress left many Victorians believing that the world was becoming automatically a better and better place. As Charles Darwin concluded, after expounding the theory of evolution: 'As natural selection works solely by and for the good of each being, all environments will tend to progress towards perfection.' By then most white-collar workers enjoyed a week or two's holiday which they often spent at the seaside. Working-class families had to rest content with day trips to the sea.

But all did not wait for perfection to come unaided. Reports of, for instance, semi-clothed men and women sleeping and working together in crowded rooms did shock some wealthy Christians into campaigning to improve their conditions. At the same time criminals were treated more humanely and townspeople in particular condemned cruelty towards animals.

Progress also brought its shocks, as the Reverend F. Kilvert was disgusted to find when on holiday in the Isle of Wight in the 1870s:

'At Shanklin one has to adopt the detestable custom of bathing in drawers. If ladies don't like to see men naked why don't they keep away from the sight?' But his was a losing battle. By then public opinion was committed to universal respectability.

The beach at Yarmouth in 1890. Only hands and some faces are exposed to the sun.

Wealthy business and professional men who longed to be accepted as the equals of landowners in the nineteenth century usually sent their sons to public schools, but often their wives were more affected by a craving for respect. Some therefore drew attention to their wealthy relatives' possessions at every opportunity, like this parson's wife in Jane Austen's *Emma*, who wanted everyone to know that they owned more than one carriage:

My brother and sister have promised us a visit in the spring or summer and that will be our time for exploring. They will have their barouche-landau, of course, which holds four perfectly. They would hardly come in their chaise, I think, at that season of the year. Indeed, when the time draws on I shall decidedly recommend their bringing the barouche-landau; it will be so very much preferable.

The rapid growth of trade and industry in the nineteenth century left more and more who could not aspire to being taken for ladies and gentlemen feeling that they were entitled to respect. Few clerks, shopkeepers, engineers or craftsmen could impress others with their material possessions, yet most were aware of their own importance. They therefore tended to tell others about their virtues: they worked hard and long, saved their money, did not drink and so on. Stories, like this one, about two bankrupt farmers who became printers, implied that the less successful were less virtuous:

They commended themselves to their employers by their diligence, sobriety and strict integrity. They plodded on, rising from one station to another, until at length the two men themselves became employers, and after many long years of industry, enterprise and benevolence, they became rich, honoured and respected by all who knew them. Out of their abundant wealth they gave liberally to all worthy objects, erecting churches, founding schools, and in all ways promoting the well-being of the class of working men from which they had sprung.

People were constantly encouraged to stand on their own feet, backed up by proverbs like: 'Heaven helps those who help themselves.'

Such were the fundamental if somewhat conflicting virtues of the Victorian Age.

The 'Age of Optimism', generated by the splendour of the British Empire, is reflected in tableau form.

Part 3 The twentieth century

Introduction

Tuesday, 1 January 1901, was no ordinary New Year's Day, because it heralded the dawn of a new century. Then, three weeks later, the old queen died and with her passing came a new king, her son Edward VII. But was this new era really so different from the old one? And had not the twentieth century, perhaps, begun already in 1900, as some contemporaries thought?

Whichever day they should have celebrated matters little to us now. But we must take care not to overstress the importance of the line which divides the two centuries. Eventually the twentieth century took on a character all of its own and those who survived had to adapt themselves to a style of life that was increasingly unfamiliar – but only eventually. For a whole decade the Edwardians lived out their lives in a pattern very similar to the one they had known as Victorians. And not until Europe was engulfed by the First World War (1914–18) did many Britons become aware that time could not stand still.

Therefore a book which describes the principal changes in how people lived cannot end one section neatly in 1900 and start the next in 1901. Already we have followed into the early twentieth century some developments, like the expansion of industry. Soon we shall be glancing back to others, like electricity and the motor car, which began under Queen Victoria, but at the time affected only a minority of her subjects.

The move to the towns, by far the most important of all nineteenth-century changes, was over by 1910. Since then about one Briton in five has continued to live in the countryside. After 1910 the very rapid rate at which the population had been growing slowed down markedly. But in most other ways the transformation of life continued. Our standard of living, for example, has gone on rising during the present century and so has the expansion of education and the improvement of medical knowledge. And they came either along lines familiar to the Victorians or else built directly upon their advances.

At first sight some other recent changes, like the development of the welfare services and the reduction in the gulf separating rich and poor, appear to belong entirely to the twentieth century. But on closer examination they were made possible only by earlier developments and so are really their delayed results. Thus, although by the end of the nineteenth century society had been transformed only in part, there is clearly a danger that we might, on the other hand, exaggerate the extent to which subsequent changes have altered people's lives. And so anyone who wants to understand why we live the way we do now should have turned first to the nineteenth century for most of the explanations, before learning about more recent times.

The visual record of this century is photographic. The range and advantages of this over drawing and painting used by magazines and newspapers in the last century are obvious. As well as people and events being instantly recorded by the camera and relayed through television to every home, the camera is available for everyone to record their own lives.

George Eastman introduced his first Kodak camera in 1888 with the slogan 'You press the button – we do the rest.' The camera was factory-loaded with film and had to be returned for processing and reloading. In 1899 he introduced film which the amateur could process and make prints. Prospective buyers of Kodak cameras were informed, 'a collection of these pictures may be made to furnish a pictorial history of life as it is lived by the owner, that will grow more valuable every day that passes'.

This is still true. A great deal of information as well as amusement can be got from the family photo album. These photographs all come from such a collection. They show: the wedding in 1926; the family house being built; a trip into the country (the early motorist could not rely on finding a garage and carried petrol with him); an airport in 1927 (even London Airport once looked like this); a 'modern' pram in 1935.

Chapter 9
Industry and agriculture since 1910

The changing pattern of industry

The development of electricity has played a leading role in the continuing changes in British industry in this century. Vital though the steam engine was, it had several disadvantages. For instance it had to be used where the power was wanted, coal was a bulky fuel and it took time to get the steam up. Electricity had none of these snags, but it took a long time to adapt it for industrial use.

As long ago as the eighteenth century some scientists had known that lightning was an electrical force which gave off light and could be conducted through metals. But, even though they discovered how to store electricity in batteries, they found no practical use for it until the 1830s. Then they discovered how to send messages along telegraph wires with electricity.

In the 1830s they discovered also that electricity could be produced by moving a magnet rapidly inside a coil of wire. However, it took many inventors another fifty years to generate large quantities of electricity, transform it to over 100,000 volts so that it could be conducted long distances along copper wires and then step it down to about 200 volts to drive electric motors safely.

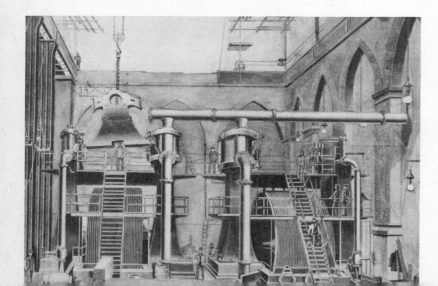

A Victorian power station being built.

Many more uses were devised for it in the later nineteenth century, especially in the USA. They included telephones, electric lighting, carpet cleaners, hot-plates, motors for driving trains and trams and small machines in factories.

Without fast-flowing rivers the British could not make electricity cheaply. They therefore generated most of theirs from coal by steam engines, and until later developments cut its price they used it mostly for lighting. The steam turbine, which rotated continuously like a windmill, was much faster and more efficient than a piston engine. Since the larger power stations produced much cheaper electricity, the country gained when most of the smaller ones were closed in the 1930s. At the same time the remaining stations were linked together with a network of cables, known as the National Grid, so that extra power could be sent to most places in Britain.

By the 1930s the cost of electricity in Britain had fallen by nine-tenths since 1900, and improved motors and equipment made further savings. In industry electric motors at last replaced steam engines as the main source of power. They were not only smaller and cleaner but were also available at the flick of a switch. The amount of electricity consumed in Britain has risen very rapidly.

The rotor blades of a large steam turbine used for generating electricity.

In the nineteenth century large quantities of gas were made quite easily from coal when it was turned into coke. It was therefore used widely to light streets. The main problem was that the holders in which it was stored and the pipes which carried it tended to leak. Later, when it became safer, it was piped into some houses — first for lighting and then for cooking and heating.

Subsequent improvements in the making and using of gas in the twentieth century have enabled some large factories to drive their machines with gas, but in general it has not become a major source of power for industry. From the 1960s, however, the exploitation of natural gas from the bed of the North Sea began to alter this.

The figures opposite reveal the fortunes of the major nineteenth-century industries during the present century.

The triumph of electricity over steam explains most of the reduced output of coal, even though coal also made much gas and electricity. Most pits have installed electrically driven machinery for cutting and moving coal during the present century, but many seams were so narrow that they were unable to take full advantage of it. Countries like the USA with considerably larger seams could therefore mine coal more cheaply.

By the 1930s Britain's share of the world's export of cotton goods had fallen from a half to a quarter in less than twenty-five years.

An early gasworks. A retort in the building was stoked with coal to produce the gas, which was then stored in the gasometer on the left.

Industry in the twentieth century

coal mined

1910   260 m tons
1938   230 m tons
1966   175 m tons

cotton cloth made

1910   7500 m sq. yds
1938   3500 m sq. yds
1966   1000 m sq. yds

224

Butane gas stored in pressurized containers, in Kent, 1957. High pressure ensures that the gas remains as liquid, which takes up less space than in its gaseous state.

wool and worsted made

1910	700 m sq. yds
1938	475 m sq. yds
1966	300 m sq. yds

ships built (3 yr av.)

1910	1·3 m tons
1938	0·8 m ton
1966	1 m tons

steel produced

1910	6⅓ m tons
1938	11 m tons
1966	25 m tons

The Lancashire mills were equipped with many out-of-date machines, while their chief rivals, the Japanese and Indians, not only installed more automatic looms and mules but also paid their workers lower wages.

In contrast the woollen industry declined more slowly. This was partly because Britain exported fewer woollens, which were also more difficult to mass produce than cotton. The output of some products, like carpets, even grew. From the 1950s wool also suffered less from the large-scale use of man-made fibres. Terylene is normally mixed with wool, but nylon, for example, began to replace cotton, which therefore slumped faster. Clothing made from these materials usually wears longer, costs less, dries more quickly and does not crease so easily.

Shipbuilding suffered most from the collapse of world trade in the 1930s (see page 246). However, it does not explain why Britain was building only ten per cent of the world's merchant shipping in the 1960s compared with sixty per cent in 1910. While the British shipbuilders kept to their well-tried ways, the Japanese and Germans in particular tended to use larger shipyards, equipped with modern cranes and pneumatic and electrically driven tools. They could therefore build oil-burning ships and large tankers more cheaply. The British employers had more troubles with their workmen and had to pay more for their steel.

225

Steel-making flourished in wartime, but between the wars the industry changed slowly. Since Britain was heavily committed to producing acid steel from non-phosphorous iron ore, it was expensive to turn to basic steel-making. Most British steelworks were smaller and rather scattered so that much iron ore and coal had to be transported. Some important centres like Sheffield and Ebbw Vale were also handicapped by being away from the sea. Not until the 1940s did Britain begin to follow Russia and the USA in building large modern plants. Most of the pioneering work in making specially tough steel was done abroad. It was alloyed with small quantities of other metals, like nickel, in very hot electric furnaces. Despite considerable progress, by the 1960s Britain had fallen to the position of the world's fifth largest steel producer.

Many new industries have also grown up in Britain, of which motor manufacture is the most important. It developed from bicycle-making around Coventry and Birmingham early in the present century and spread later to other parts of the midlands. At first many firms made the vehicles singly or in small batches, constructing most parts by hand. By the 1920s, however, most British cars were mass produced by six main firms. Led by William Morris, they had adopted the American system of making them in large quantities from standard parts, most of which were produced by smaller specialist firms.

The motor-body shop of William Morris of Oxford in 1913. Each car is assembled separately, employing techniques resembling those used in a nineteenth-century coachbuilding workshop.

Cars and commercial vehicles
produced in Britain

1910	15,000
1938	450,000
1966	2,000,000

Morris Eights being produced
in 1946. The assembly line
has greatly speeded production
as each man adds one new
part to every car.

As the demand for motor vehicles built up they were assembled on a conveyor belt which moved across the factory floor. From the 1950s some parts were both made and assembled by very expensive machines, which were controlled by computers. The equipment which made the Ford Anglia, for example, cost over seven million pounds. In the early 1960s the Mini was made from 14,000 different parts supplied by 4000 firms. By then, its makers, Morris and Austin, had joined to form the British Motor Corporation, which subsequently expanded into British Leyland. This firm and Ford now make about three-quarters of all British cars. And yet, impressively though the motor industry has grown in Britain, recently it has expanded even more quickly in Germany, France and Japan.

At first many small firms also assembled aeroplanes, receiving their engines and other components from firms like Rolls-Royce. The aircraft industry flourished most from the 1930s, when its demands for electrical equipment, rubber and petrol stimulated further other new industries which had already grown with the motor car. Most aeroplanes were made from aluminium, which is a very light and tough metal. Because it could not be extracted from bauxite clay without electricity, large quantities were not available before the twentieth century. Other uses were soon found for aluminium because it conducts electricity well. By the 1960s, however, the British aircraft industry had run

into serious difficulties, partly because the Americans found it easier to sell more of these very complex machines at a lower price. In an attempt to solve its problems it then started to cooperate with the French.

Electrical engineering also expanded very rapidly in the 1930s to meet the demand for generators, cables, light bulbs, radios, cookers and so on. Since then this trend has continued, partly as the result of new developments like the computer. By the early 1960s it produced three million radios, one and a half million television sets and one million washing machines every year as well as many other appliances. However, Britain exported very little because Japan made better transistor radios, for example, more cheaply.

Innumerable other machines and equipment are now made. The chemical industry, for instance, produces medicines, soap, dyes and paints in growing quantities. It has also developed plastics. In the 1930s Britain only produced brittle bakelite, but by the 1950s her chemists made plastics which did not break and resisted higher temperatures. By the early 1960s (when two-thirds of a million tons were made annually) plastics had become even more indestructible. Now they are often used as cheap substitutes for iron, wood or leather.

The milling of flour, making of clothes, boots and shoes, and other important industries have developed from mechanical inventions made or applied in the last twenty years of the nineteenth century. Since then factories have also produced cakes, biscuits, jam, chocolates, tinned fruit and vegetables, and cigarettes in increasing quantities. Since the machinery in these lighter industries has usually been driven by electricity, they have not had to operate near the coal-fields.

Britain now has a very complex and constantly changing economy.

Census of production
(net output) 1968

	£m
engineering	6,70
construction	2,85
food/drink/tobacco	2,00
textiles/leather/clothing	1,70
gas/electricity/water	1,55
chemicals	1,50
metals	1,10
mining	75
others	3,00
	21,15
agriculture	90

Compare with 1907 on page 71.

The first vacuum cleaner produced in 1900 looks similar to a modern one. Few rich households then really needed a vacuum cleaner as this work was done by servants. Today, with mass-production technique, approximately 85 per cent of homes have a vacuum cleaner.

This could be the control panel of a missile base or a rocket station. It is, in fact, the 'process control area' of a modern food factory.

The machine hall of an underground power station in New South Wales, Australia; the four water turbines were produced by an English manufacturer.

Big businesses

By the 1930s most firms had become limited liability companies and very few partnerships were left in industry. Since then businesses have gone on growing in size.

The quickest way to create a big business is when several firms amalgamate to form one company. This began to happen at the end of the nineteenth century when some shipbuilding and steel-making firms joined together. So did rival companies in tobacco and chemicals. Similar mergers have occurred in motor manufacture and almost every other industry throughout this century. Often the firms have joined up willingly, but sometimes a big company has taken over control of a smaller one against its wishes by buying more than half its shares.

Normally large firms enjoy several advantages. They can afford to install advanced and costly machinery more readily and to mass produce goods in vast quantities. They can also employ more scientists to research into new processes. When they have few rivals, there is less need for them to keep their prices as low as possible and in bad times competitors can more easily settle prices and the quantities they sell.

Lever Brothers is one of the most successful twentieth-century firms. They started in Lancashire in the 1880s as grocers and had become a leading soap-making firm by 1900. Then they bought up many of their rivals and produced two-thirds of all British soap by 1920. To help ensure a constant supply of fat and oil, they next acquired a whaling company, but Macfisheries, the chain of fish shops which they developed in the 1920s, was not connected with soap. Nor was the

sausage firm of T. Wall and Son, which later made ice cream to keep its employees occupied in summer.

In 1929 Levers merged with their chief Dutch rivals, who also produced margarine, to form the huge Unilever combine. By the late 1960s it controlled nearly 600 companies all over the world. Their vast array of products include Omo, Lux, Stork, Echo, Bird's Eye, Batchelors and many other names which people often think are made by separate firms. Companies like Unilever, which produce a great variety of goods, are now amazingly secure because a slump is most unlikely to affect them all at the same time. But these vast international companies are so rich and powerful that there is also a danger that while promoting their own interests, they may harm those of individual nations or people.

Many industries which provide us with important services are no longer run by ordinary companies. The government (and not shareholders) appoint the members of the Boards which control them. They have few or no rivals and do not attempt to make large profits.

The British Broadcasting Corporation was one of the first of these. Another was also established in 1926 to organize the generating of electricity. Since the 1940s BOAC and BEA have flown passengers abroad. At the same time the supplying of electricity was also nationalized and the declining railways and coal-mines were also run by government-appointed boards. Although these nationalized industries do not have to pay dividends to shareholders and can tap the government for the money they need, they are normally expected to pay their way. And since shareholders rarely have any say in how huge companies like Unilever are run, they are similar in practice.

Unilever today is a large combine producing many products. But it started out with W. H. Lever selling soap. He called on the Bolton grocery store, shown far left, to launch Sunlight Soap, and told the manager, 'You stock it, we'll sell it.' The early 1930s map shows operating units all over the world.

Working conditions

At the beginning of the century working conditions had already been improved in many industries, but, particularly in small factories or workshops employing only a few operatives, things were often still very bad. However, by 1910 there were 200 inspectors at work studying the causes of industrial diseases like poisoned lungs and deformed spines. They gradually forced the employers to improve ventilation and unhealthy working conditions. They also made them place guards round their machines and take similar precautions, as well as fining them for breaking the factory regulations.

The proportion of injuries fell at last in the early twentieth century. And yet over 500 people are still killed and perhaps 250,000 injured in all industries every year. Electricity, more powerful machinery and higher temperatures have made some jobs even more dangerous, but too often employers and their workers also neglect vital safety precautions.

Nowhere was the work more dangerous and more difficult than in the mines. There, the miners' burden was lightened only slowly. Most owners introduced electricity and machinery for cutting and hauling very reluctantly. When George Orwell visited several mines in the 1930s, only half the coal was cut by machine. He described a Lancashire pit in *The Road to Wigan Pier*:

Coal-miners in 1908 tackling a large seam, which has been undermined with picks, shovels and crowbars.

232

Mechanization has been brought to mining. The telescopic pit-props make tunnels safer and the shearer-cutter makes the large-scale work easier. But mining is still a dangerous, unpleasant job and the small-scale work must still be done by hand.

Nowadays the preliminary work is done by an electrically driven coal-cutter. Incidentally it makes one of the most awful noises I have ever heard, and sends forth clouds of coal dust which make it impossible to see more than two or three feet and almost impossible to breathe. The machine travels along the coal face cutting into the base of the coal and undermining it to the depth of five feet; after this it is comparatively easy to extract the coal to the depth to which it has been undermined. Where it is 'difficult getting', however, it has also to be loosened with explosives. After the blasting has been done the fillers can tumble the coal out, break it up, and shovel it on to the conveyor belt.

By the 1950s nearly all pits had coal-cutting machines and were loading more coal mechanically on to conveyor belts. The National Coal Board provided many more pit-head baths so that almost all miners could wash before they went home. But, even though wages have risen rapidly and hours of work have shortened, coal-mining is still a hard and unpleasant job. The miners continue to work in cramped conditions and in a hot and dusty atmosphere, some at night. The manhandling of heavy machinery in a confined space is always difficult and, despite more and better equipment, the pick and shovel are still used, especially in the narrow seams. Nor can the inspectors prevent many miners from suffering from deformed bodies, diseased lungs and weak eyesight, and hundreds from dying in accidents. Few are now killed in prominently reported major explosions. Most casualties occur in ones and twos, victims of falling rocks.

The large-scale production of chemicals and motor cars, for example, led to much larger factories in the twentieth century. By the 1930s most industrial workers were employed in businesses of at least 500 people and today firms with several thousand employees are common.

A whole range of faster and more automatic machinery has also altered profoundly the work inside the factories. From about 1900 more employers tried to make their men work harder by paying overtime or piece rates. At the same time, workers in the larger factories concentrated increasingly on just one or two processes before passing the work on to their neighbour to save time and raise their output. Recently this subdivision of labour has become so specialized that some men and women do the same small task up to a thousand times every day. These very repetitive jobs are not interesting and usually require little thought. 'My mind is so stunted with the sort of work we do that I could do a job on the line and, ten seconds after I have done it, I don't know what I've done,' one metal finisher told G. Turner, the author of *The Car Makers*.

Alan Sillitoe gives a good impression of factory work in the 1960s in *Saturday Night and Sunday Morning*. The hero, who began work at fifteen as a messenger boy for a bicycle firm, used to cut and drill every day 1400 cylinders accurate to within five thousandths of an inch. He could have done more, but preferred to work really hard in the morning and then take it easy in the afternoon. He started at 7.30 a.m.

The car makers.

You began the day by cutting and drilling steel cylinders with care, but gradually your actions became automatic and you forgot all about the machine and the quick working of your arms and hands. The noise of motor trolleys passing up and down the gangway and the excruciating din of flying and flapping belts slipped out of your consciousness after perhaps half an hour, without affecting the quality of the work you were turning out. You went off into pipedreams for the rest of the day. In the evening when you would be feeling as though your arms and legs had been stretched to breaking point on a torture-rack, you stepped out into a cosy world that would one day provide you with the raw material for more pipedreams as you stood at your lathe.

Since the middle of this century in particular, many factories have speeded production with conveyor belts, which bring the objects to the workers on the assembly line. There they have to complete each task in a set time because each object moves on relentlessly. Sometimes this makes them very rushed and gives them little chance to relax. Some machines are also so noisy that they are very exhausting and make conversation almost impossible. However, modern machinery has also brought many benefits. Now, for instance, very few factory workers have to lift heavy weights and their work is usually much cleaner too. Yet all do not work in pleasant conditions, as G. Turner discovered in the 1960s:

Some of the paint-shop men at one factory spend their days gazing up at the underbellies of motor-cars. Their job is to fill in gaps missed by the automatic sprayer and they work in a sunken bay above which the cars appear, one after another. Many of them hate it. 'You are stuck in that hole under the car,' said one man who worked there. 'The auto-machine does nine-tenths of it for you, so not only is it hot, not only are the fumes noxious, but it's also damnably boring.' The temperature is between 90 and 100 degrees.

Yet not all skilled crafts have disappeared. Indeed many new ones, like fitters and mechanics, have grown up in the technically advanced engineering industry. Not that work on the production line is totally unskilled. Although newcomers can often learn how to handle the complex machinery in factories and elsewhere quite quickly, they rarely perform as rapidly or as accurately as the more experienced workers. Indeed one car worker told G. Turner that it ought to take two years to learn how to build the seat of a car. 'Putting any Tom, Dick or Harry on these jobs at half an hour's notice is not fair to the public,' he insisted. Officially many factory jobs are now classed as 'semi-skilled' and it is easy to take for granted the skills and stamina which they require. Over half the manual workers are now 'skilled' and less than a quarter 'unskilled'.

Another result of the increased specialization of jobs, combined with the lengthening of life has been that more and more people have had to change their job at some stage in their careers. For example, as the steam engine became out of date, boilermakers had less and less to do and so they turned to other engineering tasks. However, until recently very little has been done to help these redundant men retrain for other jobs and so some older men have been left without any work before their retiring age.

The industrial revolution led to a huge expansion of jobs in offices,

A typing pool in 1934. Office work has become more like factory work but in much pleasanter surroundings.

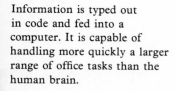

Information is typed out
in code and fed into a
computer. It is capable of
handling more quickly a larger
range of office tasks than the
human brain.

administration and the professions. Their number has risen from about half a million to four million in the last 100 years. All nineteenth-century clerks were men, but the 1901 Census reported: 'There is an increasing tendency to the employment of female clerks.' This was because the typewriter had revolutionized clerical work. More and more women have been employed as typists and secretaries and now most office workers are female. The telephone, dictaphone and other machines have transformed their work further, but they have hardly made it any easier. The faster their machinery, the more work they are expected to do, even though in many offices computers have taken over much of the calculating and other routine tasks.

The conditions of office work have improved more slowly than in most other jobs. This is partly because until recently white-collar workers have been reluctant trade unionists, disapproving of strikes. In addition their jobs are usually graded clearly according to pay and status and so most devote their energies to winning promotion for themselves. Unlike manual workers, who can rarely expect improvements unless they all agitate for them together, white-collar workers have been much more ready to put up with existing conditions, afraid that protesting may harm their own careers.

Today, even though their hours are often no shorter and their pay no higher than some manual workers, most white-collar workers retain several distinct advantages. Their conditions are usually more pleasant and they rarely lose their jobs. They are paid regularly and, in addition to getting more as they become older, they can normally expect a pension when they retire.

In the early twentieth century manual workers turned more and more to trade unions to improve their conditions. From 1910 the less skilled workers took part in many long and bitter strikes, partly because prices were rising faster than their wages. The unions were even more keen to strike in the 1920s when prices fell and some employers tried to cut their wages. However, they are at their weakest in a slump, when many unemployed are willing to replace the strikers. 'Not a penny off the pay, not a second on the day,' chanted the miners in 1926, but, although the transport and many industrial workers came out for nine days in their support, it was all in vain. The middle classes were badly frightened by this sympathetic or 'General Strike'. In the words of the *Daily Mail*, they regarded it as 'a revolutionary movement which could only succeed by destroying the government. A state of emergency and national danger has been proclaimed to resist attack.' This made the TUC call off the strike. It had intended to support the miners, not to attack the government. And so the miners struggled on alone for seven months before they were crushed. The unions continued to lose members.

Rising prices and near full employment brought revival (see pages 248 and 264). Trade unions are always strongest in a boom, when the employers want to avoid stoppages because their order books are full and they can rarely find replacements for strikers if they dismiss

Trade-union members

1910	2·5m
1920	8·0m
1935	4·6m
1950	9·3m
1971	10·0m

Before and after the First World War there were many bitter strikes. Troops with fixed bayonets trying to scatter the strikers at Llanelly, South Wales, 1911. Two railwaymen were shot dead at this strike.

them. They are therefore most likely to give in to union demands. Thus the campaign to remove another hour from the working day made good progress, and since the 1930s industrial workers normally spent about forty-eight hours a week at work. Most had to wait until the end of the decade for a week's paid holiday and even then one-third did not enjoy it. However, since 1945 holidays with pay have been extended further. And so the unions have had considerable power and influence since the 1940s, even though the proportion of working people who belonged to them did not increase in the 1950s and 1960s. Today one employed man in two and one employed woman in four belongs to a trade union.

During the present century many other developments have also altered the trade-union movement. A few large unions have dominated it since the 1920s and over half the members now belong to eight. The Transport and General Workers Union, formed in 1922, has been the largest of all since the mid 1930s when it overtook the miners. Many small or local unions also merged into national ones and their total fell from 1300 in 1900 to 500 by 1970.

Secretaries and other elected officials cannot possibly make contact with all the members of a huge union and so workers in big factories are usually represented by unpaid shop stewards. Since the 1920s many have played an important part in negotiating with the employers. In

Troops march in to restore order during the Glasgow ship workers' strike in 1919. The leaders who were eventually imprisoned included Emanuel Shinwell, a future cabinet minister.

Dockers march in support of Covent Garden workers on strike in 1924. A march by angry strikers with banners, escorted by police, was one common form of industrial protest.

Another method used by workers is to picket their factory to prevent any 'blacklegs' – strike-breakers – getting into work. Today such demonstrations receive much wider publicity through television.

Six of Sunderland's 5700 unemployed in 1968. The past was bleak; the present is bleak; does the future hold anything less bleak than the dole?

sharp contrast with the shop stewards who devote much of their spare time to union affairs, most members rarely attend meetings or show interest in how their unions are run.

The unions have forced many employers to engage only trade-union members and some have even achieved closed shops excluding all other unions. In shipbuilding and some other industries this has led to some serious disputes as to which union's members should do exactly which jobs. The car-making industry and other modern ones have also been disrupted because the workers have joined various existing unions and not all one of their own. Individual unions are still very independent, for the TUC has little power over them.

Since government inspectors have contributed to improved working conditions and modern machinery to higher wages, it is difficult to estimate the effect of trade unions. Certainly they have played a major part in more than doubling the average wages of manual workers since 1900 (allowing for the rise in prices) and in reducing the gap between the skilled and less skilled. They have also seen that employers pay them regularly, usually once a week, and often give the same rate for one job over most of the country – apart, perhaps, from London. The unions have agitated strongly for greater safety precautions, like electric light in the coal-mines. They have prevented many employers from dismissing their workers automatically whenever they had no work. They have also made them relax their discipline in the factories. 'It was hell in those days,' recalled a Vauxhall car worker of the 1920s. 'I've seen men sacked for washing their hands as the hooter blew.'

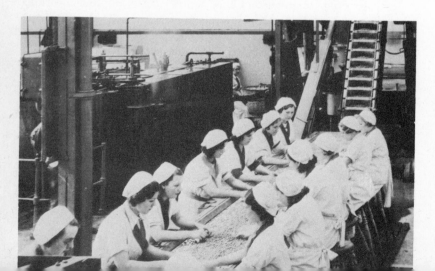

'From field to can – in a day.'
In the 1920s many people
were employed to pick, cart,
inspect and pack the peas.
Right: Pea-viners harvesting
the crop ready for freezing.
Mechanization has reduced
the number of jobs for casual
labour.

Farming in Britain

	wheat	
	acres	yield per acre
1910	1·8m	17 cwt
1939	1·8m	19 cwt
1968	2·4m	30 cwt

	barley	oats
	acres	acres
1910	1·7m	3m
1939	1m	2m
1968	6m	1m

	cattle	pigs	poultry
1910	7m	2·5m	33m
1939	8m	3·8m	64m
1968	12m	7·8m	1·25m

	tractors
1910	500 approx.
1939	55,000
1968	450,000

Farming

British farming revived temporarily during the First World War, but its decline continued in the 1920s.

By the 1930s the price of grain had fallen so low (6/- to 7/- a quarter for wheat) that most arable farmers would have gone bankrupt had the government not given them a fixed price for their wheat, even when it was cheaper from abroad. It also helped the farmers set up marketing boards to control the production of some foods, like milk and potatoes, and so keep their prices steadier. These measures staved off ruin for many farmers, but although more bought their own farms, few really prospered.

The Second World War (1939–45) changed all this. Encircled by enemy submarines, the farmers helped feed the country by producing two-thirds more food by 1945. Encouraged by the government, they began to use everywhere new machines and methods which individual farmers had tried and improved in the 1930s. These included tractors, combine harvesters, milking machines and fertilizers like lime and phosphate. By 1945 they cultivated eighteen million (instead of twelve million) acres.

After this war the government did not abandon the farmers. It continued to encourage them with special grants to buy more fertilizers and equipment and improve their buildings. With subsidies it reduced food prices and so kept many farmers in business. Altogether during the 1960s they were supported with about £300 million a year. Recently the government has also encouraged them to farm larger farms. The figures show how successful this policy has been.

To achieve this, farms have been run more and more like any other business, ruthlessly cutting costs as well as looking for new methods

which pay. Friesian cows, for example, have gradually replaced Short-horns, because they give more milk. Although there are still many farms with less than 100 acres, they are becoming larger so that they can make full use of the most efficient modern equipment. Technically British farming is now among the most advanced in the world, but our prosperity still depends less on farming than any other country's and we import half our food.

Until recently the number of farmers remained almost constant (at about 250,000), but the number of labourers continued to decline, especially with the great advance of machinery from the 1940s. Tractors, milking machines and combine harvesters led to one man doing work which had previously kept several fully occupied, and little extra labour is now needed at harvest-time. Farm work has therefore become more lonely even though it is also much less exhausting physically. Most farm workers now look after several machines and have considerable scientific knowledge, yet they are paid less than workers in most other industries.

Conclusion

The contrast between the industrial scene now and that of the eighteenth century is extraordinary. Cheap power is everywhere available – even on most farms. Factories, firms and farms alike have all increased in size and wealth. Machinery has made much work less tiring and more suitable for women, and today's worker is more secure than any of his ancestors. His pay is better, his hours shorter and his holidays longer. But all changes have not been for the best. In large concerns, for instance, individuals can easily feel isolated and unimportant. Machinery has made many jobs very repetitive and it is now common for people to do the same work throughout the year. The price of better conditions can be an unrelieved boredom.

A Labour Party poster, 1922, attacks the low pay of farm workers.

The combine harvester cuts, threshes and winnows the corn. The grain is poured into the accompanying tractor's trailer. The straw is baled later.

Will apples of the future look like a crop of tomatoes? Scientists are experimenting to develop small-size (about three feet high) heavy cropping trees that can be planted very close together. They would be harvested by a machine that cuts down the tree (leaving stumps like those in the foreground) and separates apples from branches and leaves.

Not everyone agrees with the new directions that farming is taking. 'Factory farming' worries many people, especially those concerned with animal welfare. These veal calves live their short lives in one stall without going outside into fields.

Chapter 10
Trade and communications

Britain's trade

Britain did not prosper in the first half of the twentieth century as most people expected. Since the British exported more goods than any other country, they suffered badly from a succession of events which affected world trade.

After the First World War of 1914–18, trade revived very slowly, partly because Germany's economy was ruined and also because the western countries refused to trade with Communist Russia. A big drop in the price of food and raw materials at the same time left their producers unable to buy so much from the industrial nations.

In 1929 a catastrophic fall in the price of American shares triggered off a massive slump, which spread to all western countries in the early 1930s. When Britain and the others who traded with the USA tried to protect their own industries with higher customs duties on foreign goods, they merely cut world trade further. Before it had recovered the world was fighting again, in the Second World War of 1939–45. Though the British enjoyed victory in 1945, their economy had nearly collapsed like many other European countries. However, the western ones recovered much more quickly than in the 1920s, partly because the Americans helped them. By the early 1950s Britain at last exported as much as before the First World War, while its industrial production had doubled, since 1913.

During this century Britain has exported machinery, motor vehicles and chemical products increasingly in place of cotton. At the same time, however, our share of the world's trade in manufactured goods has fallen from a quarter to a tenth. More and more exports went to countries in the Empire until 1939, when they took half. Since then, as they have become independent, Britain has traded increasingly with other industrial countries, especially in western Europe.

Our imports have also become more varied. They include raw materials like oil, iron and paper, more foods and fruit and, since the 1960s, more technically advanced machinery, clothes and other manufactured goods.

Unfortunately since the 1930s our earnings from invisible trade have fallen so much that they no longer pay automatically for the difference

On the outbreak of war in 1914 the interest rate on borrowed money was doubled.

Value of the £

1940	£1 = $4
1949	£1 = $2·8
1967	£1 = $2·4

246

Balance of trade
(annual averages)

	visible	invisible
1911–13	£140m	+£345m
1935–8	£355m	+£330m
1953–5	£255m	+£290m
1964–6	£315m	+£130m

	shipping earnings
1935–8	+£95m
1953–5	+£35m
1964–6	−£25m

government
expenditure abroad

1935–8	−£5m
1953–5	−£230m
1964–6	−£450m

between our imports and exports. The two main reasons for this have been the decline in our merchant shipping and the great increase in the money which the government spends abroad – partly on military bases, and partly as aid given to some developing countries. In addition, from the 1950s Britain has suffered, like all industrial countries, because the prices of many imported raw materials have risen faster than those of most manufactured exports. However, when allowances are made for inflation (see next page), the gap between our imports and exports has really become much smaller. And so, overall, we do not normally run into international debt. If we are left with a deficit in some years, we generally manage to cancel it with a surplus later on.

All this, however, does not describe fully Britain's position in the world today, which has continued to decline despite impressive achievements in many industries. Their total output, for example, rose by a quarter in the 1950s, but the French increased theirs by a half while the West Germans' doubled. Germany was, of course, recovering from total ruin after the war, but this trend has continued ever since. In the five years from 1963, Britain's industrial output rose by one-fifth, Italy's by two-fifths and Japan's doubled. It was this trend which finally persuaded many Britons to join in 1973 the Common Market established by six other nations in western Europe.

People have suggested many different explanations for this, like the failure of managers to modernize their factories and machinery and of their workers to work hard enough, but it is very difficult to be sure which are the most important. We may well be responsible for most of our own problems, but the second World War also contributed to them.

To pay for some of the cost of the war, Britain borrowed about £4000 million from the rest of the world, but when it was over we could not repay most of our debts. This worried few of our creditors. Gold was so scarce that, when they traded, most western countries often paid each other in American dollars or British pounds. Hence an extra supply of pounds was quite welcome. In the late 1940s this also helped the war-weary British, but in the long run it has added to our difficulties.

Since the war, continuous inflation and a large deficit in our balance of payments have forced our government to reduce the value of the pound at least twice. The foreigners who held pounds lost a lot of money on devaluation and naturally do not want to be caught again. Therefore at the first sign of a weakness which might lead to another devaluation, they usually start to sell their pounds. Since Britain has only a limited amount of gold and dollars in reserve to pay them, a big run on sterling can soon turn into a major financial crisis.

The government therefore frequently tries to check inflation and cut our imports by, for instance, leaving people with less money to spend. In these credit squeezes it may raise taxes and make borrowing more difficult. This normally strengthens the pound but restricts industry. Hard though they have tried, no government has yet found a way of both preventing financial crises and encouraging our industries to expand. At times supporting one of the western world's two international currencies has proved a very heavy burden.

Prices and shopping

No government has really found a way to stop prices going up. They have risen enormously since 1900.

During both world wars food and other materials like steel were in such short supply that they all became much more expensive. To pay for these wars the government also had to have enough money. Since 1914 paper money has not been backed by gold and so it has been able to print as much as it needed. The partial return to the Gold Standard from 1926 to 1931 concerned only Britain's dealings with foreign countries. Ever since, therefore, the value of the pound has depended not on the amount of gold held by the Bank of England, but on the wealth of the country and on the credit of the British government. The words printed on its face are meaningless.

One advantage of leaving the Gold Standard is that the government can provide the country with sufficient money to transact all its affairs, either by printing more notes or by permitting the banks to lend more. However, if it creates money faster than the rate at which industry's output increases, then the money becomes less valuable and prices rise automatically. Once prices begin to go up, people's wages will be worth less if they do not receive continual wage increases. But, whenever pay rises are given without increases in production, a further round of inflation, as a continuous fall in the value of money is called, follows inevitably.

This has happened steadily since the Second World War. Because the supply of money had been limited by the amount of gold available, it had not occurred in the nineteenth century. Instead, a shortage of money contributed to the periodic slumps from which business suffered. Now, however, once the spiral of rising prices and wages has begun, pushing each other up, it is very difficult to halt it. And so today £5 will rarely buy the same goods for which not even £1 was needed in 1913. Yet prices in the shops might well have risen even faster if the retailing trade had not been revolutionized since 1900.

In the nineteenth century most shops were run singly by one family, who knew the bulk of their customers personally. Their range of goods was narrow, partly because, like shoemakers, they often made them themselves from the raw materials. Grocers, for instance, blended their own tea and cured hams. They also weighed specially everything they sold. Drapers' shops, for example, were usually packed with boxes and

Purchasing power of £1	
1900	100p
1910	90p
1920	35p
1930	55p
1940	45p
1950	27½p
1960	20p
1970	12½p

Lyons' horse-drawn bread vans, 1919.

'The Dairy' counter at Sainsbury's branch at Croydon in 1930. Numerous assistants stand ready to weigh purchases such as butter and cheese on the large scales. Some packaged food, tea packets and tins, can be seen in the background.

bales of material. Shopkeepers rarely displayed their goods to attract attention. Markets were especially busy in the northern manufacturing towns on Saturday evenings. The stall-holders and purchasers usually haggled over prices, which were lower than in the shops.

Shopping changed gradually from the later nineteenth century when some successful drapers in large towns became department stores, selling other goods like furniture. Shops run by craftsmen disappeared as more and more goods were mass produced by machinery. Wholesale merchants then bought them from the manufacturers and distributed them to the shopkeepers.

Cooperative societies, which at first sold mainly groceries, not only did their own wholesaling but were able to reduce prices for regular customers because of their very steady sales. Co-ops spread mostly in the smaller industrial towns of Yorkshire and Lancashire from the 1860s. By 1914, they had three million members.

Later some other groups, like Thomas Lipton, followed the Co-ops' example. They graded, weighed and packaged the food at their head-quarters and then sent it to their many shops throughout the country. These multiple stores, as they were called, cut their prices, since they could afford to make a smaller profit on each article, and so increased their sales. By the early twentieth century some also made their own butter and even had their own tea plantations.

Jesse Boot, the chemist, and other shopkeepers followed this lead. Multiple stores selling shoes, hardware and men's clothes were among the most successful. Those offering mass-produced women's clothes did not catch on until the 1940s.   During the 1920 and 1930s there was a huge increase in the number of shops of all kinds. Some of the most successful were chains of department stores, like Woolworths and Marks and Spencers. They sold at very attractive prices a great variety of goods, most of which were made specially for them.

Since the 1950s many more shops have taken advantage of the increasing range and quality of ready-made and pre-packed goods to stock a much wider range. Until the 1960s all shops had to sell standard brands at the same price. Then resale price maintenance was abolished and chains of supermarkets with a much greater turnover, like Tesco, were able to cut prices on food and many ordinary branded goods. They also saved money by letting customers serve themselves – an example which many other shops have followed recently.

Small specialist shops have suffered as a result. People, of course, still patronize one-man shops, especially the general stores near their homes, but they now make most purchases in large shops and multiple stores. By cutting prices and increasing sales these shops have contributed directly to the rapid expansion of many consumer industries (page 228). Advertising has also had the same effect.

A Woolworth's store at Holborn in the 1920s. The original 3d and 6d store (nothing cost more than 6d), windows packed with goods to entice customers.

The car has changed and so have advertisements selling cars. Simplicity in 1899, holiday car in 1922, family car in 1933, and 'something very special' in 1973.

WOLSELEY

The Ideal Car for the Holidays

The motorist of moderate means, who requires a high-class but economical vehicle, will find no car so suitable as THE WOLSELEY TEN. Definitely recognised as the leader amongst small cars, it is equal in road performance and in appearance to cars of much greater horse-power.

"WOLSELEY"

It combines high road speed, great flexibility, and great climbing power with a low fuel consumption, and is particularly economical in upkeep. For holiday touring or for daily use it stands without rival.

On May 2nd and 3rd, a Wolseley TEN set up the first **Double Twelve - Hour Record** in the British Light Car Class. This was not a specially built racing car, but was a STANDARD WOLSELEY TEN, slightly modified to suit racing conditions—a striking proof of the robust constitution of WOLSELEY standard productions.

THE WOLSELEY TEN.	
TWO-SEATER (Specification B)	£440
(" A)	£475
TORPEDO (" B)	£455
(" A)	£490
COUPÉ (Fixed head)	£595
(Folding head)	£635
Dunlop Tyres fitted as standard.	

Write us for Catalogue No. 20, post free.

WOLSELEY MOTORS LTD., Adderley Park, BIRMINGHAM.
(Proprietors : Vickers Limited.)
London Showrooms: WOLSELEY HOUSE, 157, PICCADILLY, W. 1.
Indian Depot: Sandhurst Bridge Road, Chowpatty, Bombay.

More Minors to choose from
A bigger model for the family as well

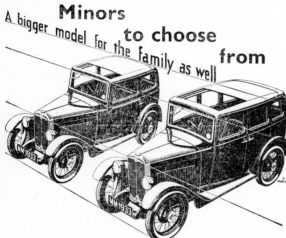

● Lots of improvements for the Minor in 1933. Four-speed gearboxes for smarter acceleration and greater flexibility. New radiator and longer bonnet to keep pace with modern body lines. And not only a *better* range but a *wider* range. Now you can have the indefatigable Minor's 'big car' performance with the body style and size to suit you. Five standard models from which to choose and a Family Minor at an astonishingly low price—a four-door saloon with surprising roominess. If you want thorough-paced motoring at 'bus-fare budgetting, your choice must fall on one of these gallant Minors. Here is the full 1933 range:

Two Seater (3-speed)	(short wheelbase)	£100
Two Seater (4-speed)	(short wheelbase)	£105
Tourer	(short wheelbase)	£115
Saloon - (fixed head)	(short wheelbase)	£122 10s.
Saloon - (Pytchley sliding head)	(short wheelbase)	£125
Family 4-door Saloon (long wheelbase)	(Pytchley sliding head)	£145
Special Coupe (long wheelbase) (Pytchley sliding head)		£165
		Ex works

Triplex Glass throughout. Dunlop tyres and Magna type wire wheels standard. Guaranteed for 2 years. Backed by Morris Universal Service.

Heard about "Morris 1933", the fascinating 56-page book that's more than a catalogue? You must read it. Your copy's waiting you at any Morris Dealer. Or send direct to us

MORRIS
MORRIS MOTORS LIMITED, COWLEY, OXFORD

Something very special

FIAT 128 SPORT COUPE

1290cc front wheel drive engine with overhead camshaft. 0-50 in 7.6 100 mph. GT instrumentation. Generous 2+2 seating with matt black interior. Special steering wheel trim. Carpeting throughout. Styling which will do wonders for your ego. And a price that's not likely to give your bank manager a heart attack: £1398.40. Take a test drive.

By 1910 they also agreed that pistons which moved four times to each explosion used the fuel most efficiently.

Even though pneumatic tyres made of rubber were soon devised for the wheels, the motor vehicle did not lead immediately to a revolution in transport. The early ones carried only people, because they were not powerful enough to carry goods in bulk. These early motor cars were uncomfortable and very unreliable. Punctures, boiling radiators and other mechanical failures happened so frequently that long journeys felt rather like adventures. There were very few garages or mechanics to help when they ran into trouble like this:

I was driving down a main road in Somerset when, before anything could be done about it, I noticed a small open drain about two inches deep and four inches wide, running across the road. On crossing it, perhaps doing a gallant twenty-five, both the front wheels came off simultaneously, the car came to its knees with an abrupt jerk, and slid some yards along the road. I remember seeing the spare wheel leave its moorings and disappear down the road round a corner.

However, from the 1920s motor vehicles were greatly improved. Experiments on precisely when the fuel should be ignited at the end of the piston's second stroke made their engines more powerful. Lighter bodies made them faster. By lowering their centre of gravity and increasing the size of their tyres, they also held the road much better. When brakes were put on all the wheels they could be stopped more abruptly. Gradually the engines were kept cool more efficiently until the radiators rarely boiled. Dynamos and more suitable oils also contributed to making the internal combustion engine much more reliable in both hot and cold weathers.

From the 1920s motor cars became much cheaper and more comfortable, but as their numbers increased they badly needed better roads.

Picnic in the car park in 1923.

Left: Rolls-Royce Tonneau, 1905. Below: The Austin Seven was the first small popular car and gave the families able to buy them their first chance to motor. Between 1923 and 1938, 350,000 were sold at about £150 each.

Harvesting by motor. Lorry loaded with potatoes in Lincolnshire 1907.

In the towns these were usually made up by the early twentieth century, but most country roads were suitable only for horses and foot travellers. Motor vehicles found them narrow and winding and either muddy when wet or dusty when dry. They were soon coated with tar, but few dangerous bends were remodelled or by-passes built before the 1930s. Then traffic lights were also installed at town crossroads and roundabouts at some busy road junctions. Unlike Germany and the USA, however, Britain did not build special motorways until the 1960s.

The number of vehicles licensed records the fantastic growth of motor transport in the twentieth century. By the 1920s lorries proved to be ideal for carrying bulky liquids like milk and petrol, while vans delivered the more fragile and perishable goods. Increasingly from the 1930s heavy and bulky goods were sent by road. Travel by rail was rarely so quick or so convenient. By the 1930s, therefore, trains carried little more than half the freight and two-thirds of the passengers of 1910.

The railways played a crucial part in the Second World War, but by the mid 1960s the volume of their traffic had fallen to the level of the 1930s. By then the railways had also closed many of their least used lines, but in other ways they were considerably improved. For instance the steam engine was replaced mostly in the 1950s by faster electric and diesel locomotives. The diesel engine, which burns a heavier oil than petrol and was first installed in ships, also drove many large lorries.

Experiments in America and France in the early twentieth century developed another use for the internal combustion engine: the aeroplane. Judged by modern standards, aeroplanes in the 1920s and 1930s were small and the journeys were slow, uncomfortable and infrequent.

Great technical improvements from the 1940s altered all this. The piston engine was replaced by the faster turbine, driven by a jet of gases, so that today people can reach most important towns in the world in less than twenty-four hours. Aeroplanes can also fly safely in most weathers and the dark. The larger planes take some freight

Number of vehicles licensed

	cars	goods
1910	0·05 m	0·03 m
1930	1 m	0·35 m
1950	2·3 m	0·92 m
1970	11·5 m	1·62 m

Numbers travelling by air between Britain and foreign countries

1938	70,000
1948	900,000
1958	4,250,000
1968	14,200,000

255

and have also reduced their fares considerably. Ocean liners have suffered directly as the numbers travelling by air between Britain and foreign countries have risen continually.

Even though the airlines carry more and more passengers on the longer routes inside the British Isles, the rather strange situation has developed in which it is usually quicker to travel from London to New York than to the remoter parts of Scotland. Indeed in many ways the aeroplane now holds a position similar to that of the stage coach in the 1830s. A comparatively small number of people use it very frequently while the majority fly very occasionally or not at all.

The first air postal delivery. An aeroplane of 1911 carrying mail.

Two passenger planes in 1935.

B-R-R-R-R-R-R-R!

This cartoon suggests several reasons why the GPO took over private telephone companies in 1912. Hull, however, has continued to run its own independent system.

The communication of ideas

The transmission of news and ideas has speeded up enormously in this century. The telephone service has been improved and extended beyond recognition. By the early twentieth century, people other than Alexander Bell, the original inventor, had developed better microphones and receivers and extra equipment like amplifiers. It had become possible to ring someone anywhere in Britain. However, when the Post Office finally took over the telephone system from many small companies in 1912, it was very backward in comparison with the USA. Since then Britain has also been slow to install automatic switchboards, which connect two callers without an operator, and telephoning has remained rather expensive. Even so it has enabled business men to speed up their transactions and in the more isolated parts of the countryside in particular people have come to treat the telephone as a necessity. By the 1930s many public call-boxes were erected and, as the British telephoned more, the Post Office delivered letters less frequently. And yet most other industrial nations still made greater use of the telephone in the 1960s.

The wireless telegraph, which the Italian, Marconi, developed around 1900, transformed communications at sea. Because it transmitted messages (in Morse code) on radio waves, it was soon used by ships. When they needed help, for instance, they could send out the distress signal, S.O.S. (. . . − − − . . .). Then, from the 1920s, the human voice was transmitted on radio waves through a microphone. This made it possible to telephone people abroad and for aeroplanes to contact the ground.

Phones in Britain

1912	0·7 m
1939	3·25 m
1971	13·5 m

With electricity, therefore, we can now send a message to or from most parts of the world and receive an answer almost instantaneously. Yet it is still expensive. To talk to someone in America, for example, costs over a pound a minute.

On a larger scale, the way news is broadcast has altered too. At the end of the nineteenth century British newspapers consisted of column after column of small print, which put off all but the keenest reader. All this changed when the British began copying many features of the American press. They moved their main news to the front page in the early twentieth century and used increasingly larger headlines. Articles became shorter and were written in simple and arresting language designed to hold the attention of a person who knew little about the subject. They described disasters and dramatic rescues in detail, often stressing the fact that they had engulfed the lives of people as ordinary as their readers. They also included many stories which, though trivial, had human interest.

Should sun-bathing and undressing on the beach be allowed? These two questions have divided Brighton into two camps, and for the moment the sun-bathers are carrying the day. Today there was a general undressing on the beach, and several who did not venture into the water lay half-clothed on the shingle all day. Women in pleasure boats have often complained of seeing men more or less unclothed sun-bathing in canoes.

The mayor declares that there is nothing of which to complain. Both he and his wife, he states, undress on the beach, and they have seen nothing that could give rise to complaint. After all, he states, it is quite easy to undress under a bathing wrap or a mackintosh without giving offence to anyone.

The *Daily Mail* was the first morning daily paper to adopt popular techniques. It included articles on food and clothes as well as gossip about famous people. Selling at a halfpenny from 1896, its circulation soon rose to over a million. Around 1930 the other leading papers

NEWS FROM LADYSMITH.

FIERCE FIGHTING ON TWO DAYS.

INFANTRY DUEL.

CRUSHING BLOW TO THE RAND VOLUNTEERS.

COLLAPSE OF AN ATTACK ON ESTCOURT.

SHARP FIGHTING AT KIMBERLEY.

RELIEF COLUMN ABOUT TO ADVANCE.

BOERS VERY ACTIVE.

MAFEKING AGAIN SERIOUSLY MENACED.

FATE OF WINSTON CHURCHILL.

General Buller's original plan was understood to be for an advance by three columns upon Bloemfontein and Pretoria. The three columns would have landed, one at Capetown, another at Port Elizabeth,

In this cutting from the *Daily Mail*, 1899, the complete day's news can be read from the headlines.

The *Sunday Times* being printed in 1969.

Daily Mirror	4·4 m
Daily Express	3·4 m
Sun	2·7 m
Daily Mail	1·8 m
Daily Telegraph	1·4 m
Financial Times	0·2 m
The Times	0·3 m
Guardian	0·3 m

Front-page headlines, 1918
and 1945.

tried to attract more readers by offering them free insurance, cameras
or books as well as making the news appear more exciting than it
really was. The *Daily Express* was the most successful in presenting
events and people as larger than life. The fact that its readers increased
after it announced confidently in 1939: 'There will be no War this
year or next year either' indicates that they read it more for entertainment than for news. The *Daily Mirror*, which gave less space to news
and more to headlines, photographs, strip cartoons and human stories,
became even more popular in the 1940s. As in the Sunday papers,
many of its stories were about trivial events, but it often placed them
close to items of important news which it discussed seriously.

By the 1960s these last two sold over nine million copies a day
between them. This meant that every weekday at least half the population saw either the *Mirror* or the *Express*. Most of the rest also read
a paper produced in London. Many families bought an evening paper
regularly too. Together the papers printed thirty million copies every
day in the 1950s, with even more on Sundays, but the total has fallen
somewhat since. This is partly because many papers with a small circulation cannot charge so much for their advertisements and have closed
down, but mainly because of the appearance of television. Even so
the British still read more papers than people in any other country.

A radio picture of 1926 showing the queen of Rumania driving through New York. With radio pictures like this newspapers could include up-to-date photographs of foreign events as well as of home affairs.

Regular programmes were first broadcast on the wireless in the USA in the 1920. There, advertisements were included to pay for them, but in Britain they were kept off the air. Instead those with radio sets had to buy a licence. At first the BBC broadcast only news of important events and so sometimes the newsreader announced: 'There is no news tonight.' During the 1930s, when most homes acquired a set, the BBC expanded its news service. It started to broadcast regular bulletins throughout the day and employed reporters to gather news from all parts of the world. Since then, therefore, most people have been able to hear reports of general elections and important sports meetings, floods and similar disasters almost as soon as they have happened.

Radio licences

1929	3 m
1939	9 m
1949	12 m
1971	2 m

This crystal radio set cost 7/6 in 1924.

Television broadcasting started at the end of the 1930s, when screens were seven inches wide. Most families did not own a set until the 1950s, when ITV was set up to rival the BBC. For a long time Britain suffered from being a television pioneer, receiving inferior pictures on only 405 lines rather than on 625. Even so, moving pictures have influenced viewers much more than sound alone. Although devoted mainly to entertainment, television has also shown a great variety of news and events, and satellites now bring us live pictures from the other side of the world.

These revolutionary developments were made possible only by the great expansion of industry and the nation's growing wealth. As one result of them our ideas and opinions about what is happening in the world now depend very much on what a few men decide to tell us in their newspapers and broadcasts. And yet one can easily exaggerate the extent of their influence. A survey in the USA, for example, showed that one hour after a news bulletin two-thirds could not remember anything they had seen or heard.

Yet nobody today can be unaware that we are part of a world community. The British depend on other countries for much of what is consumed and we cannot prosper unless they buy our industrial products in return. Foreign products line the shelves of the supermarkets and we take it for granted that we can see and hear events on the other side of the world. If an international business deal is going wrong, then a transatlantic telephone call may put it right, or perhaps an executive might have to make a five-hour air trip across the Atlantic. It is a far cry indeed from the days in 1805 when it took seventeen days for the news of Trafalgar to reach London.

A 1935 television receiver developed by John Baird, showing a perennial favourite – Mickey Mouse.

Chapter 11
Living standards and health

Introduction

The expansion of trade and industry during the twentieth century led to a continuing increase in Britain's wealth. The growth in the nation's total income, of course, wildly exaggerates this rise because it ignores both the rapid inflation of prices and the rise in population, although in Britain the latter has increased much more slowly since 1910. And so the average income per head, recalculated at 1913–14 prices, is a much more reliable guide. It shows that whereas in the fifty years before 1901 people on average had become more than twice as wealthy in the twentieth century it took longer for their wealth to double again and most of this increase occurred in the 1930s and after 1950.

And yet, despite this great increase in wealth, a huge gap has remained between the living standards of rich and poor. When Sir W. Crawford surveyed the nation's eating habits in 1936, he estimated carefully how much money the individuals in five different groups had to spend on average.

family income per annum	percentage of population	income per head per week
over £1000	1%	£8·00
£500–£1000	4%	£4·40
£250–£500	20%	£2·15
£125–£250	60%	£1·00
under £125	15%	62½p

Recently the gap between the earnings of skilled and unskilled workers has been reduced, but still the differences in family incomes are very great. Unfortunately this is difficult to prove because the available information gives individual, and not family, incomes. However, the richest five per cent of the population still own at least seventy-five per cent of the nation's property and the proportion of all taxes paid by the rich has not increased since the 1930s.

The huge growth in the country's wealth has had all kinds of consequences – lengthening of life, expansion of education and the reduction of poverty, to name but three.

British national income

1910	£2000 m
1937	£4500 m
1965	£28,000 m
1971	£38,600 m

Average annual income per person (at 1913–14 prices)

1901	£47
1911	£49
1921	£44
1931	£49
1939	£61
1959	£61
1959	£78
1965	£93
1971	£94

This photograph (*above right*) was taken in 1933. Even then some poor families still lived in one room and conditions hadn't improved much since the nineteenth century. In contrast to the very poor; the very rich (*right*).

Reduction of poverty

Low wages were the main cause of poverty in the nineteenth century, but there was no noticeable decline in the number of poor between the two world wars, because so many people were out of work. In this period the proportion of unemployed rarely fell below one in ten and in the early 1930s it rose to over one in five.

The explanation was the decline which afflicted some of the traditional industries like cotton, shipbuilding and coal-mining, so that parts of the industrial north, and South Wales, were worst hit. There, some towns had up to half their men out of work. In these areas the Labour Exchanges, which had been established early in the century to help the unemployed find work, served little purpose because there simply were no vacancies to fill. And so the unemployed felt increasingly helpless and degraded, as well as poor, as a journalist discovered in 1931.

I gazed out of my hotel bedroom in South Wales. The sight was one of the most doleful I have ever seen in my life. It consisted chiefly of this: miners — obviously dressed in their Sunday best — standing with their hands in their pockets along the street kerb. Just standing. I knew that if I asked some of them, they would tell me they were 'waiting for something to pass by' — a chance to run an errand, or do something to earn a few pence. Others, especially the men over 35, would answer they were waiting for the Old Age Pension to come along.

DOOR-KEEPER for " Social Club," hours 3-5 p.m. and 7-11.45 p.m., Sundays, 7-11 p.m.; wages £2 per week. Apply by letter only, giving full particulars, Secretary, Bridgeway Club, Bridge-rd., W.6.

The response to an advertisement for a job in London, 1933.

The Secretary,
Bridgeway Club,
Bridge Road, W.6.

requests us to announce that he had

1,425 APPLICATIONS

in response to a position advertised in the "News-Chronicle" on Tuesday last.

The vacancy has now been filled, and the Committee of the Club in thanking all disappointed applicants trusts they will soon obtain employment.

In 1940, at the start of the Second World War, almost everyone found work and the number of poor fell rapidly as a result. Until the 1970s comparatively few people were unemployed for long, apart from the sick, the disabled or the ageing.

Large families were another cause of Victorian poverty and during the present century they have become significantly smaller. Women who were married in the 1860s eventually had families of six or seven children on average. From then the number fell rapidly until the 1930s when the average was little more than two. By 1950 well over two-thirds of the boys and girls in Britain belonged to families with three children or less. Because adults lived longer there were also fewer orphans.

Furthermore, from 1946 mothers received 5/– a week for every child after their eldest. Soon these family allowances were paid for over four million children. Most parents spent well over 5/– a week on each child, but family allowances helped in particular the lower-paid workers with large families to see that all their children were properly fed and clothed.

Old people have been helped in a similar way since 1909. Then old-age pensions of 5/– a week were first paid to those over seventy who did not have an income of more than 8/– from other sources. The rest had a smaller pension unless their income was 12/– a week or more, when they got nothing. Despite this means test, a million people were soon receiving a pension and this small sum removed the fear of dying in the workhouse for even more.

'When the Old Age Pensions began,' wrote Flora Thompson, 'life was transformed for such aged cottagers. They were relieved of anxiety. Independent for life! At first when they went to the Post Office to draw it, tears of gratitude would run down the cheeks of some, and they would say, as they picked up their money, "God bless you, miss!" and there were flowers from their gardens for the girl who merely handed them the money.' As prices rose the government gradually increased the value of the pension. By the 1940s it stood at 26/– a week (42/– for a married couple). By then it was paid to most women over sixty and men at sixty-five. Widows also received small pensions.

Since 1913 the government has also organized an insurance scheme to help the unemployed. Those who are working pay a small contribution which finances those who are out of work. However, in the 1920s and 1930s the government saved money with devices like the means test so that, although no unemployed became destitute, many still lived in poverty.

Even though the workhouses were run in a more friendly atmosphere, old-age pensions and unemployment benefit reduced the numbers who turned to the Poor Law for assistance. The Poor Law was finally replaced in 1948 by the National Assistance Board (since absorbed by the Ministry of Social Security), whose duty was to pay out money to all 'without resources to meet their requirements'. However, the disgrace of asking for help was so ingrained that many had to be persuaded to claim their new rights. Within a few years well over a million were receiving national assistance.

Since the 1940s few people have been really poor, but these welfare services have not eliminated poverty as many hoped, partly because the benefits they pay have been set so low. Some of course, waste or mismanage their money, but many families still live crowded together in two or three rooms for other reasons. Indeed the evidence suggests that poverty probably increased in the 1950s and 1960s, even though it is now judged by higher standards.

Insurance stamps for health and unemployment.

In 1960 two professors calculated that about one person in seven was living below the income level which the National Assistance Board set as necessary for food, rent, clothing and fuel. They included three million old people and two and a quarter million children. Slightly larger families and somewhat longer life are two explanations for this unwelcome development. Inflation is another. Despite the growing national income, the wages of the lowest-paid workers do not always rise as fast as prices, and in the large cities especially, where rents are high, some become worse off. In addition family allowances and pensions do not rise automatically with the cost of living; the government is usually reluctant to increase them.

There is great concern about the continued rise in population and the consequent pressures on housing and welfare facilities. One hope is the spread of morally acceptable and realistic approach to population control. There is a real need for information about contraception and several towns and boroughs produce their own propaganda as well as offering advice and free contraceptives.

Ribbon development in the 1930s. Many houses were built beside main roads like this.

A housing estate of the 1950s. Though rather drab from the outside, such houses are often very comfortable.

Towns and houses

Almost all the increase in population during this century has been absorbed by the towns, which have continued to expand, especially in the south-east and midlands, where most modern industry has settled away from the coal-fields.

Late nineteenth-century builders usually erected their housing estates within easy reach of a railway station or a road with a good tram service, where the houses fetched the highest prices. And so most towns had not spread out evenly. 'Good train services have a powerful effect in promoting the development of residential districts,' explained a civil servant about London in the early twentieth century. 'Examples of this are to be seen at Wembley Park and at Harrow where there is now a ten minute service of trains.'

Until motor buses were improved in the 1930s, some districts quite close to the centre of a town remained badly served by public transport. Then areas which had previously been difficult to reach, like Wythen-shawe to the south of Manchester, were built up rapidly. Since the 1920s few new houses have been erected in terraces. Instead, estates of semi-detached houses with gardens have been built in most suburbs. The main snag of living in a well-spaced housing estate is, of course, the distance from many of the houses to the nearest shops, post office or public house, but the motor car has overcome this.

In the present century expanding towns have covered much more land and so people who visit a town which they once knew well often find they barely recognize it. This happened in the 1930s to a character in one of George Orwell's novels, who explored what had once been a small market town.

I don't believe anyone who hadn't happened to be born here would have believed that these streets were fields as little as twenty years ago. It was all houses. There were little knots of houses dumped here and there, wherever anybody had been able to buy a plot of land. The pond where I had caught my first fish had been drained and filled up and built over. For hours on

end I'd be walking through a world that wasn't there. I'd count my paces as I went down the pavement and think 'Yes, here's where so-and-so's field begins. The hedge runs across the street and slap through that house. That petrol pump is really an elm tree. And here's the edge of the allotments. And this street, which was a dismal little row of semi-detached houses, is the lane where the nut-bushes grew on both sides.'

Some towns, which were originally several miles apart, have spread so much that their suburbs eventually joined up. Stoke was formed in this way from what had previously been six towns. However, the boundaries of some built-up areas, which looked like one town with several centres, were not changed and so they were administered as separate towns. These areas are called conurbations and mean that some of the figures for the growth of towns are rather misleading. In the twentieth century, for instance, Manchester has not only been a town of about 700,000 inhabitants but also the centre of a conurbation containing nearly two and a half million people.

British population

	1910	1966
country	9 m	10 m
London	7·25 m	8 m
other towns	24·75 m	35 m
	41 m	53 m

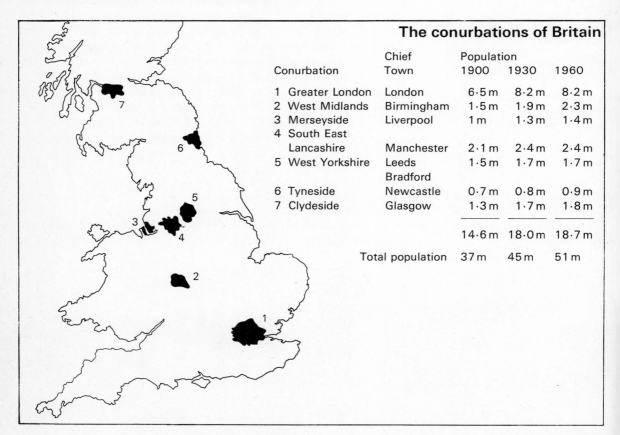

The conurbations of Britain

Conurbation	Chief Town	Population 1900	1930	1960
1 Greater London	London	6·5 m	8·2 m	8·2 m
2 West Midlands	Birmingham	1·5 m	1·9 m	2·3 m
3 Merseyside	Liverpool	1 m	1·3 m	1·4 m
4 South East Lancashire	Manchester	2·1 m	2·4 m	2·4 m
5 West Yorkshire	Leeds Bradford	1·5 m	1·7 m	1·7 m
6 Tyneside	Newcastle	0·7 m	0·8 m	0·9 m
7 Clydeside	Glasgow	1·3 m	1·7 m	1·8 m
		14·6 m	18·0 m	18·7 m
Total population		37 m	45 m	51 m

Since the 1950s the centres of many towns have been altered out of all recognition. Parts of some, particularly in the Midlands and the South, were destroyed by German bombs in the Second World War and have been rebuilt with attractive shopping centres and spacious streets. Many others, which suffered little bomb damage in the war, have pulled down streets of terraced houses to make room for large shops and/or blocks of offices and flats. Many families have therefore had to move away to housing estates on the outskirts or even to specially created new towns like Stevenage and Chelmsley Wood.

At the start of this century two Britons in every five lived in one of the country's seven largest conurbations (see the diagram opposite). The Birmingham conurbation is the only one which has increased much since the 1930s, mainly because people have not been allowed to build on most of the land around big cities. This protected countryside is called 'Green Belt'. Nevertheless, even though its expansion has been halted, about one Briton in seven still lives in London. During this century the number of towns with over 50,000 inhabitants has risen from eighty in 1900 to more than 200 today (although only twenty-five of these contain over 200,000 people).

In recent years most country dwellers have been able to reach a large town fairly easily by bus or car. Indeed many villagers now travel

A pearly king and queen pose in front of the flats to which they had recently moved. The old street-life, the life-style they grew up in, has gone for ever.

At the start of this century
a working-class family would
use outside toilets, a stone
sink, a tin bath; but by the
1950s they had become evils
to be eliminated as quickly as
possible.

to work or shop in a town almost as frequently as those who live
in the suburbs. Because those who live outside towns enjoy most of
their advantages, many of the differences between life in the town
and in the countryside have disappeared.

Living conditions in the towns themselves have improved. Much
of the worst housing disappeared in slum clearance schemes, especially
in the 1930s and 1950s, The larger and better-spaced houses which
replaced them were usually semi-detached with two or three bedrooms.
Recently many families have also moved into flats. Altogether the
number of dwellings has risen very rapidly. And so very few houses
now remain with two inhabitants per room. In most the average is
about two people for every three rooms.

In the nineteenth century most people rented the houses in which

Dwellings in Britain

1900	7·5 m
1930	10·5 m
1965	17·0 m

they lived from a private landlord, but this too has changed. Few people can ever raise the cash to buy a house, but building societies, which originally assisted builders to put up houses in the nineteenth century, have lent more and more money to the purchasers since then. Now nearly half the families live in their own house. However, since it usually takes at least thirty years to repay the loan on a mortgage, building societies normally lend only to younger men with a good steady job. Local councils therefore started to build decent homes for the families of unskilled and semi-skilled workers from the 1920s. By 1970 the councils owned about a quarter of the country's housing. Only a minority still rent their dwelling from a private landlord. They include many of the poorer unskilled workers, recent immigrants, older couples and young single persons, most of whom are ineligible for a council house.

Despite all this progress, however, some families still lack indoor flush lavatories or fixed baths with running water. Often, but not always, they are in older houses which have been subdivided into several apartments and rented. Since the nineteenth century people's idea of what is a satisfactory house has changed remarkably.

Since the mid-twentieth century people have taken it for granted that houses should have carpets, upholstered furniture, wallpaper and electric gadgets.

With rising standards, a good water supply became essential. And so, since 1900, increasing quantities of water have been pumped from the Welsh valleys and Lake District into towns like Birmingham and Manchester. In the towns running water was at last laid on to the homes of most workers in the early twentieth century, but country-dwellers did without it for another generation or more.

Diet

The great increase in wealth and foreign trade led directly to a continuing improvement in the standard and variety of people's diets.

The cost of most imported foods continued to fall in the twentieth century, so that by the 1930s most of the butter and cheese, sugar, flour and fruit eaten in Britain, together with more than half the meat, was produced abroad. Some fruits, like bananas and oranges, which grew in warmer climates, were shipped in fresh, but more perishable ones like peaches and pineapples usually came in tins. The canning of British fruit and vegetables, like peas, as well as of all sorts of meats, fish and soup, gave most Britons a much more varied diet in winter and spring by the 1930s. In addition many ate fresh apples, tomatoes and other fruit and vegetables out of season because they were imported.

The upper classes had shorter and better-balanced meals by then, with less meat and more vegetables and fruit. This tendency was quickened by the Second World War, which created such a shortage in the 1940s that the government was forced to ration much of the food. For a time the wealthiest third of the population ate less, while the poorest third were better fed than they had ever been.

Since the war, the subsidies paid to farmers have helped keep prices down and the wealthy have not returned to eating huge meals regularly.

Average British weekly diet

	1910
bread/cakes/biscuits	6 lb
potatoes	4 lb
other vegetables	1 lb
fruit	1 lb
meat/fish	2½ lb
sugar/preserves	1½ lb
fats/margarine	2½ oz
cheese	2 oz
tea	2 oz
eggs	2 oz
milk	2½ pt

Note If you compare these diets with those on page 186 remember that the latter are not for the whole population, just some labourers. In the twentieth century meat consumption has not increased; poorer people have bought better cuts instead.

A communal feeding centre in wartime, 1940.

1960

4 lb
3½ lb
2 lb
2 lb
2½ lb
1¼ lb
12 oz
3 oz
3 oz
4½ oz
5 pts

By 1960 therefore nearly everyone ate between 30/– and 35/– worth of food a week and all but the poorest could afford to feed themselves adequately. As a whole we are now better nourished than ever before and those who eat an unbalanced diet do so either because they like it or because they do not know how much milk, eggs, fruit and other foods they need or how harmful too much sugar can be.

In the present century more and more foods have been sold which are ready to serve as soon as they are boiled or heated. At first most of these convenience foods came in tins, but others were sold in packets, like custard and jelly powders. By the 1920s porridge could also be made in two minutes and cornflakes started to rival it very successfully with other American-style breakfast cereals. From the 1950s many more convenience foods have caught on, including powdered coffee and cooked meats, deep-frozen vegetables and fish. These ready-to-serve foods not only save time, they can also be bought at all times of the year. However, they rarely have a strong flavour and many do the eater little good. Most meringues, for example, are not made from white of egg but from a cellulose material, and 'orangeade' is not necessarily made from oranges.

Nevertheless the vast improvement in people's food has not only removed most of the difference in size between richer and poorer children, it has also contributed directly to the falling death rate.

A can of oyster soup, 1890.

A tempting display of packaged and convenience foods.

Health and medicine

It is not until the early twentieth century that we can get any reliable idea of the extent of ill health among the people. For then the army rejected as unfit to fight in the Boer and First World Wars about forty per cent of the men it examined. Of two and a half million men who ought to have been in the prime of life in 1917-18 it concluded:

Of every nine men of military age in Great Britain, on the average three were perfect, fit and healthy; two were on a definitely inferior plane of health and strength, whether from some disability or some failure of development; three were incapable of undergoing more than a very moderate degree of physical exertion and could almost be described with justice physical wrecks; and the remaining man was a chronic invalid with a precarious hold on life.

At the same time children were first examined medically in elementary schools. A quarter of those without spectacles could not see properly, 20 per cent suffered from diseases in their ears, nose or throat and 10 per cent were clearly underfed. In extreme cases they had bandy legs or pigeon chests because their bones were not properly formed. Three-quarters had decaying teeth and over half the girls had nits or lice in their hair.

This situation was due partly to ignorance and bad living conditions, but some were ill only because they could not afford to consult a doctor.

'The doctors weren't for the likes of us,' wrote the daughter of a farm labourer at the end of the nineteenth century:

They would be sent for when folks were dying and it were too late anyway, but there were all sorts of reasons for not sending for them. For one thing there was no such thing as telephones, and somebody had to go the four or five miles to fetch the doctor. But it were the paying for him that were the worst difficulty of all, because he charged so much for a visit, and when it were the father of the family that were bad, there'd be no money coming in for food, let alone to pay the doctor with. My poor old mother died at sixty-two with cancers all over her and suffered cruelly. But she suffered as well from knowing how much she owed the doctor who attended her.

Many doctors tried to overcome this by treating some patients free, but there were always many more whom they never saw. In addition they rarely gave them the same care and attention as their paying patients.

This situation was improved in 1913. Then, by paying small weekly contributions, most wage-earners became entitled to see a doctor free. But they still had to pay for the treatment he prescribed and for all medical attention to their wives and children.

Proportion of those aged 0–4 at first date who survived

	20 years	40 years	60 years
1841	85%	65%	40%
1881	90%	75%	60%
1921	92%	85%	

From the early twentieth century many towns supplied mothers with pure milk and also copied the French and Belgians in setting up infant welfare centres. There, mothers were taught how to feed their babies properly and how to keep them healthy. Health visitors also visited them to give further advice in their own homes. From the 1920s at school a small bottle of milk was given free to the poorest children every day. All received one in the 1940s, when many more also ate a cooked dinner at school. Since then under-fives and expectant mothers have also been given free milk, orange juice, cod-liver oil and vitamin tablets. Regular ante-natal check-ups have also reduced the risks of childbirth.

Meanwhile the knowledge and efficiency of nurses, doctors and surgeons have continued to increase. Hospitals have been transformed since the later nineteenth century, partly because they have been staffed with more and more trained nurses. In the twentieth century some surgeons discovered that if they kept their operating theatres so clean that germs could not reach their patients, they did not need an antiseptic like carbolic acid. They therefore wore masks and rubber gloves and soon took other precautions like sterilizing dressings with steam. The Americans made further progress in anaesthetics by using cocaine. A German developed the X-ray, which enabled a surgeon to examine broken bones or a patient's insides before he opened him up.

One of the main dangers of a long operation – that the patient would collapse from loss of blood – was also removed in the earlier part of this century. After the four main groups of human blood were identified everyone could receive a blood transfusion, although hospitals did not learn how to store enough for all emergencies until later. Recently, therefore, operations to the lungs, womb, heart and even the brain have become quite common.

An early X-ray being taken with apparatus developed by W. Röntgen. It played a crucial role in detecting T.B. early enough so that it could be treated.

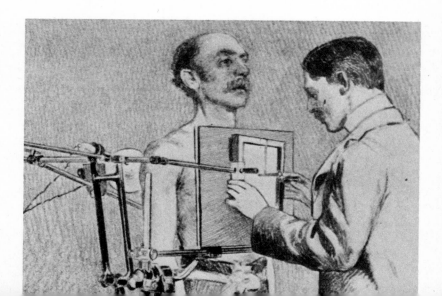

Many more discoveries, like the fact that those suffering from diabetes need insulin, have made the doctors increasingly effective. From the 1930s they could cure their patients of some diseases with various drugs which prevented some germs from spreading in their blood. The first one was originally used for dyeing wool red before it was discovered that it had more beneficial uses. One of the most important, known popularly as 'M & B', dealt with pneumonia.

Throughout the 1930s some scientists also worked on Alexander Fleming's discovery that a mould called penicillin killed some bacteria as well as stopping them from growing. They mass produced it hastily during the Second World War and since the 1940s doctors have used it to cure patients suffering from blood poisoning for instance, or infections that give them sore throats. They have also discovered more and more drugs (or antibiotics) which destroy other bacteria.

These advances saved many lives, but they also meant that medical treatment became vastly more expensive. This could have meant that only the rich benefited, but in 1948 the National Health Service was created. At last all women, children and old people were able to see a doctor and receive any treatment, however costly, free of charge. By the 1950s nearly a third of the women and a quarter of the men consulted a doctor during the course of a year. The hospitals were also reorganized. Formerly some had been run privately while others had been in the charge of the Poor Law or local council. Then all were grouped together and everyone was entitled to free treatment within them. Even so those who paid were still likely to be treated better for minor complaints, if not for serious ailments.

Since the 1950s people have also visited dentists free or at reduced costs. By the late nineteenth century dentists were able to save some teeth by drilling away the bad parts and filling the holes, but they

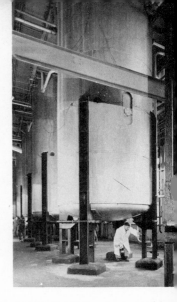

Antibiotics being fermented on a vast scale.

The laboratory of one of the manufacturers of the contraceptive pill. The workers are wearing protective clothing against the effect of hormones. The pill has given women a new freedom.

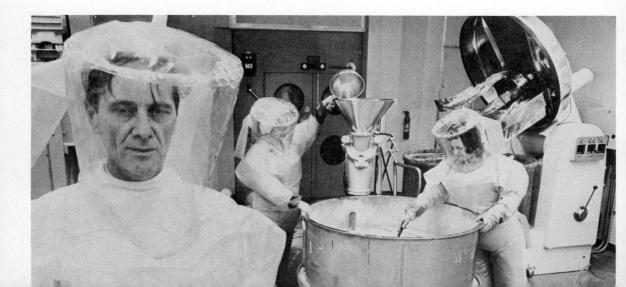

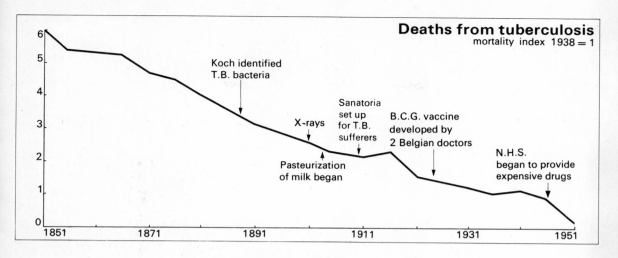

Deaths from tuberculosis
mortality index 1938 = 1

Koch identified
T.B. bacteria

Sanatoria
set up
for T.B.
sufferers

X-rays

B.C.G. vaccine
developed by
2 Belgian doctors

N.H.S.
began to provide
expensive drugs

Pasteurization
of milk began

did not kill the pain with gas or injections until later. With more
and more adults living longer and children eating sweets and foods
containing sugar, the number requiring dental treatment has risen continually during the twentieth century.

It is impossible to say which of all the developments described so
far played the greatest part in making people more healthy. The graph
of deaths from T.B. helps explain why. Medical advances did not become effective until the twentieth century so gradual improvements in
housing and feeding must account for much of the fall in deaths from
T.B. before 1900.

Such medical progress was being made towards the end of the nineteenth century that many people assumed that doctors would soon
be able to prevent or cure nearly every disease. Today, even though
very few die from infectious diseases, we know that they were too
optimistic. This is partly because the doctors still cannot cure cancer
and rheumatism, for example. It is also because more and more people
have died from heart diseases as they have lived longer and become
wealthier. In addition the causes of some illnesses are very complex
and difficult to diagnose.

Asthma, for example, is obviously a physical complaint which affects
the lungs, yet doctors have discovered during the present century that
attacks of it are usually brought on by worry and similar emotional
upsets. Worry is also a major cause of stomach ulcers. In addition
some people can feel pain when they have nothing physically wrong
with them, and others suffer from a whole range of mental illnesses
which may have no physical symptoms at all.

Of course some nineteenth-century doctors realized that if someone
brooded for days on end or screamed and burst into tears when there
was apparently nothing to upset him, there must be something seriously

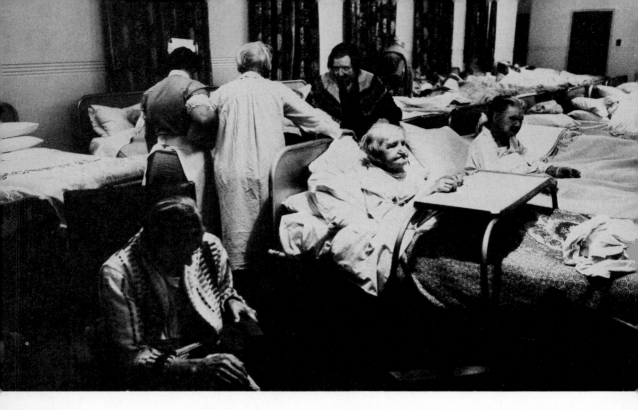

wrong. In their way these people's minds were just as ill as the bodies of those who suffered from T.B. or rheumatism. Most doctors, however, did not come to see it like this until after Sigmund Freud (1856–1939), who worked in Vienna, helped open their eyes. Gradually they came to accept that there were many mental illnesses in addition to depression and hysteria, which were usually caused by serious worry, frustration or stress.

Until quite recently the only mentally ill patients who received any attention were the wealthy and those who were a danger to others. Since doctors have come to recognize much milder forms of mental disturbances, it is now believed that they cause, either directly or in part, perhaps a third of the suffering in the world, especially among women. It is therefore hardly surprising that people should think that there has been a great increase in mental illness recently, whereas all that may have happened is that doctors now recognize it when they see it. Indeed one modern doctor has written of the eighteenth century: 'the proportion of the population afflicted with mental illness was probably not a great deal smaller than it is today', and because there are no records it is impossible to prove him wrong.

Since the mid twentieth century doctors have often managed to relieve the sufferings of those with acute depression. Recent methods of treating the mentally ill with drugs and electricity have not always

Overcrowding is becoming a major problem in our mental hospitals.

Lengthening of life has increased the proportion of the elderly. As families become more dispersed the grandparents are no longer part of the family set-up. The state has had to step in and organize old people's homes.

been completely successful. The limited progress in this field contrasts sharply with the huge advances made in physical medicine in the last hundred years.

These developments have had a profound effect upon people's thinking. Freud and other writers, for example, have gradually persuaded us that our upbringing, environment and physical condition strongly influence the views we hold and the way we behave. Opinions, of course, differ widely as to how much these pressures are beyond the control of each individual and how free we are to determine our own destinies. However, there is now no doubt that a 'normal' or mentally healthy person is far from responsible for all his words and actions.

Summing up

Without any doubt both the wealth and the health of the nation have continued to improve greatly during the present century. And yet the rich and poor are with us still.

So far as health is concerned, progress has been very marked. By the 1960s the average expectation of life for men was sixty-seven and for women seventy-three, and only 2 per cent of all babies died before they were one. What is more, town-dwellers now live as long as country folk and noticeably higher death rates are found only among the families of the poorest unskilled workers.

Chapter 12
Education and social customs

Education

'I well remember the attitude of the staff of an old grammar school to which, in 1904, I with five others was fortunate enough to proceed by means of a scholarship examination,' recalled a former elementary school boy some time later. 'We were constantly reminded by the masters that we were scholarship pupils and were looked upon in the light of poor relations. This attitude passed over from the staff to the boys, who showed that in every way they regarded scholarship pupils as belonging to an inferior category.'

The boy eventually became a university professor. Of course, few have climbed so far during the present century, but an increasing number of working-class children have been given similar opportunities to advance themselves. At first this was achieved by the grammar schools taking more and more pupils free, in return for substantial grants from the government. But, as we have seen, they normally did so most reluctantly.

At the same time many more grammar schools were built for girls. In the countryside they were often admitted to the boys' school, although at first they were taught in separate classes. Soon it was as easy for a girl to win a grammar school place as a boy.

Most counties selected their scholarship pupils with the aid of an intelligence test, but some, whose parents wanted them to start earning as soon as possible, never went. In some towns up to a quarter of those offered a grammar school place turned it down. Even so, the proportion of elementary school children who went to grammar schools at about eleven rose rapidly. In Wales twice as many went to a grammar school by the 1930s as in England. The proportion was also much higher in Scotland, where secondary education began at twelve and lasted five years. And so considerable progress was made towards educating children according to their own abilities rather than their father's wealth.

In the 1920s the government decided that all children, and not just a small minority, should receive secondary education. Their plan was to turn the top forms of elementary schools into senior schools (later called modern schools), and to rename the junior forms primary

Proportion of elementary school children going to English grammar schools

1890s	1 in 200
1914	1 in 40
1930	1 in 11

schools. By then everyone stayed at school until they were fourteen and so, to give them a four-year course, the government decided to raise the school leaving age to fifteen and to start secondary education at eleven.

These decisions were carried out only gradually. The Second World War, for instance, delayed raising the leaving age until 1947. However, by the end of the 1930s two-thirds of the elementary school children had been transferred to modern schools. Many of the rest attended rural schools run by the Church of England, which could not afford to build the new schools and refused to let its older pupils move to modern schools run by the county councils. This deadlock was not resolved until 1944, when an Act was passed making all state schools teach religion according to an agreed syllabus and start each day with a brief act of worship. In addition, the religious schools (Roman Catholic as well as Anglican) received more money from the government. In return the Church let the county councils build the remaining modern schools and by the 1950s very few children were left in all-age elementary schools.

Because they tried to teach almost as many subjects as the grammar schools these modern schools needed at least several hundred children before they could employ a wide range of specialist teachers. And so children often had to travel some distance every day to their nearest school. Without buses and motor coaches, secondary education for all would not have come so quickly.

A cookery class, Clapham, 1900s. The girls are preparing a dinner for a family of seven whose income is under £3 a week.

The county councils also took over all but about 200 grammar schools in England and Wales after 1944. Those which remained independent of the local councils included most of the best-known city grammar schools. They continued to charge fees to about half their pupils, many of whom came from professional and comfortably-off middle-class homes. All fees were abolished in the other (maintained) grammar schools.

Most English counties sent a fifth to a quarter of their children to grammar schools, although in Wales it was often more than a third. Since the 1950s an increasing number have stayed on until seventeen or eighteen, especially in the south and Wales. As their academic standards have also risen many of the differences between grammar and public schools have been reduced. The number of teenagers has hardly altered in the twentieth century, but the total receiving grammar school education in England and Wales has shot up.

Some people were already criticizing the new system when it finally emerged in the 1940s. The education at many modern schools was hardly different from that given to senior classes in elementary schools. In addition it was difficult to explain why the proportions of grammar and modern school children varied so much in some counties. Furthermore, the intelligence tests by which they were selected tested mainly their ability to use words and not other types of intelligence. Children of well-educated parents and from small families had a marked advantage. Also one could not always tell how eleven-year-olds would develop later on. Finally children who went to modern schools were frequently regarded as having failed, and a system of education which made people treat two-thirds of the eleven-year-olds in the country as failures was obviously most undesirable.

Children at grammar schools
England and Wales

	total number	those not paying fees
1895	35,000	2,500
1930	400,000	175,000
1965	900,000	865,000

Despite such demonstrations, most councils moved slowly towards abolishing the 11-plus completely.

Tulse Hill School. Large school buildings were erected to house comprehensive schools in big cities.

Comprehensive schools therefore appeared in some towns like London and Coventry, designed to take all the children over eleven from one area. They were teaching about 250,000 children in the mid 1960s when the government at last encouraged the county councils to provide comprehensives for all their children. It also decided that from the early 1970s they should stay at school until they were sixteen.

These two decisions set the county councils many problems. With very little extra money, they often created comprehensives from schools some distance apart. To reduce this disruption some counties like Leicestershire first sent their children to junior comprehensives from which some or all transferred at about fourteen to senior schools. Recently many more counties have tried to produce comprehensive education on the cheap with variations of such schemes.

Although about one child in twenty over the age of eleven now attends a private school, the sons and daughters of manual workers are no longer educated in inferior schools of their own. In theory indeed, all have enjoyed equal opportunities since secondary school fees were abolished in 1944, but in practice this is not so. A report at the end of the 1950s showed that half the country's most gifted children had left school by the age of sixteen. This was partly because some fathers believed that education was wasted on their daughters, who therefore took a job as soon as possible. In addition children whose parents had left school at fourteen or younger could rarely help them with decisions like which subjects to study. Lacking support on such problems, many left before they need have done. On the other hand, those who stayed on often developed interests different from their parents' and became aware of a gulf opening up between them.

At the end of the nineteenth century most children in elementary schools were taught in classes of seventy or more. Even then they were often taken by unqualified teachers, some of whom were teenagers in training. A few were in their seventies, because all the older teachers did not receive a pension until the 1920s.

Qualified women teachers usually received between £40 and £80 a year in the later nineteenth century, while male elementary school teachers were paid from £60 to £120. But this was not the main reason for the shortage of teachers. Those in charge of the schools generally managed to run them as cheaply as possible by employing very few teachers, and so under 3000 new teachers were trained every year. In the early twentieth century the government helped the county councils build more training colleges which, together with the smaller families, left few classes of more than fifty children by the end of the 1930s.

This situation was worsened temporarily by the Second World War and the unexpected number of children born after it, but it has improved slowly since. After a great expansion of the training colleges in the 1960s, more than 30,000 people were trained as teachers every year. This achievement was not so effective as first appears because most new teachers were women who left after a few years to raise their own families. Nevertheless, though classes vary in size, teaching groups of about thirty-five to forty are probably the most common in junior schools today.

After 'Payment by Results' was abandoned in the 1890s, most teachers in elementary schools continued to teach mainly facts, partly because it helped pupils win grammar school scholarships. However, teachers have gradually come to realize that the younger children are, the more effectively they learn through experience rather than by memory. And so infants who appear to be playing are often learning too.

These ideas have greatly influenced the junior schools which have devised more imaginative and stimulating methods of learning to read and to understand mathematics. Recently teachers have also come to regard painting, music and physical training as opportunities for children to express their feelings as well as skills for them to acquire. With more money to spend they have used films, radio and other audio-visual equipment in addition to more models, pictures and books.

With smaller classes, teachers can give each child individual attention and some divide them into several separate groups. Because they are now more concerned that children should understand what they study they have mostly abandoned learning by heart. At the same time, however, some teachers may have neglected to teach their pupils spelling, how to write legibly and similar basic skills.

Secondary education has been dominated in this century by exams, usually taken at sixteen and eighteen. (In Scotland the Leaving Certificate was taken at seventeen). Before 1917 there was a great variety of exams. Then they were replaced by the School Certificate in which candidates had to pass five key subjects at one sitting. Those who failed in one subject had to sit them all again. After 1950 it and the Higher Certificate gave way to the more flexible G.C.E., although the syllabuses were still rigidly prescribed. In the mid 1960s another examination was provided – the C.S.E.

Methods of teaching, however, have altered little, since candidates have had to remember so much detailed information and the junior forms of most secondary schools have been set regular exams as well. Perhaps the main change in secondary education has been the introduction of subjects like German, physics, chemistry and even economics to replace the classics. The content of most other subjects is also changing. History, for example, is becoming the study of how people lived and worked as well as of the battles they fought and the men who ruled them. Some secondary schools have also begun to teach several subjects combined together and to use methods which allow pupils to work more on their own.

A class studying in a language laboratory. This kind of learning enables pupils to work at their own pace.

This picture of Birmingham university reflects the growth of higher education since 1900, when only 20,000 students attended university. Within the next seventy years the number studying for degrees rose about ten times. This was achieved first by expanding greatly the civic universities and then by founding new ones and colleges of advanced technology. Even so, from the 1930s, the proportion of university students who were children of manual workers remained at a quarter and this figure is much the same even today.

Proportion of people attending church 1960s

	regularly	at least once a year
C. of E.	5%	25%
R.C.	5%	7%
Presbyterian	1·5%	4%
Nonconformists	2·5%	6%
others	1%	2%

With fewer children to control, teachers have become less strict. This partly explains why children are now beaten less often, but ideas on how they should be brought up have also changed. Adults today are less certain about how people should behave and what they should believe, so that children are rarely given moral lessons. Also, apart from the Roman Catholics who ran one state school in fifteen by the 1960s, few people now think that learning about Christianity is one of the main purposes of education.

In fact in the present century the number of churchgoers has fallen sharply. By the 1950s and 1960s only about 15 per cent went to church on an ordinary Sunday and nearly sixty per cent did not attend a single service during the year. The Nonconformists have suffered most. Only the Roman Catholics have gained support. A higher proportion of country dwellers still go to church, while in the towns the wealthier and better educated, teenagers and over-forties tend to worship more.

It is impossible to show with any precision how religious beliefs have changed, for, according to recent surveys, people's beliefs are usually much more vague than their clergyman's and some are even quite different. In the 1940s, for instance, they discovered that a quarter of those who attended Church of England services in London did not believe in a life after death. Now about two Britons in three believe that Jesus Christ is related to God, a half accept the likelihood of life after death, a third say daily prayers, one in six believes in hell, one in ten accepts the literal truth of the Bible and only one in twenty is a complete atheist.

Nor is it easy to determine how much influence the great expansion of education has had on the way people think or whether it now equips children better to cope with the stresses, complexities and challenges of modern life than it did in Victorian times.

Pin-ups of the early cinema

Left: Rudolph Valentino. When he died in 1926 at the age of thirty-one, several girls committed suicide.

Right: Mary Pickford, who nearly always played the part of a poor-but-honest working-class girl.

The cinema has tried to stop declining audiences by showing films you would not see on television.

Cinema admissions

1939	1,000 m
1949	1,430 m
1959	580 m
1969	215 m
1971	3·5 m

Records sold

1939	14 m
1949	37 m
1959	67 m
1969	170 m
1971	200 m

The first gramophones played revolving cylinders, not flat discs.

Leisure

Music halls still flourished during the early twentieth century. Their audiences were better behaved, the stars better paid and their performances, which were becoming more like modern pantomimes and variety shows, were more respectable. But much of the spirit and uninhibited enthusiasm of the music halls was also dying.

The cinema killed the music halls in the 1920s. At first silent films were shown in gyms, church halls and other available buildings, and a pianist often tried to match the action with suitable music. The films flickered and the actors moved in jerks, but the public flocked to see them, especially the young adults. From the 1920s sumptuous picture palaces were built all over the country, often with an electric organ instead of a piano.

Most films shown were American. Westerns, thrillers and gangster films were all popular. Comedies were also well liked. All invariably had simple plots in which the characters were either good or bad. The slapstick farces were much influenced by the English, and the most famous comic actor of all, Charlie Chaplin, first appeared in the English music halls before he went to Hollywood.

Animated cartoons also had large followings, especially those which portrayed the fantastic adventures of Felix the Cat. Nothing could destroy Felix. After dynamite or earthquakes had blown him to pieces, his scattered limbs were soon reassembled. Travel films depicting jungles and romantic scenery were almost as sure of success. The cinema gave people a welcome contrast to their mundane lives, and actors and actresses with obvious sex appeal made a deep and immediate impact.

The sound track transformed the cinema in the 1930s, when films became known as 'talkies'. Colour caught on more slowly. Walt Disney was one of the first producers to use it successfully. The cinema grew in popularity until the 1950s, when it was partly eclipsed in its turn by television. Since then many cinemas have either been closed or turned into bingo halls.

People's increasingly comfortable houses have recently become more and more places of entertainment. From the 1930s the radio (page 260) has entertained most households with light, cheerful music and sometimes with plays, talks and classical concerts. But television has had an even greater influence on the lives of most families, partly because they use it less as a background to something else. By the 1950s it was not at all unusual for adults to watch television for more than two hours most evenings in the week. At the same time long-playing records increased the popularity of the gramophone enormously and helped arouse a greater interest in music of all kinds.

The number of books and magazines of all kinds which are read at home has grown throughout this century. Thrillers have always been popular, but a new development, the detective story, appeared in the 1920s. Spy and war stories and science fiction also have acquired many devotees. During this century people have been able to borrow more and more books from their local library, but since the 1930s, when cheap paperbacks were first produced, many have preferred to buy their own. Since the 1920s people have also spent countless hours trying to solve crosswords. They were an American invention which the newspapers popularized in England.

Gardening has become another very popular hobby with both sexes. (In the 1960s ninety million pounds a year were spent on it. As the number of house-owners has increased, so many more have taken up do-it-yourself hobbies. Children have also enjoyed a much greater variety of toys and games, not only because their parents' standard of living has risen, but also because they have been mass produced in cheaper materials like plastic. The spread of crazes for collecting objects like cigarette cards, stamps and autographs has further reduced the difference between the amusements of richer and poorer children.

At the same time all kinds of clubs and organizations have grown up for adults, like Townswomen's Guilds, Women's Institutes and evening classes catering for a wide range of interests. Together with all the other forms of entertainment which have become so popular in the twentieth century, they help to explain why, since the First World War, people have continued to drink little more than half as much alcohol as they did in the nineteenth century.

Recently there have also been significant changes in the way in which we entertain ourselves out of doors. The number who play football and cricket has not altered much since the last war, but their regular spectators have declined steadily. Television has made them more critical of their local games and has fostered an interest in minor sports, like wrestling, motor racing and show jumping, whose leading performers usually display astonishing skills.

Football and cricket were designed for men, but as the pressures preventing women from taking strenuous exercise gradually disappeared, the demand for more suitable sports like tennis, swimming and golf has grown. However, most towns lack adequate facilities for them and so people have gone increasingly (in their cars) to the countryside for their recreation. The law still restricts organized games on Sundays, but the hills and rivers are always available. Fishing, sailing, potholing and climbing, for example, have all boomed recently as well as touring in cars.

Among the working classes in the north and midlands, cycling and pigeon racing had many devotees. Boxing was also cheap and had a strong appeal for some healthy manual labourers. Gambling games like pitch-and-toss became very popular among miners and other manual workers after cock-fighting died out. Betting on football

Loans from public libraries in UK

1896	25,000
1911	55,000
1924	85,000
1939	245,000
1962	460,000

Spectators at Football League matches

1939	29 m
1949	41 m
1959	33·5 m
1969	29·5 m

Active sailors

1949	30,000
1959	250,000
1964	500,000

matches developed in a big way from the 1920s when the pools were introduced. Greyhound racing also started in the 1920s. The chief attraction of horse racing had always been the chance to bet and, as wage packets rose, so did the amount staked with bookmakers on both dogs and horses.

As wages have increased and paid holidays have lengthened, more and more people have gone away for holidays. Before the 1930s few manual workers enjoyed more than day trips to the sea. For many these were made possible from the 1870s by improved standards of living, cheaper railway excursion fares and bank holidays on Whit Monday and the first Monday in August. Generally the working classes went to those resorts nearest to their homes, like Margate and Blackpool. There piers and promenades were erected and the resorts began to provide their visitors with pleasure gardens, tennis courts and so on. Brass bands and donkey rides along the beach became two more attractions of the seaside. Until the 1920s people paddled and sat there, but they rarely sunbathed or even swam. Then as both became popular, swimsuits changed markedly (see page 258).

To cater for the growing number of regular holiday-makers since the 1930s, villages like Clacton have grown into large resorts and special holiday camps have been built by William Butlin and others. Both these pictures were taken at Skegness in 1939.

Saluting the flag, 1922.

Inland holidays have also become more popular during this century. The Boy Scouts and Girl Guides have organized many camps since the beginning and the rapid spread of Youth Hostels in the 1930s enabled more young people to escape from their town on bicycles for more than a day. Since then many more people have also toured in regions like the Lake District and North Wales, sometimes sleeping in tents or caravans and walking or climbing.

Few people other than landowners visited the Continent in the early nineteenth century, but then the railway and steamship reduced the time spent on travelling and made continental holidays cheaper and more comfortable. Later in the century, therefore, many of the English middle classes visited the cathedrals and other places of interest mainly in France and Italy, often on tours run by Thomas Cook. The upper classes amused themselves at pleasure resorts like Monte Carlo where they could gamble. Until the 1950s France remained much the most popular country visited by the British, but since then they have gone further and further afield.

No longer does a small minority enjoy most of the opportunities and wealth for pleasure and recreation. And so the ways in which the British people spend their leisure have continued to change profoundly.

Holidays abroad

1835	50,000
1900	500,000
1965	5,000,000

Women

Women have gained more than men from some of the main developments of the twentieth century. For instance, they now live about six years longer on average than men and in addition childbirth is no longer such a danger for women as it once was. Machinery has also created more and more jobs requiring little physical strength that women can do just as well as men.

As standards of living have risen, housewives have had to struggle less to make ends meet. Since women spend more time at home, they have also gained more from hot-water systems, modern cookers and other improvements to houses. Thanks to soap powders and washing machines, washing is not such hard work nor does it dominate their Mondays. Tinned, frozen and packaged foods have saved them much time too.

In the first half of this century, the work of domestic servants also became easier in various ways. However, even though their wages rose, the number of servants declined very rapidly, especially in the 1940s. Working-class girls have rarely put themselves voluntarily at the beck and call of other women to do their personal work. When given a choice, they have preferred their independence. Now less than one family in a hundred has a living-in maid. And so women who require domestic help have to make do with part-time assistance or the services of a foreign *au pair* girl and take full advantage of all the latest labour-saving devices.

The decreasing size of the average family has also eased women's work. This trend continued in the twentieth century because more and more couples took deliberate steps to conceive less often. Contraceptive practices seem to have started on a significant scale among the middle classes in the 1870s. At first the most widely used method was withdrawal or interrupted intercourse. Despite the mass production of rubber, only a minority used the sheath until the middle of the present century, when it was supplemented by more satisfactory contraceptives, like the pill, which depended on the woman.

Illegitimacy rate

1950	4.5%
1960	6%
1966	8%

Until the early twentieth century, those who advocated publicly the use of artificial methods risked imprisonment. The churches also condemned them as wicked and unnatural, but since 1930 when the Church of England first supported birth control, the Roman Catholic church alone condemned it. Although the proportion of illegitimate babies, which remained constant at about one in twenty until the 1950s, has risen since, most women in theory can now have as few or as many children as they choose. In consequence few women now suffer from dropped wombs and similar ailments caused by having too many children or doing heavy work within a few days of their birth. At the same time the idea that sex is something which respectable women should enjoy, and not just endure, has been generally accepted.

Since the 1930s people have also tended to marry younger. This is partly because girls who are fed better are reaching earlier the age of puberty, when they are first able to have children. Nearly a third of the brides were teenagers by the 1960s.

In 1923 women were given the same rights as men in divorce cases. Since then the grounds upon which either can sue for divorce have been further extended. The result has been that at a time when fewer and fewer marriages are ended prematurely by death, an increasing number is dissolved by man. Now about one marriage in ten ends in divorce. Since, however, there is no way of measuring how many couples continued to live together unhappily in the nineteenth century nor how many husbands deserted their wives, by itself this information does not prove that the modern family is breaking up. Indeed some would argue that since people now expect more happiness and companionship from marriage, they no longer tolerate unsatisfactory relationships as they used to.

All these changes taken together have produced a new pattern of life for most women. Instead of working for nearly fifteen years before they marry and then often not going out to work again, girls generally work for about three to five years after leaving school. Then, after having a smaller family early, they will be approaching forty, not fifty, when their youngest child is growing up. They will not be worn out

Liverpool women in a biscuit factory. There seemed to be no objection to women doing such dull and repetitive work for little pay.

Women aged 20–24 married

1891	30%
1911	25%
1931	25%
1951	45%
1970	60%

Divorces in Britain

1913	1000
1938	7000
1961	25,000
1969	50,000

from rearing a large family nor will they feel they are nearing the end of their active life. On the contrary most can expect about another thirty-five years of fairly healthy life.

Despite such progress and the much greater freedom which they enjoy in their behaviour, however, women have still not attained full equality with men. Many parents, for example, still think their sons need a better education than their daughters. Boys are more often encouraged to stay on at school and only one girl goes to a university for every three boys.

None the less the opposition of well-to-do parents to their daughters taking jobs has been worn down gradually. At first they were allowed to become private secretaries (but not typists) and serve as assistants in high-class dress shops in the west end of London. Thanks mainly to the efforts of Florence Nightingale well-born girls who became nurses in the large London hospitals were not considered to have disgraced their families either. Nor were those who taught in the leading girls' schools.

Young women who travelled to work daily by themselves could hardly be said to need an escort in the evenings and so they soon went to cinemas and other places of entertainment by themselves. They were also admitted to public houses, but for long most women felt uncomfortable in them, except perhaps in one special room. The convention that women should not pay for anything when they are out with men has taken even longer to die. So has the idea that men should not swear in the presence of ladies nor discuss distasteful subjects with them.

In the 1920s British women also began to follow the Americans in breaking down the ban on smoking in public. At first only Egyptian and Turkish cigarettes were considered respectable, but eventually they

Women entertainers, 1920.

Women's Auxiliary Air Force. During the two world wars women tackled a number of jobs previously reserved for men.

smoked even Virginian ones in buses, restaurants or other public places.

At the start of the century lipstick, rouge and eye shadow were regarded as the trade mark of prostitutes and actresses. By the 1920s, however, smart ladies were wearing them in the evenings. Eventually girls from the skilled working classes and suburban middle-class homes also took to make-up. These two groups have generally been the slowest to change their minds on what they consider to be acceptable conduct.

Few jobs are now closed to women by law, but in practice they rarely occupy the best-paid and most important positions. For instance, a very small proportion of solicitors, engineers, chartered accountants and directors of companies are women. Part of the reason is that most mothers do not work continuously in their twenties and thirties when men are building their careers and so are left behind in the race for promotion. They therefore rarely rise above the lower-grade jobs, and even when they do the same work as men in factories, shops and offices they are usually paid less.

It is impossible to say if women are now happier than they were in earlier generations. Like modern girls, they adapted themselves to life as they found it and, knowing what was expected of them when they married, devoted themselves to running a home and bringing up their family. Today, in comparison, women have to try to be good at many things — looking after children, cooking, organizing a home, dressing fashionably and often doing a job as well.

Conclusion

Women are still 'second-class citizens' in many ways but are becoming increasingly aware of their rights on such matters as equal pay and the legal control of their children. Perhaps the kind of demonstration shown here will reduce discrimination.

With increased material wealth during this century snobbishness about material possessions seems to have grown. As one lady complained when interviewed in Woodford, a London suburb, in 1959: 'People seem to think that if they've got something you haven't got they're better than you are.' 'During the course of a conversation a neighbour told me they were getting a new car,' said another. 'Then she mentioned someone else in the road who's just got a new car, and she said: "That'll be a knock in the eye for them."' Advertising is one explanation, but the disappearance of many obvious differences between white-collar and manual workers is another.

And yet, in spite of the great increase in material possessions and the many other ways in which our lives have improved, the comforting belief in the inevitability of progress has been rudely shattered in the twentieth century. It made little sense to those who survived the First World War (1914–18). Subsequent atrocities like the Nazis' massacre of the Jews, the development of atomic weapons and wars in Vietnam, Nigeria and elsewhere have undermined it further. However, confused though many of us are about where we are going, we have come to accept that to improve the standard of living the government should interfere more in our daily lives and in the running of the economy.

The Second World War
(1939–1945) affected and
changed the lives of everyone
in Britain. Homes were no
longer safe from attack. People
survived air raids by using
shelters – one kind was the
Anderson metal shelter usually
built partly submerged in the
garden. In London the
Underground was used.
People slept on the platforms
and lines – and even concerts
were given to raise morale.
The war meant new
organizations to combat the
effects of bombing and other
possible attacks – the ARP
and the Home Guard.
Everyone had identity cards
and ration books, clothes, food
and petrol were all rationed.
Most other things were in
short supply as all production
concentrated on winning the
war. These photographs are
from *Picture Post*, an
illustrated magazine which
employed brilliant
photographers to cover all
aspects of the war.

Chapter 13
Government in the nineteenth and twentieth centuries

Local government

The very rapid growth of towns in the nineteenth century made the existing system of local government increasingly unfit, and so it was gradually overhauled to meet the situation with which it had not been designed to cope.

The first change came in the 1820s when Nonconformists and Roman Catholics were allowed to sit on town councils. Then Parliament reformed the government of the Scottish towns in 1833 and the English and Welsh ones two years later. The householders who paid rates elected their councillors for three years – a third every year. The council also chose a third of their own number for six years (aldermen) and the mayor. A close check was kept on how they spent their money by auditing their accounts regularly. Large towns without charters soon acquired them. The councils could also take over from their Improvement Commissioners, but most waited for fifteen years or so before claiming these powers because ratepayers were usually more keen to save rates than to improve public health. Some soon provided themselves with water and gas works, parks and trams and also started to tackle their slums (page 101), but the smaller towns especially postponed most of these schemes until about the 1870s.

In the 1830s and 1840s police forces were established in the larger towns under Watch Committees. Most counties waited until the later 1850s for their force, which was run by a chief constable. Their efficiency varied considerably. Originally the police were agile young men who patrolled regular beats of about twenty miles every day. By this means they scared off some criminals and protected property better than the old constables and watchmen. Their other duties included controlling rioters and demonstrators, fighting fires, checking weights and measures in shops and seeing that publicans obeyed the licensing laws. Much later they began to use forensic science to detect criminals with fingerprints and similar evidence and enforce orderly behaviour on the growing number of motorists.

From the 1830s various elected bodies were set up to provide other services. In 1835 the country was divided into about 700 Poor Law Unions, each of which elected regularly a Board of Guardians who took over responsibility for the poor from the J.P.s. Separately elected Boards of Health appeared for a few years from 1848, Highway Boards supervised roads from 1862 and School Boards were established after 1870. Each board employed a number of officials, but because many authorities were very small they carried out their duties most unevenly. This system was very complex. Not only were the different boards elected separately, but they raised separate rates and rarely had common boundaries too. This hotch-potch was simplified at last from 1888, when all the counties were given their own councils with members elected by the ratepayers. They took charge of main roads and bridges, public health and housing, libraries and lunatics, among other responsibilities. With the J.P.s they appointed separate committees to run the police. London was governed by a single council for the first time too. Most towns with over 50,000 inhabitants continued to control their own affairs as newly christened County Boroughs. Education and child welfare were added to the duties of these councils early in the twentieth century and relieving poverty in the 1930s.

Elected Urban District Councils governed the smaller towns after 1894. They disposed of sewage, collected refuse, lit streets and so on, but were supervised by the County Councils. Rural District Councils had similar powers in the countryside together with oversight of the small and almost ineffective Parish Councils. The activities of J.P.s were finally reduced to little more than licensing and minor infringements of the law. Although established before the motor car, this system of government remained almost unaltered until the 1970s.

The Pontefract (Yorkshire) Fire Brigade in 1900. In the late nineteenth century most towns established their own fire-fighting service, but their equipment was very limited.

Central government

In the mid nineteenth century the national government's influence declined in one important way. After sweeping away most customs duties it retained little control over foreign trade (page 133). Until the early twentieth century at least, the government in Britain interfered little in other economic matters. Many other states, for instance, ran their railways, but the British government merely kept their prices down and imposed regulations making them safer.

Since the First World War, however, the government has assisted many struggling industries and helped organize several new ones. It has also taken steps to reduce unemployment, assist those out of work and settle disputes between employers and their workers. With old-age pensions, national insurance and national health, family allowances and social security schemes, the government has become involved more and more directly with raising people's standard of living. Nor has it left the local authorities free to run housing, health and education as they like. More and more Acts have instructed them what to do. And, as these services have expanded, the government has contributed

One cartoonist's view of the conflict of democratic government and the trade unions in 1920.

POTATOES
are
PRECIOUS
DON'T
WASTE
THEM

Wartime poster from the
Ministry of Food.

Because the population increased
threefold between 1845 and 1965
and the value of the pound fell to
about an eighth total taxation per
person rose less than seven times.
Customs duties are paid on
imports. Excise is a tax on goods
sold in this country, like beer and
tobacco. Income tax rarely rose
above 5 per cent in the nineteenth
century, but much higher rates
have been introduced since then.

more to their cost and appointed more inspectors to keep them up
to the mark.

At first the responsibility for supervising domestic affairs was shared
between the Home Secretary, Privy Council and Board of Trade. The
former, for example, took charge of the police and inspecting factories,
the second, schools, and the third, safety on the railways. However,
there was no logic in this division and in the later nineteenth century
Prime Ministers began to resolve the muddle by creating more ministries. They were usually called Boards at first and the minister in charge
was paid only a small salary, but they became full ministries later.
Thus the Local Government Board, which was set up in 1871, became
the Ministry of Health in 1919. Several other new ministries were
created at the same time – for instance, in 1916 Labour and Pensions,
and in 1919 Agriculture and Transport – and more have emerged
subsequently, while others have also been reorganized. During this
century the number of full ministers has grown from thirty to over
fifty, but the Cabinet has included only about twenty of them.

The government has employed more and more people as its work
has expanded. In theory, for example, the Minister of Transport decides
when and where to build motorways, with what surface and how many
lanes. This work is so complicated, however, that many civil servants
have to make detailed studies first. They also organize many less
important matters like the siting of road signs and the introduction
of new one-way traffic schemes. Hospitals and schools are run in a
similar way. Together Whitehall and the local authorities now employ
directly over two million people. They include not only soldiers and
sailors, doctors and teachers, but firemen, policemen and postmen, tax
collectors, customs officers, clerks, inspectors and many other civil servants.

Information about the expansion of the civil service is not very
reliable, partly because the jobs are so varied. Finance probably
records better the increasing scope of government. Not only has the
amount spent on the social services and education shot up, but aeroplanes, submarines and modern weapons are so expensive that the cost
of defence in peacetime has also soared – from £60 million in 1905
to £2000 million in 1965.

Government income

	rates £m	total taxes £m	customs and excise £m	income tax £m	death duties £m	motor tax £m
1845	10	55	40	5	3	0
1905	50	150	70	30	20	0
1965	1,000	9,000	3,500	3,900	300	200

Parliament

To help persuade the king appoint them as ministers, some leading landowners had groups of friends and followers in the eighteenth century House of Commons. However, no group was large enough to control Parliament by itself and so the governments were always coalitions of several groups. When William Pitt and Charles Fox died in 1806 their parties did not disband. Other leaders took them over and in the next twenty years more M.P.s joined what became the Tory and Whig parties. Although party members normally voted together, their leaders had little hold over them, for all M.P.s paid for their own election campaigns.

When one party won a clear-cut majority in the House of Commons, like the Whigs in 1830, the king had no option but to appoint their leader Prime Minister. Since then the sovereign has exercised less and less political power, becoming little more than a referee who helped resolve the deadlock when no one party dominated the Commons. The government's work has also become so complicated that the monarch could not possibly supervise most of it. In the nineteenth century he (or she) generally took a particular interest in the army and foreign affairs and left the ministers to settle other matters on their own.

As the Prime Minister acquired the king's power to appoint and dismiss his colleagues, Parliament also underwent far-reaching changes.

The House of Commons at the beginning and end of the nineteenth century. This building was burnt down in 1834.

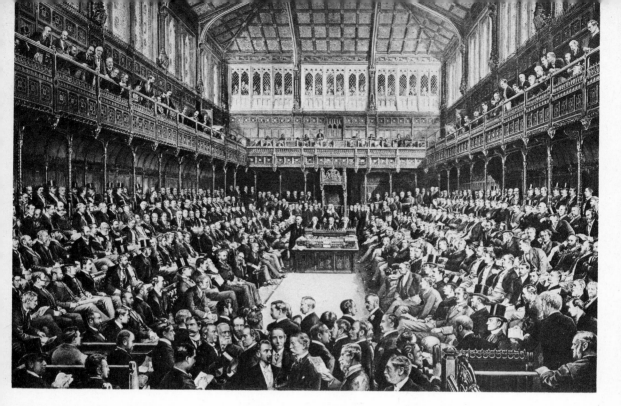

In the new chamber there were still only enough seats for two members in three. Some are therefore standing to hear an important speech by W. E. Gladstone. After the second building was destroyed in 1940 by German bombs, the present chamber was modelled very closely on it.

As the right to vote has been extended since 1832, the number of electors in Britain has increased nearly 100 times (see page 304). In the nineteenth century it depended mostly on the value of people's houses and until 1885 was different in town and country. Until 1948 some could vote twice. They included those educated at certain universities or who owned property in two constituencies. In 1832 and 1867 some seats were given to the new industrial towns, but the country districts were heavily over-represented until 1885 and most M.P.s remained landowners. After 1885 no borough with less than 15,000 inhabitants had an M.P. to itself and few constituencies had two seats either. By 1948 each constituency had about 50,000 electors. Other changes eventually made it easier for non-landowners to become M.P.s. They included:

1858   M.P.s no longer had to own property.
1872   Electors at last voted in secret.
1883   Candidates' election expenses restricted for first time. (They have spent about £700 each at twentieth-century elections.)
1912   M.P.s were paid. £400 p.a. at first. Increased from 1937.

Electors have continued to prefer candidates with some wealth, education and administrative experience. Most twentieth-century M.P.s have come from the professions and business. Those who were manual workers were almost all trade-union officials.

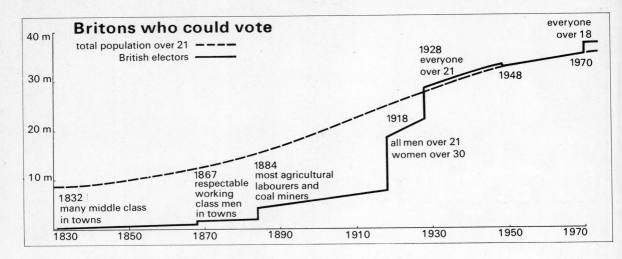

Britons who could vote

total population over 21 — — — —
British electors ————

40 m
30 m
20 m
10 m

1832
many middle class
in towns

1867
respectable
working
class men
in towns

1884
most agricultural
labourers and
coal miners

1918
all men over 21
women over 30

1928
everyone
over 21

1948

everyone
over 18

1970

1830 1850 1870 1890 1910 1930 1950 1970

The landowners have also lost most of their power in the House of Lords. Until the later nineteenth century all peers owned land, but many businessmen, politicians and others without land have been ennobled since. All were hereditary and male until 1958, since when life peers and some women have been admitted. By the 1960s over 1000 lords could sit, but most hardly ever attended.

As the House of Commons came to represent the ordinary people more, the Lords continued to alter and delay Acts, but they rarely killed them. In theory they could do this until 1911 and they did reject the Secret Ballot in 1870, for example, but when the Commons was very keen on a measure the Lords almost always let it pass a few years later. When they became more obstructive after 1906, the Commons forced through an Act which limited their powers from 1911 to postponing non-money bills for two years. They were reduced further to one year in 1949.

Political parties

Political parties did not develop continuously from the 1830s. In 1846, for instance, the Tories split over Free Trade and for twenty years the political situation became confused. However, party agents and societies were established particularly in the towns where the parties were evenly matched. They devoted themselves to registering as many of their own supporters and excluding their opponents' as possible, because the right to vote then depended mainly on the value of people's property and there was often considerable doubt as to who was qualified. Most grocers, shoemakers, publicans, Scots and Nonconformist ministers voted for the Whigs, and Anglican clergymen and butchers for the Tories, but otherwise there were few occupational differences between their supporters.

By the 1860s the two main parties often called themselves Liberals and Conservatives and they dominated Parliament again. Although prominent landowners were among the leaders of both parties, the Liberals, especially under Gladstone, tried to remove many restrictions preventing the Nonconformists and middle classes from sharing the privileged position of the landowners. As the defenders of the landed interest and Church of England, most Tories did not oppose all changes, but tried to delay them. Since some of their leaders realized that many manual workers preferred to be ruled by landowners than by business and professional men, they too introduced some changes, like the county councils and the 1867 Reform Act. During the later nineteenth century the Conservatives opposed granting independence to Ireland (part of UK since 1801) and came out very strongly in favour of expanding Britain's Empire. Both issues divided the Liberals and help explain why the Conservatives governed for most of the twenty years after 1885.

Feasting and similar methods of winning support became less effective as the number of electors increased. From the 1860s, therefore, the Liberals especially publicized their policies in the newspapers and copied other means from the Americans. They founded branches in the constituencies so that ordinary electors could join the party. Both parties also opened working men's clubs and ran fêtes and garden parties to involve as many as possible in their activities. They also helped raise funds and at election time keen members distributed leaflets. In some towns like Birmingham the Liberals in particular also strove to win control of their council and school board. This increased party rivalry and led to fewer M.P.s being returned to Parliament unopposed.

By the 1880s both parties were well organized on a national scale. At an annual conference representatives from the constituencies met some of their parliamentary leaders, who usually thanked them for their help and encouraged them to work harder. Sometimes they also explained what they were doing in Parliament, but the rank and file never discussed their policies. Their M.P.s chose the party leader, whose influence was limited because most M.P.s still paid their own expenses and therefore felt free to vote according to their consciences when they conflicted with the party line.

As the electorate increased, however, both parties took little interest in the problems of the poorer town-dwellers. Improvements for them generally stemmed from the campaigns of dedicated individuals like Lord Shaftesbury, whose speeches, meetings and letters to the press against various abuses often roused the middle classes into demanding action from Parliament. Then it would probably appoint a Select Committee or Royal Commission to investigate the problem, but weaken the Acts designed to enforce some at least of their recommendations.

Eventually the reports of the inspectors and civil servants who had to implement these Acts prompted the government to take more effective action against, for instance, the worst landlords or employers. On balance the Conservatives probably improved ordinary people's health and housing more; but even so, few politicians were keen on social reform in the nineteenth century.

The Liberals revealed new-found concern for working-class welfare between 1906 and 1914, but it benefited them little. They were never returned to power again. In 1900 some trade unions had decided to form their own party, and this Labour party replaced the Liberals as the second party in the Commons in the 1920s. In 1924 and 1929–31 it formed two brief minority ministries. The Labour party was the first committed to pressing for shorter hours of work and higher wages and welfare benefits too. It was also organized very differently. At their annual conferences the representatives of the unions and other party members not only discussed, but also decided, the policies which their M.P.s should support in Parliament. In the House of Commons they were all expected to vote together, even when they disagreed with their colleagues, and since few could afford to fight an election without help from party funds, rebels were rare. The party leader, who was elected by the M.P.s, was also expected to follow the decisions of the party conference rather than his own ideas.

In all this they were influenced strongly by socialist ideas, many of which stemmed from the writings of Karl Marx. 'The bourgeoisie is unfit any longer to be the ruling class in society', he had announced as long ago as 1848. 'Its fall and the victory of the proletariat [manual workers] are equally inevitable.' The working men needed merely to unite to bring it about. However, their plans for when they finally attained power were always rather vague and the Labour party had no

Sir John Simon, a future Foreign Secretary, addressing an open-air election meeting in 1910.

Ernest Bevin, Foreign
Secretary in 1945,
campaigning for election.

more effective cure for massive unemployment, for instance, than any
other party.

The more definite programme which their leaders devised in the
1930s accounted for much of their work when Labour won its first
majority (1945–51) after the war against Hitler. It included completing
the National Health Service, nationalizing several industries and giving
independence to India – the heart of the British Empire. By then Wales,
industrial Yorkshire and the north-east were the main Labour strong-
holds. In the Commons the party was represented by many teachers,
journalists and lawyers as well as trade unionists. The M.P.s no longer
followed slavishly the annual conference's decisions and the Prime
Minister ran the government in the way he wanted. In opposition
Labour continued to express sympathy towards the poor, but when they
returned to power (1964–70) persisting economic problems left them
performing less than they promised.

In general the Labour party has found it easier to put its ideas
into practice in local government than in central government. Early
in this century many Labour members were elected to town councils
in south Wales and east London and by the 1930s they goverened
all London and Sheffield too. There and elsewhere they built houses
for the needy and improved many other amenities because they were
not afraid to spend money. Soon after the vote was given to all adults
in local elections in 1945, Labour controlled most large cities. This
roused the Conservatives, who reversed the situation in the 1960s.

Since the later nineteenth century, when the Liberals became more
radical, almost all landowners and most farmers have supported the
Conservatives. From the 1880s, too, more and more business men and
bankers have been elected as Conservatives, who have also dominated
the Lords. The emerging trade unions and Labour party then frightened
many suburban and small property owners into deserting the Liberals
for the Conservatives, whom they expected to resist change more firmly.
Since then the political allegiance of most voters has depended largely
on their social class. In addition the south of England has remained
overwhelmingly Conservative. Women have favoured them too. In
1959, for instance, more men voted Labour than Conservative, yet
the latter still secured one and a half million more votes. Clearly the
Conservatives have been the chief gainers from female suffrage, for
since the 1920s out of over 600 M.P.s not even five per cent have
been women.

Conservative politicians have governed the country for long periods
from 1918, helped on three occasions by Liberal and Labour leaders
(1918–22, 1931–5 and 1940–5). However, when in power, Conservative ministers paid less heed to the old Liberal principles of low taxation
and freedom for the individual from state control which they cham-
pioned in theory. This naturally disappointed many of their reactionary

How the different classes
voted in 1964

Class and percentage of electorate	Lab %	Cons %	Lib %
Managerial middle class (12%)	10	75	15
lower middle class (18%)	25	60	15
skilled manuel workers (35%)	55	35	10
other working class (35%)	60	30	10

supporters, especially since the Conservatives adopted eventually many of their opponents' policies. These included concern for the unemployed, support for state education and the National Health Service and the need to finish dismembering the Empire and join the European Common Market. (On the latter issue the Labour party remained much more deeply divided.) However, because over half their M.P.s had business connections, and many of the rest were farmers, lawyers and army officers, it is not surprising that the Conservatives were a practical party concerned with survival.

The Conservative organization has also developed more like the Labour party's. Their annual conferences have held increasingly serious debates on their policies and since 1965 the M.P.s have officially elected their leader. The party whips in the House of Commons have also ensured that on most occasions the M.P.s do not vote independently. With this discipline, once a party wins a working majority in the Commons, its leaders can normally expect to govern the country for the next five years. (Since 1911 elections have been held every five years at the most — except in wartime.) With television, general elections have become more than ever a battle to decide which of the two party leaders will become Prime Minister. Now the victor enjoys greater powers than an eighteenth century king. And yet the well-drilled parties have not reduced their backbench M.P.s to mere robots. Their opportunities to influence their leaders' policies are much greater than those of the party members and, above all, the electors.

Conservative Party Conference in Blackpool, 1972. Party conferences are the focal point of political life, where any factions with a variety of opinion can try to consolidate their views.

Conclusion

Many people dislike some at least of the policies of both major parties or else they feel frustrated because neither will take up a particular issue. Although they can vote, from time to time they feel so powerless to influence party policies that some resort to marching in the streets, for example, to register their protest. However, the police now control most demonstrations so skilfully that, if they want to, the politicians can normally ignore them.

Before capable police forces were formed in the mid nineteenth century, rioting and looting were much more likely to break out, especially in the towns. The J.P.s could not call in troops to quell disturbances until after things had got out of hand. By contrast civilian policemen armed only with truncheons can be summoned before violence breaks out and are then on hand to pounce on the trouble-makers. By such means they made harmless most protests by trade unionists, suffragettes and others against the country's government.

Our continually expanding police force can, therefore, pose a serious dilemma. The stronger and more efficient it becomes, the more it may tempt the government to ignore, or even crush, the discontented.

Just how powerful the modern state can be was shown during the two world wars. Then, from about 1916 to 1918, and 1940 to some time after 1945, the government exercised vast powers. It could force civilians to fight or to work in particular jobs, turn them out of their homes and imprison them without trial. The government also pegged prices and wages, nearly trebled the taxes and rationed scarce supplies of food, clothes, petrol, etc. It controlled the use of wood, paper and other essential materials too. Though reduced, the government's powers in peacetime are still very great, and there is always a danger that ambition, laziness or stupidity will lead it to misuse them.

Policemen

1855	15,000
1910	55,000
1965	95,000

Belfast, 1970. From 1969 such scenes became common in the streets of Northern Ireland. They provided disturbing proof of just how quickly a peaceful community can be overwhelmed by violence and disorder — especially when the policies and actions of the government persistently annoy a sizeable minority.

Chapter 14
The problems of today and tomorrow

Some are obvious — and terrifying. Mankind now possesses weapons which are capable of destroying most of the life on this planet. There is no guarantee that they will never be used. The world's population now increases every year by more than the number of people in Britain. The time could come when all cannot be fed. People in most other countries are much poorer than we are and at the moment we give them little assistance. Ought we to increase it for our sakes or theirs and, if so, to whom should we give the most help?

Other problems do not threaten such dire consequences, yet many are still very pressing. During our lifetimes the pound has steadily

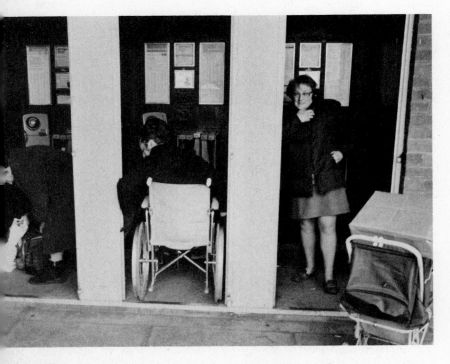

For most of us, making a telephone call presents few problems provided we can find the right change and an empty telephone booth. But for the woman in the middle, struggling to get her wheelchair through the doorway, it is a major undertaking. If only they had made the entrance three inches wider! Nevertheless, here she is fortunate. There is a step up into many phone boxes which means she can't get into them at all. Nor can she use many public and private buildings without help, because they have not been designed with her disability in mind.

Are we helping these disabled people as much as we should, not only to move around, but also to find work and to look after themselves at home? How many are handicapped physically, and are they being given enough money to overcome their disabilities as well as possible?

lost value. Inflation could increase very rapidly. Can anything be done to halt it? Our government is committed to providing almost all of us with jobs. Is it possible to do this and really modernize our industries at the same time? If not, what would be the cost of making the country's wealth grow faster? Are we perhaps too concerned with material possessions? Will extra money really leave us better off?

Are we the best judges of our own interests? Do we eat wisely and take sufficient exercise? Are we genuinely interested in our poorer neighbours? Is our wealth distributed satisfactorily? If not, what can we do about it? What consequences might follow from its present uneven distribution? Is everyone paid as they deserve? Does anyone receive so little that they would be justified in disrupting the country in order to secure more?

Are we sufficiently free to spend our money and our time as we like? Are modern governments too powerful? Ought the Prime Minister be allowed to decide the date of the next general election? Should the government provide us with more sports facilities or help for artists and musicians? Education is changing rapidly. Ought we to help or hinder its changes?

In ten or twenty years' time, what appears satisfactory now may be out of date. Should we wait for this to happen before taking action or can we ease the problems of the future?

Other people, like drug addicts, cannot always look after themselves for different reasons. Should they be given more help? What effect does the regular taking of hard drugs have on people? Has the number of drug addicts increased recently? Why do people take drugs anyway — and why do some of them not stop at the soft drugs, like cannabis? Is it simply because they cannot cope with life, or can it be that, despite all the improvements of the last two hundred years, for them the world remains a frightening and unpleasant place from which they yearn to escape? Drug addiction is, in fact, not a new problem. Laudanum — a liquid form of opium — was a common medicine in the nineteenth century, and led to the same addiction as heroin.

Living near a busy airport can make even a simple job like hanging out washing in the garden a noisy task likely to cause a headache. Providing earmuffs may be one solution but is it the only way to make life bearable for people affected by aircraft noise?

If special precautions are not taken against them, many of the impressive achievements of science and industry will harm unexpectedly innocent people (and animals). Loud noises are not the only form of pollution or even the worst. Smoke and poisonous fumes can pollute the atmosphere, old bottles, cans and plastic containers spoil the land, while sewage, oil and industry's chemical wastes endanger the rivers and the sea. And all the time our society produces more and more rubbish for disposal.

Poisonous fumes are not the only harmful effect of the motor car. Tens of thousands are killed and injured on roads every year and, as more cars are driven, traffic jams regularly paralyse the centres of towns. To cope with this situation many new roads have been thrust through towns – at great cost in money and to the environment. Attractive or satisfactory houses have often been pulled down (which does nothing to help the housing shortage), and formerly quiet and peaceful areas subjected to the roar of traffic day and night.

Are we paying too high a price for the car's convenience? Has it got out of control and, if so, what action can we take?

Undoubtedly the last century has been an age of unprecedented material progress, but has our extra wealth definitely improved the quality of life? Can people devoted, for example, to drinking and gambling confidently answer 'Yes'? And are those who enjoy their summer holidays in caravan camps like this in any sense better-off than their ancestors who never had a holiday? Or can they be held responsible in any way for scenes like the one below? The more people who can get out of cities to the countryside and seaside, the better, but is it worth ruining places . . .

These lads, like many others
one Easter weekend, were
visiting a seaside resort intent
on enjoying themselves. But
the police suspected that their
idea of fun would end in gang
warfare, throwing of bottles
or bricks, breaking of
windows and injuries to
people, and so they took
precautions. Youths without
bootlaces, belts and braces
could hardly terrorize the
neighbourhood.

But why should boys want
to behave like this? Is it the
fact that so many youth clubs
are so dull that they felt
driven to make their own
excitement? Or were these
well-fed and healthy boys
simply indulging in high
spirits, like previous teenagers?
(See picture, p. 178.)
Is it possible that however
much our environment may
have changed during the last
two centuries, human nature
has not changed at all?

Further information

Many topics in this book are covered so briefly that readers will want to
discover more about them. Fortunately a wealth of books exist, written at
a level comparable to this one. Someone wanting to study the improvement
in health, for example, will find something of interest in most of the
following volumes:

Health and medicine

R. K. Allday, *The Story of Medicine*, Ginn – Aspects of Social and Economic
   History.

J. M. Calder, *The Story of Nursing*, Methuen – Outlines.

R. Calder, *From Magic to Medicine*, Macdonald.

R. J. Cootes, *The Making of the Welfare State*, Longman (with 7″ record).

G. R. Davidson, *Medicine through the Ages*, Methuen – Outlines.

K. Dawson and P. Wall, *Public Health and Housing*, Oxford University Press
   – Society and Industry in the Nineteenth Century.

A. Delgado, *A Hundred Years of Medical Care*, Longman – Then and There.

M. N. Duffy, *Medicine*, Blackwell – Twentieth Century Topic Books.

I. Eberle, *Edward Jenner and Smallpox Vaccination*, Chatto & Windus.

M. St J. Fancourt, *They Dared to be Doctors*, Longman.

A. and G. Howat, *The Story of Health*, Pergamon.

E. Jenkins, *Joseph Lister*, Nelson.

R. W. Johnson, *Disease and Medicine*, Batsford – Past into Present.

N. Longmate, *Alive and Well*, Penguin – Topics in History.

T. B. McCulley, *Man against Disease*, Pergamon.

I. Martin, *From Workhouse to Welfare*, Penguin – Topics in History.

B. Read, *Healthy Cities, a Study of Urban Hygiene*, Blackie – Topics of
   Modern History.

J. Rowland, *Chloroform Man: Dr James Simpson*, Lutterworth Press.

E. J. Trimmer, *I Swear and Vow: The Story of Medicine*, Blond Educational –
   Today is History.

R. Watson, *Edwin Chadwick: Poor Law and Public Health*, Longman – Then
   and There.

Inevitably, all these books are not of equal value. Some are better
illustrated or written in a simpler style, others are more detailed or more
accurate or stress differently the roles of particular individuals.
However, most of these volumes belong to a series in which the publishers
try to maintain uniformity in both treatment and format, so that once one

knows two or three of its books one normally has a reliable idea of the rest of the series. For this reason I have listed below selected books, not on particular topics, but in several of these series. The current catalogues of each publisher will show what other titles are available.

Series of topic books

Allen & Unwin, *Understanding the Modern World*
  The Industrial Revolution (1760–1860). The Scientific and Industrial Revolution of Our Time. Yesterday – A History of the Times of Your Parents and Grandparents.
Batsford, *Past into Present*
  (This series is splendidly illustrated, but the texts sometimes lapse into inadequacy partly because they cover such a long period in time.)
    Clothes; Country Life; Entertainment; Factories; Home Life; The Post; Poverty; Ships; Shops; Town Life; Transport.
Blackie, *Topics in Modern History*
  The Trade Union Story.
Blackwell, *Pocket Histories*
  Cricket; Football; Railways; Schools.
Blackwell, *The Twentieth Century Topic Books*
  Emancipation of Women; Fashion and Dress; Flight.
Blond Educational, *Today is History*
  Glasgow; Manchester; The Press; Strike or Bargain.
Faber, *World Outlook 1900–1965*
  British Democracy in the Twentieth Century; 1897; the Edwardians; English Society between the Wars.
Ginn, *Aspects of Social and Economic History*
  Press; Railways; Women.
Harrap, *As They Saw Them*
  F. Nightingale; E. Pankhurst.
Longmans, *Then and There*
  (This outstanding series is one of the few cheap enough for schools to be able to buy in sets, but some volumes are easier to read and others concentrate on one locality. It is also accompanied by source books and filmstrips.)
    Eighteenth Century: London; Edinburgh; Scotland; Roads and Canals.
    Nineteenth Century: Agrarian Revolution (S. Yorkshire); Railways (1825–1845); Galashiels (Wool), Belper (Textiles) and South Yorkshire (Coal and Iron) in the Industrial Revolution; London (1851); Sir R. Hill and Post Office; Learning and Teaching (Northampton); Sailing Ships and Emigrants.
    Twentieth Century: Edwardian England; Motor Revolution; Suffragettes; General Strike; Glasgow in the Tramway Age.
Macmillan, *Signposts to History*
  Emancipation of Women.
Macmillan, *Sources of History*
  The Trade Unions.
Methuen, *Brief Lives*
  Brindley and Telford; G. and R. Stephenson.

Methuen, *Outlines* (ideal for the library)
   Aircraft; Boxing; Coal Mines; Football; Forge and Foundry; Glass;
      Inland Waterways; Kitchen; Mechanical Power; Railways; Ships;
      Spinning and Weaving; Talking Machines; Wheels on the Road.
Methuen, *Story Biographies*
   Mrs Pankhurst.
Murray, *The Changing Shape of Things*
   Britain's Food; Dress; Houses; Interiors; Transport by Land.
Oliver & Boyd, *History Topic*
   Men and Machines; Transport and Communications; Trade Unions.
Oxford University Press, *Clarendon Biographies*
   W. Cobbett; C. Darwin; K. Hardie; G. and R. Stephenson; Queen
      Victoria.
Oxford University Press, *Lives of Great Men and Women*
   Great Inventors; Social Reformers.
Shire, *Lifelines*
   I. K. Brunel; J. Wedgwood.
University of London Press, *It Happened Round Manchester*
   Canals; Entertainments; Railways; Textiles.
Ward Lock, *How Things Developed*
   Furniture; Games and Sports; Inland Waterways; Railways; Roads;
      Wireless.
Ward Lock, *Our Modern World*
   Hairstyles and Hairdressing; Shops and Shopping.

These two series examine the problems of today in very different ways:

Oxford University Press, *The Changing World*
   Urban Growth in Britain; Agriculture in Britain; Transport in Modern
      Britain; Britain's Changing Countryside.
Penguin, *Connexions*
   Food; Lawbreakers; Out of Your Mind?; Shelter; Standards of Living;
      Violence; Work; Fit to Live In?

Readers can also consult with profit more general books like these:

History textbooks

B. Catchpole, *A Map History of the British People 1700–1970*, Heinemann.
D. Thompson, *The British People: 1760–1902*, Heinemann.
P. Mauger and L. Smith, *The British People: 1902–1968*, Heinemann.
J. and M. Ray, *The Victorian Age*, Heinemann.
A. J. Patrick, *The Making of a Nation: 1603–1789*, Penguin, chapters 12–15.
A. M. Newth, *Britain and the World: 1789–1901*, Penguin, chapters 9–11.
E. N. Nash and A. M. Newth, *Britain in the Modern World: The Twentieth
   Century*, Penguin, chapters 1, 10–12.
R. Hart, *English Life in the Eighteenth Century*, Wayland.
R. Hart, *English Life in the Nineteenth Century*, Wayland.

Many excellent books have had to be omitted from these lists, but anyone
wanting further recommendations should consult: W. H. Burston and C. W.

Green (eds.), *Handbook for History Teachers*, Methuen. The Historical Association's biennial magazine *Teaching History* also includes book reviews and ideas for studying history.

Reading what people alive today have written about the past is not the only way of discovering how our ancestors lived, nor even perhaps the best. What previous generations wrote about themselves can often be more fascinating and instructive.

Some books collect together selections from contemporary writings, but though convenient, these brief extracts can have several disadvantages. They may not reveal the writer's circumstances or opinions, for example, and so his pronouncements can be taken as almost infallible. To the list of source books, therefore, I have added a few complete contemporary writings and when I have quoted from them myself I have shown the page references in this book.

Original source books

Allen & Unwin: E. Royston Pike: *Human Documents*
    Industrial Revolution; Victorian Golden Age; Age of the Forsytes.
Allen & Unwin: *Picture Source Books for Social History*, edited by M. Harrison
    Eighteenth Century; Early Nineteenth Century; Late Nineteenth Century; Twentieth Century.
Blackwell: *They Saw it Happen*: 1689–1897; 1897–1940.
    How They Lived: 1700–1815.
Evans: *History at Source*: Agriculture 1730–1872; Children 1773–1890; Entertainments 1880–1900; Factory Life 1774–1885; Law and Order 1725–1886; Shopping 1721–1900.
Macmillan: M. W. Flinn: *Readings in Economic and Social History*
    P. Lane: *Documents on British Economic and Social History*, 3 vols: 1750–1870; 1870–1939; 1939–67.
Oxford University Press: *Society and Industry in the Nineteenth Century*, edited by K. Dawson and P. Wall
    Education; Factory Reform; Poverty; Trade Unions.
    Transport Revolution in the Nineteenth Century (3 vols), edited by R. Tames

Complete memoirs, etc.

W. Cobbett, *Rural Rides* (1821–32), p. 114.
M. Vivian Hughes, *A London Family 1870–1900*, p. 175.
J. London, *The People of the Abyss* (London poor in 1902), pp. 105 and 109.
H. Mitchell, *The Hard Way Up* (leader in suffragette and labour movements in N. England from 1890s).
G. Orwell, *The Road to Wigan Pier* (poverty and unemployment in the north in 1930s), pp. 96 and 233.
M. Powell, *Below Stairs* (servant in Brighton and London between wars).
G. Raverat, *Period Piece* (upper middle-class childhood in late nineteenth-century Cambridge), p. 200.
F. Thompson, *Lark Rise to Candleford* (late nineteenth-century childhood in North Buckinghamshire village), pp. 128, 152, 168 and 265.

Also available are many packs of facsimile documents, which include reproductions of letters, newspapers, posters, maps, pictures and so on. Many of these archive teaching units are produced by non-profit making organizations and cover local themes well. A few representative ones are listed below, but any attempt to summarize them all is soon out of date. In *Teaching History* no. 6 (1971) and no. 7 (1972) G. R. E. Wood gives a good idea of the full range.

Archive teaching units

Jackdaws (Cape): Cricket; Christmas; Clipper Ships and the Cutty Sark; Early Trade Unions; Faraday and Electricity; General Strike; Motor Industry; James Watt and Steam Power; Women in Revolt.

Sheffield University Institute of Education: Apprentices in the Eighteenth Century; Barnsley in 1869; Charity School in the Eighteenth Century; Election in 1807; Enclosure in 1791; Police and Crime in the Mid-Nineteenth Century; Turnpike Road.

Newcastle University Department of Education: Coals from Newcastle; Election in 1826; Popular Education 1700–1870; Railways; Turnpikes; The Tyne 1800–50.

Buckinghamshire, Hertfordshire and Warwickshire Record Offices have each produced a unit on enclosure of an eighteenth-century village.

Scouse Press: Genuine Liverpool Street Songs and Broadside Ballads.
Manchester Manuscripts (Historical Association): The Princes of Loom Street (1800–50).

Recently some publishers have started to produce more ambitious project kits, but as yet they are not always as rewarding to follow as their authors intended. They include:

Macmillan: *Exploring History*
Industrial Revolution; Transport; Victorian Britain.

Historical novels can bring the past to life vividly and develop the reader's understanding. All these books are first-class stories:

Historical novels

H. Burton, *Time of Trial*, Oxford University Press (London and Suffolk in 1801).

F. Grice, *Aidan and the Strollers*, Penguin (actors in the early nineteenth century).

L. Garfield, *Black Jack*, Penguin (thieves in early nineteenth-century London).

M. Trevor, *The Rose Round* and *Lights in a Dark Town*, Collins (Victorian Birmingham).

G. Avery, *A Likely Lad*, Collins (Edwardian Manchester).

F. Grice, *The Bonnie Pit Laddie*, Oxford University Press (Durham mining village in the early twentieth century).

G. Symons, *The Workhouse Child*, Penguin (early twentieth century).

G. Symons, *Miss Rivers and Miss Bridges*, Macmillan (suffragettes).

K. M. Peyton, *Flambards*, Oxford University Press (society before 1914).

G. Cooper, *An Hour in the Morning* and *A Time in the City*, Oxford University Press (domestic service in the early twentieth century).

F. Grice, *The Oak and the Ash*, Oxford University Press (Durham mining village in 1920s).

H. Burton, *In Spite of All Terror*, Oxford University Press (evacuation from London in the Second World War).

J. Kamm, *No Stranger Here*, Longman (adoption and drugs today).

Contemporary illustrations

Books containing photographs and other contemporary pictures include:

I. Doncaster, *Evidence in Pictures*, Longman.
  Social Conditions in England (1760–1830).
  Changing Society in Victorian England (1850–1900).
  Social Changes in Twentieth Century England.
G. Winter, *A Country Camera (1844–1914)*, David & Charles.
G. Winter, *Past Positive*, Chatto & Windus (early photos of London).
J. Simmons (ed.), *A Visual History of Modern Britain*, Studio Vista.
  Education.
  Government.
  House and Home.
  Industry and Technology.
  The Land.
  Recreations.
  Town.
  Transport.
Victorian and Edwardian Photographs, Batsford.
  Brighton.
  Cambridge.
  Liverpool and the North-West.
  London.
  Norfolk.
  Oxford.
  Scotland.
  Surrey.
  Wales.
  Yorkshire.

Filmstrips

The available filmstrips include:

Common Ground, Longman
  Introduction to the Industrial Revolution (12 parts).
Educational Productions, East Ardsley, Wakefield, Yorks
  The Agrarian and Industrial Revolution; Twentieth Century Britain
  (2 parts); The Changing Style of Costume.
Hulton
  Social Life in the Eighteenth Century; Victorian Social Life; English

Social Life 1902–18; Telford; Story of a Railway; Milestones of Aviation 1903–53.

Films

Some films can be hired:

British Film Institute, 42 Lower Marsh St, London SE1, hires:
  Aberdeen 1906 (10 minutes); Children at School 1938 (20 minutes); Coalface 1935 (10 minutes); Enough to Eat 1936 (20 minutes); Housing Problems 1935 (18 minutes); The Oxford & Cambridge Boat Race 1911 (4 minutes).
Rank Film Library
  The Changing World of Charles Dickens (37 minutes); The Growth of London (23 minutes); The Lady with the Lamp – Florence Nightingale (106 minutes).
H. Harrison Films
  English Costume 1740–1920 (39 minutes).

This list does not include dramatized fiction. Further films from these and other companies are given, with the addresses, in *History Films for Hire* obtainable from Film Service Office, Main Library, University of Birmingham, P. O. Box 363, Birmingham B15 2TT.

Gramophone records

Records of the popular music and songs of previous generations can be bought from:

Topic Records, 27 Nassington Road, London NW3. They have a long list of industrial, mining and sea songs, including: *The Iron Muse*; *Along the Coaly Tyne*; *Steam Whistle Ballads*; *Men at Work*.
Fontana. Their records include *Music Hall*; *Scrapbook for 1914*; *Scrapbook for 1940*.

Museums

Museums vary greatly in the range and quality of their material. Most larger towns have a museum with at least one section portraying life and work during the last two hundred years. Very few, however, can match the Castle Museum in York and St Fagan's in Glamorgan (see the picture on p. 35) or the Geffrye Museum, London, for its reconstructed rooms.
  Specialist museums include:

Rural life
Reading, Berkshire; Hartlebury, Worcestershire; Stowmarket, Suffolk.

Childhood and toys
Edinburgh; Brighton; Bethnal Green, London; Blithfield, Staffordshire; Warwick.

Golf
Dundee.

Staffordshire County Council
Education Department
produce very useful local
history source books which
can be obtained from the
County Record Office.

Cricket

Lord's, London.

Costume

Manchester; Bath; Victoria and Albert, London.

Transport

General: Glasgow; Beaulieu, Hampshire.
Railways: York; Leicester; Stockton.
Tramway: Crich, Derbyshire.
Horsedrawn Vehicles: Maidstone, Kent.
Canals: Stoke Bruern, Northamptonshire.
Ships: Greenwich, London.
National Postal Museum, London.

Medicine

Wellcome Institute, London.

Science and industry

General: South Kensington, London; Birmingham; Newcastle; Salford;
    Swansea.
Textile Machinery: Bolton, Lancashire.
Glass: St Helens, Lancashire.
Iron Founding: Coalbrookdale, Shropshire, where the whole area is worth
    visiting.
Sheffield has an eighteenth-century scytheworks and water-powered grinding
    shop.
Birmingham has an eighteenth-century watermill.

Museums and Galleries in Great Britain and Ireland (normally available from
    W. H. Smith's) provides the details and opening times of these and many
    other museums.

Buildings and field studies

Our environment contains many buildings, earthworks and so on, which
were often created for purposes different from their present uses. The
following books should help the reader detect and understand some which
were erected originally in the eighteenth and nineteenth centuries.

Methuen, *Get to Know*
    Factories and Workshops; Farms; Houses and Flats; Inland Waterways;
    Railways; Shops and Markets; Village Survey.
Routledge & Kegan Paul, *Local Search*
    The English Home; the English Village; the Post Office.
Shire, *Discovering*:
    Bridges; Canals; Schools; This Old House; Towns; Watermills;
    Windmills.
Rivingtons, *Field Studies for Schools*
    Purpose and Organization: Field Excursions in N.W. England, E.

Scotland, N. Wales, E. England, W. Scotland, E. Midlands, S.W. England.

(These volumes contain very practical suggestions for particular excursions.)

J. N. T. Vince, *History All Around You*, Wheaton.

T. Corfe (ed.), *History in the Field*, Blond Educational.

Local history

G. A. Chinnery, *Studying Urban History in Schools*, Historical Association, and A. Rogers, *This Was Their World*, BBC, should help anyone trying to discover more about the history of their own locality.

Statistics

Additional statistics can be found in:

R. Mitchell and P. Deane, *Abstract of British Historical Statistics*, Cambridge University Press.

A. F. Sillitoe, *Britain in Figures*, Penguin.

Annual Abstract of Statistics, HMSO.

Social Trends, HMSO.

The current numbers of the last two volumes will supply the up-to-date information. If you compare it with the earlier figures in the text, remember that the latter cover Britain (England, Wales and Scotland), but not Northern Ireland.

Some suggestions for things to do

1   Topic books, like those recommended on pp. 317–318, can be read straight through, but sometimes a better way of using them is to concentrate on specific aspects of a topic, like discovering what you can about the measures taken to ensure comfort or safety on the railways or what kind of songs were most popular in the music halls.

2   Alternatively you can take a particular individual and see how much you can find out about his or her schooling, family life, ideas, beliefs and so on.

3   You can also pose problems for yourself. Just how bad were living conditions in the mid-nineteenth-century towns, for example, were they equally bad for everyone and is it possible to exaggerate them? Then try to find the answers.

4   Occasionally you could start with a statement in the text, such as drink not being a main cause of poverty (p. 108), and then look elsewhere for information which either refutes or substantiates it. Then you can try to decide which interpretation seems most plausible and why.

5   If you find it difficult to understand statistical information, try turning the lists of figures in this book into graphs or diagrams, but before you begin think carefully about the best scale and shape to use. You could start, for instance, by copying out the graphs on p. 91 and then add in these figures for 1950 (figures are in thousands):

Birmingham	1113	Glasgow	1090	Manchester	703
Blackpool	147	Leeds	505	Sheffield	513
Bolton	167	Liverpool	789	Sunderland	182
Bradford	292				

6   Talk to older people, like your parents and grandparents, about what life was like when they were young. Ask them what they learned at school, how they were treated as children, how many brothers and sisters they had, what games they played, what clothes they wore, how their houses were furnished, what their first job was and how they found it, and so on. What do they remember about important happenings, for instance the Second World War?

7   In this book you have read brief extracts from some novels written by Jane Austen, Arnold Bennett, Mrs Craik, Mrs Gaskell, H. G.

Wells and others. If you found them interesting you could look for some of them in a library as well as for novels by other writers, like George Eliot.

8 Novels by such authors are often made into television serials and films. Many portray very well what life was like for a particular class in the eighteenth, nineteenth or early twentieth centuries. The *Forsyte Saga* was one famous TV serial, while films have been made of the *Go-Between*, *Tom Jones*, *Far From the Madding Crowd*, and so on. After you have seen films or programmes like these, try discussing with someone else what you have learned about the ideas, assumptions and ways of life of the characters involved.

9 You can also learn a lot about the life of earlier generations by studying contemporary pictures. This book contains drawings, paintings and cartoons by Hogarth, Rowlandson, Gillray, du Maurier, Scharf and other artists, and if you have enjoyed them you can find more of their work in other books. Those listed on p. 321 contain mostly photographs.

10 Like other historical documents, drawings and photographs often need interpreting. Therefore study them for some time to see if they are deliberately putting over a particular point of view, whether the people portrayed are wearing their best or worst clothes, and so on. Did the sun always shine in Victorian England?

11 Everyday objects used by the Victorians or Edwardians can often be obtained privately or from local Schools' Museums Services, and can make you curious to discover what they were used for, and by whom. Why not see what you can find?

12 In addition you can visit a museum, perhaps one of those mentioned on p. 323. Before you go it is usually best to know in advance what you are looking for. In the large national museums you can easily be overwhelmed by the number of objects on display, so small museums with thoughtfully laid out collections can provide just as satisfactory visits – see B. Winstanley, *Children and Museums*, Blackwell.

13 The houses of landowners, famous writers and artists are often preserved almost as they used to be. London has Chiswick House, Osterley Park House and the homes of Carlyle, Dickens and Keats, for instance, and similar houses exist all over the country. See if you can find any near where you live, perhaps by consulting *Historic Houses, Castles and Gardens in Great Britain and Ireland*. When you visit one, try to imagine what life in the house must have been like when the original owners resided there.

14 If you enjoy model-making, you can buy kits of accurate-scale models of old locomotives, engines, cars and aeroplanes. On completion, find out something about the life and times of the people who used the real things.

15 In your local environment you will find many buildings and earth-works which were created originally for all kinds of purposes. Helped by some of the books listed on p. 323, see if you can detect former farm-buildings, toll-houses, warehouses, factories, chapels or cinemas. Can you also estimate when they were first erected?

16 You can add a new dimension to the study of a familiar area by looking at old maps, which are normally kept in county (or city) Record Offices and large Public Libraries.

17 You could also get the first edition of the One Inch Ordnance Survey Map (mostly mid-nineteenth century) which has been re-published by David & Charles, Newton Abbot, Devon. It covers England and Wales in ninety-seven sheets.

18 Look at some nineteenth-century Directories (kept by Record Offices and Central Libraries) which list all the shopkeepers, crafts-men and professional men in each town and show where they lived, as well as the schools, churches and local arrangements for travel and post. David & Charles have republished a few Directories from the mid-nineteenth century.

19 Many Record Offices also have copies of the census enumerators' notebooks for at least one of the censuses between 1841 and 1871. These record the occupation of each householder, how many ser-vants, children and other relatives lived with them and also people's ages and where they were born. From these you can discover where the servant-keeping or wealthier classes lived, the age structure of the population, how many had moved into the community and from where, and so on.

20 Ask in your Central Library and Record Office for old copies of local newspapers whose articles and advertisements will give you an insight into local life.

21 Discovering history for yourself is much more time-consuming than reading about it in a book, but it can be much more exciting. If you have found a topic really interesting you could even assemble your own collection of documents, like those listed on p. 320. If you decide to do this, you will find that John West, *Archives for Schools*, Schoolmaster Publishing Co, contains much helpful advice.

22 Why not trace your own family history? You can follow your family back through the female line as well as the male, and when you have learned where some of your ancestors lived and what they did, uncover what you can about these localities and occupations. At some stage you will almost certainly come across a country family moving into a town and other information which should make you realize just how much some of the developments described in this book relate directly to you. These two books should prove helpful: D. Iredale, *Your Family Tree*, Shire. D. J. Steel and L. Taylor, *Family History in Schools*, Phillimore.

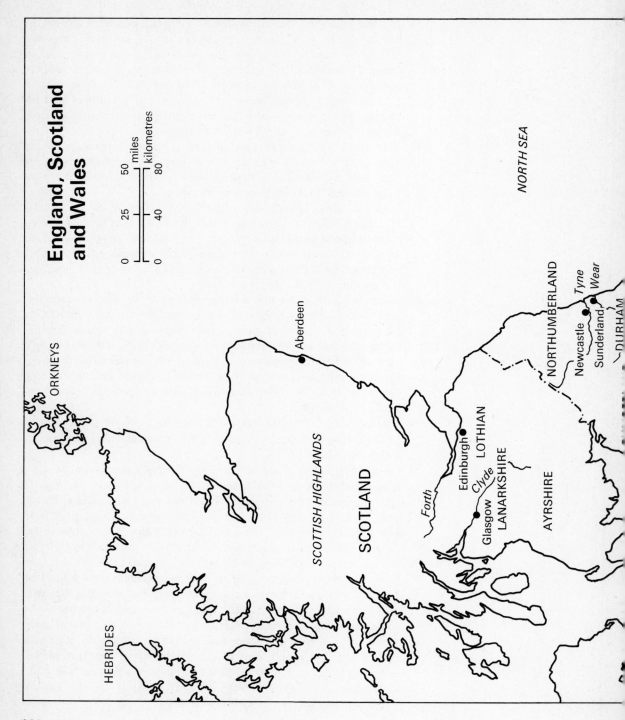

England, Scotland and Wales

miles
0 25 50

kilometres
0 40 80

ORKNEYS

HEBRIDES

SCOTTISH HIGHLANDS

SCOTLAND

Aberdeen

Forth

Edinburgh

LOTHIAN

Clyde

Glasgow

LANARKSHIRE

AYRSHIRE

NORTH SEA

NORTHUMBERLAND

Newcastle

Tyne

Wear

Sunderland

DURHAM

Scarborough

THE WASH

NORFOLK

Norwich

Yarmouth

EAST ANGLIA

Newmarket

Margate

Dover

KENT

London

ESSEX

Kingston

SURREY

Brighton

Tunbridge
Wells

Hull

YORKSHIRE

York

WEST RIDING

Leeds

Bradford

Doncaster

Rotherham

Trent

Sheffield

RUTLAND

Peterborough

NORTHAMPTON–
SHIRE

Cambridge

BEDFORDSHIRE

Stevenage

MIDDLESEX

Burnley

Halifax

Oldham

Manchester

Preston

LANCASHIRE

Bolton

DERBYSHIRE

Nottingham

STAFFORDSHIRE

Stoke

Wednesbury

LEICESTERSHIRE

Dudley

Coventry

Birmingham

WARWICK–
SHIRE

Oxford

Thames

BERKSHIRE

Reading

HAMPSHIRE

Southampton

Portsmouth

ISLE
OF WIGHT

ENGLISH CHANNEL

DISTRICT

Blackpool

Mersey

Liverpool

CHESHIRE

Chester

Severn

SHROPSHIRE

Coalbrookdale

Redditch

WALES

Ebbw Vale

Cardiff

WILTSHIRE

Bristol

Bath

SOMERSET

Taunton

DORSET

Bournemouth

Weymouth

NEW
FOREST

DEVON

Exeter

CORNWALL

329

Index

Acknowledgements

Access: 251
Aerofilms: 267, 313, 314
Architectural Press Ltd: 244
Associated Electrical Industries
    Ltd: 223
Bankfield Museum, Halifax: 68,
    70, 72–3
Bethnal Green Museum,
    photographs by John Webb: 202
British Museum: 10, 32, 52, 55,
    87, 88–9, 126, 137
British Petroleum Co Ltd: 225
British Rail: 121
County Record Office, Stafford,
    and Rev James Sankey, M.A.
    B.Sc., the Methodist Church,
    Leek Circuit, and the Trustees
    of the William Salt Library and
    Mr G. S. McCann, photographs
    by Peter Rogers: 119, 138,
    160–61, 193, 242, 294
Daily Express: 309
Daily Mirror: 259
Dudley Library: 30, 59, 63, 67,
    96, 188, 232
Euan Duff: 235, 267, 279
Mark Edwards: 294, 310–11
Findus Ltd: 243
Fox Photos: 272
John Freeman: 11, 55, 88–9
G.L.C. Library: 198, 281, 283
Glaxo Laboratories: 276
Guardian: 282
Hammersmith Health Education
    Service: 266
Nick Hedges: 315
Thurston Hopkins: 263

Hoover Ltd: 288
Illustrated London News: 78, 82–3,
    84, 103
Keystone Press Agency Ltd:
    218–19, 290
Leeds Central Library: 38, 69, 71,
    90, 95, 97, 104, 148, 172–3,
    217, 252, 270, 299
D. F. Lockwood: 221
London Transport Executive: 123
Mansell Collection: 42, 107, 109,
    110, 181, 207, 210, 238–9, 263,
    275
Museum of English Rural Life,
    Reading: 12, 20, 26, 36, 142,
    144, 147, 149, 150, 154, 155,
    157, 158, 200, 209, 224
National Coal Board: 233
National Museum of Wales: 23
Northampton Public Library: 75
Nottingham Local History Library:
    30
Observer: 251
Paul Popper: 313
Post Office: 115, 126, 237, 256
Punch Publications: 300
Radio Times Hulton Picture
    Library: 13–20, 22, 23, 24–6,
    29–30, 33–5, 37, 43, 46, 48–9,
    53–4, 56–7, 61–2, 64, 73, 86–7,
    92–3, 98, 100–103, 105–6, 112,
    117, 119–20, 122, 125, 128,
    130, 134–5, 139–40, 143, 144,
    149, 152, 154, 159, 162, 165,
    167, 169, 171, 185, 187, 189–90,
    193, 195, 197–9, 200–201,
    203–4, 206–9, 212–16, 236,